THE GERMAN HANSA

THE GERMAN HANSA

PHILIPPE DOLLINGER

TRANSLATED AND EDITED BY

D. S. AULT and S. H. STEINBERG

STANFORD UNIVERSITY PRESS

STANFORD, CALIFORNIA

1970

Stanford University Press
Stanford, California
© Philippe Dollinger 1964
Translation © Macmillan and Co Ltd 1970
Originating publisher: Macmillan and Co Ltd, London and Basingstoke, 1970
Printed in Great Britain
ISBN 0–8047–0742–1
LC 77–120697

PREFACE

There has been no general study of the Hansa in England since A. Weimers' contribution to volume VII of the *Cambridge Medieval History* (1932), despite the importance of Anglo-Hanseatic relations for nearly five hundred years. I hope, therefore, that this book will be of use to everyone with an interest in the history of trade in northern Europe. This edition is essentially the same as the original French version (*La Hanse*, Paris, 1964) although it does incorporate corrections and additions which were made in the German translation (*Die Hanse*, Stuttgart, 1966). In addition it has been read and edited by Dr S. H. Steinberg in association with Professor A. von Brandt of Heidelberg University, the leading authority at present on the history of the Hansa. Dr Steinberg also supervised the work of translating the book, and for all his efforts I should like to express my deepest gratitude. To his name also should be added those of Miss Phyllis Hartnoll, Mr P. D. Whitting and Mr P. A. S. Evans for their general assistance on literary and historical matters.

CONTENTS

Part Three: *Crises and Decline*

Documents

LIST OF MAPS

List of Hansa Towns

Towns whose merchants shared in the Hanseatic privileges abroad, from the fourteenth to the sixteenth century (in some cases only for a short period), are listed in geographical groups, and in alphabetical order within each group, except in the coastal districts. The list is based on the paper by W. STEIN, in *Hansische Geschichtsblätter* (1913–15), the map designed by W. VOGEL, in *Propyläen-Weltgeschichte*, vol. 4 (1932) p. 296, and in the case of Westphalia, on the list given by L. VON WINTERFELD, in *Der Raum Westfalen*, II 1 (1955) pp. 345–52.

IN CAPITALS: chief towns of thirds or quarters: e.g. COLOGNE
In italics: towns which played an important part in Hanseatic affairs: e.g. *Deventer*
200 towns are listed below.

RHINE–MEUSE: COLOGNE, Dinant, Duisburg, Düsseldorf, Emmerich, Grieth, Neuss, Nijmegen, Roermond, Tiel, Venlo, Wesel, Zaltbommel.

IJSSEL AND ZUIDERZEE: Arnhem, *Deventer*, Doesborg, Elburg, Harderwijk, Hasselt, Hattem, *Kampen*, Ommen, Stavoren, Zutphen, Zwolle.

NORTH SEA COAST: Groningen, *Bremen*, Stade, Buxtehude, *Hamburg*.

WESTPHALIA: Ahlen, Allendorf, Altena, Arnsberg, Attendorn, Balve, Beckum, Belecke, Bielefeld, Blankenstein, Bocholt, Bochum, Bödefeld, Borgentreich, Borken, Brakel, Breckerfeld, Brilon, Coesfeld, Dorsten, DORTMUND, Drolshagen, Dülmen, Essen, Eversberg, Freienohl, Fürstenau, Geseke, Grevenstein, Hachen, Hagen, Haltern, Hamm, Hattingen, Herford, Hirschberg, Hörde, Hüsten, Iburg, Iserlohn, Kallenhardt, Kamen, Langenscheid, Lemgo, Lippstadt, Lüdenscheid, Lünen, Melle, Menden, Minden, *Münster*, Neheim, Neuenrade, Neustadt (Hesse), Nieheim, Oldenzaal (Netherlands), Olpe, *Osnabrück*, Paderborn, Peckelsheim, Plettenberg, Quakenbrück, Ratingen, Recklinghausen, Rheine, Rüthen, Schwerte, *Soest*, Solingen, Sundern, Telgte, Unna, Vörden (Westphalia), Vreden, Warburg, Warendorf, Warstein, Wattenscheid, Werl, Werne, Westhofen, Wetter, Wiedenbrück.

LOWER SAXONY: Alfeld, Aschersleben, Bockenem, BRUNSWICK, Einbeck, Gardelegen, *Goslar*, Gronau, Halberstadt, Hameln, Hanover, Helmstedt, *Hildesheim*, *Lüneburg*, *Magdeburg*, Osterburg, Quedlinburg, Salzwedel, Seehausen, Stendal, Tangermünde, Ulzen, Werben.

CENTRAL GERMANY (between the upper Weser and the Saale): Duderstadt, Erfurt, Göttingen, Halle, Merseburg, Mühlhausen (Thuringia), Naumburg, Nordhausen, Northeim, Osterode, Uslar.

BRANDENBURG: Berlin, Brandenburg, Cölln-on-the-Spree, Frankfurt-on-the-Oder, Havelberg, Kyritz, Perleberg, Pritzwalk.

BALTIC COAST, WEST OF THE ODER: Kiel, LÜBECK, *Wismar*, *Rostock*, *Stralsund*, Greifswald, Demmin, Anklam, *Stettin*.

FURTHER POMERANIA, EAST OF THE ODER: Belgard, Gollnow, Greifenberg, Kammin, Kolberg, Köslin, Rügenwalde, Schlawe, Stargard, Stolp, Treptow-on-the-Rega, Wollin.

PRUSSIA, SILESIA, POLAND: Braunsberg, DANZIG, Elbing, *Königsberg*, Kulm, *Thorn*, *Breslau*, *Cracow*.

LIVONIA: *Dorpat*, Fellin, Goldingen, Kokenhusen, Lemsal, Pernau, *Reval*, *Riga*, Roop, Wenden, Windau, Wolmar.

SWEDEN: Kalmar, Nyköping (?), *Stockholm*, VISBY.

Chronology of the Hansa

General History		Hanseatic History	
First half of 12th century	Beginning of German colonisation in the east		
1125–1137	King (from 1113 Emperor) Lothair III		
1142–1180	Henry the Lion Duke of Saxony	1143–59	Founding of Lübeck
1152–1190	Emperor Frederick I		
1154–1189	Henry II King of England	c.1157	Henry II grants privileges to the Cologne merchants in London
		c.1160	Formation of the Community of German merchants visiting Gotland
1189–1192	Third Crusade	End of 12th century	Founding of the German *Kontor* in Novgorod
		1201	Founding of Riga
1202–1242	Valdemar II King of Denmark		
1213–1250	Emperor Frederick II	1226	Lübeck granted imperial charter, becomes an imperial city
1216–1272	Henry III King of England	1227	Victory at Bornhöved over the Danes
1230–1283	Conquest of Prussia by the Teutonic Order	c.1230	First alliance between Lübeck and Hamburg
1237	Livonia becomes subject to the Teutonic Order and Estonia to Denmark (until 1346)	c.1250	Founding of Stockholm
		Second half of the 13th century	Building of the *Marienkirche* in Lübeck
1253	Founding of the archbishopric of Riga	1252–1253	Privileges granted to Hanseatic merchants in Flanders
1254	Rhenish town league		
		1256–1264	Formation of the League of Wendish towns
1273–1291	King Rudolf of Habsburg	1280–1282	First transfer of the Bruges *Kontor* to Aardenburg

		1281	Organisation of the London Steelyard
1285–1314	Philip the Fair King of France	1284–1285	Hanseatic blockade of Norway
		1293	Control of the Novgorod *Kontor* passes from Visby to Lübeck
1286–1319	Eric Menved King of Denmark	1307–1319	Danish protectorate in Lübeck
1309	Teutonic Order moves its headquarters to Marienburg	1307–1309	Transfer of the Bruges *Kontor* to Aardenburg
1327–1377	Edward III King of England	1347	Statutes of the Bruges *Kontor*
1337–1453	Hundred Years War		
1340–1375	Valdemar IV Atterdag King of Denmark	1356	First general Hanseatic diet. The Hansa of the towns begins to develop
1346–1378	Emperor Charles IV	1358–1360	Embargo against Flanders
		1361	Visby captured by Valdemar IV
1346–1384	Louis de Male Count of Flanders		
1348–1350	The Black Death		
1356	Golden Bull, constitution of the Empire	1367–1385	Cologne Confederation formed against Denmark
		1370	Peace of Stralsund
1375–1412	Margaret Queen Regent of Denmark, Norway (1380) and Sweden (1389)	1388	Trade broken off with Flanders, England and Novgorod
1384–1404	Philip the Bold Duke of Burgundy and Count of Flanders	1388–1392	Embargo against Flanders
1386–1434	Vladislav II Jagiello King of Poland and Grand Duke of Lithuania	1392	Peace of Niebur with Novgorod
1397	Union of Kalmar unites the three Scandinavian kingdoms	1390–1401	The *Vitalienbrüder*
1400–1410	Emperor Rupert	1408–1416	Overthrow of patrician regime in Lübeck
1411–1437	Emperor Sigismund	1410	Defeat of the Teutonic Order at Tannenberg

1412–1439	Eric of Pomerania King of the Scandinavian Union	1418	Hanseatic statutes against trouble-makers
1419–1467	Philip the Good Duke of Burgundy	1419	Founding of the University of Rostock
1422–1471	Henry IV King of England		
c.1428	Introduction of the Sound dues	1426–1435	War between the Hansa and Denmark. Peace of Vordingborg
1428–1430	The Low Countries united under Philip the Good	1419–1441	Conflict between the Hansa and Castile
1439–1448	Christopher II (of Bavaria) King of the Scandinavian Union	1438–1441	War between the Hansa and the Dutch. Peace of Copenhagen
		1436–1438	Transfer of the Bruges *Kontor* to Antwerp
1455–1485	Wars of the Roses		
1461–1483	Louis XI King of France	1451–1457	Last embargo against Flanders
1461–1483	Edward IV King of England		
1467–1477	Charles the Bold Duke of Burgundy	1454–1466	War between Poland and the Teutonic Order
		1466	Second Peace of Thorn: the towns on the Vistula come under Polish sovereignty
		1470–1474	The Hansa at war with England
1477–1493	Maximilian Regent of the Low Countries (Emperor 1486–1519)	1471	Cologne excluded from the Hansa
1478	Conquest of Novgorod by Ivan III	1474	Peace of Utrecht
1470–1503	Regency of Sten Sture in Sweden	1483	Perpetual peace between the Hansa and France
		1489	The St George statue by Bernt Notke
1509–1547	Henry VIII King of England	1494	Ivan III closes the Novgorod *Kontor*
1513–1523	Christian II last king of the Scandinavian Union	1522–1531	Lutheranism spreads throughout north Germany
1523–1533	Frederick I King of Denmark	1525	Albert of Hohenzollern secularises Teutonic Prussia

1519–1556	Emperor Charles V		
1523–1560	Gustavus Vasa King of Sweden	1533–1535	Wullenwever burgomaster of Lübeck
1547–1584	Tsar Ivan IV (the Terrible)	1534–1536	The Counts' War
1556–1598	Philip II King of Spain	1556–1591	Sudermann syndic of the Hansa
1558–1603	Elizabeth I Queen of England	1557	Diet at Lübeck, reorganisation of the Hansa
1561–1581	Estonia under Swedish protectorate, Livonia under Polish protectorate	1558	Capture of Narva and Dorpat by Ivan IV
1562	Secularisation of the Teutonic state in Livonia by Ketteler, who becomes Duke of Kurland and Semigallia, and a vassal of Poland		
1563–1570	Nordic Seven Years War between Sweden and Denmark, the latter in alliance with Lübeck	1564–1568	Building of the Hansa's house in Antwerp
1566	Beginning of troubles in the Low Countries which lead to the ruin of Antwerp	1566	Lübeck suffers a naval defeat off Gotland
		1567	Hamburg grants privileges to English merchants
1581	United Provinces proclaim their independence	1579	Elbing grants privileges to English merchants
1588	Destruction of the Invincible Armada	1598	Elizabeth I closes the London Steelyard
1588–1648	Christian IV King of Denmark and Norway	1601	Stade excluded from the Hansa
		1607	Hanseatic embassy to Spain
1609–1621	Truce between Spain and the United Provinces	1616	Alliance between the Hansa and the United Provinces against Denmark
1611–1632	Gustavus Adolphus King of Sweden	1621	The Swedes land in Livonia and capture Riga

1618–1648	Thirty Years War		
1625–1629	Danish War against the Habsburgs; Peace of Lübeck	1626	Conquest of Prussia by Gustavus Adolphus
		1628	Wallenstein besieges Stralsund
1630	Gustavus Adolphus lands in north Germany	1630	Alliance between Lübeck, Bremen and Hamburg
		1631	Sack of Magdeburg by Tilly
1648	Peace of Westphalia		
		1669	Last Hanseatic diet at Lübeck

INTRODUCTION

THE German Hansa, which began as an association of north German merchants, and developed in the mid-fourteenth century into a community of cities, is a creation unique in the history of the Middle Ages. It is true that city leagues were not uncommon in this period, in Germany as well as in Italy; but none of them lasted so long or spread so wide as did the Hansa. In its heyday it comprised nearly 200 maritime and inland towns, stretching from the Zuyder Zee in the west to the Gulf of Finland in the east and from Thuringia in the south to the Baltic in the north. The other city leagues, moreover, were set up for political ends, to defend the autonomy and constitution of their members, whereas the Hansa was formed and maintained to protect its merchants in foreign parts and to extend their trade. This did not prevent it from replacing the feeble imperial authority and thus becoming a front-rank political power in northern Europe, capable of conducting victorious wars against neighbouring states, though these always served economic objectives.

The Hansa remained, however, an anomalous institution which puzzled contemporary jurists. It was not a sovereign power, for it remained within the framework of the Empire and its members continued to owe some measure of allegiance to many different overlords, ecclesiastical or lay. It was an amorphous organisation, lacking legal status, having at its disposal neither finances of its own nor an army or a fleet. It did not even have a common seal or officials and institutions of its own, except for the Hanseatic diet or *Hansetag*, and even that met rarely, at irregular intervals and never in full strength.

But in spite of these structural weaknesses and the conflicting interests inevitable in an association of towns so different and so distant from one another, the Hansa was able to hold its own for nearly five hundred years. The secret of its long life is to be found not in coercion, which played no appreciable role, but in the realisation of common interests which bound the members of the community together. This sense of solidarity was founded on the determination to control the commerce of northern Europe. The historical function of the Hansa was in fact to furnish western Europe with those products of eastern Europe which it needed and in return to provide eastern Europe with some basic necessities, above all cloth and salt, from western Europe. As long as this economic interdependence continued, the Hansa survived.

The history of the Hansa can be dated with a fair degree of precision, from the middle of the twelfth century to the middle of the seventeenth century. Its beginning is marked by the founding in Wendish territory in about 1159 of the city of Lübeck, a western European gateway to the east. Lübeck soon became, and thereafter remained, the head of the Hansa, not only because of its favourable situation on the Holstein isthmus, between the two northern seas, but also because of the enterprise of its citizens. German merchants from Lower Saxony, Westphalia and the Rhineland soon settled in the new town and, following the example of the Scandinavians, began to trade overseas. To the people of that period the Baltic was not a cul-de-sac shut in by ice-bound shores: it was a trade route, giving easy access to the Russian rivers and leading to the great markets of Novgorod and Smolensk, to which came by long and weary roads rare and precious goods from distant countries, from the shores of the White Sea as well as from Byzantium and Moslem lands.

German merchants not only traded all round the Baltic, but also cooperated actively in the founding of new towns dedicated to trade, in which they secured for themselves a preponderant influence. At the same time they were spreading along the shores of the North Sea, in Norway, in the Low Countries, and in England, where they strengthened the long-established commercial links between Cologne and London. By the middle of the thirteenth century the Hanseatics already held a near-monopoly of trade in the two seas, and their commerce was organised around the great axis Novgorod–Reval–Lübeck–Hamburg–Bruges–London. In the fourteenth century they extended and developed their dealings with southern Germany and Italy by land, and with the Atlantic ports of France, Spain and Portugal by sea.

However it was at this time that there also appeared in many countries the first signs of resistance to the economic ascendancy of the Hansa. New competitors, especially the Hollanders and the south Germans, successfully attacked the Hanseatic monopoly. It was mainly in order to meet this threat that the Hansa transformed itself during the third quarter of the fourteenth century into an association of cities, which could more easily protect the interests of its merchants abroad. But in spite of some outstanding successes, its efforts, not only on the economic but also on the political plane, failed to check the progress of its rivals. By the beginning of the sixteenth century the decadence of the Hansa was obvious to all. It is, however, important to define precisely the nature of this decadence. There was no question of a decline in the fortunes of the towns themselves; certain of them, such as Hamburg and Danzig, even experienced a remarkable increase in prosperity at the beginning of the modern era. Nor was there any falling off in the volume of trade, which on the whole showed a considerable increase. To give only one example, the exports of grain from Pomerania, Prussia and Poland reached unprecedented figures. But the newcomers took an ever-increasing share in this larger volume of trade. The economic system of the Hansa was not adaptable to new conditions, and it no longer had the political power to stand up to the monarchies of the time. Thus each member was driven to ask itself if adherence to the community, with the sacrifices that it implied, did not involve more disadvantages than advantages. From that time on, despite praiseworthy attempts to recover lost ground, the Hansa was doomed.

The date of its dissolution can be fixed at 1630, when a closer alliance was set up between Lübeck, Hamburg and Bremen, which in fact took the place of the Hansa. However it is usually brought forward to the year 1669, when the Hanseatic diet met for the last time and a final attempt at restoration proved unsuccessful.

This great association, first of merchants and then of towns, gave itself the name which it has kept throughout history – the German Hansa, *Hansa Theutonicorum, dudesche Hense.* Already in the Middle Ages there was speculation about the meaning of the word Hansa, and the most fanciful derivations were proposed. The word is Germanic and very ancient, appearing in Wulfila's Bible, where it is used in the sense of a warrior band. In the twelfth and thirteenth centuries it is found in a wide area, stretching from the Seine to the Elbe, and also in southern Germany; it means a tribute paid by merchants, sometimes a group of merchants abroad. It is in this sense that it was applied in England at the beginning of the thirteenth century to the members of the Flemish Hansa in London, itself first an association of merchants, then of towns.

It was not until fairly late that associations of north German merchants were in their turn described as Hansas. It first occurred in England, in a royal charter dated 1267: it seems clear that they were so called because their statute was analogous to that of the Flemish Hansa in London. Soon after, small groups of Hamburg merchants in Utrecht and Ostkerke, and of Lübeck merchants in Hoek on the Zwijn, were also called Hansas. From the west the term spread to other Hanseatic regions, but it was not until 1343 that the king of Norway and Sweden, writing to the *universos mercatores de Hansa Theutonicorum*, provided an example of the term being used to mean the entire community of north German merchants and no longer merely a single group in some foreign country. Soon afterwards the Hansa developed as a league of towns, and the expression *stede van der dudeschen hense* became current. So it seems as if the German Hansa did not acquire its definitive title until long after its formation; but this did not prevent it from becoming, as its insignificant precursors were rapidly forgotten, the Hansa *par excellence*, the one and only Hansa.

A minor problem of terminology may be mentioned here, namely what word should be used to describe the bond, both loose and difficult to define, which bound the members of the Hansa together. In German, English and French the term Hanseatic 'League' is used. This is misleading, since 'league' implies a relatively precise organisation, which the Hansa lacked; moreover within the Hansa there were in fact a number of leagues, both general and local, which were formed for particular ends and for predetermined periods. But they were never identical with the Hansa, and it is necessary to make clear the difference between the two kinds of institution. Moreover even in the Middle Ages the Hansa expressly rejected such descriptions as 'society', 'league', or 'corpus'. It is possible to employ such vague terms as Hanseatic union or corporation; but the best solution is undoubtedly to adopt the term 'Hanseatic Community', noting that it translates various expressions current in medieval times, such as *communis mercator, der gemene kopman, die gemene stete*.

By the end of the eighteenth century, the Hansa was almost entirely forgotten. Interest in its history was revived in the early years of the nineteenth century with the publication of the first great monograph on the community, by Georg Sartorius (1803–8). But it is mainly in the last hundred years that Hanseatic studies have been systematically pursued, with the publication of the great collections of sources such as the Cartulary of Lübeck, the collection of *Hanserezesse* and the *Hansisches Urkundenbuch*. Perhaps even more important has been the publication from 1871 onwards of the review *Hansische Geschichtsblätter*, the real backbone of

Hanseatic historiography, which has appeared regularly since the date of its foundation, with the exception of the period of the Second World War. Finally during the last hundred years a veritable galaxy of historians have devoted themselves, either exclusively or principally, to the history of the Hansa, among them Karl Koppmann, Wilhelm Stieda, Dietrich Schäfer, Ernst Daenell, Walther Stein, Walther Vogel, Fritz Rörig and Paul Johansen, to mention only the best-known of those no longer alive.

There is no need to point out that during this period the accepted picture of the Hansa, or at least of certain aspects of it, has varied a great deal. This is largely because of the inorganic, almost indefinable structure of the community; for example at one time the Hansa of the towns was held to be the true Hansa and everything that preceded its formation was looked upon as a sort of pre-history, a process of gestation. Today it is recognised that in the twelfth century the association of merchants embodied the Hansa as much as did the community of towns in the fourteenth. Similarly the zenith of the Hansa has been assigned to various dates. Fifty years ago historians fixed it a little before the middle of the fifteenth century: at that time the community did indeed comprise the largest number of towns, while its trade was being extended as far as Portugal. Nowadays, however, we tend to shift it back to the last third of the fourteenth century, immediately after the formation of the Hansa of the towns and the victorious Peace of Stralsund, for from this time onwards the Hansa was more intent on conserving the advantages already gained, by creating an elaborate set of regulations, than on making fresh acquisitions. Its rivals were already beginning to contest its predominance not only in their own countries but also in the Hanseatic domain itself. In short, in dating the zenith we rely nowadays more on internal criteria. Finally if economic history, as was only natural, has always been in the forefront of Hanseatic studies, attention has nevertheless been concentrated principally on economic policy, made more easily accessible by the study of charters and ordinances. But for some time now a strong interest has developed in quantitative values, which help to assess precisely the volume of trade. The result has been a revival of interest in the final phase of the history of the Hansa, hitherto relatively neglected, since documents relevant to this field of study, outstanding among which are the famous accounts of the Sound customs dues, are more numerous for this period.

Hanseatic studies have not failed to mirror the ideological conflicts of our time. Thirty years ago the quest for economic facts was censured as being tainted with materialism, and researchers were invited to devote more attention to political factors. At the moment historians beyond the Iron Curtain show a preference for the study of the social structure of the towns, and of the economic, political and social conflicts which arose in the fourteenth to sixteenth century, subjects which are neither new nor their exclusive domain. In addition they are endeavouring to pinpoint the traces of Slav urban foundations, prior to the wave of German colonisation in the twelfth and thirteenth centuries, and to evaluate their role in the urban history of the region. These researches are one aspect of the interest shown everywhere at present in the study of medieval urban topography.

Finally there is a general feeling that the subject should not be studied from a too narrowly national point of view, and that the Hansa should not be considered exclusively from the German angle. An effort is being made to discover what it brought to the peoples with whom it traded, and what part it played in their cultural development.

PART ONE

From the Merchants' Hansa to the Hansa of the Towns

(12th–14th Century)

CHAPTER ONE

Northern Europe in the First Half of the Twelfth Century

I. TRADE IN NORTHERN EUROPE

THE North Sea and the Baltic may be said to form a northern counter-part of the Mediterranean. The three seas provided an established route between West and East, obstructed however in the north by the configuration of the coasts, which forced ships to make a long detour around the Skaw and through the Danish Straits.

In the first half of the twelfth century the Germans had still only a fairly modest share in the commerce of these two seas, which a few years later were to fall entirely under their domination. In both the Scandinavians were still the leading traders. The Norwegians had perhaps developed their commerce most fully. It was with England – especially with Boston – that their trade was most active, thanks to the many colonies which the Vikings had founded there; the same was true of the Irish Sea, which the Scandinavian settlements on both shores of the Bristol Channel had transformed into a Norwegian lake. But the Norwegians and Danes were also regularly trading with the Continent, visiting Bremen and Utrecht, where their presence is noted in 1122, Cologne and probably, even farther afield, Flanders and Normandy. In the west they had reached Iceland and Greenland, in the east they roved almost the whole Baltic sea. In their swift narrow-beamed vessels they carried the products of their country, especially stockfish, hides and leather, salt butter, timber and also oriental products, brought back from the Baltic ports. This trade, which does not seem to have been declining at the time, still retained a semi-rural character, though it was beginning to centralise itself in the newborn towns, in Bergen and Trondheim on the Atlantic coast, and in Oslo and Tönsberg on the Skagerrak.

On the southern shores of the North Sea the most active groups were the Flemings, whose trade was expanding, and the Frisians, who were in something of a decline. The Flemings traded principally with

I   Expansion of Hanseatic trade

Map legend:

Principal routes of regular traffic:
before 1250
1250 – 1350
1350 – 1500

600 kms
400 miles
0

Locations labeled on map: Novgorod, Pskov, Vitebsk, Smolensk, Reval, Dorpat, Polotsk, Kovno, Lemberg, Åbo, Visby, Riga, Cracow, Stockholm, Danzig, Thorn, Oslo, Rostock, Magdeburg, Erfurt, Nürnberg, Bergen, Lübeck, Cologne, Frankfurt, Venice, Hamburg, Lüneburg, Strasbourg, Milan, Genoa, Boston, Bruges, Paris, London, Bourgneuf, La Rochelle, Brouage, Bordeaux, Barcelona, Edinburgh, Lisbon, Setúbal, to Iceland

England. From the ports of Wissant, Bruges and Aardenburg they sailed for London, where they had their own association, the London Hansa. They sold mainly their own cloth, whose production was greatly increasing, and perhaps, even as early as this, French wine. They brought back the wool needed for their textile industry as well as tin, lead, hides and skins, all purchased direct from the producers. From this time onwards Bruges became the most important commercial centre of the Low Countries. Alongside the Flemings merchants from the Meuse, that is to say, from Huy, Liège, Nivelles and Dinant, were no less active, taking to England Rhenish wine, metal manufactures, precious stones, luxuries from Regensburg or even Constantinople, and armour from Mainz. An English regulation of about 1130 laid down the conditions under which these 'Lorrainers' might import and sell their merchandise in London.

The Flemings also traded with the northern Low Countries, with northern Germany, with Schleswig, and perhaps with Scandinavia. But in this area the Frisians were still dominant, extending their trade right into the Baltic. By the end of the eleventh century there was a Frisian guild in Sigtuna in Sweden. But their influence was declining, for reasons not yet fully determined. Possibly the main reason was the Frisians' aversion to urban life at a time when the town was becoming the mainspring of economic activity. At all events the eclipse of the Frisians for a period of two hundred years – after which the Hollanders took over their role – gave the Hanseatic merchants their great opportunity. They were able to take advantage of the Frisians' decline to usurp their position as the dominant maritime and commercial power in the north. Tiel, still prosperous in the eleventh century, was sinking into decay in the twelfth, as is shown by the transfer of the imperial customs house in Kaiserwerth. It succumbed to the competition of Utrecht, better situated for inland navigation and increasingly frequented by Flemings, Rhinelanders, Saxons, Danes, Norwegians and even by the Frisians themselves. In addition Stavoren on the Zuiderzee also captured part of Tiel's trade.

It was now that German sailors and merchants, especially those from Cologne and Bremen, began to take a steadily increasing share in the North Sea trade. At the beginning of the eleventh century King Ethelred II accorded his protection to the merchants of the Empire, putting them on an equal footing with the Londoners as 'worthy of good laws'. These *homines imperii* were for the most part merchants from

Tiel, but some were from Cologne, which had long traded with England, and some from Bremen, whose commercial relations with England are attested before 1100. The Cologne merchants, having increased their trade, were granted, in 1130 at the latest, the right to reside in London, an advantage refused to the merchants of Tiel and Bremen. At some time – the date is unknown – they acquired a house on the Thames, upstream from London Bridge, the Guildhall, which they made their business headquarters and which was the cradle of the future Hanseatic factory (*Kontor*). In 1157 Henry II granted his special protection to the Cologne merchants, their goods and their settlement, allowing them the privilege of selling their wine in the same market – that is to say, under the same conditions – as French wine.* At this time Rhenish wine was in fact already the staple of Cologne trade, but to it should be added metal manufactures and armour produced in Cologne. The return freight was mainly wool, and to a lesser degree metals and foodstuffs.

The trading voyages of the Cologne merchants took them not only towards the west but also towards the north-east, to Denmark, where they bought eastern products and sold their wine and, it may be assumed, Flemish cloth, and also tufa from Andernach, which was used in the building of several Danish churches, notably the cathedral of Ribe. Their trade was carried on increasingly in their own ships, instead of using those of the Frisians. The great increase in the maritime interests of Cologne is shown by its participation in the twelfth-century crusades. In 1102, among the Christian fleet anchored before Jaffa, mention is made of ships from the lower Rhine under the command of a certain Hadewerk, a native of Westphalia. In 1147 ships from Cologne formed the bulk of the German contingent which joined the English and Flemish squadrons at Dartmouth and took part in the capture of Lisbon before sailing on to the Holy Land.

Bremen was hardly less active than Cologne. In about 1075 Adam of Bremen, who was somewhat prone to exaggeration, wrote that 'merchants from all over the world meet in Bremen'. Trade was particularly brisk with Scandinavia, part of the ecclesiastical province of Bremen. Even after the creation of the archbishopric of Lund in 1104 commercial relations continued: at the end of the twelfth century the king of Norway was complaining of the inordinate quantities of wine which Germans were unloading at the port of Bergen.

* Document No. 2.

During the same period the Baltic was also the centre of a flourishing trade linked with that of the North Sea, not by the long route round the Skaw, but across the isthmus of Schleswig. Ships from the west sailed up the river Eider and discharged their cargoes at Hollingstedt; these were then carried overland to Schleswig, or else the vessels themselves were dragged overland for about fifteen kilometres to the estuary of the river Schlei. Since the destruction of Hedeby (Haithabu) by the Wends in the middle of the eleventh century, Schleswig had become the great trading centre of this area. It was in a way an early prototype of Lübeck as the western European port on the Baltic coast. Here Frisian, Saxon and perhaps Flemish merchants met merchants from Denmark, Sweden and Russia.

Trade in the Baltic was, however, principally in the hands of the inhabitants of Gotland, which in the eleventh century, after its conversion to Christianity, had acquired great naval and commercial importance. This had not yet led to the setting up of an urban centre: agriculture and sea trade were still more closely connected here than elsewhere. Commercial activity appears to have been confined to a number of sites which were occupied intermittently and protected by earthworks, and shared by several villages. One of these was located on the site of the future Visby, the best harbour on the western shore.

The sea-going farmers of Gotland seem to have sailed in every direction. They were to be found in central Sweden, where they paid regular visits to Sigtuna, which had taken the place of Birka on Lake Mälar. But it was above all towards Russia, by the traditional route of the Varangians, that they extended their activities. The Viking raids had come to an end after the eleventh century; Scandinavian trade was now concentrated mainly in Novgorod, then rising towards the height of its prosperity. The Gotlanders had founded a trading centre there and endowed it with a church dedicated to St Olaf, which is mentioned first around 1080. This 'Gothic Court' was soon to be sheltering Germans too, who would then create a similar establishment of their own, the *Peterhof* or 'Court of St Peter'. The Gotlanders took to Novgorod western products, including Flemish cloth – Ypres cloth is mentioned in about 1130 – and brought back furs and wax as well as oriental luxury goods exported through Byzantium, Kiev and Smolensk. They may also have found these articles in the trading centres of the southern Baltic, in Stettin and Jumne on the river Oder, where Adam of Bremen mentions the presence of Greek merchants, or at Truso at the mouth of the Vistula. They probably ranged the coast of Samland in search of amber. They also trafficked in Saxony, doubtless in steadily increasing numbers, since in 1134 the Emperor Lothair III granted them exemption from customs duties and his protection 'throughout the whole Empire': these journeys were made either through Schleswig or directly through Wendish territory, when the latter was not troubled by domestic disturbances. It is certainly true that the Gotlanders travelled as far as England, as is shown by the quantities of English coins buried on the island in the eleventh century.

The Scandinavians were not, however, the only people trading in the Baltic. In the first half of the twelfth century there was a marked, though short-lived, increase in Russian trade, due to the rise of Novgorod. Russian merchants were particularly active in Gotland, where traces of their Orthodox churches have been found, and also in Stettin, which a group of merchants from Novgorod had made their goal. Moreover the Chronicle of Novgorod mentions the plundering of Russian merchants in Denmark in 1134; the same thing happened again at the time of the dynastic troubles twenty years later. In addition to the Russians, mention may be made of the trading voyages of the Wends of Rügen and of the Prussians and the Estonians, which were, however, confined to their respective coasts. The Germans, although their presence in Stettin and Schleswig is well attested, seem to have had no great share in the Baltic trading before the foundation of Lübeck.

In contrast, overland trade in the north German plain was principally, as was surely natural, in the hands of the Germans. However in the north-west they were meeting stiff competition from the Flemings and the merchants from the Meuse. The most active traders were doubtless the merchants of Ghent, who came to Cologne to exchange their cloth for grain and wine. Often they went beyond Cologne, either eastwards to fetch copper from the Harz, or southwards towards Coblenz to buy wine directly from the producers. But from the middle of the twelfth century onwards, when the archbishop made Cologne a staple-market, their journeys up the Rhine were stopped. The merchants from the Meuse, from Liège, Huy and Dinant also came to Cologne for the fair in August, bringing the products of their metal industry. The presence of merchants from Verdun has also been noted, but nothing is known of the nature of their business; their main preoccupation, the slave trade, had come to an end at the beginning of the eleventh century.

Among the Germans the merchants of Cologne were the most

adventurous. If they rarely ventured towards the west as yet, they were nevertheless very active in the south and east. The purchase of wine, on which their prosperity was founded, led them towards the middle Rhine and Alsace. But they were also to be found in Austria, at the market in Enns, selling stockfish and cloth, and buying hides, wax and perhaps even ore from Hungary. In the east they were principally attracted, like the Flemings, by the copper and silver of the Harz. These metals, which were in great demand, were exported to all parts, some by the Saxons themselves, mainly towards the west, by the great route Magdeburg–Goslar–Soest–Dortmund–Cologne. By the end of the eleventh century Goslar, as well as other rising towns in Lower Saxony and Westphalia, had developed a metal industry whose products were dispatched to distant markets. Further to the north the salt-works of Lüneburg, which had existed since the tenth century, were sending their salt to the Rhineland; but it is impossible to estimate the volume of this trade. Then again merchants from the Saxon towns were making regular journeys to Schleswig. In Soest at the end of the thirteenth century a 'Schleswig fraternity' is mentioned: such a term could only have been coined before the foundation of Lübeck.

On the river Elbe, right on the frontiers of the Empire, there were two towns of some importance to traders. One was Bardowiek, where Saxon merchants forded the river at the last practicable point before it joined the sea on their way to Wendish territory, particularly to the island of Rügen, to buy fish; their customs dues, imposed by the emperor and levied by the duke of Saxony, brought appreciable revenues to the imperial exchequer. The other was Magdeburg, important as a centre for missionary activity in the heathen countries beyond the Elbe, and headquarters of an inland water transport system which played an important part in the wars against the Wends; its flourishing merchant quarter provided a meeting place for Saxon and Slav traders. It was obviously a busy commercial centre, although there are very few precise details as to the type of business transacted there.

To sum up: shortly before the middle of the twelfth century north European trade was still shared between merchants drawn from many different nations; and the Germans, although displaying some signs of initiative, were playing only a relatively modest role in commerce. Only the very perspicacious could have foreseen that in a hundred years' time the circumstances were to be completely transformed in their favour.

2. POLITICAL, RELIGIOUS AND DEMOGRAPHIC FACTORS

At the beginning of the twelfth century the boundary of the Empire and of Christendom still followed approximately the line of the rivers Elbe and Saale, as it had done three centuries before. After temporary successes, all the attempts made in the tenth and eleventh centuries to subjugate and convert the eastern territories had been held in check. To begin with, Otto the Great had organised marcher-provinces beyond the Elbe; he had created the bishoprics of Brandenburg and Havelberg, suffragan dioceses to Magdeburg, which became an archbishopric in 968; on the Baltic, in Holstein, the bishopric of Oldenburg had been created, suffragan to the archbishopric of Bremen. But all this had fallen into ruins before the end of the tenth century, when the defeats suffered by Otto II in Italy encouraged the Slavs in their great rebellion.

Between the Elbe and the Oder various Wendish tribes were settled, who had never combined in any comprehensive political unit: the Wagrians in eastern Holstein, the Obotrites in Mecklenburg, the Pomeranians on the Oder, the Liutizi, the most numerous and the most turbulent, in Brandenburg, the Hevellians on the Havel. These primitive pagan tribes, torn by civil strife but inured to war by their constant battles with the Saxons, were very jealous of their independence. When conquered, they submitted to Christianity and the payment of tribute: as soon as the danger was past, they rejected both.

Throughout the eleventh century the Germans made little or no progress, the more so because after the extinction of the Saxon dynasty the emperors lost interest in these regions. The Franconian dynasty, native to south Germany, was deeply involved in Italian affairs and the Investiture struggle: neither Henry IV nor Henry V could or would intervene beyond the Harz mountains.

The only lasting result of the work of the Ottonian emperors was the creation of the Polish Church, which survived thanks to the conversion of the ruling dynasty. Politically, however, this offered only slender advantages, since the founding of the archbishopric of Gniezno in 1100 freed the Polish Church from German influence. Throughout the eleventh century and the early years of the twelfth the Polish princes, some of them tributary vassals of the Empire, others independent, sought to obtain the royal title and to extend their influence over the peoples living between the rivers Oder and Elbe, which occasioned frequent clashes with the Empire. In the north the situation was not very different. The kingdom of Denmark, which included Schleswig, Jutland, the islands and Skania, had been subject to German influence as long as the Danish Church was part of the archbishopric of Bremen–Hamburg. This dependence ceased with the creation of the archbishopric of Lund (1104), but relations between the two realms remained cordial as they continued to make common cause against the predatory Wends.

Nevertheless from the early years of the twelfth century onwards conditions favoured a permanent German advance beyond the Elbe. Missionary efforts were redoubled. In the region of the Oder, Bishop Otto of Bamberg, at the instigation of Boleslav of Poland, undertook between 1124 and 1127 two missions to the Pomeranians: his efforts were crowned with success; thousands of people were converted and churches were built for them. At the same time the archbishop of Bremen sent missionaries to Holstein, principally to Old Lübeck. Although their success under their leader Vicelin was jeopardised by a pagan reaction, Christianity nevertheless took a decisive step forward, thanks to the arrival of numerous German settlers after 1140. It was even possible for a moment to believe that a full-scale military expedition would result in complete conversion. In 1147 Bernard of Clairvaux authorised the north Germans to direct their crusade, originally planned for the Holy Land, against the pagan Slavs. Two sizeable armies, supported by the Poles and the Danes, crossed the Elbe, but failed to seize the fortified places of the Liutizi and the Obotrites. They were forced to beat a retreat, and the great crusade remained an isolated episode.

However from the political point of view the reign of Lothair III, undistinguished in other respects, was to be of decisive importance in this region. Duke of Saxony since 1106, Lothair's extensive possessions enabled him to act with an authority which his predecessors had lacked. When he became king in 1125, he did not neglect the interests of the Saxons. He intervened successfully in the dynastic struggles in Denmark; he obtained the submission of the rebellious Obotrite princes, Pribislav and Niclot, and he finally forced Boleslav to come to Merseburg and do homage for Pomerania and Rügen. But above all he took important decisions which resulted in the consolidation of the eastern German territories. As duke of Saxony, he had in 1110 granted the countyship of Holstein to Adolf I of Schauenburg, whose son was to be the founder of Lübeck. In 1134, as emperor, he entrusted the Northern March to Albert the Bear, who methodically set about its conquest. Finally by giving his daughter's hand in marriage to the Guelph Henry the Proud, he secured for his son-in-law the succession as duke of Saxony, which in 1142 passed to Henry's son, Henry the Lion. In this way three dynasties were founded which were to devote all their energies to the German colonisation of the east. When we add that Lothair III granted the merchants of Gotland privileges in the duchy of Saxony, probably on reciprocal terms, it becomes evident that he was the main originator of the political and commercial expansion of the Germans.

However neither the royal will nor princely ambition nor the sermons of the missionaries would have been enough to alter the character of the age-long conflict between Slavs and Germans. The decisive factor was the immigration, in successive waves from the twelfth to the fourteenth century, of hundreds of thousands of Germans. The overpopulation of western Germany, the growing scarcity of arable land, the excessive fragmentation of farms, as well as the emancipation of the peasantry from the manorial system, all combined to set in motion and maintain emigration from all the western regions. Saxons, Westphalians, Rhinelanders, Hollanders, Flemings and Franconians all took part in it, attracted by the promise of land and the prospect of quick prosperity. The first wave of immigrants, which began in the middle of the twelfth century, turned principally towards Holstein and Brandenburg. In a famous passage, written in about 1170, Helmold of Bosau describes this brilliantly successful colonisation: 'God having abundantly granted good fortune and victory to our duke and other princes, the Slavs have been put to flight on every hand. From the confines of the Ocean valiant and innumerable multitudes of people have been called in; they have occupied the lands of the Slavs, they have built towns and churches and have increased their wealth beyond all expectation.' The occupation of the land by the peasants was accompanied everywhere by the establishing of merchant towns, which later were to make possible the foundation and expansion of the Hansa.

3. THE RISE OF THE TOWNS

It is obvious that the development of the Hansa was in fact closely linked with that of the towns. In its essence, and in all its activities, the Hansa was urban. Its birth, in the second half of the twelfth century, occurred at a time when the long evolutionary process of the older towns was coming to an end and a start was being made in the founding of new towns, whose number was to show an extraordinary increase in the thirteenth century.

In north-west Germany the future Hansa cities of any importance were almost all old-established towns, whose urban character had developed slowly from the tenth to the thirteenth century, in the way so often described, but with a number of local variations. This entailed an increase in population in certain favourably situated settlements as artisans moved in from the country and merchants set up permanent establishments; the amalgamation, within a single fortified area, of a merchant quarter – called *wiek* in north Germany – and an older administrative centre, either ecclesiastical or lay; the development of a uniform code of law, peculiar to the town and its inhabitants and dealing especially with matters of real estate and trade; the creation of a community of burgesses, often bound together by oath; the preponderant influence in this community (at least in the more important centres) of the merchants, sometimes grouped together in a guild; the annexation of the government by the richest families, or patriciate; the growing independence of the town in relation to the local feudal lord; and finally the development of administrative institutions controlled by the burgesses, among which the council (*Rat*) – which does not appear until the very end of the twelfth century – became everywhere the controlling organ in the now fully developed town.

In the area under discussion the oldest town, the only one dating back to the Roman period, was Cologne. Because of its economic importance and its early development, Cologne played an important part in the rise of the towns of north-west Germany. It deserves the name, given it by Planitz, of the 'mother of the German towns'.

During the whole of the Middle Ages Cologne continued to be the focal point of intense commercial activity. A new phase in its development had begun with the Carolingian epoch and the Norman invasions. A colony of merchants, in which Frisians no doubt played the leading role, had been set up between the Roman wall and the river Rhine around a vast rectangular market-place, which was to become the model for many other trading cities. By the middle of the tenth century this quarter was linked with the town by a surrounding wall. As the population grew, a second enclosure, taking in other new districts, was built at the beginning of the twelfth century, and the area of the town was increased to 197 hectares, a figure unsurpassed by any other contemporary European town except Constantinople. A new wall, the last to be built in the Middle Ages, was constructed towards the end of the century, again considerably increasing the area of the town (401 hectares). At the same time Cologne's political organisation was perfected. Its inhabitants, grouped in parishes, were united under the direction of the merchant guild into a single urban community, with the jurymen (*Schöffen*) of the archiepiscopal court as its executive organ. This community rose against the archbishop in 1074; in 1106 the common bond among its members was confirmed by the taking of a mutual oath, and six years later it was recognised by the archbishop. From this time on the city was responsible for its own administration under the direction of the powerful 'Rich Men's Club' (*Richerzeche*), which comprised the great merchants and property-owners. It had its own seal and, by the middle of the twelfth century, a townhall; the town council (*Rat*) did not, however, appear until 1216. Finally the early and important economic development of Cologne accounts for the formulation of a code of civic law as early as the eleventh century, much earlier than anywhere else. The principles which governed the organisation of the merchant guild, their rights over the market buildings and the laws concerning real estate greatly influenced the law codes of newer towns all over Germany. The role played by Cologne in the development of urban institutions in other towns must not, of course, be exaggerated. Its law code did not inspire that of Soest to the extent that used to be believed; the guild did not by any means always play a decisive role, nor did the college of *Schöffen*; above all several Rhenish towns, as well as Soest and Lübeck, had a town council before Cologne. It is nevertheless true that in all essentials Cologne initiated urban life in north-west Germany.

The towns on the right bank of the Rhine had no Roman antecedents. Usually they rose around fortified places erected after Charlemagne's conquest of Saxony. The cathedral and the episcopal castle, or a royal palace, as in Dortmund and Soest, became the nucleus of the future city. Many of these urban settlements were endowed, from the ninth to the eleventh century, with the right of holding markets, which made a greater or smaller contribution to their development depending on how favourably they were situated for economic growth.

Like the towns to the west of the Rhine, but at a later date, these medieval towns were formed by the amalgamation of a lay or ecclesiastical nucleus and merchants' quarter. The earliest example is Magdeburg: the wall around the town, begun by Otto the Great, was finished in 1023. Elsewhere the amalgamation did not take place until the twelfth century, as at Goslar (1108), Dortmund, Hildesheim, Bremen and Erfurt (about 1150). Also during the first half of the twelfth century there appeared, following not long after that of Cologne, a community of burgesses, sometimes in possession of important administrative functions. At Soest and at Halberstadt, as early as 1105, the burgesses controlled food supplies and weights and measures, and exercised jurisdiction in cases of fraud arising from these matters, electing their own judges and jurymen.

The formulation of an urban law code, in which local customs were combined with royal and seigniorial rights and borrowings from foreign codes, was a decisive factor in urban evolution. Although these codes were not usually written down before the thirteenth century, several go back to the first half of the twelfth. In Westphalia the oldest is that of Soest (*c.* 1100), which was passed on to various neighbouring towns. Introduced, with modifications, in Lübeck, it was taken from there along the Baltic shores as far as Estonia. The Dortmund code, in which more markedly Flemish and Rhenish influences can be detected, was adopted by most Westphalian towns, Dortmund remaining the supreme court (*Oberhof*) dealing with appeals and legal interpretation. Similarly in Saxony the Goslar code was adopted by several towns north and south of the Harz. But the Magdeburg code had the most far-reaching sphere of influence; from the end of the twelfth century it was adopted, with variations, by hundreds of eastern European towns where it was considered to be 'the German law' *par exellence*.

The end of the twelfth century saw the rise of the new towns, founded at a definite date and acquiring in a few years all the urban characteristics. Topographically they can be distinguished from the older towns by a more regular plan and the checker-board pattern of their streets. Although the ambition of lay and ecclesiastical lords caused them to be in excessive numbers, few of them on this side of the river Elbe were able to rival the older towns in importance. Among the more successful ones may be mentioned Lippstadt in Westphalia, founded in 1168 by a vassal of the archbishop of Cologne, which adopted the Soest code, and Stendal in the Altmark, founded by Albert the Bear.

One must not, however, make too sharp a distinction between old and new towns. Several of the former were stimulated in their development by the later foundation at their very gates of a new suburb, of a twin-town in fact. This was the case with Lüneburg, and above all with Hamburg, which became a busy seaport only when Adolf III, count of

Holstein, founded a merchant town opposite the archiepiscopal city in 1188.

One of the peculiar characteristics of north Germany is the large number of double or even multiple towns. Two or three urban establishments were often founded on the same site at different times, and their functions were not always clearly distinguished. Instead of joining together in a single town, they developed independently, each one retaining its own city wall, its citizen community, even its own council; amalgamation came very slowly, and was sometimes interrupted by periods of regression. The most remarkable example of this is Brunswick, which in medieval times was the largest town in Lower Saxony. On the right bank of the river Oker a trading-post, the *Alte Wiek*, was in existence as early as the tenth century, while on the left bank the scene was dominated by a ducal castle and a fortified church, in whose neighbourhood in the eleventh century a merchant quarter (*Altstadt*) was set up around a rectangular market-place. In the second half of the twelfth century two new towns were founded, Hagen on the right bank and Neustadt on the left. Up to 1269 Altstadt, Hagen and Neustadt each had their separate councils, and later on Alte Wiek and Sack also had their own. Although in 1269 a single council, common to all five towns, was set up to deal with matters of common interest, the older organisations still continued to exist, wielding powers about which we have little detailed information. At Hildesheim, similarly, there were three towns each with its own council, Altstadt (eleventh century), Dammstadt, the Flemish weavers' quarter (late twelfth century) and Neustadt (early thirteenth century). At Osnabrück the Old Town and the New Town (mid-thirteenth century) did not unite until 1306, though at Hamburg the amalgamation took place as early as 1215, less than twenty years after the foundation of the New Town. In eastern Germany, later on, this pattern was frequently repeated as at Brandenburg, Berlin-Cölln, Danzig, Königsberg and Reval.

To what extent was this urban development paralleled in Slav territory, prior to German colonisation? The earlier theory, that urban life in its entirety was brought into these lands by the Germans, who founded cities in virgin territory or beside simple fishing villages, has now been abandoned. Recent studies have shown that not only in Poland but also in Mecklenburg and Pomerania urban centres were growing up between the tenth and the twelfth centuries, by a process similar to that found in western Europe.

From archaeological researches, and from the narratives of Adam of Bremen (*c.* 1075) and Helmold (a century later) it can be deduced that the Slav towns were essentially fortified places, but that in addition to their military and religious institutions they might also include one or more unfortified trading centres where foreign merchants – Frisians, Germans or Scandinavians – stayed from time to time. Little beyond their military role is known of such places of the Obotrites as Oldenburg, Demmin or Ratzeburg; however there was a colony of 400 Frisians living at Süsel, and at Old Lübeck the Slav Prince Henry installed, at the beginning of the twelfth century, a number of merchants and craftsmen outside the walls of the eleventh-century fortified settlement.

We are somewhat better informed about the Pomeranian towns. Besides Belgard and Kolberg, mentioned as fortified places, both Jumne, on the island of Wollin at the mouth of the Oder, and Stettin were very busy commercial centres. According to Adam of Bremen the former was the 'largest city of all Europe'. The settlement was four kilometres long and its extensive commercial relations explain the alleged presence of 'Slavs, Greeks, Barbarians and Saxons'. The town was already declining at the beginning of the twelfth century, but the fact that Christian missionaries set up a bishopric there in 1140 (soon transferred to Kammin on the other shore of the strait) proves that it retained a certain importance. Jumne has been identified with the fabulous Vineta of the Scandinavian sagas. It is said to have been engulfed by the sea as a punishment for the immorality of its inhabitants, but sailors sometimes heard its church bells pealing under the water.

At this time Stettin was the most densely populated of the Pomeranian towns. In about 1160 the chronicler Herbord counted there 900 heads of families, that is to say about 5,000 people. It was under the protection of a ducal castle, around which no doubt some nobles (*primates*) had settled, dominating the town and summoning the assembly of the 'people' at their pleasure. Alongside the city walled merchant colonies had been set up, in which, since the missionary expeditions of Otto of Bamberg, Germans had become ever more numerous. Similar urban settlements with wooden walls have been discovered particularly in Poland, at Poznan, Gniezno, Kalisz, Breslau and Cracow, and also in Prussia, at Truso near Elbing. The great weakness of these Slav towns appears to have been the lack of a law code protecting the merchants, which accounts for the popularity of the German codes, adopted from the thirteenth century even by purely Slav towns. This lack, together with the influx of German settlers summoned by local lords because of their superior commercial technique and greater skill as craftsmen, explains why, in the Hanseatic area, new foundations have almost completely effaced all traces of this early urban development.

CHAPTER TWO

The Founding of the German Cities of the East and the Gotland Community (c.1150–c.1280)

I. THE FOUNDING OF LÜBECK

TOWARDS the middle of the twelfth century German migration towards the east, which had begun fifty years before, suddenly intensified. Like other great lords, Adolf II of Schauenburg, count of Holstein and vassal of Henry the Lion, duke of Saxony, wished to populate his lands and finally subjugate the pagan Obotrites, still masters of the eastern shore of Holstein. For this reason, says Helmold, he sent recruiting agents as far afield as Holland and Flanders to invite peasants to settle in great numbers in Holstein. His summons met with a ready response.

At the same time the count decided to found a trading establishment on the Baltic coast. The site of the future town was carefully investigated. It is probable that the choice first fell on Oldenburg, an important Wagrian centre and an episcopal see founded by Otto the Great, which had been destroyed and, though rebuilt, was now vegetating quietly; but the site was too out of the way. Old Lübeck, on the Trave, a little further downstream than the future city, was better situated; half-christianised, the place had enjoyed a certain prosperity a few years back. But the destruction of the town in 1138 had shown that the site was difficult to defend against a determined enemy.

Finally Adolf II decided on the confluence of the rivers Wakenitz and Trave, about five kilometres from the ruined township. The site was well chosen. In their winding courses the two rivers almost entirely surrounded an oblong peninsula about 135 hectares in area, whose marshy shores made defence easy. Situated about twenty kilometres from the mouth of the Trave, the town ran little risk of falling victim to a surprise attack by pirates. The Trave was deep enough for the ships of that period, and the chosen site was almost at the narrowest point of the Holstein isthmus, about fifty kilometres from Hamburg: it was bound to attract the merchants.

Helmold has left us a colourful account of the exciting beginnings of the new town.* The rapid rise of Lübeck aroused the jealousy of Henry the Lion, who did his best to ruin it, first by hostile measures, then by the foundation of a rival town, which he called *Löwenstadt*, 'Lion's Town'. But this was laid out on an unfavourable site; and the duke eventually forced his vassal to cede his rights. From that time the new Lübeck, founded definitively in 1158–9, quickly prospered, thanks to the many privileges conferred upon it.

Although Helmold's narrative goes into considerable detail, he sheds no light on many problems which have fascinated modern historians. For the actual particulars of the foundation contemporary sources give no clues at all, and we have to rely on documents of a considerably later date to study the layout of the town, and to have recourse to a comparative study of the foundation charters of other twelfth-century towns. Fifty years ago Fritz Rörig published his famous theory of 'a consortium of entrepreneurs'. He suggested that, as in the case of Freiburg in Breisgau, a group of great merchants had jointly received from the duke the entire urban area of Lübeck on condition that they established there a merchant city. This group is then thought to have divided up the land among themselves, including the small plots round the market, which were rented to craftsmen. This opinion was supported by a study of the ownership of the plots round the market, as far as this could be reconstructed with the help of the land-register of the town, which, however, dates only from 1285, more than a century after the foundation. Finally Rörig suggested, still on the basis of the distribution of property at the end of the thirteenth century, that the patriciate, that is to say the families represented on the council at that period, were descended from these founding fathers.

This thesis was at first widely accepted but today has been in part refuted. It still seems probable that the foundation of Lübeck resulted from a grant of the site to a group of settlers or to their leader: the founding charter of the New Town of Hamburg (1188) provides us with an exact account of this process. On the other hand the idea that the land was once held in common is now unanimously rejected. It is much more likely that the lots – each about 100 feet by 25 – were from the very beginning privately owned, on payment of a quit-rent which rapidly fell into abeyance. Moreover Rörig failed to demonstrate conclusively any continuity between these original settlers and the patriciate at the end

* Document No. 1.

of the thirteenth century: there is no proof that the vast urban properties of the great families as we find them around 1300 had been built up as early as the middle of the twelfth century, and in certain cases it has been proved that they were definitely of more recent formation. Nor is it probable that, as Rörig maintained, so large an area as Lübeck – 135 hectares – should have been the subject of a formal town-planning scheme agreed upon by the consortium. The foundation of 1159 doubtless involved only a limited area around the great rectangular market, which was surrounded by shops and had the cloth-hall, soon to shelter the townhall as well, in its north-east corner. The primitive settlement of 1143 remained separate, on a site which cannot be identified exactly – perhaps near the Church of St Peter. Other separate settlements were built, in the north of the peninsula around the ducal castle, facing the isthmus, and an ecclesiastical quarter in the south, near the confluence of the Wakenitz and Trave. Finally Rörig showed a tendency, especially at first, to exaggerate the dynamic role played by the founders, spurred on by the desire to found an entirely new type of town devoted to long-distance commerce on a grand scale (*Fernhandelsstadt*). In contrast his critics laid great emphasis on the considerable role played in the foundation by the duke and his officials, and also on the influence of Westphalian models and the many and various features borrowed from earlier towns. Despite these emendations, Rörig's views, still valid on many points, form one of the great creative hypotheses which for a long time have stimulated research into an important aspect of medieval history, and whose repercussions are still felt today.

The population of the new town increased rapidly. The inhabitants who returned from Löwenstadt were joined by those of Old Lübeck, which now ceased to exist; also perhaps by the German merchants of Schleswig, destroyed in 1156, as well as by those of Bardowiek, deliberately ruined by the duke himself, who now resolved to favour Lübeck by all the means in his power. As early as 1160 he caused the bishopric of Oldenburg to be transferred to Lübeck, and shortly afterwards there began almost simultaneously the construction of the Church of St Mary, near the market, and of the cathedral, both in brick. From this time on there was a steady increase over the centuries in the number of inhabitants, as craftsmen and merchants came from the west, principally from Westphalian towns. These immigrants either settled in Lübeck or, after a shorter or longer stay, set off again for the new towns of the Baltic, for Gotland or Sweden. The town being essentially a trading centre,

Henry the Lion lost no time in granting his protection to the Russian and Scandinavian merchants who frequented it, as well as exempting the merchants of Lübeck from dues throughout the duchy of Saxony.

If Lübeck was to prosper, it was important to achieve the pacification of Holstein and to put an end to the incursions of the pagans. In 1160 Henry the Lion subdued the whole territory of the Obotrites, whose chief, Niclot, was killed. He also conquered Schwerin, where a bishopric was established. However four years later Niclot's son Pribislav, despite his conversion to Christianity, was again stirring the country up against the Germans. But this was a final challenge. In 1167 he resigned himself to paying homage to the duke, who enfeoffed him with Mecklenburg, the country of the Obotrites. This fief, raised to a duchy in 1348, was to remain in the hands of the descendants of the Slav prince until the twentieth century. From now on Lübeck's link with the sea was assured, and the way made easier by the acquisition of rural territory, principally along the Trave, whose extension the town was to pursue with deter-mination over the centuries.

The urban institutions of the emergent town are known principally from the 'most honourable privileges' (*jura honestissima*) confirmed in 1188 by Frederick Barbarossa. It does not seem as if the burgesses formed a sworn association. The duke granted certain economic and adminis-trative powers, notably supervision of the recently founded mint, to a body of burgesses. From this the council originated, though its existence can be proved only from 1201. The burgesses received the right to develop the Soest law code, which the duke had granted to the town, to collect part of the profits of the administration of justice, and to be judged only by the town judge (*advocatus*) appointed by the duke, privileges which were later to be increased.

However the revolt of Henry the Lion against the emperor, and his fall in 1180, placed Lübeck in a delicate situation. As it remained faithful to the duke, Frederick Barbarossa came to besiege it in person; never-theless he accepted its submission and confirmed its privileges. The imperial protection was a first step towards the status of imperial city, granted by Frederick II in 1226. But the emperor was far away, and the count of Holstein, taking advantage of the partition of the duchy of Saxony, re-established his authority over the town in 1192. His ambitions were to be a constant threat to the independence of Lübeck.

An even more serious danger appeared suddenly at the end of the century. The Danish kingdom had been consolidated under Waldemar the Great and now, under his two sons Knut IV and Waldemar II, embarked on conquest. These two, taking advantage of the weakness of the German crown, imposed their overlordship on the princes of Mecklenburg and Pomerania. Lübeck resisted at first, although her territory was conquered. But when the news came that a merchant fleet on its way to the fair in Skania had been captured by the Danes, the town yielded. In return for the confirmation of its privileges, it recognised Waldemar 'the Victorious' as its lord. The latter then conquered Holstein, imposed his lordship on the town of Hamburg and the archbishop of Bremen, and embarked on the conquest of Estonia. Danish dominion over northern Europe seemed assured, the more so as the young Frederick II, who had other troubles, recognised Waldemar's rule over all the territories beyond the Elbe.

However Danish hegemony was fragile. When Waldemar was kidnapped and imprisoned by the count of Schwerin, all the conquered countries rose in revolt. Liberated, the king tried in vain to re-establish his position. His troops were defeated in a great battle at Bornhöved in 1227, in which the citizens of Lübeck seem to have played an important part, and at one blow his power was destroyed. In our days the battle of Bornhöved has sometimes been celebrated as an event of capital importance, which is supposed to have determined the course of history in northern Europe for centuries, comparable to the battle of Bouvines, where at about the same time the future of western Europe was decided. This is an exaggerated view. Danish power was subject to periodic prolonged eclipses throughout the Middle Ages, and a victory would not have changed matters for long. But it is certain that this feat of arms gained increased prestige for Lübeck in the countries on the shores of the Baltic.

In the previous year the city had obtained a charter from Frederick II, extending its privileges and granting it the status of a *civitas imperii*. This rank of imperial city, which was to be awarded to no other town beyond the Elbe, gave Lübeck an ascendancy which, together with its material prosperity, secured leadership in this part of the world. Less than a century after its foundation its predominance was manifest. It was the most populous and thriving city of northern Europe, its ships sailed the Baltic and the North Sea, its merchants traded in Russia, Scandinavia and England. In medieval urban history there is hardly another example of a success so sudden and so brilliant.

2. THE GOTLAND COMMUNITY

Lübeck had been founded essentially with seaborne commerce in the Baltic in view. Its inhabitants began immediately to build ships, so that its merchants, and also those from the interior, might all sail for Gotland and Russia. Perhaps as early as this, certainly only a few years later, the first cogs (*Kogge*) were being built in Lübeck harbour. It was actually in the second half of the twelfth century that this new type of ship was developed, which in the thirteenth and fourteenth centuries was to be the standard vessel of the Hanseatic fleets. Owing to the width of its hull and its ease in handling, the cog was to prove better adapted to the methods of commerce and colonisation than Scandinavian vessels.

All who wished to trade in the Baltic had to come to an understanding with the Gotlanders. Henry the Lion realised this. He reconciled the warring Germans and Gotlanders, made them swear to keep the peace (1161) and confirmed the privileges granted to the latter in the duchy of Saxony by Lothair III. From this time on the German merchants could travel to the island of Gotland. After the foundation of Lübeck they formed themselves into a sworn association at the instigation of Henry the Lion, who recognised their leader Olderic as his representative and granted him judicial powers over them, similar to those accorded the Gotlanders in Saxony.

In this way was founded the Community of German merchants regularly visiting Gotland (*universi mercatores imperii Romani Gotlandiam frequentantes*), which may be regarded in some sort as the birth of the Hansa. The Community contained merchants not only from Lübeck but also from Westphalian and Saxon towns. As early as 1165 merchants from the insignificant little town of Medebach were trading in Russia. Gradually they were joined by merchants from the new towns founded in Slav territory on the Baltic coast. Unfortunately our sources give very little indication of the constitution of the Community. It seems that each year merchants from various towns elected their 'alderman' (*Oldermann*) and swore an oath of obedience and mutual aid. It may be that the oldest Lübeck seal (first preserved on a document of 1226), which shows two men on board ship taking an oath, is a representation of this scene. In the thirteenth century there were four aldermen at the head of the Community, elected respectively by the merchants of Lübeck, Visby, Soest and Dortmund. They had the same powers as those enjoyed by the later heads of the Hanseatic *Kontore*, exercising jurisdiction over their companions and acting as their representatives to foreign powers as need arose. The Community had its own seal, adorned with a fleur-de-lis. This perhaps symbolised the royal protection which the community enjoyed, since some seals of Henry the Lion and the Emperor Henry VI also bear this emblem.

Despite the fall of Henry the Lion and the growing weakness of the imperial power, the Gotland Community, with the support of the interested towns, developed rapidly. Although the island was at first, and long remained, the principal centre of their activities, its members were not slow in following the Scandinavians to the coastal countries first of the Baltic, then of the North Sea, trading, founding settlements, obtaining privileges from princes and concluding commercial treaties with them, confirmed with the seal of the community.

However the very importance of Gotland explains why many German merchants soon decided to make their homes there rather than visit it periodically. They settled in Visby, on the west coast, where there was already a Scandinavian settlement and which by the middle of the twelfth century had several churches. Thus, at a date and by a process unknown, a German town was set up, whose seal also displayed a fleur-de-lis, but with the inscription: *Sigillum Theutonicorum in Gutlandia manentium*. A distinction was in fact being made between those Germans who merely visited the island (*frequentantes*) and those who were domiciled there (*manentes*).

In its turn the Scandinavian settlement became a town with its own seal, representing a lamb. Visby was thus a double town, in which each community had at first its own council; the two soon amalgamated, but it was taken for granted, as it was in Swedish towns later on, that the councillors should be chosen from among both nations. On the other hand the urban code of law appears to have been common to the entire town from the very beginning.

Visby was the centre of a very active trade, stimulated, apparently, by fairs, where merchants, settlers, missionaries and crusaders took in stores before setting out for Russia or Sweden. Its development was very rapid, and comparable to that of Lübeck. By the middle of the thirteenth century it was surrounded by a stone wall, 11,200 feet long, enclosing an area of about 90 hectares. Today the ruins of eighteen medieval churches still remain. The largest, that of St Mary of the Germans, built between 1190 and 1225, was the parish church of the German community. Because of its material prosperity Visby's political influence was increasing also. The town endeavoured to take the place of the Gotland Community in their role as protectors and directors of the Germans trading in Russia. The latter deposited each year at Visby the treasure-chest of the *Kontor* established in Novgorod, and the town council set itself up as court of appeal in disputes which had arisen within the *Kontor*. But these pretensions were in conflict with those of Lübeck, which from the end of the thirteenth century had been enforcing recognition of her superiority from nearly all German towns. The prosperity of Visby was thus as short-lived as it had been sudden.

3. EXPANSION TOWARDS RUSSIA AND LIVONIA

At the same time as the German merchants began to frequent Gotland, some of them followed the Scandinavians towards Russia, attracted as they were by Novgorod, an important market for oriental goods, furs and wax, just at the height of its prosperity. Here the Germans were at first associated with the Gotlanders in their 'Court of Olaf'. The text has been preserved of a commercial treaty concluded in 1189 by Prince Jaroslav with the Germans and Gotlanders jointly: stipulating similar privileges for Russian merchants, he granted them his protection for their persons and their goods, as well as legal guarantees. But in some articles, even at this early date, the Germans are referred to separately. This is the oldest known treaty made by the Hanseatics with a foreign prince, but mention is made in it of an earlier treaty.

As the Germans became more numerous they acquired, on the edge of the market-place, an establishment of their own, the *Peterhof*, granted privileges in the years 1205–7 by Prince Constantine. Even before the end of the twelfth century they had built a stone church there. The speed with which the German merchants penetrated into Russia is surprising. It can only be explained by the complaisance of the Gotlanders who, at least at first, kept strictly to the terms of the pact with Henry the Lion; acting as guides, hosts and fellow-traders in Novgorod to those who were later to oust them entirely.

The earliest regulations for the *Peterhof*, drawn up soon after the middle of the thirteenth century, afford us some details on the first organisation of the *Kontor* and on the difficulties of the passage to Novgorod. Ships and merchants coming from Gotland assembled at the mouth of the Neva, at the island of Kotlin (Kronstadt). Here an alderman was chosen, who acted as the leader of the group during the journey, and the goods were usually transferred to smaller vessels. Russian pilots took charge, and the Germans sailed up the Neva, through uninhabited lands threatened by Swedish and Karelian pirates. They emerged into Lake Ladoga and stopped at the port of Ladoga, near which they owned a church and a cemetery. A second transfer of cargo was necessary, as the Volchow was interrupted by rapids. These were negotiated with the help of a corporation of boat-towers (*vorschkerle*) and at last they arrived at Novgorod.

It seems that from the beginning two distinct groups of merchants made this journey annually, the first travelling in winter (*Winterfahrer*) and the second in summer (*Sommerfahrer*). Those arriving in autumn spent the winter at the *Peterhof*, this being the best season for obtaining the finest furs. They set out again in the spring with the first thaw, usually before the arrival of the summer merchants, who made a shorter stay, only until early autumn. There was accordingly an interval during which the court was empty: the two keys which gave access to it were entrusted, one to the archimandrite of Novgorod, the other to the abbot of the Monastery of St George. On the other hand the merchants took away the chest, which they deposited at Visby, the four keys which locked it being entrusted to the four aldermen of the Gotland Community from Visby, Lübeck, Soest and Dortmund. At first Novgorod could be reached only by this river route. But in 1201 the chronicle of Novgorod records as a heroic feat the arrival of a group of German merchants who had travelled overland from the Dvina. Thereafter groups of both winter and summer merchants, setting out from Riga or Reval and travelling via Pskov (*Landfahrer*), regularly reinforced the groups of merchants travelling by water (*Wasserfahrer*), who seem, however, to have retained a certain pre-eminence over the others.

Novgorod was not the only eastern objective of the German merchants frequenting Gotland. Still following in the steps of the Scandinavians, they were eager, as soon as Lübeck was founded, to extend their activity towards the Baltic countries and, beyond these, up the Dvina to the Russian markets in Polotsk, Vitebsk and above all Smolensk on the upper Dnieper. But here conditions were quite different from those in Novgorod. The Baltic countries were inhabited by tribes who were still pagan, Lithuanians in the south, Livonians and Letts on the lower Dvina, Finnish Estonians on the shore of the Gulf of Finland. This made commercial enterprise very risky, and commercial penetration went hand in hand with conversion, conquest and the founding of new cities.

From 1184 Meinhard, a missionary who had come from Gotland with several companions from Holstein, had converted a number of Livonians and built a church in Üxküll on the lower Dvina. The archbishop of Bremen, who dreamt of continuing the great tradition of ecclesiastical expansion in the north, consecrated him bishop of Livonia two years later. But it soon became evident that only a full-scale crusade could ensure the christianisation of the country. The new bishop, Albert (1199–1229), proved his worth by undertaking this task and bringing it to a successful conclusion. He obtained the support of Pope Innocent III, the German King Philip of Swabia, the king of Denmark, master of northern Germany at this time, the archbishop of Lund, and the city of Lübeck. Above all he enlisted the active co-operation of the Gotland Community, who equipped hundreds of crusaders and made possible their transport to Livonia.

The expedition was successful. In 1201 Albert founded Riga, settling merchants in the town and fortifying it. He also introduced the Visby code of law, later replaced by that of Hamburg, which in turn was related to that of Lübeck. Riga was made the see of a bishopric, which was detached from the province of Bremen and in 1245 raised to an archbishopric. To complete the conquest and ensure the defence of the country, he created in 1202 a military order, the *Fratres Militiae Christi*, commonly called the 'Brethren of the Sword' because of the badge which adorned their cloaks. It was significant that the new order was open not only to nobles but also to merchants. Despite the resistance of the pagans, the conquest of the Baltic countries was relatively easy. Everywhere it was accompanied by the foundation of trading establishments: for example at Dorpat, which became a city and the seat of a bishop in 1224, and at Reval, where 200 German merchants settled in 1230 side by side with Danish and Swedish colonists.

In this work of colonisation German merchants, whether as soldiers or as traders, played a highly important part. They had no intention of allowing the archbishop or the Brethren of the Sword to take over all their political rights. For example in 1226, when a crusade was undertaken against the island of Ösel, the papal legate decided that the city of Riga should receive a third of the booty. The town handed over to the Gotland Community half of its share, comprising lands to the south of Riga, on the coast of Courland, on Ösel and in Estonia.

However the preponderant influence of the travelling merchants was to be short-lived. As in Gotland the Livonian towns, having granted them equal rights with their own citizens, gradually imposed restrictions on them. In this area the need for strong defences was paramount. In 1236 the Lithuanians inflicted a crushing defeat on the Brethren of the Sword, and the whole work of conversion and colonisation appeared to be in danger. It was saved by the pagans' failure to pursue their advantage, and by the intervention of Hermann von Salza, Grand Master of the Teutonic Order, who had just embarked on the conquest of Prussia. He dispatched in haste a contingent of knights, who restored the situation. The surviving Brethren of the Sword were incorporated in the Teutonic Order, who, under a Land Master, gradually extended their conquests as far as Lake Peipus. However their work was never completed. In the south the expeditions undertaken against the Lithuanian Samogites failed to subdue them, with the result that the Teutonic state remained cut in two sections, Prussia and Livonia, between which even at a later date the only sure communication was by sea. To the north the Order was obliged for the next hundred years to recognise Danish sovereignty over Estonia as well as the subordination of its bishopric to the archbishop of Lund. Danish domination did not, however, interfere with the rising prosperity of the German towns of Reval and Narva, both endowed with the Lübeck law. Reval became more and more a base for operations and an assembling-point for German merchants travelling to Novgorod either by sea or by land.

The Teutonic Knights were less ready than their predecessors to countenance a division of authority, and they restricted considerably the powers of both the bishops and the towns. Riga and the Gotland Community lost the vast territories they had acquired, and Riga was put under the law of Hamburg instead of that of Visby – the Lübeck law was unacceptable, as the town was suspected of using the spread of its law for political ends. However trade in these regions was now assured of efficient protection.

In the eyes of the German merchants Riga was principally a base from which to develop their trade in the Russian towns of the upper Dvina. In 1212 an expedition led by Archbishop Albert compelled the prince of Polotsk to recognise the Germans' right of free passage on the river. Taking advantage of this privilege, the merchants pressed on as far as Vitebsk, then to Smolensk, a market of the first rank, which maintained commercial relations with the Black Sea, the country of Suzdal and

Novgorod. As a privileged community they bought houses in Smolensk and built their own church. They even obtained the right to sell on credit – which was later strictly forbidden by the Hansa itself – and to trade outside the town. The treaty of 1229,* from which this information is taken, is interesting because of the names of the German witnesses who guaranteed its authenticity. They included four merchants from Riga, three from Gotland, two each from Lübeck, Soest, Münster, Dortmund and Groningen, and one from Bremen. This list affords us valuable proofs of the variety of origin of the merchants in the Gotland Community and of the multiplicity of towns interested in trade with far-off Russia.

However the prosperity of the German establishment in Smolensk was in no way comparable to that of Novgorod. The Russian towns on the Dvina, Vitebsk and above all Polotsk, soon insisted on their rights as staple-markets, which forced the German merchants to remain within their walls. As a result, from the second half of the thirteenth century onwards, the latter ceased to frequent Smolensk, and Polotsk became the furthermost point at which Germans and Russians met to trade.

The energy with which the Germans pressed forward into Russia in their quest for wax and furs can easily be explained by the large demand for these commodities in western Europe. However in this period – the end of the twelfth and beginning of the thirteenth century – it is difficult to determine which were the main outlets: certainly the German towns, possibly already Flanders and perhaps the Champagne fairs. Yet the Hanseatics did not themselves take the eastern goods to these emporia but left their conveyance mainly to Flemish traders, who bought them in Saxon and Westphalian towns. There is, however, no exact evidence for this carrying trade.

4. THE FOUNDING OF GERMAN TOWNS ON THE BALTIC

While German colonisation was pushing towards Gotland and Russia, progress was also being made in eastern Germany. But here the process, though somewhat slower, was much more thorough. Military conquest, conversion and commercial penetration were accompanied by an influx of peasant settlers, especially numerous in the last third of the thirteenth century. The result of this was the Germanisation of the country up to

* Document No. 3.

and beyond the river Oder, while even further afield many Germans were helping in the creation of new towns and settling there.

Between the Elbe and the Oder all the princes, German and Slav alike, welcomed the arrival of colonists and the foundation of towns. The latter were conceived as fortresses, regional markets, trading and supply centres. With local variations, the general process was as follows: on the invitation of a local lord, a settlement was founded around a rectangular market-place, near which a parish church and town hall were built. From the beginning, or after only a few years, the settlement was recognised as a city and received a constitution and a code of law: Lübeck law on the coast, Magdeburg law or one of its derivatives in the interior. Subject at first to a seigniorial bailiff (*Vogt*), the town was soon administering its own affairs through its council (*Rat*), which was composed of members of the most influential families among the burgesses. Protected by a seigniorial castle, the town was surrounded by a palisade, replaced sooner or later by a stone wall. If the foundation prospered, a second or even a third town was soon set up alongside it. This 'new town' (*niuwe stat*), at times scarcely younger than the 'old town' (*olde stat*), was granted in its turn a constitution, a separate council and a rampart of its own. The fusion of the two towns into one institution and the building of a single wall around them usually took place much later.

It was rare for these new towns to be established on virgin soil. They were usually placed near a fortified place, a castle or an existing Slav village. At first the new settlement would include a Slav population, whose status varied from place to place, but the Slavs, whether in law or in fact, were not eligible for citizenship, which was reserved for Germans only. Even in distant Cracow, a future Hansa city, the town charter granted in 1257 by Duke Boleslav to the German colonists withheld the freedom of the city from Poles, and this ban remained in force for more than fifty years.

In the thirteenth century a series of new towns appeared along the Baltic coast which were to attain great commercial prosperity. In the planning and preparation of these Lübeck played a prominent part, and the founding merchants too came from that town. The first of the new towns was Rostock. It was founded on a site where a Slav settlement with a market of its own, frequented by the Scandinavians, had prospered in the twelfth century; but its inhabitants had been decimated by war. A colony of German merchants settled there around 1200, and in 1218 the village was recognised as a town by the princes of Mecklenburg, who granted the inhabitants the Lübeck law, a council of ten members and exemption from customs dues throughout the principality. In about 1230 a second settlement grew up around the market-place and a church dedicated to Our Lady, and later two more smaller towns arose. In 1262 the prince amalgamated them all so that there should be in future only one council and one law throughout the town, and in about 1300 a stone wall was built around the entire complex.

Wismar, though nearer to Lübeck, developed more slowly than Rostock. Here it was not the oldest German settlement of about 1200 but the second, centred on the Church of Our Lady, which in 1228 was granted the status of a city. Another new town was added to it in the middle of the thirteenth century, and the whole was then surrounded by a palisade, which was not replaced by a stone wall until about 1400. The oldest surviving town-register reveals, for the period 1250–70, the origin of the inhabitants as shown by their names: half of them came from the surrounding district, nearly a third from Holstein, Saxony, Westphalia and the Low Countries, but these had come via Lübeck.

In Pomerania, Stralsund presents the rather unusual picture of a town built directly on the coast, facing the island of Rügen. It too resulted from the fusion of three German settlements, of which the second, built around the Church of St Nicholas, became a city in 1234, under Rostock, that is to say Lübeck, law. On the Oder, Stettin, a great Slav town, contained two German quarters as early as the twelfth century, and these probably increased considerably in the thirteenth. Accordingly the duke of Pomerania decided in 1237 'to grant the city German law instead of the Slav law', to which the inhabitants were then subject. This may have been the Lübeck code, but six years later it was replaced by that of Magdeburg. The creation of these two great ports, which were to play an important role in the Hansa, was accompanied in the thirteenth century by several more modest foundations, such as that of Greifswald (1241), a future university town, Kammin, an episcopal see, Anklam, Kolberg, etc.

On the left bank of the Vistula there was Danzig, whose early history as a town is little known; but it certainly reached far back into the past. By the end of the tenth century a castle is mentioned there, in whose neighbourhood in the following century a native merchant quarter grew up. A German settlement, doubtless originating from the end of the twelfth century, was raised to the status of a city by Duke Svantopolk in 1238 and probably endowed with Lübeck law, replaced in 1343 by that of Kulm, derived from Magdeburg. But another fourteenth-century foundation, the *Rechtstadt*, around the Church of Our Lady, was destined to become the active business centre of Danzig, which was thus composed of at least five nuclei.

Inland, colonisation was vigorously pursued by the margraves of Brandenburg. But in this region the towns, even those which became members of the Hansa, developed more slowly, because of their less favourable situation. One of the oldest, Brandenburg, founded in 1170, a double town on the Havel which was not united until the eighteenth century, was the seat of a bishop and of a court of appeal for the towns of the margraviate. On opposite banks of the Spree, Berlin (about 1230) and Cölln, after an abortive attempt at fusion in the fourteenth century, were not united until 1709. Berlin, though more important than is usually supposed, thanks to its trade in grain and timber, became of real consequence only in the fifteenth century, when it became the residence of the Hohenzollerns. Finally Frankfurt-on-the-Oder (1253), despite its bridgehead situation on the river, remained quite insignificant. The towns in this area, like all those created in Silesia and Poland, with or without the aid of German settlers, were granted Magdeburg law.

Had German colonisation been limited to its first spontaneous burst of energy, the Germanisation of the country would have come to an end well to the west of the lower Vistula. But an almost fortuitous event, which was to have incalculable consequences, enabled it to extend farther east. This was the conquest of Prussia by the Teutonic Knights.

The Prussians, a branch of the Lithuanian people, had remained fiercely attached to their gods. Though Pomerellia and Danzig, on the left bank of the Vistula, had been converted to Christianity as early as the eleventh century, all the efforts of Polish missionaries on the right bank had been in vain. In 1222 a great insurrection swept away all that had been achieved, and the bishop of Prussia, appointed by Innocent III, was taken prisoner. From then on the Prussians intensified their devastating raids into Christian territory, until the duke of Masovia, vassal of the king of Poland, appealed in desperation to Hermann von Salza, Grand Master of the Teutonic Order. Hermann was searching for a new field of activity for his Order, which had been withdrawn from the East, and protracted bargaining eventually led to an agreement in 1230. The Teutonic Order was granted the district of Kulm and all the territories to be conquered from the Prussians as an independent and autonomous property.

So the foundations were laid of a new German state, of a great continuous lordship – further augmented after 1236 by the acquisition first of Livonia and then of Estonia – in which the Teutonic Order exercised almost absolute authority, apart from certain rights conceded to the bishops. However more than fifty years of warfare were needed to ensure the security of the state and the final subjugation of the Prussians, who with the help of the Lithuanians put up a desperate resistance. Their resistance explains why the conquest was carried out so much more brutally in this region than anywhere else. The inhabitants were for the most part killed or deported.

Simultaneously with the pacification of Prussia, the Teutonic Order tackled the rural and urban colonisation of Prussia in a more systematic fashion than any other rulers. Settlers were drawn for the most part from Silesia and central Germany, the principal recruiting area of the knights themselves, and later on from various parts of northern Germany.

As soon as operations began, two cities, Thorn and Kulm, were founded on the right bank of the Vistula, with castles to protect them. In 1233 Hermann von Salza granted them a charter (*Kulmer Handfeste*), on which those of other Prussian towns were later to be based. They were also granted extensive landed property, part of the revenues of the administration of justice, the urban law of Magdeburg, and a certain degree of administrative autonomy, though the Order retained control of the fortifications and placed a heavy burden of military service on the shoulders of the citizens. The two towns were to have very different destinies. The Grand Master had intended Kulm to become the capital of Prussia. He made it the seat of a bishop and gave it a court of appeal. But his plans came to nothing, and Kulm remained an insignificant townlet. In contrast, Thorn, on the border of the kingdom of Poland, was to enjoy a rapidly increasing prosperity, thanks to traffic along the Vistula, and in the fourteenth century was to become the most important Prussian city after Danzig.

Although Lübeck had played an almost negligible role in this area, it took an active part in the creation of coastal cities. Its ships supported the expeditions of the Teutonic Order and its merchants made an important contribution to the foundation of Elbing (1237), on the eastern arm of the Vistula, near ancient Truso; as a result it was granted Lübeck law, the only example of this in Prussia. Up to about the middle of the fourteenth century, when it was overtaken by Danzig, Elbing was the principal

Prussian port. In 1337 it was expanded by a new foundation, which was not incorporated until 1478. Finally in Samland, the last region to be conquered by the Teutonic Order, Königsberg was founded on the river Pregel, apparently receiving its name in honour of King Ottokar of Bohemia, who in 1255 took part in a crusade. It consisted of three townships, those of the Order, the bishop and the merchants, and was not unified until 1724.

The circumstances of their foundation explain the special characteristics of the Prussian towns. Their layout is even more regular than that of the towns lying between the Elbe and the Oder, their streets forming an impeccable checker-board pattern, a feature also found in Breslau and Cracow. Again, these towns retained for a long time a pronounced military character, with their castles and strong fortifications. Finally their strict subjugation to the Grand Master of the Teutonic Order explains why the latter was later accepted as a member of the Hansa – the only territorial prince to enjoy this privilege.

5. EXPANSION INTO SCANDINAVIA

The activity of the Lübeck merchants and the Gotland Community was directed first and foremost towards Russia. But it was soon extended also towards Scandinavia, where considerable German immigration, principally into the towns, took place during the thirteenth and fourteenth centuries. The extent of the 'eastward expansion' and its political consequences should not lead us to forget the scarcely less marked 'northward expansion'.

Almost as soon as Lübeck was founded, commercial relations were established with Sweden. Henry the Lion had concluded a treaty with Knut Eriksson (after 1173), granting the Swedes exemption from customs dues in Lübeck. From this time onwards German immigrants began to settle in Sweden, where they seem to have played an important part in urban development. Before their arrival towns had begun to develop in Sweden, the members of settlements as yet quite small forming embryonic urban communities under a royal bailiff (*gälkare*), assisted by ward leaders. The Germans introduced everywhere the institution of the council, modelled on that of their own towns. As in the east, they generally settled in groups, either in an existing town or in the immediate neighbourhood, around a rectangular market-place near which they erected their church. Not only merchants but also German craftsmen settled in Swedish towns. The importance of this influx is shown by the numerous German loan-words to be found in Swedish designations of particular trades.

At first Germans migrated into southern Sweden, especially to Kalmar, which became quite German in character, but from the middle of the thirteenth century onwards they settled principally in central Sweden. Summoned by the regent, Birger Jarl, the Germans seem to have played an important part in the foundation of Stockholm (about 1251). The creation of this town had a double objective: political, to reinforce the new Folkun dynasty; and economic, to revive commerce in the district ruined by the destruction of Sigtuna in 1187. Birger Jarl and his successors made every effort to attract German merchants and craftsmen, so that the new town might benefit from their wealth, their energy and their technical experience. In the Swedish chronicles King Magnus is blamed for the excessive favour he showed to foreigners.

The rise of Stockholm and central Sweden was encouraged in the second half of the thirteenth century by the opening of the copper mines at Falun. Here also the Germans seem to have played an important part. Miners from the Harz settled in the region and even Swedish historians agree that the organisation of the mines was probably based on that of the Rammelsberg near Goslar. German names are to be found in this period in all the little towns of the mining district. In Västerås in particular, the centre of the copper trade, the council was composed of six Germans and six Swedes. In the fourteenth century Lübeck citizens are known to have owned shares in Swedish mines.

Although Germans do not seem to have formed a majority of the population in any Swedish town, their influence was for a long time predominant in the artisan guilds and in commerce, and therefore in municipal administration. As late as 1345 a royal ordinance laid down that town councils should be composed half of Swedes and half of Germans, a rule which even in later years was still being broken in favour of the Germans.

The number of German immigrants and their leading role in commerce constituted a serious threat to the national development of Sweden, whose economy was in danger of becoming too narrowly dependent on the Hansa. However this did not happen, firstly because Sweden, unlike Norway, was able to maintain a prosperous agricultural and stock-breeding industry, so that its population did not need to rely on the import of German cereals; secondly, and principally, because the Swedish royal house from the outset tried to assimilate the foreigners, instead of granting them privileges harmful to their own subjects. As early as 1251, in the treaty concluded by Birger Jarl, it was specified that natives of Lübeck settling and living in Sweden 'should be subject to the laws of the land and should henceforward be called Swedes'. The effect of this wise enactment was to prevent the formation of German communities privileged in law if not in fact, and to encourage the fusion of the two nationalities. This fusion was complete in the small inland towns as early as the fourteenth century, but in the larger towns was not realised until the end of the fifteenth century.

In Denmark, as was only natural, German immigrants were even more numerous than in Sweden. In Schleswig in particular Germans at times formed the majority of the town populations: the code of Tondern (1243), based on that of Lübeck and written in Low German, is an indication of this. Even in the islands, and especially Copenhagen, the German element became preponderant in the artisan class and in commerce. However this did not make Denmark proper a region of more than minor importance for the Hanseatic merchants, who could buy little but cattle there.

The position was very different in Skania, owing to the herring fishery. On the western shore of the peninsula herrings were to be found in such abundance, according to Saxo Grammaticus (late twelfth century), that one could catch them by hand and they were a hindrance to navigation. The fisheries here were certainly very ancient, but it was not until the Lübeck merchants arrived, bringing salt from Lüneburg, that a great trade in salt fish developed. Practically nothing is known of the early stages of this trade, which centred on the fair at Skanör, in the peninsula of the same name: it probably belonged to the earliest years of the thirteenth century. The merchants from Lübeck were soon joined by others from Saxon and Westphalian towns, and then from ports established along the Baltic shore as far away as Danzig and Riga. Several of these towns acquired plots of land near Skanör – Danish *ved*, Low German *vitte* – where the salting was done and business transacted at the time of the fair.

Towards the middle of the thirteenth century the Skania fair became international, as Norwegians, Englishmen and Dutchmen began to attend it. In the texts they are described as 'circumnavigators' (*umlandsfarer*) because their ships sailed round Jutland. Although salt fish remained the most important commodity, woollen and linen textiles, salt, grain, hides and beer were also sold. Skania's prosperity was, however, short-lived, for when the Germans realised how much its international fair was competing with their own east–west trade, they became uneasy. By the end of the thirteenth century they had succeeded in preventing Flemish, Frisian and English ships from penetrating into the Baltic, and the Skanian fairs gradually became nothing more than a herring market, monopolised by the Hanseatics.

In Norway merchants from Lübeck are first to be found towards the end of the twelfth century. Here again it was hard on the heels of the Scandinavians that the Lübeck merchants arrived at Bergen, the country's busiest port, which had long enjoyed commercial relations with Bremen. They traded rye, flour and malt for dried cod, fish-oil, butter and hides. We do not know how relations were initiated, but a letter of Haakon IV (1248), in which he begs Lübeck for a shipment of grain to avert a grave famine, shows us that by this time western Norway was already dependent on food supplies from north Germany. When one remembers that in the twelfth century the Norwegians were carrying on a flourishing trade with all the North Sea countries, this may cause some surprise. It seems that since that time the population had greatly increased and Norwegian farmers were not only unable to increase their productivity but also because of the competition from foreign grain, were turning to other activities, which a royal ordinance (1260) tried in vain to prevent. Moreover Norwegian vessels of traditional design were incapable of transporting bulk products in sufficient quantities.

Lübeck did not fail to exploit this favourable situation. Important privileges were obtained for Lübeck and the other Wendish towns, facilitating their wholesale and retail trade, exempting their merchants from public duties and granting them legal safeguards. The German ascendancy was already so marked that the kings attempted to shake it off, but the trial of strength (1284) led only to a consolidation of Hanseatic supremacy in Norway.

6. COMMERCIAL EXPANSION TOWARDS THE WEST

From the thirteenth century onwards German trade began to expand across the North Sea, towards England and the Low Countries, though it did not take the form, as it did in the east and north, of massive immigration and colonisation. It remained strictly commercial in character, with groups of merchants establishing increasingly close relations with English ports and with Bruges.

As we have seen, trade had already been carried on for a long time between Cologne, Bremen and England. The new factor in the thirteenth century was the appearance in the North Sea, in rapidly increasing numbers, of merchants coming from the east – later to be called 'Easterlings' or 'Osterlings' – principally from Lübeck, but also from Visby, from Baltic ports such as Rostock, Stralsund, Elbing and Riga, and from Saxon inland towns. They were not yet making the sea passage direct from the Baltic. The journey round Jutland seemed too long and dangerous, so they crossed the isthmus from Lübeck to Hamburg, where they embarked for England or Flanders. Regular travel by sea from the Baltic to the North Sea did not develop until the second half of the thirteenth century, following the example of English and Flemish ships visiting the fairs in Skania.

Since obtaining their first privileges in London in 1157, the Cologne merchants had considerably increased their business in England, taking advantage of the political alliance between the Guelphs and Plantagenets. In 1175 they had obtained the right to trade freely throughout the kingdom, and Richard Lionheart, in gratitude for the three ships which they fitted out for his crusade, freed their London house from all imposts. Lübeckers and other merchants from the east seem to have begun to visit English ports regularly at the beginning of the thirteenth century, first going to Yarmouth, Lynn, Hull and Boston and then to London; perhaps here too they were following in the footsteps of the Gotlanders.

The Cologne merchants were naturally enough not very pleased when these new arrivals appeared on the scene, and looked on them as intruders. Their ill-will was so evident that Frederick II thought it necessary to intervene, and in the charter which he granted to Lübeck in 1226 he called on them to cease persecuting the citizens of the town of Lübeck, to whom he granted privileges equal to those of the Cologne merchants. The concessions were of no great practical value, but the kings of England could not but be well-disposed towards these foreigners who were bringing eastern products, wax and furs into their country. In 1237 Henry III conferred his protection on the merchants of the Gotland Community and exempted them from customs dues on all goods bought and sold by them within the realm. Thirty years later, as the affairs of the Easterlings prospered, the king granted them equal rights with the Cologne merchants. In 1266 the merchants from Hamburg, and in the following year those of Lübeck, were given the privilege of forming a

Hansa of their own on the model of that of the merchants of Cologne. It is in these two documents that we find for the first time the word 'hansa' applied to groups of merchants from north Germany.

For a long time these privileges were not sufficient to put an end to the feud between Cologne and Lübeck. It was certainly not easy to establish harmony between the interests of the long-established Rhineland commercial axis and those of the new east–west traffic, the true Hanseatic highway. However the existence of three competing associations was soon felt to be harmful to all of them. The disadvantages were most keenly felt by the Westphalians, who shared in both the Rhenish and the eastern trade. They therefore acted as intermediaries and in 1281 managed at last to effect a reconciliation. From now on there officially existed in London a single 'German Hansa', under the authority of an alderman, elected by the merchants and confirmed in his office by the city. It is significant that the alderman in that decisive year and three of his successors were natives of Dortmund. A privilege granted in that same year by the mayor of London tells us what obligations were imposed upon the Germans: they paid an annual rent of forty shillings for their Guildhall and shared in the guard duties and maintenance of one of the city gates, Bishopsgate.

What the three rival groups of German merchants had formed was, in effect, a federation. A true amalgamation was not achieved until the fifteenth century. The merchants of Cologne – together with those of Dinant – retained exclusive control over the Guildhall, and after 1324 they no longer admitted merchants from other towns, who had to establish their own buildings in the Steelyard. Nevertheless it can be said that 1281 saw the foundation of the Hanseatic *Kontor* in London.

It was not until fairly late, in the early years of the thirteenth century, that German merchants, even from Cologne, appeared in Flanders. This is something of a paradox, considering the short distance from the Rhineland and the unique place held by Bruges in the history of the Hansa. It is evidently to be explained by the activity of the Flemish merchants, whose business was still expanding, not only in Cologne, but in Bremen and Hamburg, and in Saxon and even Baltic towns.

However during the second quarter of the thirteenth century the number of German merchants regularly visiting Bruges and other ports on the Zwijn increased considerably. Merchants from Cologne and Westphalia doubtless came overland, while most of those from Bremen,

Hamburg and Lübeck came by sea. In contrast to what had happened in London, no conflict arose between merchants from Cologne and Lübeck. The former had no long-established privileges to defend and were principally concerned with retailing their wine in the Flemish towns; and for buying cloth for resale in England other Flemish and Brabantine towns were more suitable.

The growing importance of the German colony in Flanders is shown by the curious project, approved by Margaret, countess of Flanders, in 1252, of founding a privileged merchants' quarter near Damme, in which all the German merchants were to be grouped together. This 'New Damme' would have been the Flemish counterpart of the London Steelyard and the Novgorod *Peterhof*. However the plan came to nothing, perhaps because of excessive demands made by the Germans and a lack of enthusiasm on the part of the citizens of Bruges, who might well be perturbed by the establishment of a group of privileged foreigners. Perhaps too the Germans, scattered about the various ports on the Zwijn, found that their dispersion had definite advantages. Whatever the reason, the outcome was that Bruges was the only one of the four great foreign *Kontore* where the Germans, instead of being secluded in a separate quarter, lived among the native population. This could not fail to be of great consequence, not only for their trade, but also for their cultural contacts.

In 1252 and 1253 the countess of Flanders conferred a series of privileges on the German merchants, one of which was granted expressly to those 'who are of the Roman Empire and frequent Gotland'. They obtained legal security, reductions of the customs dues in Bruges and Damme, laid down in the greatest detail, and in the latter town a weigh-house of their own. These privileges, later increased, were the foundation of the prosperity of Hanseatic commerce in Flanders.

In the following years Hanseatic trade increased, though it is not possible to quantify it statistically. This boom was matched by that of Bruges, rapidly becoming the central market of the western world, where merchants from every country were to be seen. Englishmen, Scots and Irishmen brought the wool essential to the textile industry; Hollanders and Frisians brought their cattle; merchants from La Rochelle and Bayonne brought their wine. All the Iberian peoples were represented, Basques, Navarrese, Castilians and Portuguese, bringing wool and Mediterranean fruit. As the Champagne fairs declined in importance, Italians came and settled in great numbers, making Bruges the principal financial centre of northern Europe. From the end of the thirteenth century onwards Genoese and later Venetian galleys took their cargo of spices directly to the Zwijn.

Attracted by the almost boundless commercial opportunities which Bruges offered, Germans came in increasing numbers. The natives of Bremen brought with them their beer, much in demand at this time. Merchants from Lübeck and Hamburg were the most numerous, and two streets in the town were called after them (1282, 1306). A privilege of Philip the Fair, granted to the German merchants in Flanders, makes special mention of those from the Wendish towns, from Elbing, Gotland and Riga: these Easterlings brought furs, wax, ashes and cereals. Among the Saxon towns Brunswick was the most active, several aldermen of the *Kontor* coming from there. In Westphalia Dortmund was indisputably the most important, so long as Cologne remained aloof. All these merchants came thronging above all to buy Flemish cloth, whose infinite variety could satisfy any clientele.

Although Bruges was the main centre of their activity, they also frequented other Flemish towns and especially the fairs, notably those of Thourout and Ypres. For the years 1272–86 there are still in existence bills of exchange in which Germans appear as creditors: 16 from Lübeck, 9 from Cologne, 2 each from Hamburg, Brunswick and Dortmund. Finally the Hanseatics were to be found also at the Champagne fairs, where in the second half of the thirteenth century there is mention of merchants mainly from Cologne but also from Westphalia, and of one merchant from Magdeburg. But here again Lübeck seems to hold first place, for a charter of Philip the Fair (1294) authorised its citizens to return by any route they pleased if they were carrying German goods, but only through Bapaume if they had bought goods in Flanders. There is even a record of a citizen of Lübeck settled in Troyes acting on behalf of his native town.

7. DECLINE OF THE GOTLAND COMMUNITY

Thus in little more than a hundred years Hanseatic trade developed with extreme rapidity in the northern seas. Everywhere Germans were ousting their competitors, particularly in the Baltic but also in the North Sea. They went so far as to stop the Gotlanders passing westwards through the Danish straits, and the Frisians, Flemings and English eastwards. They even got hold of the trade between Norway and

England. In all the coastal countries they had acquired important privileges which gave their commerce a fresh impetus.

The motive power for this expansion had been provided by the Gotland Community. However by the mid-thirteenth century this organisation was declining. The paradox is only apparent. It was difficult for a simple fraternity of travelling merchants to deal with problems which became steadily more complex as their business expanded. In addition the authority and strength of this fraternity rested in the last resort on the support given to it by the towns, especially Lübeck, where most of the merchants started their journeys, and Visby, the principal centre of their trade. As the towns developed, establishing contacts among themselves and increasing in political power, they were bound to look askance at an association which claimed to be a separate authority and whose decisions might drag them into costly and dangerous enterprises.

It follows therefore that the Gotland Community was bound to disappear. From the middle of the thirteenth century onwards it no longer had any real existence, as can be seen in an agreement concluded in 1280 between Lübeck and Visby, to which Riga acceded a little later. These cities undertook to combine their powers and resources to protect against all attacks and losses the German merchants trading from the Sound to Novgorod. This had previously been the responsibility of the Gotland Community, but it is not even mentioned.

One would have expected a new organisation for the protection of the merchants, in the form of an association of the interested cities, to have taken the place of the older one. But at the time when the first regional town leagues were only just being formed, so vast a combination would have been premature. Instead Visby and Lübeck seemed ideally suited to undertake the task together. But as each of them wished to be the sole authority, a conflict broke out between them. The struggle was brief, for the power and widespread influence of Lübeck gave it an incontestable superiority. In 1293 an assembly of Wendish towns resolved that the court of appeal for the *Kontor* in Novgorod should be transferred from Visby to Lübeck, and asked all the towns concerned to give their verdict. Almost without exception the towns from the Rhineland to Prussia agreed to the move. Only Riga, Osnabrück and perhaps one or two other Westphalian towns, jealous of the supremacy of Lübeck, voted for Visby. The pre-eminence of Lübeck was patent: as two towns* on the Zuiderzee wrote enthusiastically at the time, Lübeck

* Document No. 15 (*a*).

was recognised as the leader of the merchant towns of northern Germany.

However the Gotland Community still existed in theory. Lübeck seems to have been afraid that Visby would use it in an attempt to restore its own influence, and consequently, in 1298, moved the assembly of Wendish towns to decree that the Gotland Community should no longer have a seal of its own, which might be used to seal a document unwelcome to the other towns. Thus, long after it had ceased to function, the legal existence of the Community was brought to an end.

It had nonetheless been of considerable importance, uniting the merchants of some scores of German towns, both ports and inland cities, from Cologne to Riga, co-ordinating their activities and obtaining for them privileges in foreign countries. When it disappeared, the common interest which had caused it to come into being, and which it had strengthened, continued to exist, but it was not until the middle of the fourteenth century that this first form of Hanseatic organisation was succeeded by another, the Hansa of the towns.

CHAPTER THREE

Towards the Hansa of the Towns
(c.1250–c.1350)

I. THE FIRST URBAN LEAGUES

As early as the mid-thirteenth century the cities tried to take over from the Gotland Community the protection of German merchants abroad. Although a comprehensive union was delayed by political circumstances, it was facilitated and brought nearer by the creation of regional urban leagues. Throughout Germany the towns, newly come to power, were faced by the anarchy resulting from the failure of imperial power, and so formed alliances destined to safeguard peace and defend their own privileges. In the north no association attained the size of the ephemeral Rhenish Town League (1254). Here, on the other hand, smaller groups showed greater efficiency and stability than was found in the south. Neither then nor later, however, were these leagues specifically Hanseatic, since the defence of political interests and the struggle against the encroachments of territorial rulers took precedence over commercial objectives.

In 1246 two urban leagues appeared simultaneously, one in Westphalia, the other in Lower Saxony. The first included Münster, Osnabrück, Minden, Herford, Coesfeld 'and the other affiliated towns'; its aim was to ensure free access to their markets and to make common cause against all aggressors. Seven years later another league was formed, linking Münster, Dortmund, Soest and Lippstadt. These coalitions were several times renewed and resulted in an almost permanent association of the Westphalian towns, in which the most important, Dortmund, played the leading role. The Saxon town league originated as an alliance between Münden and Northeim and became effective twenty years later, when the town of Ghent, exasperated by the indignities suffered by its merchants, announced that in retaliation the goods of all Saxon merchants within her borders would be seized. A protest was immediately made by Lüneburg, Quedlinburg, Halberstadt, Helmstedt, Goslar,

Hildesheim, Brunswick, Hanover and Wernigerode, to which Hamburg, Stade and Bremen, and later Magdeburg, acceded. After a period of weakness at the beginning of the fourteenth century this league of Saxon towns, under the leadership of Brunswick, became one of the best organised of all.

However for the history of the Hansa the formation of the league of 'Wendish towns' is more important. Strictly speaking, this term, encountered for the first time in 1280, is applicable only to the new towns in Wendish territory, that is to say to Lübeck, Kiel, Wismar, Rostock and later Stralsund, though Hamburg and Lüneburg are normally included, as they were closely connected with the others in most matters. The league was based on the association initiated in 1230 between Hamburg and Lübeck, when the former told her neighbour that she was granting equal rights to the citizens of Lübeck passing through her territory and expressed the wish that the traditional friendship between the two cities should be maintained. In 1241 they concluded a formal treaty, agreeing to share the expense of keeping the roads between Hamburg and Lübeck free from brigands. It was also agreed that any criminal banished from one city would be banished from the other. A new agreement was made in 1259, preceded four years earlier by a monetary convention fixing an equal par value for the pfennig minted in both cities. From this time on consultations on matters of all kinds were frequently held, and despite inevitable disagreements, the alliance, based on the complementary interests of the two towns, went from strength to strength.

It was not so easy at first to bring about a *rapprochement* with the new Baltic towns. Lübeck seems to have been troubled by the rising prosperity of her neighbours, who might well become her rivals. Stralsund was sacked in 1249 by a Lübeck fleet and we know, though without any of the details, that at this time relations between Lübeck and Rostock were also very strained. However a reconciliation was arranged by Wismar in 1256, both cities surrendering all claims to compensation for the damage inflicted. Three years later the three cities agreed to join together to combat piracy, and in 1264 a formal alliance was concluded at Wismar for one year. The treaty dealt with piracy, as before, but also with mutual assistance in case of war against a territorial prince, and with points of civil law. An interesting detail is that all decisions of the league were to apply to towns using Lübeck law, of which there were so many all along the shores of the Baltic. Obviously Lübeck's intention was to use the wide diffusion of its law for political ends. But the attempt was unsuccessful, no doubt because of the resistance encountered in the east, and Lübeck had to be content with the support provided by the Wendish towns. In 1265 these reaffirmed their alliance, this time without limiting its duration, and pledged themselves to annual consultations on matters of common interest. From now on the Wendish League may be considered a permanency: it was reinforced by the more or less constant adherence of the Pomeranian towns, which in addition to Stralsund included Greifswald, Stettin and Anklam.

The Wendish, Saxon and Westphalian leagues were separate entities, but soon showed a tendency to act together in important matters. For example in 1280, when the Wendish towns decided to transfer the Bruges *Kontor* to Aardenburg, Lübeck asked the other cities to agree to it. Various consultations of this kind strengthened the link between the groups of towns in different areas, and it was in this way that the regional leagues contributed to the foundation of the Hansa of the towns. All the same, we must be careful not to look on it as the result of the amalgamation or fusion of regional leagues. For the Hansa of the towns differed from them both in its structure and in its aims. It arose from the identity of interests of towns which were willing to act together in protecting their merchants, who had themselves at first been grouped together in the Gotland Community.

Other leagues were set up later in various parts of the Hanseatic domain. For instance at the end of the thirteenth century one can discern a grouping of Prussian towns, which became a firm association in the fourteenth. Unlike the earlier leagues, whose members were subject to a variety of overlords, the Prussian towns were all subjects of the Teutonic Order. For this reason the Grand Master exercised a great influence over their meetings and their decisions, especially at first. For their part the Livonian towns, less strictly supervised by the Order, began to act together as early as the end of the thirteenth century, but did not form an organised group until the second half of the fourteenth.

2. THE FIRST TRIALS OF STRENGTH: FLANDERS AND NORWAY

Reinforced by the urban leagues, the Hansa in the last quarter of the thirteenth century began active intervention abroad to protect the interests of its merchants. The chosen weapon, which proved very effective, was the blockade, that is, the suspension of all trade. In actual fact this form of retaliation was already long-established, but up till now it had been used rather as a matter of prudent reaction in the face of attacks or persecution suffered by Germans. Henceforward joint action was to be undertaken with the intention of forcing concessions from the town or country at fault.

As early as 1277 this plan of action can be seen developing in the east. After Livonia had been attacked by the Russians and Lithuanians, the German merchants, Lübeck and the other towns concerned, acting in concert with the Teutonic Order and the Livonian bishops, decreed that no more journeys should be made to Novgorod. Anyone going against the interdiction was to suffer the death penalty and the confiscation of his goods. But we do not know what the results of this venture were.

The suspension of Hanseatic trade with Bruges in 1280 was of far greater significance. Discontent had been growing within the German colony for several years. It seems that the citizens of Bruges, irritated by the privileges granted to foreigners by the counts of Flanders, were constantly trying to whittle them down. Also the foreigners, as their numbers increased, were less ready to observe the obligation to trade only with Bruges citizens. Eventually riots broke out, and both persons and property were endangered.

No doubt the Hanseatics would not have dared to take action by themselves. But other foreigners, the Spaniards in particular, were no less alarmed. So Lübeck sent a representative to Bruges, the town councillor Johann Doway, to consult with them. There was no question of forbidding trade with the whole of Flanders – which would have damaged the interests of the foreigners too – but only with Bruges. In this way the goodwill of the count of Flanders, essential to the success of the operation, would be assured. The choice of a new trading centre fell on the neighbouring town of Aardenburg. Lübeck took the precaution of asking the principal Saxon, Westphalian and Prussian towns, and Visby, for their verdict. All, with some reservations in matters of detail, pronounced in favour of the transfer. Thereupon the Hanseatics and most of the foreign merchants established themselves in Aardenburg, which hastened to grant them generous privileges.

In Bruges the departure of those who had assured its prosperity at once made itself painfully felt. The city, resigned to the necessity for sweeping concessions, started negotiations, and two years later the German and other foreign merchants returned there. In addition to their former privileges they had obtained concessions regarding weights and measures, and the right to deal directly with other foreigners. The economic weapon, in the form of a transfer of the *Kontor*, had shown itself to be very effective. The Hanseatics were not to forget this, and in the next hundred and fifty years the operation was repeated four times, with varying success.

Two years later, in 1284, the Hansa, encouraged by its success, embarked on a fresh trial of strength, this time with Norway, where the Hanseatic privileges were also considered to be excessive. The king endeavoured to restrict them, and the German merchants complained of the 'injustices' which they were compelled to suffer. On learning that a ship had been attacked and pillaged by the Norwegians, the assembly of the Wendish towns, meeting at Wismar, resolved on a blockade. The export to Norway of grain, flour, vegetables and beer was prohibited, on pain of fines and confiscation of the goods. Ships were posted in the Danish Straits to prevent smuggling. The Wendish towns obtained the support of the Pomeranian towns, Riga, Visby and even certain North Sea towns. On the other hand Bremen refused to co-operate, and her merchants were thereafter excluded from Hanseatic privileges. This attitude is symptomatic of the conflict between the interests of the old and new commercial practices, of which the quarrel between the merchants from Cologne and Lübeck in England had already provided an example. Bremen had long had commercial relations with Bremen, and did not choose to take part in measures which would have the effect of favouring the Baltic towns.

The blockade was a complete success. Deprived of grain from Germany, the Norwegians were unable to obtain it from England or elsewhere. 'Then', the chronicler Detmar reports, 'there broke out a famine so great that they were forced to make atonement.' With Sweden acting as mediator, peace was concluded. Not only did Norway have to pay indemnities for the financial losses which had been caused, but she was also forced to grant the Hanseatics extensive privileges. These, written into the treaty of 1294, allowed them to trade freely in Norwegian ports as far north as Bergen; to buy, sell and set up warehouses inland, without paying either royal or local duties; and to transport their goods exclusively in their own ships. The only restriction imposed was that Germans were forbidden to trade north of Bergen, a stipulation which was always observed.

In the years which followed, the Hanseatics exploited these privileges to consolidate their domination. Abroad, they got all the trade with the eastern ports of England into their hands, for the English merchants did not enjoy similar privileges. Inland they acquired numerous premises and ousted the native merchants, even obtaining a large share of the retail trade. In addition many German craftsmen, particularly shoe-makers, settled in Bergen and supplanted the Norwegian craftsmen. Faced with this disturbing situation, King Haakon V towards the end of his reign (1316–18) attempted to put an end to it. He would have liked to forbid the Germans to trade outside the towns or to settle in them for the winter, for it was principally the *vintersitteri* who were taking over the retail trade both in the towns and in the countryside. He also taxed the exporters of cod and butter, and limited the export of these commodities to the importers of flour and barley (for brewing). This measure was intended to prevent famine, but its only effect was to make the Norwegian economy even more closely dependent on the German. The regulations were never enforced, and failed to achieve their purpose. The instability of the royal house, the weakness of the middle class, the eager welcome extended by the nobility to foreigners, above all the imperative need for German grain, guaranteed the Hanseatics a stronger hold over Norway than over any other country.

In Flanders, however, the blockade of 1280, though it had been extremely successful at first, had little effect in the long run. The German merchants in Bruges soon raised further complaints of restrictions on their freedom of activity. After 1305 a second transfer of the *Kontor* to Aardenburg was being considered, for the difficulties complained of, the worst of which was the losses involved in the exchange of money, had not been rectified. Two years later, negotiations having broken down, the decision was taken. This time the German merchants were the only ones to emigrate from Bruges to Aardenburg, but once again they enjoyed the support of the count of Flanders, Robert of Béthune, who granted them an important charter, containing above all legal guarantees. The Germans did not wish to set up their *Kontor* permanently in Aardenburg, any more than they had done twenty-five years before. Bruges was irreplaceable. Consequently painstaking negotiations were opened, conducted not by the Wendish towns, owing to some temporary disagreement, but by the Saxons. The bargaining dragged on and on, until the count of Flanders himself brought it to an end by forbidding foreigners in Aardenburg to weigh goods in lots larger than sixty pounds. The Germans then returned to Bruges (1309), which granted them a comprehensive privilege, regulating both fiscal and commercial matters and defining in detail their rights concerning the staple, weights and measures, exchange and transport, and the rights and duties of brokers and landlords.

This second trial of strength thus resulted in another undoubted triumph for the Hanseatics. The charters of 1307 and 1309, confirmed in 1338, were to remain for nearly two hundred years the basis of their claims and the foundation of their commercial prosperity in Flanders. Although we have no figures to prove it, it is certain that their trade increased notably in the next fifty years. The Westphalian merchants in particular were to play a large part in the export of English wool to Flanders.

We have little information about the internal organisation of the Bruges *Kontor* at this time. We do not even know if merchants were grouped within the community according to their town or origin. It was not until 1347 that the *Kontor* drew up its first constitution,* in which the community of German merchants in Bruges was divided into three sections, or 'thirds' (*derdendeel*), each of which had two aldermen and its own treasury. The first comprised the merchants from the Wendish and Saxon towns, the second those from the Westphalian and Prussian towns, and the third those from the Livonian towns and Visby. Later on, in the Hansa of the towns, this same rather unusual division into three thirds is to be found.

3. THE DANISH OFFENSIVE AND THE CRISIS OF THE HANSA AT THE BEGINNING OF THE FOURTEENTH CENTURY

As the thirteenth century came to an end, it seemed as if the Hansa, strengthened by its successful interventions abroad, was about to assume a definite organisation under the direction of Lübeck and the other Wendish towns. But this did not happen. A serious crisis arose at the beginning of the fourteenth century, which severely tested the solidarity of the Wendish towns. The cohesion of the Hansa itself was threatened and the formation of the Hansa of the towns was delayed.

The crisis arose principally because of the determination of the princes of north Germany to re-establish their authority over the towns, which had become practically independent. The counts of Holstein, among others, had never, since the time of Henry the Lion, resigned themselves to their entire exclusion from Lübeck. But for a hundred years their efforts to re-enter it remained without success. In the same way the

* Document No. 17.

princes of Mecklenburg wanted to recover their rights over Wismar and Rostock. But to carry out their plans the princes needed money and troops. The king of Denmark, Eric VI Menved, was now to provide them with both. A series of confused hostilities resulted, in which the Wendish towns frequently found themselves divided between the opposing camps.

Eric Menved in effect revived the policy followed a hundred years before by Valdemar the Victorious of expansion into northern Germany. In about 1300 the prince of Mecklenburg, whose treasury was empty after his conflict with the margrave of Brandenburg, ceded his rights over the town of Rostock and its territory to Denmark. Eric immediately took possession of the town, unopposed. Two years later he obtained from the Habsburg King Albert I confirmation of the charter granted by Frederick II, recognising Danish sovereignty over the regions east of the Elbe. Lübeck, as an imperial city, was excepted, but this had no practical effect.

Lübeck was at the time engaged in a bitter struggle with the counts of Holstein, allies of the prince of Mecklenburg. In her turn, she formed an alliance with the dukes of Saxony and Schleswig and with Hamburg, appealing to the other Wendish towns for help, but received only a letter of sympathy from Rostock. In 1307, with her outlying districts laid waste and the city besieged, she was forced to call upon the king of Denmark for help. The latter hastened to impose peace on the belligerents, but Lübeck had to recognise him as her protector (*Schutzvogt*) for ten years and pay him an annual tribute of 750 marks. All the Wendish towns thus found themselves under the direct or indirect rule of Eric. But this state of affairs did not last long. Stralsund, Greifswald, Rostock and Wismar, resolved to resist the claims of their overlords, formed a defensive league in 1308. Lübeck, invited to join them, refused for fear of attracting Eric's wrath, and when two years later she agreed to join, it was only on the express condition that the league was not directed against the king of Denmark.

This policy 'which', as the chronicler Detmar wrote, 'was greatly to her profit', struck a serious blow at Lübeck's prestige. By accepting Danish protection and refusing aid to her neighbours in their struggle for independence, the 'head of the Hansa' was showing herself unworthy of the leading role which she had hitherto played so brilliantly. The consequences were soon apparent. In the negotiations which were being conducted at this time with the count of Flanders to bring back to Bruges the German merchants who had emigrated to Aardenburg, Lübeck took no part. At the other end of the Hanseatic world, Visby took advantage of the situation to regain her right of appeal over disputes in the Novgorod *Kontor*. Finally a few years later Haakon V initiated a series of measures intended to weaken the position of the Hanseatic merchants in Norway.

In the meantime Eric IV and his vassal, the prince of Mecklenburg, had decided to reduce the towns by force. The first to be attacked was Wismar. In spite of the help sent by Rostock and Stralsund, she was forced to capitulate after a siege lasting several months and to submit to the conditions laid down by the prince (1311). Then it was the turn of Rostock, which offered a desperate resistance to a coalition of princes. After the initial defeats the council showed a willingness to make peace, but a revolt broke out, instigated by the craft guilds, who were in favour of resisting to the utmost. Some members of the town council were massacred, others exiled and a new council took the place of the old. This was the earliest of those 'democratic' revolutions which were later to be so frequent in the maritime towns. Surrender was, however, inevitable (December 1312). Rostock had to pay a heavy fine of 14,000 marks and swear fealty to the king of Denmark, with the prince of Mecklenburg acting as his proxy, and a short while later re-established the old council. A few years later Stralsund was also attacked (1316). But thanks to the intervention of the margrave of Brandenburg the town defended itself successfully and obtained confirmation of its privileges.

In spite of this success, the situation remained serious and the future of the Hansa seemed to be threatened. Materially, the towns were impoverished by warfare. Politically, nearly all had had to agree to restrictions on their independence. Morally, the abdication of Lübeck and the lack of solidarity among the Wendish towns revealed the weakness of the Hanseatic bond. It seemed that each town would now have to come to terms with its territorial ruler and give up the co-operation with other towns. This would have brought about the end of the Hansa.

However the situation improved rapidly after the death of Eric Menved in 1319. Denmark had exhausted both her financial and her military resources, and the crown lands had for the most part been sold to native or foreign noblemen. The crown being powerless, the kingdom sank into anarchy and there was now no question of pursuing a policy of expansion. On the contrary the north German princes were quick to see their opportunity and to attack Denmark. This meant that they gave up trying to assert authority over the towns in their domain, and instead endeavoured to engage their help in their undertakings. For twenty years Denmark became a field of expansion for the Germans, especially for the nobles, in whose train came merchants, artisans, even peasants. Since the causes of dissension had disappeared, the Wendish towns could once more act together and re-establish their former authority over the Hansa.

The principal role in the history of this penetration of Denmark, with all its confusing ups and downs, was played by the more active of the two counts of Holstein, Gerhard, called the Great. For fifteen years he was *de facto* king of Denmark, the more so as the country remained without a ruler for eight years. He even caused himself to be invested with the duchy of Schleswig, which thus for the first time in history was united with Holstein under the rule of a German prince.

The German influx into Denmark was not without unhappy consequences for Hanseatic interests. The excesses committed by the immigrants provoked nationalistic reactions, and in 1332 hundreds of Germans, many merchants among them, were massacred in Skania. Above all, general lawlessness provoked a dangerous recrudescence of piracy and brigandage. Gerhard did his best to keep them in check with the help of Lübeck and Hamburg, but had only partial success; a grand alliance, formed in 1338 between the towns and thirteen princes of north Germany, was equally ineffective.

The death of Gerhard, who in 1340 was assassinated by a Danish nobleman, seemed likely to increase the confusion. The new count of Holstein was unambiguously hostile towards the towns and, supported by Sweden, attacked both the ships and the territory of Lübeck. Alarmed by this aggression and fearing the spread of piracy, Lübeck supported the accession of the new Danish king, the young Valdemar IV Atterdag. In the state of anarchy into which Denmark, dominated by German noblemen, had been plunged, it was impossible to foresee that Valdemar, after twenty years of patient hard work, would become a powerful ruler and a redoubtable enemy of the Hansa. For the moment he showed himself full of goodwill, granting privileges to Lübeck and promising his assistance to the Wendish towns. In 1343 he ceded Skania to Sweden; three years later he sold his possessions in Estonia to the Teutonic Order for 19,000 marks, and so appeared to renounce the expansionist policies in this area which had so often alarmed the Hansa towns. In reality he was thus obtaining the resources necessary for re-establishment of the royal power, so that he could later resume his predecessors' designs on north Germany.

However in the mid-fourteenth century this danger was not yet apparent. After a long period of tribulation the Hansa was once more flourishing, in spite of continual piracy. Solidarity between the members of the community had been restored and Lübeck had resumed her dominant role. As a result of the crisis the towns retained a justified distrust of the princes, who were ambitious to subjugate them, placed obstacles in the way of their association and dragged them into adventures which were contrary to their interests. The prudent policy which the Hansa later adopted towards Denmark was to be based on experience.

4. ECONOMIC EXPANSION IN THE FIRST HALF OF THE FOURTEENTH CENTURY: ENGLAND

Despite the political crisis the first half of the fourteenth century was characterised by the steady economic advance of the Hansa. Unfortunately little is known about this period, which immediately precedes that in which the community achieved its greatest prosperity. Statistics are still rare, the *Rezesse* of the few regional diets are not very informative, and the texts of the privileges granted afford few precise details.

However almost everywhere one can discern signs of growing activity. As more immigrants arrive, the towns continue to increase in population and many of them extend their city walls. We have already noted the activity of the Hanseatics in Flanders and their growing influence in Scandinavia. In the east in 1311 the town of Pskov is mentioned as having seized nearly 50,000 furs belonging to German merchants, and in the winter of 1336–7 the presence of 160 merchants at the *Peterhof* is an indication of the prosperity of the Novgorod *Kontor*. In Prussia, after the last vestiges of resistance had been stamped out, the Teutonic Order set up its headquarters in Marienburg in 1309; this cannot have failed to stimulate trade, which became very important at the end of the fourteenth century. But all this remains very fragmentary.

There is, however, one region where the economic progress of the Hansa can be studied in somewhat greater detail, and that is England. Here too the Germans were able to extend the privileges which they had been given in the thirteenth century. In 1303 Edward I granted all foreigners, whatever their nationality, the important privilege known as the *carta mercatoria*, to compensate them for the rise in customs dues on the export of wool and hides. They were exempted from all taxes and services within the kingdom and were permitted to settle in any part of the realm and there deal wholesale with both foreigners and natives. They also obtained legal guarantees and protection against infringements by royal officials. It is true that these exceptional advantages roused bitter opposition among the English merchants and had to be revoked by Edward II. But this repeal was directed principally against the Italians, the most influential of the foreign groups. The Germans, on the other hand, were able to obtain confirmation of their privileges, and eventually became the only group to benefit from the *carta mercatoria*. Also, as far as they were concerned the principle of collective responsibility in the case of debts contracted or crimes committed by one of them was abandoned. Finally Edward III, whom the Hanseatics, by their loans, helped to obtain the throne in 1327 in place of his father, was kindly disposed towards them, and throughout his long reign hardly ever failed to further their interests.

The increasing volume of business conducted in England by the Hanseatics in the first half of the fourteenth century is shown, among other things, by the large number of them who settled permanently in the country. The acquisition of English nationality, of which the earliest known example goes back to 1309, at first took the form of admission to citizenship in a certain town. As this raised practical difficulties, the crown from 1324 onwards took the step of conferring 'denizenship' upon foreigners, granting them equal rights and economic privileges with English merchants throughout the realm. This favour was first granted to the most influential of the Hanseatics, above all to the king's creditors, among them two members of the powerful Sudermann family of Dortmund, and later on to many others. At this time, and even well into the second half of the fourteenth century, English citizenship was not incompatible with enjoyment of Hanseatic privileges, and this form of naturalisation, which encouraged closer relations with both English merchants and the court, greatly extended the influence and activity of the Hanseatics.

From this time on the goods imported by the Hanseatics into England consisted for the most part of Rhenish wine, brought in by the merchants from Cologne, wood and grain from Prussia, and furs and wax from Russia. The following incident shows how important the English considered the import of wax, which was a monopoly of the German merchants. In 1309 it was in short supply, and the price doubled. The

Hanseatics were accused of having instigated a plot against the crown by suspending the import of this commodity. Brought before a commission of inquiry, they had great difficulty in establishing their innocence.

wool trade 1273

English exports at this time consisted primarily of wool and secondarily of metals. Thanks to the system of export licences, established by Henry III at the time of a conflict with Flanders, and also the accounts of the customs houses, we have some statistics – the first available – on the German share in the wool trade. In 1273, out of a total of 32,784 sacks of wool, each of about 166 kilogrammes, exported by 681 merchants, 1,440 were exported by 49 Hanseatic merchants. They were fifth on the list, far behind the English (11,415), the Italians (8,000), the French including the Flemings (7,150), and the merchants of Brabant (3,678). Their share was 4·4 per cent of the total value of exports, or 6·7 per cent, if one considers foreign merchants alone. This is modest; but we should not forget that wool was for them only a marginal trade. Three years later the figures were still much the same. In 1303 at Boston the Hanseatics were paying 33 per cent of the 'new custom' on the export of wool, and in 1310–11, 54 per cent. The maximum was reached in the exceptional years 1339–42, when the annual export rose to 3,500 sacks.

From the end of the thirteenth century onwards, following the example of the Italians, certain Hanseatics, especially Westphalian merchants from Dortmund, were also acting as credit bankers, lending either small sums to unimportant Londoners or considerable sums to the crown. The earliest known example goes back to 1299, when Edward I borrowed 500 marks sterling from a group of Hanseatics, which included one man from Lübeck, one from Cologne and one from Dortmund. Similarly in 1317 Edward II borrowed several sums, amounting to £416, from various members of the Revele family of Dortmund.

But it was under Edward III that German loans became important. To go to war with France the king needed large sums of money. His principal creditors were English or Italian, but he did not disdain to appeal for financial help to the Hanseatics. In exchange he granted them export licences for sacks of wool, reduced their own customs dues and farmed out to them the collection of customs dues from others. In 1338 he borrowed £1,200 from four Dortmund merchants, two of whom belonged to the Sudermann family, in return for which he granted them export licences for 400 sacks of wool. In the same year, during a triumphal journey up the Rhine, he obtained £750 from four Cologne merchants. A little later he borrowed various sums, in one case £5,000, from some Dortmund merchants. These were relatively small sums when one remembers that in 1339 he owed £210,000 to the Bardi and Peruzzi and £76,000 to the Englishman William de la Pole. In February he pledged his great crown to the archbishop of Trier for 50,000 guilders, and later his little crown and that of the queen to various Cologne financiers for nearly 10,000 guilders (more than £1,500).

In order to protect their interests more effectively, his German creditors formed, in 1339, a consortium comprising at least thirteen members, most of them great Westphalian merchants. With them was a newcomer, Tidemann Limberg, the boldest and most active of these speculators. In its first year the consortium lent the king more than £18,000, payable for the most part in various towns in the Netherlands. In May 1340 there was a new loan of £8,300 in exchange for export licences for 3,386 sacks of wool and the right to collect customs dues in fifteen English ports as long as the debt remained unpaid.* More loans amounting to about £10,000 were granted in the next two years. Perhaps the greatest service the Westphalian consortium rendered Edward III was to redeem the royal crown, which his creditors threatened to sell: 45,000 guilders were advanced to the archbishop of Trier, 4,400 to the Cologne creditors, and in 1344 the regalia were recovered.

At this moment the German consortium was dissolved because the king, yielding to pressure from the English merchants, withdrew from it the right to collect customs dues. Moreover most of its members had taken fright at the risks entailed in these operations, and were inclined to give up financial speculation. The bankruptcy of the Bardi and Peruzzi, which occurred in 1345, and the growing hostility of the English merchants merely confirmed them in their resolution, and their business was gradually restricted to purely commercial enterprises. Limberg was one of the last to withdraw. The great financial role which the Westphalian merchants played in England, modelled on that of the Italians, remained unique in the history of the Hansa. Nevertheless it shows how much influence the Germans had acquired in this country, an influence which was maintained in the following centuries largely through being limited to commercial activities.

* Document No. 6.

5. THE BLACK DEATH (1350)

Just at the period of their most rapid expansion the Hansa towns, like all Europe, were struck by the catastrophe of the Black Death. In the autumn of 1349 the plague appeared in Sweden and Prussia, doubtless carried there from England. It moved down the valley of the Rhine, from one bank of the river to the other, and reached Cologne in December. For the Hanseatic area as a whole, 1350 was the year of disaster. The epidemic spread from the west in Frisia, and from Jutland and Gotland into north Germany, reaching its climax in the summer. Brandenburg was the last district to become its victim, in the early months of 1351.

It seems probable that north Germany was one of the worst-affected regions of all Europe. To be sure, many of the fantastic figures advanced by chroniclers bear witness only to nightmare memories of the scourge: one survivor out of ten in a good number of towns, according to Detmar (late fourteenth century); 9,000 dead in Elbing, 11,000 in Münster, 90,000 (!) in Lübeck, according to Reimar Kock (sixteenth century). But certain details are more convincing. According to Heinrich of Lamspringe, only three monks survived in the Franciscan monastery of Magdeburg, and in his own convent only two out of ten; according to another writer on an estate in East Prussia, one serving woman, strutting about in her mistress's finery, was the sole survivor.

Of the towns, Bremen appears to have been the worst sufferer. A roll of the victims, drawn up by order of the council, contains 6,966 names, to which must be added 1,000 unidentified dead. Unfortunately we do not know the population of the town at this period, but it can scarcely have been more than 12,000 to 15,0000, so we must accept that more than half the inhabitants perished, perhaps as many as two-thirds. In Hamburg 12 master bakers died out of 34, 18 master butchers out of 40, 27 officials out of 50, 16 members of the council out of 21. In other towns, we know only the number of councillors who died: 11 out of 30 in Lübeck, plus 2 town clerks out of 5, 42 per cent in Wismar, 36 per cent in Lüneburg, 30 per cent in Bremen, 27 per cent in Reval. We cannot assume that these percentages apply also to the total population, since the councillors might be either more exposed to contagion or, on the other hand, in a position to make good their escape. However we may suppose that in the Hansa towns the number of victims was rarely less than a quarter of the population.

It is easier to imagine the catastrophic upheaval caused by the plague than to unearth contemporary evidence of it. But there must have been a decline in agricultural and industrial production, paralysis of land and sea transport, and business recession caused by the death of leading businessmen and their associates. It is even more difficult to appreciate both the immediate and the long-term consequences of the catastrophe in the development of the Hansa towns.

From the demographic point of view it seems that the decline in urban population was made up fairly rapidly by immigration from the country-side. It is probable that for some years admission to citizenship was made easier. In any case an increase in the number of new citizens is to be seen everywhere. In 1351 there were 422 admissions to citizenship in Lübeck, against an average of 175 for the period 1317–49. In Hamburg and in Lüneburg the figures are respectively 108 against 59 and 95 against 29. For a decade the influx remained sizeable, and then slackened. One may assume that within fifteen years populations had risen to their former levels or often surpassed them. The city councils, forced to replace their dead members, seem to have made their choice almost ex-clusively among the leading families of the town. In Lübeck no more than two or three new names appear. Generally speaking, the plague does not appear to have resulted in any modification of the patrician structure of the town councils.

As far as landed property is concerned a similar upheaval took place immediately after the disaster, but settled conditions returned after a few years. Everywhere the plague gave rise to numerous transfers of property. In Lübeck, where at least 27 per cent of property-owners had perished, the yield of the 10 per cent death duties was ten times higher in 1351 than in 1350, and was still eight times higher in 1353. The transfer of property was given added impetus by the fact that heirs were often compelled to sell the property they had inherited because they were unable to pay the interest charges with which it was encumbered. There can be no doubt that the plague resulted in the concentration of greater wealth in fewer hands. This in turn may have given rise – though there is no proof of it – to an increase in the demand for luxury goods and at least a temporary reduction in the demand for everyday consumer goods.

Finally from the financial point of view the plague caused a crisis of some gravity. Money became scarce and the rate of exchange went up. It was mostly small businesses which were affected by the upheaval, but the larger commercial undertakings also suffered, investors preferring to put their money into annuities, which they considered a better risk: indeed the market in annuities does not appear to have been affected by the depression. However here too the crisis was of short duration, and in Lübeck at least the situation had returned to normal by about 1355.

One question remains: what were the long-term consequences of the Black Death for the Hansa? It is clear that the depopulation of western Germany meant the halting of emigration towards the east – or at least accentuated a decline already perceptible in the first half of the fourteenth century; the more so as from now on epidemics, often devastating, broke out every ten or fifteen years. It is equally clear that this halting of emigration was highly prejudicial to the extension and consolidation of German settlement in the east, now deprived of the influx of peasants which had been its strength. It is less certain that the repercussions were equally disastrous for the towns, and therefore for the commercial development of the Hansa, since the inroads of the epidemics into the urban population were usually made good fairly rapidly by immigration from the rural areas. Although we lack precise statistics, the population of the Hansa towns in the fifteenth century was probably larger than in the middle of the fourteenth. One can therefore assert that the Black Death was nothing more than a dramatic episode in the history of the Hansa.

CHAPTER FOUR

The Hansa of the Towns: A Great Power in Northern Europe (c.1350–c.1400)

IN the third quarter of the fourteenth century the Hansa, having recovered its temporarily disrupted unity, was faced by two decisive ordeals: economic conflict with Flanders and war with Denmark. In the course of these struggles it developed a new organisation, which had been in preparation for a long time. The community of German merchants was replaced by, or rather subordinated to, an association of Hanseatic towns, which would in future protect the interests of merchants abroad and at the same time assume control of the activities of the component parts. Victorious abroad, the Hansa of the towns was now attaining the position of a great power in northern Europe, which it was to keep for about a hundred and fifty years.

1. THE CONFLICT WITH FLANDERS AND THE FORMATION OF THE HANSA OF THE TOWNS

Even before 1350 relations between Bruges and the Hansa had once more deteriorated. The principal cause of this was the war between England and France. On land and at sea the merchants were suffering serious losses, and on the strength of the privilege of safe conduct they demanded indemnities from the city of Bruges and from the count of Flanders. They met with either refusals or delays. In addition they complained of having to pay customs dues contrary to their exemption therefrom. Consequently Lübeck, even more determined than the other towns, was considering the possibility of once again moving the *Kontor* away from Bruges.

An incident in 1351 embittered the conflict. A ship from Greifswald had been seized at the estuary of the Zwijn by an English privateer, towed into open waters and there looted. The pirate, arrested a little later off Sluys, was tried and, as a result of pressure from the Hanseatic *Kontor*, executed. In reprisal Edward III seized the property of the Hanseatic merchants in England. But he later revoked this measure and, angered by the evasive diplomacy of Bruges, brought the wool staple back from there to England.

Not satisfied with this, the *Kontor* made further demands, chiefly to have its own weigh-house, a right already enjoyed by the English and Spaniards. This was granted, but the only effect of the concession was to provoke further demands, especially for the payment of indemnities to the victims of piracy.

These disputes had great repercussions in Germany. For good relations with Bruges were of vital importance to almost all the Hanseatic towns, and the general feeling was that intervention in defence of the threatened privileges was essential. On the other hand many towns were perturbed to see the *Kontor* taking the initiative in negotiations with Flanders, without mandate and at the risk of dragging the towns unwillingly into international conflicts. The old distrust of the independent position of the merchants, which had manifested itself in the suppression of the Gotland Community, reappeared with regard to the *Kontor* at Bruges. Lübeck decided to convoke delegates from the towns in order to deal with the affairs of Flanders. This assembly, which met in 1356, can be considered the first full diet of the Hansa towns. Unfortunately we do not know its composition, but there can be no doubt that the assembly was well attended and that all sections sent representatives.

The most important decision made by the diet of 1356 was to send an embassy to Bruges. Led by the Lübeck councillor Jakob Pleskow, it comprised delegates from the three Hanseatic thirds, Wendish–Saxon, Westphalian–Prussian and Gotland–Livonian. It does not appear to have achieved any substantial results in its negotiations with the city of Bruges and the count of Flanders. On the other hand it intervened decisively in the affairs of the German *Kontor*. It confirmed, in the name of the towns, the constitution which the *Kontor* had set up in 1347, but defined in even greater detail the powers and competence of the six aldermen. This may not appear to be a step of any great importance, but in effect it established the fact that the *Kontor*, hitherto independent, was now subordinate to the authority of the combined towns, and its decisions in future would be valid only if approved by the towns. In law, and no longer only in fact, the towns, acting through the general diet, were establishing their authority over their merchants in foreign parts. This became evident ten years later when the Bruges *Kontor*, having on its own initiative legislated in monetary matters, was immediately called to order by the diet at Lübeck and instructed to take no action without the approval of the towns.

In the course of the next twenty years the other three *Kontore* were similarly brought under control. In Novgorod in 1361 an embassy led by two councillors, one from Lübeck and the other from Visby, informed the merchants of the *Peterhof* that in future no regulation was to be issued without the consent of Lübeck, Visby and the three Livonian towns. This decision affirmed not only the subordination of the *Kontor* to the Hansa, but also the growing influence of the Livonian towns, which had originally been very weak. The *Kontor* in Bergen, composed for the most part of merchants from Lübeck, was less able to manifest an independence which had never really existed. In 1343 King Magnus Eriksson, while confirming the Wendish towns in their former privileges, officially recognised the statute of the *Kontor*. In 1365 the *Kontor* requested approval of a certain number of regulations and Lübeck's detailed reply bears witness to the authority which it enjoyed over the *Kontor*. The London *Kontor*, like that in Bruges, had drawn up its own constitution before the end of the thirteenth century; towards the close of the reign of Edward III it became anxious about the new 'subsidies' levied on German merchants. They were considered an infringement of the Hanseatic privileges. Negotiations achieved nothing. In 1374 therefore the *Kontor* appealed to the towns. An embassy, led by one councillor from Lübeck and one from Elbing, travelled to London, negotiated and obtained satisfaction, though not without some difficulty. We do not know if the *Kontor* presented its statutes for approval on this occasion, but it probably did so. In any case from now on submission was complete, the more so as its privileges were constantly threatened during the reign of Richard II.

In short the subordination of the four great *Kontore*, so important in the final structure of the Hansa, was achieved without any serious difficulties and there were very few occasions on which any one of them later tried to shake off the tutelage. This was only to be expected. When foreign states attempted to restrict their privileges, the German merchants needed the support of the towns, who alone could protect them efficiently. The authority of the Hanseatic diet over the foreign-based merchant communities was felt to be both a necessity and a benefit.

However the Hanseatic embassy to Bruges in 1356 had not cleared up the matters at issue between Flanders and the German merchants. In the months which followed, relations became even more strained. The city of Bruges, in urgent need of money, levied new duties on business transactions. Depreciation of the currency caused the prices of landlords, brokers and carriers to rise, and the staple was extended to salt and grain, which foreigners had hitherto been allowed to sell freely among themselves, 'from ship to ship'. All these measures were considered to be infringements of the Hanseatic privileges, but the chief cause of complaint remained the refusal to pay indemnities. Lübeck in particular pressed for extreme counter-measures, and summoned another Hanseatic diet which was to decide upon the transfer of the *Kontor*. This diet, which met on the date fixed (January 1358), was not, however, fully representative. The Wendish, Saxon and Prussian towns were represented, but not the Westphalian and Livonian towns, which apparently hesitated to risk a trial of strength. However Lübeck's authority was strengthened by the written approbation of Visby and the Swedish towns, and the assembly decreed a blockade of Flanders.

This was a bold step to take, particularly when compared with the earlier blockades. For there was no longer any question of making a distinction between the city of Bruges and the count of Flanders, since both were considered jointly responsible for the infringement of the Hanseatic privileges. The ban was therefore aimed at the whole of Flanders, including Antwerp and Malines, recently acquired by Count Louis de Male. The German merchants were asked to leave Flanders before 1 May and to take up residence in Dordrecht. Hanseatic ships were forbidden to sail beyond the Meuse. Goods might be sold only to the north of this line, and even then not to Flemings or to merchants on their way to Flanders. Conversely, no merchandise originating in Flanders might be bought from anyone at all. On their return home German merchants had to produce certificates issued by the authorities of towns in the Low Countries where they had been doing business. This obligation was extended even to ships sailing for England, Scotland or Norway, since they might be tempted to put in at Flemish ports. The case of vessels driven into the prohibited zone by contrary winds or tempest was foreseen: they, too, were forbidden to dispose of their cargoes in Flanders. Finally any disobedience, whether by a town or by an individual, was to be punished by perpetual exclusion from the Hansa.

The blockade, which was harmful to both sides, was particularly hard on Bruges, which made energetic attempts to end it. But the stakes were so high that negotiations dragged on for two years. The Flemings attempted, unsuccessfully, to minimise the effects of the blockade by granting the city of Kampen all the privileges enjoyed by the Hansa, on condition that Kampen supplied them with German goods. They tried to win Cologne over to their side; but contrary to their expectation, that city pressed for an even stricter application of the blockade. The interruption to trade was, however, slow to produce its full effect, particularly as it was impossible to prevent smuggling entirely. However the dwindling flow of merchandise from the east led to a serious recession in Flemish trade. In 1359 the harvest in the Low Countries was poor, and the shortage of grain from Prussia was keenly felt. During the winter of that year heavy rains made it impossible for the grain carts from Picardy to ford the Somme. In the spring of 1360 the Wendish towns decided to close the Danish Straits to prevent the ships of Prussian smugglers carrying grain to the Low Countries.

In the end the Flemings resigned themselves to accepting, more or less in their entirety, the claims of their adversaries. Peace was concluded in the summer of 1360, the blockade was lifted, and by September German merchants were again settling in Bruges. The Hanseatics obtained confirmation of all their privileges, defined in such detail as to prevent any one-sided interpretations. In some respects these privileges were even extended. For example the right to carry on retail trade was granted for the first time. Moreover the charters bore the seals not only of Bruges, but also of Ghent, Ypres and the count of Flanders, which guaranteed their validity throughout Flanders. Finally agreement was reached on the bitterly contested question of indemnities. The count's share was fixed at 1,500 guilders, that of Ypres and Bruges at 155 pounds groschen. Payments were made punctually during the next three years.

So this economic war ended with a resounding success for the Hansa. It had now been demonstrated that a closer union between the towns and the sacrifice of local interests would bring their reward. It is significant that the town of Bremen, whose merchants had remained outside the community since the end of the thirteenth century, chose this moment (1358) to change its mind and to ask for and obtain readmission, though on rather harsh terms.* Throughout northern Germany it was now

---

* Document No. 18. Some historians seem reluctant to accept the idea that the Bremen merchants, excluded from the community in 1275 for having refused to participate in the blockade of Norway, should have remained outside the Hansa up to 1358. Basing their opinion on an obscure passage in a chronicle, they suggest readmission before the end of the thirteenth century, followed in about 1350 by a second exclusion, for which, however, no plausible reason can be found. It seems quite natural that the Bremen merchants, relying

accepted that to belong to the Hansa was the only way to ensure the prosperity of the individual towns.

However the situation was still precarious, and the advantages won in Flanders were soon to be called in question again. Here as elsewhere the Hanseatics were condemned to a perpetual struggle in order to maintain their privileged status, as much against the authorities in foreign countries as against potential rivals. Doubtless no one at the time took particular notice of the fact that the Flemings had granted to two non-Hanseatic towns, Kampen and Nürnberg, the same privileges as the Hanseatics. This was, however, an omen of the rise to power of the most redoubtable of the future rivals of the Hansa, the Dutch and the south Germans.

2. THE DANISH WAR, THE COLOGNE CONFEDERATION AND THE PEACE OF STRALSUND

Only a few months after their success in the west, serious news brought consternation to all the Hansa towns. Valdemar IV Atterdag had suddenly landed on Gotland, defeated a hastily assembled army of peasants, and seized and sacked Visby. For nearly three hundred years the island was to remain a Danish possession.

Since ascending the throne twenty years earlier Valdemar had been patiently at work, restoring his finances, redeeming crown lands, reducing some of his nobles to obedience and rebuilding his army. In the spring of 1360 he had recovered Skania from the Swedes, and even then the Hanseatics had been perturbed at the high price demanded for his confirmation of their charters. The conquest of Gotland swept aside all their illusions. This was a direct challenge to the Hansa. Certainly the king was quite ready to renew Visby's charter, and made no objection to her remaining in the Hansa. And certainly for the last fifty years the town had lost the leading position in the Baltic which it had enjoyed in the thirteenth century, and its decline was already apparent. Nevertheless it

on their long-standing connections with Scandinavia, Flanders and England and the special privileges accorded them there, should have seen no point in joining the Hansa so long as the latter was without a fully cohesive organisation. This is one example of the reserve shown by merchants of the old towns towards the 'Easterlings', the newcomers; another example is the attitude of the Cologne merchants settled in England. Cf. H. SCHWARZWALDER, 'Bremens Aufnahme in die Hanse 1358 in neuer Sicht', in *Hansische Geschichtsblätter*, 79 (1961).

was one of the great Hansa towns of the time, and retained a certain commercial and strategic value for the Wendish towns because of its position on the route to Stockholm. Above all by this act of aggression Valdemar was asserting his intention of resuming the project of Danish hegemony in the northern seas. War was inevitable.

A diet of the Wendish and Pomeranian towns, meeting in Greifswald, resolved on a suspension of commercial relations with Denmark. To finance the war it imposed a levy of fourpence per pound on ships and merchandise exported from the Hansa towns. Alliances were formed with the kings of Norway and Sweden, the duke of Schleswig and the counts of Holstein. But this auspicious start led nowhere. The Grand Master of the Teutonic Order, who had pledged his participation in the war, contented himself with sending financial aid, as did the princes. Kampen and the other towns on the Zuiderzee continued to trade with Denmark, thus rendering the blockade ineffective, and the whole burden of the war fell on the Wendish towns. In April 1362 a fleet of 52 ships, including 27 cogs, set sail for Copenhagen. But its leader Johann Wittenborg, burgomaster of Lübeck, made the mistake of landing part of his troops in order to besiege Hälsingborg. Valdemar seized his opportunity, attacked the Hanseatic fleet and captured twelve large ships. Wittenborg was only too glad to accept an armistice which allowed him to take the remains of the expedition back to Germany: a little later he paid for his defeat with his life.

This setback created unrest in the Hansa which lasted several years. Consultations about a second expedition led to nothing. Negotiations with Denmark were begun, dragged on for three years and resulted in an uneasy peace. Dissension broke out even among the Wendish towns about apportioning the costs of the campaign. It was an open question whether – as had been the case fifty years before – the solidarity of the towns was not about to be seriously impaired.

However this did not happen. Times had changed. The cohesion of the community had been strengthened by the conflict with Flanders and was no longer to be destroyed by one setback, however serious. In 1366 a general diet met in Lübeck and adopted a series of measures intended to reinforce the authority of the towns, notably by restricting the management of the *Kontore* to citizens only.* Moreover Valdemar IV, instead of encouraging disunity among his adversaries, was inept enough to unite them in opposition to himself by seizing Prussian vessels in the Sound

* Document No. 19.

and by harassing the Prussian merchants equally with the other Hanseatics. As a result the Grand Master Winrich von Kniprode himself came to Lübeck to propose a military alliance. Valdemar also adopted a less lenient attitude than hitherto towards the towns on the Zuiderzee, which soon showed themselves ready to participate this time in an attack upon Denmark. Moreover in February 1367 the king of Sweden, Magnus Eriksson, was deposed by his nobles and replaced by Albert, son of the duke of Mecklenburg, who was equally in favour of intervention. Valdemar's sole remaining ally was Haakon VI of Norway, to whom he had given his daughter in marriage.

At first the Wendish towns hesitated to resume hostilities. They showed little enthusiasm for the Grand Master's offer, and it was not until an alliance had been concluded between the Zuiderzee and Prussian towns that they again took the initiative in the attack against Valdemar and Haakon. A general diet was summoned to meet in Cologne to make the final decisions.

This great diet of 1367 is in many ways exceptional in the history of the Hansa. To begin with, the meeting place was unusual as this was the only time the Hanseatic diet met in Cologne, whose outlying situation was clearly inconvenient. But in this case it had the advantage of being easily accessible to the Dutch, whose participation was essential for success. Also it was evidence of the intention to deal tactfully with the Rhenish metropolis by not stressing the primacy of Lübeck.

The participation in the assembly of three groups of towns which were not members of the Hansa was also unusual. They were towns on the Zuiderzee, represented by delegates from Kampen, Elburg and Harderwijk, and the towns of Holland and Zeeland, represented by delegates from Amsterdam and Briel. All agreed to accept the decisions of the assembly.

Finally, in order to intensify the war effort, the towns decided to form a much closer alliance than in the past, a true league (*verbund*) which took the unusual name of the 'Confederation' of Cologne. This was set up not only for the duration of the war, but also for three years afterwards. It was in fact prolonged until 1385. These dispositions seemed to be preparing the way for changes in the structure of the Hansa.

The diet laid down minutely detailed financial and military measures. As in 1361, but under more rigorous control, poundage was to be levied on all merchandise and all ships entering or leaving a Hanseatic port. To simplify collection, the rate – variable within narrow limits – was specified in the various currencies in use: those of Flanders, Lübeck, Pomerania, Prussia and Livonia. In the military sphere the diet fixed the number of ships and soldiers to be provided by each member, and decided on the departure date from the North Sea and the Baltic of the fleets which were to assemble in the Sound for the final assault.*

At first adherence to the league was limited, even within the membership of the Hansa. Only the Wendish and Prussian towns were represented at Cologne. But during the months that followed, most of the seaports from the Gulf of Finland to the mouth of the Rhine gave their assent more or less explicitly. Some, it is true, showed no great enthusiasm, among them Bremen and above all Hamburg, whose possible exclusion from the Hansa was mooted. On the pretext that they were exhausted by local wars, they refused to take part in military operations and offered financial aid only. The inland towns, which took little interest in a maritime war, were even more apathetic. The Westphalian towns did not even provide a subsidy. This is only one example of the serious disagreements within the Hansa which were so frequent in the course of its history, and which were indeed inevitable in view of the differences in the situation and interests of such a large number of towns.

The coalition was very much strengthened by alliances with Sweden, Mecklenburg and Holstein, and with the Danish nobility who had rebelled against Valdemar. The king does not seem to have realised the extent of his peril. At the decisive moment of the Hanseatic attack, he saw fit to leave his realm to seek for allies in northern Germany. He found none, and a Danish defeat became inevitable. The Wendish and Dutch fleets razed Copenhagen, putting its port out of action, and ravaged the Danish and Norwegian coasts, while the count of Holstein raided Jutland. With the help of the Swedes Skania was overrun, Hälsingborg alone offering resistance. Soon Norway, on whom the blockade fell particularly heavily, solicited and obtained an armistice. In Skania operations dragged on until the capitulation of the castle of Hälsingborg on 8 September 1369, which induced the Danish state council to sue for peace. The Hansa agreed to a suspension of hostilities, in spite of the opposition of the German princes who wished to take full advantage of the situation and continued the war.

Peace with Denmark was concluded the following year at Stralsund (24 May 1370). The Hansa demanded no new privileges in matters of

* Document No. 7.

commerce, but was content with confirmation of the previous charters. These allowed for complete freedom of trade and the abolition of the increased dues levied on German merchants in Skania since 1361. But strategically the Hansa obtained the conveyance to the Confederation for a period of fifteen years of the four fortresses which guarded the Sound – Hälsingborg, Malmö, Skanör and Falsterbo – as well as two-thirds of the revenues derived from them. This gave the Hansa mastery of the Sound for many years. Finally the Danish state council promised that when Valdemar IV died, they would not elect a successor without the consent of the confederated towns.

This new trial of strength culminated therefore in a triumph for the Hansa; and this time victory had not been achieved simply by economic measures. On the contrary the towns had shown that they were capable of raising battle-fleets and armies. They had been supported by powerful princes, but they were no longer the latter's retainers as they had been fifty years before. They had directed the essential operations themselves, and they had always retained the initiative in both war and peace. Finally they had abandoned their allies and made a separate peace with the enemy, as they were to do again in the war of the Danish succession. The Peace of Stralsund marks the emergence in northern Europe of a new power, which here replaced the lapsed imperial authority. It was not a sovereign power, since the towns which composed it remained legally subject to many different territorial rulers. Its only basis lay in the will to defend its commercial interests, if need be by force of arms. It was a strange phenomenon, unique in the Europe of those days.

The clause in the Peace of Stralsund relating to the Danish succession was to be invoked five years later. Valdemar IV died in 1375, leaving only two daughters, Margaret, who had married Haakon VI, king of Norway, and Ingeborg, wife of Henry of Mecklenburg, brother of the king of Sweden. The Hansa, having to choose between a union either of Denmark and Norway, or of Mecklenburg, Denmark and Sweden, came down on the side of the former, unlike the German princes, who favoured the latter. The Danish state council therefore decided in favour of the young Olaf (1376–87) under the regency of his mother Margaret. In acknowledgement of the league's support, Norway also signed the peace treaty, and confirmed the Hanseatics in all their privileges.

The Hansa had certainly chosen the lesser of two evils, for the power of Denmark was less dangerous than the ambition of the German princes. All the same its vigilance was not relaxed, and the Cologne Confederation was several times renewed. There was even reason to suppose that it might become a permanent organisation, identified with the Hansa. However the only reason for its existence had been the threat from Denmark. Once peace had been established, its only firm basis lay in its control of the Danish fortresses and their revenues. When, in conformity with the treaty, the castles were handed back to Denmark in 1385, the question arose of whether the Cologne Confederation should be renewed or replaced by a different form of alliance. The general opinion, which was not that of the Grand Master of the Teutonic Order or of the Prussian towns,* was that there were no grounds for pursuing either course. Obviously the towns were reluctant to enter into too close an alliance, with too clearly defined political and military clauses which might entail great sacrifices, except when it was absolutely necessary. The Cologne Confederation had therefore no lasting influence on the organisation of the Hansa, although it did help to strengthen its internal cohesion. It was, however, remembered as an impressive institution, and was taken as a model by those who endeavoured in the fifteenth century, but with no great success, to set up the leagues known as *tohopesaten*.

3. THE EMBARGOES OF 1388

It would be a mistake to think that the Hanseatic victory had eased the position of the German merchants abroad. On the contrary a continuous state of tension was to be found in many parts towards the end of the fourteenth century. The Hanseatic merchants endeavoured to exploit their success by strict insistence on the recognition of their privileges, while the foreign towns, under pressure from their own merchants, were reluctant to countenance for ever the privileged position of the Germans, which seemed to them unjustified. Even the princes, though more ready to favour the Hanseatics, were bound to regard certain legal and fiscal exemptions as a threat to their own sovereignty. Finally the continual demands for indemnities could not fail to poison relations. As a result there were frequent disputes, swift to arise and difficult to resolve, particularly with England, Flanders and Russia. Matters came to a head in 1388, when an embargo was in simultaneous operation in all three areas. Nevertheless the Hansa managed to avoid open warfare. Indeed the leading Hanseatics of this period, particularly Jakob Pleskow

* Document No. 22.

of Lübeck and Wulf Wulflam of Stralsund, refused to allow themselves
to be seduced by the memory of past victories, and opposed those who
clamoured for war. In so doing, they displayed to the full that Hanseatic
common sense which consisted in combining firmness with a profound
desire for peace, the only policy, in fact, which could ensure the prosperity of the community.

By the end of Edward III's reign relations with England were strained,
and the increase in English trade in the Baltic was already causing
concern in Germany. From about 1350 onwards the English Merchant
Adventurers had been visiting the ports of Elbing, Danzig and Stralsund,
unloading English cloth and taking on board timber, grain and copper
from the Carpathians. They rented houses and shops, and were at first
well received, especially by the Teutonic Order, who were by tradition
friendly towards England because of the many English knights who
fought in the crusades against the pagan Lithuanians. But soon English
trade threatened to become so extensive that English merchants were
forbidden to sell retail, to trade outside the towns, to trade directly with
other foreigners, or to charter Hanseatic ships. Conversely, Germans
were no longer allowed to export their products in English ships, and
after 1370 the Hanseatics, having complete control of the Sound, were
able to oust their competitors almost entirely from the fairs in Skania.
All these measures could not fail to worsen relations between them,
particularly in view of the Hanseatics' main grievance, the obstacles
placed in the way of their trade in England. As the Prussians had the
predominant share in this trade, the Teutonic Order soon pronounced
itself in favour of energetic measures, while the Wendish towns coun-
selled moderation. It has already been noted that as early as 1357 the
London *Kontor* had to appeal to the towns in order to obtain the abrogation of additional 'subsidies'. Two years later the accession of Richard
II aggravated the situation, for the new king was more susceptible than
Edward III to pressure from merchants and from Parliament. He began
by refusing to confirm the charters, setting out a whole series of conditions, among them the listing of the Hansa towns, so that the benefits
might be strictly limited to those entitled to them. This request was
refused. But instead of breaking off relations, as the Teutonic Order
wished to do, Lübeck again sent Jakob Pleskow to London, where he
succeeded in obtaining the desired confirmation of the privileges. He
failed, however, in part of his mission, as the request for indemnities
met with no success, nor was there any improvement subsequently. The

Hanseatics were obliged to pay additional poundage and tonnage, chiefly on imports, but also on certain kinds of English cloth when exported, particularly kersey. The situation suddenly took a turn for the worse in 1385, when an English fleet attacked German ships, including six Prussian vessels, in the Zwijn. The Grand Master broke off commercial relations between Prussia and England. But once again the Wendish towns were more conciliatory, and English merchants in the Baltic were allowed to settle in Stralsund. However as complaints of abuses committed by the English continued to pour in, the Wendish towns themselves decided in 1388 to seize the English goods warehoused in Stralsund. Richard II retaliated by taking similar steps in England. War seemed imminent. But negotiations were begun and soon led to an agreement, as neither party had anything to gain by open conflict. The confiscations were repealed, the Hanseatic charters were confirmed, and the English were authorised to carry out wholesale transactions in Prussian seaports, even with foreigners.

This settlement seems to have been more profitable to the English than to the Germans. The Merchant Adventurers settled in Danzig, formed an association under the authority of a 'governor' and acquired a house there. Despite protests they continued to sell retail, and entered into commercial partnerships with Hanseatics, thus extending their trade. By contrast the Germans in England remained subject to imposts which they considered iniquitous and their ships suffered attacks from pirates. As a result in 1398 the Grand Master denounced the agreement which had been reached ten years earlier. Although hostilities did not break out immediately, Anglo-Hanseatic relations remained troubled, and from time to time some incident would cause further deterioration. Experience had shown that it was impossible to regulate these relationships by means of a detailed legal instrument, and that an unstable *modus vivendi* would have to be accepted, varying according to circumstances and the current degree of mutual goodwill. It had also become apparent that the lack of co-operation between the Wendish and Prussian towns had been prejudicial to German interests.

After the treaty of 1360 relations with Flanders remained almost cordial for about fifteen years. However German merchants were soon formulating an increasing number of complaints. The *Kontor* sent a list of grievances to the Hanseatic diet, pointing out that Bruges had refused to impose penalties in cases of assault and damages, or to act as guarantor for its landlords; duty had been levied on imported cod; the import of beer from Hamburg had been forbidden; certain types of cloth had proved to be of poor quality, etc. The Hansa merely sent an embassy to Bruges, which achieved nothing. The *Kontor*, feeling it had been abandoned to its fate, attempted to act independently and without consulting the towns, secretly instructed all German merchants to leave Bruges during the winter of 1377–8. But the plan became known, and Count Louis de Male was so enraged that he arrested the Hanseatics and seized their goods. With no expectation of outside help, the *Kontor* had to submit to the count's demands, promise that its merchants would remain in Flanders, and answer the accusation of having exceeded its privileges. It was with great bitterness that the *Kontor* informed the Hansa of these events: 'Seeing that the citizens of the towns are our masters, let them consider the humiliation which has been inflicted upon us because we were not willing to give up our privileges!'

The Hanseatic diet was not entirely unmoved by this unfortunate state of affairs. It addressed a protest to the count of Flanders, refused to acknowledge the agreement reached without prior consultation, and began to negotiate. But the moment was badly chosen. Flanders was in a profoundly unsettled state. The weavers were in control of Ghent, Bruges and Ypres. Civil disorders, the insecurity of the Zwijn, the contributions levied by Bruges upon the merchants, all these led the Hanseatics to emigrate for the first time to Dutch ports. Things became much worse when Philip van Artevelde, having seized power in Ghent, occupied Bruges. The crushing defeat of Artevelde at Westrosebeke in 1382 by a French army which had hurried to the count's aid resulted in a general flight of foreign merchants from Bruges, which continued for several months until not more than twenty Hanseatics remained. For several years trade between the German towns and Flanders was almost completely at a standstill.

The death of Louis de Male in 1384 opened the way for negotiations with his successor, Philip the Bold. But the Hanseatics put forward exorbitant conditions, demanding not only high indemnities but also the erection and maintenance of a chapel of expiation, as atonement for the arrest of their merchants in 1378, and the endowing of three perpetual masses in memory of the victims of the troubles. The negotiations came to nothing, especially as the Hansa was suffering from internal dissension. The Grand Master and the Prussian towns, who were at this very moment behaving so aggressively towards England, wanted to continue the talks, while the Wendish towns had decided to move the

Kontor from Bruges. Lübeck eventually won the day: on 1 May 1388 the general diet decreed a blockade of Flanders.

The techniques employed were pretty well the same as thirty years before. Orders, kept secret as long as possible, were sent to the Bruges *Kontor*, instructing it to move to Dordrecht in Holland. Hanseatics were again forbidden to cross the line of the Meuse, and to trade with Flemings or others in the prohibited zone. To prevent smuggling, the presentation of certificates of origin for merchandise imported into Germany again became obligatory and neutrals attempting to unload Flemish products at a Hanseatic port were no longer simply refused entry, as in 1358, but had their goods confiscated – thus demonstrating beyond question how much more powerful the international position of the Hansa had become.

However one great difference between the two embargoes should be noted. In 1358 the Hanseatics had unanimously agreed that all trade with Flanders should cease. This time the Teutonic Order and the Prussian towns, already unwilling to break off the negotiations, opposed the prescribed measures with such determination that they had to be granted special concessions. They were authorised to continue selling to the Flemings the amber of which they held the monopoly. They could also buy the Mechlin cloth needed for the knights' clothing, and they were allowed to frequent the fairs of Brabant although these were held in the prohibited zone (1390). The towns of the Zuiderzee, especially Kampen, also showed little eagerness in implementing the blockade or taking action against the many smugglers, especially Prussians, who put in at their ports. The ambiguous attitude of Kampen was made a matter of reproach when a few years later it applied for admission into the Hansa.

All this explains why four years of negotiation were needed to restore peace, in spite of the accommodating attitude of the Flemings, who were often supported by the Grand Master. The Hanseatics, who were at first adamant, finally gave up their demand for a chapel of expiation, on condition that pilgrimages were made to Rome, Compostella and the Holy Land, and in return for an official apology for the arrests of 1378, presented by the four 'leaders of Flanders'. The most bitterly contested questions were those of indemnities, finally fixed at £11,000, and of responsibility for losses suffered by Hanseatics. It was decided that in the event of an attack by a Fleming within the boundaries of the countship, Ghent, Bruges and Ypres should pay compensation if the criminal were insolvent. If the damage was caused by a foreigner, even outside the boundaries of the countship (this provision was especially aimed at acts of piracy on the high seas), and if attempts to obtain compensation from the aggressor's home town proved fruitless, then the duke and the three towns were to arrest all the citizens of the town refusing compensation within their boundaries. This was a considerable extension of the Hanseatic privileges.

By the autumn of 1392 half the indemnity had been paid. Lübeck had been confirmed in her old privileges and had obtained new ones from Philip the Bold. The German merchants then returned to Bruges. Once again the Hansa had triumphed. But the victory was even more elusive than before. The Flemish towns were not disposed to countenance indefinitely privileges which they considered excessive. Even before peace had been signed they had agreed among themselves to act in concert to oppose any fresh claim made by the Hanseatics. For his part the duke of Burgundy was in a better position than the towns or even his predecessors to resist Hanseatic pretensions. The progressive extension of his sovereignty over the greater part of the Low Countries would soon blunt the economic weapon, hitherto so effective, by obliging the Hanseatics to transfer the *Kontor* to a place too remote from Flanders to be economically useful. Finally the attitude of the Teutonic Order showed how difficult it was to achieve the union which was essential to the success of the Hanseatics. Thus the blockade of 1388 marks the last great Hanseatic victory in the Low Countries.

In Novgorod at this time the situation was equally tense. Infringements of privileges, incidents and attacks were continually occurring, the more so as the Russians were inclined to obtain compensation from the Hanseatics for the invasion of their territory by the Teutonic Knights from their bases in Livonia. As early as 1367, when the knights ravaged the region of Pskov, Novgorod arrested German merchants, a step which led to reprisals against Russian merchants in Livonia. The Order forbade the export of salt and herring into Russia, a prohibition which the Hansa likewise enjoined.

Normal relations were resumed in 1371, but deteriorated fifteen years later when war broke out again. In 1388 the Hansa decided to act. In normal times she might perhaps have hesitated, but at this moment the blockade of England and Flanders was depriving Russian products of their most important outlets; and it was a good opportunity to interrupt Novgorod's trade as well. In order to make the embargo effective, the Hansa negotiated first with the Land Master of the Order, then with

Sweden and the Prussian towns, so as to prevent supplies reaching Russia via Finland, Livonia or Lithuania. Although the blockade does not seem to have been strictly enforced, it achieved its purpose. In 1392 a Hanseatic delegation, under the leadership of the Lübeck councillor Johann Niebur, went to Dorpat and then on to Novgorod to conduct peace negotiations. The grievances of both sides were settled. The former treaties, based on reciprocity of rights for Germans in Novgorod and Russians in Gotland and Livonia, were renewed and clarified. The freedom and safety of the Hanseatics were guaranteed even in the event of war between Novgorod and Sweden or the Teutonic Order.

This agreement, called by the Russians 'Niebur's kissing of the cross', remained for a century the charter of Russo-Hanseatic relations, to which reference was made when disputes arose – and disputes were just as numerous as they had been in the past. At the same time the delegation took advantage of its presence in Novgorod to demonstrate the authority of the Hansa over the *Kontor*. Without consulting a single member of the *Kontor* the delegation levied a tax on business transactions which was used to repair the *Peterhof*, then in a dilapidated state, and drew up a revised version of its statutes.

4. THE 'VITALIENBRÜDER' AND THE SUPPRESSION OF PIRACY

In the last quarter of the fourteenth century the Hansa had to face a danger which, if not new, was at least more acute than in the past: piracy.

The sudden reappearance of this scourge in northern waters was the result of the lawlessness provoked by the ambitions of the house of Mecklenburg. In 1364, as we have seen, Albert, son of the reigning duke, had been elected king of Sweden. He hoped to turn Valdemar's defeat to account by supplanting him on the throne of Denmark. The Mecklenburgers therefore refused to join the Hansa in the Peace of Stralsund. But this did not help them. Five years later they suffered another setback. On the death of Valdemar, Albert was passed over in favour of Margaret, whom the Hansa recognised as regent of Denmark. From this time on they committed acts of piracy against their rival, and naturally Hanseatic vessels were not excepted. In 1376 therefore a general diet declared war on piracy. Poundage was to be levied for a period of two years in order to equip warships. But it is significant that Rostock and Wismar, both in Mecklenburg, shirked their obligations, and Lübeck and Stralsund were left to carry on the war more or less on their own. Soon the Prussian towns backed out as well, and the great campaign which had been envisaged came to nothing.

In the following years the position of the Mecklenburgers deteriorated, while Margaret's authority was reinforced. After the death of her husband Haakon VI in 1380 she was recognised as regent of Norway on behalf of her son Olaf. In 1389, when a rebellion of the Swedish nobility drove Albert from his throne and put him in prison, she became also queen of Sweden. Stockholm, however, remained loyal to Albert, thanks to the support of the German population of the town.

In their almost desperate situation the Mecklenburgers decided to wage the war of piracy with added vigour. In a sensational proclamation they promised to open their ports 'to all those who at their own risk would go to sea to harm the kingdom of Denmark'. The appeal was highly successful. Knights, townsfolk, peasants and gallows-birds hastened to enlist under the leadership of the Mecklenburg nobility. Rostock and Wismar became pirate bases, where ships were armed and equipped, raids planned and booty safely stored and divided up. Piracy soon made navigation almost impossible in the Baltic, for the corsairs did not confine their attacks to Danish ships. The Hansa not only suffered material loss in the war, but was once again torn by an internal crisis, when two of the Wendish towns, through self-interest and loyalty to their overlord, dissociated themselves from the common cause.

It was in this period that pirates were first called *Vitalienbrüder*, a name which has remained associated with them. It is of French origin. At the beginning of the Hundred Years War the *vitailleurs* were the soldiers responsible for supplying the armies, which they eventually did by brigandage pure and simple. At sea the name was given to ships carrying supplies to fleets and ports, and finally it reached the Baltic, where it became synonymous with pirate.

Piracy enabled the Mecklenburgers to win some resounding successes. They were able to succour the garrison of Stockholm on several occasions, to carry out devastating raids along the Danish and Norwegian coasts, and to inflict serious losses on the Danish fleet. In 1391 the Mecklenburgers captured Bornholm, Visby, which provided them with an excellent base for their operations, Åbo, Viborg and various strongholds in Finland. Two years later Bergen was sacked, and its inhabitants took an oath of loyalty to Albert of Sweden. In the following year Malmö too was pillaged.

The Hansa tried to bring pressure to bear on Rostock and Wismar to stop them sheltering the pirates, but the two towns made the loyalty due to their overlord an excuse for refusing to take any action against the pirates or even to return goods which had been looted. The insecurity at sea was such that the diet of 1392 had to order a suspension of all trade with Skania for a period of three years. As a result, according to Detmar, the price of herring rose, in Prussia to three times its previous level and in Frankfurt ten times. Lübeck and Stralsund fought a hard battle with the pirates simultaneously. But if the seaways were to be made safe the co-operation of the Teutonic Order was indispensable. However the Grand Master, Conrad von Jungingen, was dreaming of further territorial expansion in the Baltic; he intended to profit by the war and did not choose to further the cause of Denmark.

A great step forward was finally achieved in 1395, when the Hansa induced the belligerents to accept its mediation. By the Peace of Skanör Albert was set free, and Stockholm was handed over to a group of seven Hansa towns – Wendish, Prussian and Livonian – to be ceded to Margaret after three years against a ransom of 60,000 marks, which however was never paid. This treaty ensured Margaret's triumph over her enemies. In 1397 she caused a proclamation to be made at Kalmar establishing the union of the three Scandinavian kingdoms under her grand-nephew, Eric of Pomerania. This union was to remain in existence, at least in theory, for more than a hundred years. A year later, in 1398, the queen made a triumphal entry into Stockholm, after confirming the Hanseatic privileges in all three kingdoms.

The Peace of Skanör removed the justification for piracy, but it remained rampant in the area around Gotland and would have persisted even longer if the Grand Master had not at last decided to co-operate with the Hansa in putting a stop to it. He may have been afraid that if he refrained from doing so he would lose to Denmark all the benefits of pacification. So he assembled 84 ships and 4,000 men at Danzig, and captured Visby without difficulty. The combined fleets of Lübeck and the Prussian towns then pursued the pirates so energetically that by 1400 the Baltic was entirely free of them.

However most of the *Vitalienbrüder* had merely moved on to another theatre of operations. They took refuge in the North Sea, where they met with a friendly reception from the count of Oldenburg and the minor lords of east Frisia. Bremen and Hamburg only got the better of them by a considerable effort, but in 1400 the pirates suffered a serious defeat in Frisia, and in the following year the last of their leaders, Godeke Michels and Klaus Störtebeker, were captured and beheaded in Hamburg, together with hundreds of their companions, whose heads were displayed to the people. The terror that they had inspired for more than twenty years, the boldness of their raids and their dramatic end, all help to explain how the *Vitalienbrüder* came to be regarded as legendary figures. Some were believed to have made distant expeditions, visiting strange tribes, even as far afield as the 'Caspian Mountains'. Störtebeker especially – only the end of whose life is historically attested – became the great commander-in-chief of all the pirates, directing their exploits on the high seas and amassing fabulous treasures. The account of his death was, of course, embellished with edifying details.

Thus the Hansa finally emerged triumphant from yet another ordeal, having defeated a threat to the prosperity of its trade scarcely less grave than those previously encountered. After two hundred years of more or less steadily increasing prosperity the 'community of the merchants of the Empire', now a community of merchant towns, was again demonstrating its strength and its vitality. It had obtained for its members, in all the countries on the shores of the Baltic and the North Sea, from Russia to England, extensive privileges and a near monopoly of long-distance trade in the two seas. The preceding hundred years had shown that it could surmount, if need be by embargo or even by war, any obstacles placed in the way of its economic dominance. The years which followed the Peace of Stralsund may therefore be considered the heyday of the Hansa.

However events had also shown that Hanseatic successes were always precarious, and that advantages won were always liable to be challenged. In foreign countries growing resistance could be discerned against privileges which were considered excessive. The Hansa was also beginning to feel the threat within its own domain of commercial rivals who were technically superior and increasingly enterprising. This is why, from the beginning of the fifteenth century onwards, the Hansa is seen to be on the defensive, preoccupied with retaining the advantages it had secured rather than with gaining new ones, even though it was still extending its field of action. Its greatest asset was still its role as intermediary between eastern and western Europe for the exchange of products vitally important to both. Its weakness, evident in the moment of its greatest achievements, lay in the divergence of its members' interests, which was tending to increase, particularly as between seaports and inland towns, or Wendish and Prussian towns. Thus the decline of the Hansa may be said to have begun in the fifteenth century. It was slow at first and hardly apparent, but it became more and more obvious in spite of the many appreciable successes still to come, and in spite of repeated though fruitless efforts at revitalisation.

PART TWO

The Hansa in the 14th and 15th Centuries

CHAPTER FIVE

The Organisation of the Hansa

I. MEMBERSHIP

Up to the middle of the fourteenth century, that is to say in the period before the formation of the Hansa of the towns, there is no real difficulty in deciding who was a member of the community. All German merchants who enjoyed the Hanseatic privileges when abroad were assumed to be members. What procedure had to be followed by candidates for membership we do not know. In a *Kontor* the alderman probably held an inquiry and gave a decision; or perhaps the candidate was accepted by his companions when the company set out from a Hanseatic port. But the problem appears to have caused no difficulties. Neither the first three *schra* of Novgorod nor the 1347 regulations of the Bruges *Kontor* make any reference to it. It seems likely that there was a ready acceptance of applicants, provided they were natives of north Germany, or of any Baltic maritime town where there was a group of Hanseatic merchants. The statute of the Bruges *Kontor*, for instance, lists members from Swedish towns.

When the Hansa of the towns had been formed, after the middle of the fourteenth century, enjoyment of the Hanseatic privileges was conditional on citizenship of a member town. It seems that there was at first some doubt about the position of merchants who were citizens of small towns not recognised as Hanseatic, and hitherto not admitted into the community, but in 1366 the diet of Lübeck made a ruling that only citizens of Hansa towns could enjoy the privileges of the 'common merchant'. Thereafter outsiders were probably obliged to acquire citizenship of a Hansa town.

The inadequacy of this ruling became apparent in the fifteenth century, when it was noted that many foreigners were becoming citizens of Hansa towns merely in order to enjoy commercial privileges. To put a stop to this, the diet of 1434 restricted membership of the Hansa to merchants born in Hansa towns. But this ruling must have been difficult to enforce, for it was reaffirmed more than once. Towards the end of the century

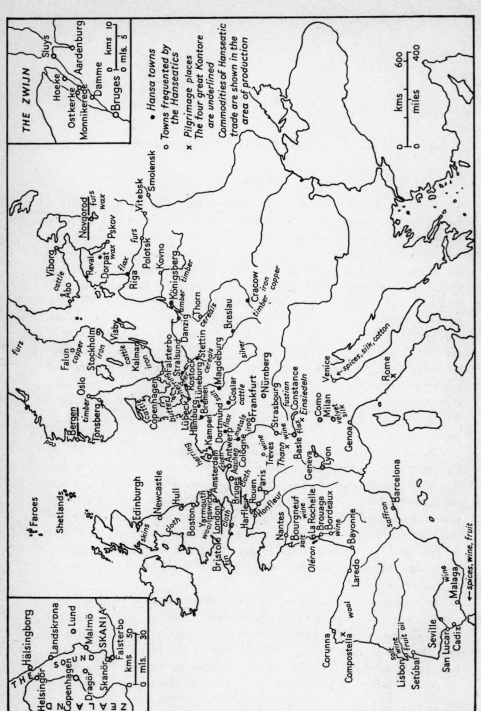

2   Hanseatic trade in Europe (15th century)

the more important towns, at least in the Westphalian third, were instructed to issue certificates attesting citizenship of a Hansa town.

But which towns were members of the Hansa after the middle of the fourteenth century? This is one of the most difficult problems in the history of the community. The answer varies according to the definition given to the phrase 'Hansa town', which can mean either a town whose merchants when abroad were admitted to the *Kontore* and enjoyed the Hanseatic privileges, or a town actively participating in the organisation and operations of the community and taking its share in the resultant expenses – in other words, a town which, directly or indirectly, received a summons to the Hanseatic diets.

One might have expected the Hansa to take the trouble to draw up an official list of member towns and keep it carefully up to date. But nothing of the sort can be traced, and it seems that the need for such a list never made itself felt. At the time of the first Hanseatic diets it was apparently taken for granted that towns interested in protecting their merchants abroad were automatically members of the Hansa, and no one thought of enumerating them. Only in very rare instances was the matter discussed. This was done in the case of Bremen, for example, which had remained outside the Hansa for a long time, applied for membership in 1358, and was accepted only after due deliberation. Later on, other towns whose earlier membership of the community was doubtful or disputed did the same. But for most of the original Hansa towns nothing of this kind was necessary and often it is only in a late document that we find them mentioned as members of the Hansa.

The Hansa was reluctant to draw up a list of its members for another reason. Periodically such a list was demanded by foreign governments, especially by England, who wished to put an end to the abuses resulting from uncertainty on this point. These demands were always met with evasive replies, on the pretext that it was impossible to present an exact list. The real reason was that the Hansa was not anxious to furnish its adversaries with a document which might be used as a basis for collective claims for compensation and demands for indemnities.

However lists of Hansa towns do exist, inserted in official documents of the fifteenth and sixteenth centuries and drawn up for various purposes: assignments of quotas in military contingents or fiscal levies, convocations of diets or rolls of absentees. Naturally these lists differ considerably, presenting what are often intentional omissions or additions. Although they are of no great value in themselves, they do at least afford us a rough estimate of the number of Hansa towns. According to the most reliable, these varied between 55 and 80. This is confirmed by certain other estimates, emanating from various sources. For instance in a petition addressed to Pope Urban VI (1378–89) mention is made of 'Lübeck, the head and leader of 77 great cities, long united in a league or association called the Hansa'. This figure, which might seem suspect because of its symbolic character, is however corroborated by other estimates made by the Hanseatics themselves. For example the Bruges *Kontor* in 1469 spoke of 'the Hansa, which comprises 72 good towns, not counting all those which look to them'. At this period the figure 72 was almost official, accepted even by foreign chancelleries: Louis XII, in 1507, wrote to 'the 72 cities of your community and confederation'.

Modern historians, however, following Walther Stein, have rejected this figure as meaningless and much too low. Taking 'Hansa town' to mean a town whose citizens enjoyed commercial privileges abroad, they have drawn up a list and arrived at a figure of more than 180. It is probable that detailed research based on the above criterion would permit the addition of several dozen more, if all member towns, whatever their importance, are regarded as of equal standing.

But we must ask whether this is a valid criterion, and whether in the fifteenth century every town whose merchants enjoyed the Hanseatic privileges was actually accepted as a member of the Hansa. According to Luise von Winterfeld's researches on Westphalia it seems that it was not so. It is evident from the documents that the only towns to be accepted as 'towns of the Hansa' were those which were summoned to the Hanseatic diets and which were represented there either directly, or indirectly by the delegate of another town. Only these towns were called upon to furnish financial or military contributions when the need arose. The 'associate towns' (*Beistädte*), although they shared in the commercial privileges, were not regarded as full members. There are therefore grounds for making a distinction within the Hansa itself between two classes of town of unequal status, the active members, of which there were about 70, called 'towns of the Hansa', and the passive members, of which there were about 100, usually very small, called 'Hanseatic towns'. The total of about 180 Hansa towns represents in some sort the survival of the Hansa of the merchants, with the organic grouping of the Hansa of the towns superimposed upon it.

It is difficult enough to list the towns which were members of the Hansa at any time between 1350 and 1450. It would be futile to try to draw up a list giving exact dates. For that one would need to know for each town the date of entry and the date of withdrawal. In most cases this is impossible. For a convincing demonstration of this fact one has only to take a close look at how a town was admitted to the Hansa – in its wider sense – and how it ceased to be a member.

There were three ways in which one could be or become a member of the Hansa: by being accepted from the beginning, that is, from about 1358, as a town of the German Hansa; by being officially admitted on request; by slipping in unofficially, which was only possible in the case of small towns.

It has been said that when the Hansa of the towns was formed, no list of members was drawn up. Obviously the most important towns figure among the original members but there are a number of doubtful cases which cannot be cleared up even by later documents.

For towns not recognised as Hanseatic from the beginning a formal request for admission was necessary. In general the application laid great stress upon the fact that the town's merchants had in former times enjoyed the privileges of the 'common merchant' and that it was therefore a Hansa town. The application was examined and accepted or rejected in a Hanseatic diet. We know of only one exception to this procedure. The town of Neuss was admitted in 1475 by imperial decree, after successfully withstanding the siege by Charles the Bold of Burgundy. Sometimes an application was refused because the applicant town was too remotely situated. Constance, for instance, was refused admission in 1417. But more often it was through fear of unfair competition, or a suspicion that the candidate was trying to extend the benefit of the commercial privileges to foreigners, especially to the Hansa's dreaded rivals, the Dutch. The applications of Utrecht, presented in 1422 and 1451, were both rejected for this reason. Arnhem, which first applied in 1380, was admitted as late as 1441, in the same year as Kampen, which had been a candidate for a similar length of time. It was, however, simply jealousy of the Livonian towns which caused the rejection of Narva's application in the sixteenth century.

As there was no authoritative list of the original members, a number of small towns, whose membership of the Hansa was, to say the least, doubtful, were able to assert their Hanseatic status and usurp the benefits of the community's rights without applying for membership. In Westphalia in particular there were constant complaints about this abuse in the second half of the fifteenth century. Eventually in 1494 it was decided that only the leading towns were competent to issue certificates of Hanseatic membership to individual merchants, which in effect made them the final judge as to which towns were members.

Similarly membership of the Hansa could be terminated in three ways: by exclusion; by withdrawal; by tacit renunciation of the rights and duties of a Hansa town.

Exclusion, although it always created a great stir, was only a minor factor in the numerical decline of the Hansa. There were relatively few exclusions, and except in the final years they were always temporary. They were most often justified by civil disorders resulting from revolution. The dispossessed council, in whole or in part, lodged a complaint with the Hanseatic diet, which then took the decision. This happened in the case of Brunswick in 1375, Bremen in 1427, Münster in 1454. Violations of the fundamental principles of the community were less common, though it was on these grounds that Cologne was excluded, since it had obtained special privileges in England in 1471.

Rather more numerous, and often permanent, were the official withdrawals. One of the reasons for these was pressure from the territorial overlord, anxious to strengthen his authority over the town. This was the case with Northeim in Saxony as early as 1430, Berlin in 1452, Halle in 1479. More common, though not openly admitted, was the desire to escape the expense of membership. Breslau announced in 1474 that her commercial interests were taking her away from the Hansa.

Much more common were *de facto* but undeclared withdrawals. A growing number of small towns could no longer fulfil the financial burdens of membership, notably the costs of delegations to the diet. Their merchants no longer frequented the *Kontore* and therefore no longer needed to take advantage of the privileges. In these circumstances their adhesion to the Hansa was meaningless and purely theoretical. After many vacillations the diet decided in 1514 to face the implications of these cases of absenteeism and about thirty towns were declared excluded from the community. Several of them, however, later applied for re-admission and were again counted as Hansa towns.

In view of all these uncertainties it would be meaningless to draw up lists of member towns for various periods. One can only say in a general way that the number of Hansa towns increased notably during the first half of the fifteenth century. Cologne in particular, hoping to strengthen her influence in the Hanseatic diet, favoured the admission of several neighbouring towns. During this period exclusions and tacit withdrawals were still rare, though later they become more numerous. Thus the Hansa appears to have attained its largest membership shortly before the mid-fifteenth century. This, then, marks the peak of the Hansa as an institution, fifty years after its zenith as an economic force.

Though fundamentally an association of towns, the Hansa counted among its members one sovereign prince, the Grand Master of the Teutonic Order. The considerable part played by the Teutonic Knights in the colonisation and development of German towns in Prussia and Livonia explains this anomaly, as it also explains the authority he exercised over the Prussian towns, which was greater than that of any other territorial ruler. One would expect the Grand Master's membership of the Hansa to have led to all his subjects being considered Hanseatics, but in fact only the citizens of six Prussian towns were considered full members, though the Order's own merchants appear to have enjoyed the Hanseatic privileges everywhere except in Novgorod. Their status was, however, somewhat ambiguous, as can be seen from a letter dispatched by the Grand Master in about 1390 to the *Kontor* at Bruges. The *Kontor* had excluded from the benefits of the Hanseatic privileges the Head of the Trade Department (*Grosschäffer*) of Königsberg and his agents, because of some flagrant violation of these privileges. The Grand Master argued that the *Grosschäffer*, being a member of the Order, could not be a member of the Hanseatic community and therefore could not be excluded from it; but, of course, he ought to respect its regulations.

There can be no doubt that the Teutonic Order, famous for its christianising influence, in which knights from far-off countries played their part – Marshal Boucicault, for example, from France, and the Earl of Derby, the future Henry IV, from England – conferred upon the Hansa in the eyes of feudal Europe a prestige to which a community of merchants could never have laid claim. The Grand Master is even described as 'chief of the Hansa' (*caput Hansae*) in certain English sources. It is also evident that the naval and military strength of the Teutonic Order was often very valuable to the Hansa. But this very strength was not without its disadvantages. The Order had its own objectives, and often involved the Hansa in enterprises that damaged its commercial interests and embroiled it in quarrels with foreign powers. Although the Order at first contributed to the prosperity of the Hansa, it was later one of the factors in its decline.

Finally there should be mentioned the strange case of the peasant community of Dithmarschen (on the west coast of Holstein), which may have joined the Hansa at a late date. In 1468 the community concluded an alliance with Lübeck, which, frequently renewed, lasted until 1558. The resounding victory which these peasants in 1500 won over the Danes strengthened the alliance, and from then on delegates from Dithmarschen appeared regularly at the Hanseatic diets. The peasants of Dithmarschen had been trading by sea since the fifteenth century, particularly with Livonia, but the Livonian towns were suspicious of these peasant traders who, with the support of Lübeck, laid claim to the Hanseatic privileges. In 1554 the Hanseatic diet decided that the inhabitants of Dithmarschen were not members of the Hansa but that their participation in the Hanseatic privileges was to be tolerated. This decision reflects the ambiguity of their status. Five years later this peasant community was overrun by the Danes and the alliance with Lübeck lapsed. The case of Dithmarschen, like that of the Teutonic Order, reveals the diversity and flexibility possible within the Hanseatic organisation.

2. HANSEATIC DIETS AND REGIONAL DIETS

From 1356 onwards the *Hansetag*, the general assembly of the Hansa towns, was the controlling organ of the Hansa. It might even be said that it was the only institution which could strictly be called Hanseatic, since the Hansa had no administrative apparatus of its own, and the regional diets took counsel also on matters which did not concern the Hansa.

The *Hansetag* was the supreme authority within the community. It decided, in principle without appeal, all important matters of concern to the whole community: the ratification of treaties or commercial charters, negotiations with foreign towns or rulers, the dispatch of embassies, questions of peace, war or blockade, financial and military measures, economic regulations of all kinds, the exclusion or admission of members, mediation in disputes between Hansa towns, and so on.

All this constituted a heavy task which, one might have thought, would have made frequent and regular meetings essential. But in fact meetings were never held at regular intervals, in spite of attempts to set up such a system in the fifteenth century. If one enumerates the assemblies which can properly be termed general, that is, those at which the towns of all three thirds were represented, one arrives at the following figures: 27 between 1356 and 1400, 12 between 1400 and 1440, and 7 between 1440 and 1480. If those diets at which only two of the thirds were represented,

but which could, at a pinch, be called general, are added, the figures become respectively 41, 14, and 17, that is, less than one per year in the
fourteenth century and scarcely one every three years in the fifteenth.

These figures are astonishingly low, and are in marked contrast to the
frequency of the regional diets, which often met several times a year. The
explanation is quite simple. The towns shrank from the high cost of
sending delegations to distant cities. Also, as some of the questions to be
debated were of interest only to certain towns, it was preferable to
summon all the towns only when questions of a truly general character
were to be discussed. This helped to cut down the number of absentees.
Finally the community relied on Lübeck to take all the necessary decisions,
except in matters of major importance, since Lübeck was in fact in
charge during the intervals between diets. The leadership of Lübeck
had become firmly established as early as the thirteenth century. In the
fourteenth it had become even more marked, and it was officially
recognised in 1418, when the town was asked, in association with the
Wendish towns, to take charge of the interests of the community.* This
decision accounts in part for the dwindling number of general assemblies
held in the fifteenth century, though it does not follow that the controlling function of Lübeck was always accepted without demur.

Because of its pre-eminence and its geographical situation Lübeck was
the normal meeting place of the general diet. Of 72 diets held between
1356 and 1480, 54 met in Lübeck. Ten were held in Stralsund, out of
consideration for the Prussian towns which put forward a plea for a less
distant meeting-point, three in Hamburg, two in Bremen, and one each
in Cologne, Lüneburg and Greifswald.

It was also Lübeck, except in very special circumstances, which took the
initiative in summoning a Hanseatic diet. Its council sent the summons to
the other Wendish towns and to the principal towns of the thirds, which
in turn passed on the invitation to the other towns in their area. That at
least was the procedure in theory, as set out in a regulation sent to the
Saxon towns in 1426. In actual fact the list of towns to which Lübeck
directly addressed the summons was continually changing.

The date fixed for the meeting was sufficiently far ahead – several
months – to allow groups of towns to agree beforehand on the agenda, to
define their point of view on certain matters and to allow their delegates,
furnished with a strict mandate, to arrive at the assembly at the time
fixed. Travelling expenses were largely the responsibility of the town

* Document No. 15 (*b*).

sending a delegate but also partly of the towns indirectly represented by it, calculated according to a scale which gave rise to fierce bargaining. In order to cut down costs, certain towns at the beginning of the fifteenth century asked if they could be represented by their syndics, who were doubtless familiar with the diplomatic and legal affairs under discussion. But the *Hansetag* of 1418 ruled that only councillors were competent to represent their towns at the diet.

The Hanseatic diet was attended by far fewer members than the total membership of the community would suggest. Ordinarily ten to twenty towns alone were represented, though often, it is true, by two or three delegates each. The highest figure, reached in 1447, was 39 delegations, scarcely half the effective total. This means that no assembly was truly representative. In addition to the delegates of towns, who alone had a vote and a choice in the drafting of the ordinances (*Rezesse*), distinguished guests were sometimes present, among them the emperor, the archbishop of Bremen, princes, either in person or by proxy, and delegates from the *Kontore*, invited for matters which concerned them.

Seen from the outside the Hanseatic diet was an impressive institution, but it suffered from internal weaknesses, some of which were rather foolish. The principal one was absenteeism,* caused by a desire to avoid the cost of sending a representative or of being involved in unpopular decisions. When there were too many absentees, it became necessary to summon a second assembly, to the great annoyance of the delegates present, who had been put to needless trouble. Unsuccessful attempts were made to enforce attendance. In 1430 it was laid down that anyone absent without good cause was to be fined one gold mark. Confiscation of goods was envisaged, and even exclusion from the Hansa. In 1457 the diet ordered thirty towns to pay the fine, unless speedy and valid excuses were proffered. But all such measures remained ineffective, mainly because no one was eager to apply them strictly.

Often the diet could not begin its work until long after the date which had been fixed, because of having to wait for the late-comers. Here again a system of fines did little to improve matters. No less irritating was the common practice of leaving the diet before the end of the session, when discussions appeared to be turning to the disadvantage of their own town. Delegates preferred to slip away before a decision was taken: this made it easier for their council to refuse to accept it. It was therefore decreed that all delegates were to present their excuses publicly before

* Document No. 21.

leaving and to subscribe in advance to the decisions arrived at after their departure.

In the council chamber the position of each delegate was fixed according to an order of precedence which naturally gave rise to frequent disputes. The chief seat, at the centre of a horseshoe-shaped table, was the prerogative of Lübeck, although it was repeatedly claimed by Cologne. Cologne took the second seat, on the right of the representative of Lübeck. The third seat, on his left, was occupied by the representative of Bremen – the seat of an archbishop – but Hamburg also laid claim to it.

Debates went on for a long time and agreement was often difficult to come by. Delegates often argued that they had no authorisation to pronounce on the matter under discussion, and that they must refer it back to their town, whose views would not be known until long afterwards. Sometimes they lodged a protest on behalf of their mandators, and their disapproval had to be inserted in the *Rezess*. After the discussions, resolutions were voted on under a simple majority rule. Those sponsored by Lübeck were usually carried. They were then inscribed on parchment in the form of a *Rezess*, to which was affixed the seal of the town in which the session had been held. Each delegate received a copy, and on his return home had further copies made and dispatched to the other towns for which he had been acting. These ordinances in their entirety represented the collective legislative and diplomatic records of the Hansa and were presumed in principle to be accepted and applied by all its members. But there was a great gap between theory and practice.

The difficulty of bringing together delegates representing all sections of the Hansa in part explains the existence of assemblies of the 'thirds'. The 'thirds' are mentioned for the first time in the 1347 statutes of the Bruges *Kontor*. Within the *Kontor* merchants were grouped according to their country of origin in one of three 'thirds', Lübeck–Saxony, Westphalia–Prussia and Gotland–Livonia. Each 'third', as the names indicate, consisted of at least two groups. The first, with Lübeck as its principal town, comprised the Wendish, Saxon, Pomeranian and Brandenburg towns. The second, led first by Dortmund and later by Cologne, included the Westphalian, Rhenish and Prussian towns. Geographically this was a strange grouping, since no community of interests can be discerned. It was no doubt established in the hope of counterbalancing the powerful Wendish–Saxon 'third'. The principal town of the remaining third, which was the least powerful, was sometimes Visby and sometimes

Riga. It is surprising that the Livonian towns did not form part of the same 'third' as the Prussian towns, particularly as they had the same overlord. No doubt the existence of this 'third' was due to the reluctance of Visby, which was still very influential in the mid-fourteenth century, to join either of the other two. These groups which developed within the Bruges *Kontor* were not found in the other *Kontore*, where the German merchants grouped themselves differently. As a result the assemblies of the 'thirds' concerned themselves almost entirely with Flemish affairs, their usefulness being to complement the badly attended *Hansetage*.

The division into 'thirds' meant that the principal town of each 'third' acted as intermediary and was therefore more influential within the Hanseatic organisation. Consequently competition for the rank of chief town of a 'third' was keen. Cologne, disregarded at first because there were not many Cologne merchants in Bruges, soon laid claim to first place in the Westphalian 'third' and by taking advantage of the decline of Dortmund, which had been weakened by warfare, succeeded in obtaining it in the middle of the fifteenth century. Brunswick was very unwilling to submit to Lübeck and eventually succeeded in obtaining a reorganisation of the 'thirds', officially adopted by the Lübeck diet in 1494. From then on there was a Lübeck 'third'(principal town Lübeck), a Westphalian 'third' (principal town Cologne) and a Saxon third (principal town Brunswick) which also included the Prussian and Livonian towns. The town of Danzig was naturally not content to take a subordinate place, and after fifty years of competition between Danzig and Brunswick for direction of the 'third' there came into existence a Saxon 'quarter' headed by Brunswick, and a Prussian–Livonian 'quarter' headed by Danzig. The three 'thirds' were thus replaced by four 'quarters'.

In the functioning of the Hanseatic organisation the diets of the 'thirds' were less important than the regional diets. The community of interests was obviously greater between towns in the same area, especially when they were under the same territorial prince. This was the case in the east with the towns of Brandenburg, Prussia and Livonia, and in the west with the towns of the countships of Cleves and Guelders. Being near each other they could meet and consult together at frequent intervals without incurring any great expense. These regional diets played a great part in the preparatory work for the Hanseatic diets* as well as in the execution of decisions taken there. They were, however, not specifically

* Document No. 22.

Hanseatic. More important to them were the decisions of a political nature relating to the maintenance of their legal status and their relations with their overlord. The groups also comprised towns which were not members of the Hansa, and their delegates apparently left the assembly when Hanseatic matters were discussed.

Among the regional diets those of the Wendish towns had the greatest influence on the policy of the Hansa. They met often, several times a year. Situated at the very centre of the Hanseatic network, owing allegiance to different territorial rulers, comprising both Baltic and North Sea ports, counting one Saxon town (Lüneburg) and at least one Pomeranian town (Stralsund) among their members, and being under the direction of the 'head of the Hansa' (Lübeck), the Wendish towns were an epitome of the whole community. They had, of course, their own interests, which were in many respects distinct from those of either the eastern or the western towns. Often they had to face charges of self-interest. But the question of repealing the mandate to direct the affairs of the Hansa which had been granted them in 1418 was never seriously considered – proof that in all essential matters they embodied the will of the Hansa as a whole.

The Hanseatic community was based ultimately on the councils of the individual member towns, which, especially in the case of the larger towns, played a decisive role. They called meetings of regional diets, discussed questions to be brought before the general diet, sent off their representatives, assumed responsibility for the cost of delegations, carried on correspondence with neighbouring towns and with Lübeck, and saw that the Hansa *Rezesse* were carried out. One need hardly stress the exceptional role played by the council of Lübeck, which often had to take serious decisions on behalf of the Hansa and to commit itself to expenditure in the common interest with no certainty that its actions would later be approved by the general diet.

Thus the administrative and political functioning of the Hansa was assured by three types of assembly, superimposed one above the other. At its base were the councils of the separate towns. Above them came the regional diets, sometimes with extended membership. And at the top there was the *Hansetag*, the only institution which was specifically Hanseatic, with the council of Lübeck acting as its permanent representative.

3. THE FOUR *Kontore* AND THE OTHER SETTLEMENTS ABROAD

The *Kontore*, or associations of German merchants abroad, were the backbone of Hanseatic trade. Founded spontaneously at different times and accorded special privileges by the ruling powers wherever they settled, they were governed by regulations which became progressively more rigorous, and came under the jurisdiction of the Hanseatic diet after the mid-fourteenth century. They were known officially as 'the community of merchants of the German Hansa in . . .' (for example *communis mercator hanse Theutonice Bergis existens*) and, more briefly, as 'the common merchant at . . .' (*der gemene kopmann to . . .*). The word *Kontor* was not used until the sixteenth century.

If one were to count up all the German merchant settlements, not only those in northern and eastern Europe but also those on the Atlantic coast as far south as Portugal, the total would be several score. Legally they were all of equal status, but obviously some were more important than others. Four of them were the mainstay of the Hansa, and fundamental to its prosperity. These were the *Kontore* at Novgorod, Bergen, London and Bruges. It is perhaps surprising that there was none in countries like Denmark, Sweden or Poland, with which the Hansa carried on an active trade. But the rise of a great *Kontor* was possible only under certain conditions which did not obtain everywhere. It was essential that there should be an important commercial centre, at a considerable distance, relatively speaking, from north Germany, where Hanseatics could make large purchases of products for which there was a big demand. It was also essential that the local authorities should be willing to grant privileges. In Denmark the Germans found only a limited quantity of saleable goods. Skania would have been more suitable, because of its dried herring, but there were no big towns there and foreigners made only short visits, when the fairs were being held. In Sweden, Stockholm seemed well adapted for the development of an important *Kontor*, but although German merchants were very numerous, they were awarded no special privileges there. Finally in Poland trade was carried on by the Hansa towns of Thorn, Cracow and Breslau, so that the need for another settlement was never felt.

The organisation of the *Kontore* was much more rigorously regulated than that of the home towns. Each had its own leaders, tribunal and treasury. Unlike the community of Hansa towns, each *Kontor* had the legal status of a corporation. It had its own seal, which in the case of London and Bruges bore a two-headed eagle, in Bergen a cod-fish, and in Novgorod the key of St Peter. All merchants visiting the town were obliged to present themselves to the authorities of the *Kontor*, to submit to the strict discipline prescribed by the statutes, and to lodge within the walled precinct (except in Bruges). Each year the assembly of all the merchants elected a variable number of aldermen, who were obliged to accept the appointment, which was not rendered any more attractive by the fact that it was unpaid. Even with the help of assessors, the administration of a *Kontor* was a heavy task. It entailed jurisdiction over the members, administration of the funds drawn from fines and from a turnover tax (*schoss*), commercial, legal or diplomatic negotiations with the local authorities, correspondence with the towns, and perhaps attendance at the Hanseatic diet to furnish information (the *Kontore* were not members of the Hansa, and were not normally called in to attend). Although they were in general administered along the same lines, there were quite noticeable differences between the various *Kontore*, which deserve to be studied.

Novgorod. The Hanseatic *Kontor* at Novgorod (*curia sancti Petri, Peterhof*) is one about which we know most, owing to its statute (*schra*) which appeared in seven successive revisions between the middle of the thirteenth century and the beginning of the seventeenth. Situated on the right bank of the river Volkhov, at the corner of the market square, it covered a fairly spacious site, surrounded by a palisade with only one entrance gate. The principal building, the stone-built Church of St Peter, was not used only for religious purposes. It housed the treasury, the archives and the weighing machines, and also served as a depot for goods of the most varied kinds. At times so much was crammed into it that it became necessary to forbid the stacking of goods on the altar. Finally in case of attack the church was the ultimate refuge for the merchants. Around the church there were hutments which served as living quarters for the merchants (*Meistermänner*), their assistants and apprentices, and also the great meeting-hall, business premises and administrative offices, stalls, malt-house, presbytery and prison. Since the fourteenth century the Germans had also been in possession of the Court of St Olaf, or Court of the Goths, originally the settlement of the Gotlanders, situated near the river, where some of the merchants lodged when accommodation was short.

The importance of the Novgorod *Kontor* explains the bitter rivalries which it provoked among the Hansa towns, as each was anxious to gain control of its administration. Visby, heir to the Gotland Community, re-tained its influence over the *Peterhof* until about 1293. Then for over a hundred years Lübeck and Visby contended for control, until the Livonian towns, especially Dorpat and Reval, entered the field and from 1442 onwards prevailed.

The principal peculiarity of the Novgorod *Kontor* lay in the alterna-tion, more clearly marked than elsewhere, between the winter merchants (*Winterfahrer*) and the summer merchants (*Sommerfahrer*), travelling by both land and water. They seldom met, and each group had its own separate organisation. Over a period of two hundred years this underwent a series of transformations. Up to the middle of the fourteenth century the general assembly of the merchants (*Steven*) had complete liberty to elect the alderman (*Oldermann*) of the *Hof*, who appointed four assessors. His powers seem to have been more absolute than elsewhere, as was only natural in a *Kontor* so isolated and remote. However appeal might be made against his decisions to the council of Visby, and later to that of Lübeck: the two councils quarrelled over this prerogative from the end of the thirteenth century and throughout the fourteenth. The alder-man also administered the *Kontor* funds which the merchants took with them when they departed and deposited at Visby. The revenue was derived partly from fines and the letting of buildings and stalls, but mainly from the dues on exported goods, originally paid to the prince of Novgorod. The priest of the Church of St Peter came with the mer-chants and returned with them. For hundreds of years his salary was a bone of contention. In addition to his ecclesiastical functions, he dealt with the correspondence of the *Kontor*, a duty which carried with it in the mid-fourteenth century the privilege of summoning the assembly of merchants.

When the *Kontor* became subordinate to the towns, the latter inter-vened to restrict its independence. From 1346, if not earlier, the priest was appointed by Visby and Lübeck in turn and later on by Dorpat and the Livonian towns. The *Steven* lost its right to elect the alderman, a func-tion which also fell to Lübeck and Visby, who exercised it in turn. Then the office of 'alderman of the *Hof*' was abolished in favour of two aldermen of the church (*Olderlude von St Peter*), who in their turn resigned the direction of the *Kontor* to lower officials (*Vorstender*). In the fifteenth century a completely new official, the *Hofknecht*, appointed by the Livonian towns, became the actual head of the *Kontor*. His authority rested on the fact that he alone resided permanently in Novgorod, sometimes for several consecutive years. This, together with the fact that he spoke Russian and was in constant communication with the local authorities, led him, in spite of his title – the literal meaning of which was 'servant of the *Hof*' – to be widely respected and to play an important role in politics. Nevertheless the Novgorod *Kontor*, which in the early part of the fifteenth century had often been visited by more than 200 merchants and their assistants at a time, declined rapidly as the century progressed, until it was finally closed in 1494.

Bergen. The Bergen *Kontor*, called by the Norwegians *Tyskebrygge*, the 'German quay', consisted, like the *Peterhof*, of an enclosed and privileged site on the fiord. It contained about twenty adjacent plots (*gaarden*), at first rented, later gradually purchased outright. Each of these sites was rectangular in shape, 18 to 20 metres wide and about 100 metres deep. The front faced the sea where the ships docked. At the back there were wooden buildings – up to fifteen in each *gaard* – assembly-halls (*Schüttinge*), living quarters and business premises, some that could be heated, some occupied only in summer. The whole, periodically destroyed by fire and rebuilt, still exists and gives a fairly accurate idea of the appearance of the 'German quay' in the Middle Ages. The church of the Germans, St Mary's, stone-built and partly Romanesque, which remained the property of the *Kontor* from the fifteenth to the eighteenth century, is also still standing.

The organisation of the *Kontor* is not known in any great detail. The main lines appear to have been laid down in 1343, when the king of Norway confirmed the Hanseatics in their former privileges. A little later it was made subordinate to the towns, which in fact meant Lübeck. Indeed, of the four great *Kontore*, the 'German quay' was certainly the least open to all Hanseatics. Although merchants from Westphalia and the Wendish towns were to be found in Bergen, the overwhelming majority were always from Lübeck, and the preponderance of Lübeck was never called in question, at least up to the sixteenth century. Only a merchant from a town administered under Lübeck law could be elected alderman, and Lübeck had the right to nominate the priest of St Mary's Church. The number of aldermen appears to have varied. Six are mentioned in 1388, but only two in the fifteenth century, assisted by eighteen jurors.

The German colony in Bergen included not only the non-resident merchants but also a group of craftsmen who far outnumbered them. The latter had settled there as early as the thirteenth century and lived outside the *Tyskebrygge*. Among them were to be found furriers, tailors, goldsmiths, barbers and bakers, but all were known by the generic name of *Schomaker*, since the great majority of them were in fact shoemakers. These German craftsmen were originally subject to a Norwegian bailiff, but at the end of the fourteenth century they were placed under the jurisdiction of the *Kontor*, whose principal concern was to prevent them from engaging in trade, which occasioned frequent disputes. The German merchants and craftsmen together accounted for perhaps quarter of the total population of the town.

London. The London *Kontor*, situated on the bank of the Thames a short distance upstream from London Bridge, was called the *Stalhof*, in English the 'Steelyard'. The name is not derived, as was once believed, from the steel imported by the Cologne merchants, but comes from the word *stal* and simply means a place where goods are offered for sale. The *Stalhof* was located between the river and Thames Street, being approximately square in shape and surrounded by a wall. It comprised the original settlement of the Cologne merchants, the Guildhall, fronting on Thames Street, where the merchants held their general assemblies, and some adjacent plots which were acquired later. At first the Germans rented the land and the main buildings, but they were gradually able to buy up the freeholds, and their ownership was confirmed by the Treaty of Utrecht (1474). As elsewhere the yard contained a number of buildings, both business premises and living quarters, but there was no church, only a chapel. The Church of Allhallows the Great, which was frequented by the Germans, lay outside the enclosure.

Only the broad outlines of the organisation of the Steelyard are known up to the beginning of the fifteenth century. The Cologne merchants, who had been granted privileges as early as the mid-twelfth century, were joined during the thirteenth century first by Westphalians and then by 'Easterlings'. After a temporary secession of the merchants from Lübeck and Hamburg, caused by the chicaneries of the Cologne merchants, the various groups banded together in 1282 to form a 'Hansa of the Germans'. They did not, however, amalgamate completely. The statute of 1437 shows that the merchants of the Steelyard were divided according to their origin into three thirds, though these were different from those of the Bruges *Kontor*. The first, led by Cologne, included the Rhinelanders. The second comprised the Westphalians, the Saxons and the merchants from the Wendish towns. The third, led by Danzig, covered the merchants from Prussia, Livonia and Gotland. This separation appears to have counted for very little, however, being invoked only for the election of assessors. The control of policy, of the assemblies, the treasury and the tribunal, was common to all three thirds. Each third appears, however, to have had its own salaried secretary or *clerc*, whose importance increased in the fifteenth century as the volume of correspondence grew. These clerks were sent sometimes on diplomatic missions, not only to Hansa towns but also to foreign courts.

As in the other *Kontore*, the general assembly of the merchants of the Steelyard elected its leader, the 'German alderman' (*aldermannus Theutonicorum*), annually at the beginning of January. From among the Council of Twelve the alderman chose two, not from his own third, as his assessors; and the three formed the executive committee of the *Kontor*. The peculiarity of the Steelyard, however, lay in the existence of another alderman, the 'English alderman'. Proposed by the merchants and installed by the king, the English alderman had to be a citizen, sometimes the mayor, of London and a member of the city council, to which he swore an oath of loyalty on taking up his duties. He was usually a native of Germany who had acquired English nationality. His authority was not limited to the Steelyard but extended to all Hanseatic *Kontore* in England, for which reason he was sometimes referred to as the 'supreme alderman of all England' (*overste alderman van al Engellant*). His function was both judicial – to act as mediator in disputes between Hanseatics and Englishmen – and diplomatic – to represent and defend the interests of the Germans before the native authorities. This curious integration of the Hanseatic organism into existing English institutions, which certainly had its advantages, led also to an obligation which has no equivalent in any other *Kontor*. From the end of the thirteenth century onwards the merchants of the Steelyard were responsible for manning and maintaining Bishopsgate, one of the entrances to the city.

Bruges. The *Kontor* at Bruges was exceptional in that it did not have a self-contained site at its disposal. The German merchants therefore lodged with landlords or in rented houses. They were also to be found in Damme, a wine staple, in other ports on the Zwijn, and especially in Sluys, particularly favoured by the seamen. Since 1442 the *Osterlinge*, as the Hanseatics were called, had possessed a house of their own, and another, larger one was completed in 1478. It was situated on the square, which was their favourite meeting place. Previously they had held their assemblies in the refectory of the Carmelite convent, whose church was their official religious centre.

The *Kontor* was granted its first privileges in 1252 and soon became prosperous. But it was not properly organised for another hundred years, and then probably only after serious disagreements among its members. According to the statute of 1347,* the merchants were divided into three thirds, Lübeck–Saxony, Westphalia–Prussia and Gotland–Livonia, a grouping which seems to reflect that of the Hansa towns. The thirds had a considerable degree of autonomy. Each elected annually two aldermen (who named six assessors chosen from among their third), held separate assemblies, and appointed delegates who negotiated with the town in matters concerning their third, and controlled its own treasury. Funds were derived principally from the *schoss*, a sales tax of a third of a groschen per pound, that is, 1/720 of the value. The Gotland third, however, being poorer, was obliged to charge a higher rate, which led it in the mid-fifteenth century to demand and obtain the amalgamation of the three treasuries. In 1486 the decline in the *Kontor*'s fortunes caused the number of aldermen to be reduced from six to three, one for each third, and the number of assessors from eighteen to nine. Even when most of the Hanseatics had emigrated to Antwerp, the aldermen continued for a long time to stay at Bruges, maintaining the fiction that the *Kontor* was still active.

The Bruges *Kontor* was incontestably the most important of the four, both because of the volume of business transacted there and because of the number of merchants from all Hanseatic regions who frequented it. The general assembly of 1457 brought together about 600 people, probably including assistants, servants and seamen. For a ceremonial procession in 1440 in honour of Philip the Good, the Hanseatics provided 136 horsemen (compared with 150 Italians and 48 Spaniards), which would give about the same total figure. The diplomatic role played by the aldermen was exceptionally important, as they maintained diplomatic relations not only with the rulers of the Low Countries, the counts of Flanders and the duke of Burgundy, but also with the French and Spanish sovereigns, since they were the natural spokesmen of the Hanseatic establishments scattered along the Atlantic coast. Lastly the cultural influence of the *Kontor* was considerable. It was there that the Hanseatics perfected their commercial and financial techniques, and from there that the literary and artistic movements of the west penetrated into north Germany.

Other settlements abroad. However important the four great *Kontore*

* Document No. 17.

may have been in the organisation and business life of the Hansa, the part played by more modest establishments, scattered throughout the countries bordering on Germany, must not be overlooked. Legally, these factories were no different from the *Kontore*. Their organisation was the same and their merchants enjoyed the Hanseatic privileges. According to an instruction sent by Cologne to her citizens in England, as soon as four merchants found themselves together in a foreign town, they were to elect an alderman and obey him. A similar stipulation was made by Lübeck. This means that Hanseatic communities abroad must have been more numerous than is generally known.

The most prosperous of these settlements probably contained as many merchants as did the *Kontore*. This may be presumed to have been true of Pskov, especially when trade with Novgorod was interrupted. It was certainly true of the 'company of the common merchant from German towns in Copenhagen', founded in 1378 by citizens of the Wendish and Pomeranian towns. This company owned several houses in the town, and obtained the lion's share of Danish trade until its privileges were suppressed in 1475. Some of these establishments possessed an enclosed site, as at Polotsk, where the Germans had their own church, at Tönsberg and doubtless at Oslo, and at Boston, where it was called the *Stalhof*, as in London.

Like the *Kontore*, these settlements, autonomous at first, were brought under the control of the towns after the mid-fourteenth century. This usually meant that they were controlled by the town whose merchants were present in the greatest number, a process which was accentuated in the fifteenth century with the development of the staple. In this way Pskov came to depend closely on Dorpat, Polotsk on Riga, Kovno on Danzig, Tönsberg and Oslo on Rostock. In the west geographical factors led to these settlements being made subordinate to the great *Kontore*. Thus the Bruges *Kontor* – with the support of the Hansa, which was anxious to establish there the staple for all the commerce of the Low Countries – asserted its authority over the factories in Antwerp, Dordrecht, Utrecht and many other towns. Towards the south it exercised control over the settlements along the Atlantic coast, notably those at Nantes, Bourgneuf, La Rochelle, Bordeaux and Lisbon.

In the same way the London Steelyard never relaxed its efforts to bring all the Hanseatic settlements in England under its control, and even destroy their independent organisation. The most active establishments were those at Ipswich, Yarmouth, Lynn, Boston, Hull, York and

Newcastle. From the fourteenth century onwards they sent delegates to the Steelyard in London to co-operate in working out a common policy. They were also obliged to send to London the dues levied on their merchants. When in the mid-fifteenth century certificates of Hanseatic membership were required, the Steelyard reserved to itself the exclusive right to issue them for England. But it did not succeed in suppressing the independent organisations of the factories, which retained their own aldermen. Boston in particular resisted its interference strenuously, being frequented mainly by citizens of Lübeck coming from Norway, and dependent on the Bergen *Kontor*, which on occasion spoke of 'our alderman of Boston in England'. In 1474, however, the Steelyard succeeded in obtaining recognition of its authority over Boston, conjointly with that of the Bergen *Kontor*.

4. CHARACTERISTICS AND RESOURCES OF THE HANSA

One of the most striking features of the history of the Hansa is the contrast between the breadth of its activities and the amorphousness of its structure. The community, made up of towns none of which was fully sovereign, did not even rank as a corporation. After it had forbidden the use of the seal of the Gotland Community, it did not even have a seal of its own. It had no common institution other than the *Hansetag*, no permanent officials (at least not before the mid-sixteenth century), no regular financial resources, no fleet and no army.

It would be reasonable to expect that such an organism, which had none of the traits characteristic of a state, but which nevertheless wielded the power of a state, should have perplexed jurists steeped in the principles of Roman law. However in the Middle Ages there is little trace of any desire to define the legal character of the Hansa. The question only arose in certain special cases. For example in 1418, a dispute at law having arisen between Hamburg and Bremen, the latter town asked Cologne for a copy of the foundation charter of the German Hansa. Cologne replied, with good reason, that no such charter was to be found in her archives. Fifty years later, after the arrest of the German merchants in England, the Privy Council tried to justify the measure by enunciating the principle of the collective responsibility of the Hanseatic merchants. In reply it received a vertitable treatise on the nature of the Hansa.* It was neither a society (*societas*), nor a college (*collegium*), nor

* Document No. 26

a corporate body (*universitas*), but a permanent federation (*firma confederatio*) of towns, owing allegiance to various princes, having no common institution – even the Hanseatic diet was not admitted as such – and consequently not responsible for the acts or undertakings of any of its members.

Such a loose organisation had its advantages but also entailed certain drawbacks, especially in the event of serious difficulties. In certain quarters, notably in Lübeck, this had not gone unnoticed. It was for this reason that attempts were made in the last third of the fourteenth and throughout the fifteenth century to strengthen the Hansa by means of leagues, with precisely defined financial and military obligations, concluded for a fixed number of years and often renewed. The earliest was the Cologne Confederation, formed in 1367 to intensify the war effort against Denmark. This included Holland and Zeeland towns which were not members of the Hansa. Though it was extended several times beyond the original date, it was not maintained after 1385, by which time all the clauses of the Peace of Stralsund had been fulfilled.

In the fifteenth century the increasingly alarming pressure exerted on the towns by the princes gave rise to new leagues, called *tohopesaten* ('standing together'). In 1418 Lübeck, which had just been officially recognised as the head of the Hansa, put forward a plan for a league based on the organisation of the Wendish league. It was to comprise about forty Hansa towns from the various regions and in case of aggression provided for measures of mediation followed, if necessary, by military action. The size of the military contingent and of the financial subsidy to be contributed by each town were laid down. This plan appears to have been approved in principle, but subsequently no trace of its activities can be found. However the *tohopesate* was renewed in 1430 and again in 1443, restricted this time to the towns of the Lübeck third, and on several later occasions.

In the attempts to bring all the Hansa towns into a closer union with precise obligations, the *tohopesaten* were only moderately successful, since they aroused the mistrust that the towns always showed towards commitments of a political or military nature. They were much less effective than the regional leagues, in which the feeling of solidarity was strengthened by the threat of oppression from an overlord common to all the members. It was also always recognised that these leagues were clearly distinct from the Hansa proper. The hope, cherished for a time by Lübeck, of turning the Hansa into a true league was disappointed, and it was never anything more than a community devoted to exclusively commercial ends.

Yet in spite of its structural weaknesses the Hansa was not without the means to make its own members, as well as foreign states, adhere to its decisions. In dealing with a single town, persuasion, mediation and finally sanctions were used. If a town was recalcitrant, submission was often achieved by means of letters, verbal messages, exhortations and threats. Disputes arising between two Hansa towns were more serious, and it was important to achieve a settlement without allowing any outside intervention. The *Hansetag* of 1381 gave precise instructions on this subject. Neighbouring towns were encouraged to meet to attempt a reconciliation between the opposing parties, but any participation by a territorial ruler in this mediation was to be avoided. If they were unsuccessful, the matter was to be brought before the Hanseatic diet, which gave a final decision, appeal to any prince or to the emperor being forbidden. Naturally the efficacy of this procedure varied a good deal. Usually, after much close bargaining and a hard-won compromise, the differences were settled. Occasionally, however, a prince, jealous of his authority, would forbid towns owing him allegiance to take their disputes before the Hanseatic diet, as did the Grand Master in 1426 in the case of a dispute among the Prussian towns. And occasionally the *Hansetag*, faced with a refusal to acquiesce in its judgement, would have to have recourse to sanctions. In minor cases, such as negligence in carrying out Hanseatic obligations, the offenders were fined. In serious cases, especially when a duly constituted council was overthrown by violence, the diet decreed the exclusion of the rebel town, thus depriving its merchants of the benefits of the privileges abroad and of all commercial relations with other towns. We have seen that Brunswick (1375), Bremen (1427) and Cologne (1471) submitted to such an exclusion, which was, however, temporary. Enforcing the obedience of a recalcitrant town by military action was never contemplated.

Exclusion could, of course, also be used against individuals guilty of having transgressed the 'law of the common merchant'. Sentence was pronounced either by the town of which the merchant was a burgess, or by the *Kontor* where the offence had been committed. It involved his banishment from all Hansa towns and the confiscation of his goods, a certain proportion however being left for the heirs. In times of war this penalty was inflicted on all those smuggling goods into the blockaded country. An exclusion which attracted much attention was that of

Christian Kelmer, a great merchant from Dortmund and former alderman of the London Steelyard, which took place in 1385. Having imported furs into England and paid the customs duty demanded, he had re-exported the unsold furs and paid customs duty again, not bothering about the customs exemption enjoyed by the Hanseatics in England and so running the risk of calling this exemption in question.* Since he was highly regarded at court, Kelmer had no difficulty in obtaining English nationality and he took frequent advantage of it to make trouble for his former compatriots: proof that exclusion, even of one individual, could be a two-edged weapon.

In dealing with a foreign power, the Hansa had in essence three weapons at her command with which to press her claims: negotiation, suspension of trade and war.

When a dispute arose, usually as a result of attacks upon merchants or some violation of the Hanseatic privileges, an attempt was first of all made to reach a friendly settlement. Negotiations with the foreign town or prince were conducted by the heads of the *Kontore*. If these led to nothing, the diet sent an embassy, formed, at least on important occasions, of delegates from various towns, which shared the cost among themselves. In actual fact it was often Lübeck which took on the burden and expense of providing these embassies.

In the thirteenth and fourteenth centuries the delegates were always members of a town council, and usually merchants. In the fifteenth century it became more and more common to employ jurists, university graduates well-versed in Roman law. Officials, notably the syndics of the towns, were also entrusted with diplomatic missions. However the councillors retained their prestige, and their participation was essential to any important embassy. For example in 1476 the Bruges *Kontor* wrote to Lübeck about a proposed embassy to Louis XI of France, saying that the king would consider himself insulted if the leader of the delegation were a mere secretary without a doctor's degree.

Hanseatic diplomats had a reputation for skill and tenacity in negotiation. One of the English negotiators of the Peace of Utrecht said that he would prefer to treat with any prince in the world rather than a Hanseatic councillor. As was only natural, certain members of the council made a speciality of diplomatic work and were constantly on the move. One of these was the Lübeck councillor Johann Doway, who undertook several missions in Flanders, Denmark, Gotland and Livonia.

* Document No. 23.

These missions were not without their dangers. Apart from the perils of travel by sea, the ambassadors risked imprisonment and even assassination. In treaties signed with the rulers of Novgorod and Smolensk in the thirteenth century, the murder of an ambassador was listed as entailing liability for a double indemnity.

When negotiations were unsuccessful, and if the stake was worth it, the Hansa decreed a suspension of trade with the offending country. For a long time this economic weapon was the most effective in its armoury, and was employed in the thirteenth, fourteenth and fifteenth centuries against various countries, and at times simultaneously against several. These included Poland, Novgorod, Norway, England, Scotland, Flanders, France, Castile and even Venice (in this case, it is true, on the orders of the Emperor Sigismund). An embargo was obviously damaging to the Hanseatics themselves, but its effects were usually felt even more severely by the country concerned, which suffered not only a decline in its trade but the loss of essential foodstuffs, grain in the west and in Norway, salt and herring in the east. An embargo, therefore, though its effects were not immediately apparent, soon led to negotiations which ended, after two or more years, by restoring peace.

In Flanders the Hansa used a more flexible form of embargo, transferring the *Kontor* from Bruges to another town in the Low Countries. This avoided the disadvantage of a complete cessation of the Hanseatics' trade in an area vitally important to them, and Bruges, alarmed at the prospect of being supplanted by a rival, soon showed itself more accommodating. As a result the earliest transfers of the *Kontor*, the first in 1280, the second in 1307, from Bruges to Aardenburg, carried out with the approval of the count of Flanders, were a complete success. Two subsequent moves, in 1358 and 1388, to Dordrecht, aimed at Bruges and at the count of Flanders simultaneously, were still effective. But the extension of Burgundian rule over the greater part of the Low Countries rendered the system ineffective, as it involved the transfer of the *Kontor* to a port too remote from Flanders. The last transfer, to Deventer and Utrecht in 1451, was a partial failure.

It was difficult to enforce the strict application of an embargo. The Hansa tried to achieve it by rigorous and minutely detailed regulations. Merchants were required to swear an oath promising not to frequent the forbidden zone and certificates had to be produced attesting the origin of all goods transported. Offenders were punished by banishment and by confiscation of their goods. Smuggling could never be entirely eliminated but up to at least the fifteenth century it did not prevent an embargo being successful.

For the Hanseatics themselves, however, embargoes entailed serious and cumulative disadvantages. Not only did they hinder Hanseatic trade in one area, but their repercussions weakened it elsewhere. Also they put a heavy strain on Hanseatic solidarity. The various groups of towns never had identical interests, and in applying a blockade they showed varying degrees of enthusiasm. Because of this there was almost constant bad feeling between the Wendish and Prussian towns during the fourteenth century. For the Hansa's competitors, the Hollanders and south Germans, an embargo provided an excellent opportunity to take their rivals' place. In these circumstances the economic weapon, highly effective in the period of Hanseatic expansion, quickly became blunted when the period of decline set in.

The ultimate sanction was war. Again and again the Hansa had to resort to war, either to safeguard her independence or to protect her merchants. Although the community had no financial resources of its own, no fleets, no soldiers other than those of the towns and of the Teutonic Order, it nevertheless managed to cope with the situation. The financial difficulties were surmounted by levying duties on goods (*Pfundzoll*) and using the funds so obtained to equip warships and maintain the contingents put in the field by the towns. The military resources of the Hansa always remained modest, and she was obliged to seek allies not only among the German princes but also among foreign states. In fact Hanseatic military action was essentially a war of piracy – large-scale naval operations were rare. Except in Denmark and Norway the Hanseatics did not risk incursions into enemy territory.

The principal adversary of the Hansa was Denmark, whose designs upon north Germany, periodically revived, constituted a threat to the very existence of the community, while its control of the Sound made it capable of striking heavy blows at Hanseatic trade. War with Denmark is a constantly recurring feature of the history of the Hansa. Mostly it was waged for political reasons, usually involving the other Scandinavian states; but there were also many conflicts – with England, Holland, France, Castile, not to mention the pirates – which arose from commercial matters. On the other hand there were no land wars which can properly be called Hanseatic, not even those waged by the Teutonic Order against the Russians, to which the Hansa sometimes contributed a financial subsidy. Disputes with ruling princes never gave rise to concerted action by the community. The most serious effort in that direction was the dispatch of contingents to the siege of Neuss by various towns in 1475, to reinforce the imperial army in its struggle against Charles the Bold of Burgundy.

It is not surprising that in spite of the number of wars in which it became involved the Hansa, being a society of merchants and having as its objective the prosperity of their trade, should always have been very reluctant to have recourse to arms. War implied great financial sacrifices, interruption of trade, loss of ships and goods; it entailed dangerous concessions to allies always greedy for their own advantage; it brought back the scourge of piracy. Finally, even more than an embargo, it accentuated the lack of unity within the community, as a great number of towns tried to evade the burden of heavy military commitments. In fact most of the Danish wars were waged by the Wendish towns alone. The only wars that one might truly call Hanseatic were those fought against Valdemar IV from 1361 to 1370 and against England from 1470 to 1474. The most clear-sighted of the Hansa's leaders, especially in Lübeck, were fully aware that war endangered the very existence of the community, and they had recourse to it only in the last extremity.

5. THE HANSA, THE EMPEROR AND THE PRINCES

The Hansa towns, with the exception of Visby, Cracow and the Swedish towns, were all situated within the territory of either the Holy Roman Empire or the Teutonic Order. Even as late as the fourteenth century the Hanseatics called themselves 'the common merchants of the Roman Empire of Germany'. But in reality the Hansa and the Empire were two quite distinct political entities which made only a few tentative and short-lived attempts to act in concert.

In the early days, it is true, Lothair III, and especially Henry the Lion, who was as much the emperor's deputy in north Germany as a territorial prince, gave decisive encouragement to German commercial expansion in the Baltic. The privileges conferred on Lübeck by Frederick I and Frederick II can also be regarded as evidence of a positive policy in this direction. But after the decline of imperial power in north Germany in the mid-thirteenth century, the emperors concentrated all their efforts on restoring their power in south Germany. The Hansa developed independently of them, and indeed by assuming responsibility for the protection of German commerce in northern Europe, took their place.

When the emperor did intervene in the north, it was as lord of the imperial cities rather than as emperor. But there were very few imperial cities in the area. Apart from Lübeck there were only Dortmund and Goslar and, in an already marginal zone, Nordhausen and Mühlhausen in Thuringia.

In the Middle Ages only one emperor, Charles IV of Luxembourg, showed any real interest in the Hansa. At the beginning of his reign he had seemed hostile rather than friendly. He refused to support the Hansa against the Danes, and the clause in the Golden Bull which forbade the formation of urban leagues gave cause for anxiety. But his attitude changed after the Hanseatic victory over Denmark. In 1375 he went in person to Lübeck and stayed there for ten days, presiding over a session of the town council and addressing the councillors as 'my lords'. He appears to have envisaged a strengthening of the bonds between the Hansa and the Empire. His acquisition of Lusatia and the march of Brandenburg seemed to presage a more active policy in north Germany, manifesting itself on the economic front in a closer relationship between Bohemia, the North Sea and the Baltic by way of the Elbe. Lübeck seems not to have welcomed these projects, which were in any case abandoned on the death of Charles IV three years later. None of his successors implemented his plans, and Lübeck had to wait five hundred years for the honour of a second imperial visit, in the person of William I.

In the fifteenth century the Emperor Sigismund also intervened in Hanseatic affairs, but only as mediator in the conflict between Lübeck and the Hansa which broke out after the setting up of a town council hostile to the patriciate. Peace was restored but no further collaboration took place. Sigismund later appealed to the Hansa for help against the Hussites, but he himself never thought of supporting the Hansa in any way. Finally in the sixteenth and seventeenth centuries the Habsburgs tried to make the Hansa a partner in their European policy, in collaboration with Spain. But the Hanseatics were reluctant to participate, especially as by this time the political situation had been embittered by religious differences. It is therefore probably true to say that throughout the centuries the Empire and the Hansa never managed to co-operate.

But as nearly all the Hansa towns were situated within the territory of some lay or ecclesiastical prince and were subject in some degree to his authority, one of the major problems which the Hansa had to solve was that of the relationship between town and prince. In the thirteenth and fourteenth centuries the principalities were still too weak to prevent the emancipation of the towns or to oppose effectively the formation of urban leagues. The great strength of the towns lay in their wealth, which enabled them to make loans to the princes, who were always short of money, and to obtain in exchange the attributes of sovereignty, among them the right to levy tolls and market dues, to fortify the town and to exercise criminal jurisdiction. The homage rendered to the prince was usually balanced by the confirmation of privileges, and there was a strict protocol governing his right of entry into a town. Only in the lands of the Teutonic Order was the situation different. Up to the battle of Tannenberg (1410) the Prussian towns were kept in fairly close subjection by the Grand Master and could only carry out the decisions of the Hansa with his approval.

But after the mid-fourteenth century the progressive strengthening of the German principalities modified this equilibrium. The princes did all they could to reassert their authority over the by now almost independent towns and to impose on them an economic policy which favoured the interests of their own territory and thus called in question the towns' relationship with the Hansa. This gave rise to many confused conflicts, connected sometimes with similar disputes in the Low Countries and south Germany. In 1388 the archbishop of Cologne, encouraged by the overwhelming defeat of the Swabian Town League, attacked Dortmund, but without gaining any decisive success. Similarly in 1396 the duke of Brunswick, supported by the duke of Mecklenburg, made an abortive attempt to take by force the town of Lüneburg, which was aided by Lübeck, Hamburg and several Saxon towns. Aware of their peril, the Hansa towns tried to organise their defences against the ambitions of the princes. But as we have already seen, the attempt to strengthen the Hansa with a *tohopesate*, a military and political league, had very little practical result. More effective were the regional leagues, especially those of the Wendish and Saxon towns. Within this framework the principle that military or financial aid must be given to any town attacked by a prince, and that princes should be excluded from the settlement of any dispute between towns, was often applied.

Happily for the towns, solidarity between the princes was no stronger than that between the towns. In 1443 consultations took place between the king of Denmark, the dukes of Mecklenburg and Brunswick, and the margrave of Brandenburg, with a view to finding some means of subduing the towns, but no common action resulted. The struggle became particularly fierce towards the middle of the fifteenth century, when the princes achieved some measure of success. The most marked was that of the margrave of Brandenburg, who forced the cities within his electorate, notably Berlin and Frankfurt-on-the-Oder, to withdraw from the Hansa. In the west the duke of Guelders seized Arnhem in 1466. However the towns usually emerged victorious from these attacks, in spite of their marked military inferiority. From 1440 onwards the Prussian towns allied themselves with the nobility against the abuse of power by the Teutonic Order and forced the Grand Master Paul von Russdorf to abdicate. This humiliation inflicted on a powerful prince had widespread repercussions. Stettin, with the aid of the Wendish towns, repulsed the attack of the margrave of Brandenburg. In the west the archbishop of Cologne, despite great efforts, failed to seize Soest (1444–7). Above all the defeat under the walls of Neuss of Charles the Bold, the ally of the great German lords, was taken as symbolising a defeat for the princes and a victory for the towns.

Nevertheless there can be no doubt that these fifteenth-century struggles against the princes were in the long run very damaging to the Hansa towns. Certain of them, for example Dortmund and Brunswick, took a long time to recover from their ruinous effects. Nearly all were weakened by the considerable expenses involved in strengthening their walls and paying their mercenaries. Their influence declined sharply while that of the princes increased. The latter developed not only their military power but also their economic ascendancy, taking the grain trade into their own hands and controlling the agricultural markets. It is obvious that one of the essential factors in the decline of the Hansa in the fifteenth century was the exhausting struggle carried on by the towns against the princes.

CHAPTER SIX

The Towns

1. THE TOWNS AND THEIR PLACE IN THE HANSA

THE 180 to 200 towns which are known to have been members of the Hansa were grouped in clusters of varying density across an area bordered by the Zuiderzee, the Meuse, Thuringia, Brandenburg, Poland and the Gulf of Finland. It is important, however, to remember that even in this Hanseatic zone a great number of small towns never formed part of the community. This is also true of a few relatively important towns, notably the capitals of some principalities, such as Oldenburg, Verden, Schwerin, and Marienburg in Prussia. To these may be added the Frisian port of Emden, which rose to great eminence in the sixteenth century.

It goes without saying that in the history of the community each Hansa town occupied a place of varying importance depending on its geographical position, its size, its changing interests and the rise or fall of its fortunes. Some were members of the Hansa from the beginning and remained members to the end. Others joined later, at different dates and sometimes for a short period only. Others again withdrew sooner or later. Finally there are a number of doubtful cases. It is therefore necessary to survey at least the most important Hansa towns and to attempt a brief characterisation of each.

Wendish and Pomeranian towns. To begin with, the core of the Hansa was made up of the so-called Wendish towns, those of the Lübeck third. These were Lübeck, an imperial city, Wismar and Rostock in Mecklenburg, and Hamburg. Also connected with this group, though not so closely, were Stralsund in Pomerania, the Saxon town of Lüneburg, and Kiel, an insignificant town in Holstein. Kiel was the most northerly of the Hansa towns in this group. None of the smaller cities of the duchy of Schleswig was ever a member of the community, although the majority of its inhabitants were German. They probably wished to avoid disputes with the king of Denmark. It should be noted that the Wendish group, with the exception of Kiel, included only important cities. The smaller towns of Holstein and Mecklenburg were kept out by the seaports, who doubtless wished to make them economically dependent.

Strengthened by special alliances, which were often extended to more distant towns, the Wendish group did in fact assume leadership of the Hansa, long before the *Hansetag* of 1418 conferred this role officially upon it. This does not mean – and the fact is typical of the Hansa – that its members did not have frequent and serious differences of opinion among themselves. For example in 1367 Hamburg showed some un-willingness to join the Cologne Confederation. At the end of the century Rostock and Wismar supported the *Vitalienbrüder*. At the beginning of the fifteenth century Lübeck, having changed its political administration, was in conflict with the other towns. Many other examples could be cited. However, common interests were so strong that these crises were soon over and the union of Wendish towns remained one of the founda-tions of Hanseatic greatness.

There is no need to emphasise at length the special role of Lübeck, the history of the town being so inextricably bound up with that of the Hansa as a whole. From the thirteenth to the fifteenth century Lübeck was the largest town in north Germany after Cologne, having about 15,000 inhabitants in 1300 and nearly 25,000 in the fifteenth century. Its ex-ceptional role was due mainly to its favourable situation on the isthmus of Holstein, midway between the Rhenish and Prussian towns. Even the opening of the direct maritime links between the Baltic and the North Sea by way of the Sound did not for some time diminish its importance. As an assembling-point for emigrants from the west, it imparted a continuous impetus to the foundation and expansion of the maritime towns of eastern Europe. But its leadership rested primarily on the activities of its merchants, who are to be found in all the countries border-ing the northern seas, along the Atlantic coasts, all over Germany, and in Italy. Lübeck imbued the Hansa not only with its own energy but also with its conservative spirit, being careful to maintain the traditional principles on which its prosperity had been established and to repress any tendency towards innovation. Both in its strength and in its weakness Lübeck was the embodiment of the Hansa.

The town owed its prosperity also to its relations with its neighbours, whose economy was often complementary to its own. This was par-ticularly true of Hamburg, which was in some sort its outer harbour on the North Sea, at least until the sixteenth century, when the roles of the two towns were gradually reversed. Hamburg was slow to increase in size. From a population of roughly 5,000 around 1300 and 8,000 around 1375, it reached 16,000 by the mid-fifteenth century and more than 50,000 by the mid-seventeenth. In spite of the common interests which it shared with Lübeck and their long-standing and lasting friendship, Hamburg managed to preserve its individuality. Very few natives of Hamburg achieved success in Lübeck or vice versa; very few families had members in both towns. The economic structure of Hamburg was moreover more complex than that of its neighbour, which was based entirely on long-distance trade. Hamburg combined an extensive sea trade with many close links with the hinterland via the Elbe. Manufacturing enterprises too were very important, and in contemporary eyes Hamburg was above all the city of beer. This diversity of function appears to have resulted in a less rigid mentality than was the case in Lübeck, more opportunist, more open to new ideas: thus its development ran a smoother course, and its expanding economy was in no way affected by the decline of the Hansa.

In the south, Lüneburg (with some 10,000 inhabitants) was a member both of the Wendish and of the Saxon group, which gave it an important role as intermediary between the inland towns and the seaports. Its rich salt-pans were the foundation of its prosperity, as they were of Lübeck's, and it was this that gave Lübeck the monopoly of the salt trade in the Baltic, at least up to the mid-fourteenth century. Lüneburg salt was also the decisive factor in the development of the herring trade in Skania, another bastion of Lübeck's wealth.

The development of the Baltic ports, Wismar (8,000 inhabitants at the end of the fifteenth century) and Rostock (15,000 around 1400), ran parallel to that of Lübeck, but without arousing her hostility. Their prosperity was based on their sea trade, particularly with Scandinavia, and on their considerable output of beer. As early as the fifteenth century, however, signs of decadence can be seen, evidenced by the decrease in size in the military contingent specified in successive *tohopesaten*. The same development is discernible in Stralsund (10,000 inhabitants around 1400), whose maritime relations were even more important, extending not only to Scandinavia but also to England, Flanders and Poitou. Among the Wendish towns of the Baltic only Lübeck had a greater volume of trade with western Europe.

In the east, Stralsund maintained the link with the Pomeranian towns on both sides of the Oder. Apart from Stettin these were, unlike those so far mentioned, modest little towns, about fifteen in number. Most of them, especially those in Further Pomerania, were not accepted as

Hansa towns until the last quarter of the fourteenth century – Rügenwalde in 1379 and Stolp three years later. The Pomeranian towns did not
play an important role in the Hansa. Although they occasionally held
regional assemblies of their own, they followed for the most part the
directives of the Wendish towns, on which they were economically
dependent. After Stralsund the most important was Stettin (9,000 inhabitants in the fifteenth century), which dealt principally in herring from
Skania and profited from the conflicts between the Teutonic Order and
Poland by diverting part of the trade from the Vistula to the lower Oder.
Stettin then became a grain-exporting centre, but this did not lead to
any notable increase in her growth.

Saxon, Thuringian and Brandenburg towns. To the south and west
of the Wendish group, in Lower Saxony, there were about twenty-five
Hansa towns scattered over an area between the Elbe and the Weser,
from the North Sea to south of the Harz. In spite of the dismember-
ment of the duchy of Saxony at the end of the twelfth century, regional
leagues bound these towns more closely together in the thirteenth. Nine
of them had been members of the Hansa since the middle of the fourteenth century: Brunswick, Goslar, Lüneburg, Hameln, Hildesheim,
Göttingen, Magdeburg and Hanover. Bremen was admitted in 1358,
while most of the other cities, especially those furthest south, did not
become members until the fifteenth century.

Among the Saxon towns Bremen, with about 12,000 inhabitants before the Black Death, 17,000 fifty years later, held a position which was
in every way unusual. Situated at some distance from the main group, in a
zone with only a few Hansa towns – the nearest, Buxtehude and Stade,
were about fifty miles away – this great archiepiscopal city, which in
modern times was to call itself a 'free Hansa town', seems to have been
singularly headstrong. On three occasions, in 1285, 1427 and 1563, she was
excluded from the community, the first time, apparently, for a period of
more than seventy years, a most unusual event. The prosperity of
Bremen was founded less on the transport of goods between east and west
than on her dealings, initiated in the twelfth century, with Norway,
England and the northern Low Countries, as well as with the hinterland
of the Weser, Saxony and part of Westphalia. In short Bremen, together
with the Rhenish towns, participated in the flow of trade from south to
north which had existed before the Hansa and which always found
difficulty in adapting itself to the new conditions created by the German
expansion into the Baltic region

In the large group of inland towns in Lower Saxony, Brunswick and Magdeburg played the leading part. Brunswick, one of the great cities of northern Germany in the late Middle Ages – when it had about 17,000 inhabitants – was always the unchallenged head of the Saxon 'quarter' of the Hansa, extending its influence in particular over the towns between the Harz and the lower Elbe: Hildesheim (6,000 to 8,000 inhabitants in the fifteenth century), Hanover, Göttingen and Goslar (about 10,000) – this last an imperial city, owing its prosperity to the copper and lead mines of the Rammelsberg. Brunswick, an industrial town, was frequently troubled by revolts against the patriciate. One of them, in 1375, caused her to be excluded from the Hansa for a period of five years. Like nearly all the inland towns, Brunswick began to decline in the fifteenth century, the more so as she had to defend herself against the machinations of her own duke. But she managed to retain her independence – even claiming the title of free town – and her leading role until the seventeenth century.

Magdeburg, which probably had about 20,000 inhabitants, does not appear to have occupied the dominating position within the Hansa which one would expect in view of her considerable role in German expansion towards the east. However she fulfilled a useful function as the link between the Saxon towns proper and other groups more or less closely connected with them: for example towards the south Halle (7,000 inhabitants around 1500) and the Thuringian group, containing Erfurt (16,000) and Naumburg, as well as the imperial cities of Nordhausen and Mühlhausen (8,000). Except for Halle none of these southern towns ever sent a representative to a Hanseatic diet or shared the costs of an embassy. However their merchants are found occasionally in Flanders, in company with the Hanseatics, as early as the end of the thirteenth century. A league formed with the Saxon towns in 1426 to guard against the Hussite danger accentuated their Hanseatic character, which however always remained fairly vague, and these contacts seem to have been abandoned after the mid-fifteenth century.

More important was the link that Magdeburg maintained with the Brandenburg towns, which because of their common dependence on the margrave formed a group of their own with their own assemblies. Five of them (including Salzwedel and Stendal), situated on the left bank of the Elbe in the Old March (*Altmark*), were more closely connected with the Saxon towns than the five beyond the Elbe, which included Berlin–Cölln and Frankfurt-on-the-Oder. Except for the latter they all seem to have been members of the Hansa of the towns from the beginning. By the end of the Middle Ages Berlin–Cölln, contrary to what is often believed, was already a town of some importance, with about 6,000 inhabitants. Since the end of the thirteenth century its merchants had been active in Hamburg and Flanders, profiting from the grain and timber trade down the Havel to the Elbe. But in the mid-fifteenth century the town came under increasing pressure from the margrave of Brandenburg. Because of this no delegates were sent to the Hanseatic diet of 1450; threatened with exclusion as a result, Berlin gave official notice in 1452 of her withdrawal from the Hansa. In the course of the second half of the fifteenth century the other Brandenburg towns also ceased to be active members.

Westphalian towns. Westphalia, lying between the Weser and the Rhine valley, was the zone with the largest number of Hansa towns. If all the urban centres, large and small, whose burgesses shared in the Hanseatic privileges when abroad are included, the total is nearly eighty. However among this number only about fifteen, grouped around the four main centres – Dortmund, Soest, Münster and Osnabrück – were active members of the community in the middle of the fifteenth century. The large number of towns is explained by the great enterprise of the Westphalian merchants, from the mid-twelfth century onwards, in all spheres of Hanseatic activity. They were to be found everywhere, in the eastern towns, in the four great *Kontore* and in countries beyond the sea. We have already seen, for example, the considerable share that they had both in the founding of Lübeck and in German trade with England.

As in Lower Saxony, by the middle of the thirteenth century the towns had combined in leagues, some great, some small, all with varying memberships, which strengthened their feeling of solidarity. Soest, owing obedience to the archbishop of Cologne, seems to have been at first the richest and most influential town in this area, with perhaps 13,0000 inhabitants at the end of the thirteenth century. In the fourteenth century leadership passed to Dortmund (about 10,000 inhabitants), an imperial city. Dortmund was recognised as the head of the Westphalian quarter of the Hansa, within which the northern towns were grouped around the episcopal cities of Münster (8,000 inhabitants in the fifteenth century) and Osnabrück (6,000).

The preponderant role played by the Westphalians in the merchants' Hansa enables us to understand their attitude, which at first seems strange, towards the Hansa of the towns. For a long time they maintained a very reticent attitude towards the new organisation which the community had adopted in the middle of the fourteenth century, mainly because the leadership had been seized by the seaports. Despite pressing invitations no Westphalian towns sent delegates to the diet of 1358 held in Lübeck, which decreed the blockade of Flanders, nor to the diet held in Cologne in 1367. The towns of this area refused to bear any part, even a financial one, of the burden of the war against Valdemar IV, asserting that this maritime war was no concern of theirs. It was not until 1379 that Dortmund first sent a delegate to a *Hansetag*, and not until 1418 that all four principal towns were represented there. Later, however, the opposition grew weaker, in part no doubt because of the general decline of the Westphalian towns, which suffered very severely in the feudal wars. This is especially true of Dortmund and Soest but applies also to Minden, Herford and Lippstadt, whose expansion came to an end in the late fourteenth century. Their decline gave Cologne the opportunity to become the head of the Rhenish–Westphalian third. Cologne endeavoured to summon assemblies of the third with greater frequency and to increase the number of active member towns, which did indeed rise to fourteen; but an unusually large number of small Hansa towns, which took no active part in affairs, continued to exist – persistent proof of the commercial initiative of the Westphalian merchants.

Netherlands and Rhenish towns. In the mid-fifteenth century there were about twenty Hansa towns in the Low Countries, attached to the Cologne third. Except for Groningen, isolated in the north, they were strung out along the eastern shore of the Zuiderzee (Stavoren, Kampen, Harderwijk), the Ijssel (Zwolle, Deventer, Zutphen) and the lower Rhine (Arnhem and Nijmegen).

In this region membership of the Hansa was not taken for granted, and the credentials of each town were carefully studied before it was admitted to the community. By the end of the thirteenth century, apparently, the merchants of the towns of the eastern Zuiderzee were enjoying the privileges of the 'common merchant'. The enthusiastic letter addressed by Zwolle and Kampen to Lübeck, recognising the latter as the head of a body of which they were members, appears to confirm this. But the crisis of the Hansa in the first half of the fourteenth century weakened these ties. According to the founding charter of the Cologne Confederation (1367) the towns of the Zuiderzee formed a group apart, outside the Hansa, like the Holland and Zeeland towns. However a little later

Harderwijk, Zutphen, Elburg and above all Deventer (roughly 10,000 inhabitants around 1400), important for its fairs where merchants from the Rhineland, Westphalia and Holland met and exchanged their goods, were all members of the Hansa. Other towns, among them Nijmegen, Stavoren (at the beginning of the fifteenth century) and Arnhem (1441), found it more difficult to obtain admission.

The negotiations with Kampen were particularly intricate. In the Middle Ages this town, situated at the mouth of the Ijssel, was the busiest port in the northern Low Countries, with a population of about 12,000 in 1400 (at the same period, Amsterdam had less than 5,000 inhabitants). Ships and merchants from Kampen had been trading in the Baltic as early as the thirteenth century; they then extended their trade to Norway, England and the shores of France as far as Bourgneuf, which they reached before the Hanseatics. The latter were offended by the special privileges which Kampen had managed to obtain in Bruges, as well as by the blockade-running of which her merchants were guilty in 1388. But eventually after she had shown herself hostile towards the Hollanders in their war with the Hanseatics in 1438, Kampen was admitted into the community in 1441. The Hansa was to regret this decision on many occasions, as Kampen remained very independent and her merchants secretly favoured the Hollanders. In fact Kampen, like other towns of the Zuiderzee, felt she had common interests with the Hansa through her links with Cologne and her trade in the Baltic, in opposition to Denmark; but in the west she had her own interests, and was particularly reluctant to take part in the blockade of Flanders.

It may be asked why, in this region, the Hansa reached its western boundary at the Zuiderzee and on the Ijssel. Why did the Holland and Zeeland towns not join the Hansa? They too were within the Empire; their interests often coincided with those of the Hanseatics, as is proved by their joining the Cologne Confederation and, later on, the alliance of the Hansa and the Low Countries in 1616. But because of their relative unimportance in the thirteenth century they could not claim that long-standing connection with the Hansa which appears to have been a necessary condition for admission into the community. Above all the rapid expansion of their industry and of their seaborne trade encouraged them to reject the commercial monopoly of Bruges, to which the Hanseatics remained steadfastly attached. Finally the incorporation into Burgundy of the north-western Low Countries underlined the separation between the two groups. It is debatable, however, whether the

Hansa, by systematically opposing the Hollanders instead of trying to enter into partnership with them, did not throw away a golden opportunity of increasing her prosperity and strength.

When we come to consider the Rhineland, a curious fact immediately emerges. Until the second half of the fourteenth century, except for Emmerich, a place of no importance, Cologne was the only Hansa town. It was only later on, and often at her instigation, that about a dozen other Rhenish towns were admitted, among them Wesel and Duisburg in 1407, followed by Düsseldorf and Solingen, and finally Neuss in 1475. The most westerly town, Roermond on the Meuse, was added in 1441. Further to the south, Dinant appears as the only non-German Hansa town, but its relationship with the community is not absolutely clear. The English and Burgundian authorities regarded Dinant as a member of the Hansa, and during the fifteenth century the town itself repeatedly asserted that this was the case. In fact Dinant participated in the Hanseatic privileges in England but nowhere else, and even in the Steelyard occupied a separate building. However Dinant was never represented at a *Hansetag* and should therefore be described only as a passive member of the Hansa. Finally Aachen, like the towns of the middle Rhine, was never a member of the Hansa.

In every respect Cologne, the largest town of medieval Germany, with nearly 30,000 inhabitants in the fifteenth century, occupied a special place within the Hansa, so special that certain modern authors tend, more or less consciously, to consider Cologne as less Hanseatic than the seaports. This was not so. Except for Lübeck no other town held so important a position within the community, from the beginning right through to the end. At all times her merchants were to be met with everywhere, from Russia to Portugal. But it is true that Cologne was not only a Hansa town. Long before the emergence of the Hansa she was already the great Rhenish metropolis, enjoying active commercial relations with the whole of southern Germany and with England, where she was the first to be granted special privileges. She was able to retain and even augment this position within the Rhineland – notably by developing her trade with Italy – and become a Hansa town at the same time. More than any other town Cologne shared simultaneously in the two great commercial routes of northern Europe: the Rhenish one linking Italy with England, and the Hanseatic one along the axis Novgorod–Lübeck–Bruges.

Cologne is about 200 kilometres from the sea. From the thirteenth century onwards large sea-going vessels were no longer able to reach it. Nevertheless Cologne merchants continued for a long time to trade beyond the seas: a remarkable fact, when compared with the narrowing horizons and creeping atrophy of other inland towns of north Germany such as Dortmund, Brunswick and Thorn. The persistence of Cologne's maritime interests was due, it is true, to the dynamism of her merchants; but it also owed much to a natural geographical feature, the fact that the Rhine, unlike other rivers, debouches into the sea at many different points, thus preventing the rise of a great estuarial port which might have cornered the seaborne trade and the transhipment of cargoes. After Tiel, whose attempts in this direction had been abandoned by the end of the eleventh century, neither Dordrecht on the Waal, nor Utrecht on the Old Rhine nor Kampen on the Ijssel was in a position to aspire to the function which is discharged today by Rotterdam. Cologne was therefore able to fulfil satisfactorily her double mission as a Rhenish and a Hansa town, not to mention her considerable inland trade in all directionus. If it was at times difficult for her to reconcile these very diverse interests – as is shown by her exclusion from the Hansa in 1471 – she nevertheless succeeded in maintaining, down to the seventeenth century, economic activities which linked her with all parts of Europe.

Prussian, Livonian and Swedish towns. Although the towns of Prussia and Livonia were all situated within the territories of the Teutonic Order, they were in different Hanseatic thirds. The former were grouped with the Westphalian towns, and the latter, together with Visby, formed the Gotland–Livonian third.

The six Prussian Hansa towns, Danzig, Elbing, Braunsberg and Königsberg on the coast, and Kulm and Thorn on the Vistula, were unique within the Hansa in owing allegiance to a prince who was himself a member of the Hansa, the Grand Master of the Teutonic Order.

In the fourteenth century they were kept in stricter subjection to their feudal lord than any other towns in the community, the Order retaining everywhere complete military control. Even the assemblies of the six towns, which go back to the thirteenth century but became particularly frequent from the second half of the fourteenth onwards, were supervised by the Grand Master, as were also the votes of their representatives at the Hanseatic diets. The towns tried to extend their privileges by invoking sometimes the help of the Order, sometimes that of the Hansa, as seemed best at the time. They became more independent in the period after the battle of Tannenberg (1410), conducting a series of bitter struggles, together with the Prussian nobility, against the domination of the Order. In 1466 the towns of the Vistula passed under the less rigorous suzerainty of the king of Poland.

On the economic front the Prussian towns, mainly concerned with the export of the bulk products of their area – timber and grain – endeavoured to develop their direct maritime links with the west through the Sound, to the detriment of the Lübeck–Hamburg route, and to remain on good terms with England, their principal customer. As a result they were almost constantly on bad terms with the Wendish towns. This put a heavy strain on the internal cohesion of the community and lessened its power.

Situated at the mouth of the eastern arm of the Vistula, Elbing was the first of these towns to expand and until the middle of the fourteenth century it remained the most important Prussian port. But Elbing was soon outstripped by Danzig, which cornered most of the traffic along the Vistula and monopolised relations overseas. In 1300 Danzig was still a small town, with perhaps 2,000 inhabitants, but by the end of the four-teenth century she had become a great city, with about 10,000 inhabitants, a figure which had doubled fifty years later. Her expansion was held in check for a while by local wars, but was resumed at an even more rapid rate towards the end of the fifteenth century. Inland, Kulm began to vege-tate almost as soon as it was founded, and its economic weakness was so pronounced that it had ceased to be a member of the Hansa by the second half of the fifteenth century. In contrast Thorn became the scene of intense commercial activity in the fourteenth century, trading with Poland and the Ukraine on the one hand and with the west on the other, down either the Vistula or the lower Oder. But this expansion was brought to an end in the fifteenth century by competition from Danzig. Lastly Königsberg, originally chiefly a bastion of the Teutonic Order against the still-pagan Lithuanians, grew more slowly. The export of amber and forest produce, and later on of grain, allowed it to outstrip Elbing (about 10,000 inhabitants) at the beginning of the fifteenth century. This expansion was to continue in the sixteenth century, when Königs-berg became the capital of the secularised Prussian state.

Attached to the Prussian group were two very far-off towns, Cracow and Breslau. Their membership of the community, despite their remote-ness from the Hanseatic zone, is to be explained by the long-standing activity of their merchants in the west, particularly in Flanders; by the importance to the Hansa of Slovakian copper; and by the economic pre-ponderance of the German population in the early stages of the towns' development. Cracow, where up to 1316 only Germans could become citizens, is mentioned as a Hansa town in 1387, but it was certainly considered to be a member long before then. The strengthening of the Polish element in the population and the increase in trade towards the west along the Leipzig–Nürnberg route, to the detriment of trade on the Vistula, progressively weakened the Hanseatic character of the town, which ceased to form part of the community in the last quarter of the fifteenth century. Much the same thing happened with Breslau (about 20,000 inhabitants in the fifteenth century) which is also mentioned as a Hansa town in 1387. Having complained on several occasions of the vexations inflicted on her merchants in Flanders by the Hanseatics, Breslau officially announced in 1474 her withdrawal from the community, stating that its privileges were no longer any advantage to her. The two towns had never sent delegates of their own to the Hanseatic diets, where they seem to have been represented by those of Thorn or Danzig.

In the Baltic countries there were about a dozen so-called Livonian Hansa towns, but only three of them were economically and politically important, Riga, Reval and Dorpat. All three had been members of the community from the beginning, and this may also have been true of Pernau, a busy port in the middle of the fourteenth century but soon afterwards in decline. The others, such as Wenden, Fellin, Wolmar and Windau, were not considered to be Hansa towns until the fifteenth century, in some cases quite late in the century. Cohesion among the Livonian towns was ensured by regional diets, which met fairly regularly from the mid-fourteenth century onwards.

Riga (8,000 inhabitants in the fifteenth century?), the seat of an archbishop, was the most influential of the Livonian towns, and often at loggerheads with the Teutonic Order. She had long enjoyed commercial relations with the west, and her expansion depended on trade along the Dvina, which she gradually made her monopoly. Reval (Tallin), in Danish hands up to 1346, prospered because it was the assembling-point for ships and merchants making the journey to Novgorod (6,000 inhabitants around 1500). This function would more naturally have been discharged by Narva, also a German town, on the eastern frontier of the Teutonic Order territory and nearer to Novgorod, whose merchants enjoyed the Hanseatic privileges in Flanders. But Reval, an older town, was selfish enough, even as late as the sixteenth century, to rigorously oppose the admission of Narva into the Hansa. The ambiguity of its status thus makes Narva comparable to Dinant in the west. Lastly the inland town of Dorpat (Tartu), through which merchants passed on the overland route to Novgorod, had close business connections with Pskov, and was a great market for Russian products until its destruction in 1558.

On the island of Gotland, Visby was still claiming in the second half of the fourteenth century the leadership of the Gotland–Livonian third, basing this claim on the great role it had played in the extension of German commerce towards the east and on the still considerable volume of its trade with England and Flanders. But by this time its decline was patent, the process being hastened by the sack of 1361. Once Visby had passed under Danish control, it could no longer sustain its pretensions, and although it remained a Hansa town up to the sixteenth century, it occupied an increasingly unimportant place in the community.

Finally there is the question as to whether certain Swedish towns were members of the Hansa. In the statutes of the *Kontor* of Bruges it is laid down that merchants from Gotland, Livonia and Sweden form the third Hanseatic 'third'. It is clear that at this period Swedish merchants – nearly all of them, no doubt, of German origin – were recognised as members of the community. But what was their position after the formation of the Hansa of the towns? There is evidence that a delegate from Stockholm was present at the *Hansetag* of 1366, and in 1388, in a letter addressed to Reval, the Swedish capital spoke of Visby as the 'head of our third'. It therefore seems indisputable that Stockholm (6,000 to 7,000 inhabitants around 1500) was a Hansa town, at least in the fourteenth century. It is more difficult to know what to say about other towns, but it appears that the same conclusion may be drawn about Kalmar and Nyköping, both of which in 1362 levied the *Pfundzoll* on behalf of the Hansa. In the fifteenth century there is no comparable evidence, so there is reason to believe that the Swedish towns were by that time no longer considered to be Hanseatic. It is probable that the decline of Visby, which had been particularly interested in bolstering up its third in order to maintain its influence, contributed to this premature withdrawal.

This survey of the Hansa towns will have made plain their differences of status and diversity of functions. It may be noted in passing that the desire to characterise so many different towns succinctly is a very old one. It inspired a popular saying, probably dating from the fifteenth century, which offers the following definitions – sometimes rather unexpected – of a dozen Hansa towns: Lübeck, a warehouse (*Kaufhaus*); Cologne, a wine-cellar (*Weinhaus*); Brunswick, an arsenal (*Zeughaus*); Danzig, a granary (*Kornhaus*); Magdeburg, a bakery (*Backhaus*); Rostock, a malt-house (*Malzhaus*); Lüneburg, a salt store (*Salzhaus*); Stettin, a fish shop (*Fischhaus*); Halberstadt, a brothel (*Frauenhaus*); Reval, a depot of wax and flax (*Wachs- und Flachshaus*); Cracow, a copper warehouse (*Kupperhaus*); Visby, a warehouse for pitch and tar (*Pech- und Teerhaus*).

2. POPULATION

The demographic history of the Hansa towns in the last three centuries of the Middle Ages is in all essentials akin to that of the west as a whole. It is characterised by a more or less rapid increase in the urban population, due to immigration, up to the mid-fourteenth century. The Black Death caused an abrupt fall in numbers which was, however, made good by increased immigration during the following years; this process was repeated roughly once every ten years, as successive outbreaks of the plague decimated the population. Finally in the fifteenth century the population of many towns ceased to grow or actually decreased, though a few continued to expand.

Within this general scheme, however, the Hansa towns present three particular traits: immigration was usually from west to east; the proportion of immigrants from distant regions was larger than elsewhere; the German towns beyond the Elbe contained a Slav minority of varying sizes.

There are few documents on which to base a study of these facts. They consist principally of lists of new admissions to citizenship, and few go back beyond the fourteenth century. Immigrants bearing names which are also place-names, the only ones of value in this context, do not usually constitute more than half the total. Even so they do not indicate the origin of the immigrant, but only the original home of his family, at least in the great majority of cases. Consequently they make possible only a fairly vague estimate of the shift of population.

The great migratory movement towards the east is reflected in the population of all Hansa towns, even as late as the fifteenth century. The Westphalian towns were strengthened by Rhenish, Franconian and even Walloon elements. Bremen owed its development to the Dutch and the Frisians. Hamburg grew with the arrival of immigrants from Saxony, while those from Holstein were relatively few. For Lübeck and all the eastern towns, overpopulated Westphalia supplied the life-blood which ensured their growth. Setting out from the many tiny Westphalian cities, the immigrants spread out into all the Baltic coastal towns, as well as into the inland regions of Poland, the Baltic countries and Sweden. Certain names bear witness to this dispersal. For example the Warendorps, who bore the name of their place of origin near Münster, were one of the most powerful patrician families of Lübeck, at least from the thirteenth century onwards. Their relatives are to be found in the other Wendish towns, in Danzig, Elbing, Visby, Riga and Dorpat, often as members of the town council. Similarly the Attendorns, who came from the Ruhr, can be traced in more or less the same towns, as well as in Stockholm. There can be no doubt that the common origin of the immigrants scattered in distant cities, whether there was a family relationship or not, was one of the strongest bonds holding the Hanseatic structure together, particularly in the case of the Wendish towns on the Baltic.

The flow of population towards the east also explains the high proportion of citizens in the eastern towns who came from distant parts, more especially in the thirteenth century, but much later as well. In Danzig in the last third of the fourteenth century, for example, immigrants coming from west of the Elbe still represented 25 per cent of the total, while in the same period in Dortmund people born in the immediate neighbourhood formed almost 90 per cent of the population.

The great part played by immigration in the peopling of the towns, particularly after the recurrent epidemics, led Heinrich Reincke to a surprising conclusion. He suggests that in all the Hansa towns, up to and including the seventeenth century, immigrants outnumbered natives among the burgesses. If this is so, it is easier to understand how so many first-generation citizens were able to rise to the highest offices within the city. It then becomes less surprising to note that of the four great burgomasters of Lübeck at the end of the fourteenth century two were natives of Visby, one of Brunswick and one of Hildesheim; that of the four burgomasters of Hamburg in office in 1490 none was born in the city and none was the son of a burgess; that Wullenwever, a native of Hamburg, was able to dominate Lübeck, even though he had not become a burgess until he was nearly forty; and so on.

West of the Elbe the population was wholly German, but to the east the Hansa towns included Slav (Wendish) elements, varying in importance according to the area concerned, but always much smaller in the towns than in the surrounding countryside. The Germans prevailed by virtue of their wealth, their technical superiority as businessmen and craftsmen and, almost everywhere, by virtue of their numbers. The Hansa towns were therefore centres of Germanism in the east.

Naturally it was between the Elbe and the Oder, and in Pomerania, that the Slavs were less numerous in the towns, while maintaining their numbers in the countryside right up to modern times. In Magdeburg as early as 1290 the use of the Slav language in courts of law was abolished as no longer necessary. During the same period it is still possible to trace in Rostock and Stralsund the existence of a special bailiff (*Vogt*) with jurisdiction over the Wends, who disappears later on. Even when reinforced to some extent by the immigration of peasants who settled together in a suburb – as happened notably in Stettin and Frankfurt-on-the-Oder – this Slav element appears to have become insignificant by the fifteenth century.

Further to the east, in the Prussian towns, the Germans were also strongly in the majority. In Danzig in the fourteenth century Kashubians and Poles do not appear to have exceeded 10 per cent of the total. The proportion was doubtless higher in Thorn and Culm. From the middle of the fifteenth century onwards Polish immigration into the towns of the Vistula intensified.

The situation was noticeably different in the Baltic countries. Although the Germans still had a large majority in Riga (70–80 per cent) they were in the minority in Estonia, probably also in Dorpat and certainly in the smaller towns. Reval is unusual in that it had in the fifteenth century a not inconsiderable Swedish population; here Germans, Swedes and Estonians formed respectively, at the beginning of the sixteenth century, a third, a sixth and a half of the total. A recent study, based on tax registers for the year 1538, affords some interesting glimpses of the distribution of nationalities among the various social classes. The upper class, consisting of merchants and property-owners (18 per cent), was wholly German and had probably been so since the mid-fourteenth century. The middle class, consisting of craftsmen in easy circumstances (22 per cent), contained 59 per cent Germans, 23 per cent Swedes and 18 per cent Estonians. Finally in the lower class, consisting of day-labourers (60 per cent) paying only a very small scot (*schoss*) or even nothing at all, the nationalities were respectively 2 per cent, 25 per cent and 73 per cent. These figures show the overwhelming social preponderance of the Germans, which one finds paralleled in other towns, even where they were in a minority.

Lastly in foreign countries – Poland, Denmark and Sweden – Germans appear to have been always in the minority, except in the towns of Schleswig, and increasingly so from the fourteenth century onwards. Generally speaking, in all regions where the rural districts had not been

Germanised, the proportion of Germans in the towns was at its highest at the beginning of the fourteenth century, and then decreased owing to the immigration from the countryside.

The regulations governing the legal status of Slavs in Hansa towns appear to have been fairly liberal up to about the middle of the fourteenth century. After the introduction of 'German law' they were not excluded from urban citizenship; or at least one may assume so from the names of certain burgesses which indicate a Wendish origin. In Lübeck, even in the town council, one finds such names as Ruce or Went. In Stendal, on the left bank of the Elbe, similar names are found in the merchant guild. In contrast nothing comparable can be found in Stettin and Elbing, even though they were important commercial centres before the conquest.

After the mid-fourteenth century restrictive measures became more and more frequent, especially with respect to the guilds. Slavs were excluded in 1323 by the drapers of Brunswick, in 1350 by the grocers of Lüneburg, in 1400 by the goldsmiths there. In Lübeck it is not until the fifteenth century that one finds similar ordinances, of an economic rather than a nationalistic character. The main issue was overcrowding of the guilds. In the Prussia of the Teutonic Order, on the other hand, the exclusion of the Slavs, decreed as early as 1309, was probably more the result of nationalist apprehension. But the rule was not strictly applied, for we find Slav names among the burgesses of various towns. In Livonia the administration was less severe. Up to the mid-fourteenth century the Slavs in Riga were free to trade, but after 1354 they were excluded from the 'great guild' of merchants and in 1399 it was forbidden to form a commercial partnership with a Slav. One after another the guilds too were closed to them. It is difficult to determine how far and for how long these restrictions were maintained.

3. SOCIAL STRUCTURE: THE PATRICIATE

The internal history of the Hansa towns, like that of other German towns, is marked by recurrent and often violent conflicts between the great families (*Geschlechter*) and the guilds (*Handwerker*). It would be wrong to regard these disputes as nothing more than a conflict between the merchant class, who controlled the council and the government, and the artisans, who were trying to take over at least some measure of power. Such a theoretical approach would grossly oversimplify a complex social structure and misrepresent the true character of the disputes. A more useful approach to the social realities of the situation is to try to group the urban population according to their degree of wealth. It is evident that such a study of the medieval period can lead to only very tentative results and is moreover possible in only a few cases, by making use of tax registers and sumptuary laws. Any delimitation of social groups based on this criterion must be somewhat arbitrary.

Heinrich Reincke distinguished in the population of Hamburg at the close of the Middle Ages five classes according to wealth: 1. The rich, with more than 5,000 Lübeck marks (some, by about 1500, had managed to amass 40,000), comprising the great merchants and *rentiers*. 2. The upper-middle class, with 2,000 to 5,000 marks, comprising the richest of the brewers and ship-owners, the middle-rank merchants and the drapers. 3. The middle class (600 to 2,000 marks), comprising most of the brewers and retailers and the most prosperous craftsmen, particularly butchers and goldsmiths. 4. The lower-middle class (150 to 600 marks), comprising most of the master craftsmen and the small brewers, tenants rather than property-owners. 5. Finally the most impoverished category, comprising municipal employees, small craftsmen, journeymen and, poorest of all, the day-labourers, porters and domestic servants.

It is obvious that this classification cannot be applied to other towns. Each had its own economic characteristics. In less flourishing towns, such as Lüneburg, the great fortunes were smaller, and the middle class tended to be more differentiated. However as far as the growth of wealth from the fourteenth to the sixteenth century is concerned, there is a certain analogy between Hamburg, still increasing in prosperity, and Rostock, already declining. In the latter town the middle class grew weaker, dwindling from 74 per cent to 59 per cent in 1454, while the poorest class increased from 25 per cent to 38 per cent. In Hamburg the number and wealth of the most heavily taxed rose slightly and the gap between rich and poor tended to widen, thus explaining in part the increased violence of social unrest and the success of Luther's doctrines.

The members of the great families, the patriciate, were known by various names according to the district concerned. In Westphalia they were often called 'the hereditary proprietors' (*erfsaten* in Dortmund), in Lower Saxony 'knightly companions' (*kunstabelen*), in the Wendish towns, at least in the fifteenth century, 'squires' (*Junker*). Whatever its name, the patriciate was made up of the richest and most influential families in the town. According to the Lübeck Chronicle, it consisted of 'the rich merchants and the wealthiest proprietors' or 'the merchants and the richest men in the city'. After the revolution of 1408 it was decreed that in future 'merchants and *rentiers*' should be entitled to only half the seats on the council. As in Lübeck, the patriciate in most Hansa towns was made up essentially of merchants and *rentiers* – the two groups could hardly be separated. The wealth of both groups was based on urban and rural property, participation in commercial and manufacturing enterprises and ownership of shares in ships and movable goods. Furthermore the wealth of the *rentiers* was most commonly derived from trade. In the seaports the great merchants were necessarily even more influential than in such inland towns as Osnabrück, Soest and even Cologne, where property-owners were numerous and powerful. It seems moreover that, generally speaking, the influence of *rentiers* within the governing class increased during the fifteenth century, even though the patriciate normally recruited its new members from among the newly rich merchants. But it may be safely asserted that the most striking characteristic of a Hansa town in all periods was the marked preponderance of the mercantile element, which remained unshaken even in the face of repeated rebellions.

It is almost always impossible to determine the origin of the great urban families. A few noblemen, such as the Mörders of Stralsund, are to be found among them, as are *ministeriales* (especially in the small episcopal towns of Lower Saxony) such as Evert van Holthusen, a great merchant, diplomat and member of the council of Hildesheim in about 1400. Not very numerous are craftsmen who had grown rich and whose name betrays their origin: in Bremen the Pellifexes, in Erfurt the Goldslegers, Kupferslegers, Murers, Zieglers, etc. In some towns the composition of the patriciate reflects certain specific activities. For example in Goslar there are the owners of silver or copper mines (*montani*) and the smelters (*silvani*), in Lüneburg and Halle the owners of salt mines (*sodemester*) and salt-refiners (*pfänner*), in Wismar and Rostock the brewers, and in Danzig the ship-owners.

Almost everywhere the patriciate had its own associations which, though established at different times, enabled it to extend its influence over the town. In Cologne the oldest society of this sort was the merchant guild, which can be traced as far back as the eleventh century. In the mid-twelfth century it was replaced by the *Richerzeche* ('Rich Men's Club'), comprising the great merchants and property-owners. This exercised absolute control over the government of the town up to the end of the fourteenth century. In Dortmund there was in the thirteenth century a 'great guild' under the patronage of St Reinhold (*Reinoldi-gilde*), later called the *Junkergesellschaft*. There was a similar club in Riga, and in Danzig in the fourteenth century there was a Brotherhood of St George. Quite often, as in Bremen, Münster, Osnabrück, Magdeburg and Stendal, the association was called the *Gewandschneidergilde*, testifying to the outstanding importance of the trade in Flemish cloth. In certain towns, however, for example in Hamburg and Stralsund, no patrician association existed. In Lübeck it was not until 1379 that the 'Circle Society' was formed (*societas circuliferorum, Cirkelselschop*), when a contract was agreed between nine patricians and the Convent of St Catherine, which allotted them a chapel in its church. Recruited by co-option, administered by four elected *Schaffer*, holding two general assemblies a year, it had between thirty and fifty members in the fifteenth century. All the great families of the city were represented. In 1429 among its 52 members there were 19 councillors and 3 burgomasters. In 1483 there was only one councillor who was not a member. The Circle Society survived as the social centre of the Lübeck patriciate up to the beginning of the nineteenth century. Its last co-opted member became mayor of the town in 1813, under French rule. It was so exclusive that in 1450 a junior society was formed, the 'Society of Merchants' (*koplude kumpanye*), which accepted the newly rich, of whom an appreciable number were eventually admitted to the Circle Society.

In all towns the solidarity of the patriciate was reinforced by inter-marriage. In Lübeck in about 1380 a petition pointed out that most of the members of the council were cousins to the third degree. For them government was almost a family business, and they took care that craftsmen and the 'unworthy' should not intrude. On the other hand they were quite ready to welcome foreigners, provided they were rich, respected and married one of their daughters. It was in this way that in the fifteenth century Nürnbergers found it quite easy to infiltrate into the council, at Lübeck and elsewhere.

Despite its exclusiveness the patriciate was continually compelled to take in fresh blood, owing to the rapid extinction of its families as they were thinned out by epidemics, emigration and degeneration. As a rule the prosperity of a great family was unlikely to extend over more than three or four generations. However in this respect there are considerable differences between different towns.

The most stable and exclusive patriciate was that of Cologne. Within the *Richerzeche* descendants of families already powerful in the twelfth century were still dominant in the fourteenth, among them the Judes and the Lyskirchens, who were to retain an important role as late as the seventeenth century. The refusal to admit new elements explains the violence of the opposition at the end of the fourteenth century, which destroyed the pre-eminence of the patriciate as a body without, however, abolishing the political and economic influence of the richest families, now divided into corporate groups (*gaffeln*). On the other hand in Hamburg and Stralsund renewal within the patriciate was particularly rapid, the great families maintaining their position for only two or three generations. Lübeck and most of the Hansa towns represent an intermediate type. Alongside a small number of families which remained influential for centuries – the Warendorps from the twelfth to the sixteenth, the von Lüneburgs from the fourteenth to the seventeenth – the ruling families usually disappeared after three or four generations and were replaced by *nouveaux riches*. One such was Hinrich Castorp, one of the great Hanseatic burgomasters of the fifteenth century, a merchant from Dortmund who became a burgess of Lübeck in 1445 and seven years later was admitted to the Circle Society and the council.

Below the patriciate there was a middle class, not quite so rich but more numerous. This class also engaged in commercial activities and as a result remained outside the craft guilds. In Hamburg this group formed Reincke's second category. It too contained great merchants, some of them occasionally engaged in retail trade as well, brewers or exporters of beer (not members of the craft guilds), ship-owners, drapers and some horse-dealers. The importance of this class varied a great deal from town to town. Its members were excluded from the more important public offices and in particular from the council. Naturally this middle class aspired to play its part in political life and often sided with the craft guilds in their rebellion against the patriciate. Its aims were achieved in some towns, for example in Brunswick and Dortmund. But often, too, its interests and its matrimonial connections bound it to the great families, to whose level its most active members could hope one day to rise. This explains why the dominance of the patriciate was never seriously challenged in most Hansa towns.

4. THE GUILDS

In the Hansa towns, as elsewhere, the greater part of the urban population was grouped into craft guilds, which went under various names (*Ämter*,

Innungen, Gilden, Gewerke). This was true even in the great commercial towns: 62 per cent in Hamburg in 1379, if one includes the small brewers. As elsewhere, all trades were represented: food, metal, textiles, leather, wood. Certain trades, however, were particularly popular and flourishing, maintaining close contacts with the maritime trade, like the coopers, who were to be found in large numbers in the Wendish towns. Other trades, by contrast, were highly specialised, such as the makers of amber rosaries in Lübeck, the anchor smiths in Danzig, and the linen weavers of the Westphalian towns.

Up to the sixteenth century the important guilds were gradually granted a series of charters, laying down their professional organisation and guaranteeing them a monopoly (in Cologne and Magdeburg these begin as early as the mid-twelfth century). The most influential guilds generally formed a privileged group, which might acquire political rights and representations on the council. This was true of the five *grosse Innungen* of Magdeburg (weavers, mercers, furriers, cordwainers and tanners, and clothiers), the six 'guilds' of Dortmund, and the *Vier Gewerke* of Berlin, Frankfurt, Rostock and Greifswald, which usually comprised the butchers, the bakers, the cordwainers and the weavers or smiths. Rarely, as in Münster, the prominent guilds were associated in a larger group under the direction of two aldermen.

The internal organisation of the guilds of the Hansa towns presents no original features. As happened everywhere, the guilds became 'closed shops' in the fourteenth century by the limitation of the number of apprentices to two or three per master, an increase in the number of journeymen, and progressive difficulties in becoming a master. In addition to the high fees charged for admission to the guild and to the freedom of the city, a masterpiece had to be produced; this was made a requirement as early as 1313 for the smiths of Stettin, in 1360 for the goldsmiths of Riga, and ten years later for the cordwainers of Lübeck. These regulations had the effect of reducing the membership of the guilds at a time when the number of merchants remained stable or even increased. This is one of the reasons for the failure of the political claims put forward by the guilds in the Hansa towns.

The control and organisation of its guilds was the affair of the town council. In such matters the Hansa rarely intervened. In 1417, however, immediately after the troubles in Lübeck, the Hanseatic diet decreed that any craftsman settling in a Hansa town was to have his proficiency certificate attested both by the town from which he came and the town in which he wished to settle. It was no longer enough merely to present it to the aldermen of the guild. This was a political measure, designed to keep a closer check on craftsmen suspected of a seditious temper. More frequently the regional diets issued regulations dealing with the guilds. As early as 1321 common regulations were laid down for all Wendish towns, dealing with journeymen coopers. This fixed their maximum wages, forbade them to undertake any private work, and enjoined them not to leave their masters in order to attend the fair in Skania. Other ordinances enjoined the use of the Rostock ton for the consignment of herring, and of the Lüneburg ton for salt. In the middle of the century the same towns fixed common regulations for their boilermakers and pewterers. Other regulations, concerned mainly with goldsmiths, were issued for the Prussian towns as a whole.

As everywhere in western Europe, the urban guilds tried to acquire political rights and representation in the governing corporations. Disputes, which at first, in the late thirteenth century, were only sporadic, had become both more serious and more widespread by the second half of the fourteenth century. They broke out continually during the fifteenth century and became even fiercer at the beginning of the sixteenth with the spread of the Reformation.

Magdeburg was the first to become the scene of serious troubles. In 1301 ten leading guildsmen were burned alive after an uprising. After 1330, however, the great families lost control of the town and were obliged to acquire membership of the five 'great guilds'. In the same year a revolt in Bremen was quickly suppressed. In the last quarter of the fourteenth century civil disorder in Brunswick caused the Hansa serious alarm for the first time. The announcement of new taxes aroused the fury not only of the artisans but also of certain elements in the mercantile class, and eight burgomasters were massacred. Brunswick was excluded from the Hansa, but was readmitted in 1380, although the patrician hegemony had not been restored. Indeed the new constitution of 1386 distributed the 103 seats in the council between 25 representatives of the great families, 31 drapers, money-changers and goldsmiths, and 47 craftsmen. In Lübeck, in 1384, under the leadership of an ambitious merchant, Paternostermaker, a butchers' revolt broke out, which was suppressed with much bloodshed. Shortly afterwards in Stralsund an opposition party led by a rich non-patrician merchant, Karsten Sarnow, quickly got rid of the council, a task made that much easier by the general resentment of the Wulflam family's tyrannical exercise of power. But the threat of expulsion from the Hansa provoked an immediate reaction, and in 1391 Sarnow was executed. Lastly in Cologne the guilds, whose first revolt in 1370 had been brutally repressed, carried the day in 1396 and put an end to the rule of the *Richerzeche*. The most formidable of these outbreaks was the one at Lübeck lasting from 1408 to 1416, all the more so as it had repercussions in other Wendish towns. This crisis, which shook the Hansa to its foundations, ended in almost total victory for the patricians.

The causes and circumstances of these struggles were very diverse and it would be wrong to make generalisations about them. The exclusiveness of the patriciate, the ambitions of certain powerful personalities, the political aspirations of the guilds and the merchants kept out of the government, rivalry between the great families, discontentment with taxes and bad financial administration – all these were factors of varying importance in the uprisings, which were further enflamed by the disturbances in Flanders. Historians of both east and west agree in denying these conflicts the character of a genuine class warfare. It is not permissible to talk of a revolt of the poor against the rich, nor even to distinguish a clear opposition between patriciate and guilds. Indeed the grouping of the antagonists varies considerably according to the circumstances. While the first revolt of the butchers at Lübeck in 1380 can be seen as a conflict between certain craftsmen and the patriciate, the revolt at Brunswick in 1374 was characterised by an alliance between the artisans and the middle-rank merchants, and the revolt at Stralsund seems to have received the support of some members of the patriciate, who were disgusted by the tyranny of the Wulflam family.

In general all these revolts failed to seriously weaken the status of the patrician class in the Hansa towns. Its domination was broken only rarely, as in Magdeburg and Cologne. Even when the commune succeeded in unseating the established regime, they could usually maintain themselves in power for only a few years. This was the case in most of the Wendish towns. Nearly everywhere, however, the patriciate had to admit some – though very few – representatives of the guilds to the councils, or agree to the formation of a people's assembly, which in the event had no real power.

The Hansa could not remain indifferent to these urban conflicts, which threatened its existence and favoured the designs of the princes. The identity between the interests of the great families and the interests of commerce usually led the Hansa to intervene on behalf of the existing authorities against the rebels, in favour of the 'old council' which had been driven out by a 'new council'. The first time this happened was in Brunswick in 1374. After an appeal from the fugitive patricians the Hanseatic diet decreed the exclusion of the rebel city. But the latter was not to be intimidated, and finally obtained readmission without completely restoring the patrician hegemony which had originally been demanded. This partial failure made the Hansa more prudent. It took no action at all when the patriciate was overthrown in Cologne in 1396, in Dortmund in 1399, in Danzig in 1416 and in Breslau in 1418, and intervened to only a limited degree in the troubles in the Wendish towns. However the crisis in Lübeck from 1408 to 1416 highlighted the very real dangers to which these revolts exposed the Hansa. Accordingly the *Hansetag* of 1418 resolved to oppose them in future with the greatest firmness. A series of exclusions followed: Stade in 1419, Stettin in 1420, Bremen in 1427, Rostock in 1439, Münster in 1454. All these towns, however, were readmitted fairly quickly after various concessions had been made.

There is no doubt that the maintenance of the patrician regimes in the Hansa towns resulted in some measure from pressure exercised by the Hansa. But it was due principally to the economic and social preponderance of the mercantile element and the relative weakness of the guilds, particularly those of the textile industry. This is in striking contrast to the towns of the Low Countries, where during the same period the weavers were displaying their revolutionary ardour to far greater effect.

CHAPTER SEVEN

Ships, Shipping, Ship-owners

I. SHIPS

THE rapid expansion of German trade in northern European countries from the mid-twelfth century onwards is, of course, bound up with the development of Hanseatic shipping. For at least two hundred years German vessels seem to have been better adapted to the new conditions of trade than those of their competitors. A technical superiority of this kind, although difficult to demonstrate in detail, can alone explain the pre-eminence which the Hanseatics retained up to the fifteenth century.

When Lübeck was founded, two different types of ship sailed the northern seas: the Viking longship, narrow-beamed, fast, driven by oars and sail, and drawing very little water; and the western sailing ship, shorter, broader, but more seaworthy. Both these types had a limited cargo-carrying capacity, scarcely exceeding 15 lasts,* or 30 tons. It is obvious that the work of colonisation, and the crusades in the east, in so far as they involved seaborne expeditions, made larger ships essential.

Accordingly there appeared in the north towards the end of the twelfth century a larger ship which soon became universally known as the cog (kogge, coggo). There is an account of the departure from Cologne in 1188 of four great ships, each reckoned at more than 80 lasts, which were carrying crusaders to the Holy Land. The chronicler Henry of Latvia records that in the year 1206 the city of Riga was saved from famine by the arrival of two cogs. The carrying capacity of the new ship soon exceeded 100 lasts, that is, eight to ten times as much as its predecessors. An average cog probably measured about ninety feet from stem to stern, about twenty in the beam, and drew about ten feet of water. The hull was made of planks overlapping one another like the tiles of a roof; keel and stern-post were rectilinear. With only one sail,

---

* In medieval times the size of German ships was always measured in lasts. The last was a unit not of volume but of weight, applied to the cargo which the ship could carry. The value of this varied according to the goods involved, but generally speaking a last is roughly equivalent to two metric tons.

she was relatively easy to handle, capable of working to windward, and fast – four to five knots in a good wind – especially when, after 1200, the quarter-rudder was replaced by the stern-rudder.

The origin of the cog, whose method of construction differed notably from that of previous ships, is still a matter of debate. It may be that the new technique was perfected by Hanseatic shipwrights, basing their design on the local timber-framed houses. It is more likely, however, that it was developed by the Frisians in the Low Countries, where dues payable by cogs (*cogscult*) are mentioned in the statutes of Nieuport in 1163, and in the bishopric of Utrecht as early as the tenth century. This implies that broad-beamed ships appeared in the west earlier than in the east. In any case it is certain that the Hanseatics gave a great impetus to the building of the new type of ship, which ensured them a clear superiority over their competitors, especially in the Baltic. In the thirteenth century, and in the fourteenth as well, the cog is the typical Hanseatic ship.

However in the fourteenth century another type of ship, the hulk (*Holk*), appeared in the Hanseatic area. This was at first a cargo boat of modest dimensions, flat-bottomed and broader in the beam than the cog. But it grew progressively larger, and because of its superior cargo-carrying capacity completely supplanted the cog in the course of the fifteenth century, all the more easily in that it borrowed some features from the cog itself, in particular the keel. The hulk could transport 150 lasts (300 tons) or more. Its superstructure, fore- and stern-castles (one or two storeys high) steadily increased in size.

Finally from about 1450 onwards an even larger vessel made its appearance, the caravel (*Krawel*), first built in Mediterranean and Atlantic ports. It was characterised by three masts instead of one, and by a smooth hull, with planks laid edge to edge and no longer overlapping. The caravel allied speed to a greater carrying capacity, at times exceeding 400 tons. It was sheer chance that ensured the success of this new type of ship. In 1462 an exceptionally large French caravel, the *Saint-Pierre de La Rochelle*, was abandoned in the port of Danzig by its captain. Fitted out by the town as a privateer against the English, it created a sensation everywhere by its enormous size, even though it was not a very efficient fighting ship. Other caravels were then built; but up to the seventeenth century the hulk remained the chief type of large Hanseatic ship.

Generally speaking, the dimensions of ocean-going ships continued to increase during the last three centuries of the Middle Ages. The growing importance of the bulk products they transported – salt, cereals and timber – were a contributory factor. On occasion, for instance at the *Hansetag* of 1412, opposition to this development was voiced. The excessive draught of the new ships greatly increased the risk of their running aground in harbour. In this matter, standard practice varied from one to another. While the Wendish towns and Bremen preferred to use ships of medium tonnage, the Prussian and Livonian towns concentrated on the construction of large vessels to transport the bulky products of their hinterland. In comparison with the merchant marines of other nations, the Hanseatic fleet seems on the whole to have been characterised at all times by an exceptional number of large ships.

In addition to these the Hanseatic fleet also included many smaller ships, which went by a great variety of names. Among the deep-sea vessels of medium tonnage the most commonly mentioned are the *Kraier* and the *Ewer* (25 to 50 lasts). More numerous were the small coastal vessels. Designed originally also for the high seas, these had gradually been relegated to more modest duties. Occasionally they were used also for river traffic. The *Schute* and the *Schnigge* (the latter could if necessary be worked with oars) were small, fast sailing boats (10 to 25 lasts), which could in case of danger be used as reconnaissance vessels ahead of the larger ships. Smaller even than the *Schute* and the *Schnigge* were the flat-bottomed prams, used for transporting salt and timber, the *Balinger* and the *Busse*, and the numerous barks and barges used to unload cargo from sea-going vessels which circulated in ports and up rivers.

In medieval ships there was as yet no specialisation, no particularity of construction according to function. All were designed principally as cargo ships. At first, in the colonising and crusading period, the transport of passengers may have been fairly usual, but later it was rarely necessary, except in the case of embassies or pilgrimages to Compostella. On such occasions travellers had to manage as best they could with temporary accommodation rigged up for the passage. Nor were warships – called 'peace ships', *vredenschepe* – in any way different from other ships. In wartime a city would hire from private citizens any vessel available, which it would then man and equip with engines of war at its own expense. It is possible, however, that in the fourteenth and fifteenth centuries military needs encouraged the general development of the forecastle. The higher it was, the easier it became to board or to repel boarders.

It would be interesting to know the size of the Hanseatic fleet in the

Middle Ages. Walther Vogel risked an estimate, necessarily approximate, for the end of the fifteenth century. According to his calculations the Hanseatic ocean-going fleet – excluding coastal vessels – probably numbered 1,000 ships, with a carrying capacity of 30,000 lasts, distributed as follows: 10,000 for the Baltic fleet trading through the Sound with the Low Countries, England and Poitou; the same for trade within the Baltic; 2,000 for trade with Norway and Iceland; and finally 7,000 or 8,000 for the North Sea, though here evaluation is particularly difficult. With 60,000 tons the Hansa would have been the leading naval power of the period, outranking Holland and England and also perhaps France and Spain.

The expansion of sea trade led naturally to an accelerated programme of ship-building in all seaports. Since ships wore out rapidly and many were lost by shipwreck or piracy, constant replacements were needed. The shipyards, set up along the rivers and leased out to the builders, were called *Lastadie*, a word of Flemish origin meaning a place where merchandise was unloaded. Oddly enough, right up to the end of the Middle Ages, ship-builders did not form a separate guild in any town, but remained associated with the carpenters. But they enjoyed a certain prestige, and a few of them, notably in Stralsund, were able to join the town council.

We have no figures at all on which to base an estimate of the amount of ship-building in the Middle Ages. It seems that next to Lübeck, Danzig was the most active centre of the industry, at least until about 1450. The proximity of vast forests, providing not only timber but also tar and pitch for caulking, favoured its development. Here and at Elbing there appeared within the smiths' guild a specialised group of anchor smiths, using iron imported from Sweden.

The shipwrights did not work exclusively for Hanseatic owners. They sold boats to foreigners – Englishmen, Dutchmen, even Italians. However when Dutch ships plying in the Baltic became more numerous, the Hanseatics were alarmed to see that they were themselves contributing to their rivals' rising prosperity. Restrictive measures were considered from about 1412 onwards and in 1426 the Hanseatic diet forbade the sale of ships to foreigners, a decree which was periodically renewed. There was little hope of the measure proving effective. Its only result was to stimulate naval construction in other countries and at the same time to deprive the Hanseatic yards of valuable customers. It was therefore badly received by the interested parties, especially by the Teutonic Order.

Danzig did not apply the ordinance until 1441, and even then normally only in time of war. It was usually considered enough to make delivery subject to fairly illusory conditions. For instance a group of Genoese ship-owners, when placing an order for a ship in 1473, had to undertake that no enemy of Danzig, particularly Thomas Portinari – one of whose galleys had just been captured by a corsair – would be allowed to acquire a share in it. It sems probable that the marked decline in Danzig ship-building in the second half of the fifteenth century was accelerated by these prohibitions.

2. SEAFARING

As was universal in the Middle Ages, Hanseatic ships were slow, and the duration of a voyage varied considerably according to the winds. Average speeds were in the order of four to five knots, ten at the most with a good wind. Ships were capable of tacking, but they usually did so only in emergencies, preferring to wait in port for more favourable conditions. It took four days to sail from Lübeck to Danzig and nine from Lübeck to Bergen, though in fact two or three weeks were often required. The journey from Livonia to the Bay of Bourgneuf usually took two months or more. The shores of Jutland were particularly dangerous, as ships driven by the west wind risked running aground on sand-banks. These perils, together with the length of the detour, explain why the direct sea route was never able to supplant entirely the overland Hamburg–Lübeck route, which was quicker despite the two transfers of cargo involved.

Travelling as they did across the narrow seas, Hanseatic sailors were never long out of sight of the coast, except on the run from Norway to England. On the open sea they usually estimated their position by dead-reckoning, setting a course by the stars. If they wished to take an exact bearing, experienced pilots put their trust principally in the lead, since they knew the exact depth of the sea along all their routes. It was less than 100 metres nearly everywhere. The Italian Fra Mauro, on his world chart (1458), noted of the Baltic: 'In this sea one navigates neither by chart nor by compass, but by the lead.' The configuration of these coasts and seas explains why the new nautical instruments were not widely used there until comparatively late. The compass and theodolite, common in the Mediterranean as early as the thirteenth century, were not habitually used in the north until the beginning of modern times, and the chart even later.

Along the coasts sailors took their bearings from various landmarks – islands, woods and the towers of town churches, which, it seems, were built especially high with this in mind. That of St Peter in Rostock, rising to about 132 metres, was visible at sea over 50 kilometres away. A few wooden towers were used to mark reefs. Lighthouses, notably at the entrance to the Trave – they were lit only when visibility was bad – are mentioned in the fifteenth century.

A body of navigational lore arose which was handed on orally from generation to generation. It was eventually written down, at the latest in the second half of the fifteenth century, in the 'Book of the Sea' (*Seebuch*). In all essentials this was a translation into Low German of a Flemish compilation, composed a century earlier in Bruges, with additional information relating to Hanseatic waters. Here everything which might be of use to the navigator from Cadiz to the Gulf of Finland was recorded: the times of tides, distances, soundings, landmarks, dangers of certain coasts, etc.* In order to use the Book of the Sea it was obviously necessary to be able to read; and this probably meant that its use was at first somewhat restricted and became general only in the sixteenth century.

In order to guarantee the security of ships at sea the Hansa found it increasingly necessary to issue various regulations, dealing especially with two points: winter voyages and sailing in convoy.

It had become customary to suspend sea traffic in the winter, as the ports were frequently icebound. At the end of the fourteenth century, probably after accidents had occurred, the diet debated the matter at length and resolved to change the custom into a compulsory regulation. In 1403 it decreed that navigation was to be prohibited between Martinmas (11 November) and St Peter's Day (22 February). Any ship, of whatever nationality, entering a Hanseatic port after 11 November had to produce a certificate attesting that it had started its return journey before that date, failing which it would be confiscated, along with its cargo. Ships of less than 30 lasts were exempt, as well as those coming from or sailing to Norway. Wismar succeeded in gaining the additional concession that for ships carrying herring and beer – that is, trading with Skania – the period of the ban would be reduced, running from St Nicholas's Day (6 December) to Candlemas (2 February).

These ordinances were resented by the Prussian towns. Their larger ships were subject to discrimination in favour of those from the Wendish

* Document No. 28.

towns. In 1425 they obtained a ruling that winter traffic would only be authorised between Lübeck, Denmark and Rügen. The Dutch also protested, but in vain. For all practical purposes traffic in the Baltic was suspended during the winter. In the North Sea, where the ban was also in force, it was less strictly observed. Moreover it did not apply to ships coming from the Channel or the Atlantic, as long as they had not taken in or discharged cargo in the Zwijn.

These measures certainly prevented shipwreck, but they were also a brake on Hanseatic trade. Many German ships were obliged to winter at great cost in Flemish or English ports, being unable to get back to their home port before the date fixed.

Even more difficult to apply were the regulations about sailing in convoy. Before the mid-fourteenth century sailing alone or in small groups of two to five ships had been normal practice. However the war against Denmark and above all the recrudescence of piracy caused the diet to advise navigation in large convoys. In 1392 the Prussian towns decreed that a group of at least ten was essential for passage through the Sound. Five years later they limited passage of the Danish Straits to three voyages, fixed for 22 April, 10 May and 15 August. This was obviously unsatisfactory, as in the following year the entire Prussian merchant fleet traversed the Sound on 13 July under the escort of two warships carrying eighty men-at-arms. It appears to have been the custom from then on for all the Hanseatic ships leaving the Baltic for the North Sea and the Bay of Bourgneuf to join up in a single fleet protected by warships financed by the members of the convoy, each vessel providing one or two soldiers. Even in the North Sea sailing in convoy became more common, especially in time of war or for long voyages. It was not only as a safety precaution that the Hansa favoured this practice. It had the further advantage of ensuring equal opportunity for all merchants, both as buyers and sellers. Travelling alone ensured high profits for some to the detriment of others and occasioned disastrous price fluctuations on the home markets.

Of course sailing in convoy also presented serious disadvantages. In addition to the increased risk of collision, ships were obliged to assemble at a predetermined rendezvous and wait, often a long time, until all the other ships had arrived. Often there were complaints about convoy commanders who refused to give the signal for departure. Acts of insubordination became frequent. To put a stop to all this, an oath of obedience was required from the skippers. Leaving the convoy was punished by a fine and even exclusion from the Hanseatic privileges. Conversely some contracts for freight-carrying included sanctions against skippers who missed the date of departure. It is easy to understand that although the merchants insisted on sailing in convoy as a safety precaution, the ship's captains on the whole preferred to take the risk of travelling alone.

The whole body of regulations dealing with navigation, maritime trade and sailors gradually developed into a Hanseatic maritime code, for which three distinct sources can be discerned.

Originally each town had its own customary law. The oldest known in Germany is that of Hamburg, first written down in 1292. It detailed certain rules, dealing notably with freight, and was intended for use mainly by the Hamburg merchants in Bruges and Utrecht. This code was adopted, with modifications, by Lübeck (1299), Bremen, Oldenburg and Riga. An amplified version, called the *Ordonancie*, was drawn up in the second half of the fourteenth century.

A more important source for the Hanseatic maritime code was the *Rôles d'Oléron*. Drawn up around the end of the thirteenth century at Oléron, this customary was intended for use principally by the merchants of La Rochelle and Bordeaux trading in wine with the ports on the Zwijn. It laid down procedures in case of collision or disputes with the crew. In the fourteenth century it was translated into Flemish under the title 'Customary of Damme' (*Vonnesse van Damme*). This version, translated in its turn into Low German and combined with the *Ordonancie*, became, under the title of *Waterrecht*, the sea-law first of the Hansa towns of the North Sea, then, after its adoption by Lübeck, of the Baltic towns. Visby being the seat of the most important naval court in the Baltic, the collection gradually became known as the 'Sea-Law of Gotland' (*Gotländisches Wasserrecht*), a title which became definitive with the first printed version, which appeared at Copenhagen in 1505. A strange progress for a code devised to meet the needs of the French wine trade!

Finally a third source for the code, dating from the second half of the fourteenth century, was provided by decisions of the Hanseatic diet on maritime matters. A partial collection of these was made in 1482, but it was not until 1530 that a comprehensive codification was printed, under the name of 'Regulations for skippers and crews' (*Ordonancie van den schipperen unde Boozluden*). Based on such diverse sources, the Hanseatic sea-law certainly lacked uniformty. At the end of the sixteenth century the syndic Sudermann was invited to produce a unified revision, but unfortunately he never completed the task.

3. INLAND NAVIGATION

Inland navigation was almost as important to Hanseatic trade as navigation on the high seas. With a few exceptions, such as Bergen in Norway and perhaps Danzig, the great ports could not be reached by large or medium-sized ships. Cargoes had to be transferred in the estuary to smaller vessels which could navigate upriver.

River navigation required vessels of various kinds depending on local conditions, from simple open boats to small covered sailing ships. On the fast-flowing middle Rhine, for example, flat-bottomed barges were used. These were easily manoeuvrable and had reinforced bulwarks to withstand collisions. On the other hand below Cologne, where transhipment took place, the broader, slower and deeper lower Rhine allowed the use of larger craft, possibly using sail on occasion. Some, like those which can be seen in Memlinc's *Shrine of St Ursula*, differed very little from deep-sea vessels. Everywhere the maintenance of a sufficient depth of water was one of the major concerns of the urban authorities. In harbour it was strictly forbidden to throw ballast or rubbish overboard. Even in the rivers, especially near the mouths, ambitious engineering projects were undertaken in the fifteenth century. At attempt was made, for instance, to deepen the channel of the Trave by reducing its width, but without much success. The unsuccessful attempts to counteract the silting up of the Zwijn are further proof that at this period man was quite helpless when faced with this problem.

Throughout Germany river navigation was in the hands of urban guilds of boatmen. The ship-owners and councils of the seaports do not appear to have shown any interest in this branch of business. With the development of the staple in the fourteenth and fifteenth centuries, the rivers were divided up into sharply defined areas in which the guilds of the great riverside cities arrogated to themselves a monopoly of navigation. Examples of this are the *gylda nautarum* of Berlin on the Spree and the Havel, and the Brotherhood of St James in Hamburg on the lower Elbe. The Vistula is the only exception to this fragmentation. In 1375 the Teutonic Order set up over the guilds of each riverside city a committee of elders (*Oldesten*), who drew up regulations valid for all boatmen and all cargoes in Prussian towns, thus establishing an association which was professional as well as religious.

River travel, though less dangerous than sea travel, nevertheless exposed sailors to similar risks. In the event of war between the rulers of lands bordering the river, boats were often attacked. Again it is only on the Vistula that a systematic defence organisation existed, at least in the mid-fifteenth century, at the time of the Thirteen Years War between Poland and the Teutonic Order. The Prussian towns and nobility having placed themselves under the protection of the king of Poland, the Order attempted to interfere with river traffic. Danzig and Thorn then decided to organise convoys, escorted by warships and provided with cannon and mercenaries. Several times in 1459 and 1460 fleets of more than 100 barges travelled from one town to another, skirmishing all the way.

The importance of inland navigation is shown by the attempts which were made to enlarge certain stretches of water and to dig canals. At times these projects aroused bitter rivalry between the towns. In 1377, for example, Lüneburg, which profited greatly from the overland route that linked her with Brunswick, obtained a ducal ban on the construction within the duchy of any navigable waterway prejudicial to her trade. Fifty years later, when Brunswick began to canalise the Oker, which would have directed trade towards Bremen, Lüneburg allied herself with Magdeburg and forced Brunswick to suspend the work for a period of seven years (1440). However a few years later Brunswck was able to resume the discontinued project and constructed a navigable waterway, with locks, as far as the Weser. Similar works were undertaken by Hanover, Soest and Herford.

Of all the canals two in particular played an important role in Hanseatic trade. One was constructed in East Prussia under the direction of the Teutonic Order in the late fourteenth and early fifteenth century, joining the Pregel and the Kurisches Haff and thus creating a water-link, entirely inland, between Danzig and Kovno, along the two Haffs (lagoons) and the river Niemen. This canal favoured the economic expansion of Danzig, which became the principal outlet for Lithuanian products.

Of more far-reaching importance was the canalisation of the Stecknitz, a tributary of the Trave, which linked the latter via Mölln with the Delvenau, a tributary of the Elbe: it thus provided a water-link between Lübeck and Hamburg, that is, between the Baltic and the North Sea. As early as the mid-fourteenth century there had existed a rudimentary canal there, which allowed the salt-prams of Lüneburg to reach Lübeck. But it soon proved inadequate, and between 1390 and 1398, after long-drawn-out negotiations with the local rulers, a canal with locks was constructed which was navigable by lighters. It is difficult to assess the economic importance of this canal in the fifteenth century. Its principal function was still the transport of salt from Lüneburg to Lübeck, but it also made possible the transport of bulk products – wine in particular – from the Elbe to the Trave and vice versa. It was especially valuable during the frequent wars with Denmark, when the route through the Sound was cut. Thus for instance in 1428–9 when Lübeck was defeated in the Sound, the canal dues doubled. In peacetime it was less useful, and there is little evidence that it diverted to Lübeck any sizeable pro-portion of the sea trade through the Sound. One of its main disadvantages was that the Lübeck–Hamburg waterway route was twice as long as the overland route via Oldesloe. Accordingly in 1448 Hamburg pro-posed to Lübeck the digging of a more direct canal, linking small tributaries of the Alster and the Trave – a genuine anticipation of the Kiel Canal. Work was begun, but the project was never completed. The attempt, however, shows the importance that the two towns attached to an inland waterway, and suggests that the Stecknitz canal, despite its imperfections, helped to uphold the economic primacy of Lübeck.

4. SHIP-OWNERS, SKIPPERS, CREWS

In all Hanseatic ports owners of ships and of shares in ships formed a respected though fairly heterogeneous group. Up to the thirteenth century, however, they could hardly be said to form a separate profession. The same man could be both owner and skipper of his ship and own the greater part of the goods he transported and sold at the end of his voyage. But as ships grew larger and it became customary to divide the ownership into an increasing number of shares, a certain degree of specialisation took place among ship-owners, skippers and freighters.

By the end of the thirteenth century it was not uncommon for a ship to be owned jointly by two people. At the beginning of the fourteenth century a division into four shares is mentioned for the first time (though a similar division is recorded in England 200 years earlier), and this soon became current practice with ships of any size. In the fifteenth century division into eight shares was common, but in the case of larger ships we also find examples of sixteen, thirty-two, even sixty-four shares. To give one example: a Lübeck ship, engaged in the salt trade and sailing in 1449 to Bourgneuf, was divided between eight owners, of whom five owned a sixteenth each, one a sixteenth and a quarter, one an eighth, and the skipper a quarter. One of these ship-owners, Hermen Meyer, in addition owned in the same salt fleet shares in five other ships, of an eighth, three-eighths or three-sixteenths.

This splitting up into small shares was the result of the division of inheritances, of the anxiety of ship-owners to spread their risks, of the increase in tonnage, and of the wish to make it possible for more people to acquire shares and so make the financing of ship-building easier. Ship-owners were usually, of course, merchants, but some were also shipwrights, some even artisans. Many retired skippers, being nautical experts, put nearly all their money into ships. For example Hermann Mesman of Lübeck at the end of the fifteenth century estimated his wealth at 3,900 marks, in the form of three complete ships and shares, ranging in size from an eighth to a half, in six others.* The biggest ship-owner in the Hanseatic world was – obviously – the Teutonic Order, at least at the beginning of the fifteenth century. In 1404 the two treasuries of Marienburg and Königsberg possessed four complete ships and shares in thirteen others, representing nearly 900 lasts valued at 10,000 Lübeck marks. But after the defeat at Tannenberg this investment quickly dwindled away.

The proprietors of a ship formed a partnership whose members were often citizens of different towns. They met regularly, or at least kept themselves scrupulously posted on their share of the expenses of fitting out the ship and the receipts from freighting.† They gave their instructions to the skipper, examined the written or oral log of his voyages and, if need be, discharged him.

The most important of the ship-owners was the master or captain (*schep-herr*, whence *schepper*, *Schiffer*, 'skipper'). In the Middle Ages the captain was hardly ever a paid employee. He usually owned a share in the ship he commanded – generally a quarter or an eighth. He received no special payment for his duties as captain. As one of the owners he received the proportion of the profits to which his share entitled him, but in practice he made extra profits by transporting cargo on his own account. He had to be a married man and a father, his stake in the town being a guarantee of his honesty. The precaution was not

* Document No. 41.
† Document No. 34.

unreasonable. Far more than merchants, ships' captains had a predilection for a roving life and thanks to their many contacts abroad were easily able to emigrate in case of difficulties.

In theory the captain had only to carry out the instructions given him by the owners. In fact he was usually left to handle matters on his own. He recruited, paid and discharged his crew. He settled contracts of freightage with the merchants, supervised the loading and unloading of the cargo and gave the order to weigh anchor. At sea his authority was absolute. If the actual navigation and handling of the ship were not his job but the coxswain's, the captain nevertheless had the final responsibility. He decided at what ports the ship would call, how long it would stay there, whether local pilots should be engaged for passing dangerous channels. In cases of extreme danger he determined, after consulting experienced members of the crew and those freighters present, what merchandise should be jettisoned. For the information of his partners he was obliged, at least after the fifteenth century and in the case of long journeys, to keep a written log, for which purpose he was often accompanied by a scrivener.

Among the ship-owners the captains formed a highly respected group, mainly because of their responsibilities, their close relationship with the freighters and the growing importance of their commercial operations. Since they were themselves merchants, many of them were admitted into the patriciate and occupied the highest public offices, though their promotion did not always mean that they had to give up the sea. Among the captains of a fleet which set sail for Flanders in 1422 was von Doetinchem, the burgomaster of Danzig, and in 1436 the councillor Heinrich Buck. It is interesting to note that many of these Hanseatic captains were of Dutch origin. This is already noticeable in the third quarter of the fourteenth century in ships plying between Lübeck and Stockholm, and even more apparent in the North Sea. The later Dutch supremacy at sea was already foreshadowed. Simon van Utrecht, from Haarlem, had perhaps the finest career of any ship's captain of this type. He became a burgess of Hamburg in 1399, he commanded ships belonging to the city in the struggle against the *Vitalienbrüder* and covered himself with glory; in 1426 he became a member of the council, and six years later burgomaster.

The crew (*Schipkindere*) were recruited by the captain for the duration of the voyage. They might be either townsfolk or peasants. The usual number was a dozen sailors for a ship of 150 tons, twenty for a larger vessel of 250 tons, that is, one man for every twelve tons. Up to the four-teenth century there was hardly any specialisation of function among sailors. The first to emerge as a separate figure is the coxswain. He was responsible for navigation, which implied long experience of the sea, expert nautical knowledge, the ability to calculate the altitude of the stars, and on occasion the use of the compass. The function of the medieval coxswain was more or less equivalent to that of the modern captain, except that it did not involve – at least in theory – any authority over the crew, who were subject to the captain alone. Besides the cox-swain fifteenth-century records mention carpenters, cooks and scriveners. Lastly below the sailors properly so-called (*Bootsmanns*, *Schipmanns*) there is occasional reference to ship's boys (*Jungens*, *Jungknechte*).

Among the crews there was a development somewhat akin to that of the guilds. At first when ships were small a patriarchal regime obtained, and members of the crew could hope to become captains themselves one day. But as ships grew larger a class of sailors developed, similar to the journeymen of the guilds, who could scarcely hope to become captains. As they became more numerous, sailors became less docile and more demanding in the matter of pay. The Hansa was alarmed by this ten-dency and tried to suppress it. The diet of 1418 decreed that insubordina-tion and desertion should be punished by imprisonment and in the case of a second offence, by branding with a hot iron. On several occasions the necessity for absolute obedience to the captain was stressed, but apparently to no effect.

One of the principal sources of conflict between captain and crew evidently arose from rates of pay and methods of payment. In general the towns tried to impose strict regulations in this matter, but the cap-tain was usually obliged to discuss rates of pay directly with the men when he took them on. According to the sea-law of Hamburg a sailor received at the moment of sailing on a voyage to Gotland or Norway ten English shillings, representing a wage for twelve weeks, and after that tenpence for each additional week. On a voyage to Flanders he received first twelve Hamburg shillings, for seven weeks, and then nine English pence for each extra week. In Lübeck, on the other hand, wages might vary according to the profit made on the cargo.

It is almost impossible to get a clear idea of how rates of pay increased. Walther Vogel, basing his estimate on a few scattered examples (and reckoning in grammes of silver), suggested that they may have gone up by 50 to 100 per cent between the thirteenth and fifteenth centuries. He reckoned that pay remained low, roughly equivalent to that of a labourer. It is true that the basic rate of pay could be increased in various ways, above all by the seaman's right to transport and sell goods on his own account, sometimes merchandise chosen by himself, but more often prescribed. He was also entitled, if he did not exercise this right himself, to concede it to a third person. In addition he might receive from the freighters a small payment for the ventilation of certain goods (*Kühlgeld*), as well as for loading and unloading in port (*Windegeld*). Finally during the four winter months when he was not at sea he could accept paid work on land. As a result a sailor's life does not appear to have been one of great hardship. The curious case of the crew of a Prussian ship, who took aboard, on their own account, a hundred tuns of wine at La Rochelle with the intention of selling them in Sandwich, paying the captain two nobles per tun as the cost of freightage (1455), illustrates the opportunities for profit open to simple sailors. Certainly the Hanseatic marine does not appear to have suffered from a shortage of man-power at any time.

As in the trades, brotherhoods were formed in the fifteenth century of which all seamen, captains and crew alike, were members. Their activities were religious, social and charitable. Such was the Brotherhood of St Nicholas, founded at Lübeck in 1400. In the same town there was founded at the end of the century a Brotherhood of St Anne, of which only sailors might be members and from which captains were excluded, analogous to the associations of journeymen. But this seems to have remained an isolated case.

5. FREIGHTAGE

The captain's major concern was obviously to charter his ship to merchants on the best possible terms and then to bring his cargo safely to its destination. Though there were still occasionally cases, even in the fifteenth century, when the skipper was also the owner of most of his ship's cargo and himself undertook its sale at the end of the voyage, he had by that time become for the most part just a carrier, fulfilling contracts concluded with freighters. The latter tended to form an increasingly large group. The cargo of a Hanseatic ship lost in 1345 belonged to 26 merchants. That of another lost in 1430 to 39; that of a third lost in 1468 to 62. This increase was due not only to the greater cargo-carrying capacity of the vessels but also to the desire to limit risks by spreading consignments among several ships. This is apparent, to give only one example, from the inventory of the cargoes of a fleet of ten ships which entered the harbour of Reval towards the end of the winter of 1430. The three biggest freighters had distributed their shipments among nine, eight and seven ships respectively. Marine insurance, a common commercial practice in the Mediterranean and Portugal from the middle of the fourteenth century onwards, remained unknown to the Hanseatics up to the second half of the sixteenth century. The only way to avoid serious losses was therefore to disperse consignments. This had the disadvantage of making trade more complicated, regulations more cumbersome, and of putting a brake on enterprise. The lack of any form of marine insurance was certainly one of the great weaknesses of the Hanseatic commercial system.

At the beginning of the navigation season, captains and merchants in all seaports would be discussing contracts for carrying cargo. Up to the thirteenth century these took the form of an oral agreement, concluded in the presence of witnesses over a glass of beer. In the fourteenth century the oral contract was replaced by a written document, but the oldest ones still extant do not go back beyond the fifteenth century. They took the form of a chirograph. Two identical texts were written out on one sheet of paper, which was then cut in two along an irregular line marked by the first few letters of the alphabet.* One copy was handed to the merchant, who usually deposited it in the townhall, and the other to the captain. In the event of a dispute the authenticity of the two texts could be checked by seeing if they matched exactly. This procedure, which had been used in the Mediterranean in the twelfth century but had been abandoned in favour of a notarial deed, remained in use in the Hanseatic world up to the sixteeth century.

There was a risk that individual bargaining of this kind could lead to dangerous inequalities. In the thirteenth century an attempt was therefore made in certain cities to regulate the freightage. In Lübeck a delegate of the Company of Bergen Merchants collected all requests for cargo to be shipped to that port and distributed the merchandise among the ships available, giving priority to members of his company. They drew up a list of freighters for each vessel, supervised the loading of the cargo and its stowage in the hold, checked the fitting out and arming of the crew, etc. After 1445 four officials were elected to this office. Lübeck even tried to centralise in its own port all the Bergen shipments from the Wendish towns on the Baltic, but opposition from Wismar

* Document No. 39.

caused the scheme to fail. However it seems that in the sixteenth century the Lübeck officials went to Wismar and Rostock in order to supervise these operations. In the same period a similar control was set up for trade with Livonia and even for charters from Hamburg to Flanders: this is another example of the way in which Lübeck exercised authority over the Wendish towns.

There is no need to stress the fact that disputes between captains and freighters were never-ending. The Hanseatic sea-law did its best to be fair to both parties. The captain had the right to keep the merchandise on board if the freight charges had not been paid. The freighter was responsible for delays in delivering goods for loading, and half the freight charge remained due if the goods contracted for were not delivered in time. In the event of shipwreck or seizure by pirates, the captain was absolved from all responsibility. In stormy weather he had the right, even if the freighters present objected, to jettison all or part of the cargo, after consultation with the more experienced members of the crew. In case of damage to the ship while at sea the freighters had to bear their share of the losses involved. The same rule applied to damage caused when docking, to ransoms payable to pirates, and even to the cost of a pilgrimage vowed in a moment of extreme peril. In the case of accidental collision the damages were borne equally by the two ships, the captains bearing the cost of repairs and the freighters that of the goods lost.

Since travel by sea involved heavy risks, it is not surprising that freight charges were extremely high. The few surviving records which touch on this point do not go back much beyond the fifteenth century and show considerable variations. In general the transport of cheap bulk products was much more costly than that of expensive products. At the beginning of the fifteenth century the freight charge from Danzig to Bruges of a cargo of corn was equal to 48 per cent of the price; of rye, 68 per cent; of salt, 66 per cent; of timber, 79 per cent. On dangerous journeys the charge might be much higher, 85 per cent for instance for Portuguese salt shipped to Bruges. In contrast the cost of shipping spices, cloth and wine was only 10 per cent. It was reckoned that carrying a ton of wax brought in double the profit made on a ton of grain.

It is almost impossible to give a figure for the average profit on a cargo as a percentage of the value of the ship. There were considerable variations, but it has been established that the profit was usually between 50 and 100 per cent of the value of the ship, though a voyage especially favoured by the gods might bring in a profit of over 200 per cent. It is even more difficult to estimate the net gain to a ship-owner, since there is no precise information about the pay of crews, the cost of repairs – which varied considerably from year to year – or the rate of depreciation of the ships, which wore out very quickly. Walther Vogel estimated that after all expenses had been paid, the revenue from a ship can be reckoned to average 10 to 15 per cent of its capital value, and that a quarter-share, or even an eighth, was ample for the support of a family. In fact the profession of ship-owner, even more than that of merchant, was extremely chancy. Though at times it brought in large profits, it could, in the face of persistent bad luck, lead to ruin. In addition the profits appear to have dwindled in the fifteenth century, especially in the eastern Baltic, as a result of competition from the Dutch. The latter were able to operate with freight tariffs definitely lower than those of the Hanseatics and consequently, in spite of the rise in the volume of trade and the ban on chartering foreign ships, they succeeded in capturing some of the Hanseatic trade. The decline of the commercial fleets of Danzig and the Livonian towns followed as a result.

CHAPTER EIGHT

The Merchants

I. OCCUPATIONAL GROUPS AND ASSOCIATIONS

THE history of the Hansa is practically identical with that of the *mercator hansae Teutonicorum*, more often called 'the common merchant' (*der gemeene copman*). It was he who by founding the Gotland Community created the Hansa, and the Hansa of the towns had no other objective than to ensure the merchant's prosperity.

To speak of *the* Hanseatic merchant would be to substitute an abstraction for the reality. A number of different categories of merchant may in fact be defined, however roughly, on the basis of wealth, business activities and social status.

At the top there was the great merchant, who was almost exclusively concerned with long-distance wholesale trade, relying largely on credit, and active in many geographical and economic spheres. Until the beginning of this century it was thought that the great merchant banker of the Italian or south German type was unknown or very rare in the Hanseatic domain, since there were no large well-organised firms with numerous branches comparable to those of the Peruzzi, the Medici or the Great Trading Company of Ravensburg. Rörig and his pupils, however, have completely demolished this erroneous concept and shown that the great merchant was a type of businessman characteristic of Hanseatic commerce in the fourteenth and fifteenth centuries, not only in Lübeck but in every other important town of north Germany too.

If one refers to the five classes of tax-payers proposed by Reincke for Hamburg, the great merchants naturally appear in the first class, with a capital of between 5,000 and 25,000 Lübeck marks at the end of the fourteenth century and possibly about 40,000 at the end of the fifteenth. This was the figure reached by Johann Bussmann, the richest citizen of Lübeck at the beginning of the sixteenth century. In Hamburg the burgomaster Henning Buring, of the Company of England traders, left a fortune of 46,000 marks at his death in 1499. But however impressive these figures may be, they are considerably inferior to those of the big firms in south Germany in the same period, for example the Fuggers (375,000 Lübeck marks in 1511), the Welsers (486,000 in 1515), the Great Company of Ravensburg (198,000 in 1496) and even Claus Stalburg of Frankfurt (82,500 in 1515).

The wealth of these great merchants was derived in varying proportions not only from the profits on commercial operations but also from interest on loans, shares in firms and ships, and ground-rents, annuities, etc. It comprised also landed property, both urban and rural, precious objects, cash, etc. Their commercial activity was characterised by the multiplicity of the enterprises in which they were engaged, always in the form of wholesale trade, either buying or selling. Dealing in Flemish cloth was often an important part of their business.

Socially, these wealthy merchants were nearly all members of the patriciate. Either they belonged to one of the great families or, having recently been made burgesses, were received into patrician society because of their wealth and matrimonial connections. They were often to be found on the town council and in the highest municipal offices. Such were the burgomasters Johann Wittenborg (mid-fourteenth century) or Hinrich Castorp (late fifteenth century) in Lübeck, Hans Hüge and Henning Buring (late fifteenth century) in Hamburg, Eberhard Ferber (early sixteenth century) in Danzig and so on.

Below them in a second category came those whose fortune was between 2,000 and 5,000 marks. These middle-rank merchants dealt generally with one foreign country only – Flanders, Sweden, England or Russia – and their business affairs were less complex. In addition many of them were not exclusively wholesalers but also sold retail at least part of the merchandise they imported. Vicko van Geldersen, of Hamburg, and Johann Tölner, of Rostock, both of whom left account-books, are representative of this category in the second half of the fourteenth century. They both imported large quantities of Flemish cloth, which they sold retail to their customers, the first in the little towns of the Elbe and the lower Weser, the second to the noble families of Mecklenburg. These middle-rank merchants, with some exceptions, were not members of the patriciate, unless they were eventually admitted because of the prosperity of their business. Along with the ship-owners, drapers and the richest of the brewers, they constituted that middle class which was often irritated at being excluded from high public office and which on occasion made common cause with the guilds against the great families.

Lastly those who may be called the small merchants possessed a capital not exceeding 2,000 marks. They were divided into two quite distinct categories. One group, consisting of shopkeepers and retailers of all kinds, does not present any distinguishing Hanseatic characteristic. As in any other medieval town they were organised in corporations and were closely dependent on the great merchants. They were not admitted into the associations of long-distance traders, as expressly laid down in the oldest statute of the *Artushof* of Danzig. The other group, however, the most modest of the oversea traders, were wholesale dealers on as large a scale as their small means allowed. Among them were the numerous Lübeck traders who travelled to Skania, and most of the *Bergenfahrer* who bought just one or two lasts of herring. Like the merchants who dealt on a much larger scale, they were admitted to the *Kontore* and the merchant associations. They were therefore Hanseatics on an equal footing with their richer colleagues, and resembled the retailers only in the slenderness of their means. Some of them, though of humble origin, became very wealthy. An example is Bertold Rucenberg, who in 1364 wrote in his will: 'From my parents I received nothing which puts me under an obligation to anyone at all; all that I possess I have earned since my youth by patient hard work.'

Much more clearly than this division into classes by wealth corresponding to modern concepts, the contemporary texts display the social groupings of the merchants. Like all medieval associations, and in particular the trade guilds, they were both professional and religious, charitable and recreational. As headquarters they had a house with an assembly hall, and were administered by aldermen elected by all the members.

In certain towns the long-distance merchants were all members of a single society, sometimes old-established, sometimes not founded before the fourteenth century. There were merchant guilds in Bremen and Goslar as early as the thirteenth century, in Stettin and Riga by the fourteenth. There was an association of 'seafaring merchants' under the patronage of St Nicholas in Stendal, Lüneburg and several towns on the Zuiderzee. One of these associations, best-known because of its statutes, is the 'Court of Arthur' (*Artushof*) in Danzig. The house where the members met, originally the headquarters of the patrician Brotherhood of St George, was in fact by the end of the fourteenth century open to all long-distance merchants and by the end of the fifteenth century to foreigners and ship-owners as well.*

* Document No. 24.

More characteristic, however, of the Hanseatic world – although similar societies existed in Italian cities – were societies of merchants all of whom traded with a particular foreign port or country. The oldest was the *fraternitas danica* of Cologne, mentioned in 1246 and comprising probably all the merchants engaged in the Baltic trade. Merchants dealing with England formed another group, as can be seen from a charter conferred upon them by the town in 1324. By the end of the fourteenth century societies of this sort, called *Fahrer Kompanien*, appear in a number of ports and inland towns. The name *Fahrer* ('sailors') here means merchants, not boatmen or ships' captains, although occasionally some of these were admitted. These groups were particularly active in Lübeck. The oldest, that of the 'sailors to Skania' (*Schonenfahrer*), first mentioned in 1365, was the largest and most influential. Somewhat later there appeared the company of the *Bergenfahrer* (which, however, may go back to 1343), then the companies of the sailors to Riga, Novgorod, Stockholm, England, Spain, etc. By the end of the fifteenth century there were ten such companies in Lübeck and six in Rostock. By contrast there were only three in Hamburg, founded at the end of the fourteenth century, one, the richest and largest, for Flanders, one for England and one for Skania. It was trade with Scandinavia which gave the main impetus to the founding of these societies. *Schonenfahrer* are to be found in eight Hansa towns, including Dortmund and Deventer, and *Dänemarkfahrer* or *Dragörfahrer* in various Baltic ports. But there is also mention in the fifteenth century of a society of merchants in Cologne trading with Venice (*Fenedierverder*).

These companies do not seem to have enjoyed a monopoly of trade with any particular country. In Hamburg at any rate not all those trading with England were members of the *Englandfahrer*. Conversely, membership of one society did not exclude membership of another, and it is probable that most merchants, particularly the wealthier ones, belonged to more than one. The organisation of the companies was strict or lax according to the town in which they were situated. In Lübeck they provided a rigid framework regulating the activities of the long-distance merchants.

One of the most closely studied of the Lübeck companies is that of the *Bergenfahrer*. It came under the patronage of St Olaf and had its own chapel in the Church of St Mary. It was managed by three or six aldermen elected for life at a general meeting (*Schütting*), and in the fifteenth century had between 100 and 200 members. These were all of equal status and fell into two groups: the *borger to Lubeke*, rich and elderly merchants, heads of business houses, who lived in Lübeck; and the *Kopgesellen to Bergen*, younger men, sailing regularly to Norway and staying for long periods in Bergen, trading in dried fish. Nearly 200 wills which have survived from the fourteenth and fifteenth centuries give interesting glimpses of the origin and social status of the *Bergen-fahrer*. Only about a quarter of them were natives of Lübeck, and 30 per cent were from Westphalia. Nearly all were of humble origin. After 1409, 78 per cent of the testators are careful to point out that having amassed by their own efforts all that they possess, they are free to dispose of it as they wish. The exacting nature of their work explains the small proportion of married men. Out of 187 members for whom this information is available, only 82 were married, and of these only 43 had legitimate offspring. Trading in cod rarely led to a high social position. Generally these merchants achieved only a modest competence and few of them entered the council, unlike the merchants trading with Skania, Russia and Flanders. The exceptions, however, show how the Lübeck citizenry renewed its strength by admitting men from the lower social strata.

2. THE MERCHANT'S OCCUPATION: TRADING ON HIS OWN ACCOUNT AND IN PARTNERSHIP

Up to the mid-thirteenth century the average Hanseatic merchant was an itinerant trader, such as was to be met with everywhere at that time. Assisted by one or two servants, he travelled abroad with his goods, disposed of them when he reached his destination, usually by barter, and returned home, there to sell the goods he had acquired abroad. Because of the dangers faced on land and at sea, these merchants nearly always travelled in groups (*cohors institorum*, as Helmold says in the twelfth century), often made up of men from the same town. They were armed, as they were authorised to be by imperial edicts, perpetually on the alert and ready to fight brigands, pirates or even dissatisfied customers. Often they were accompanied by a priest, itinerant like themselves. Such were the original merchants of the Gotland Community, and certain characteristics of this early stage persisted for a long time, especially among the Hanseatic groups making the journey to Novgorod. Not being able to either read or write, these itinerant traders kept only rough accounts, and their commercial usages were necessarily rudimentary.

In the course of the thirteenth century this primitive type of itinerant trader was replaced by the independent entrepreneur in charge of his own firm. When his destination was relatively near at hand and the route safe he no longer accompanied his merchandise himself, a clerk being entrusted with this duty. As land and sea routes became safer, this practice was gradually extended to long-distance commercial enterprises. The merchant, no longer compelled to be continually on the road, could now conduct several enterprises at the same time in different areas. Thus by the fourteenth and fifteenth century the top- or middle-rank Hanseatic merchant had become a sedentary worker. He conducted his business at home, from his office (*scrivekamere*). Surrounded by a small staff – a scrivener, two or three servants, journeymen or apprentices – he sat at his own desk, corresponding with his business associates, representatives or clerks in other Hansa towns or the *Kontore* abroad. He still travelled occasionally, mainly to deal personally with important matters. But normally the goods he dispatched, stamped with his own trade-mark, were entrusted to a clerk or to the captain of the cargo vessel, and were accepted at their destination by a representative or agent.

This transformation was made possible only by the development of education, the stages of which are obviously difficult to trace. In Lübeck up to the mid-thirteenth century there was only the cathedral school, whose pupils were nearly all destined for the Church. But in 1262 a second school was founded near the Church of St James, a 'school of the liberal arts'. In 1300, despite the opposition of the chapter, the council set up an elementary school in each of the four parishes of the town and appointed the masters. It may be assumed that these foundations permitted laymen to receive the rudimentary instruction necessary for their trade.

A great step forward was made towards the end of the thirteenth century by the institution of registers whose entries were publicly authenticated. In 1270 there appeared for the first time, in Hamburg, a 'Book of Debts' (*Schuldbuch*). Seven years later in Lübeck there appeared the *Niederstadtbuch* (as opposed to the property register, known as the *Oberstadtbuch*), followed by similar registers in Riga in 1286, Stralsund in 1288 and Lüneburg in 1290. The recording by merchants of their debts and contracts, with a municipal guarantee, was a decisive factor in the development of credit and commerce in the fourteenth and fifteenth centuries.

Now that the merchant could read and write he began to keep accounts. In the Hanseatic area the oldest surviving account-book is a fragment from the end of the thirteenth century, followed by that of the Lübeck councillor Hermann Warendorp (1330–6). It is written in Latin, sometimes by Warendorp himself, sometimes by his brother-in-law, Johann Clingenberg, who in Warendorp's absence acted as his business representative. The entries are somewhat miscellaneous. In addition to commercial affairs there are lists of ground-rents, building operations and domestic expenses. After the mid-fourteenth century account-books were written in German and became more common, each merchant probably having several. Those still extant were intended to serve many different purposes but show a growing tendency towards specialisation, which was not, however, based on any clear system. Some contain only credit operations; but most contain commercial dealings as well, sometimes classified under special headings. For example in the book of Johann Piesz of Danzig in about 1430, sales, purchases and commission business are kept separate. As a rule it was customary in the fifteenth century to separate receipts and expenditures. This can be seen in the account-book of the 'Company of Venice' founded by the Veckinchusen brothers. For the period from 1 May 1407 to 15 March 1408 there are four pages giving particulars of goods dispatched, with their prices, then another four pages listing receipts of cash or goods; after which the balance is shown and an entry is made recording the dispatch of the accounts to a partner. It can be deduced from this book, as from others, that transactions were not usually posted as they took place but were written up from separate notes when accounts had to be rendered.

Although the Hanseatics made some definite progress in the keeping of accounts, they did not adopt all the improvements introduced by the Italians. Thus double-entry book-keeping remained unknown until the sixteenth century. Similarly there is no manual of accounts comparable to the *Tractatus computis scripturis* by Luca Paccioli, or of commercial usage like that by Pegolotti in Bruges (1315). No doubt apprentices learnt commercial practice under the direction of a merchant when working in one of the *Kontore*, particularly that of Bruges.

The municipal registers of debts, the account-books and the correspondence of Hanseatic merchants show clearly the extensive use of credit in the fourteenth and fifteenth centuries. It was through the Italians in Flanders and England that the Hanseatics became familiar with the bill of exchange, which some of them used frequently. In Bruges Hildebrand Veckinchusen in little more than two months at the beginning of 1408 drew nine bills of exchange for a total of 216 pounds groschen on his brother Sievert, payable at Hamburg or Lübeck. At the same time he effected in one year (1408–9) five transfers, amounting to 3,979 ducats or 576 pounds groschen, in favour of his partner Karbow in Venice. Does this mean that the bill of exchange was common practice among most Hanseatic merchants? It would be going too far to say that, for in the few cases where the wording of the bill has survived we can see that it was not cast in the laconic form used by Italian financiers. It was a relatively detailed missive, and the 'order to pay' is wrapped up in prolix circumlocutions which suggest that this method of payment was exceptional. In addition bills of exchange are nearly always mentioned in connection with Bruges. In the east merchants seem hardly to have used them at all. Even in the west the steps taken by the Hansa in the fifteenth century to limit credit must certainly have restricted the use of bills of exchange.

There were two ways in which a Hanseatic merchant might conduct his business: either on his own account (what German historians call *Eigenhandel*) or in partnership. An individual business employed only the capital and agents of a single merchant, who would do business personally or on commission (*sendeve*). Usually the master (*Herr*) entrusted his clerk (*Diener*) with goods, which the latter disposed of according to precise instructions, or with a sum of money with which to buy goods.* The agent was considered legally responsible for the merchandise but had nothing to do with the payment for it. Should the validity of the operation be questioned, responsibility fell entirely on the master, if the clerk took an oath that he had acted for the best according to instructions. A commission could not properly be called a business partnership and was not usually based on a contract, since the clerk acted only as an agent. The *sendeve* was similar to the Italian *commenda*, except that it seldom gave the clerk a share in the profits but only a fixed salary. The agent, moreover, was not necessarily an employee of the master. He might be a correspondent, a citizen of another town, carrying out the commission gratis in exchange for similar services. Although widely used, the *sendeve* has left hardly any traces, not even in the account-books, since no rendering of accounts was necessary.

A partnership had the advantage that it made more capital available and divided the risks. It was therefore the standard form of commercial enterprise. Usually it brought together a small number of associates,

* Document No. 33 (*a*).

two, three or four, rarely more, for a limited period of years and for a particular type of operation. It was often a family business. Johann Tölner, of Rostock, whose account-book dating from the mid-fifteenth century is still extant, was in partnership with his father, son-in-law and his son-in-law's son-in-law. Often the members of a partnership lived in different towns, which was an advantage to the business but complicated the rendering of accounts.

Partnerships were known by the most varied names, none of which was restricted to a clearly defined type of association. Among them were *vera societas* (*vrye selschop* or *kumpanie*) or *contrapositio* (*wedderlegginge*), implying an equal capital investment by each partner. A clearer picture results from a tripartite classification based on the source of the capital invested.

In the first type, which was closest to the *sendeve*, only one of the contracting parties provided capital. The other was content to carry out the commercial operations. Usually profit and loss were shared equally, but there were cases in which the risks of the business were covered entirely by the sleeping partner.

In the second type, which was the most common, each partner brought in his share of capital and one or two of them conducted the business as well. Profits were shared in proportion to the capital invested. In case of loss each partner was responsible only for the original amount invested. The partnership could be extended beyond the date fixed in the contract, until such time as one of the partners wished to withdraw.*

Finally the third type was the *vulle mascopei* or 'complete partnership', in which the partners pledged in common all or the greater part of their fortunes. Such an association, implying the right of one partner to draw on the funds of the other, was scarcely conceivable except between two brothers who were in fact carrying on their father's business undivided. Examples of this are particularly frequent in the trade between Lübeck and Bergen.

Every great Hanseatic merchant was an associate in many partnerships which were linked together only through him. In each of them his rights were the same as those of his partners. However extensive his business may have been, he figured less as the head of a great commercial undertaking than as a participant in a number of separate businesses. The unusual structure of the great Hanseatic undertaking has led some historians to doubt its very existence. It is true that in the area with which

* Document No. 33 (*b*) and (*c*).

we are concerned there was no single large commercial firm, permanent, centralised, having its headquarters in a special building, with subsidiary firms, its own clerks and agents and surviving through several generations – the sort of business represented for example in Italy by the Peruzzi, Datini and Medici families, in south Germany by the Great Trading Company of Ravensburg or the Diesbach–Watts, and later on by the Fugger and Welser families. This more sophisticated type of commercial enterprise was not developed by the Hanseatics, or at least not until the sixteenth century, when the firm of Loitz of Stettin came into being. But this in no way precludes the existence of merchants operating on a large scale, investing large amounts of capital, carrying out large-scale and complex financial and commercial operations in various geographic regions; among them the Gallin, Warendorp and Limberg families in the fourteenth century and the Veckinchusens and Castorps in the fifteenth.

There is one exception – a very unusual one – to this absence of large firms, and that is the Teutonic Order, which was a member of the Hansa. The Order was engaged in commercial activities certainly from the end of the thirteenth century onwards. Its organisation at the end of the fourteenth and beginning of the fifteenth century is fairly well known, thanks to accounts which have been preserved. At this period it had a capital of about 35,000 pounds of Flemish groschen, and possessed two 'great treasuries' (*Grosschäfferei*) at Marienburg and Königsberg, whose directors, monks or laymen, were appointed and controlled the first by the Treasurer (*Ordenstressler*) and the second by the Marshal of the Order. Subordinate to the treasuries were representatives (*Lieger*), usually appointed annually, in Bruges, London, Scotland, Lübeck, Danzig and Riga, who had full authority to accept goods, sell them as they thought best, and buy and dispatch other goods. They were obliged to present their accounts on demand. More numerous were the depositaries (*Wirte*), who, independent of the Order, were responsible for the goods deposited with them, but not authorised to transact business on their own initiative. Lastly general liaison was maintained by the clerks (*Diener*), who accompanied the goods, made purchases on behalf of the Order and were also empowered to do business on their own account. Up to the battle of Tannenberg the commerce of the Order flourished; afterwards it declined, though it did not disappear entirely. It is obvious, however, that the trade organisation of the Order, which lasted for more than 200 years, cannot be considered typical of Hanseatic undertakings.

3. SOME GREAT MERCHANTS

The business activity of certain Hanseatic merchants of the fourteenth and fifteenth centuries is revealed to us – though in only a fragmentary fashion, of course – by entries in public documents such as municipal registers of debts, land registers and various customs accounts. Their personality comes through more clearly in such private documents, business letters, wills and account-books as have survived; unfortunately family chronicles are almost completely lacking. For none of the merchants is there full and satisfactory documentation, abundant though it may be in certain cases: in particular, we know nothing about the merchants' youth, that important period when the foundations of their fortunes were laid.

It is at the end of the thirteenth century, when the registers of debts were instituted, that the Hanseatic merchant ceases to be anonymous. Among the operations entered in the *Schuldbuch* of Hamburg, one of the names which recur most often is that of Winand Miles. A native of the Old March of Brandenburg, son of a burgomaster of Salzwedel, brother of a burgomaster of Hamburg, he was himself a councillor in Hamburg, where he died in 1301. The register contains entries of 54 transactions carried out by him between 1288 and 1301, usually short-term loans, the total involved being 3,350 marks. He appears to have grown rich by dealing principally in timber and grain, both imported down the Elbe from the region of Brandenburg and Berlin. These products, or at least some of them, were no doubt sold in Flanders, for Miles is mentioned as an importer of cloth and as debtor to two cloth merchants of Ghent, Guillaume Better and Gislebert van Hove. There is no indication of commercial relations with England or with Lübeck and the Baltic. Miles normally did business on his own, but he also figures in partnership with his brother, the burgomaster. This is the sum total of the information available about a great Hamburg merchant in the closing years of the thirteenth century, the basis of whose business was trade with the hinterland of the Elbe.

Johann Wittenborg, fifty years later, is better known, mainly because of his tragic death in 1363. He typifies the great Lübeck merchant, member of a patrician family, a great property-owner, and a politician of the first rank in his city's service.

Johann Wittenborg's affairs are known to us mainly through his account-book, begun in 1338 by his father, also a merchant. It covers

the years 1346 to 1359, though most of the entries are undated. Wittenborg's business interests extended to almost every corner of the Hanseatic
world: Flanders, England, Skania, Prussia, Livonia and Russia. He
dealt principally in cloth, usually from Flanders but also from Valenciennes and Louvain. There are entries for 32 purchases of cloth, involving 308 pieces valued at 2,620 Lübeck marks. In furs, bought in
Livonia and dispatched to Bruges, the turnover varied from year to
year, reaching a maximum of 1,300 marks in 1358. In the same region in
1358 he bought wax to the value of 727 marks. In Danzig he bought large
quantities of barley and malt to be used in the brewing of beer – he
owned a brewery in Lübeck – which he then exported to Skania.

It is not possible to estimate even approximately the volume of business
carried on by Johann Wittenborg, but for the years 1357–8 his credit
purchases of cloth, grain, malt, furs and wax amounted to 6,776 marks.
A striking characteristic of his business is the frequent dispatch of silver
bullion to settle outstanding accounts, particularly to Dorpat and
Livonia, but also to Danzig and even Bruges, where Laurent van der
Burse received from him commission amounting to nearly 200 Flemish
guilders. It is therefore interesting to note that all the merchandise
Wittenborg bought in either eastern or western Europe was sold in
Lübeck. Wittenborg shipped neither Flemish cloth to Livonia nor wax
to Bruges. His trade centred on Lübeck rather than on the great Hanseatic routes. He made at least three long journeys, one before 1348 to
England, a second 'overseas' in 1354, and a third to Bruges in 1356, when
he travelled via Aachen, doubtless to make a pilgrimage at the same time.
A large number of clerks and associates were active in his affairs, of
whom at least two, mentioned in the book, were related to him.

Like all merchants who had become rich, Wittenborg also dealt
largely in property, the transactions being entered in the *Oberstadtbuch*.
In the last years of his life he bought a great many annuities, and
according to his will he owned four houses in Lübeck.

His success as a businessman ensured him a brilliant career as a
politician. In 1350 he became a member of the council, perhaps to fill a
gap left by the Black Death. Soon after he was playing an important role
in diplomacy. In 1358 he represented Lübeck at the Hanseatic diet in
Rostock. Two years later he was head of a mission to the duke of Saxe-
Lauenburg. He became burgomaster in 1360 and in the following year
represented Lübeck at the diet in Greifswald, when war against Denmark was decided upon. As supreme commander of the Hanseatic fleet

dispatched in 1362 into the Sound, he committed the fatal blunder of landing troops to lay siege to Hälsingborg, thus allowing Valdemar IV to surprise his fleet and capture twelve of his cogs. On his return to Lübeck he was arrested. His friends did their best to have him tried by the Hanseatic diet, but he was brought before the council of Lübeck, condemned to death on a charge which remains unknown and beheaded in the market square.

More or less contemporary with Wittenborg was Tidemann Limberg, or Lemberg (1310–86), a man of quite different character, a typical parvenu and speculator. As a young man he left his native village and moved to nearby Dortmund, a nursery of great merchants which had been a centre of the English wool trade for more than fifty years. He came of a humble stock and did not owe his rise to influential relations. This makes it all the more regrettable that nothing at all is known about his early years in business and his first transactions, doubtless carried out at the London *Kontor*. By 1340 he was established in England, already rich and influential. In partnership with a merchant from Ghent he lent £1,000 to Edward III: this was the first of a long series of credit operations, and also the first indication of that royal favour which was to continue for more than twenty years. Within a few months Limberg was admitted into the great consortium formed by the king's Westphalian creditors. He soon became their syndic, with a colleague, and thereafter played a leading role. It was with him that Edward III negotiated the return of his great crown, pledged to the archbishop of Trier for 45,000 guilders.

After the break-up of the consortium in 1344 Limberg formed another, in which his associates were Hanseatics, mainly in order to redeem the smaller crown, which had been pledged to certain Cologne merchants, and he also entered into various partnerships with English merchants. During the siege of Calais he lent the king a further £10,000. In return for a loan of £3,000 to the Black Prince in 1347 he obtained the revenues of the Cornish zinc mines for three years and three months, which gave him a monopoly in the export of this mineral. He also undertook, among other things, the shipment of grain to Bordeaux for the English troops. The remarkable thing about him is that he always seemed to have considerable sums of money available to make advances when other Hanseatic merchants were in grave financial difficulties.

Around 1350 Limberg was at the height of his success. He had fallen out with most of his Westphalian colleagues, who were jealous of his

success and alienated by his ruthless business practices. He seems to have
thought nothing of acquiring English citizenship, for he obtained from
the Abbey of Wilmington vast royal fiefs in eight southern counties.
Edward III still had complete faith in him and protected him against
the attacks of his numerous enemies. In 1351, when the king ordered the
arrest of all Hanseatics in England and the seizure of their goods, he
excepted Limberg. Two years later he consulted him before re-establish-
ing the wool staple in England. Limberg also effected transfers of funds
to the papal court at Avignon, and in 1351 Clement IV granted him the
privilege of taking a portable altar on his travels.

However Limberg had to face increasing hostility from the English
merchants. It was probably this that induced him to leave England in
1354, later than most of his colleagues, and to settle in Cologne. Here he
bought many municipal annuities and became a burgess in 1358. He
dreamt of setting the seal on his success by making a brilliant marriage
with the daughter of some patrician house. But the moment was ill-
chosen. The great families, whose hegemony was threatened by the
democratic party, were in no mood to welcome a parvenu. Disappointed
in his matrimonial ambitions, Limberg returned to England in 1359,
where he leased the silver, lead and copper mines of Alston Moor and
made a further loan of £1,000 to the king. But his enemies were watch-
ing him. Accused of complicity in the murder of a London citizen, he
escaped with difficulty to the Continent. This time Edward could no
longer protect him and decreed, though only after a long interval, the
confiscation of his goods. England being closed to him, Limberg settled
in Dortmund, where he married the daughter of a burgomaster. There
also he was coldly received, and in 1367 he returned to Cologne, where he
spent the last years of his life, still actively engaged in business, dealing
mainly in wine and cloth. He gave financial support to the opponents of
the great families, but with sufficient prudence to avoid trouble at the
time of the patrician reaction in 1370. He was buried, in accordance with
the wish expressed in his will, in the monastery of the Austin Friars, to
which he had made several donations. The settlement of his estate – he
had no children – caused serious difficulties between the city of Cologne
and the neighbouring rulers.

By his individualism, his audacity and his speculations under the
protection of a foreign monarch, Tidemann Limberg is closer in spirit to
the Italian financiers than to the Hanseatics of his period, even though
to some extent he may be regarded as representative of the Westphalian

merchants grown rich on the proceeds of the trade in English wool. But he was a lone wolf who never managed to find a footing in any social group. It is significant that in spite of his wealth he never held public office in any town, except perhaps once, when he may have been an alderman of the London *Kontor*. He remains an exceptional personality in the history of the Hansa.

In general the information about individual merchants is only fragmentary. It is, however, possible, with the help of a few entries in the account-books of the Lübeck custom-house (*Pfundzollbücher*), to attempt a sketch of a certain Johann Nagel, who was typical of the great Swedish merchants of German origin. The Nagels were one of those families, originating from Dortmund, who had proliferated in various Hansa towns. They were to be found in Lübeck, Rostock, Linköping in Sweden and Åbo in Finland, though their exact degree of relationship can seldom be determined.

Johann Nagel was a native of Västerås, the principal town of the mining district of central Sweden, where numerous Germans had settled. In 1365 he took up residence in Stockholm so as to be able to operate over a much wider field. From 1368 to 1371 he journeyed to Lübeck every Easter with a consignment of copper worth approximately 200 marks, and probably also with other Swedish products such as butter. His wares were not sold in Lübeck but dispatched to Flanders, where cloth, spice and oil were bought for shipment to Sweden, where they were joined by linen and salt bought in Lübeck. It is impossible to establish precisely the volume of his trade. It was certainly more modest than the similar business carried on by Lübeck merchants dealing with Stockholm. After 1376 Nagel's commercial dealings with Flanders diminished, as is known from loans of some hundreds of marks which he granted to Lübeck merchants. This development in Nagel's activity was probably the result of his increasing importance in public affairs. By 1385 at the latest he was burgomaster of Stockholm. First commerce, then finance, combined with high municipal office – here again is the classic life pattern of a great merchant, of which unfortunately all too little is known.

Of all the Hanseatic merchants of the Middle Ages, the brothers Hildebrand and Sievert Veckinchusen left behind them the most abundant documentation. Eleven of their account-books and hundreds of their business letters are preserved in the archives at Reval. But even so not very much is known about their lives. Even the place where they were born, around 1370, is unknown. It may have been Dortmund, since the family was of Westphalian extraction, but was more probably some Livonian town. A third brother, Caesar, became councillor and burgomaster of Reval, and it was in this town that Hildebrand and Sievert probably started their business. During the last decade of the fourteenth century they travelled regularly to Bruges. Twice, in 1394 and 1398, Hildebrand was elected alderman of the Livonian third of the *Kontor*. Sievert held the same position in 1399. Hildebrand was married first to the sister of a burgomaster of Dortmund, then, in 1398, to the daughter of a rich Riga merchant. But he quarrelled with his father-in-law, went to Lübeck and became a burgess of that town. Soon – though still retaining his Lübeck citizenship – he settled in Bruges, attracted by the vast possibilities of the 'medieval world market'. Except for a few short voyages he was to remain there almost until his death in 1426. As for Sievert, he set up in Lübeck in about 1400; but when serious political trouble broke out in 1408, he made common cause with the patriciate, left the town and lived for the next ten years in Cologne. He returned to Lübeck in 1418 and remained there until his death in 1433.

Although they each had their own business, the two brothers were often partners in large-scale enterprises. Their letters show that their business relations extended not only throughout the Hanseatic zone from Novgorod to London, with the exception of Scandinavia, but also into southern Germany, Italy, northern France, Bordeaux and Bayonne. At the beginning of the fifteenth century their trade was principally with Livonia, to which they exported cloth, salt and spices, and where they bought wax and furs. The fur trade seems to have been particularly prosperous around 1400. The two brothers were continually expanding this branch of their business, in which, however, they suffered serious losses. In 1406 they entered into partnership with Heinrich Tyte of Reval and Woesten of Dorpat with a capital of 100 pounds groschen. At the end of six years their takings came to 673 pounds as against purchases to the value of 621 pounds, which, taking their investment capital into account, represented a loss of 48 pounds.

Their most important undertaking, the 'Venetian Company', was equally unsuccessful. The company was set up in 1407 with a capital of 5,000 marks (800 pounds groschen), divided into five shares. The chief partners were Hildebrand Veckinchusen in Bruges and Peter Karbow in Venice. The latter exported to the north – by both land and sea – spices, cotton and silk, and received from his partner English cloth, amber rosaries and above all furs.* At first the company prospered. In 1409 the capital was raised to 11,000 marks. In 1411 Karbow wrote to say that he had dispatched goods to the value of 70,000 ducats (the ducat was roughly the same value as the mark) and that he had received goods to the value of 53,000 ducats. But after that there were many reverses. Carried away by success, Karbow made rash purchases of spices, drawing too many bills of exchange on his partner. He was swindled by a supplier and lost 1,500 ducats. In Germany one of the partners was robbed of 1,700 guilders and imprisoned. The partners quarrelled among themselves, there was a lawsuit, and the partnership was wound up on conditions which are not perfectly clear but which certainly involved losses.

Hildebrand, in spite of his brother's warnings, continued to launch out into new enterprises. In October 1418 he bought on credit more than 11,000 furs in ten days. In 1420, hearing that there was a shortage in the east, he made massive purchases of French salt, a project which does not appear to have brought him the profit he expected. He also suffered losses on damaged consignments of figs and rice. In 1417 he contributed to a loan of 3,000 crowns to the Emperor Sigismund, the repayment of which was long delayed.

If Hildebrand's projects usually turned out badly, his imprudence was primarily to blame. But matters were made worse by the particularly unfavourable state of affairs in the second decade of the fifteenth century, accentuated by such political events as the internal crisis in the Hansa itself, caused by the overthrow of the patriciate in Lübeck, the ban on trade with Venice decreed by Sigismund in 1417, and after 1419 the Hispano–Hanseatic conflict. Everywhere the market was saturated. The Veckinchusens' letters are forever complaining of the difficulties encountered in selling their goods: furs and amber in Venice; Russian wax and Norwegian fish in Frankfurt, which the clerks had to try and sell further afield, in Mainz and Strasbourg; southern fruits and spices in Reval and Novgorod; cloth and alum in Lübeck and Danzig.

In 1419 Hildebrand's credit must still have been good, as in that year he was elected alderman of the Bruges *Kontor* for the Lübeck third. But his situation deteriorated rapidly and he had to borrow from Lombards resident in Bruges. Sievert begged him in vain to return to Lübeck, hoping that there he might cure him of his propensity for speculation. In 1422, on a complaint brought by his landlord, Hildebrand was arrested and imprisoned for debt. Neither his family nor the *Kontor* nor Lübeck

* Document No. 37.

appear to have been ready to go bail for him, and he was not released until three years later. Ruined and embittered against his relatives, he returned to Lübeck, where he died a short time later.

That Hildebrand was largely responsible for his own misfortunes is shown by the career of his brother, a much more circumspect person. On his return to Lübeck in 1418 he bought investment property, a share in a salt mine at Oldesloe, and made a number of profitable business deals, in particular by joining the monopolistic guild of rosary-makers. He became so prosperous that he was admitted to the patrician Circle Society in 1431. If he had not died shortly afterwards, he would certainly have become a member of the council.

In Hinrich Castorp (*c.*1420–88) we encounter once again the classic type of the great Lübeck merchant, holding the highest office and playing an important part in politics. He was born in Dortmund and did not settle in Lübeck until he was thirty years old. He is thus one of the many examples of a recent immigrant who by reason of his wealth and business contacts reached the highest rank in his adopted city. Castorp also began his business career with a long period of residence in Bruges (1441–50), moving to Lübeck in 1450. His rise was rapid. Having married the daughter of Engelbrecht Veckinchusen, a nephew of Hildebrand, he was admitted to the Merchants' Company, then into the Circle Society. From 1462 he was a councillor, and ten years later he became burgomaster, taking as his second wife a Kerckring, daughter of one of the most respected families. Of a religious turn of mind, cherishing a special devotion to St Anne, Castorp is distinguished by his intellectual preoccupations, hitherto unusual in Hanseatic merchants. He read and collected chronicles and history books.

His business activities, less extensive than those of the Veckinchusens, are also known in less detail, for none of his account-books survives. He was particularly active between 1450 and 1470 in three main areas: Flanders, the east (Prussia and Livonia) and Brandenburg. Usually he traded in partnership with his brother Hans, who was a burgess first of Reval and then of Lübeck. Hinrich grew rich in the typically Hanseatic trade between east and west via Lübeck. Flemish, Dutch and English cloth, oil and southern fruits, and salt from Bourgneuf were bought and exported to Danzig, Reval and Novgorod, where they were exchanged for wax and furs. There are indications of trade with Erfurt and Nürnberg, and the Castorps were also associated with a company in Brunswick which dispatched English cloth into Brandenburg and brought back wax in return. The seizure of a consignment valued at more than 5,000 marks gave rise in 1463 to a lawsuit which dragged on for twenty-four years, apparently without the Castorps ever obtaining the compensation they demanded.

Following the classic line of development of the newly rich merchants, the Castorps gradually abandoned the trade which had been their chief interest in favour of investments in credit and annuity operations. In 1461 Hinrich, Hans and four other Lübeckers formed a partnership with the intention of founding a municipal bank. The council demanded a guarantee of 6,000 marks, and the enterprise seems to have turned out badly, for it was wound up ten years later. In the same year Castorp and two other Lübeckers lent 3,000 marks to the king of Denmark, who handed them his crown as a pledge. Other loans, one for 2,600 marks, were granted to various merchants. The purchase of annuities, begun in 1456, increased steadily up to 1473. Forty houses in the town were involved, representing an income of 716 marks. At the 5 per cent interest rate normal in Lübeck these investments represented a capital outlay of 14,330 marks. An approximate estimate of the value of his other revenues, property, chattels and capital tied up in commercial undertakings gives a figure of 25,000 marks for Hinrich Castorp's fortune. It is certain that at the time few citizens of Lübeck were richer than Castorp.

Castorp played an important part in political and diplomatic affairs, especially in the later years of his life. But even as early as 1447, when he was alderman of the Bruges *Kontor*, he had been delegated to the diet at Lübeck, and he was also intimately concerned in the negotiations with Flanders and the duke of Burgundy in the following years. In 1464 he was in Danzig and Thorn with the Hanseatic delegation which acted as mediator to bring to an end the war between Poland and the Teutonic Order. Convinced that peace was essential to the prosperity of Lübeck, he tried to prevent war with England, but when war was declared he prosecuted it with the utmost energy. He was the leader of the Hanseatic delegation which negotiated the Peace of Utrecht in 1474. His clear vision, characteristic of the merchant turned statesman, and his profound attachment to the cause of peace, joined with his dogged tenacity in time of war, make Hinrich Castorp a perfect embodiment of the Hanseatic virtues. One of his sayings is often quoted as expressing the whole spirit of the Hansa: 'Let us meet and talk; for though it is easy to hoist the ensign, it is difficult to lower it with honour.'

At the end of the fifteenth century and in the early years of the sixteenth the four Mulich brothers (Kunz, Hans, Paul and Mathias) represent a new type of merchant, showing how the Hanseatic domain was invaded by south German business interests. The Mulichs were in fact natives of Nürnberg and did not become citizens of Lübeck until later, between 1476 and 1514.

Already the father of these four men is mentioned as being in Lübeck on several occasions between 1436 and 1474, the year of his death. It was he who established the commercial relations between Nürnberg and Lübeck which his sons were to develop. Hans and Kunz are the first of them to appear in Lübeck, but Hans remained a citizen of Nürnberg all his life, whereas Kunz became a burgess of Lübeck in 1476. He had married a rich widow, the daughter of a councillor, who brought him a dowry of 6,500 marks in cash and 500 marks in annuities. Thereafter the trade carried on by the Mulich brothers between Lübeck and Nürnberg was greatly extended. Proof of this can be found in an invoice-book which lists the purchases made at the Lent Fair in Frankfurt in 1495 by Paul Mulich, acting as agent for his brother Mathias, resident in Lübeck. The total amounts to 7,655 Rhenish guilders (11,483 Lübeck marks). Luxury goods are by far the most important items in the list: pearls, brooches, chains, gold rings, goblets and other silver articles (3,040 guilders); luxury cloths, especially velvet from Milan and Genoa (1,720 guilders); refined silver (1,481 guilders); weapons and coats of mail (505 guilders); spices (315 guilders); and paper from Lombardy (116 guilders). Among Paul's suppliers were some of the great south German firms of the period: 850 guilders went to the Great Trading Company of Ravensburg, 700 guilders each to George Fugger and Peter Watt. Less is known about the goods sent from Lübeck to Frankfurt. They were principally Norwegian cod, Skanian herring and amber chains. The Mulichs also appear to have dealt with Livonia and Scandinavia, but of these transactions no details are known.

Of the four brothers the richest was probably Mathias, especially after he inherited his brother Paul's estate in 1520. He settled in Lübeck in 1490 but became a citizen as late as 1514. In addition to the property in Nürnberg which he inherited from his father, he bought thirteen houses in Lübeck, some of which he resold, as well as three estates in the neighbourhood. He supplied arms and jewellery to princely courts, dealing with the dukes of Schleswig and Mecklenburg and especially with the king of Denmark, from whom he received in fief an estate in Oldesloe, where he built a copper foundry. Although he was admitted to the patrician Circle Society in 1515 and was connected by his two marriages with the Kerckrings and the Castorps, he did not become a councillor. But at his death in 1528 this native of Nürnberg was certainly one of the most prominent personalities in Lübeck. Unfortunately we do not know the size of his fortune, though it was probably over 25,000 marks.

These few examples of the lives of great Hanseatic merchants hardly permit the pinpointing of any general characteristics, but they make clear the recurrence of certain features: the frequency of Westphalian origin, the ease with which immigrants could carve out a career in their adopted towns, the importance of the family as a basis, at least in part, for commercial activities, and the role of marriage in their success. Normally after the years of apprenticeship the merchant devoted himself almost exclusively to commerce, in which the cloth trade was usually very important. Later on he loaned money and bought property and annuities. In his last years he became increasingly absorbed in official civic duties. This is particularly true of the lives of the two most successful merchants, Johann Wittenborg and Hinrich Castorp.

4. THE MERCHANT'S LIFE

The principal aspects of the fifteenth-century merchant's life can be gleaned to some extent from the statutes of the merchant associations and the *Kontore*, from demands for compensation for damage suffered, and above all from letters. Family chronicles would be invaluable, but only two survive: those of Jakob Lubbe, a Danzig businessman, born in 1430 in a village near Marienburg, and Franz Wessel, burgomaster of Stralsund, born there in 1487.

It is about the early years of these merchants that least information is available. At about six years old the child would go to the parish school. It is remarkable that young Lubbe, a peasant's son, learnt to read and write in his native village. As for Wessel, he got beyond this elementary stage and learnt 'to decline and conjugate, so that he was able to understand a little of the Latin tongue'. Schooling ended between the ages of twelve and fifteen, and hardly any merchant-to-be went to a university, though a good knowledge of law was becoming increasingly necessary to a man who might one day reasonably expect to hold public office.

The young man now embarked on his commercial apprenticeship

under the direction of a merchant, usually a relative. During the years spent in different countries the young man became familiar with book-keeping, accounts, inspection of merchandise, buying and selling and the system of credit. After two or three years he became a clerk and began to trade on his own account while undertaking missions on his master's behalf. He might remain a clerk for the rest of his life, but normally, after a period of time which varied considerably according to his personality and achievements, he became the head of his own firm.

From now on the merchant was settled in a town and travelled less often, managing his affairs from his office. The letters of the Veckin-chusen brothers give a lively picture of his pursuits and preoccupations. He accepted delivery of goods dispatched by his clerks or associates, examined their quality with a critical eye and also arranged for the dispatch of other goods, negotiating contracts with carriers and skippers. The letters give an important place to information. In almost every one the merchant writes about political events, about wars and their repercussions in the world of commerce. He gives the price of various goods, works out the amount of imposts and expenses, discusses the margin of profit, the tastes and the financial standing of his customers. If, as is very often the case, there are no buyers for the goods, he gives orders that cargoes should be sent to another destination, sometimes to be disposed of at any price that can be obtained, and countermands the dispatch of certain goods. Often he tells his partners how anxious he is about the approaching rendering of accounts, about the payment of his debts, about his lack of ready cash. A score of letters from merchants in Riga in 1458 all betray similar anxieties. The Russians are refusing to buy cloth, especially Flemish cloth, preferring the cheaper English cloth. Furs are finding no buyers in Bruges. There is great anxiety about attacks from pirates based on Danzig during a war with the Teutonic Order. Thus it is with relief that they see ships from Lübeck and Flanders come safely into port, especially the salt fleets from Bourgneuf, for now they can reckon on satisfactory profits – on condition, however, that a Dutch salt fleet does not put in an appearance, which would lower the price and compel them to sell at a loss. These letters give the impression that the typical Hanseatic merchant of the fifteenth century lived in perpetual anguish, obsessed more with the superabundance of goods to be sold than with the fear of losses from shipwreck or seizure. The invocations of divine aid, with which the letters are studded, were certainly not mere stylistic flourishes.

Outside the office the merchant spent his time within the framework of the trade associations, similar in spirit and organisation to the trade guilds. Almost every day he would go to the headquarters of his association, where in the common-room (*Schütting*) he would meet his fellows, sit in his usual place, talk about public and private matters, gather information, take part in the drinking, banqueting and, on occasion, the welcoming of foreign guests, and the voting in the general assemblies which elected aldermen and jurors.

The statutes of the *Artushof* of Danzig, more detailed than those of any other merchant association, show a proper concern for preserving the good name of the association, maintaining a fitting standard of behaviour and avoiding extravagance. It was forbidden, under pain of fines or even exclusion, to throw plates and dishes at other members, to draw a knife, to play at dice for money, to pour into one's neighbour's glass a mixture likely to make him drunk, to talk scandal, particularly about women, or to utter abuse, especially of the authorities. The number of courses at a meal was strictly limited, as was the number of mountebanks. Wine was reserved for guests. The company was expected to break up at ten o'clock when the 'beer bell' was rung, and so on. One of the favourite amusements was betting, of which a careful record was kept, the stake being usually a sum of money or a length of cloth. The merchants betted on anything: an approaching marriage, the duration of a war, the price of herring, the result of an election or a tourney. The subject of some bets was preposterous. For example, one man betted that a certain cook would acknowledge that her master was the father of her two children; another undertook for ten guilders not to comb his hair for a year. Feasts, celebrated with splendour, occasionally enlivened the rhythm of the daily round.

A merchant could not always pursue the even tenor of his life within this peaceful framework. At times, especially while he was young, he had to embark on arduous and perilous journeys. When he was no more than twelve, Franz Wessel had been sent to the fair in Skania. During the next eight years, in spite of an illness which periodically immobilised him, he went twice to Holland, twice to Skania, and also to Gotland and Riga. Even when they reached riper years, most merchants undertook long business journeys. Some of them, settled in Scandinavia or the Baltic countries, came to Lübeck almost every year to buy goods.

Before starting on a journey the merchant felt the need to put his temporal and spiritual affairs in order. He often chose this moment to make his will, in which he never failed to make a number of pious bequests. These were intended, as was sometimes pointed out, to contribute to the salvation of the testator's soul if the journey resulted in his death. 'Let those about to embark go to confession. It took so little time for us to lose our lives', is written under the picture in a chapel of the Church of St Mary in Lübeck representing the shipwreck of a *Bergenfahrer*. Indeed during the long weeks of monotonous sailing the fear of tempest or attack by pirates never ceased to haunt the traveller, who did not feel safe until the ship entered port.

Most of the Hanseatic merchants travelled to one of the four great *Kontore*, where their business would keep them for several months. Here, under the protection of charters granted by foreign sovereigns, they found security. But charters were not worth much when a country was racked by civil strife – not uncommon in Flanders – or when the local authorities were in conflict with the Hansa. The history of the Hansa is marked by a series of arrests and seizures, often involving violence, particularly at Novgorod. In 1424 all the Germans in the *Kontor* were thrown into prison and thirty-six died. In 1494 Ivan III deported to Moscow the forty-nine merchants of the *Peterhof*. They were not freed for three years, and all perished at sea on their journey home.

Official violence of this kind was, however, rare. Much more common were individual injuries resulting from assaults or quarrels concerning the price and quality of goods, or payment for them.* The demands for compensation contain long lists of such grievances and make very clear the hazards of the merchant's life.

It was partly in order to guarantee the protection of its merchants that the Hansa imposed a strict discipline upon them when abroad and tried to isolate them as much as possible from local contacts. The pattern of life, however, varied greatly from *Kontor* to *Kontor*. In Bruges, where the Hansa had no house of its own, the merchants, living in rented houses in the town among a population whose language differed little from their own, could feel as free as in their own homeland. It was not so in the other three *Kontore*, where they were subject to constant supervision and were obliged to lodge and eat inside their own concession. It was in Novgorod that living conditions were most austere, especially for those who spent the winter there. Because of the differences in language, religion and manners the Germans lived there even more retired than elsewhere, in constant fear of attack and robbery. By day Russians were allowed with-

* Document No. 9.

in the walls of the *Peterhof* to buy or sell, no commercial transaction being permitted outside. But at night the entrance gate was hermetically sealed, guard dogs roamed within the walls and watchmen were locked into the church where the most valuable merchandise, the archives and the treasury were kept. Masters on the one hand, and clerks and apprentices on the other, formed separate societies, each with their own dormitories and refectories. There were few amusements available to this purely male group of a few dozen or hundred inhabitants. All they could do during the long evenings of the Russian winter was to talk and drink in the great heated common-room. Even so, any excessive indulgence was kept strictly in check by the threat of fines or imprisonment.

The austere routine of the *Kontore* was enlivened from time to time by a few traditional festivals. Among these the Bergen 'games' were famous throughout northern Europe, as much for their brutality as their splendour. They took place every year shortly after the arrival of the Hanseatic fleets, and combined a springtide festival with pageants, masquerades, dances and carouses. The chief attraction was the torturing of the young journeymen of the *Bergenfahrer*, before they were admitted as full members of the groups. This involved three ordeals. The first was by smoke. The candidate was hoisted up on the end of a rope to a chimney-vent pouring forth pungent smoke and had to undergo a burlesque cross-examination before he was let down, half-asphyxiated. The second was by water. The candidate was thrown three times into deep water in the harbour and then had to climb back into his boat while older members in other boats belaboured him, his only defence being a friend armed with a stick. The third and worst ordeal was by whipping. Drunk, blindfolded and naked, the sufferer was brought into 'paradise' and whipped till he bled, his screams being drowned by a great clatter of cymbals and drums, after which he still had to sing a comic song for the members as they sat at table.

At the beginning of the sixteenth century the roughness of these 'games' brought protests from the Church (the ordeals were sometimes enlivened by blasphemous confessions) and the Danish government and even from the Hansa itself. The games were criticised for their brutality, for the accidents they caused – though these were apparently rare – their high cost and their immorality. But the principal cause of complaint was that the games were damaging to trade, since these frightening ordeals discouraged the sons of rich merchants. But this was just what the

Bergenfahrer wanted. Most of them were of humble origin and they had no desire to take into their community members of wealthy families who might seize control of it. Consequently the complaints, the exhortations and the regulations intended to subdue the high spirits of the games remained ineffective for some time. It took the disappearance of the Hansa itself to put a stop to them. During the seventeenth century the number of Hanseatic merchants in Bergen declined. In 1671 – two years after the last *Hansetag* – a Danish edict forbade the games under severe penalties. This time it was obeyed. The Bergen games, which in a way reflected the rise and fall of the Hansa, disappeared for ever.

There was hardly one medieval merchant who did not at some time in his life go on a pilgrimage. This was undertaken as a penance, to cure an illness or to fulfil a vow made in a moment of extreme peril. Among the Hanseatics the most popular shrine was that at Aachen, where they were drawn not by the tomb of Charlemagne but by the relics of the Virgin. Many other shrines also attracted them, especially those at Thann in Alsace,* Einsiedeln in Switzerland, Rome and Compostella. The chronicle of Franz Wessel describes a veritable odyssey, the pilgrimage of the future burgomaster of Stralsund to St James of Compostella, undertaken in 1506 when he was nineteen. The ship in which he was sailing contained 500 pilgrims, not counting the women and girls. It called at about fifty ports in Norway, Scotland, Flanders, England and France. At Plymouth a pilgrim was stabbed by two of his companions, who were hanged. Although forbidden to do so, the ship left port and had to fight a running battle at sea with two English ships sent in pursuit. At last Wessel arrival at Compostella, where he was present at the coronation of King Philip the Fair. He returned safe and sound to Stralsund, to be joyfully welcomed by his parents, 'for he was their only son and they were convinced that he had perished at sea or elsewhere'.

Perils, journeys and anxieties of this kind were the common lot of all medieval merchants. The Hanseatics were perhaps somewhat different from their fellows in that their life and thought were contained within a more rigid framework. This discipline, which weighed particularly heavily on them in the *Kontore*, had one advantage. It developed in them a keen community spirit, more pronounced than that of merchants of other nations. But it also weakened their initiative, lessened their ability to adapt themselves to circumstances and condemned any individual action which ran counter to the rules of the group. They were pain-

* Document No. 25.

fully intent on maintaining a rigorous equality between members of the community and enforcing the strict regulation of their rights and their activities. In his chronicle Wessel relates an incident symptomatic of this lack of initiative. In 1485, because there was no salt for sale in Bourgneuf, the entire Danzig fleet returned home with empty holds. Thus neither the agents in Bourgneuf nor the skippers had dared to take it upon themselves in these unforeseen circumstances to override their freighters' instructions and load up with other merchandise in order to make some profit from their journey. One can hardly imagine Italian or even English merchants submitting so tamely in a similar situation. Because of the rigid framework of rules within which he had to work, the Hanseatic merchant lost some of his taste for risks, a failing which was bound to have an adverse effect on the destiny of the community as a whole.

CHAPTER NINE

Economic Policies of the Hansa:
Its Competitors

CREATED for the protection of its merchants, the Hansa never ceased to employ what political power it had, both in Germany and abroad, in their best interests. At first and up to about 1350 its principal task was to obtain privileges for the merchants and to ensure that these privileges were respected by foreign towns and rulers. It succeeded in this task so well that in northern Europe its merchants enjoyed what was practically a monopoly of the trade between east and west.

But by the second half of the fourteenth century competition from foreign merchants, especially Hollanders and south Germans, was developing inexorably, and after a long period of economic liberalism the Hansa turned to issuing regulations which became increasingly severe; they were designed to reserve exclusively for its members the privileges already won, and to prevent or at least to limit the expansion of foreign trade within the Hanseatic orbit, especially in the Baltic. This policy, often ill-advised – for it endangered Hanseatic interests as well – achieved some successes in the fifteenth century, but failed in its main purpose, since it did not succeed in checking the rise of the Hansa's rivals.

I. THE FOREIGN PRIVILEGES

The granting of royal protection in 1157 to the Cologne merchants who had settled in London opens the long series of privileges conceded to Hanseatic merchants by foreign rulers, lords and cities. At various times during the next two hundred years German merchants gradually obtained more or less equal concessions in all countries, though greater perhaps in Flanders than elsewhere. 'Our people have greater liberties and privileges there than in any other country', affirmed Prussian envoys to England in 1386.

In what did these famous privileges, so avidly sought after, consist?

Chiefly in political and legal guarantees of security for the person and possessions of the merchant on the one hand and exemptions from dues and imposts on the other. From the beginning the privileges recognised the right of the Hanseatic merchants to form an organised group, to elect their own aldermen and to hold meetings. Wherever the Germans owned an enclosed site, as for example in London, Bergen and Novgorod, it enjoyed a form of diplomatic immunity, and local officials had no power within its boundaries. Everywhere the community's own court dealt with lawsuits and offences in which only its members were concerned, awarding prison sentences and confiscating possessions. In Novgorod the court was even competent to deal with crimes punishable by death or mutilation, though in Bruges and London such cases had to be referred to the local courts.

When a Hanseatic merchant caused loss or injury to a native or a non-German foreigner or vice versa, the matter was brought before the local court by one of the aldermen, who acted as spokesman for the plaintiff or defendant, as the case might be. The charters all abound in precise guarantees granted to the Germans. By the thirteenth century they were exempt from trial by combat – a very important concession. In the event of a Hanseatic being found guilty, the principle of strictly individual responsibility prevailed. Neither the Hanseatics as a body nor the fellow-citizens of the delinquent could be arrested in his place or deprived of their possessions. Furthermore if the guilty man was a clerk, goods belonging to his master could not be confiscated. Finally, contrary to general usage, the possessions of a Hanseatic who died in a foreign country, even if he were a bastard, were returned to his heirs and could not be seized and appropriated by the local ruler or the crown.

Hanseatics who were attacked or robbed were quick to insist on immediate satisfaction of their claim, and the local court had to investigate the matter within eight days. For murder or mutilation, it was permissible to apply the *lex talionis* to the culprit. In the case of theft, the thief was imprisoned until compensation had been paid. If he had absconded and his possessions remained in the country or had been brought back to it, they were seized and used to compensate the victim. In Flanders in 1389 the Hanseatics were given an unusually extensive privilege. Ghent, Bruges and Ypres gave a joint guarantee that any object stolen from a Hanseatic by a Fleming within the countship, or even outside it, would be restored or replaced. If the theft had been committed by a foreigner, the count and the cities were to bring pressure to bear upon the town where the thief had taken refuge. If restitution was refused the arrest of all the merchants of that city and the seizure of their goods was decreed.

For debt, the procedure differed according to whether the creditor was a Hanseatic or a native. In the former case, the Germans obtained a ruling, applicable originally only in Bruges, later throughout Flanders, that the debtor should be constrained by the local courts to pay up within three days, under pain of imprisonment and confiscation of goods. If he died, the creditors had first claim on his estate. As debtors, the Hanseatics were again able to ensure that the principle of collective responsibility was set aside. None of them was answerable for a colleague. The most that was agreed was that the native town of the defaulter should pay the debt, if the town in question had caused a contract to be drawn up in due form. If not, the German could extricate himself by a simple oath. However the Germans were not able to exempt themselves from imprisonment for debt, as is shown by the arrest of Hildebrand Veckinchusen in 1422; but they could avoid imprisonment by producing sureties.

The Hanseatics were particularly anxious to insure themselves against risks consequent upon war breaking out between the country with which they were trading and any other. They were not to be implicated by delivering to either side or to suffer wrong or loss as a result of the hostilities. Certain clauses concerning escorted convoys show that they also claimed that the foreign power was responsible, even outside its own boundaries, if their merchants were attacked on either their outward or return journey.

One of the privileges claimed most insistently by the Hansa in every country was exemption from the law concerning flotsam and jetsam on sea-shores and river-banks. It was obviously very important for its members to be able to recover the cargoes of ships wrecked or run aground. This claim caused more legal wrangling than any other, firstly because of the infinite diversity of circumstances, secondly because of disputes about whether a particular wreck came under the jurisdiction of the royal bailiff or that of the agent of the local ruler, and finally because of the traditional notion, firmly embedded in people's minds, that wreckage belongs to the man who finds and seizes it.

The Hanseatics laid down as a general principle that any wreck which was salvaged should be kept by the shore-dwellers for a year and a day and then handed over to the owners or their heirs on the payment of salvage dues. Moreover the only flotsam which was to count as a wreck was that on which no living creature, not even a domestic animal, was to be found. However when all the passengers had perished it was often difficult to identify the owners of a ship. Even when inquiries were successful, the shore-dwellers and the royal or seignorial bailiffs often refused restitution. Payment of salvage dues (*Bergelohn*), especially, led to the most complicated disputes. Although in principle the rates were fixed, the salvagers never failed to demand an exorbitant sum. When a ship was wrecked on the coast and the crew survived, it was conceded that the latter should have three days in which to salvage the ship. But the shore-dwellers often refused to help so as not to be deprived of their rights to flotsam and jetsam, or even actively opposed any attempt at recovery by the owners or their compatriots. Another source of conflict arose when the disaster occurred on the high seas and the wreckage was washed ashore. Local authorities would claim the right to seize it, on the grounds that its Hanseatic origin was not certain. In short although the charters proclaimed the abolition of the right to flotsam and jetsam, this was constantly being claimed, to the detriment of the Hansa.

It was without doubt their fiscal privileges which were most precious to the Hanseatics and which aroused the most jealousy. They demanded and obtained in all countries considerable reductions in customs dues, a precise determination of the imposts to be paid – as in the tariff granted in 1252 by the countess of Flanders – as well as the assurance that these dues would not be increased, and that no new ones would be imposed. This was almost tantamount to limiting the authority of the foreign ruler in fiscal matters, and it is understandable that such prerogatives were only granted with great reluctance. For example when in 1347 Edward III raised the export duty on English cloth, the Hanseatics refused to pay, invoking their charters; and the king finally agreed that they were right. Twenty-five years later there arose a fresh series of disagreements. The Hanseatics again refused to pay the 'subsidies' demanded by the crown, and the situation was exacerbated by the death of Edward III, which happened at a very opportune moment for the Hansa. Disputes about the levying of dues poisoned Anglo-Hanseatic relations throughout the whole of the fifteenth century. In fact the fiscal privileges enjoyed by the Hanseatics in England were particularly generous. On certain articles they paid less than the English themselves. For example on a length of bleached cloth a Hanseatic paid 12 pence, an Englishman 14 and certain foreigners 31 pence.

Another special privilege claimed by the Hanseatics was the right to re-export unsold goods without paying dues. This seems to have been sometimes disregarded, but the Hanseatics were very strict about it. Thus when in 1385 a rich Dortmund merchant, Christian Kelmer, ventured to pay a few shillings to the English customs when re-exporting a consignment of unsold furs, the London *Kontor* at once excluded him from the Hansa.*

Various other advantages were conceded to the Germans to help their trade: the right to have their own weigh-house – a right which they renounced in Bruges because of the high cost; to verify weights and measures by means of officially gauged standards given them by the authorities; to have a precise tariff of charges payable for porters, brokers and the use of the town crane; to load and unload their vessels at night, and so on. How exorbitant their claims could become can be seen by their attempt in 1339 to have the chain which barred access to Sluys harbour at night removed so that they could make their ships safe there at any time. Philip the Bold, in an outburst of rage, declared at first that this request was '*chose pas honneste et non raisonnable*'. But he soon agreed that the harbour-master should remove the chain at night, free of charge, at the request of a Hanseatic ship.

No doubt the privileges granted to the Hanseatics were often ignored, evaded or openly violated, especially in wartime. If such was the case, energetic demands for compensation were made as soon as peace was declared, which foreign governments were obliged to satisfy, at least in part. On the whole there can be no doubt that their numerous charters assured exceptional opportunities for Hanseatic trade and contributed to its triumph over its competitors. But it is also certain that they provoked a growing resentment among foreign merchants, and also among foreign rulers, who were reluctant to accept the limitation of their authority. It is understandable that throughout northern Europe they were very ready to welcome the Dutch in order to free themselves from these fetters. In this sense the policy of privilege helped to undermine from the fifteenth century onwards the commercial supremacy of the Hansa.

All Hanseatic merchants, whatever their town of origin, enjoyed the privileges when abroad on an equal footing. This was one of the fundamental principles of the community. One might have expected the towns within the borders of Germany to grant other Hanseatics, if not complete equality with their own burgesses, at least a preferential treatment in comparison with aliens. But nothing of this kind can be found, nor

* Document No. 23.

does the Hansa seem to have attempted to set up such a system. Each town remained mistress of her own commercial organisation and was only interested in furthering the interests of her own merchants. It was not uncommon for a town to offer special advantages to the merchants of a neighbouring one, but there was no question of extending these favours to all Hanseatics. The protest made by Hamburg to Lübeck in 1418 is significant. The exemption from harbour dues granted to Lübeck merchants was applicable to them alone, and no goods belonging to Prussians or Livonians were to be treated like those of a Lübeck merchant. Discrimination of this kind increased with the passage of time. In the fifteenth century the staple regulations were continually being tightened up in every town, and were often used as much against merchants from other Hanseatic towns as against non-Hanseatics. It almost seems as if on the plane of economic policy the German Hansa had no reality except outside Germany.

2. THE COMPETITORS

From the middle of the twelfth century onwards the trade of the Germans' rivals in northern Europe, the Scandinavians, Russians, Frisians and Flemings, had steadily declined. The Hansa, thanks to the size of its merchant marine, the dynamism of its merchants and the extent of its privileges in foreign countries, had gradually obtained a *de facto* trade monopoly. This favourable trend began to be reversed during the second half of the fourteenth century. New competitors appeared, of varying degrees of dangerousness. They established themselves in the Hanseatic orbit, and in spite of obstacles put in their way continued to increase their trade in the fifteenth century, thus putting the Hansa on the defensive.

It was the Italians who first alarmed the Hanseatics. In northern Germany the small amount of business they transacted, either as money-lenders or as merchants, was confined to Cologne; but the Germans were constantly meeting them abroad, first at the Champagne fairs, then in Flanders, England, Frankfurt and even in Poland. They recognised the financial power of the Italians and the superiority of their commercial techniques, and seem to have feared the extension of Italian business interests into their own area. In 1397 the Prussian towns begged the Grand Master of the Teutonic Order to refuse the 'Lombards' entry into the country. In 1412 the Hanseatic diet at Lüneburg forbade them to carry on business of any kind, either as merchants or as financiers, especially in the seaports. It was a draconian measure, unparalleled in any other nation. It was not strictly enforced, as is evident from the establishment of the Baglioni–Bueri bank in Lübeck at the beginning of the fifteenth century. In fact the Germans' fears had been groundless. No great Italian firm seems to have attempted a full-scale extension of its activity into the Hanseatic zone of influence. It was not from this quarter that danger threatened the Hansa.

At the end of the fourteenth century the English appear to have been more formidable rivals. The Merchant Adventurers were appearing in greater numbers in the Prussian towns and in Stralsund, bringing their cloth there and taking back grain, timber, resin and metal from Slovakia. Along with them came Scottish merchants, carrying on very much the same trade. It was not long before the Hansa was thoroughly alarmed at the attempts of both groups to penetrate into the interior and sell their cloth directly to their Prussian and Polish customers. After the crisis of 1388 an English settlement had even been officially established in Danzig, with the approval of Richard II. Like the German *Kontore* in foreign countries, it brought together all the Englishmen resident in Danzig and was placed under the direction of an elected 'governor', who presided over their meetings. The merchants bought or rented houses in Danzig and entered into partnerships with Danzig citizens. But unlike the Germans they brought their families with them, thus giving rise to fears that they might stay permanently in the country.*

However this promising beginning came to nothing, at least during the fifteenth century. The English complained on several occasions of the obstacles put in the way of their business and of the violent attacks made upon them not only in Prussia but also in Skania and Norway. They were unable to penetrate into Livonia or any Wendish town other than Stralsund. Even in Prussia their trade was strictly supervised and in spite of the goodwill shown by the Master of the Teutonic Order made no appreciable progress. Throughout the fifteenth century the Hanseatics managed to prevent the English trade from causing them serious losses by limiting its development. The time for the great expansion of English trade in Germany had not yet come.

The Dutch, on the other hand, were to prove themselves the most dangerous competitors of all. Their progress was irresistible, and between the fifteenth and seventeenth centuries they gradually outdistanced the

* Document No. 10, §§ 6 and 9.

Hanseatics. Up to the mid-fourteenth century they did not appear very dangerous. The Dutch towns had hardly begun to expand: around 1400 Amsterdam and Leiden had barely 5,000 inhabitants each; Dordrecht, in spite of the advantages of its situation, could not eclipse Bruges; maritime trade hardly extended beyond the Low Countries and England. Competition from the populous cities on the eastern Zuiderzee and the Ijssel, such as Zwolle and Deventer, might well appear more dangerous. This was particularly true of Kampen, whose merchants had been encountered by the Hanseatics in Norway and Skania since the thirteenth century, and which did not become a member of the community until 1441.

At times the interests of the Hollanders and the Hanseatics were identical. For instance in 1367 Amsterdam, Briel and other towns joined the Cologne Confederation against Denmark and Norway. But this was the last manifestation of solidarity. From then on, in all circumstances and in all areas, the Hollanders appeared as enemies of the Hansa. What made them particularly dangerous was that, unlike the English, they were not content with claiming a share in the trade traditionally regarded as Hanseatic within a given area. On the contrary, by developing their industry and their merchant fleet and by transporting their products in their own ships in the northern seas, they dealt a blow to the basic commercial organisation of the Hansa.

In this process the expansion of the textile industry was of particular importance. From the second half of the fourteenth century onwards the manufacture of cloth, hitherto an essentially rural occupation satisfying local needs, was concentrated in towns, principally in Leiden, but also in Amsterdam, Haarlem and Rotterdam. Thanks to the privileges conferred by the counts of Holland, the textile industry, supplied with English wool and further stimulated at the beginning of the fifteenth century by the immigration of Flemish weavers, developed rapidly. Soon Dutch cloth made its appearance in all the Hanseatic markets. The most serious consequence was the threat to the trade in Flemish cloth, centred in Bruges, which was the foundation of Hanseatic prosperity.

The Dutch towns also began to produce beer. In the fourteenth century the northern Low Countries were an important market for German beer. In 1347, of 457 brewers in Hamburg, 127 exported their production to Amsterdam and 55 to Stavoren. But afterwards Dutch beer was increasingly to oust German beer, even outside the Netherlands.

Lastly in the same period herring-fishing developed in the North Sea while decreasing on the coasts of Skania. Originally herring-fishing had taken place only offshore, but in the fifteenth century, owing to the production of large nets and the building of specialised boats, it was extended to the open sea. The centre of the new fishing industry was Briel, where the fish were salted and put in barrels. Although Dutch herring did not equal the Skanian in quality, it was cheaper: thus it replaced the latter in the Rhine valley and could be sold widely even in the Baltic.

Even more alarming to the Hanseatics than this blow to certain vital sectors of their trade was the extension of Dutch sea traffic. Dutch ships had always been busy, but in the thirteenth and even the fourteenth century they were found only in the coastal and inland waters of the Low Countries. Unlike the Hanseatic marine, which was basically urban, Dutch shipping retained a pronounced rural character. Even in the fifteenth century, when there was a tendency towards centralisation in a few big towns, the building and fitting out of ships continued to flourish in the smaller ports of Zeeland and Holland.

The expansion of maritime trade was favoured by the rise of the textile industry, as the Hollanders themselves fetched the indispensable English wool either from England or from the staple towns of the Continent. Following the example of the Flemings, their ships also penetrated into the Atlantic, to fetch salt, increasingly in demand in northern Europe, from Bourgneuf, and wine from France. Above all they began to appear in greater numbers in the Baltic, bringing grain from Prussia and Poland. Previously their occasional appearances in the Baltic, from the thirteenth century onwards, had been confined to times when there was a shortage of grain. As the population of the northern Low Countries increased and the export trade of the Flemings decreased, the Hollanders regularly visited the Prussian ports and soon the Livonian ones as well. In Novgorod they are mentioned for the first time in 1432, selling herring, cloth and French salt, and buying wax and flax. In Prussia and the Baltic countries they met with a friendly reception, especially from the nobility, since their presence gave a fresh impetus to trade. It was even more natural that they should be eagerly received in Denmark and Norway, countries which were resentful of the Hanseatic monopoly.

Lübeck and the Wendish towns were the first to be alarmed by Dutch expansion. If the newcomers had been content to share in the export of Prussian grain, less harm would have been done, for the Hanseatic fleets were not large enough to handle all the west-bound trade. But they were soon acting in flagrant violation of the regulations of German commerce.

Their ships not only called at recognised ports but dropped anchor in small, unfrequented harbours, where they could deal directly with peasants and big landowners, thus depriving the towns of their role as intermediaries. Even in the towns they acquired a share of the trade, chiefly because their freight charges were lower than those of the Hanseatics. Like the English, but on a larger scale, they extended their business by entering into partnership with burgesses of German towns. Finally the growth of Dutch trade increased the importance of the direct sea route through the Sound, to the detriment of the Lübeck–Hamburg land route.

The Hansa was successful in limiting the growth of English trade in the Baltic, but it found itself powerless in the face of the Hollanders' irresistible expansion. Neither progressively stricter regulation nor open warfare (1438–41) could put any permanent obstacle in the way of these new rivals. The Hollanders seized every opportunity to consolidate the advantages they had gained in eastern Europe, profiting from the internal troubles of the Hanseatic community in 1408–18, the blockade of Flanders in 1451–7 and the war between Poland and the Teutonic Order in 1454–66. The main cause of the Hanseatics' failure to avert the danger of Dutch rivalry was their lack of unity. The Livonian towns and the Teutonic Order in particular were not prepared to oppose the Dutch advance, which brought them considerable advantages. In 1411, in spite of the embargo decreed by Danzig, the Grand Master authorised the Dutch to export grain from the town. In 1438, in defiance of the ban imposed by the Prussian towns, he allowed them to trade in Poland. The noblemen paid no heed to any urban regulations and demanded that, 'in accordance with ancient custom', the Hollanders and the English should be allowed to purchase grain freely in the interior. How far dissension among the Hanseatics could go was shown during the war of 1438. The Grand Master refused to take part in it, and when the Wendish towns barred the passage of the Danish straits to Dutch ships he sequestrated the possessions of Lübeck merchants in Prussia. All this explains the steady progress of the Hollanders, and contributed to the fact that by the mid-fifteenth century the trade monopoly of the Hansa in northern waters was at an end.

Besides the Hollanders, the south Germans, particularly the Nürnbergers, became the Hanseatics' most dangerous competitors in the fifteenth century. Since they were Germans – although treated as foreigners – this rivalry did not lead to political incidents, seizures of goods, or war, but it would be a mistake to regard German competition as less important than any other. The expansion of the south Germans' trade was at least as harmful to the economic system of the Hanseatics as that of the Hollanders.

The Hanseatics had come into contact with their German rivals as early as the thirteenth century, at the Champagne fairs. But it was during the fourteenth century that the Nürnbergers spread out all over southern and western Germany, into Italy and the Low Countries. In almost seventy cities, notably in Lübeck, they were exempted from the payment of market dues. Since 1311 they had been granted privileges by the duke of Brabant, and in 1361 Louis de Male granted them benefits in Flanders roughly equivalent to those enjoyed by the Hanseatics. But they were still content in general to trade only between south Germany and the Low Countries, and although Cologne's trade with Frankfurt and the countries along the Danube suffered from their competition, Hanseatic interests were not yet gravely threatened. However by the end of the fourteenth century the Nürnbergers had gained a firm foothold in Lübeck. One of their great houses, that of the Pirkheimers, was represented there by one of its most influential partners, Johann Lange, who had married into a patrician Lübeck family. He traded with Visby, Reval and Danzig and carried out financial operations linking Sweden, Frankfurt, Prague and Italy. At the beginning of the fifteenth century the firm of Kress appears to have been the most important. The volume of trade now carried on by south Germans is reflected in a complaint from the retailers of Lübeck, in which they maintained, doubtless with some exaggeration, that a single Nürnberger sold as much in one day in the town as the Lübeckers did in a year.* Their business was in direct competition with that of the Hanseatics. They exported furs, amber and preserved fish to the south and supplied the north with spices, metalwares and luxury goods, and even with goods from Cologne and Flanders, thus, like the Hollanders, dealing a blow to the Hanseatic trade centred on Bruges.

Although the retailers of Lübeck called for energetic measures against these competitors, the great merchants were reluctant to follow suit, fearing reprisals against their own activities in Nürnberg. But at the beginning of the fifteenth century the council decided to take action. On several occasions the Nürnbergers were forbidden to enter into partnership with Hanseatics or to sell retail. They were also ordered to sell only

* Document No. 36 (*b*).

articles manufactured in Nürnberg, and a tax was put on spices. These measures had little effect, as the Nürnbergers had already had frequent recourse to a device employed earlier by Hans Lange. They married Lübeck women and thus acquired Lübeck citizenship, while continuing to trade on behalf of their original firm. Some of the patricians were quite willing to ally themselves with rich and respected Nürnberg families and become agents for the foreign firm. With their help the south Germans penetrated into the most exclusive circles, notably into the charitable Brotherhood of St Leonard. Some were even admitted into the Circle Society. Through these family connections the Nürnbergers were easily able to evade the regulations intended to limit their activities. They increased in numbers during the second half of the fifteenth century, thus preparing the way for the Fuggers, whose business interests in the Hanseatic orbit were to extend more widely still.

It was not only into Lübeck that the Nürnberg merchants infiltrated. From the fourteenth century onwards they were to be found in Leipzig, Breslau, Cracow, Lemberg and especially in Posen. The Polish kings and nobility gave them a warm welcome, not fearing from them the political meddling indulged in by the Prussian merchants. From Poland they penetrated into Prussia and Livonia and were well received by the Teutonic Order, whose revenues they increased. But the Prussian and Livonian towns took fright and adopted a series of measures against the intruders, who by using the same methods as in Lübeck rendered them for the most part ineffective.

Undoubtedly the most dangerous aspect of this expansion was the development, to the benefit of the Nürnbergers, of a commercial west–east axis, Frankfurt–Nürnberg–Leipzig–Posen, along the southern border of the Hanseatic zone. Instead of being brought by river to the sea and so along the maritime axis Bruges–Lübeck–Reval, the products of central Europe were being diverted to the new route, along which south German and Italian goods moved in one direction and Russian and Polish in the other. It is significant that in 1474 Breslau announced that she was retiring from the Hansa. The change in commercial routes meant that her interests no longer orientated her towards the north. The danger seems to have been recognised in Lübeck. The lack of zeal displayed by the council in combating the activities of the Nürnbergers makes it seem likely that they preferred to suffer competition from them within the city (which brought in some profit), rather than to drive them out and so encourage them to establish commercial relations outside the Hanseatic orbit, where they would have been safe from interference. It is nevertheless true that from the fifteenth century onwards the south Germans, who had already captured a share in the spice and cloth trade of the Low Countries, were beginning to invade the fur trade, one of the basic commodities of Hanseatic activity.

There is one more group of rivals to the Hansa, whose activities made themselves felt from the mid-fifteenth century onwards and above all in the sixteenth century – the great landed proprietors of the eastern regions, from Mecklenburg to Livonia. The land-owning noblemen had not thought of organising the sale of their produce over long distances – with one exception. The Teutonic Order, as mentioned above, had developed into a powerful business concern, employing its own agents to the detriment of the merchants of the Prussian towns. Other princes and lords, however, left it to the Hansa towns to take care of the disposal of their agricultural surpluses. Moreover they were far more interested in buying cloth and other western goods than in exporting grain. One has only to look at the ledgers of a few Hanseatic merchants, such as those of Vicko van Geldersen in Hamburg and Tölner in Rostock, to appreciate the important place occupied in these merchants' affairs by their noble customers in the hinterland.

This situation changed in the course of the fifteenth century. Recognising the steadily increasing demand for grain in the Low Countries and elsewhere, the great landowners of the east intensified their agricultural production and set about organising its sale on their own account. Dutch ships were becoming increasingly numerous, and it was easy for the noblemen to get in touch with them directly in ports 'banned' by the Hanseatics. Cereals were not the only commodity involved. For the sale of Polish and Prussian timber, peasants formed associations to deal directly with foreign merchants. Some towns no doubt managed to make a profit from the general increase in agricultural production. The astounding rise in the prosperity of Danzig on the threshold of the modern age is, for example, bound up with the increase in cereal production on the estates of Polish and Ukrainian noblemen.* On the whole, however, the co-operation between the landed proprietors and foreign merchants was prejudicial to Hanseatic trade, as it excluded the town merchants, thus depriving them of their middleman's profit.

The increase in the numbers of south Germans in the east had a similar effect. Even if few of them bought grain or timber, they nevertheless

* Document No. 44.

supplied the nobility with Flemish and Italian articles which had formerly been furnished by the Hanseatics. It is understandable that the measures decreed by the towns in defence of their merchants' trade were mainly ineffective, since they conflicted with the interests of the big landowners. From the middle of the fifteenth century onwards the Teutonic Order and the Prussian nobility, for once acting together, laid open claim to the right to trade freely with foreigners. Some townsfolk managed to cope with this difficult situation by marrying into the rural nobility, but this was exceptional; generally speaking, there was a constant weakening of the towns' hold over the cultivable countryside, to the benefit of the nobility. This is not the least important aspect of the Hanseatic decline at the end of the fifteenth and throughout the sixteenth century.

3. REGULATION OF TRADE

Faced with increasing competition, the Hansa endeavoured to marshal her defences. She does not seem to have envisaged defeating her rivals in a freely competitive market, and indeed the rapid progress made by the Hollanders and the south Germans offered very little hope of doing so. Moreover the basic principle of the Hansa was that all its members were assured strictly equal rights, and this was not compatible with a system of economic liberalism. There remained only one way in which the Hansa could fight back: by regulation. Although never systematised, regulations became increasingly strict in the fifteenth century, dealing especially with three points: the exclusion of all non-Hanseatics from sharing in the Hanseatic privileges; the limitation of the activity of non-Hanseatics in Germany by various measures which together were labelled 'guest law' (*Gästerecht*); and the strengthening of the Hanseatic staple at Bruges, in order to hinder Dutch trade.

When trading abroad, the Hanseatics could not avoid entering into close business relationships with merchants from other countries. One result of this inevitable collaboration was that there was no very clear distinction between Hanseatics and non-Hanseatics, and even less between German capital and foreign capital, when both were invested in a Hanseatic enterprise. As long as the Hansa was in a state of expansion this interpenetration had brought its members more advantages than disadvantages, since it made their transactions easiers. A broad tolerance seems to have prevailed in the *Kontore*: at times non-Hanseatics even held office in them.

But when foreign competition developed, that is to say from about 1350 onwards, this situation was seen to be prejudicial to the community's interests, and the Hansa decreed a series of measures to deal with it. Some of these were of a legal nature, intended to clarify the distinction between Hanseatics and non-Hanseatics. The main ones have already been noted: enjoyment of the privileges to be restricted to the burgesses of Hansa towns only, office in a *Kontor* to be open only to Hanseatics (1366); a ban on the acquisition of nominal citizenship in a Hansa town or being a citizen of two towns at once (1417); and enjoyment of the privileges to be restricted to citizens by birth only (1434). It was soon found that these prescriptions were being evaded by means of foreign clerks being taken into the service of German merchants, especially in England. The diet of 1447 tried to put a stop to this by decreeing that in future foreign clerks would benefit from the privileges only after they had been in the service of a Hanseatic merchant for seven years and had themselves become burgesses of a Hansa town where they owned a house and hearth of their own. Unless these conditions were fulfilled they could neither invest funds in a Hanseatic enterprise nor share in its profits nor enter into partnership with their master. In addition the following were excluded even if they fulfilled these conditions: the English, the Hollanders, the Zeelanders, the Flemings, the Brabanters and the Nürnbergers, that is to say all their most dangerous rivals.

These prohibitions show clearly that the aim of the legal measures was to prevent foreigners and foreign capital from reaping the benefit of the Hanseatic privileges. Thus a particularly vigorous attack was made on partnerships between Germans and foreigners. This practice had been an early cause of alarm, especially in the east. By the end of the thirteenth century the Novgorod *Kontor* had written into its statutes a ban on business associations with Russians, either in the form of a partnership or of a commission agency, under pain of a fine of fifty marks. The same sanction was applicable to Hanseatics who transported goods on behalf of Italians, Flemings or Englishmen. For a long time this measure was peculiar to the *Peterhof*, but in 1360 the Bruges *Kontor* in its turn forbade all business partnerships with Flemings, and in 1405 the diet at Lübeck promulgated a general ban on all partnerships between Hanseatics and non-Hanseatics. In 1418 the measure was extended to ship-owners. Foreigners were forbidden to own a share in a Hanseatic ship and Hanseatics were forbidden to own a share in a foreign ship.

These prohibitions were periodically renewed during the fifteenth century, though it is difficult to say how strictly they were applied. It seems that the Teutonic Order and the Prussian towns made little effort to conform. In Bruges protests were made, but in vain, and as a result a good many merchants and an even larger number of ships' captains repudiated their Hanseatic citizenship and became naturalised in the country where they conducted their business. The Hansa took strong measures against them, barring them for ever from citizenship in a Hansa town and forbidding its members to trade with them. But here again sanctions appear to have been applied more strictly in some areas than in others, despite the exclusions and official threats. However the desired end seems on the whole to have been achieved, and it soon became difficult for foreigners to trade under the protection of the Hanseatic privileges. The renewal of the restrictive measures shows that the great majority of the Hanseatics thought them necessary, however much harm they did them individually. It was obviously the only way to counter foreign competition.

The regulations which constituted the 'guest law' (*Gästerecht*) dealt with trade carried on by foreigners in Germany. One might have thought it simpler just to forbid foreigners access to all Hansa towns, but so radical a measure was never envisaged, except against the Italians. Nor was it desired. Municipalities and individual merchants had no wish to be deprived of the profits to be gained from trading with foreigners, and most important of all, the Hanseatic marine was not large enough to handle all the freight trade, particularly in Prussia and Livonia. This shortage of ships became more acute in the fifteenth century. The need to ensure transport for an increasing quantity of cereals, urgently needed in the west, and to satisfy the demand for salt in the east, obliged the Hanseatics to make room for foreign trade. It was principally as a result of these new conditions that the great increase in Dutch maritime trade in the Baltic took place. Consequently the 'guest law' began to favour the foreigners' trade wherever it offered advantages to the Hansa towns, and to hinder it wherever it threatened their interests.

The legal status of foreigners was not everywhere the same. In Prussia the English complained of being victimised by ordinances which were applied to them alone. In Livonia the towns resolved in 1450 to admit in future only Hollanders and Zeelanders into the country. All other foreigners, that is, the French, Walloons, Italians, Scots, English, Spaniards and Flemings, were to be expelled. Five years previously the

Prussian towns, with the exception of Danzig and Marienburg, had refused entry to Nürnbergers. But such measures were not observed for long.

Other ordinances of a more general nature, issued by the Hanseatic diet of 1417 and renewed regularly thereafter, laid down that foreigners were to frequent only Hansa towns and there to sell only wholesale and only to burgesses. Although Hanseatics claimed in all foreign towns the right to sell directly to foreigners, they had no intention of granting reciprocal rights in this respect. Above all they were anxious to prevent competitors from penetrating inland and dealing directly with their customers. Diets, both general and regional, frequently repeated the ban on frequenting ports other than those which were 'customary'. This was evidently aimed at the Hollanders, who were accused of carrying off the grain which should have flowed through Hanseatic ports. In Livonia on several occasions foreigners were forbidden to learn the Slav language, so as to prevent all dealings with the natives. Their stay in the country was limited to four, three or even two months so that no colony could be formed. They were also forbidden to remain during the winter or, of course, to become citizens of any Livonian town.

It is difficult to assess the results of all this legislation. The 'guest law' seems to have operated unevenly. English merchants in Prussia were seriously hampered by it and their trade failed to develop. On the other hand neither the Hollanders nor the south Germans appear to have encountered any insurmountable obstacle to the expansion of their trade in Prussia and Livonia, thanks no doubt to the favour shown them in the countryside, and especially by the nobility.

The strengthening of the Hanseatic staple in Bruges was one of the essential features of the struggle against competition from foreign trade, especially that of the Hollanders. In the fourteenth century Bruges had been the staple-market for the whole of the Low Countries, not only for the import of the principal products of the east – wax, furs, metals – but also for the export of cloth. By the end of the century, however, as other centres in the Low Countries offered increasing competition, Bruges had begun to lose her unique position. The Hansa itself, after the blockade of 1388, appeared to be attaching less importance to the Bruges staple, and the important privileges which were obtained in Antwerp in 1409 were the first step towards a decentralisation of her trade in this area. The rise of the Dutch textile industry and of Dutch trade in general called a halt to this development. Indeed the Hollanders, by bringing cloth themselves into the Hanseatic zone, where they found an ever-increasing number of buyers, and thus causing a decline in the trade of Flemish cloth, struck a serious blow at a vital sector of Hanseatic trade in the Low Countries. To counteract this the Hansa, and especially Lübeck, resolved from 1440 onwards to reinforce the staple at Bruges. In 1442 the diet at Stralsund decreed that henceforward only cloth bought in Bruges should be admitted into a Hansa town. Three years later the diet at Lübeck forbade the buying of Dutch cloth and ordered all ships sailing to the Low Countries to take their cargoes, with the exception of perishable goods (*Ventegüter*), to the staple at Bruges.

This was a serious blow to the Hollanders, who were now unable to export their cloth directly to a great many countries of eastern Europe and who feared that an appreciable number of foreign ships might cease calling at their ports. But the prohibition was also harmful to the Hansa towns on the Zuiderzee, to Cologne and to customers in the eastern countries who preferred Dutch cloth, which was cheaper than Flemish. This resulted in an unprecedented increase in smuggling, in which the Hollanders found accomplices everywhere. In addition the Hansa herself was damaged by the embargo which she mounted against Flanders from 1451 to 1457, and of which her adversaries took full advantage. This did not deter her in 1466 and 1470* from renewing the staple ordinances, but the rapid decline of Bruges at the end of the century nullified her efforts. The German merchants themselves, in defiance of the regulations, were penetrating into the towns of Holland and Brabant, and in this area too the great commercial battle between the Hanseatics and the Hollanders ended in a complete victory for the latter.

4. THE STRUGGLE AGAINST CREDIT FINANCE

The use of credit had become widespread in the Hanseatic world as early as the thirteenth century, the Germans having learnt the technique from the Italians, whom they met first at the fairs in Champagne and later in Bruges, London, Cologne and probably even in the cities of the east. Since credit, at least in the form of loans, was indispensable to the development of trade, the towns themselves encouraged the practice, setting up loan-registers at the end of the thirteenth century and thus giving credit transactions an official guarantee. Even abroad the Hansa towns supported the enterprises of their merchants in this way. There are still in

* Document No. 27.

existence some ten letters sent by a financier, Reineke Mornewech, at the end of the thirteenth century to the Lübeck council. He was the town's agent in Flanders, and carried out on his own responsibility large credit and exchange transactions, paying out considerable sums to merchants from Lübeck and Saxony and also to foreigners, negotiating loans, settling debts, selling merchandise on credit, and drawing bills of exchange on Lübeck.* As there is afterwards no mention of such town agents, carrying out temporary commissions, it is probable that the development of credit meant they were no longer needed.

In the fourteenth century credit was practised on a vast scale. The extensive operations of Westphalian merchants in London have already been dealt with. In the earliest extant account-books of Hanseatic merchants loans figure prominently together with occasional entries dealing with bills of exchange. The towns also used this method of payment. After 1361 the levying of poundage, which involved the transfer of considerable funds from one town to another, shows its use as standard practice.†

However it is apparent, from the almost total absence in the Hansa towns of banks comparable to those of the Italians with their many branches, that credit did not develop on a large scale in the area. In the fifteenth century there was, however, an Italian bank in Lübeck, founded around 1410 by Ludovico Baglioni of Perugia and his partner Gerardo Bueri (often called Gerhard the Italian) of Florence, a kinsman of the Medici. The latter, in order to overcome the difficulties caused by his foreign status, married the daughter of a Lübeck burgomaster and became a burgess in 1428. From then on his bank expanded rapidly. Like their Italian colleagues, the two partners launched out into commerce as well as banking, trading in the Baltic and holding shares in the trust controlling the sale of amber rosaries made in Lübeck. As they were in contact with the pope and the Medici family, they made large payments in Italy, Basle and Bruges on behalf of the towns of Lübeck and Danzig, made loans to churchmen and Lübeck merchants, and probably profited from deposit accounts and exchange transactions.

At this time it seemed as if Lübeck might become a great financial centre in northern Europe, but the prospect was short-lived. On the death of Bueri (1449) his bank was wound up and the interests of the Italian creditors were taken over by Benedict Stefani of Lucca, a representative

* Document No. 30.
† Document No. 35.

of Cosimo de Medici. However a few years later there was an interesting attempt by Godeman van Buren to found a genuine Lübeck bank. The town granted its protection to the enterprise on a guarantee of 6,000 marks provided by six burgesses, of whom Hinrich Castorp was one. But in 1472 van Buren went bankrupt, his bank was wound up and no further attempt of this kind was made. Banking and trade with Italy became increasingly the preserve of the south Germans.

However widespread the practice of credit appears to have been in the Hanseatic world, it encountered invincible distrust in many mercantile quarters. In the fifteenth century distrust gave way to overt hostility.* The Hansa thought it necessary to engage in a systematic campaign against the use of credit in commercial transactions. This is one of the oddest features of its economic policy.

The initiative came from the east, which was economically less developed than the west. Trade, especially in Russia, often took the form of barter or was carried on with 'fur-money', marten being the unit of currency. An attempt to introduce specie into Pskov and Novgorod had to be abandoned, as the coins were said to transmit the plague. The settlement of loans provided a further source of disputes with the Russians, which it was thought better to avoid. Thus the second *schra* of the Novgorod *Kontor* (about 1295) forbade all credit transactions (*Borgkauf*) under pain of a fine.

It is even more surprising to note that credit also became more and more unpopular among influential people in the Hansa, even in Lübeck, on the grounds that it caused instability of prices, which would upset business. Sometimes a buyer would sell at a loss in order to get ready cash to settle debts; at other times, not being obliged to pay on the nail, he would agree to an excessive credit. Credit was also accused of increasing the temptation to take risks, and even worse, of favouring the dishonest schemes of unscrupulous merchants, thus compromising the good name of the Hansa.

It was at the end of the fourteenth century that hostility to credit developed into a systematic campaign. In 1399 the Livonian towns forbade its use in trade with the Russians. More than that, they demanded and obtained the abolition of credit transactions even in Flanders. In 1401 the diet at Lübeck forbade for a period of three years all buying and selling on credit in dealings with foreigners in Flanders. This was the first general enactment of this sort, and also the first attempt to impose

* Document No. 31.

archaic commercial practices on the west. There seems to have been great consternation in the Bruges *Kontor*, which vainly pointed out the damage the Hanseatics would suffer, even though the measure appears to have been applied only to the trade with Livonia. Even there much resistance had to be broken down. In 1411 the Livonian towns decreed that all imported goods had to be accompanied by a certificate saying that they had been bought in Flanders for cash. In the years that followed trade between Flanders and Livonia degenerated into barter, with furs and wax being exchanged for cloth and spices.

The results of this regulation were evidently favourable, for the Hansa then tried to abolish credit throughout Flanders. A fundamental measure to this effect was decreed in 1417 and repeated in 1422, 1434 and 1447. In 1462 the London Steelyard called for the suppression of credit, notably for buying cloth, which seems to show that the measure had not yet been extended to England. The demand was unsuccessful. Some years later German merchants owed £5,000 to clothiers in Gloucestershire.

Again it is difficult to decide how effective legislation was. Certainly long-term credit became rare and as a result Hanseatic trade – that of the medium and small merchants rather than the great merchants – was seriously hampered. This curious and increasing hostility towards an economic practice indispensable to the trade of the period cannot be explained entirely in terms of the conservative spirit characteristic of the Hansa, nor by the effect of a few great bankruptcies, like that of Hildebrand Veckinchusen, a victim of the abuse of credit. It must be viewed within the framework of the Hansa's struggle against foreign competition. Like the ban on the formation of partnerships with non-Hanseatics, the ban on credit was aimed at preventing foreigners from participating in Hanseatic ventures, and at reserving for Hanseatics the exclusive enjoyment of the privileges, the indispensable foundation, as they thought, of their prosperity. This policy was partially successful, but it soon became evident that the Hansa could not hope to triumph over her rivals by imposing conditions contrary to the commercial practice of the day.

5. MONETARY POLICY

The variety of currencies in use certainly constituted a serious obstacle to Hanseatic commerce. From the thirteenth century onwards, as a result

of the emperor granting the princes the right to mint, appreciable variations became noticeable in the value of the pfennig – the only minted
currency of the period – in the various regions of northern Germany.
Thus when she strengthened her organisation in the mid-fourteenth
century, she was unable even to envisage the unification of the monetary
systems within her own domain. Different currencies remained in use in
different areas, among them the marks of Lübeck, Pomerania, Prussia and
Riga, and later on the Brandenburg thaler in the east and the Rhenish
guilder in the west. In the Hanseatic orbit the most widely used currencies
were, in addition to the Lübeck mark, the Flemish pound of groschen and
to a lesser extent, the English pound sterling.*

A factor favourable to commerce was the early acquisition by the towns
of the right to mint, the only exceptions being certain Westphalian and
Saxon towns where the bishops retained this right. Being in control of
their own currency and anxious to develop their trade, the Hansa towns
were careful not to exploit their coinage as a source of revenue by means
of frequent debasement. They could not, of course, prevent a general
depreciation and reduction in the fine metal content. The nominal value
of the silver mark increased five times between the beginning of the
fourteenth and that of the sixteenth century. However monetary fluctuations remained relatively limited.

After about 1350 the desire to simplify the currency led to monetary
agreements between the towns of certain regions throughout Germany.
Such groups were formed by the towns of Lower Saxony under the
leadership of Brunswick, Goslar and Hildesheim, anxious above all to
regulate the trade in silver ingots; by the Pomeranian towns; and in the
fifteenth century by the Westphalian towns, which were joined by
Bremen and the towns of the Zuiderzee.

The only important group in the Hanseatic area was the monetary
union of the Wendish towns. Formed in 1379 after the Peace of
Stralsund, it contained, strictly speaking, only four towns – Lübeck,
Hamburg, Wismar and Lüneburg. But Rostock and the Pomeranian
towns of Stralsund, Greifswald and Stettin adhered to it temporarily, as

---

* As a rough guide, here are some approximate monetary equivalents at the
beginning of the fifteenth century. Silver coins: 100 Lübeck marks=53
Prussian marks=64 Riga marks=15 Flemish pounds=13 pounds sterling.
Gold coins: 100 Lübeck marks=64 English nobles=47 Ghent nobles=92
French crowns=110 Rhenish guilders=213 Guelders guilders=100 Venetian
ducats. 1 Lübeck mark = 16 schillings of 12 pfennigs each = 192 pfennigs.

did other towns between the Weser and the Oder, and also Denmark. Although not members, they all adopted the Wendish standard, with the result that the influence of the Wendish union extended over a fairly wide area including virtually the whole of Scandinavia. In principle the monetary union was an organisation entirely distinct from the Hansa, incorporating non-Hanseatic towns and holding its meetings elsewhere and on different dates from the Hanseatic diets. In fact when the Hansa legislated on monetary matters, in particular on the melting and minting of ingots, or the import of debased currency, it was obvious that its inspiration came from the directives issued by the Wendish union.

The Wendish union did its best to maintain the monetary standard agreed on, to keep a watch on circulation, to supervise the mints, their employees and the goldsmiths, to procure the necessary silver by importing it from Bohemia and Brunswick, and to maintain the towns' monopoly of the buying and selling of precious metal. One of its greatest achievements, though it did not take place until the beginning of the sixteenth century, was the striking of a silver coin to the value of the Lübeck mark, bearing the arms of the four towns and containing eighteen grammes of fine silver. The union's task was made more difficult by the fact that it had no means of compulsion. The regular restatement of certain regulations in one ordinance after another proves that they were only very partially adhered to.

As the monetary union and the Hansa towns were tied to the silver standard, they were alarmed by the spread of gold coins in the fourteenth century. They endeavoured, though without success, to establish a fixed relationship between the value of silver and gold, but in 1340 Lübeck obtained from the emperor the right to mint gold coins. Until the sixteenth century Lübeck kept firmly to the model of the high-grade Italian florin of $23\frac{1}{3}$ carats fine, whereas the gold guilders mostly circulating in Germany, especially those minted by the Rhenish electors, had from the end of the fourteenth century shown a rapid decline in fine metal content and value. It is evident that the Hansa towns retained a certain distrust of gold coins and even tried to restrict their use, fearing fluctuations in value which might rock the silver coinage. In 1430 the Livonian towns – the most conservative in this as in every other respect – protested officially against the payment in gold for a load of French salt. In the mid-fifteenth century the Wendish towns also forbade payments in gold, even in the western *Kontore*, under the pain of confiscation of the goods sold. Here, as in other matters, the traditionalist mentality of the leading men of the Hansa led to measures which ran counter to the general economic development and even the wishes of the German merchants themselves. But although this excess of prudence had certain disadvantages, it did ensure a relatively stable monetary situation in the Hanseatic world.

CHAPTER TEN

Hanseatic Trade

I. THE SOURCES

THE study of Hanseatic trade in the Middle Ages must be preceded by an evaluation of its documentation. It goes without saying that such documentation is most unsatisfactory. The extant texts make it easy to ascertain the chief commodities, their place of origin and destination, and what types of business were carried on in various fields. But for a reasonably accurate picture quantitative data are essential, even if the figures are unreliable – as they always are. During the last fifty years Hanseatic and other historians have made a detailed study of the quantitative aspects of Hanseatic trade, both relative and absolute. Substantial though still limited results have been achieved.

From the documentary point of view, the history of Hanseatic trade can be divided into three periods.

1. Up to about 1275 there are hardly any figures at all, even for individual items. Chronicles, charters, regulations, even customs rolls such as that of Bruges for 1252, give no precise details.

2. From the end of the thirteenth century to the middle of the fourteenth century a certain amount of data begins to be available in the debtors' registers set up in various towns, notably Hamburg, Lübeck and Riga. But they only provide information about the details of certain transactions by a particular merchant, as do the earliest account-books of Lübeck merchants, dating back from the end of the thirteenth century, like those of an unknown trader around 1280, and of Hermann Warendorp and Hermann Wittenborg in the second quarter of the fourteenth century, or the first inventories of lost ships. A few figures of more general significance do, however, exist, for one country – England. From the Customs Accounts and the export licences for wool sacks instituted by Henry III we know the number of merchants, whether English, German or of any other nationality, who were engaged in the wool trade in 1273 and 1277, and also the number of sacks exported in those years. These figures concern a branch of trade which was of only secondary

importance to the Hansa, wool being exported almost exclusively to the Low Countries. But a later Customs Account gives a list of merchants and merchandise leaving the port of Boston during the summer of 1303, while another gives similar information for arrivals at the port of London during 1308–9. There is also a fair amount of other data enabling an estimate to be made of the volume of Westphalian trade in England in the second quarter of the fourteenth century.

But all this amounts to very little. It is important to note that the enormous increase in Hanseatic trade at this time, and its ascendancy in the northern seas, is not reflected in any of the figures available.

3. From about 1350 onwards the documentation becomes fuller. There is a good deal of detailed information, either of the same kind as for the previous period but more plentiful and more precise, or of a new kind, such as merchants' correspondence. But one essential source, of outstanding importance, is represented by the customs accounts (*Pfundzoll-bücher*). Poundage (*Pfundzoll*) was levied in times of war when ships and cargoes left or entered Hanseatic ports. It was levied on about ten occasions between 1361 and 1400, and frequently during the following century. The most complete list, and the one which has been most closely studied, is that for Lübeck in the year 1368. Of great value also are the lists for Hamburg in 1369, 1399 and 1400, for Danzig in 1474–6 and 1490–2, and for Lübeck in 1492–6. The last, unfortunately, are not easy to use in the form in which they have been published by Bruns.

These fiscal documents are of great interest because they give, in principle, the sum total of ships and merchandise leaving or entering a particular port in a particular year. No doubt they contain many errors and omissions. They are certainly no more accurate than the customs accounts of the Sound from the end of the sixteenth century onwards, whose unreliability has recently been established. It is nonetheless true that in comparison with the vagueness of the information available for the preceding period, they provide a considerably clearer picture.

Valuable as they are, the *Pfundzollbücher* have the disadvantage of being concerned only with exceptional years, years of war, because of course it was war that led to the levying of the tax recorded in them. Thus the figures for trade with the belligerent countries are deceptive. This explains the insignificance of Lübeck's trade with Norway in 1368, and also the small number of furs imported from Russia in that year. In addition it must be remembered that in the Middle Ages, as a result of different contingencies, it was not unusual for trade to be doubled or halved from one year to another. To obtain a clear picture identical sets of figures for consecutive years would be needed, which the *Pfundzoll-bücher* do not provide.

Only two series of continuous figures have been preserved. The first is provided by the English Customs Account and deals with the export of English cloth by Hanseatic merchants* (and others) during the years from 1399 to 1482 with hardly any gaps. This provides us with exceptionally precise information. The second set of figures has been taken from the accounts of the Teutonic Order and covers the transactions of the great treasury of Königsberg with Flanders from 1390 to 1404.† Unfortunately the corresponding figures for the other commercial office of the Order, the great treasury of Marienburg, are missing. A third though fragmentary series is provided by the *Pfahlgeld* or anchorage dues levied in Danzig. These give some information about trade in the port of Danzig for ten of the years between 1460 and 1496. Lastly from the customs accounts of the Sound there survives for the fifteenth century only the list of ships which passed through the straits in 1497.

It is evident therefore that the documentation of Hanseatic trade for the period 1350 to 1500 is extremely fragmentary and disparate. Consequently it is difficult to trace the development of trade, except in the case of English cloth, or to determine the relative importance of the principal commodities. It is particularly regrettable that in the present state of research on the *Pfundzollbücher* there are virtually no trade statistics available for the whole of the first half of the fifteenth century in any Hanseatic port. More serious still is the lack of any quantitative data for either the whole or a part of the trade by land, which was perhaps just as important as trade by sea. The most useful information surviving on this subject is provided by the memorandum book in which the merchant Paul Mulich listed the goods he bought at the Frankfurt Lent Fair in 1496 for dispatch to Lübeck.

2. MAIN CHARACTERISTICS

Hanseatic trade can be defined as essentially the trade carried on by German merchants from the towns of north Germany, transporting the products of the east towards the west and vice versa. It was this trade between eastern and north-western Europe which gave rise to the Hansa

* Document No. 47.
† Document No. 45.

and kept it in being. Hanseatic trade was thus from very early days organised on the axis Novgorod–Reval–Lübeck–Hamburg–Bruges–London, though a detour round Denmark through the Sound became increasingly common.

This main stream of trade, based principally on the exchange of furs and wax for cloth, and later salt, was fed by tributary streams from neighbouring countries: in the north from Sweden (copper and iron), Skania, Norway and later Iceland (fish) and Scotland (cloth); in the south from Prussia and Poland (grain and timber), Hungary (minerals) and southern Germany (wine) and from the shores of France and Portugal (salt). It was also augmented, though less than used to be thought, by products made or harvested in the Hanseatic zone itself (beer, linen, salt, grain). The prosperity of the Novgorod–London axis can be said to reflect the prosperity of the Hansa itself. When it was weakened by Dutch rivalry and by the development of a new east–west trade route via Breslau–Leipzig–Frankfurt, it presaged the community's decline.

In addition to this specifically Hanseatic trade axis, there was an older one of great importance: the Rhineland route linking Italy and Frankfurt with the Low Countries and England. The Hansa had a share in this trade route, principally through Cologne. But this was always a minor route for the Hanseatics, along which they had no monopoly, except in the export of wine to the north-west.

Although it formed a comparatively small proportion of their trade, the Hanseatics sometimes participated in the direct exchange of goods between two foreign countries without sending them through Hanseatic ports. Their share in the shipment of English wool to the Low Countries was considerable, and they also maintained regular contact between Norway and England, which resulted in the Boston factory becoming dependent on the Bergen *Kontor*. In the west Hanseatic ships annually brought wine to England from Poitou and Gascony during the fifteenth and early sixteenth century, while Cologne merchants traded between Frankfurt, Lyon, Milan, Genoa and Catalonia, though the last-named hardly counts as a centre of Hanseatic trade.

The establishment of regular trade routes appears to have been determined more by the desire to buy than to sell. The merchants set off mainly to fetch something their customers wanted rather than to sell the goods they had taken with them. It was the quest for furs that took the Germans to Novgorod, for fish to Skania and Bergen, for cloth to Flanders, for salt to Bourgneuf and Lisbon. The reverse is only known to apply to the Cologne merchants in their trade with England: their chief concern was to sell their wine. But this was before the formation of the Hansa.

Hanseatic trade, more than that of any other nation, is characterised by the existence of relatively well-defined trade routes. As a rule the same ships, singly or in convoy, travelled regularly to and from the same foreign ports. Most merchants – with a few exceptions among the most prosperous – preferred to confine their business activities to one and the same region. This tendency towards specialisation is reflected in the multiplicity of the typically Hanseatic *Fahrer* associations, which grouped together all the merchants of a town trading with a particular foreign country.

In the cycle of exchange it appears that, broadly speaking, the east provided raw materials, bulky and relatively low in value, while the west sent back finished articles and luxury goods in return. This accounts for an important characteristic of Hanseatic trade, the lack of balance in exchange, the merchandise moving from east to west being much bulkier and, apparently, more valuable than that going in the opposite direction. Ships which had sailed westward with full holds often returned only partly laden or wholly empty, thus setting problems in the use of freight space which the Hanseatics never managed to solve satisfactorily. The increased need for French salt brought only a partial solution to a situation which resulted from the geography and economy of the northern countries. The imbalance can be detected as early as the thirteenth century. It becomes obvious in the traffic passing through Lübeck in 1368, when a third of the ships returned to Danzig in ballast, and through the port of Hamburg, where exports were much larger than imports. Finally in the sixteenth century it can be seen most clearly in the customs accounts of the Sound.

To obtain an accurate picture of Hanseatic trade as a whole, one would need to have an approximate idea of the relative importance of the traffic through the main ports. But there are insufficient reliable figures to provide the basis of such a comparison. According to the *Pfundzollbücher* trade in the port of Lübeck from March 1368 to March 1369 amounted to 546,000 Lübeck marks, of which 339,000 marks were imports and 207,000 exports. Similar figures for Hamburg in 1369 are 235,000 marks (47,000 and 188,000); for Reval about 300,000 marks in 1379 and 1382 (years of prosperity) but not more than half this figure in other less prosperous years such as 1378, 1383 and 1384. More significant is the comparison of the yield of the *Pfundzoll* in different ports in the same year. Walther Vogel has attempted such a comparison for the period from 22 February 1368 to 29 September 1369. If Lübeck's share is reckoned as 100, that of the other Wendish ports on the Baltic amounts to 93 (51 for Stralsund, 26 for Wismar, 16 for Rostock). That of the Prussian towns, taken together, amounts to 152, which suggests that Danzig's trade was equal in importance to that of Lübeck. That of the Livonian towns was a mere 41 (19 for Riga and 16 for Reval). In the North Sea, Hamburg's share was 72 and Bremen's 10. There is no need to point out that similar figures for other periods would have to be established before the Hanseatic ports could be classified in order of importance.

It would be useful if the development of trade in any one port could be traced over a fairly long period, but there again the lack of statistics makes such a task impossible. According to F. Bruns the seaborne trade of Lübeck in the Baltic alone amounted in 1492 to 660,000 Lübeck marks, of which 218,000 represented imports and 442,000 exports, while in 1368 — when imports and exports through Hamburg were particularly high — the amount was only 153,000 (57,000 and 96,000). This comparison does no more than allow us to note that, even allowing for monetary devaluation, there was a marked increase in trade during the fifteenth century — not a very original conclusion.

These two figures for Lübeck for the years 1368 and 1492 raise the general question of how Hanseatic trade developed during this period. Was the increase more or less regular except during wars and blockades, or were there periods of depression? The fifteenth century is generally considered a period of economic recession all over Europe, marked principally by a steep fall in agricultural prices. This, of course, also affected Hanseatic commerce. According to the accounts of the Teutonic Order the price of rye (in silver currency) declined steadily throughout the century by more than 50 per cent. This does not necessarily mean that the grain trade was cut by the same amount, especially as in the Low Countries the price of corn rose slightly in the same period.

The only continuous series of figures which might be helpful is that for Hanseatic exports of English cloth. Unfortunately it cannot be regarded as typical of the general line of development, as there was an exceptional boom in English, as well as Dutch, cloth in the fifteenth century to the detriment of Flemish cloth, and it is not known how much of the latter was exported in the Hanseatic zone. The number of lengths of English cloth exported by the Hanseatics increased from about 6,000 at the beginning of the fifteenth century to 9,000 during the 1460s and reached more than 15,000 by about 1480. The only periods when there was a marked falling off coincided with the wars against Denmark (around 1430) and England (1469–74). However there was one somewhat smaller decrease – of a thousand lengths – in the 1410s, which was unrelated to war. This is confirmed by the correspondence of the Veckinchusens, which gives the impression of a marked stagnation of business during the period, of a saturation of the market which made it difficult to find buyers for the most diverse commodities, such as fish, furs, amber and spices, not only in the Hanseatic zone but as far away as Venice also. The inference is that business was extremely slack from 1408 to 1418. But the crisis does not seem to have continued after 1420. Consequently, with no indications to the contrary, it is probable that with this single exception Hanseatic trade increased more or less regularly throughout the fifteenth century, though with the fluctuations inherent in all medieval trade.

These fluctuations in Hanseatic trade bring up the question of price development. A fairly precise answer can be given only for Prussia, about which the accounts of the Teutonic Order give a good deal of information, especially for the late fourteenth and early fifteenth century.

It is evident from these accounts that prices dropped considerably during the last third of the fourteenth century and that the drop was particularly sharp during the 1390s and persisted until about 1405. The fall is most marked in the case of Brabantine cloth of medium or inferior quality. Between 1379 and 1400 the Prussian retail prices of various kinds of cloth show a drop of a third. For example Oudenarde cloth dropped from 9 marks to 6, Geraardsbergen (Grammont) cloth from 8 ½ or more to 5 ½, Dendermonde cloth from 9¾ to 6½. For many other varieties the fall was 25 per cent. A similar fall is evident in the prices of other articles of many different kinds, both imported and home-produced: cod, salt, spices, southern fruits, rye and timber. The sharpest drop was in the price of amber (80 per cent for the commonest type). This fall in prices can be explained in various ways. In the case of cloth, for instance, because of the English and Dutch competition; freight charges went down because of the increase in the number of Dutch ships in the Baltic; finally the general rise in the volume of trade, with supply outstripping demand, produced an excess of certain luxury goods such as amber.

During the early years of the fifteenth century the fall in prices was checked and even halted in the case of metals, salt, wax and timber. Soon, however, prices rose again, particularly after 1410. This rise was particularly marked in the case of rye, which in 1417 cost five times as much as in 1410, but it was also considerable in the case of timber and even cloth. In Prussia it was due largely to insecurity resulting from the defeat at Tannenberg, but it extended throughout the Hanseatic orbit and probably explains the slump which is vividly depicted in the Veckinchusen letters and which affected the most diverse wares: furs, wax, fish and spices. Customers refused to buy at the higher prices and business stagnated for several years.

From 1418 onwards it seems that prices fell again, but this cannot be traced so clearly as in the previous period. The price of wax, it is true, rose from 32 Prussian marks per *schiffpfund* to 45 between 1420 and 1460, but this increase in nominal value did not compensate for the monetary devaluation. The price of rye (in silver currency) shows in Prussia a decline of more than 50 per cent between 1405 and 1508, and a similar fall is found in Lübeck and Göttingen. This was certainly one of the causes of the increase in grain exports to the west, particularly to Flanders, where no corresponding fall in prices can be observed. On the whole it seems that the increase in the volume of Hanseatic trade between the middle of the fourteenth and the end of the fifteenth century should be related to the fall in prices.

Lastly it would be helpful if the profits made by the merchants could be assessed. There is a good deal of information on this subject in the balance sheets of trading companies and in the accounts of the Teutonic Order, but the gains vary so much and for such very different reasons that no valid conclusion can be drawn. For example in 1400 the sale of three separate consignments of herring brought the Order profits of 20, 33 and 60 per cent respectively! From a series of transactions carried out in the same year it can only be inferred that profits generally ranged somewhere between 15 and 25 per cent and that the most profitable sales were usually of salt, herring and Ypres cloth. But for other commodities an entirely different state of affairs might be revealed.

In any survey of Hanseatic trade the principal commodities transported must be enumerated. The available statistics are not sufficient to enable us to range them in order of importance, and in any case the order would vary in different periods. But among the innumerable articles which we know of, there are eight that may be called fundamental and typically Hanseatic: cloth, furs, wax, salt, dried or salted fish, grain, timber and beer.

During the last three hundred years of the Middle Ages the cloth trade occupied first place, in terms of value, in the transactions of Hanseatic merchants. It was by far the most important commodity imported into the German towns and into the eastern countries too. In Lübeck in 1368 cloth represents more than a third of all imports and more than a quarter of the total trade. The enormous demand, the wide range in quality and price, the more or less certain profit, varying from 15 to over 30 per cent, explain its importance. In the thirteenth and the first half of the fourteenth century the Hanseatics dealt almost entirely in Flemish cloth, and they remained faithful to Flemish fabrics longer than any other foreigners. However in the fifteenth century the English and Dutch cloths, despite the regulations designed to exclude them, increasingly gained ground, though it is not possible to estimate their proportion of the total. Cloth from other sources – France, the Rhineland, the Hansa towns themselves – never played anything more than a modest role. The rising importance of Polish textiles from Silesia must not be overlooked. Their competition became so alarming that by the end of the fourteenth century the Novgorod *Kontor* forbade their sale. At the same time luxury Italian cloths, transported mainly through Frankfurt, were increasingly in demand in the north.

Trade in furs and wax, both eastern products, formed a kind of counterbalance to trade in cloth, a product of the west. The demand for furs in western and Mediterranean countries was considerable, and the multiplicity of varieties and prices made it possible for the merchants to adapt their trade to the most diverse needs. Furs were imported mainly from Russia, especially from Novgorod, but also from Livonia, Lithuania, Poland, Prussia and Sweden. Lambskins, on the other hand, travelled in the opposite direction, from England and Scotland to the Baltic. The fur trade was thought to be the foundation of Hanseatic wealth, though its importance is not always borne out in the figures as clearly as might be expected. At Lübeck in 1368 it takes only fifth place, after Swedish butter, though this may be a result of exceptional circumstances. On the other hand fur occupies an unrivalled place in the affairs of certain great merchants, such as the Veckinchusens, and there is mention of ships transporting more than 200,000 pelts valued at tens of thousands of marks.

The fur trade was always considered extremely profitable, as it still is, but careful research has recently shown that it was not always so. The Veckinchusens in particular met many disappointments in their business, in both Venice and Bruges. They often had to keep consignments in stock for a considerable time, or were obliged to sell at a loss or for a very small profit. In 1411 in Frankfurt a consignment valued at a thousand marks was disposed of at a profit of only 1·5 per cent. This transaction took place in the period of economic recession and therefore does not provide a basis for generalisation; the fact that the two brothers continued to deal in furs on a large scale perhaps indicates that normally they could expect more substantial profits.

Wax was produced in very much the same countries, Russia, Livonia and Prussia. Trade in wax was less speculative than that in furs, since its use as a source of lighting throughout the west assured a steady sale at a moderate profit, averaging from 10 to 15 per cent. There are no figures which would allow the volume of trade to be reckoned precisely except at the beginning of the sixteenth century, when imports into England rose to several thousand hundredweights,* but as early as the thirteenth century the Hanseatics had established a monopoly in the import of wax from the east, which they retained longer than their monopoly of furs.

If wax, furs and cloth played an essential part in the early development of the Hansa in the thirteenth and fourteenth centuries, it is impossible to exaggerate the importance of salt in the commercial expansion in the fourteenth and fifteenth centuries. The demand for salt was substantial. According to extant accounts from Upper Saxony the average consumption per person in the mid-fifteenth century was about 15 kilogrammes a year. When food was salted down, a barrel of salt was required for four or five barrels of herring or for ten barrels of butter. This precious commodity was almost completely lacking in the east. The low salt content of the Baltic prevented the exploitation of sea-water. As for rock-salt, in the whole of eastern Germany, apart from the mines at Lüneburg, only the modest salt-pits at Kolberg were of any value. Being both bulky and cheap, salt had to be transported by water if it was to travel any distance. It was therefore an ideal commodity for maritime trade, and as the movement of the salt trade was always eastward, salt formed the principal return freight for ships bringing to the west such bulky products as grain, timber and ash.

Up to the mid-fourteenth century the east was supplied almost exclusively by Lübeck with Lüneburg salt – one of the foundations of its wealth. In 1368 it was by far the most important article exported from the town. Soon, however, French salt, less pure but also less expensive, was arriving in the Baltic in larger quantities and by the end of the

* Document No. 48.

fourteenth century 'Bay salt' was commoner than salt from the Trave. French salt was at first bought in Flanders, but the Hanseatics soon began to fetch it themselves from Bourgneuf and Brouage. In the fifteenth century they also began to make regular journeys to Lisbon to bring back Portuguese salt from Setúbal. Salt from other sources – Scotland, Frisia, Kolberg, Halle and Galicia – played only an insignificant role in Hanseatic trade. There are no overall figures for the Hanseatic salt trade, but in some years during the fifteenth century more than 100 ships – some of them Dutch – carried cargoes of salt through the Sound. In Reval 1,350 lasts of Bay salt were imported in 1383, and nearly double that amount each year in the second quarter of the fifteenth century. Demand was continually increasing, probably because the Russians and Lithuanians were selling salt further and further afield. Taking advantage of the urgency of their requirements, the Teutonic Order occasionally placed an embargo on shipments in order to put pressure on the Russian government. The vital importance of salt in the east had moreover a further effect: it made it much easier for the Hollanders to increase their trade with the Baltic countries and Prussia.

The fish trade – dried cod from Norway and salt herring from Skania – was rather different from other branches of Hanseatic commerce because of the multiplicity of its outlets. Fish was brought from the north to the Wendish ports on the Baltic and thence redispatched to both the east and the west, and also, indeed mainly, into the interior, even as far as south Germany and beyond. Herring was imported in far larger quantities than cod, although the latter apparently had the advantage of keeping better. The import of salt herring into the Wendish ports at the end of the century has been estimated at 150,000 barrels, of which half went to Lübeck. It would hardly be an exaggeration to say that, long before Amsterdam, Lübeck was built on herring-barrels. However this trade received a severe blow in the fifteenth century, when the North Sea fisheries were developed. Dutch herrings were not so good as the Skanian ones but they were cheaper and almost completely supplanted their rivals in north-west Europe, even penetrating into the Baltic to offer competition there too.

Together with salt, grain – especially rye – was the commodity which the Hanseatics distributed the most widely at the end of the Middle Ages. Unfortunately the lack of reliable figures for the period before 1550 makes it impossible to estimate the increase in the grain trade. Rye, barley and wheat were grown everywhere. By the thirteenth century the countries of the middle Elbe, Brandenburg and Mecklenburg, were exporting grain to Norway and the Low Countries, but in the fourteenth and especially the fifteenth century it was Prussia and Poland who became and remained the great grain-producing regions, exporting principally via Danzig to the whole of the west, in response to an ever-increasing demand. Though figures are not available, the importance of the export of grain can be clearly seen from the political influence which the Hansa acquired through it. The pressing need for grain and flour had by the end of the thirteenth century reduced Norway to close economic dependence on the Wendish towns. Later on, the decreasing yield of corn in Flanders, and its growing cost, made it possible for the Hansa to obtain substantial advantages on many occasions. Finally in post-medieval days France, Spain and even Italy began to buy Hanseatic grain. The export of cereals was therefore one of the firmest foundations of the community's power, and even caused its temporary revival in the sixteenth century. But even more than was the case with salt, the increased demand for cereals offered the Hollanders the surest means of establishing themselves in the Baltic.

The Hanseatic east was also the west's great source of timber. Various regions specialised in its export, notably the hinterland of the Weser, Pomerania and Norway. But it was the vast forest areas in the basin of the Vistula and in Lithuania which made Danzig the leading exporter of timber, as well as of such highly valued by-products as ash, pitch and resin. The principal customers were England and Flanders, who needed timber for their ships. In the fifteenth century Prussia was exporting oak beams and planks (*Wagenschoss*) in thousands, and boards of varying thickness (*Klappholz, Dielen*) in hundreds of thousands. Yew from the Carpathians was widely required in England for the manufacture of bows, and it has been said that the Hundred Years War was won with the aid of Prussian wood. Unlike the export of grain, the trade in timber seems to have slackened off at the end of the fifteenth century, perhaps as a result of competition from Norway. By-products were less affected, as can be seen from the customs accounts of the Sound.

One of the most important exports was beer, the only one produced within the Hanseatic zone and not in a foreign country. In the thirteenth century Bremen was the chief exporter of beer to the Low Countries, but it was later supplanted by Hamburg. According to the *Pfundzoll* of 1369 beer represented a third of Hamburg's total seaborne exports, to the amount of 62,000 marks. It was thus as valuable to Hamburg as the salt trade was to Lübeck in the same period. In the fourteenth century the Baltic ports, especially Wismar, Rostock and Danzig, became great brewing towns which exported large quantities of beer to Norway, Skania and eastern Europe.

Besides these basic commodities there are a further ten which did not equal the first group in value or bulk, but which were nevertheless important in Hanseatic trade. Wine ranked highest among them, and if figures were available for the total trade in wine, it might even be found to be one of the chief commodities. But although mention is made in some instances of consignments or purchases exceeding 1,000 hectolitres, and wine is found in every Hansa town, in Scandinavia and even as far afield as Moscow, the quantities imported were nearly always fairly modest (800 hectolitres annually in Reval between 1426 and 1436) and wine does not play a great role in the affairs of any one merchant. But it must be remembered that no account-books survive for the great Cologne merchants. In the Hanseatic zone people drank mostly Rhenish wine, which was cheaper than French wine; it was handled by Cologne and Frankfurt. The sales of French wine from Poitou, La Rochelle, Bordeaux and Orléans increased rapidly in the fifteenth century, as did those of Spanish and Portuguese wines (Osey, Rumanie, Algarve) and the sweet Greek or Greek-type wines (Malmsey). Unfortunately there is no way of judging the relative importance of these various vintages. The wines of the north German plain, from Guben (south of Frankfurt-on-the-Oder) and the lower Vistula, were of only minor importance.

Trade in English wool, even more than the trade in wine, was of a marginal character, as most of it went exclusively to Flanders. In Lübeck in 1368 wool came only thirty-second in the list of imports. After being very important in the first half of the fourteenth century (3,000 sacks were exported by the Hanseatics in 1340) it later became insignificant, nor did the Hanseatics participate much in the export of Spanish wool to the Low Countries.

Among metals, iron and copper took first place. Swedish and Hungarian copper, brought to Lübeck from Stockholm and Danzig, was almost entirely re-exported by sea to the Low Countries and England, while copper from the Harz was transported overland to Cologne. Iron, though handled in larger quantities, was dealt with in the same way. It came mainly from Sweden and Hungary, but also from the Rhenish Slate Mountains, the Siegerland, from where it was shipped to western Europe.

The only textile industry of any importance in the Hanseatic zone was the linen-weaving of Westphalia. This gave rise to a considerable volume of trade, especially with the west, as can be seen from the export figures for Hamburg in 1369: linen was in second place, with a value of 30,000 marks. The production of flax seems to have increased remarkably in the fifteenth century in north Germany, Prussia and especially Livonia, where it gradually became the principal article of export.

Spices, principally pepper and ginger, do not seem to have bulked as large in Hanseatic trade as might have been expected, though they probably played an important part in the business of certain great merchants such as the Veckinchusens. Of the imports into Lübeck in 1368 they accounted for only a few hundred marks, and in 1495 they represented only 4 per cent of Paul Mulich's purchases in Frankfurt, although by that time the demand had increased considerably. Trade appears to have been brisker in foodstuffs from the Mediterranean countries – figs, raisins, rice, saffron and especially oil, all of which were dispatched to the east from Bruges and Frankfurt.

All other commodities were of secondary importance, even if at times they occupied a considerable place in the business of certain merchants. They include the products and by-products of stock-farming, oxen, horses, salted meat, butter and fats from Scandinavia and Pomeranian honey; among mineral products, silver, zinc, lead, alum; textile fibres, such as silk and hemp, and fustian; metal goods, wood and leather wares from Nürnberg, Cologne and Brunswick; Prussian amber, and gold or silver luxury articles, pearls, coral, etc.

What emerges clearly from this list is the extreme variety of Hanseatic trade. It would obviously be wrong to say that it consisted only in the exchange of raw materials from the east for expensive goods from the west. The diversity of goods dispatched to the west is evident. They were mainly foodstuffs, but also included raw materials for industry and such luxury products as furs and amber. It is the diversity of its trade which explains the key role played by the Hansa in the European economy.

Such is the Hanseatic trade in outline; but to understand its complexity it is necessary to examine, as far as possible, the conditions, nature and volume of trade in each of the regions.

3. NORTH AND SOUTH GERMANY

The vast German region of Hanseatic trade can be divided into two parts: north Germany from Frisia to Pomerania, the area of the Hansa towns, and south Germany, its hinterland.

Within this area the four great rivers Rhine, Weser, Elbe and Oder were the principal trade routes, along which the products of inland Germany moved towards the north-west and the maritime ports. Among the innumerable land routes the most important for large-scale trade were those which linked Lübeck with her markets and her sources of supply. The route from Lübeck to Lüneburg led from the latter town in three directions: towards Nürnberg, via Magdeburg; towards Frankfurt, via Hanover and Göttingen or Hameln; and towards Cologne, via Minden and Dortmund or Hanover and Hameln. In addition the routes along the coast – Lübeck–Danzig via Rostock and Stettin, Lübeck–Bruges via Hamburg, Bremen, Deventer, Nijmegen and Antwerp – were by no means negligible, since traffic could move along them much faster than by sea. The frequent reports of vehicles being robbed along these coastal roads prove that they offered considerable competition to the sea routes, especially for the transport of small articles of high value. The land routes were probably even more important to Cologne, in particular the route linking her with Frankfurt and beyond Frankfurt with Constance or Augsburg, or the route which led via Dortmund, Goslar and Magdeburg towards Brandenburg and Poland, both extending westwards towards Bruges via Aachen and Antwerp.

Unfortunately it is not possible to make even an approximate estimate of the volume of Hanseatic trade inside Germany, since there are no overall accounts such as are provided by the *Pfundzollbücher* and the customs accounts for seaborne trade. But this is no reason for underestimating it, as has been done. It is now admitted that the value of Lübeck's inland trade with Cologne, Frankfurt and Nürnberg equalled, if it did not exceed, that of her maritime trade, especially in the fifteenth century. Certain goods were moved through ports as well as overland and figures for exports by sea are provided by the *Pfundzollbücher*. But it is impossible to estimate the amounts of these same products dispatched by other routes in other directions, and all that can be done is to enumerate the commodities which played an appreciable part in Hanseatic overland trade.

North Germany produced grain on a large scale. It has already been noted that by the thirteenth century Hamburg was exporting rye from the middle Elbe and from Brandenburg. This trade was also a factor in the prosperity of Magdeburg. In spite of the rise in Prussian production, Hamburg became in the fifteenth century a great centre for the redistribution of cereals. It was for the most part corn from the hinterland of the Wendish towns that was ground into flour for dispatch via Lübeck to Norway. Pomerania also exported grain as early as the thirteenth century, through Stralsund. At the end of the fifteenth century production increased noticeably at the instigation of the nobility, and Stettin became a great centre for the export of rye and barley, though its trade never rivalled that of Danzig. Flax also was cultivated everywhere, especially in Westphalia, and most of it was woven locally. The remainder was exported towards the Rhine valley and the Low Countries.

Honey from Pomerania, Mecklenburg and the neighbourhood of Brunswick in Lower Saxony was sent mainly to Livonia and Novgorod. This is somewhat surprising in view of the fact that wax was one of the major Russian exports to the west. Probably the German flower-honey was purer and sweeter than the pine-honey of Russia; its most viscous part was sometimes marketed separately under the name of *seem* (strained honey). This honey was probably much in demand in the east and was sent there from Novgorod along the Russian rivers. In 1427 Reval imported more than 3,000 lasts (60,000 kg.) and on a single day a honey fleet of ten vessels, belonging to seventeen different exporters and each carrying more than 200 lasts, sailed into the port. The honey trade must have been very lucrative, for companies were formed which dealt in it exclusively.*

Far more extensive was the trade in Rhenish wine. Under the general heading of *Rheinwein* were grouped not only the wines produced on the banks of the middle Rhine from Cologne to Speyer, but also those from the Moselle and frequently those from Alsace as well. The last were the most esteemed, and in the fourteenth century perhaps the most plentiful: the region around Colmar alone produced 100,000 hectolitres around 1400, though by the second quarter of the fifteenth century this had decreased by about half. The bulk of the wine passed through Cologne, whose merchants often went and bought it on the spot. A few big consignments are known, such as one of 120 hogheads (1,400 hectolitres) sent in 1421 from Strasbourg to Cologne, of which half was

* Document No. 33 (c).

bought by the Veckinchusen brothers. From Cologne the wine was re-exported in all directions: westward to the Low Countries and England, both very good customers; northward via Dordrecht or Kampen to Hamburg and the Baltic (one consignment of 57 tuns sent to Reval in 1387 by a Cologne merchant was worth 4,400 guilders); and eastward to the Westphalian towns. Another great market for Rhenish and especially Alsatian wines was Frankfurt, from where it was sent, often by Hanseatic merchants, to the Saxon towns, Lüneburg and Lübeck. Lack of data makes it impossible to trace the evolution of the traffic in Rhenish wine. It is tempting to postulate a decline in the fifteenth century when the production of Alsatian wine is known to have decreased, but it would be risky to generalise from this one piece of information.

The most important mineral product was salt. The great salt works of Halle, which supplied central Germany and the most southerly of the Saxon towns, were of no great account in Hanseatic trade. On the other hand, as has been shown already, the salt works of Lüneburg were extraordinarily important. They are mentioned as early as the tenth century and were at first the property of the dukes of Saxony. By the thirteenth century they had passed into the hands of the burgesses of Lüneburg. It has been estimated that production there was about 50,000 tons in 1205 and 60,000 in 1350. The brine was drawn up in buckets and distilled in about fifty great vats. The salt obtained was either put in barrels on the spot or dispatched in bulk in flat-bottomed barges, either along the Elbe to Hamburg, or through the Stecknitz canal to Lübeck. Up to the mid-fourteenth century Lüneburg salt was in general use throughout north-west Germany, but later the importation of vast quantities of salt from Bourgneuf deprived it of its western outlets. Because of its superior quality, however, it continued to find ready buyers in the Baltic and remained one of the great sources of Lübeck's wealth. In 1458 one of the reasons given by the Lübeck ambassadors to the pope for the impossibility of breaking off relations with Lüneburg, at the time under the papal interdict, was that salt was in demand 'in all the countries with which the Lübeck merchant trades'. Four years later the same argument was advanced before the imperial council. Lübeck, it was said, lived only by trading and would perish if she were deprived of salt from Lüneburg. Although somewhat exaggerated these arguments expressed an undoubted truth.

Among the other mineral products of north Germany perhaps the most important, at any rate up to the fourteenth century, was copper from the Rammelsberg near Goslar. Harz copper was dispatched partly to Hamburg, where it was re-exported to Flanders and England, and partly to the industrial centres of Cologne and Dinant, or even further afield. In 1358 the town of Valenciennes bought Goslar copper for the casting of a bell for its belfry.

Lübeck generally relied on Swedish and Carpathian copper and does not seem to have been interested in copper from Goslar. But she was intent on acquiring the silver production of the Harz, both for her mint and for trade with the east. But from the fourteenth century onwards most of the silver she needed was supplied from the lodes in Mansfeld and Bohemia. Iron was exploited principally in the Rhenish Slate Mountains. The ore of Siegerland and Westerwald was smelted on the spot and the steel sent to Cologne, a great centre for this product. From there large quantities were re-exported to England. In the mid-fifteenth century 100 tons of steel were dispatched to London by Johann Questenberg.

Of all the manufactured products of north Germany, beer was most important in the trade of the seaports. Although very popular throughout northern Europe and because of its low price assured of vast sales, beer was perhaps the most easily damaged of all wares and the most difficult to transport. The various processes, the malting, brewing and fermentation, demanded the utmost care and attention if the product was to be of high quality and keep well. The trade also needed pure water. There was a great temptation to reduce costs by substituting oats for barley or by putting in fewer hops, which could not fail to impair the flavour and the keeping qualities of the beverage, as Bremen learnt to her cost. In the thirteenth century her breweries were flourishing and she was exporting beer on a vast scale to the Low Countries. But insufficient supervision of the brewing processes and a drop in quality caused a rapid drop in the number of her customers. By the beginning of the fourteenth century she had been supplanted by Hamburg, who took drastic steps to retain her supremacy. In 1376 Hamburg had 457 breweries, and by the beginning of the fifteenth century the number had increased to well over 500. Production amounted to 200,000 barrels, that is, about 400,000 hectolitres per annum. In 1369 beer formed a third of the town's exports, mostly to Amsterdam and Stavoren. The rest went to Flanders and England, with some going to Prussia or Livonia. On the shores of the Baltic, Wismar, even more than Hamburg, lived by the brewing of beer. In about 1460 there were nearly 200 breweries there, and brewers were in the majority on the town council. Wismar beer was exported to all Baltic countries, where its sale was sometimes hindered by prohibitions designed to protect local production; it was to be found also in Bergen, Kampen and in Flanders. Nearly all great towns had their own breweries, notably Lübeck, Rostock, Danzig and Elbing. The little Saxon town of Einbeck (from which the word *Bock*(*bier*) may perhaps be derived) specialised in the production of beer for export as early as the thirteenth century. Its quality was such as to ensure a demand for it throughout the Hanseatic world and as far away as south Germany.

The textile industry was unable to develop in north Germany because of the import of Flemish cloth by the Hanseatics. Some coarse fabrics were woven there, it is true. In the customs accounts there are occasional mentions of cloth from the Rhineland, from Wesel, Dortmund, and even from Lübeck, Rostock or Wismar. But such cloth had only a negligible share in Hanseatic trade. Linen was a different matter. It was much in demand in Europe because of its cheapness and its usefulness for clothes, sails and as a packaging material. The manufacturing centres were in Frisia and Westphalia, in the neighbourhood of Osnabrück and Münster, and later on in Saxony, as well as around Lake Constance in south Germany. Westphalian linen, woven in both villages and towns, was exported in many directions, but especially to Hamburg, from where it was re-exported to the Low Countries and England, and also to Lübeck, which dispatched it to all the Baltic countries. Production and trade appear to have increased considerably in the fifteenth century.

The other products of urban craftsmen in north Germany were less important: silks, goldsmithery and weapons from Cologne, iron tools from Brunswick, Dortmund and Cologne, bronze wares from the Harz towns and Magdeburg, amber rosaries from Lübeck, furniture and other wooden articles, and so on.

By the thirteenth century the Hanseatics had begun to penetrate into south Germany. In the fourteenth century their business in this region expanded, especially with Nürnberg and Frankfurt. The former attracted them by its production of metal goods and by its far-ranging commercial contacts, the latter by its fairs, where, as in Bruges, the merchants and products of Mediterranean countries could be found. But the Hanseatics also extended their business as far as Prague, Constance and Augsburg, with Cologne merchants travelling up the Rhine valley buying wine as has already been mentioned. Hanseatic trade in this area was mainly in the hands of merchants from Lübeck and Cologne.

How important the activities of the Lübeck merchants were can be clearly seen from the trading company formed by two of them in 1366, with a capital of 7,600 guilders; they dispatched 7,000 pelts to Frankfurt and imported in return 14 bales of fustian, valued at more than 1,600 guilders. Similar partnerships, like that of the Veckinchusens, show that the Lübeckers were taking cod, herring, grain and amber jewellery to south Germany and bringing back luxury cloths, spices, metals and wine. The Cologne merchants appear to have traded on an even larger scale. They did not only visit Frankfurt during the fairs: some of them had settled there, buying houses and shops. They took to Frankfurt cloth from the Low Countries and England, Dutch herring and metalwares from Cologne itself, and bought there metals and spices. In the fourteenth century they are to be found in Austria also, competing with merchants from Regensburg.

However the great feature of this period was the irresistible advance of the south German merchants, who to a great extent superseded the Hanseatics. The Nürnbergers especially broke into the markets of north Germany, a domain hitherto reserved exclusively for Hanseatic merchants. By the beginning of the fifteenth century the retailers of Lübeck had taken fright.* The newcomers not only brought with them the products of their native town, but also made massive sales of articles hitherto supplied by the Hanseatics. Nothing could halt the Nürnbergers' progress. At the end of the fifteenth century the list of Paul Mulich's purchases at the Frankfurt fair shows how extensive was the business carried on by one of them, now firmly established in Lübeck.† By this time the Lübeckers had for all practical purposes been ousted from south Germany.

The merchants of Cologne put up a better defence, and kept a tight hand on the wine trade. Though they were displaced in Austria, they remained in business in Frankfurt and even in Upper Saxony, frequenting the Leipzig fairs and buying and selling Zwickau mining shares. The Nürnbergers also cornered an increasing share of the trade between Frankfurt and Antwerp and between Italy and the Low Countries. There is no doubt that during the fifteenth century Hanseatic trade suffered a serious set-back in south Germany as well as in eastern Europe.

* Document No. 36 (*b*).
† See above, p. 178.

4. EASTERN EUROPE: PRUSSIA AND POLAND, LIVONIA AND RUSSIA

Hanseatic trade in the eastern Baltic, from Danzig to Reval, displays certain common features. These towns were subject to the Teutonic Order; they all exported to Lübeck, Flanders and England practically the same products – wax and furs. They all imported cloth and salt. All were interested in direct relations with the west, and from the fourteenth century onwards all had helped to develop the maritime route through the Sound, to the detriment of the overland Lübeck–Hamburg route, used almost exclusively in the previous century. The interests of the eastern towns were therefore largely opposed to those of Lübeck, a fact which had frequent repercussions in the political field. But on the whole their similarities were less important than their differences. The Hanseatic area in the east comprised two quite distinct sections: Prussia, with its Polish, Hungarian and Lithuanian hinterland, and Livonia, with its hinterland of the upper Dvina and Novgorod.

The structure of Prussian commerce underwent a profound transformation in the fourteenth and fifteenth centuries. Around 1300 most of the traffic flowed through the towns of Elbing and Thorn. Fifty years later Elbing was supplanted by Danzig and never regained her former importance. Thorn, expanding rapidly in the thirteenth century, was unable in the long run to exploit her favourable situation on the Vistula close to the Polish frontier. Caught between the staples of Danzig and Cracow, she saw the greater proportion of her trade diverted towards the Oder and Stettin. She suffered greatly during the wars between Poland and the Teutonic Order and throughout the fifteenth century showed a noticeable decline. The commercial activity of the Order, so considerable in the fourteenth century, did not survive the disaster of Tannenberg. The Grand Master declared sadly in 1440 that it no longer amounted to a tenth of its former value.

On the other hand Danzig experienced an almost uninterrupted rise in prosperity. The *Pfundzollbücher* show that by the second half of the fourteenth century she was handling two-thirds of the Prussian external trade and an increasing share of the traffic coming down the Vistula and of the seaborne trade with Lübeck and the west. Königsberg, too, the headquarters of one of the commercial offices of the Order, was expanding, if somewhat slowly, and should not be overlooked.

The prosperity of Prussian trade depended on the enormous and steadily widening hinterland. From the fourteenth century onwards the merchants of Thorn were in continuous contact with Cracow, a Hansa town through which flowed the mineral products of the Carpathians, especially copper from Neu-Sandec (Nowy Sacz, Poland), Göllnitz (Gelnica) and Schmöllnitz (Smolnik, Slovakia). From here other traders pushed on to Lemberg (Lvov), where they met Venetian and Genoese merchants coming from their factories on the Black Sea, from Tana, Caffa and Constantinople. They sold them cloth, amber, hides and herrings, and bought from them silk and spices. In Lemberg the Teutonic Order owned an amber depot, and in 1400 its assets in the town, in property and outstanding debts, represented a value of 3,200 Prussian marks. But at about this time the commercial current towards the south-east ceased to flow as a result of Timur's invasion. This, together with the discovery that seaborne trade with the west was more profitable, ruined the market for the Italians. The Teutonic Order sold its property in Lemberg in 1400.

At the same time, however, Prussian trade with Lithuania was developing. This new trade route seems to have resulted from the disappointment which the Prussian merchants experienced at Novgorod, where the Wendish and Livonian towns refused them equal rights and even denied them access to the *Kontor*. Since they were determined to share in the profitable trade with Russia, the Order in 1398 obtained from the grand duke of Lithuania permission to trade in his dominions and the right to found an establishment at Kovno. This factory expanded despite initial difficulties, and from the beginning was dominated by the Danzig merchants. By way of the Pregel canal they brought in salt and took back wax, furs and timber for naval construction. In spite of competition from the local merchants Kovno became one of the essential centres of Danzig's trade.

The seaborne commerce of Prussia, concentrated principally in Danzig, was based primarily on relations with Lübeck, Flanders and England. In the fifteenth century these were extended to Holland, Scotland and above all to the Bay of Bourgneuf. The salt fleet which sailed from Bourgneuf to Danzig every year sometimes exceeded fifty vessels. But trade with the Baltic countries was also considerable. In addition to long-standing relations with Skania there were brisk exchanges with Sweden, Finland and Riga in the fifteenth century, so that Danzig soon became the redistribution centre for salt, cloth and wine for the whole of eastern Europe.

The economic prosperity of Prussia was based mainly on the export trade of two articles fundamental to Hanseatic trade, timber and rye. Oak, beech and pine were brought mainly from the duchy of Mazovia, floating down the rivers Memel, Bug and Vistula. Ash and yew came from the Carpathians. The steadily increasing demand for timber in the west – in England, the Low Countries and even in Portugal – seems to have occasioned increased felling and traffic up to about 1450. There are figures only for the second half of the fifteenth century. In 1460 Danzig was exporting 3,161 'hundreds' of planks (*Wagenschoss*), in 1475 2,160, in 1491, 1,466, and over the same period between 265 and 400 'hundreds' of boards (*Klappholz*). These figures make it clear that the Prussian timber trade was already declining, a process which continued during the sixteenth century.

In contrast, the by-products of the Polish forests appear to have enjoyed an ever-increasing demand. Perhaps the most important was ashes, used mainly for the bleaching of western textiles. In the same years towards the end of the fifteenth century exports exceeded 1,000 lasts, and they increased considerably in the sixteenth. The production of pitch and tar, used in caulking, was not quite so high. About 1,000 lasts were exported of both products together.

But it was grain which was the foundation of Prussia's wealth and which made Danzig a great export centre. The demand for it throughout Europe increased all the time, not only in the Low Countries but also in Germany, England, northern France and Spain. It was the Teutonic Order which promoted large-scale production of cereals for export. The harvests of its vast domains in Prussia were gathered into granaries all over the country, particularly at the castle of Marienburg. Around 1400 the stores amounted to 463,000 *Scheffel* of rye (about 15,000 tons), 203,000 of oats, 47,000 of barley and 24,000 of wheat, of which only a small proportion was intended for export. Up to about 1450 exports of corn seem to have been mainly from east and west Prussia. But thereafter corn from Poland, the Ukraine and Lithuania took first place, as the great landowners intensified production and organised the flow of grain from their domains towards Danzig.*

It is not possible to follow exactly the development of this important trade. It certainly impressed the chroniclers, who remarked on the number of ships which came to load grain: in 1392 300 English ships, in 1481 1,110 ships are said to have left Danzig for Flanders. The chronicler Caspar Weinreich noticed the effect of the arrival of consignments of

* Document No. 43.

Prussian rye on prices in the west.* But the only surviving export figures for Danzig relate to the end of the fifteenth century: about 2,000 lasts of rye in 1470 and 1475, and more than 10,000 (20,000 tons) in 1490 and 1492. These quantities were to increase fivefold in the following century.

A peculiar and very ancient Prussian commodity was amber, of which there were at least three kinds, varying considerably in price according to their purity. Amber was gathered on the shores of Samland, and had to be handed over to the agents of the great treasury of the Teutonic Order at Königsberg, which was alone entitled to handle its sale. Up to 1400 amber was sent not only to Lübeck and Bruges but also to Lemberg and from there further east. Sales at this date brought in 1,000 Prussian marks a year at Lemberg, 1,300 at Lübeck and 2,800 at Bruges. Even after the battle of Tannenberg the Order kept its monopoly in amber, and in the fifteenth century it represented the only prosperous branch of the Order's business.

Among other exports, the wax and furs of Lithuania, Mazovia and Podolia figured not only in the business affairs of the Order but also in those of great Lübeck merchants like the Veckinchusens. Prussia and Sweden were the principal suppliers of iron and copper in the Hanseatic zone. The scarcity of figures and the multiplicity of measures employed do not permit any evaluation of the importance of this trade. The *Pfundzoll* of 1368 indicates only that Lübeck imported in that year 1,500 marks' worth of Hungarian copper as against 5,000 marks' worth of Swedish copper. The export of Hungarian copper, carried from Cracow to Danzig down the Vistula, became more important at the end of the fourteenth century, when the Swedish copper industry was in difficulties, and again in the sixteenth century, when the Fuggers extended their business into the north. The importance of Danzig as a metal market is shown by the fact that she was already importing copper and iron from Sweden in the fourteenth century, in order to re-export it to the west.

Mention must finally be made of the part played in Prussian trade by the Danzig artisans. For instance their immense output of beer in the fifteenth century led to regular deliveries to the Baltic countries and Finland, and naval construction, which flourished at certain periods, permitted the sale of ships to other Hansa towns and also to the English, Scots and Dutch, except when a ban on such sales was in force.

The Russo–Livonian area also consisted of two complementary zones: the Russian hinterland with the *Kontore* at Novgorod, Pleskau (Pskov)

* Document No. 12, see entry for 1481.

and Polotsk (in Lithuania), where the Germans came for furs and wax; and the Baltic countries, producing mainly flax and hemp, and containing the towns of Reval, Riga and Dorpat, bases for Hanseatic merchants travelling by land or water to the eastern *Kontore*.

Whereas during the last two centuries of the Middle Ages the Hanseatics expanded their fields of activity almost everywhere else, here the situation was quite the opposite. In the thirteenth century German merchants were regular visitors to Vitebsk and Smolensk, and their privileges, of which they took full advantage, gave them express authority to trade beyond these towns. But from the beginning of the fourteenth century onwards they seldom went beyond Novgorod and Polotsk. In the second half of the fifteenth century the Muscovite advance put an end to their trade in Novgorod, and Russian goods were in future marketed in Livonian towns. This area had originally been a meeting place for merchants from the whole of north Germany, from the Rhine to the Oder. Gradually the Livonian towns were able to achieve a trade monopoly. Riga, by blocking all through traffic, succeeded in reserving trade along the Dvina for her own merchants, and although the Novgorod *Kontor* was frequented right up to its closure by merchants from Lübeck, Saxony and Westphalia, nevertheless Reval and particularly Dorpat were of increasing consequence in its affairs.

It is unfortunately impossible to establish with any precision the share of the Novgorod *Kontor* in Russo–Livonian trade; but it was certainly a large one. The only overall figure, 96,000 Lübeck marks, gives the estimated value of the goods confiscated by the Muscovites in 1494. This is not very helpful. Reval's total trade in 1368 amounted to 99,294 marks, Riga's to 93,284 and Pernau's to 48,817; of these sums, trade with Lübeck alone accounted for 48,200 marks, 24,000 marks and 22,700 marks respectively. However these figures hardly permit generalisation as to the relative importance of the three towns. Riga seems to have been normally the busiest and Pernau's trade tends to be overestimated – in the fifteenth century its trade was no longer to be compared with that of the other two towns.

Of all the products from this area, furs were undoubtedly in the greatest demand. They came to the great fur market at Novgorod from the most distant regions, notably from Jugra on the shores of the White Sea, from Karelia and from the basin of the Volga. Sold by the Russians in sacks, they were dispatched by the Germans in barrels, each barrel containing from 4,000 to 5,000 pelts, often of different kinds.

Furs varied enormously, both in quality and in kind, and were classified by value, as shown in the Veckinchusen letters dealing with the Company of Venice at the beginning of the fifteenth century. The fur most in demand was sable, which sold in Venice at 82 ducats for 100 pelts. Very dear, but sufficiently widespread to serve as a monetary unit, was marten (30 ducats). After that came beaver (12–14 ducats). These furs were generally sold in lots of forty (*timmer*), the others in lots of 250, 500 or 1,000 pelts. Medium-priced varieties were lynx (5½ ducats per 100), otter and weasel (5 ducats). The commonest sorts were the many varieties of squirrel (3–4 ducats) and rabbit.

Furs were often referred to by their place of origin, those from Lithuania, Estonia and Smolensk being less valuable than those from Novgorod. They were also classed by colour – grey, red or black (*grauwerk, rotewerk, swartewerk*) – or by quality. *Schönwerk*, or choice grey squirrel, was without rival as a 'beautiful fur' at a reasonable price (6–7 ducats). Other names, such as *lederwerk, harwerk*, probably referred to the processing, whilst others such as *schevenissen, troynissen, anighen* are of uncertain origin and may have been derived from terms used by Russian hunters.

Here again there are no statistics on which to base a satisfactory evaluation of the Russian fur trade. Imports into Lübeck in 1368 were worth only 1,331 marks, whereas cloth imports were worth nine times as much, herring four times. But it is probable that the blockade of Novgorod decreed by the Hansa in that year was responsible for such a low figure. On the other hand entries in the accounts of certain merchants show considerable imports of furs. The Veckinchusens imported into Flanders between 1403 and 1415 more than 300,000 pelts, of which 90,000 came from Reval, 67,000 from Riga and 153,000 from Danzig. Three ships, belonging to 107 merchants from Dorpat and Riga, which sailed from Riga in 1405 for Bruges contained 450,000 pelts, estimated at 3,300 pounds groschen, in addition to wax (1,435 pounds) and linen (1,125 pounds).

The other great article of Russian commerce was wax, brought to Novgorod from as far afield as Nižni–Novgorod and Karelia, and to Polotsk from Smolensk and the Lithuanian forests. There were few commodities which could so easily be adulterated and which therefore gave rise to so many complaints. The Russians mixed with it various fatty substances, as well as acorns, peas and resin, and refused to guarantee the purity of their product. The Germans therefore appointed wax-inspectors, who took samples, melted suspect consignments down and punished the adulterators. But it did sometimes happen that Hanseatic merchants were in collusion with them and were prepared to market defective products.

The trade in wax, exported for the most part from Riga to Flanders and England, may be assumed to have been as important as that in furs, although it occupies less space in merchants' accounts. The figure given by the Lübeck *Pfundzoll* for the year 1386 (7,200 marks) is abnormally low, for the reason given above.

Flax was a peculiarly Lithuanian commodity, whose cultivation in the fifteenth century was common throughout the country. It was exported, from both Riga and Reval, to Danzig, Lübeck and the west. The same is true of hemp, though smaller quantities are involved. Livonia produced great quantities of hemp and flax yarn, used in the making of cables and cords. All other commodities were of negligible importance. However it is worth mentioning the purchase of silk coverlets from Bagdad, and of Chinese silks, proof of the wide-ranging commercial relations of Novgorod, even as late as the mid-fifteenth century.

Cloth was the principal article imported into Livonia and Russia as into Prussia. It was brought either direct from Flanders or via Lübeck. More passed through Riga than through Reval. The Livonian towns remained faithful to Flemish cloth. Although they tolerated the introduction of Dutch cloth, they forbade its sale to Russians. In the same way they prohibited the sale of English cloth in Novgorod (1476). A similar ban had been placed on Polish cloth at the end of the fourteenth century.

As everywhere in the Baltic, salt was of considerable importance. Of 1,700 vessels which sailed into Reval between 1426 and 1496, 1,216 were carrying salt; of 314 between 1427 and 1433, 105, that is, about a third, came from the Bay of Bourgneuf, as well as 103 from Lübeck and 87 from Prussia; and this during a war, when the passage of the Sound was dangerous. Yet from this time onwards Lüneburg salt, which had predominated up to the mid-fourteenth century, amounted to only a sixth of the total imports. The other commodities were less important. They included herring from Skania or Holland, German honey, spices and French wine, which seems to have been preferred here to Rhenish wine: in the fifteenth century it was noted that the latter was not much esteemed by the Livonians.

Finally no consideration of the eastern zone of Hanseatic trade would be complete without mention of Finland. In the fourteenth and fifteenth centuries Germans were to be found in Vibort and Åbo, the two principal towns, in increasing numbers. Trade, which was insignificant in the four-teenth century, developed rapidly as the two towns took advantage of the blockade of Novgorod to become export centres for Russian products. They also exported horses, fish-oil and resin, which went mainly to Reval, Danzig and Lübeck, while they imported salt, cereals, and French and Portuguese wine.

5. SCANDINAVIA

Hanseatic trade with the various Scandinavian countries has only one trait in common: the preponderance of Lübeck. Otherwise trade with the three kingdoms, Sweden, Denmark-Skania and Norway, had each its own characteristics.

In the case of Sweden it is rather surprising that the western shore, facing the North Sea, played only a minor role in the Middle Ages. The whole economy of the country was orientated towards the Baltic. Southern Sweden, containing the ports of Kalmar, Nyköping and Söderköping, was a stock-rearing country, though there were a few iron mines. Al-though the Germans went to this region earlier than to the north, it was of only secondary importance during the great period of Hanseatic trade in the fourteenth and fifteenth centuries. The same can be said of the island of Gotland, which gradually lost its importance as a port of call for those going to the east – the original basis of its prosperity. The sea-borne trade of southern Sweden, originally orientated almost exclusively towards Lübeck, turned markedly towards Danzig in the fifteenth cen-tury. Around 1500 about thirty vessels sailed every year to each of these two German ports.

From the thirteenth century onwards central Sweden was essential to Hanseatic trade. The port of Stockholm handled the products of the stock-rearing industry and of the Norrland forests, and above all copper from Falun and iron from widely scattered mines. The vital artery of foreign trade was the Stockholm–Lübeck route, served by about twenty vessels in the fourteenth century and by about thirty in the fifteenth. Most of this trade was in the hands of the Lübeckers. At the end of the fourteenth century not more than a quarter of it was handled by Stockholm mer-chants, who themselves were of German origin. From 1368 to 1370, when exports greatly exceeded imports, nine Lübeck merchants handled 60 per cent of the trade between Stockholm, Lübeck and Flanders.

Minerals were the most valuable products exported by Sweden. Almost all the copper from Falun was dispatched to Lübeck, mostly for re-export to Flanders. In 1368 these exports were worth about 5,000 Lübeck marks, and 84 per cent of the trade was controlled by no more than fourteen of the wealthiest merchants. However a sharp drop in production at the end of the fourteenth century, due to political and administrative causes which have not yet been properly investigated, led to a severe crisis in the copper market. Fifty years later there were signs of a recovery, and by the end of the fifteenth century the amount of copper exported to Lübeck greatly exceeded that of the previous century.

Iron was produced by many mines in the district of Falun, and also in central and southern Sweden. It was referred to by two different names, *yser* and *osmund*, the latter being applied only to the Swedish product. The two varieties differed only in appearance, the result perhaps of the smelting technique used. *Osmund*, unlike the pig-iron produced elsewhere, had a lumpy, rubble-like appearance (*in formibus ruderibus osmund*, as one text says). Actually more iron than copper was produced and exported. Lübeck received 1,680 *schiffpfund* in 1368, 3,000 in 1369, valued at 7,000 marks, and 5,000 *schiffpfund* in 1399. This caused a drop in price of nearly 50 per cent. Although most of the iron was re-exported to Flanders a good deal – unlike copper – was sent to various Baltic ports. The traffic appears to have increased in the fifteenth century (6,000 *schiffpfund* in 1492–4), a new factor being the export of ever larger quantities of *osmund* to Danzig.

As well as metals, Stockholm exported furs from Norrland, usually in the first two or three ships of the season, so as to get them on the Lübeck and Bruges markets before the arrival of the Russian furs. Swedish merchants had a much larger share in this trade, which in Lübeck in 1368 reached a value roughly equivalent to that of the copper trade (furs 2,300 marks, oxides 1,000 marks).

Perhaps the most surprising figure given by the *Pfundzollbuch* of 1368 concerns the export of Swedish butter to Lübeck. It was valued at more than 15,000 marks, and half was re-exported to Flanders. This abnormally high figure was probably due to the war, which deprived north Germany and western Europe of Danish butter. In the following years the figure dropped by more than 50 per cent and never again, even in the sixteenth century, reached the heights of 1368. Butter, like the cattle exported from south Sweden and Gotland, could not cope with the Danish competition.

Hanseatic imports into Sweden consisted mainly of cloth and salt. Cloth represented more than half, sometimes two-thirds of these imports. After 1375 the quantity of salt dispatched from Lübeck decreased, owing to increasing quantities of Bourgneuf salt being imported, especially from Danzig.

Although Denmark occupies an important place in the political history of the Hansa and had many immigrants from Germany, it was economically of secondary importance, apart from Skania. Being almost exclusively an agricultural area, it had nothing to offer to the great Hanseatic merchants. The Germans purchased from the Danes mainly oxen and horses. The oxen bought in the markets of Ribe or Rendsburg were moved on the hoof each year in thousands (about 20,000 in 1500) to the Wendish towns or to Holland. There was probably also a considerable trade in butter, and in exchange the Hanseatics sold the Danes salt, wine, cloth and iron.

The Skanian herring trade was on a far larger scale. The fish were caught on the shores of the southern Sound from July to September, almost entirely by Danish fishermen. The yield was unpredictable, as the shoals, though usually enormous, varied considerably in size from year to year. The fisheries were already very prosperous in the thirteenth century and seem to have reached their peak towards the end of the fourteenth century, after which they declined. It has often been said, without proof, that this was because the fish migrated to the North Sea, but this is only attested in the sixteenth century. It is more likely that there was a fall in demand, due to the declining popularity of the Skanian fairs.

The processing, salting and sale of the fish was no concern of the fishermen. In fact they were strictly forbidden to meddle in it. The various operations were carried out on the tiny peninsula of Skanör, south of Malmö, by merchants and their agents, in concessions granted by the king, called *ved* in Danish and *vitte* in German. About thirty of these concessions, held by Danish, Dutch and German merchants, are known, but there were many more. The Hansa towns owned about fifteen. Hamburg, Bremen and the towns of the Zuiderzee held concessions in the neighbourhood of Skanör; the Baltic towns, from Kiel to Reval, had theirs further to the south around Falsterbo. These *vitten* were not all of the same size, the largest, those of Lübeck and Danzig, measuring between 6 and 10 hectares. They included workshops, a church, and a cemetery, and each had its own autonomous organisation under the general surveillance of a Danish bailiff. Administration, justice and trade were controlled by a *Vogt* appointed by the town holding the concession; he was often a member of the town council. The *vitten* were not unlike the *Kontore*, allowance being made for their number, their rural character and their short three-month season of activity. They had one other unusual characteristic. Although women were excluded from the *Kontore*, the preparation and salting of the fish was carried out mainly by Danish and German women.

The sale of the salt herring, sometimes authorised within the *vitte*, took place mainly at the Skania fair, which was held from the end of July to the end of October, sometimes being extended to 11 November. In the fourteenth century the sale was carried on chiefly in Skanör, but in the fifteenth century it was concentrated almost exclusively at Falsterbo. Originally the fair was international in character and was frequented by Flemish, Dutch, English and Scandinavian merchants. Apart from fish, dealings also took place in textiles, timber, furs, wax and iron. In the fourteenth century the increase in German, and above all Lübeck, trade gradually transformed the fair's character. The Hanseatics were masters of Skania from 1368 to 1385 and took the opportunity to eliminate all foreigners: consequently the fair became almost exclusively a herring market.

The proximity of the Wendish towns explains why the trade in Skanian herring was on an extensive scale not found elsewhere. The large number of *Schonenfahrer* from Lübeck and other towns, even from the interior, bears witness to this fact. According to the *Pfundzoll* of 1368, 250 ships took to Lübeck herring to the value of 48,000 marks, in about the same number of barrels, although trade suffered that year because of the Danish war. In 1400 more than 550 Lübeck ships cast anchor, chiefly in Malmö and Dragör (near Copenhagen). They were for the most part very small barges (*Skuder*), especially those which put in at Dragör. Many carried only six to twelve barrels. The larger ships, which anchored at Malmö or Falsterbo, carried up to 400 barrels for a dozen or so merchants. Even this was modest compared with the ships in service elsewhere. In all in 1400 some 900 Lübeck importers – many of whom spread their purchases over several ships – took to Lübeck about 65,000 barrels, to which the amounts not entered in the customs register should be added. There are no comparable figures for other Hansa towns, but A. Christensen estimates that during this period sales at the Skania fair may have reached from 100,000 to 300,000 barrels of herring.

When the Lübeck ships sailed for Skania they carried the supplies necessary to the trade. In addition to empty barrels, Lüneburg salt was the essential import (1,400 lasts in 1400). But foodstuffs needed for this vast assembly of people, especially flour and beer, were also transported. In 1368 exports from Lübeck to Skania amounted to 32,000 marks and in 1400 to 40,000.

In the fifteenth century a slow decline in the Skanian herring trade is apparent. Precise figures are available only for the year 1494. The receipts of the Danish bailiff record that 3,943 lasts of herring (47,323 barrels) were bought by 202 Hanseatic merchants, distributed as follows: Lübeck 55 merchants and 1,284 lasts; Danzig 22 and 878; Stettin 36 and 811; Stralsund 21 and 524; six other Pomeranian towns 50 lasts; Warnemünde 30 and 48.

Even if these figures are incomplete, they bear witness to a marked decline, which was due mainly to the short-sighted policy of the Wendish towns. Their exclusion of western merchants from the fair in Skania was bound to encourage the growth of the North Sea fisheries. Also, by the middle of the fifteenth century herring from Holland and Zeeland had largely supplanted Skanian herring along the shores of the North Sea and in the Rhine Valley, and was even being shipped into the Baltic every year in increasing quantities. The spread of the Reformation caused a further fall in demand, and after 1560 the migration of the fish towards the Norwegian coasts accelerated the process. In the seventeenth century the peninsula of Skanör, at one time thronged by thousands of fishermen, workmen and merchants, was entirely deserted.

Hanseatic trade with Norway was based on three centres: first the *Kontor* at Bergen, dominated by the Lübeckers, and secondly the factories at Tönsberg and Oslo, used principally by merchants from Rostock. From these centres small merchants and chapmen from the Wendish towns spread out into the interior of the country. Buying and selling retail in defiance of royal prohibition, they soon had almost all the Norwegian retail trade in their hands. Consequently the economic domination of the Hanseatics was stronger here than anywhere else.

Foreign trade was for the most part carried on by the *Bergenfahrer* of Lübeck. Every year a score of vessels of average tonnage – between 40 and 60 lasts – sailed between Bergen and Lübeck. The basic commodity was cod, classified in many ways, notably by size, from *koningslobben*, which might weigh more than two kilogrammes apiece, down to *titlingen*, averaging 250 grammes. The fish were caught along the western shores, especially in the latitude of the Lofoten Islands. After being headed and gutted, they were dried in sheds by one of two processes: tied in pairs by the tail (*Rundfisch*) or split singly up the middle (*Rotschert*); they were then hung from wooden racks carefully protected from the sun. The Norwegian fishermen then took the fish to Bergen and sold them direct to the Hanseatics, who always respected the ban on trading north of Bergen. They were dispatched in barrels holding about 250 kg or in bales to Lübeck, where they were graded for size and repacked in barrels.

Cod accounted for nine-tenths of the exports from Bergen which in 1368, when there was a war on, amounted to 3,720 Lübeck marks. In 1370 the amount exceeded 10,000 marks. It was 18,000 marks in 1373, 19,000 in 1381 and about 20,000 by the end of the century. Lübeck was therefore importing about four times as much herring as cod. In comparison other exports were almost negligible. They included salmon, cod-liver oil, hides from Norrland and butter, which seems to have been of some account in the fifteenth century. Hides and furs appear to have constituted the bulk of the exports from Oslo and Tönsberg to Rostock.

Hanseatic imports into Norway, which were worth only half the exports, consisted mainly of rye and wheat flour, secondly malt and hops for use in brewing (many of the *Bergenfahrer* owned or rented hop-gardens in the neighbourhood of Lübeck), and lastly salt and linen. On the other hand, by an almost unique exception, the Lübeck merchants did not export Flemish cloth to Norway. Most of it was brought by ships from Kampen or, increasingly, from Holland.

During the fourteenth century the Lübeck merchants were also successful in gaining control of almost the whole of the trade between Norway and England. Some of their ships made round trips taking flour from Lübeck to Bergen, cod from Bergen to Boston and English cloth from Boston back to Lübeck.

In the second half of the fifteenth century, however, Lübeck's trade with Norway began to decline. Her merchants found it impossible to keep out the Hollanders, who were welcomed by the Norwegians because they provided an opportunity of getting rid of the economic domination of the Hansa. By 1438 there was already a company of Bergen merchants in Amsterdam.

Even more serious was the competition from Icelandic cod. At the beginning of the fifteenth century the Bergen *Kontor* was alarmed by reports of German ships trading with the Faroes, Shetlands and Orkneys. As a result the diet of 1417 forbade ships to put in at Norwegian ports which were not habitually used. In spite of this ships from Hamburg and Bremen were soon venturing as far as Iceland in the wake of the English, and the king of Norway granted them the right to sail directly to the island without calling at Bergen as had previously been obligatory. The Hamburg council encouraged these voyages by equipping in 1475 three large ships for a voyage to Iceland, an example, by the way, of the rivalries which bedevilled the Hansa and embittered relations within the community. Although Icelandic cod was coarser and less highly thought of than Norwegian cod, it was less expensive, and when a method of pounding the flesh was discovered which made it tender it became increasingly popular, especially in south Germany, and the Bergen *Kontor* for all its protests could do nothing about it.

Consequently by the beginning of the sixteenth century the prosperity of the German establishments in Norway, and of Lübeck's trade there, was seriously affected.

6. GREAT BRITAIN

The development of Hanseatic trade in England followed the opposite course from that usually taken in foreign countries. Generally the Hanseatics first established themselves in a great commercial centre and then from there went on to set up smaller centres elsewhere. In England in the thirteenth and fourteenth centuries their trading centres were very scattered and only in the fifteenth century did they become concentrated in London. The original dispersion resulted from the twofold origin of Hanseatic trade in England. To begin with, merchants from Cologne, the Meuse valley and Westphalia settled in London and made it the focus of their Rhenish trade. Then the 'Easterlings' of the Gotland Community, merchants from Hamburg, Lübeck and the Prussian towns began to arrive, and their first settlements were naturally in the east coast ports, Ipswich, Yarmouth, Lynn, Boston, Hull and Newcastle. Of all these Boston, frequented principally by the Lübeckers, was the busiest, as it was an export centre for wool and cloth, trading with the Low Countries, Hamburg, Danzig and Bergen. Up to the end of the fourteenth century the amount of English cloth exported by the Hanseatics through Boston greatly exceeded that from all the other English ports put together, including London (2,200 lengths in 1392), and this export trade flourished up to the mid-fifteenth century. Gradually, however, the Easterlings concentrated their business in the London *Kontor*. The inventory of Hanseatic goods seized in 1468 throughout England shows that two-thirds were taken from the Steelyard.

At the end of the fourteenth century a third stream of traffic, much more modest, joined those from the east and the Rhine, as the result of Hanseatic expansion along the Atlantic coasts. On their return from Bourgneuf, La Rochelle or Lisbon certain Hanseatic ships called not only at London, but also at such Channel ports as Sandwich and Southampton to sell French wine, and even went as far as Bristol.

As in Norway and Flanders the Hanseatics did not limit their trade to the ports but spread out into the interior, doing both wholesale and retail business. However there they were subject to the staple regulations if they wished to buy leather, hides or metals in addition to wool. They went chiefly to Norwich and York but also attended the fairs in Stamford, Lincoln, Westminster, Canterbury and Winchester.

Hanseatic trade in England can be studied in rather more detail than elsewhere, thanks to the Customs Accounts, but so far only the wool and cloth trades have been examined. On the basis of the two years from September 1446 to September 1448 – thought to be normal business years – Hanseatic trade has been estimated at £47,000 sterling, of which £25,900 is for exports from England and £21,100 for imports into England. This accounts for 13 per cent of England's total foreign trade, other foreigners handling 27 per cent and the English themselves 60 per cent. For the years from 1479 to 1482, when the end of the Anglo–Hanseatic war caused a boom in trade, the turnover reached £61,000 of which £32,000 represented exports. The Hanseatic share was still only 14 per cent of the total, against 19 per cent for other foreigners and 67 per cent for the English.

It is known that during this period English wool exports suffered a decline (30,000 sacks in the first half of the fourteenth century, 20,000 towards the end, 8,000 around 1450) while cloth exports rose: about 15,000 lengths in 1366, more than 40,000 in 1392–5, 53,000 in 1446–8, and finally, with certain unavoidable fluctuations on the way, 66,000 lengths in 1482. Hanseatic trade reflects this situation. Westphalian and Rhenish merchants were exporting as many as 3,500 sacks of wool in about 1340 (two-thirds of it from Boston, the remainder from London and Hull), but this traffic, nearly all of it with Flanders, fell away almost to nothing in the second half of the century.

On the other hand English cloth became an essential export commodity for the Hanseatics, both Cologners and Easterlings, and in the fifteenth century represented nearly 90 per cent of their exports from England. In the last quarter of the fourteenth century the quantity of cloth they dispatched was tripled. It varied between 6,000 and 12,000 lengths in the fifteenth century and continued to increase considerably in the sixteenth.* Their share of the total amount of cloth exported varied between 20 and 30 per cent. It was usually undyed and of medium quality. The records generally indicate the origin of Flemish cloth but rarely do so for English cloth. Most of it appears to have come from London and Colchester, some from Norwich and York. The Germans bought increasingly from rural producers, especially from Gloucestershire, where they were the best customers.†

In comparison with cloth other commodities are unimportant. Lead and tin from Cornwall, in which Tidemann Limberg was speculating in 1347, are mentioned in documents from Danzig at the end of the fifteenth century. There were also herring from Yarmouth, required mainly for Hamburg, and lamb- and rabbit-skins. Salt, wine and fruit, which are often listed among the exports, merely passed through England in transit.

Hanseatic imports into England were much more varied, but it is not possible to determine the relative importance of the principal commodities. Prussia no doubt supplied those most esteemed in England: timber and its by-products, ashes, pitch and resin; increasing quantities of grain; and copper and iron, which are mentioned from the beginning of the fourteenth century onwards. Wax was very much in demand, and the Hanseatics were occasionally accused of limiting wax imports in order to force up the price. In 1309 a complaint was made about this in which the loss suffered by the English was officially estimated at £1,000. This is an acceptable estimate of the value of the 531 hundredweights of wax which according to the Customs Accounts were imported in the mid-fifteenth century. They accounted for only 5 per cent of the total Hanseatic imports. Later figures show a notable upward trend – except during the war of 1470 – reaching 1,000 hundredweights annually from 1475 to 1479 and 2,750 from 1479 to 1483. This would indicate a value of about £5,200 and account for 18 per cent of all imports. The rise in imported wax continued during the sixteenth century, reaching a record of 8,455 hundredweights in 1528–9,‡ when it represented 25 per cent of total Hanseatic imports.

* Document No. 47.
† Document No. 40.
‡ Document No. 48.

It would be interesting to know the Hanseatic contribution to the import of wine, both French and Rhenish, but all that has so far been extracted from the Customs Accounts are the total figures for wine imports: about 6,000 tons at the beginning of the fifteenth century, more than 10,000 between 1408 and 1420, a drop to 5,000 round about 1475–80, probably as a result of the loss of Guyenne, and then a further rise. The foreigners' share in these imports dropped from about 25 per cent in mid-century to less than 15 per cent in 1480. Obviously the Hanseatics' share could not have been very large. They no doubt imported most of the Rhenish wine sold in the larger towns on the east coast and inland. There are no figures by which to estimate the proportion of Rhenish wine to French and Iberian, but there can be little doubt that it fell steadily from the beginning of the fourteenth century onwards, except perhaps just after the Hundred Years War.

As well as with England the Hansa had an appreciable trade with Scotland, and by the fourteenth century Edinburgh had established commercial relations with both Bremen and Prussia. Although ships sailing for England were often attacked by Scottish pirates, the fifteenth century saw a great increase in trade, particularly with Danzig. Edinburgh was the town most frequently visited, but German goods and agents are also found in Dunbar, Glasgow and Aberdeen. Hanseatic trade with Scotland was very similar to that with England. Cloth, wool, fox and otter pelts were bought, together with sea-salt from the Forth, in return for timber, resin, grain and iron. Rhenish wine was popular in the towns and at court. Unfortunately there are no details as to the volume of this trade, which was basically a counterpart to the activities of Scottish merchants in Prussia.

7. THE LOW COUNTRIES

Hanseatic trade with the Low Countries was centred on three very different areas: Flanders and the Bruges *Kontor* (together with Hainault and Brabant); Holland and Zeeland; and the Hansa towns of the eastern Zuiderzee.

The whole economic and political history of the Hansa in the last two centuries of the Middle Ages bears witness to the outstanding importance of Flanders. There were several reasons for this. It was from Flanders that the Hanseatics purchased the commodity most essential to their business – cloth. In addition, because of the density of their population and their industrial activities, the Low Countries absorbed large quantities of eastern products. They were undoubtedly the chief buyers of furs, grain and copper, and made substantial purchases of timber and its by-products and of wax, iron, flax, amber, wine and much else. The influx of foreign merchants – Italian, Iberian, French and English – to Bruges and later Antwerp meant that the Hanseatics could expand their business almost indefinitely. Finally the geographical position of the country made it an almost obligatory transit point for merchants from Cologne travelling to and from London, and for Easterlings travelling to and from London, Paris and the French and Iberian seaports.

It was of course in Bruges, the site of their *Kontor* and the centre of their trade, that the Hanseatics were most numerous and active from the thirteenth to the fifteenth century. Here were to be seen the merchants of the various thirds making a seasonal stay, and the agents and heads of firms who settled here for a period of years. Smaller groups were also established in the ports along the Zwijn, at Damme and especially Sluys.

It was not long before the Hanseatics spread into most of the Flemish and Brabantine towns, attracted by the development of the local weaving industry, and all attempts to prevent this dispersion by reinforcing the staple at Bruges proved unavailing. Little has survived, however, of all this activity. The towns most often visited were probably Ypres, Ghent, Aardenburg, Malines and above all Bergen-op-Zoom and Antwerp because of their fairs. Competition between Bruges and Antwerp, both anxious to become the centre of Hanseatic trade, is apparent from the early fourteenth century onwards. The Scheldt port of Antwerp was better situated than Bruges for trade between England, Cologne and Westphalia, and merchants from Dortmund were particularly in evidence. Nevertheless the supremacy of Bruges was not seriously threatened until after the mid-fifteenth century, when many merchants, following the example of other foreigners, moved their business to Antwerp. By 1500, in spite of the efforts made by the Hansa to retain the *Kontor* in Bruges, Antwerp had become the centre of Hanseatic trade in the Low Countries.

The lack of exact statistics relating to Hanseatic trade in Flanders is particularly regrettable. Walther Stein has attempted an overall estimate for 1369, based on the expenditure of the Gotland third in the Bruges *Kontor* as shown by the *schoss*, an *ad valorem* impost of 1/720 on merchandise imported and exported. According to his calculations the amount involved was 38,610 pounds groschen or 212,000 Lübeck marks, that is about 39 per cent of the trade in the port of Lübeck at the same date.

A second estimate, based on the accounts of Hildebrand Veckinchusen, alderman of the Lübeck third in 1419, amounts to 118,240 pounds groschen or 651,000 Lübeck marks for the year. In 1467, when it refused to pay the *schoss*, Cologne estimated its amount at 6,000 guilders, which would represent goods to the value of 1,440,000 guilders or 240,000 pounds groschen. Even allowing for the devaluation of the pound groschen, these figures show a considerable increase in trade. This was probably due to the fact that 1419, coming immediately after the constitutional crisis in Lübeck, must have been an exceptionally favourable year for trade, and that in 1467 the *schoss* was levied in advance on sales and purchases effected anywhere in the Low Countries, which had not previously been done.

It is equally impossible to ascertain the proportion of the trade of the principal Hansa towns with Flanders. This can only be attempted for Lübeck, thanks to the *Pfundzollbuch* of 1368. Cloth, mainly purchased in Bruges, accounted for 120,000 marks out of a total of 339,000. This means that Flanders was responsible for at least a third of the town's total imports. In Sweden and perhaps Livonia the percentage may have been even higher. The only Hanseatic area in which the Flemish trade was of no particular importance was Norway.

Cloth, the principal commodity bought by the Hanseatics in Bruges, represented more than 75 per cent of their exports from Flanders. There were innumerable varieties, classed according to provenance, quality and colour. In Flanders alone there were more than twenty-five towns from which the Germans habitually bought their cloth, and to these must be added some twenty more in Brabant and Hainault. The Hamburg merchant Vicko van Geldersen mentions in his accounts between 1367 and 1392 forty different makes. The accounts of the great treasury of the Teutonic Order at Königsberg show that around 1400 cloth came from sixteen different Flemish towns, among which Poperinghe ranked first with four different kinds, followed by Comines, Lille, Saint-Omer, Hondschoote and Ypres; from twelve Brabantine towns, among which were Malines with eight varieties and Brussels with three; from five towns in Hainault, including Maubeuge, and from three towns in Holland, Amsterdam, Leiden and Naarden. In 1469 a ship sailing from Lübeck to Reval carried 2,400 lengths of cloth, of which 360 were from Poperinghe, 300 from Aalst, 200 from Comines, 100 from Tourcoing, 300 from Naarden, 100 from Leiden and 200 from England.

Dyed cloths were the most expensive, the 'scarlet' of Ypres, Ghent,

Bruges or Malines being priced at more than four pounds groschen per length. Lighter cloths of medium quality, made in Hondschoote, Maubeuge and Comines, cost from one to three pounds. Say, a kind of fine wool serge, from Bruges was particularly sought after. Cheap cloth, costing from twelve to nineteen shillings a length, was made in several towns, but more especially in Poperinghe near Ypres, which, as far as quantity was concerned, seems to have been the Hanseatics' leading supplier.

All these cloths were of different lengths and widths (usually 30 to 45 ells long by 2 to 3 wide) and were further differentiated by the way in which they were folded and packed, a custom which gave rise to much fraudulent imitation. Cloth was sold in bales for which there was no fixed number of lengths. There were ready-made garments too, the most commonly mentioned being hose from Bruges.

One striking characteristic of the Hanseatics' buying policy in the last two centuries of the Middle Ages is their loyalty to Flemish cloth while from the fourteenth century onwards other European countries were giving preference to the Brabantine product. The chief reason for this was that their business centre was in Bruges. But differences can be noted in various areas. Flemish cloth kept its lead most successfully in Lower Saxony, Sweden and Livonia. In Prussia Brabantine cloth was more popular but did not exceed in entirely overtaking its rival, except perhaps inland at Cracow. On the other hand Cologne, the Westphalian towns and south Germany opted early on for Brabantine cloth, obviously because the source of supply was nearer to them. In the Cologne customs register of 1344 Brabantine cloth is shown clearly in the lead.

In the fifteenth century Dutch and English cloth ousted Brabantine cloth in many countries. In Cologne Brabantine cloth was relegated to second place and Flemish cloth disappeared almost entirely. In the rest of the Hanseatic orbit, however, the older cloths held their own against the newcomers, and there were even some new types of Flemish cloth. This conservatism is typical of the Hanseatics.

To facilitate their acquisition the Hanseatics, from at least the middle of the fifteenth century onwards, entered into agreements with the cloth producers of certain towns, notably Poperinghe, to take the whole of their output, to arrange for the manufacture of cloths of the kind that suited their customers and to fix the prices of these cloths, under the surveillance of a representative of the *Kontor* at Bruges. On the other hand the Hanseatics, unlike certain Italians, never attempted to become cloth producers themselves and run textile workshops in Flanders.

Probably the risk seemed to them too great, despite the advantages involved in having direct control over production.

The other articles exported by the Hanseatics were negligible in comparison with cloth. From the Low Countries there was little other than metal goods, bells, sickles and scissors, probably manufactured in Dinant and sold in Damme, the port from which the merchants of Dinant dispatched their copper and brass ware to London. Southern and oriental products, brought to Bruges by the Italians, were more varied and more important. Pride of place goes to spices, for which the Teutonic Order appears to have been a better customer than the burgesses of the cities. Mediterranean fruit and oil were almost as important, and French salt and wine, which the Hanseatics bought chiefly in France, were also obtainable in Bruges and Damme.

As far as Hanseatic imports into Flanders are concerned, it is as difficult to determine the relative importance of the various commodities as it was in the case of England. In the first half of the fourteenth century English wool headed the list of Westphalian imports. Then came furs. In times of famine, and increasingly throughout the fifteenth century, rye from Prussia was imported in considerable quantities. Rhenish wine, which was exempt from staple regulations, was sold wholesale and retail nearly everywhere by Cologne merchants. For the rest there was probably no eastern product, whether metal, linen, amber, timber or its by-products, for which one could not find a buyer in Bruges.

Hanseatic trade in the Holland–Zeeland area was markedly different from that in Flanders–Brabant. The commodities handled were much the same, for the northern Low Countries, like the southern, had been producing cloth in quantity since the mid-fourteenth century, and found themselves more and more in need of Prussian grain. But the Hanseatics encountered formidable rivals here, who competed with them on their own ground. Abandoning their usual custom elsewhere, they endeavoured to limit their purchases of Dutch cloth and even to discontinue them altogether. This meant subordinating their trade in this area to the Bruges *Kontor*, which was made responsible for its supervision.

The two principal centres of Hanseatic trade in Holland were Dordrecht and Amsterdam. The former was geographically better located than Bruges and might reasonably have expected to supplant her. Being on the Rhine, it was a natural base for traffic between Dortmund, Cologne and England, and also for small ships sailing to Flanders by way of the Zuiderzee and the Dutch canals, which took advantage of the shelter offered against pirates and other maritime risks. The town was thronged with merchants from Danzig, Thorn and Cracow bringing in timber, metals and grain. Like the citizens of Bruges, the Dordrechters were content with their role as agents and did not attempt to compete actively with the foreigners. Nevertheless from about 1400 onwards the Hansa concentrated more and more of its business in Bruges. Dordrecht lost her earlier supremacy in the field of German trade and was so short-sighted as to tighten up her staple regulations, thus putting obstacles in the way of trade between the Rhineland and England.

At the end of the fourteenth century relations with Amsterdam, a city only half the size of Dordrecht, were fostered chiefly by Hamburg. In 1369 a third of the beer exported from Hamburg, to the value of some 20,000 marks, went to Amsterdam. It was also through Hamburg that Westphalian linen and grain reached Amsterdam in exchange for salt, wine and fruit. In the fifteenth century, in spite of bitter quarrels, Hamburg merchants continued this business and began to export Dutch herring as well. But they could not deal openly in Dutch cloth, since it was obligatory to buy it only at the Bruges *Kontor*. During the same period trade with Prussia increased considerably, though it is difficult to determine how large a share Hanseatic ships and merchants had in it. Both Dutch and Hanseatic merchants brought timber and grain to Amsterdam and took back salt, herring and wine, but not cloth. As the Bruges *Kontor* declined, many Hanseatics went to Amsterdam as well as Antwerp. But there are as yet no reliable estimates of this expansion.

A third zone of Hanseatic trade with the Low Countries comprised the towns on the river Ijssel and the eastern shore of the Zuiderzee, which at various dates had been admitted to the Hansa, though not without some reservations. Their rise was due mainly to their favourable geographical position. The Ijssel gave them a route to the Rhine valley, Cologne and the Westphalian towns; on the Zuiderzee they shared in the great east-west stream of Hanseatic trade; and being in the midst of a sheep-rearing country, they became, like Holland, manufacturers of cloth, which soon became their principal export commodity.

The busiest towns in this area were Kampen and Deventer. During the fourteenth and fifteenth centuries Kampen was able to consolidate her ties with the Baltic, first formed in the thirteenth century, and from there merchants brought back grain, timber and flax. The earliest surviving record of a toll charged in the Sound, which dates from 1497, mentions the passage towards the east of 69 ships from Kampen. In 1503 48 passed through. Kampen undoubtedly inaugurated Dutch trade with the Baltic, and this helps to explain the distrust of the town which the Hansa always displayed. In addition, despite the hostility of the Wendish towns, Kampen managed to maintain her connection with Norway, taking in cloth, linen and grain. In the west the Kampen merchants traded with Holland, Zeeland, Flanders and England, and also with Bourgneuf and La Rochelle. Here they set a precedent in the development of the trade in French salt and wine which the Hanseatics were not slow to follow.

Scarcely less enterprising than the merchants of Kampen were those of Deventer, already mentioned in the customs roll of Coblenz in 1104 as herring-sellers, and fairly numerous in Norway in the fifteenth century. Their business activities in the Rhine valley appear to have been curtailed and indeed almost eliminated by Cologne. But Deventer found compensation in the development of its fair, which in the fourteenth century eclipsed those of the neighbouring towns and reached its apogee at the end of the fifteenth. Except for the one at Skania this was the only fair held in the Hanseatic zone. It took place five times a year and was mainly frequented by dealers from Holland, the Rhineland and Westphalia. The Hollanders came to sell cloth and buy timber from the neighbouring forests. The other merchants brought wine and metal goods which they exchanged for herring and the products of stock-rearing. There are no exact statistics for the volume of business done, but this regional fair undoubtedly contributed greatly to the prosperity of the neighbouring towns.

8. FRANCE, CASTILE, PORTUGAL

By the end of the thirteenth century Hanseatic merchants were already trading in France. Ships from Hamburg were sailing from Bruges to La Rochelle, and Lübeck merchants from Flanders were attending the fairs in Champagne, as were the merchants of Cologne. But this activity was intermittent. It was only in the second half of the fourteenth century that Hanseatic trade became established on the coasts of Poitou and Gascony and merchants sailed there regularly from both North Sea and Baltic ports. Later there were sometimes more than 100 Hanseatic vessels making the journey to the Bay of Bourgneuf, Brouage, La Rochelle and Bordeaux.

The basic cause of this expansion was the increased demand for salt in eastern Europe, which the salt-works of Lüneburg were not able to satisfy, and in spite of the amounts imported by the Flemings the markets of the Low Countries too were unable to supply enough of this precious commodity. French salt, bought on the spot, was cheaper – in normal times a third cheaper – than rock-salt. The Livonian and Prussian towns, too, were not sorry to see the end of Lübeck's monopoly of the salt trade. Further encouragement to expansion was given by the fact that Hanseatic ships, forbidden to navigate the northern seas during the winter, might sail beyond the Pas-de-Calais. They therefore arrived in Bruges at the end of the autumn, sailed on to Bourgneuf, stayed there during January and February, and returned to the Baltic between May and July.

The period of the Hundred Years War was not favourable to sea travel in these latitudes. Hanseatic ships were periodically attacked by English, Norman or Breton pirates, on the pretext that they were allied with the enemy – or even on no pretext at all. The kings of France, however, extended a warm welcome to the new arrivals, partly through commercial self-interest, but also in the hope of gaining new allies against the English. Charles V was the first to grant them his protection. Though his orders were not always obeyed, he forbade French raiders to attack them. In 1378 he even paid them an indemnity for the capture of twenty-three ships by the Normans. Chales VI and his successors were equally benevolent. Nor were the dukes of Brittany, within whose borders Bourgneuf lay, less forthcoming. In 1430 Jean V granted the Hanseatics their first charter, a guarantee of safe-conduct and protection, and later other privileges were granted and confirmed.

It was the Bay of Bourgneuf with its salt pits which constituted the chief centre of attraction for the Hanseatics. They called it simply 'the Bay' (*die Baie*) and the salt which they came to collect they called *Baiensolt*, to distinguish it from the *Travesolt* of Lüneburg and Oldesloe. This name was later applied to all French salt, to that from Brouage, for example, or even to that from Portugal. The salt trade of Bourgneuf was not of very ancient date. The little port was first visited by Flemish ships in the thirteenth century. After them came ships from Kampen. In the fourteenth century the English, Spaniards and Hollanders, as well as the Germans, came in great numbers. Among the Germans, the Hamburgers were the first to arrive, but it was not long before Prussian and Livonian ships became the most numerous. The Wendish towns and even Lübeck, in spite of its monopoly of Lüneburg salt, were also active. In 1438 a Hanseatic fleet in the Bay comprised eleven Wendish ships and twenty-three Prussian and Livonian vessels. In another fleet of fifty vessels, captured by the English in 1449, there were sixteen from Lübeck, two from Wismar and fourteen from Danzig. There were not enough Hanseatic ships to cope with the demand, and Dutch ships, first chartered by German merchants but later working on their own account, became a common sight in Bourgneuf, carrying much of their cargo to the Baltic.

There are no overall figures for the quantity of salt exported from Bourgneuf to Hanseatic ports, but the number of 'Bay ships' mentioned as entering various Baltic ports show how enormous it was. Out of 314 ships which entered Reval between 1427 and 1433, 105 had come from the Bay, as against 103 from Lübeck and 85 from Prussia. Every year they brought in about 2,500 lasts of salt (5,000 tons), while salt from other sources, including Lüneburg, amounted to no more than 500 lasts. Out of 403 ships entering Danzig in 1474, 71 came from the Bay and 2 from Brouage. In both Reval and Danzig Dutch ships formed the greater part of the salt fleets.

The purchase of salt in Bourgneuf was carried out by the ships' captains or by agents either living there permanently or sent from the Bruges *Kontor* for the season. These agents, who became more necessary as the trade increased, caused a rise in the price of salt, which they often bought from its producers on credit. When the influx of merchants made Bourgneuf a busy trading centre, the Hanseatics were able to buy other commodities there, among them wine from the Loire and Poitou, canvas for making sails, and spices brought in by the Spaniards. In exchange they sold their grain, herring and furs. However Bourgneuf offered only limited opportunities for business, and in the fifteenth century the Hanseatic agents preferred Nantes, a much larger market, where the business they did in 1456 brought a protest from the merchants in the Bruges *Kontor* about the massive consignments of furs dispatched to Nantes and La Rochelle, which in their opinion constituted a violation of the Bruges staple. There is, however, no further information about this Hanseatic factory in Nantes.

The demand for salt led the Hanseatics further afield to the Brouage district, opposite the island of Oléron. They may even have visited it first, for the salt pits there seem to have been exploited earlier than those at Bourgneuf, but it was not until 1450 that Brouage became as important as Bourgneuf, no doubt because of its nearness to La Rochelle. In some years – 1475 and 1476, for example – more ships sailed to Danzig from Brouage than from Bourgneuf. Bourgneuf, however, retained its lead up to the end of the Middle Ages. It was only in the sixteenth century that salt from Brouage finally dominated the market.

After salt, the principal commodity purchased by the Hanseatics in these regions was wine, which they bought in Bourgneuf, Nantes and Brouage, and above all in La Rochelle, the great export centre for wines from Poitou. In the fifteenth century they came to La Rochelle in increasing numbers, and in the privileges granted to them by the kings of France it is listed as the main centre of their business. While there they bought fruit, spices and canvas, and in 1419 the extent of their competition provoked dispute with the Spaniards. There are no figures to show how much wine they took with them from La Rochelle, but there are references to Prussian ships carrying up to 300 tons.

Hanseatic merchants also visited Bordeaux, though less regularly. In the early years of the fourteenth century a Cologne merchant sent 108 tons of wine from Bordeaux to Holland. Hanseatic trade flourished in the second half of the fifteenth century, when the merchants tried to take advantage of the loss of Guyenne by the English to usurp their place in the wine trade between Bordeaux and England. Even from La Rochelle and Bourgneuf their trade with England improved. A charter granted by the duke of Brittany in 1459 mentions 'Germans who often travel to England to trade and also come to Brittany'. But the English reacted vigorously to this competition. In 1490 the English Parliament declared that wine from La Rochelle and Bordeaux must be imported only in English ships. This measure was probably acted on at once, for a year later German merchants in Antwerp were protesting to the *Kontor* that the English were reserving to themselves the exclusive right to import Bordeaux wine into their country, as well as complaining of English competition in the trade in cloth and raw silk. For the Hanseatics were buying in Bordeaux, and even more in Bayonne, raw and woven silk and dyed Languedoc cloth. The English appear to have been successful in recapturing most of the import trade in wine, but even as late as the sixteenth century some Hanseatic ships were still regularly engaged in it. There is no way of knowing how much of the French wine carried by German ships found its way to England, or of determining the relative importance of French and Rhenish wines in Hanseatic trade as a whole. The Hanseatics seldom visited the other French coastal districts, least of all the Channel ports, which offered nothing of interest to them in the way of trade. In the fifteenth century they are occasionally found in the estuary of the Seine, at Honfleur and Harfleur, which in German texts become *Honychflor* ('Honey flower') and *Heringsfleete* ('Herring fleet')! In 1450 there is mention of a whole fleet of Hanseatic ships in Rouen, bringing grain and herring, and buying nothing but wine. The Cologne merchants appear to have been most active in this area. On several occasions Cologne asked Rouen to protect her merchants and to compensate the victims of Norman pirates. But very little came of these contacts.

There is no doubt that the Hanseatic overland trade in northern France increased in the fourteenth and fifteenth centuries. As the Champagne fairs declined, Paris became the centre of attraction for the north Germans, who came there from Bruges. In the early 1440s representatives of the Teutonic Order went there regularly to collect money owed to the Order. A big purchase of furs made in Prussia by the Parisian financier Dine Raponde and paid for by a bill of exchange was denounced in 1405 by the Bruges *Kontor* as an encroachment on its privileges. It was probably through Bruges that the 'French napery' destined for the table of the Grand Master travelled on its way from Paris.

Of greater importance was the trade between Paris and Cologne. It was not eastern merchandise that the Cologne merchants brought to the French capital but the products of their own industries: leather goods, jewellery, steel and above all metal goods, weapons and tools. In 1471 a stock of 600 Cologne sickles is mentioned. It is less clear what Paris exported to Cologne, but it was probably silks and fabrics. A similar trade may have been carried on between Cologne and Dijon, but there is no information about this, and wine from Burgundy is never mentioned in north Germany.

In their seaborne progress southwards the Hanseatics did not confine themselves to the French ports but from the end of the fourteenth century onwards made fairly regular calls along the coasts of the Asturias and especially Portugal, retracing a route already taken by German ships at the time of the second and third crusades and occasionally in the thirteenth century also.

It was once again the demand for salt which led to the establishment of regular contacts with Lisbon. The salt pits of Setúbal yielded abundant supplies of salt, of a slightly better quality than that of Bourgneuf. In the fifteenth century ships from Prussia and Kampen were the most frequently found. Vessels sailing for Lisbon left the Baltic in convoy with the Bay fleet but parted company when they were off La Rochelle and then stood out to the south-west. There was a small colony of Hanseatics in Lisbon in the mid-fifteenth century and in 1456 Alfonso V granted it the right to be governed by two German 'procurators' instead of two Portuguese. At the beginning of the sixteenth century south Germans visited the town more often, attracted by the great spice market. Hanseatic trade in Lisbon followed the same pattern as in Bourgneuf. The Germans sold grain and fish, and in addition to salt bought local wines, from 'Romania' and Malaga and Malmsey, and oil, spices, figs, grapes and sugar. A large Prussian ship coming from Portugal which was seized by the English in 1402 contained 180 tons of salt and about 50 hectolitres of wine. But the importance of Hanseatic trade in Portugal must not be exaggerated, for between 1460 and 1500 only one ship is known to have sailed from Lisbon to Danzig. It is probable that many others, entered as Bay ships, really came from Portugal. But, at least in the fifteenth century, Iberian salt represented only a very modest proportion of the total quantity of the commodity which came into the Baltic from the Atlantic ports.

It is not easy to discover the details of Hanseatic trade with Spanish ports. In 1419 a Prussian ship was in Seville, loading oil and wine, but German ships usually called at the Asturian ports, Berméo, Vivero, Laredo and probably Corunna (for pilgrims to the shrine of St James of Compostella), where they sold grain and herring and bought iron, wool, wine and fruit. A violent conflict between the Hansa and Castile, which lasted for nearly twenty-five years, shows that this trade, about which so little is known, was by no means negligible. In 1419 John II of Castile, annoyed by the competition offered to his subjects by German merchants who were selling in La Rochelle goods bought in Spain, decided to resort to force. On the pretext that the Hanseatics had aided the English when they were besieged in Harfleur by a Franco-Spanish fleet, he ordered an attack upon the Bay fleet, composed of German and Flemish vessels, just off La Rochelle. Forty vessels were captured and their cargoes sold. Hostilities in the interminable war which followed were confined to privateering. After ten years the Flemings made peace and the Hansa carried on alone. In 1433 the Hanseatics were forbidden to import Spanish wool into Bruges or Germany. This was intended not so much to intimidate the Spaniards as to force the Flemings to offer their good offices for a reconciliation of the opposing parties. A three-year truce, later renewed, was in fact negotiated at Bourgneuf and finally concluded at Bruges in 1443. The Hanseatics agreed to stop competing with the Spaniards, either in Spanish ports or in La Rochelle. They also agreed that Kampen, which had been admitted into the community only two years before and against which the Spaniards had a particular grievance, should be excluded from the truce.* These somewhat humiliating conditions can be explained by the Hanseatics' desire to re-establish security of trade in the Bay of Biscay, and to call a halt to a seemingly endless war which was being waged unusually far from their home bases. Trade with Castilian ports was in fact resumed, but there was very little expansion until the sixteenth century.

<h2 style="text-align:center">9 . ITALY AND CATALONIA</h2>

The importance of the trade between Italians and Germans at Bruges naturally induced the Hanseatics to venture into Italy. As in south Germany, it was mostly merchants from Lübeck and Cologne, and occasionally from Breslau, who went there in the fourteenth and fifteenth centuries. Business was apparently carried on mostly by land routes, via Nürnberg, Augsburg and the Brenner Pass to Venice, and via Frankfurt, Constance and the St Gotthard Pass to Milan and Genoa. But the sea route was also used, though by way of Bruges, for up to the sixteenth century Hanseatic ships were never found in the Mediterranean, nor did Genoese and Venetian vessels call at German ports.

In Venice merchants from Cologne and Lübeck had their own rooms in the *Fondaco dei Tedeschi*. Lübeck trade is known principally through the transactions of the Veckinchusens in the early part of the fifteenth century. The chief commodity sold by the Germans was always Russian furs.† In 1447 Bruges complained that 'for several years' Lübeck had been violating her rights as a staple-market by sending furs to Venice and Genoa. In her reply Lübeck admitted the truth of the allegation as far as Venice and Frankfurt were concerned, but denied it in respect of Genoa. In addition to furs Lübeck merchants took to Venice amber jewellery, which was highly esteemed, possibly some Westphalian cloth (which is mentioned even in Alexandria) and dried fish. They brought back spices, silks and Mediterranean fruits. Although Lübeckers are still to be found in the *Fondaco* at the end of the fifteenth century, they were already being supplanted by the south Germans, who in future were to handle all the trade between Venice and Lübeck.

Cologne merchants had been trading in Venice still earlier, and stayed there longer. As early as 1335 dues were being levied on goods from Cologne, in retaliation for losses sustained by Venetians trading in Ger-

* Document No. 11.
† Document No. 37.

many and Flanders. Among the commodities from Cologne gold-leaf and jewellery were apparently important. Forty years later Cologne told Venice that she was anxious to exercise strict control over these articles and was therefore sending a sample of her hallmark. In the fifteenth century cloth was also dispatched in great quantities. Venice erroneously suspected that this was harming her own merchants and levied a tax on all cloth imported by land. A delegation was then sent from Cologne, which advanced the argument that trade by land was more costly and more perilous than by sea, and that no other German town was bringing so much English cloth into Venice. The results of this representation are not known.

Cologne merchants were even more active in Como, Milan and Genoa (in the mid-fifteenth century Johann van Stralen, one of the richest Cologne merchants of the period, was in Genoa with a consignment of furs), but their business connections extended throughout the peninsula. Agents of Alf van der Burg are recorded in Messina, and those of Gerhard van Hilden in Catania, where they sold furs, metal goods, and linen from Constance, buying in exchange cotton, silk, spices, luxury articles, jewellery and silk fabrics.

In addition Cologne merchants penetrated into Catalonia and Aragon, where they bought saffron. Like the merchants of the Great Trading Company of Ravensburg, they probably travelled either by sea via Genoa or by land via the Rhône valley and Roussillon. In 1430 a certain Johann de Colunya settled in Barcelona in partnership with a Catalan; he bought saffron to the value of more than £2,200, selling other goods, including linen and metal work, to the value of £1,200. Thirty years later similar operations were carried out by the Stralens and Alf van der Burg. Unfortunately the information available is so fragmentary that no clear picture emerges of the trade carried on by Cologne merchants in Italy and Spain; in any case only the place of origin of the merchants engaged in it justifies our labelling it Hanseatic.

CHAPTER ELEVEN

Hanseatic Civilisation

(13th–16th century)

THE term 'Hanseatic civilisation' can only be used with certain reservations. The Hansa, a society of merchants, was not concerned with cultural activities, and none of its many different statutes and ordinances betrays any interest in them. It was not through its members that the noteworthy intellectual and artistic achievements of northern Germany took place. Even if the citizenry by reason of its inclinations and wealth sometimes fulfilled the function of a Maecenas, there can be no doubt that in this respect the Church and the nobility were more important. Furthermore such cultural activity as can be called north European was not limited to the Hansa towns but included the Low Countries, whose influence was considerable, and Scandinavia.

Nevertheless the Hansa played an important part in the formation and propagation of the cultural unity of northern Europe. Her ships carried intellectual and artistic ideas as well as merchandise. The new towns founded on the shores of the Baltic were Hanseatic in the style of their buildings as well as in their citizens' way of life. Various cultural trends are plainly connected with the rise and decline of the Hansa. Consequently the civilisation of the countries surrounding the Baltic and the North Sea from the early fourteenth to the beginning of the sixteenth century deserves to be called Hanseatic.

I. THE LOW GERMAN LANGUAGE

The cultural unity of the Hanseatic zone is most clearly seen in its linguistic unity. It coincides almost exactly with the region in which Low German was spoken at the beginning of the twentieth century. Low German escaped the second consonantal shift which at the beginning of the Middle Ages affected the High German dialects and partially also Central German. The southern limit of Low German corresponds exactly with the present borderline between *Dorp–Dorf* and *ik–ich*, running south of Cologne, Westphalia, Magdeburg and Frankfurt-on-the-Oder.

The Low Saxon dialects spoken between the Rhine and the Elbe constituted in the main the language of the Hanseatic world. They spread west to the Zuiderzee and north to Schleswig. Colonisation carried them eastward to the Baltic towns as far as Narva, and for a time into Polish, Danish and Swedish towns.

However there were two regions where Low German failed to establish itself. One was the Prussian towns, especially Thorn and Culm, where the numerous immigrants from central Germany brought with them a Central German dialect. The Teutonic Order, which recruited its members mainly from south and central Germany, also used this dialect in both its administration and its external communications. In the west the Rhenish–Franconian dialect, closer to Central German in some of its consonantal mutations, held its own in the Rhineland. It is significant that when the first translation of the Bible into Low German, formerly attributed to Quentell, was printed at Cologne in 1479, it was considered necessary to present two parallel versions, one in Rhenish–Franconian and the other in Low Saxon.

The diversity of dialects, even in neighbouring districts, was undoubtedly a handicap in relationships between the Hansa towns. Some attempts were made to establish linguistic uniformity, especially in law courts and chancelleries in which Lübeck, because of its power and influence, played a leading part. The need for a common language led to the adoption of the Lübeck dialect in all law courts using Lübeck law, from Holstein to Estonia. The Magdeburg law, widely adopted in the east, favoured the spread of the Magdeburg dialect into Brandenburg and West Prussia. The Lübeck dialect gained even more general acceptance as the language of diplomacy. Up to the mid-fourteenth century the *Rezesse* of the Hanseatic diets were written in Latin. From 1369 onwards they were written in Low German, and the Lübeck chancellery got its usage adopted both in the correspondence with the *Kontore* and in dealings with the Scandinavian rulers and the Flemish towns. There was, however, some resistance to this supremacy. The chancelleries of the Teutonic Order and of Cologne kept to their own languages. But for 150 years the dialect of Lübeck was the official written language of the Hansa, predominant in law, diplomacy and commerce.

Abroad, notably in Scandinavia, the Low German spoken by German communities in a number of towns exercised a profound influence on the national languages. It has been estimated that a third of the words in Swedish are of Hanseatic origin, the borrowings being particularly numerous in the vocabularies of handicrafts, mining and business. Even syntax was sometimes modified: with certain verbs, ancient prefixes which had fallen into disuse reappear in Swedish.

However the predominance of Low German was of short duration. Its southern border was continually being pushed back towards the north, and by the end of the fifteenth century and especially during the sixteenth and seventeenth centuries High German made inroads everywhere, reducing Low German to the language of the lower classes. There were many and various reasons for this decline. The commercial preponderance of the south Germans favoured the diffusion of their language in the Hanseatic zone, as did the efforts of Maximilian I and Charles V to reform and centralise imperial administration. By the beginning of the sixteenth century letters from Lübeck to the supreme imperial court and in general to all south German towns were being written in High German. Humanism also weakened Low German by restoring Latin to its former eminence as the language of instruction and literature. The diffusion of printed matter had the same effect. Although printing encouraged the production of numerous translations into local dialects, it strengthened even more the supremacy of High German. But the latter made its way principally as the language of the Church. From 1520–30 onwards it was being used in the pastoral letters of the Protestant ecclesiastical authorities. Even though there were no fewer than twenty-four Low German editions of Luther's Bible between 1522 and 1621, ministers from the seventeenth century onwards usually preached in High German. Indeed High German, adopted by the intelligentsia, graduate councillors and the secretaries of the chancelleries, became the official language even of Lübeck. From 1591 onwards it was used for entries in the protocols of the register of debts (*Niederstadtbuch*) and from 1617 for those in the land-register (*Oberstadtbuch*). It was even used after 1634 for official public readings of the police regulations (*Bursprake*). It is evident that by now High German was understood by everyone. It may even have been used in some family circles, for the diary of a Bremen councillor at the end of the sixteenth century was written in High German. There is an interesting parallel between the rise and fall of the Hansa and that of Low German.

2. LITERATURE, UNIVERSITIES

During the Middle Ages north Germany produced no genuinely original literary work. Writers were content to translate and adapt foreign works, mainly French, which in the fourteenth century reached them through the intermediary either of the Low Countries or of south Germany. North Germany, therefore, if it is mentioned at all, occupies only a small space in the standard histories of German literature.

This dearth of literary works can be explained partly by the fact that Low German never attained the eminence of a genuinely literary language. It is significant that the first of the Minnesingers, Heinrich von Veldeke, a native of the lower Rhineland, chose to write his *Eneide* ('Aeneid') (1189) in High German, though he betrays his origin by the use of certain Low German phrases. Other Minnesingers, as well as the poet Heinrich von Halberstadt, did the same in the thirteenth century. No doubt they were anxious for their works to be understood in the brilliant courts of south Germany. Later on, examples of this sort became rarer, but the opinion persisted that High German was the poetic language *par excellence*.

Epic and courtly poetry was aimed mainly at an aristocratic audience. With the exception of the episcopal cities of Lower Saxony, where Latin poetry flourished, the principal literary centres were the princely courts, among them the ducal court at Brunswick at the beginning of the thirteenth century, and later the courts of the margrave of Brandenburg and the Grand Master of the Teutonic Order. But the towns too, after some delay, were infected by the enthusiasm for chivalrous literature. The patrician associations in particular, eager to ape the nobility, were active in the dissemination of adaptations of great foreign masterpieces. The Bruges *Kontor* appears to have played a leading part in this: there is evidence that during the fifteenth century French and Flemish poems were being copied and translated there. These cultural links were responsible for that masterpiece of Low German poetry *Reynke de Vos* ('Reynard the Fox'), translated by a Lübeck cleric from a Flemish adaptation of the French *Renart*. Printed in Lübeck in 1498, this had an immense success throughout Germany and Scandinavia. It was translated into High German early in the sixteenth century, and inspired many other animal satires of the same kind.

There is plenty of evidence to show that chivalrous literature was highly esteemed in the Hansa towns. The popularity of the Nine Worthies, those oddly assorted legendary and historic heroes taken from ancient and medieval times and the Old Tetament, is particularly surprising. Their statues adorned the great hall (*Hansasaal*) of the townhalls of Cologne, Osnabrück and Lüneburg, as well as a fountain in Hildesheim and the assembly-hall of the *Artushof* in Danzig. No less remarkable was the success of the 'Courts of Arthur'. The fashion of invoking the protection of the legendary king for associations inspired by the chivalric ideals and of giving his name to their meeting places came originally from England. It was adopted in Flanders and later in Germany by various patrician groups. It was most prevalent in the Prussian towns, probably because of the close ties between the Teutonic Order and England. From the early fourteenth century onwards *Artushöfe* are found in Elbing, Danzig, Riga and Stralsund. Other patrician associations, notably those at Dortmund and Danzig, chose as their patron Renaud of Montauban (Reinhold), one of the four sons of Aymon. The popularity of the epic legends also explains why the huge statues in such towns as Bremen, Riga and Halle which originally symbolised judicial privilege or economic franchise came to be called Roland. Roland, Arthur, the Round Table and the Holy Grail were essential elements in the jousts and tourneys organised by the towns in imitation of the nobility.* In the fifteenth century many citizens were baptised with the names of the heroes of chivalry: Gunther, Rüdiger, Roland, Paris, Alexander, and so on. One burgomaster of Lübeck, Johann Roseke, took Perseval (Parsifal) as his family name.

It is hardly to be wondered at that none of the Low German poets found inspiration in the history of the Hansa. There is no counterpart to the Middle High German 'Good Gerard' by Rudolf of Ems, who made a Cologne merchant his hero. In the eyes of the nobility, the Church and the people the merchant, who was always suspected of making illicit profits, was too disreputable a person for heroic and virtuous deeds to be ascribed to him. No one thought his adventurous life, beset with perils as it was, worth celebrating in epic verse. The most one finds is a moralising ballad on the tragic fate of the pirate Störtebeker and much later, in 1618, the learned lament in High German to which the syndic Johann Doman was inspired by the irremediable decline of the Hansa.

Other forms of literature were preferred in the Hansa towns,

* Document No. 16.

especially popular plays and historical chronicles. At the beginning of the fifteenth century when, as a result of troubles in Lübeck, certain members of the council went into exile, they had an opportunity to see the mystery plays already popular in south Germany. On their return home, the Circle Society decided to elect two members each year charged with the composition or commissioning of plays, and two other members responsible for presenting them on a mobile stage. Only the titles of these plays are known. Some were Christian mystery plays, others adaptations of Germanic legends (*Frau Kriemhilt*), French cycles (*Arthur*) or mythological stories (*The Judgement of Paris*). Similar undertakings in other towns show how successful these performances were, often because they embodied satirical features.

Far more historical works have been preserved. Most of the Hansa towns had their chroniclers, writing first in Latin and then in Low German. The earliest Low German work is the 'Saxon World Chronicle' (*Sächsische Weltchronik*), written in Magdeburg around 1230 and introduced by Eike von Repgow, who about eight years before had written the famous law code known as the *Sachsenspiegel* in the Eastphalian dialect. Lübeck has a remarkable series of chronicles, mostly written by clerics. The earliest is the *Chronica Slavorum* by Helmold, priest of Bosau (Holstein), which was written between 1168 and 1172 and contains a valuable account of the founding of Lübeck. It was continued up to 1309 by Arnold, abbot of St John in Lübeck. It was not a town chronicle, the author being particularly anxious to glorify the missionary work of the Guelph dynasty. At the end of the fourteenth century Detmar, a Franciscan lector, wrote a chronicle of Lübeck in Low German, a supplement to the work of a layman, the town clerk Johann Rode, which was continued in the fifteenth century by three more secretaries. Some time after 1420 Hermann Korner wrote, in Latin and German, a 'new chronicle', conceived as a universal history. In the mid-sixteenth century the Protestant clergyman Reimar Kock wrote a colourful account of the events of the last hundred years. The history of Lübeck is thus fully documented for the first four hundred years of its existence.

As the Middle Ages drew to a close intellectual life was stimulated by the foundation of universities and the spread of printing. The University of Cologne, the oldest in northern Germany, founded in 1389, was more Rhenish than Hanseatic. Not many students from the seaports went there, preferring the University of Erfurt, as did two future burgomasters, Hinrich Rubenow of Greifswald and Hinrich Murmester of Hamburg.

On the shores of the Baltic, Lübeck, in spite of its widespread cultural influence, never had a university. It lacked the essential patronage of a prince. But in 1419 Rostock, with the help of the duke of Mecklenburg, founded the first seat of higher learning which can properly be called Hanseatic. It was frequented by students from the Low Countries and the Baltic region, as well as by Scandinavians who founded a fraternity there under the patronage of St Olaf (*Olavsburse*). Things did not go smoothly at first. Because of internal disorders Rostock came under the interdict of the Council of Basle and in 1432 under the ban of the Empire decreed by the Emperor Sigismund. The university moved to Greifswald, where some teachers remained after the conflict ended. Greifswald and the duke of Pomerania took advantage of the situation to obtain a new charter from the pope (1456). The University of Greifswald drews its pupils from a more restricted area than that of Rostock. A fairly large number came from Scandinavia, but hardly any from the western Hansa towns.

During the late fifteenth century the art of printing spread rapidly in north Germany. A printing-press was set up in Cologne in 1464, in Lübeck in 1475, in Rostock in 1476, in Magdeburg in 1480, in Hamburg in 1491, in Danzig in 1498, and in Königsberg as late as 1524. Although the Cologne press was first in the field in north Germany, its books were not as much in demand as might have been expected. Most of them were in Latin, to meet the needs of the university, and later on, the book market in Protestant towns was closed to Cologne, which remained Catholic. Once more Lübeck played the leading role in the Hanseatic world. The first of its six printers of *incunabula*, Lucas Brandis, came from Merseburg in Upper Saxony. Already the second of these printers made an attempt to spread the new invention throughout the northern countries, in Odense in Denmark, and in Stockholm (1483). Another, Bartholomew Ghotan, visited Sweden three times, then Finland and eventually Russia. There he met a violent death while trying to introduce the new invention. It was also in Lübeck that the best Low German version of the Bible before that of Luther's translation was published.

After Lübeck the most active centre of printing was Rostock, where the Brethren of the Common Life installed a press in their monastery (1476). Being a university town, Rostock specialised in humanist works in Latin and German. The visit of Ulrich von Hutten in 1509 encouraged the translation of Flemish and High German poems, among them Sebastian Brant's 'Ship of Fools'.

Thus in the intellectual history of the late Middle Ages Lübeck and the Hansa both played an important role in disseminating throughout the northern world different language forms, literary and learned works, and new techniques. They acted mainly as intermediaries, but their role was by no means negligible.

3. THE URBAN PANORAMA

Numerous north German towns still displayed at the beginning of this century an architectural homogeneity recalling their Hanseatic past. Many had ceased to expand at an early date – in the fifteenth century in Westphalia and Saxony, in the seventeenth century in the east – and consequently were not disfigured by tasteless nineteenth-century buildings. But the Second World War brought destruction on a large scale, and altered for ever the face of these historic cities. In particular the annihilation of the incomparable panorama of Hildesheim is to be deplored.

By their architecture Hansa towns fall into two groups, clearly differentiated by the building material used, which was either stone or brick. Stone was used in the area running from Cologne to Magdeburg, including nearly all the Westphalian and Saxon cities. Brick, on the other hand, was predominant in the maritime regions, from Bremen to Riga, along the lower Elbe (Lüneburg, Stendal), in Brandenburg and in Silesia. Brick buildings, of an impressive, unadorned, austere character, can be considered typical of the Hansa, which took over this form of architecture from the Low Countries, adapted it and passed it on to the countries of northern and eastern Europe. The contrast in building material is accentuated by the contrast between the original German territories to the west of the Elbe and the colonised territories to the east. In the west the Romanesque churches of Cologne and Lower Saxony, the basilicas of Hildesheim and the imperial palace at Goslar belong to the pre-Hanseatic period and give the towns in this area a character which more recent buildings have not destroyed. To the east, however, nearly all the architectural monuments are in the Gothic style, which flourished in these regions between the mid-thirteenth and mid-sixteenth century, coinciding with the great period of the Hansa.

In the typical Hansa town, with its more or less regular checker-board pattern, the townhall was the most important public building. Built on one side of the rectangular market square, next to the parish church, it was at first a modest edifice, combined with the drapers' hall. As the city expanded, it increased in size and splendour and finally was used only as the administrative centre. Except in the towns of the Teutonic Order, most of these townhalls were like that of Bruges, without a belfry.

In the region where stone was used, the oldest townhall to survive is that of Dortmund, built in about 1240. The ground floor served as a cloth-hall, the cellar as a wine depot, and the first floor as a council chamber. The most splendid townhalls are those of Münster, with its richly decorated stepped gable, and Brunswick, of which one wing dates from the end of the thirteenth century, the other from the end of the fourteenth century, with exuberant tracery along the arcades of the upper storey.

In the region where brick was used, the townhall of Lübeck, con-tinually enlarged over two hundred years, served as a model for that of many other cities. In about 1220 there were two modest buildings, one serving as cloth-hall (*Gewandhaus*) and the other as an assembly-hall. In the second half of the thirteenth century they were joined by two trans-verse façades, first on the side facing the market square, then on the side opposite the Church of St Mary. At the beginning of the fourteenth century a new wing was built on the east side of the market square con-taining the weighing-room and the banqueting hall, and this was further enlarged in the mid-fifteenth century.

In Lübeck and elsewhere builders soon learned to use brick, which is unsuitable for sculptural decoration, to the best advantage by adding blind façades which concealed even the roofs of the buildings behind. The plain surfaces were broken up by delicate conical colonnettes, by gables, and above all by apertures, either blind or open-work, in the form of rectangular or rose-windows, to which the masons devoted their finest chiselling. This technique achieved its most successful fusion of decora-tive richness and delicacy in the fourteenth-century townhall at Stral-sund.

Further to the east we meet another type of townhall, of which the most characteristic example is at Thorn. This vast, square fourteenth-century building with its interior courtyard is more akin to a fortress of the Teutonic Order or to an Italian *Fondaco* than to a communal building. It is surmounted by a belfry, like the townhalls in Breslau, Danzig and Reval, perhaps because in this area the townhall functioned for longer as a warehouse and commercial centre. Up to the sixteenth century not only the merchants but also the craftsmen, butchers and bakers of Thorn displayed their wares in the townhall.

In addition to townhalls, a few public buildings erected by municipalities from the fourteenth century onwards still survive, among them the cloth-hall and the weigh-house in Brunswick, the latter a fine half-timbered building dating from 1534, the herring-house in Lüneburg, the granaries in Lübeck and Danzig, and so on. In Cologne, when the great state-room of the townhall (the *Hansasaal*, where perhaps the Confederation of 1367 was sealed) was deemed inadequate, the municipality erected in 1441 a building specially designed for festivities, the *Gürzenich*, whose ballroom, 55 metres by 22, was the largest in Germany. In every Hansa town the merchant and craft guilds took pride in providing for their meetings stately edifices like the so-called Templars' House of the fourteenth–fifteenth century and the Butchers' Guildhouse (1529) in Hildesheim, both now destroyed, the *Artushof* in Danzig (1477), the house of the Skippers' Association in Lübeck, both still much as they were originally, and the house of the 'Great Guild' at Reval.

In the mid-sixteenth century Renaissance art, introduced by Dutch architects, spread throughout northern Germany. But its development ended abruptly with the Thirty Years War, and it produced only a few civic buildings of significance. Among them are the *Fürstenhof* at Wismar, a charming Italian palace cast up on the Baltic coast – but which has nothing municipal about it – and the townhall at Emden, witness to the little town's brief period of prosperity – though Emden was never a Hansa town. Otherwise the new style is seen only in alterations and additions to public buildings, such as the ornamental loggias of the townhalls at Lübeck and Cologne (late sixteenth century) or the façade built onto the Gothic townhall in Bremen (early seventeenth century).

In addition to its civic buildings the Hansa town was distinguished by the development, especially from the fifteenth century onwards, of its fortifications, intended to defend it against the threatening designs of the princes. The oldest and best-preserved is the wall of Visby, more than 3,000 metres long and still equipped with thirty-eight towers. In Germany the gates were often simple openings cut in a tower, but sometimes their size and decoration raised them to the level of monumental works of art. Such is the famous *Holstentor* in Lübeck (1447). In the territories of the Teutonic Order the military character was even more pronounced, each town being protected and controlled by a powerful castle of the Order, as at Königsberg and Reval.

If the civic buildings and fortifications are especially characteristic of a Hansa town, it goes without saying that as throughout medieval Europe, the most imposing public buildings are the churches, which impress their own character upon the town.

From this point of view the urban landscape of northern Europe is very different from that of other regions. With a few exceptions – such as Cologne and Magdeburg – there are no immense cathedrals, dwarfing the other churches in the town by their size and the splendour of their decoration. The primacy of the episcopal church was not symbolised in its architecture. Many of the most important Hansa towns – Dortmund, Brunswick, Rostock, Danzig – were not episcopal sees; but even in Lübeck the cathedral was inferior both in size and in prestige to the merchants' Church of St Mary, which was the most representative religious building in the city. Even as early as the Romanesque period, in the little episcopal cities of Lower Saxony and Westphalia such as Hildesheim, Münster and Osnabrück the cathedral was no more splendid than the other churches.

In the Hanseatic zone Gothic architecture was strongly influenced by French models, either directly, as in the early years, or indirectly through Flanders, as can be seen clearly in the period after 1400. The *Kontor* at Bruges probably played a large part in the Gothic influence, which, however, did not triumph as completely here as it did in the Rhine valley. The west front, for example, seldom presents that majestic aspect characteristic of French cathedrals. It remains austere, almost undecorated, with no rose-window, and is usually pierced by a single central door, unimposing in size and barely decorated. The towers (or, as was more usual, the single tower) surmounting the west front, even after allowance has been made for the material used, bear witness to a persistent loyalty to the Romanesque spirit.

Paradoxically it was at Magdeburg that the earliest Gothic cathedral was built. The archbishop Albert had studied at the recently founded University of Paris, and he brought back the elements of the new art. The choir and transept, built between 1209 and 1219, were inspired by the cathedral of Laon. It was not until later, after 1248, that the construction of the choir of Cologne cathedral, very similar to that at Amiens, was begun.

In the region where brick was used, the most imposing monument was the Lübeck *Marienkirche*, which had a great influence on many religious buildings in the east. The present church replaced an earlier Romanesque building, erected as soon as the town was founded and burnt down in 1251. It took a hundred years to build. French art was dominant at this period, and the influence of Soissons, through the mediation of Tournai and Bruges (*Notre-Dame*) – perhaps also of Visby – is apparent in the narrowness and height of the nave and aisles, in the triforium, the system of flying buttresses, the ambulatory and the chapels surrounding the choir. The two towers, substituted for the single one originally planned, were erected in the first half of the fourteenth century, and reached a height of 125 metres.* The exterior, with its great bare surfaces, its undecorated portals, its massive towers, is austerely majestic. The interior now makes a similarly severe impression, but formerly the bareness of the brick and the absence of ornament on the capitals were compensated for by paintings.

The *Marienkirche* inspired a number of churches in the Wendish towns, notably that of St Nicholas in Stralsund, which comes closest to its model but is more decorated. Often the west front is surmounted by only one tower, as at Wismar and Rostock. However this type of church embodying French influence prevailed for only about 100 years. It was then largely replaced by the 'hall-church' with nave and aisles of equal height, usually covered by a single roof-span, without flying buttresses, and with only one tower. This type of architecture originated in Poitou, and by the Romanesque period had spread into Westphalia. Neglected after the mid-thirteenth century, it returned to favour, particularly in the seaports, in the second half of the fourteenth century. Some of the Flemish brick churches, like that of St Giles at Bruges, served perhaps as a model. Together with the *Marienkirche* of Greifswald and Frankfurt-on-the-Oder, the most imposing church of this type is the Danzig *Marienkirche* (1340–1502), of roughly the same dimensions as the *Marienkirche* in Lübeck.

The rapidity with which these vast edifices were erected is surprising. On the flood-tide of prosperity the mercantile middle class shared enthusiastically in these projects, which expressed not only their religious faith but also their civic pride. In the ports the high towers of the churches were visible at sea for many miles and told the sailors, long before they arrived, that they were home again. The Hanseatics therefore regarded these churches as the very symbol of their home town.

* Principal dimensions of the *Marienkirche* at Lübeck (and of *Notre-Dame* in Paris): overall length 102 metres (130), width 32 metres (48), height of central nave 38 metres (35), height of towers 125 metres (69).

4. THE PLASTIC ARTS

The architecture of the north German towns was largely a middle-class affair, and consequently displays a markedly Hanseatic character. The same cannot be said of much of the sculpture and painting, especially in the case of masterpieces. It is more often in minor works that the participation of the Hanseatic middle class in the plastic arts can be seen.

Since the main material in the area was brick, it is not surprising that sculpture in stone is not comparable in quantity or quality to that of southern Germany. The outstanding groups of statuary are to be found in the choir of Cologne cathedral, at Halberstadt, and above all at Magdeburg. The theatrical attitudes and exaggerated gestures of the wise and foolish virgins in the west door of the cathedral, which date from about 1260, already manifest that tendency towards a mixture of pathos and caricature which is characteristic of late medieval German art. The fine equestrian life-sized statue of Otto II in the old market square, though only a few years earlier than the group of virgins, is far more classical in its serenity. It was apparently intended as a symbol of the judicial powers of the judges (*Schöffen*) of the town, reputedly granted by this emperor. It was a custom peculiar to north Germany to erect in public places symbolic statues of various kinds. One example is the great bronze lion set up by Henry the Lion in 1166 in front of his castle in Brunswick, a proud affirmation of the power of the Guelph. But the chief examples are the statues of Roland, whose obscure and varying symbolism has been interpreted in many different ways. With their raised swords, these Rolands are usually intended as an expression of the judicial powers and urban law in opposition to feudal authority. Carved first in wood, and from the fifteenth century onwards in stone, they have no great artistic merit, but are striking by reason of their monumental size. The one at Bremen (1404) is more than fifteen feet tall. Though numerous in north Germany, from Bremen to Riga, the Rolands are not particularly Hanseatic. None is to be found in Lübeck or Westphalia.

The art of the bronze-founder, a speciality of the towns of the Harz and Westphalia, was more widely disseminated than that of the sculptor, but its masterpieces belong to an earlier period. Bernward's column and the bronze doors in Hildesheim date from the eleventh century, the Brunswick lion from 1166. The bronze doors of St Sophia of Novgorod, with their twenty-six panels depicting the life of Christ, were completed by the end of the twelfth century. They were cast in a Magdeburg foundry and probably sent as a gift from Archbishop Wichmann or one of his successors to the archbishop of Novgorod, through the agency of Hanseatic merchants. From the thirteenth century onwards, in addition to bells, monumental brasses and ornaments, the bronze-founders also produced finely ornamented fonts, such as those in the cathedral of Hildesheim (about 1250) and in the *Marienkirchen* of Rostock (1290), Wismar (fourteenth century) and Linköping in Sweden (about 1440). This last was cast by a Lübeck founder. These fonts appear to have been exported to towns throughout the Baltic regions, where they supplanted the stone fonts which were an earlier speciality of the island of Gotland.

But the north German art *par excellence* was without doubt woodcarving, which flourished from the fourteenth century onwards. Municipalities, merchant and craft associations, as well as private citizens, were anxious to adorn their churches with statues, carved panels, choir stalls and altar-pieces. The most characteristically 'Hanseatic' gift of this kind was the four panels offered by the *Novgorodfahrer* of Stralsund to the Church of St Nicholas in the fourteenth century. They represent bearded Russians, wearing tall pointed bonnets and armed with bows and clubs, hunting ermine and squirrel in the woods and presenting their bag to a German merchant before the gate of the *Peterhof*. The *Marienkirche* in Lübeck had stalls in somewhat the same style, but less evocative, presented to it by the Skania, Bergen and Novgorod companies at the beginning of the sixteenth century. More distinguished is the altar-piece ordered in 1424 by the *Englandfahrer* of Hamburg from Master Francke, whose painted panel of the Nativity is one of his most charming achievements.

The altar-pieces are certainly the most remarkable artistic creations of north Germany. Carving and painting are here closely allied, sometimes executed by the same artist, and it is often difficult to distinguish the hand of the master from that of his pupils. Flemish and Burgundian influence is discernible in the degree of realism and in the colouring. The earliest of the great masters was Bertram of Minden (*c.*1340–*c.*1415), creator of the altar-piece in the Church of St Peter in Hamburg (the so-called Grabow Altar). When opened it measures 7·20 metres in width, and contains 46 carved figures and 24 scenes painted on a gold background, taken from Genesis and the childhood of Christ and his Passion. Bertram seems to have been principally a painter, as were Conrad of

Soest and Master Francke, also from Hamburg (early fifteenth century), and Hermen Rode of Lübeck (late fifteenth century), whilst the greatest of them all, Bernt Notke, was equally gifted as a painter and as a sculptor.

If any artist deserves to be called Hanseatic it is Bernte Notke (*c*.1440–1509). Born into a great Pomeranian merchant family, he went to Lübeck to learn his art and there, in 1467, he became a 'free master' and a burgess, having been released, thanks no doubt to his family connections, from the obligation to join either the goldsmiths' or the painters' guild. From 1483 to 1491 he lived in Stockholm, where he was for a time master of the Royal Mint of Sweden. He then returned to Lübeck, and from there travelled to the Low Countries, Prussia, Denmark, south Germany and even to Italy, where he came under the influence of Mantegna. He had a brilliant career, and his work can be seen in many Hanseatic cities as well as all over Scandinavia, in Finland, in the Baltic countries and in Frankfurt-on-the-Main. His outstanding achievements in painting are the *Dance of Death* in Lübeck, and another in Reval, and the *Mass of St Gregory* in Lübeck – though its attribution to Notke is uncertain – and in sculpture, the decoration of the rood-screen and crucifix in Lübeck cathedral, and above all the *St George* in the Church of St Nicholas in Stockholm (1489). This vast composition, 3.50 metres high, was commissioned by Sten Sture, the regent of Sweden, in fulfilment of a vow taken in 1471 as his troops were about to engage in a decisive battle against the Danes. It is without doubt Notke's masterpiece and also a masterpiece of Hanseatic sculpture. In Pinder's happy phrase, it is 'the northern counterpart of the Colleoni of Verrochio', of approximately the same date. Both are great equestrian statues. But here the similarity ends. The Colleoni, cast in bronze, is a product of the new art in all its austere simplicity, designed to exalt the defiant individualism, the *virtù*, of the *condottiere* of the Renaissance. The St George, in painted wood, is the work of a medieval Christian artist who wants to tell an edifying story through the medium of sculpture. Beside the central group of St George battling against the dragon, the princess destined to be the monster's prey kneels in prayer on a plinth carved in the form of a battlemented castle, while the plinth of the central group is adorned with several bas-reliefs representing scenes from the saint's life.

The execution of this central group betrays the mastery of the conscientious artist, in love with his craft, who delights in carving the smallest details of the horse's trappings and the rider's armour, both sparkling with jewels, the whole set off by gold inlays and richly varied colouring.

A little cavity cut in the hero's chest and covered by a metal sheet contains authentic relics, showing how far the passion for truth could be carried. But it was above all the dragon which allowed Notke to satisfy his love for complete realism. This is not the contemptible lizard found in so many treatments of this subject but a truly horrible monster, covered with a multitude of sharp scales, his jaws savagely agape, lying on a heap of bones, skulls and torn and decomposing bodies. The whole scene is alive with movement. The fierceness of the battle is expressed in the shattered stump of lance caught in the dragon's claws, in the saint's helmet fallen to the ground, in the brandished sword and the rearing horse. All this tumult is dominated by the impassive face of St George, sure of his victory. While Notke ministered to the glory of the Swedish national dynasty by embroidering a hagiographic anecdote, he ennobled his subject until it became an interpretation of one of the great moral themes of the Christian ideal, the triumph of Good over Evil.

As a painter, however, Notke, like other Lübeck and Westphalian masters, was inferior to the artists of the Cologne school, to the Master of St Veronica (about 1400), and above all to Stephan Lochner, a native of Constance, whose altar-piece *The Adoration of the Magi* (about 1450) has been regarded for the last 150 years as the masterpiece of medieval German painting.

In the works of artists, as in those of poets, it is rare to find a genuinely Hanseatic inspiration. The immense popularity of St George slaying the dragon may entitle it to rank as such, especially in Prussia and the Baltic countries, where it is plainly an allusion to the struggle of the Teutonic Knights with the pagan Lithuanians, which continued until the fifteenth century. St Nicholas, too, the patron saint of sailors, is portrayed occasionally, notably by Hermen Rode in the high altar of the Church of St Nicholas in Reval, where he is shown welcoming shipwrecked sailors. Even more moving is the naïve painting in the *Marienkirche* in Lübeck by an unknown artist depicting the shipwreck of the *Bergenfahrer* Hans Ben in 1489; it shows, under Christ crucified, the ship battered by the tempest and the crew trying to save themselves.

It was not only in Germany that the works of German painters and sculptors were highly thought of. Commissions came from all the Baltic countries, and as a result there was a regular trade in works of art, whose importance it is difficult to gauge. Reincke estimates that in the fifteenth century about 300 carved or painted panels were exported from Lübeck to the Baltic countries, Finland and Scandinavia. In general the only trace left of this trade is the present location of the actual works. But a lucky chance has preserved some information about the movements of an altar-piece depicting the Trinity, intended for the Dominican church at Reval. Commissioned in 1419 by the merchant association of the *Schwarzhäupter*, the carvings were executed by a local artist. Sent by sea to Lübeck – without paying freight charges, in view of the nature of the 'merchandise' – it was then taken overland to Hamburg, to the studio of Master Francke, who did the painting and gilding, for which he received in payment two lumps of wax, valued at 80 marks. The work took seven years, and it was not until 1436 that the finished altar-piece was taken back to Reval to be consecrated.

The Germans not only exported works of art, they also imported them. The prestige of Flemish artists and the close ties with Bruges led the citizens of many Hansa towns to buy works by Flemish or Dutch masters for presentation to their local churches. In this way the imposing altar-piece of the *Passion* by Memlinc was presented by the Canon Adolf Greverade to Lübeck cathedral. Even more famous is the triptych of the *Last Judgement*, by the same painter, in the Church of Our Lady in Danzig. But it did not arrive there by purchase. It had been ordered by Agnolo Tani, the agent of the Medici in Bruges, and was intended for a Florentine church. But it was captured on the high seas by the privateer Paul Beneke, who presented it to the great church of his native city. This is the only known example in the Hanseatic world of an abducted work of art, comparable to the much more extensive pillaging by the Venetians in the Near East.

In the sixteenth century, as a result of the steadily increasing influence of Flemish art, portrait-painting became popular in north Germany. As in Flanders, citizens who intended to present a picture to a church would have themselves painted in as kneeling figures. The most remarkable example of this is the altar-piece presented to the *Marienkirche* at Lübeck by the burgomaster Hinrich Brömse around 1515. It evokes admirably the main features of a local patrician family. Behind the burgomaster, who is clad in a sumptuous fur coat, are his six sons. One of them later also became burgomaster of Lübeck and even more famous than his father, a faithful adherent of the Roman faith and an adversary of Wullenwever. A second son became a councillor, a third a merchant in the Novgorod company, a fourth an alderman in the London *Kontor*. Equally informative is the portrait of Mathias Mulich by Jacob of Utrecht. Painted by a Dutchman, this portrait of a great Lübeck merchant, a native of Nürnberg, is a symbol of the Hansa in decline. But the finest surviving portraits of Hanseatics were the work of Hans Holbein of Augsburg, who painted them in 1532 while he was in England. The most evocative is that of Georg Giese of Danzig, a merchant of the London Steelyard, who is shown sitting at his desk with pen and ink, account-books and cash-box.

In the sixteenth century the art of north Germany was profoundly influenced by that of the Low Countries, to the extent of becoming little more than an extension of it. It escaped almost entirely the influence of Italy and classical antiquity. Northern artists were not attracted by profane subjects nor by the study of the human body. The nude is rarely found, and then only in conjunction with the theme of Adam and Eve. This is in marked contrast to the situation in south Germany. It may be said that artists in the north, though invigorated by Flemish influence, remained during the sixteenth century far more loyal to the medieval tradition than did those of south Germany. Here again the conservatism characteristic of the Hansa is plainly manifest.

PART THREE

Crises and Decline

CHAPTER TWELVE

Gathering Dangers (1400–1475)

I. UNFAVOURABLE CIRCUMSTANCES

THE fifteenth century is marked by the gradual decline of the Hanseatic community, at first barely perceptible in the face of a few obvious successes, but becoming only too visible by the second half of the century, when the general trend of development, both economically and politically, was almost always unfavourable to the Hansa.

During this period monarchical power was being consolidated in northern Europe. The rulers of the fourteenth century, often more hospitable to foreigners than their subjects, had loaded the Hansa with privileges and championed Hanseatic trade in their domains. Henceforth they were to favour their own merchants more and would be less disposed to limit their special rights, especially in fiscal matters, in favour of foreigners, or to enforce strict observance of the privileges granted by their predecessors. The Hansa, being unsupported by any political power, was hardly in a position to take a strong line and was reduced to deploying economic weapons, such as the suspension of trade and the transfer of the Bruges *Kontor*. These had once been effective in dealing with towns and minor principalities, but were to prove of little use against large, consolidated states.

It was especially in the Low Countries, an area vital to Hanseatic commerce, that the political trend was prejudicial to Hanseatic interests. Until the second half of the fourteenth century the Hansa had benefited from the fragmentation of the region into many lordships – the countships of Flanders and Hainault, the duchies of Brabant and Guelders, the countship of Holland, the bishoprics of Utrecht and Liège. The rise of Burgundy altered this situation. In 1384 Philip the Bold inherited Flanders, Antwerp and Malines. Six years later the Duchess Joan left him Brabant and Limburg. Burgundian expansion grew at the beginning of the fifteenth century; in its third decade, through conquest and the extinction of collateral branches, Philip the Good found himself in possession of most of the Low Countries, from Holland to Picardy. The

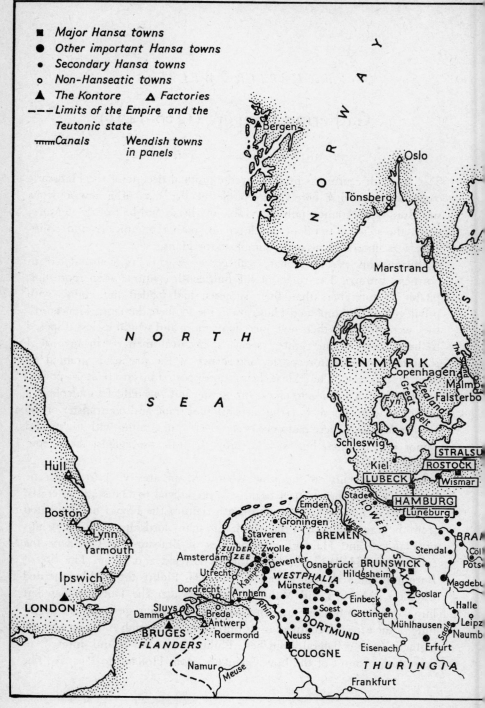

(h–15th century)

Hansa could do little against such a powerful amalgamation. It was even more serious that her most dangerous rivals, the Dutch, were vigorously supported by Burgundy, which ensured them a rapid success. The unification of the Low Countries under the house of Burgundy must be regarded as one of the principal factors in the decline of the Hansa.

Fortunately for the community, political developments in England and Scandinavia were more favourable. From 1414 to 1472 the English were weakened by the Hundred Years War and the Wars of the Roses. Although the Hanseatics suffered at the hands of privateers in the Channel and the North Sea, nevertheless the disordered state of the kingdom gave them the chance to obtain benefits from successive rulers. In spite of many vexations, it was in England that they were most successful in maintaining their position.

In Scandinavia the proclamation of the Union of Kalmar might have seemed a serious threat. The three kingdoms, now united under one queen, might well form a political and economic bloc prejudicial to the interests of the Hansa. Events were to prove that these fears were unfounded and to vindicate the wisdom of the Hanseatic leaders who had supported Margaret against her Mecklenburg rivals. The Hansa still had to contend with Danish power in the fifteenth century, but the union of the three kingdoms remained a strictly personal affair and was soon called in question. Weakness in the rulers and overriding particularist interests prevented the formation of a unified state. Thus the Hansa was able to retain her hold over Scandinavia, though here as everywhere else Dutch competition was making inroads upon her monopoly.

In the east the personal union in 1386 between the kingdoms of Poland and Lithuania made no appreciable difference to the situation. In one way the christianisation of Lithuania, the last pagan outpost in Europe, favoured Hanseatic penetration into the country. The defeat of the Teutonic Order at Tannenberg in 1410 was more serious. The prestige of the Order, in which the Hansa shared, was ruined. A long period of disorder, damaging to trade, came to an end with the Treaty of Thorn in 1466, by which Pomerella, the mouth of the Vistula, Thorn, Danzig and Elbing passed into Polish hands. But these political upheavals had no lasting effect on Hanseatic trade, as the continued expansion of Danzig makes plain.

Further to the north, in Livonia, the position of the Order and the Hansa was barely affected by the defeat at Tannenberg. But it was profoundly modified by the decline and eventual ruin of the great urban republic of Novgorod, which Ivan III annexed in 1478. The growth of the Muscovite empire, extending to the Gulf of Finland and hostile to foreigners, represented for the Hansa, as for all Germans, a grave threat, the full effects of which were to be felt less than a century later.

In the course of the fifteenth century not only the foreign but also the German principalities became more powerful. As a result the princes brought increasing pressure to bear upon the towns, which were obliged, far more than in the past, to organise their defences against the encroachments of the great lords. This constant drain on their military and financial resources was one cause of the irreparable decline of certain Hansa towns, especially in Westphalia and Lower Saxony.

Economic factors in the development of northern Europe in the fifteenth century were even more fatal to the Hansa than political ones. The most important was the expanding trade of the Dutch and the south Germans, against which the Hanseatics' only defence was an increasing regulation of their own commerce. This gave them some momentary advantages, but its main effect was to accentuate their inferiority in comparison with their rivals. Then again, the increased importance of direct relations between the Baltic and western Europe through the Sound could not fail to weaken the position of Lübeck as a transit port between east and west, controlling the traditional land route across the isthmus of Holstein. The worst consequence of this competition between the two routes was perhaps the growing divergence between the Prussian and Livonian towns on the one hand and the Wendish towns on the other. The lessening of that feeling of solidarity between towns of different areas which had been the foundation of the Hansa can be seen clearly from this time onwards. Finally the dispersion of trade among so many markets which was becoming more marked everywhere, except in England, favoured the expansion of foreign competition, and although it gave opportunities for private profit it wrecked the system of economic regulation on which the Hansa was founded.

Although circumstances augured ill for the future of the Hansa as early as the beginning of the fifteenth century, the effects were slow in making themselves felt. Both to the Germans and to the outside world the community appeared strong and prosperous. New members were being recruited, trade was being extended to Finland, Iceland and Portugal. In the fourteenth century the Hansa had been recognised as a great power, and in spite of serious signs of weakness she retained her prestige throughout the fifteenth century.

2. THE CONSTITUTIONAL CRISIS IN LÜBECK

In Lübeck the early years of the fifteenth century were dominated by a dangerous constitutional crisis, which for several years imperilled the very existence of the Hansa. In 1380 and again in 1384 the butchers' risings revealed the people's deep discontent with the exclusiveness of the patrician regime. The financial situation of the town was particularly critical at this time because of the expense of the war against the *Vitalienbrüder* and the cost of constructing the Elbe–Trave canal. In 1403 the council was forced to reveal the town's unfortunate financial position and to ask the community to approve a new tax. Rebuffed by the brewers, then by the artisans, the council finally got its way by abolishing the special oath of obedience which had been imposed upon the guilds in 1386. But two years later they were obliged to propose a new tax of a penny a barrel on beer. In return the council agreed to the formation of an advisory commission of sixty members, delegated by the community. This commission soon became the mouthpiece of the malcontents and presented the council with a long list of grievances, criticising the general policy of the town, the excessive cost of diets and embassies, the infringements of the rights of guilds, the taxes, the facilities granted to the Nürnberg merchants, and so on.

The Sixty arrogated to themselves the control of different branches of the municipal administration. The conflict grew more bitter when they demanded constitutional reforms which would have guaranteed the community a voice in the election of councillors, previously recruited by co-option. After much shuffling the council was forced in 1408 to give way to popular pressure. Immediately fifteen of the twenty-three members of the council, including the four burgomasters, went into voluntary exile. The victors proceeded to elect a new council of twenty-four members, half of whom were to be elected annually, and set up an electoral system which guaranteed the guilds a representation equal to that of the merchants and *rentiers*. The rupture was complete. For eight years the old and new councils confronted one another, each striving to achieve recognition as the rightful ruler of the town.

As Lübeck was an imperial city, the new council tried to gain the favour of the Emperor Rupert. They swore fealty to him on behalf of the town, which the patrician council had refused to do, and paid the arrears of the imperial taxes. In return Rupert granted them the right to elect their own council. But meanwhile the exiles had not been idle. Under the leadership of the burgomaster Jordan Pleskow, a skilful diplomat, they lodged a complaint with the imperial court of appeal, which a year later issued a somewhat ambiguous verdict, inviting the town to restore their rights to the exiles. The new council riposted clumsily by confiscating the exiles' property and refusing to obey further imperial summonses. Consequently, early in 1410, Rupert put Lübeck under the ban of the Empire, but as he died shortly afterwards, matters were left in suspense.

This conflict caused a considerable stir in the Hanseatic world. The very existence of the community was compromised, since its 'head' could no longer assert its leadership. 'The merchant no longer knows to whom to turn', complained the Bruges *Kontor*. But attempts at reconciliation remained ineffective. It soon became apparent that most of the towns, themselves governed by an aristocracy, were on the side of the old council. However Lübeck gained a certain measure of support from towns in which, inspired by her example, democratic factions had arisen. Wismar and Rostock remodelled their constitutions in favour of the guilds and allied themselves with Lübeck. Without going to similar lengths, Hamburg set up a commission of sixty members, who intervened in municipal affairs and engineered the expulsion of the Lübeck exiles, who went to Lüneburg. Lübeck also ensured the neutrality of the Grand Master by aiding him in the war against Poland.

The most pressing need was to ensure the continued functioning of the Hansa, since Lübeck, being under the ban of the Empire, could no longer play her traditional role. A Hanseatic diet which met in Hamburg decided that correspondence from the *Kontore* should in future be addressed to that town. When Hamburg's democratic tendencies made her suspect, Stralsund was chosen in her place, though in the event it was Lüneburg, which was both Saxon and Wendish and the chosen refuge of the exiles, which became to some extent the head of the Hansa.

The conflict was intensified when Jordan Pleskow appeared at Bruges in 1411 and, basing his claim on the decree of the imperial court which had declared the confiscation of the exiles' property invalid, requested from the *Kontor*, from the four Flemish members and from the duke of Burgundy the seizure of Lübeck property to the amount of 4,000 marks gold (256,000 guilders), the estimated value of the confiscations. The carrying out of such a measure would have meant ruin for the *Kontor*. This move on Pleskow's part, intended to compel the *Kontor* to support the exiles, was entirely successful. When a Lübeck delegation arrived to claim the *Kontor*'s loyalty to the new council, the *Kontor* broke off relations with Lübeck. Soon after, without having carried out his threat, Pleskow set off for Prussia to ask the Grand Master to ban Lübeck trade in his domain.

Meanwhile Sigismund had been elected emperor in 1411, and the exiles asked him to confirm the ban on Lübeck. The new council having again refused to obey the imperial summons, Sigismund recognised the legality of the old council but did not renew the ban. The Hansa towns, who were waiting for this to be done before excluding Lübeck from the Hansa, dared not carry out their intentions. A total impasse had been reached.

The new council did not lose heart. They asked the emperor to renew Lübeck's privileges, and offered him a present of 6,000 guilders. Sigismund demanded 24,000, and for that sum granted their request, revoked the ban imposed by his predecessor and proclaimed that he had taken Lübeck into his favour. Almost immediately these favourable omens proved false. It had been stipulated that 16,000 guilders should be paid either in Paris or in Bruges on All Saints' Day 1415. Perhaps the new council found it impossible to raise the money. The fact remains that on the agreed date no payment was made and no excuse was offered. In a fury Sigismund revoked all the privileges granted a few months earlier and summoned Lübeck to submit to her former council. Meanwhile another blow struck the town. Eric of Denmark declared against her and ordered the arrest of all Lübeck merchants in Skania.

The new council resigned themselves to failure, and in May 1416 accepted the lenient conditions proposed by a delegation of seven Wendish and Pomeranian towns. The ten surviving members of the old council, including Jordan Pleskow, returned to the city and co-opted five of their former colleagues who had remained in Lübeck. These fifteen patricians then co-opted two members from the Circle Society, five merchants, and also five members of the new council. This last concession probably did much to bring about a general relaxation of tension, but politically it was of no importance. The patriciate were once more complete masters of the council. The commons were strictly supervised and the ninety-six guilds were obliged to take an oath of obedience, giving their consent to the levying of a tax to pay the debt owing to Sigismund, now reduced to 13,000 guilders. In this way two of the measures which had most enraged the commons were reintroduced. In the neighbouring towns the former regimes were also restored, in Wismar by the duke of Mecklenburg, in Rostock and Hamburg by delegates from the Hansa.

In considering this whole matter, the striking thing is the moderation shown by both sides in the long conflict. During the eight years when it was in control of the town, the new council offered no violence to its adversaries. Similarly the patrician restoration seems to have been marked by no more than two or three executions. This is a good example of the 'Hanseatic wisdom' which avoided all excesses and was based on a profound sense of solidarity stronger than any antagonism. An unhappy contrast is provided by the massacres which took place at the same period in the Flemish towns.

The crisis had served to show the strength of the patrician system of government in northern Germany, which had gained the support of almost all the towns and also that of the rulers and princes. A Hansa drawing its strength from the guilds and the small merchants, and hostile to the great families, was unthinkable. However events had also revealed the fickleness and venality of the emperor. He had been offered a wonderful opportunity to become the leader and protector of the Hansa. He was begged to do so, even after the crisis, by the towns and by the Bruges *Kontor*. But Sigismund, caught up in a web of conflicting interests and disappointed to find that the Hansa was not going to prove a source of revenue, did practically nothing to restore its prestige abroad, and his relations with Lübeck remained strained. The leaders of the Hansa soon realised that the Empire would not provide them with the support they needed.

The crisis also tested the strength of the Hansa. As soon as it was over, the towns by common consent drew closer together. In 1417 Lübeck formed a league with the other Wendish towns, Hamburg alone holding back, which was to last five years. The Hanseatic diets which met at Lübeck in 1417 and 1418 were among the most important in the history of the community. The second was a particularly brilliant occasion. Delegations from thirty-five towns from all three thirds attended, as did representatives of the emperor, the Teutonic Order and the archbishop of Bremen. The dukes of Schleswig and Mecklenburg were there in person.

At the instigation of its president, Jordan Pleskow, the assembly drew up under the name of 'statute' a sort of Hansa charter in thirty-two articles. No particular innovations were introduced, but the statute reaffirmed earlier decrees dealing with commercial, maritime, legal and monetary matters. The first four articles were by far the most important.

In order to prevent any future attempt at insurrection, they provided for
the arrest, conviction and execution in all member towns of any agitator.
Any town in which the council was wholly or partly deprived of its
powers was to be excluded from the Hansa, if it did not submit to the
injunctions presented by the community's delegates.

It was laid down that the statute should be posted up in a public place
in all Hansa towns. The measure provoked a sharp reaction. It was in fact
an attempt to limit the towns' autonomy, since the expulsion of a single
member of the council was enough to provoke intervention by the other
towns. In Stettin popular pressure caused the council to withdraw the
announcement. In Stade the commons insisted on a revision of the constitution. In Bremen the mob tore down the proclamation and burnt it
in the market square. The Hansa took vigorous action against the first
two towns, and decreed their expulsion from the community. This soon
compelled their submission, and they were made to pay fines of 2,000 and
500 guilders respectively, and to hang up the proclamation again. The
Hansa made a more circumspect approach to Bremen, but after vain
attempts at conciliation the town was expelled in 1427 and all trade with
her suspended. As a result a burgomaster was murdered and a people's
council installed. Eventually in 1433 Bremen recalled the former council
and was readmitted into the community, without payment of a fine.
Elsewhere the statute was received without serious trouble.

The Hanseatic diet of 1418 also solemnly affirmed the pre-eminence of
Lübeck within the community. On the grounds that diets met only rarely,
owing to the difficulty of bringing delegates together, the diet requested
Lübeck and her neighbours – that is to say, the Wendish towns – to take
over the political leadership of the Hansa.* In fact Lübeck had for a
long time played the role which was now being offered to her, but it
was a great compliment to her, and helped to strengthen her authority,
to be officially chosen as head of the Hansa.

Pleskow and the Lübeck leaders had hoped for even more than this.
Aware of the weakness of the community in comparison with its enemies,
especially Denmark and the princes, they wanted to turn the purely
economic organisation into a political and military league, in which
every member would be obliged to pay a regular contribution to the
common fund and to provide a fixed number of soldiers. A plan was put
forward for such a league, to last in the first instance for twelve years,
to be led by Lübeck and to bear the new name of *tohopesate*. A list of

* Document No. 15 (*b*).

forty towns was drawn up, with the number of men-at-arms and cross-bowmen to be furnished by each and the methods of mobilisation. The plan was rejected by the Teutonic Order and came to nothing. However by 1418 the Hansa had completely overcome the grave crisis which had shaken her. The community seemed even stronger than before, and it is not without reason that historians have sometimes placed the zenith of her power at about 1430.

3. DECLINE OF THE TEUTONIC ORDER AND THE NOVGOROD *Kontor*

In the early years of the fifteenth century the Teutonic Order, a member of the Hansa, seemed to have achieved a strong and assured position. The knights held undisputed sway over Prussia and the Baltic countries, especially when in 1398 the Order obtained recognition of its rule over western Lithuania and Samogitia, which facilitated communication between the two parts of the Order's domain. In the same year, the Order gained a footing in Gotland, which seemed to presage a policy of expansion into the Baltic, aimed against Denmark, at that time an ally of the Hansa. In the economic field the Order's trade, based on the export to the west of grain, timber and amber, was in full development.

The Order's strength, however, was more apparent than real. The Prussian nobility found it difficult to submit to the tyrannic rule of the knights, who, being almost entirely recruited outside the country, were regarded as foreigners. In 1397 they formed the 'League of the Lizard', which Poland, in her own interest, supported. The Prussian towns were irritated by the commercial competition of the Order and by the special privileges granted to its merchants, which included first claim in the settlement of debts, exemption from poundage and disregard of the ban on grain exports. The Hansa herself was apprehensive of the Grand Master's intentions in the Baltic and of his selfish policy. In 1407 the Hansa was instrumental in forcing him to return Gotland to Denmark. But the most formidable opponent of the Order was Vladislav Jagiello, king of Poland and Lithuania. He supported the Prussian malcontents, and systematically obstructed Prussian trade in Poland. By recognising Cracow's position as a staple, he prevented the merchants of the Order from travelling to Hungary and dealing directly with the copper mines, and in collusion with Stettin he encouraged Polish merchants to abandon the lower Vistula route in favour of the Warthe and the Oder.

In these circumstances the Grand Master Ulrich von Jungingen declared war on the king of Poland, an action which resulted in the disaster of Tannenberg on 15 July 1410, when the Grand Master and thousands of his knights perished on the field of battle. The nobles, the bishops and the towns of Prussia immediately rose in rebellion and swore allegiance to Vladislav. The towns drove out the garrisons of the Order and solicited extensive privileges from the king. Yet the defeat of the Order did not at first seem irreparable. The new Grand Master, Heinrich von Plauen, defended the castle of Marienburg which the Poles were unable to take. In 1411 he signed the Treaty of Thorn, whose terms were comparatively favourable. The Order paid a heavy ransom for its prisoners, but lost only the small district of Dobrin (Dobrzyn) and, temporarily, Samogitia. It re-established its authority over the towns, executed the burgomasters of Thorn and Danzig and henceforth favoured the guilds against the patriciate.

In reality the power and prosperity of the Teutonic Order were at an end. Weakened by internal dissension, which resulted in 1413 in the deposition of Heinrich von Plauen, it found itself in the next fifty years at war with Poland and Lithuania, and with the Prussian nobles and the Prussian towns. These conflicts devastated the country and ruined the finances and commerce of the Order. In an attempt to restore its prestige the Order embarked on a crusade against the Hussites, with Sigismund's encouragement. This provoked a devastating counter-attack, which in 1433 brought the Hussites right up to the outskirts of Danzig. By mid-century the conflict had become desperate. In 1440 some forty Prussian noblemen and twenty towns, among which Thorn and Elbing were the most determined, formed a league in defence of their rights. The league laid before the Emperor Frederick III a complaint that gives us detailed information on the grievances of the towns, particularly Danzig: the Order was violating its charters, forbidding, quite arbitrarily, the import and export of merchandise, bestowing special favours on foreign merchants; the Teutonic government officials were abusing the right of pre-emption, exercising a tyrannous control over ships at the mouth of the Vistula and, above all, raising taxes on poundage and not passing any of this on to the towns. As the emperor did not intervene, in 1454 the league declared war on the Grand Master, threw off his sovereignty and offered their allegiance to the king of Poland, Casimir IV, who accepted it and joined the coalition. The league even attempted to win over the Hansa, which however remained neutral. The war lasted for thirteen years, and was waged both by land and by sea – Danzig pirates seriously disorganised Hanseatic trade with Livonia. It culminated in the ruin of the Teutonic state. The second Treaty of Thorn in 1466 transferred to Poland full sovereignty over the whole of West Prussia, both east and west of the Vistula, excepting Marienwerder but including Marienburg. The Order moved its headquarters to Königsberg. Nothing but part of east Prussia was left to it, and the Grand Master became the vassal of the king of Poland.

The collapse of the Teutonic Order was fatal to Germany's position in the east, but it cannot be maintained that it was altogether prejudicial to Hanseatic interests. To some extent the Hansa suffered from the backlash of the disrepute into which its most illustrious member had fallen, but she was also freed from commercial rivalry and from the selfish policies of a principality whose ambitious plans had often given her just cause for fear. To judge from contemporary chronicles, public opinion in the Hanseatic world was in general hostile to the Order. Although the Prussian towns suffered during the war, the decline of the Teutonic Order benefited them, as did the change in sovereignty. Danzig in particular gained an autonomy such as she had not enjoyed before, and received extensive commercial privileges, notably the right to determine the status of foreign merchants as she wished. With the establishing of peace her trade developed rapidly. Other towns on the Vistula, however, which received similar franchises, could not prevent their gradual decay. Thorn had blamed the Teutonic Order unjustly for its difficulties. Caught between the staples of Cracow and Danzig, it continued to decline under Polish rule, as did most of the inland towns of north Germany.

Freed from the tutelage of the Order, the Prussian towns still retained their own special preoccupations vis-à-vis the Hansa. In matters concerning passage of the Sound and relations with the English and the Dutch, their interests were often opposed to those of the Wendish towns. In 1450 a merchant from Thorn summed up the Prussian grievances when he declared bitterly: 'When the Wendish towns are at war [with Denmark], they gain by it as the whole commerce of the Baltic is diverted through Lübeck and Hamburg and thence by land to Flanders; the towns thus become rich, while we poor Prussians are brought to ruin.' The growing divergence of interests between the various groups of towns in the fifteenth century was indeed particularly obvious here.

The same is true of the Livonian and Russian areas. The trade of the Livonian towns was expanding noticeably, thanks mainly to the activity of foreign merchants, Dutchmen and south Germans. But Reval, Dorpat and Riga had no intention of allowing their own merchants to be supplanted by foreigners. Riga in particular was alarmed at the extent to which Polotsk was systematically favouring her own merchants to the detriment of the Livonians, and tried to put a stop to the penetration of Dutch merchants into the countryside, where they dealt directly with the producers of grain and flax. In 1459 Riga stopped all foreigners, including merchants from Hansa towns, from trading directly with other foreigners on her territory. This was particularly damaging to Lübeck, whose merchants had trafficked freely along the Dvina for two hundred years. Lübeck protested against this lack of Hanseatic solidarity, but obtained no effective help from the other Livonian towns. She then asked the Land Master of the Teutonic Order for support. But this caused a scandal. To call in a prince to arbitrate in a dispute between two towns was a serious infringement of the principles governing the community. Riga retorted by closing down the Lübeck depots, and in spite of continual pressure maintained the total ban on all trade between foreigners, which harmed the trade of the Lübeckers more than that of the Dutch.

The rivalry between the Livonian and other Hansa towns was very evident in Novgorod. The former did all they could to bring the *Kontor* under their control and even to monopolise trade with Russia. For example in 1416, in retaliation for infringements of Hanseatic charters by the Russians, they prohibited all trade with Novgorod by land and sea. But they authorised the Russians to trade in Livonia, thus putting the entire burden of the blockade on the other Hansa towns. The Hanseatic diet admonished them severely and ordered all its members, including Livonia, to cease trading with Russia; but without success. The Land Master of the Teutonic Order concluded peace with Novgorod on his own authority. Lübeck protested, but had to accept the *fait accompli*. In the same way she gradually lost the influence which she had exercised over the administration of the *Peterhof* since the end of the thirteenth century, and in 1422 she was forced to concede to Dorpat the control of the *Kontor* and to allow the Livonian towns to decide whether the Hanseatics should trade with Novgorod or not. The Lübeck and Westphalian merchants continued to visit Novgorod, but henceforth played only a minor role there.

In spite of the Peace of Niebur in 1392, Hanseatic relations with Novgorod during the whole period were very unsettled. Charters were violated and merchants were attacked or became involved in disputes during

which trade was suspended, sometimes for years on end. In 1424 one of
the worst conflicts, resulting from an attack upon some Russian ships, led
to the arrest of 150 Germans, of whom 36 died in captivity. In the mid-
fifteenth century war between the Teutonic Order and the Russian
princes caused a Hanseatic blockade which lasted for five years. In 1468 a
new crisis occurred when German merchants were arrested. The *Kontor*
was transferred to Narva, and it was four years before trade was resumed.

These troubles help to explain the decline of the Novgorod *Kontor*,
which is particularly noticeable after the mid-fifteenth century. But the
main cause was the decline of Novgorod itself. It was no longer the great
commercial centre which it had been for 300 years. Trade in wax and furs
was passing more and more to the Finnish and Livonian towns. The
decline was hastened by the attacks of Ivan III, who in 1471 inflicted a
serious defeat on the republic. Seven years later he seized the town, deported part of the population and brought its independence to an end.
Firm in his resolve to favour Muscovite trade, Ivan showed great
animosity towards foreign merchants, and from then on the days of the
German *Kontor* in Novgorod were numbered.

4. THE HANSA AND SCANDINAVIA

In the fifteenth century, as in the fourteenth, the major political problem
of the Hansa was still that of its relations with Denmark. The Peace of
Stralsund inaugurated a period of friendship between the two powers
which continued up to the death of Queen Margaret in 1412. The Hansa
had not opposed the union of the three Scandinavian kingdoms, and by
helping Denmark to recover Gotland had shown that it preferred the
friendship of Denmark to that of the Teutonic Order. But the policy
pursued by the peace-loving patrician councils of the Wendish towns
did not command unanimous support. In the towns themselves the guilds
were more xenophobe than the merchants, and remained at heart hostile
to the Danes. The relationship between Denmark and the Hansa was
therefore an uneasy one, and in the reign of Eric of Pomerania (1412–38),
who was less friendly towards the Hanseatics, the traditional conflict broke
out again.

The duchy of Schleswig, a Danish fief which for 100 years had been
practically independent of the crown under the counts of Holstein, was
the main bone of contention. First Margaret and then Eric tried in vain

to re-establish their authority over the duchy. Eric even sided against the rebel government in Lübeck, in the hope that the restored Hansa would recognise his rights over Schleswig and support him against Holstein. But even though his rights were recognised by the emperor, Lübeck, and especially Hamburg, had no intention of furthering his ambitions. They were content to offer their help to both parties. Eric therefore turned against the Hansa, allied himself with Poland against the Teutonic Order, welcomed Dutch and English merchants to Norway and Denmark, and harassed the German merchants. In 1426 he issued an epoch-making decree which empowered him to levy a toll on all ships passing through the Sound. With the later additions of an *ad valorem* duty on the cargoes transported, this toll remained in force for more than 400 years, and was not abolished until 1857.

As long as Jordan Pleskow was alive a precarious peace was maintained, but shortly after his death (1425) the Wendish towns declared war on Denmark and blockaded the Sound. As always, not all members supported the war. The towns of the Zuiderzee, as well as those of Prussia and Livonia, were angered by the blockade and refused to participate in it. Consequently the war was carried on almost exclusively by the Wendish, Pomeranian and Saxon towns. It began badly. A Hanseatic fleet, commanded by the burgomaster of Lübeck, Tidemann Steen, was defeated in the Sound, and the Danes were therefore able to capture a salt fleet bound from Bourgneuf to Prussia. This set-back caused popular insurrections against the patricians, who were accused of lack of zeal, in Hamburg, Rostock and in particular Wismar, where several councillors were beheaded.

The war dragged on for nine years, with varying fortunes. Lübeck benefited from it, as most of the east–west trade was obliged to follow the land route across the Holstein isthmus, and a shortage of salt gave her the chance to sell Lüneburg salt at a high profit in the Baltic countries. But the principal gainers were the Dutch, who supplied the Scandinavian kingdoms with foodstuffs, attacked Hanseatic ships and ran the blockade. In 1435 Eric, weakened by the defection of the Swedes, signed the Peace of Vordingborg, a great triumph for the Hanseatics. Count Adolf of Schauenburg kept Schleswig, and the question of homage to the king of Denmark was dropped. Eric confirmed the Hanseatic privileges within his domain, thereby accepting the commercial monopoly which Lübeck and the Wendish towns enjoyed in Norway, and agreed that although the toll on ships passing through the Sound was to continue,

Wendish ships should be exempt. The Hanseatic victory was soon seen to be even more decisive than had at first been thought. Eric, discredited, was forced to flee, and in 1438 was deposed by the Danish state council. As in 1375, the Hansa determined the succession, giving her support to the new king, Christopher of Bavaria, in exchange for important privileges. Lübeck took possession of the fortress of Hälsingborg, thus closing the Baltic to the Dutch, against whom war had recently broken out, and forced all traders to use the Lübeck–Hamburg route, much to the annoyance of the eastern towns, who were constantly reproaching Lübeck for her egotism.

The Peace of Vordingborg did not last long. Christopher and his successor Christian I soon followed the example of their predecessors and favoured native merchants and Dutch traders in an effort to break the Hanseatic monopoly in their territories. As a result the Dutch, far from being eliminated from the Baltic, continued to expand their trade there. Moreover when Count Adolf of Holstein died in 1459, leaving no direct heir, the question of Schleswig again became acute. The local nobility proclaimed King Christian of Denmark heir to both Schleswig and Holstein: suddenly the Danish frontier had moved forward to the very gates of Lübeck and Hamburg. However the Wendish towns took no action. Christian's reassurances calmed their fears, though they remained on the alert and were always ready to intervene in the affairs of the duchies, siding now with, now against the king, as best suited their own interests. But the extension of the Danish power over the isthmus of Holstein, on one of the essential Hanseatic trade routes, constituted a grave threat to the Hansa. A hundred years of endeavour had ended in a double set-back. Dutch trade was increasing in the Baltic, and Denmark's power was no less threatening than of old.

The Hansa also saw her hegemony threatened in Norway. In the mid-fifteenth century the situation in Bergen became very tense as a result of a move by the royal bailiff, Olaf Nielsson, a declared enemy of the Hanseatics. In order to protect local craftsmen from the competition of the numerous German craftsmen in the town, he brought the latter under his own jurisdiction in 1443, imposed taxes on them, fixed their prices and sought to detach them from the *Kontor*, on which they had hitherto been dependent. In 1453 King Christian tried to ease the situation by dismissing Nielsson, but two years later he was forced to reinstate him. This led to one of the bloodiest acts of violence in the history of the Hansa. In a fury the Germans broke into the monastery where Nielsson had taken refuge, burnt it to the ground and massacred not only Nielsson and sixty of his supporters but also the bishop of Bergen. Despite the intervention of the pope these crimes remained unpunished.

The Wendish towns also contrived to keep the monopoly of Norwegian trade entirely in their own hands, and had no wish to allow other Hanseatic towns a share in it. In 1446, in order to prevent the export of dried fish to Rhenish markets by ships from the towns of the Zuiderzee, particularly Kampen and Deventer, they declared Lübeck, Wismar and Rostock staples for Bergen cod. This led to continual disputes, until in 1476 the merchants from the Zuiderzee decided to set up a separate community in Bergen, with its own alderman. Here, as elsewhere, the bonds holding the Hansa together were gradually slackening.

5.　THE HANSA AND THE LOW COUNTRIES

In the fifteenth century, as in the fourteenth, the Low Countries were the main area of Hanseatic commerce and formed the major preoccupation of the community. Here, in spite of some new trends, Hanseatic policy continued along traditional lines.

Towards Flanders the Hansa maintained more or less the same attitude as in the previous century. The German merchants of the Bruges *Kontor* were careful to see that their charters were respected, and issued a constant stream of protests against infringements of them, claiming compensation for losses incurred through attacks on land or at sea, through imposts unjustly levied and through debasements of the currency. When these claims were not met, the Hanseatics again and again threatened to move the *Kontor*, and actually did so on two occasions.

The commercial and maritime expansion of the Hollanders created an entirely new situation. From the second quarter of the fifteenth century onwards the Hollanders and the Hanseatics were constantly at odds, and their antagonism soon became the determining factor in Hanseatic policy as a whole. As the Hollanders were particularly anxious to expand their trade in the Baltic, they made every effort to conciliate the Danes, who controlled the Sound. Far more often than in the fourteenth century Dutch and Scandinavian affairs were closely interrelated. As a result the Wendish towns, whose trade was seriously threatened by Dutch competition, favoured the adoption of a stern policy towards the Low Countries, whereas the Teutonic Order, the Livonian towns and Cologne were more inclined to be conciliatory. Once again a situation was developing which would accentuate the disunity within the Hansa itself.

In the Low Countries after about 1430, the struggle against Dutch competition led mainly to the strengthening of the Hanseatic staple at Bruges. By concentrating the trade of the entire area there, and by allowing into the Hanseatic zone only those wares which had passed through the staple, the Germans hoped to prevent their rivals from importing cloth into the Hansa towns, to protect their own trade in Flemish cloth and to limit and control Dutch trade in the east. But the Hansa was unlucky. Such a policy could succeed only if Bruges retained its position as the leading international market in north-west Europe. The rise of Antwerp, noticeable as early as 1450 and very evident after 1475, and the consequent decline of Bruges rendered the policy of the staple ineffective.

The agreements of 1392 had led to a fairly long period of peace between Flanders and the Hansa. However in addition to the usual complaints about violations of their privileges, the Germans accused the Flemings of frustrating the retaliatory measures which they had adopted in disputes with the Scots (1412) and the Spaniards (1419). The increase in piracy which resulted from the renewal of war between England and France, and from the activities of privateers lurking among the islands of east Frisia, also led to recriminations. As the Flemings refused to give any form of compensation and an embassy led by Jordan Pleskow in 1425 achieved nothing, the possibility of moving the *Kontor* was again mooted; but the war against Denmark caused it to be postponed.

Ten years later a series of grave events led to an acute crisis. The Treaty of Arras, which reconciled France and Burgundy, resulted first in tension and then in war between England and Burgundy, in which the Flemings were the chief sufferers. The Flemings turned on the Hanseatics, whom they suspected of sympathising with the English. In June 1436 nearly eighty Germans were massacred in Sluys. An immediate transfer of the *Kontor* from Bruges to Antwerp was decreed, and trade with the Low Countries was suspended. As Bruges and Ghent had rebelled against Philip the Good, the Hanseatics enjoyed the favour of the duke of Burgundy. They appear to have seriously considered settling permanently in Antwerp; in any case they refused to return to Bruges unless they received the satisfaction they had demanded. Their demands were reinforced by a great famine, one of the most terrible to strike Flanders in the fifteenth century. During 1438 the price of corn quadrupled. Consequently Bruges and the Flemish leaders accorded the Hanseatics an indemnity of 8,000 pounds groschen as compensation for the losses they had suffered in the town. Before the end of the year Prussian vessels laden with grain were sailing into the Zwijn and were received with transports of joy.

Scarcely had the Hanseatics raised the blockade of the Low Countries than they reimposed it, this time in order to bring pressure to bear upon the Hollanders. The latter, irritated by Hanseatic restrictions on their trade in Livonia, had been raiding Hanseatic commerce for some years, and in May 1438 they seized a dozen Hanseatic salt vessels in Brest roads. The Wendish towns closed the Sound and stopped all shipments of grain to the Low Countries. They were supported, very reluctantly, by the Grand Master of the Teutonic Order, while the Prussian towns refused them all military aid. In addition Christopher of Denmark, approached by both sides, gave preference to the Hollanders and granted them equal rights in his domains with the Hanseatics. This forced the Wendish towns to sign in 1441 the Treaty of Copenhagen, in which the two adversaries guaranteed each other's right to trade freely, and the suspension of all obstacles to navigation. This meant that the Hollanders could resume their trade in the Baltic and exploit the economic advantage they had obtained in Denmark and Norway. For them the Treaty of Copenhagen marked a decisive stage in their expansion eastwards.

The return of the Hanseatics to Bruges in 1438 did nothing to lessen the tension between them and the Flemings. The *Kontor* continued to protest against infringements of privileges, harassment and especially acts of piracy, for which no compensation was paid in spite of letters of safe-conduct. There was also a new complaint, about the formation of Flemish companies accused of monopolising trade in alum and spices with the aim of raising prices. In the hope of settling all the points at issue, Lübeck summoned in 1447 a general diet at which thirty-nine delegations were present, a record figure, thus proving how vital trade with Flanders still was to the entire community. The assembly came to the decision that the best way to safeguard Hanseatic interests in Flanders was to strengthen the Bruges staple, and a number of products were made subject to staple regulations for the first time. Furthermore the authority of the Bruges *Kontor* was consolidated by granting it the revenue of a new tax levied on all goods bought in Flanders, Brabant, Zeeland and Holland, a clear indication of the growing dispersal of German merchants and German trade throughout the Low Countries.

Behind the scenes discussions had begun with the Flemish leaders, who met all complaints with a barrage of counter-complaints: disruption of Flemish commerce by the Hanseatic regulations, defectiveness and adulteration of many articles – furs, ash, pitch, beer and Rhenish wine – dispatch of furs from Lübeck to Venice and Genoa, and from the *Kontor* to Nantes and La Rochelle, in violation of the Bruges staple. The discussions came to nothing. Those with Philip the Good a little later had no better success. There was no evading the issue: negotiations would lead nowhere, and there was no hope that the duke would now support the Hansa against Bruges, as he had done ten years earlier. Pressure had to be brought to bear on both sides, and the Hansa reluctantly decided to use the only weapon in her armoury, the transfer of the *Kontor* to some town outside the reach of Burgundy.

In 1451 the German merchants in Flanders were secretly instructed to move to Deventer. But, as always, the decision aroused protests. The Grand Master pointed out that Deventer lay too far off the main trade routes and that its port was not suitable for the large Prussian and Livonian ships. He would have preferred a reconciliation with the English first, who had just captured a great salt fleet returning from Bourgneuf. More serious was the fact that Cologne was in no hurry to apply the prescribed measures. Her merchants continued to sell their wine in Flanders without much regard for the staple regulations. The town even tried to make common cause with the eastern towns in an effort to scotch Lübeck's policy. This threatened alliance was alarming. Lübeck realised the danger and consented to a modified form of blockade, directed against Flanders and Flemish cloth only. At this price the co-operation of the Prussian towns and the Grand Master was obtained, but the blockade's chances of success were seriously reduced. The most unfortunate feature of the whole affair was that the Hollanders seized the opportunity to increase the sales of their cloth everywhere. Since most of the Hanseatic merchants had refused to move to Deventer, preferring to settle in Amsterdam, Middelburg, Antwerp or Malines, the Hansa decided to transfer the *Kontor* to Utrecht. This was more conveniently situated than Deventer, and many merchants agreed to settle there. But in 1455 Philip the Good, who considered the blockade a defiance of his own authority, sent his troops to occupy the town. The Hansa therefore resorted to negotiation. The duke agreed to set up a commission to assess the indemnities due to the Germans, nearly all of which were paid by Bruges. He also confirmed the Hanseatic charters *en bloc*, though without giving the special guarantees on monetary and judicial points which the

Hanseatics had asked for. The Hanseatics therefore returned to Bruges, re-
established the staple for their products and were granted the use of the
square of the Easterlings for the discharge of their business. On 11
August 1457 two hundred Hanseatic merchants, led by the burgomasters
of Lübeck, Cologne, Hamburg and Bremen, rode on horseback in procession into Bruges.

All the efforts of the last six years had brought the Hansa no real
advantages, and it was the general opinion that the community had
suffered a defeat. The experiment was never tried again. The unpalat-
able truth was that the transfer of the *Kontor* and even a blockade,
weapons so effective in earlier times, were useless against a power which
had control over the greater part of the Low Countries. The main effect
of the blockade was to encourage Dutch trade. It also contributed to the
departure of foreign merchants from Bruges, whereas it would have been
to the advantage of the Hansa if they had stayed. Antwerp henceforth
took Bruges's place. In 1467 the Hanseatics themselves asked for and
were granted a new charter from Antwerp, and eleven years later acquired a warehouse there on the corn market. Nor had this final blockade
increased the prestige of the Hansa. On the contrary it had revealed its
economic and political weakness, the readiness of its merchants to dis-
obey instructions and the lack of unity between the several groups of
towns. The Hanseatic *Kontor* in Bruges seemed already doomed.

6.   RELATIONS WITH ENGLAND AND FRANCE UP TO 1470

All through the fifteenth century relations between England and the
Hansa were extremely troubled. There were outbursts of persecution,
vexatious regulations, imposts denounced as iniquitous, acts of violence
and piracy. Neither side was wholly blameless, and it is hard to see why
war did not break out before 1470.

That peace was maintained in spite of all grievances can be explained
by the common interest in profitable trade relations. Also England, at
war first with France and then with Burgundy, and eventually divided
against itself by the Wars of the Roses, was in constant need of the
Hansa's commercial assistance and her diplomatic support. Within the
community the divergence of views between the various groups of towns
was even more marked in this area than elsewhere and effectively put a
stop to any attempt to take decisive action. Though Lübeck and the
Wendish towns on more than one occasion took a firm line, they were

not supported by either Cologne or the Prussian and Livonian towns, which were reluctant to go to war even to defend their own privileges and preferred when necessary to act independently of Lübeck so as to smooth things over.

In England the Hanseatics were generally supported by the king (though less whole-heartedly than in the fourteenth century), the great nobles, the clothiers, especially those from country districts who found them good customers, and the great mass of consumers. But they met organised hostility from the English merchants, who were becoming more active, the city of London and Parliament, which resented their privileged status. The Merchant Adventurers in particular were incensed by the obstacles put in the way of their Baltic trade, and were indignant at being refused in Germany the rights which their German competitors enjoyed in England.

During the first third of the fifteenth century it was the question of English trade in Prussia which did more than anything else to embitter Anglo-Hanseatic relations. As early as 1398 the Grand Master of the Teutonic Order had denounced the agreement reached ten years earlier, though he did nothing to stop the activity of the English in Danzig. But in 1420 the rapid expansion of English trade caused alarm, the factory was closed and its governor thrown into prison. Eight years later there was a volte-face and the factory was re-established. Lübeck was more concerned with infringements of the Hanseatic privileges in England, where the Germans were forced to pay the same duties as other foreigners on imports of wine, salt, herring and timber. In 1423 they refused to pay a subsidy voted by Parliament, which led to their arrest and the closing of the Steelyard. There was a fresh alarm in 1431, when duty was levied 'on pound and tun'. The Germans, convinced that war was about to break out, fled to Bruges. But it was a false alarm, and after the Treaty of Arras and the resultant hostility between England and Burgundy, the English king, hoping to reconcile the Hanseatics, confirmed all their privileges and exempted them from all taxes not provided for in the *carta mercatoria* of 1313. This victory was offset by the Grand Master's refusal to accept the agreement, which seemed to him to remove all barriers to English trade.

Hostilities flared up again in 1449, when the English captured 100 vessels in the Channel, half of them owned by Hanseatics. In reprisal the towns seized all English property in their territory. War was, however, averted once again. The English nobles urged the king to yield

Although Lübeck demanded compensation, Bremen and Cologne held back. Henry VI reciprocated by according his grace and favour to all Hanseatic merchants with the exception of those from Lübeck. Lübeck had to continue the war alone, and in 1453 Warwick, the governor of Calais, captured eighteen of her ships. Even the accession of Edward IV, who was friendly towards the Hansa, did nothing to relieve the tension. The City of London withdrew from the Steelyard the custody of Bishopsgate, a duty which it had discharged since 1282. Once again the policy of force advocated by Lübeck proved unsuccessful because of opposition from Cologne, Danzig and even Hamburg.

All attempts at moderation were in vain. The accession of Charles the Bold brought about a radical change in Burgundian policy, to the great disadvantage of the Hanseatics. The duke signed a commercial treaty with England, and Edward IV became less conciliatory. The Hansa could no longer play off Burgundy and England against one another, and war with England soon became inevitable.

From the mid-fifteenth century onwards France bulked increasingly large in the Hansa's foreign policy. Contacts between the two went back to the thirteenth century but had always been intermittent, in spite of the extension of Hanseatic trade along the Atlantic coasts. Owing to the fact that England had controlled Normandy and Guyenne from the mid-fourteenth century onwards, and that the duchy of Brittany, whose rule included the Bay of Bourgneuf, was independent, the Hansa could hardly have expected effective protection of her commercial interests from the king of France.

With the accession of Charles VII and the reconquest of France more continuous relations were established between the French crown and the Hansa, which needed the support of the French king if her ships were to be safe. For his part Charles VII was hoping to attract foreign merchants and win over the Germans in his wars with the English and the duke of Burgundy. Although there were good grounds for mutual understanding, Franco-Hanseatic relations were difficult and constantly endangered by piracy. The French privateers when harrying the English also attacked Hanseatic vessels, and since the Germans sometimes chartered English ships, the capture of a ship was followed by demands for compensation, which were nearly always refused, and reprisals. Relations between the Hansa and France were cordial only in times of truce between England and France.

The first known diplomatic contact between Charles VII and the

Hansa resulted from the seizure in 1446 of a French ship, the property of Queen Mary, by a privateer from Bremen. When the town refused to pay compensation, the king ordered that all Hanseatic ships along the coasts of France should be attacked. In 1452, however, he offered the Hanseatics his protection on condition that they broke all ties with England. This was rejected, as the Germans had no intention of taking sides. As a result Hanseatic trade, especially that of Cologne, suffered a great deal from attacks by the French, and even the intervention of the Emperor Frederick III with Charles VII was unsuccessful.

The situation improved with the accession of Louis XI, who throughout his reign displayed a steady determination to establish good relations with the Hanseatics. In 1464 they were granted a comprehensive charter – which had to be rewritten because it included *autres nacions d'Alamaigne*, i.e. their south German competitors – granting them the right to trade throughout French territory, as long as they did not trade with the English or charter English ships. They were also protected against arrest and the seizure of their goods except for debt. They were allowed to settle in France, and salvage rights were abolished in their favour.

But the good intentions of Louis XI were not sufficient to ensure peaceful relations. Piracy broke out again in the Channel, raiders from Kampen attacked French ships, and there were immediate reprisals. Even relations with the crown grew difficult after the affair of the *Saint-Pierre de La Rochelle*. This great French caravel arrived at Danzig in 1462 with a cargo of salt, and while in harbour was damaged by lightning. When its French owner died, leaving no heir, the ship became the property of the French crown. But despite Louis XI's pressing demands, Danzig refused to let the ship sail before the cost of repairs had been paid. Louis eventually grew tired of the cool reception given to his overtures, and in 1470, for the only time in her history, the Hansa found herself officially at war with France.

7. THE SECESSION OF COLOGNE AND THE ANGLO–HANSEATIC WAR

Tension between England and the Hansa, evident since the mid-fifteenth century, eventually led to open warfare between the two powers. This proved to be one of the most exacting tests which the community was called upon to undergo, since it was marked by the defection of Cologne, resolved to defend her own interests. However the energetic leadership of Lübeck and the loyalty of the other towns, especially Danzig, the most warlike of them, enabled the community to surmount a crisis which might well have been fatal.

Cologne's resentment was caused by the tax (*schoss*) levied by the Bruges *Kontor* on the import and export of Hanseatic goods. This tax had at first been levied only in Flanders, but in 1447 the diet at Lübeck extended it to Brabant and the northern Low Countries. Cologne immediately refused to pay it on the grounds of her special privileges. Since the bulk of her trade passed through Brabant and Holland, the measure hit her harder than the other towns. In addition she had very little influence in the Bruges *Kontor* and was therefore not anxious to reinforce Lübeck's pre-eminence there. At first the Hansa let the matter drop, but in 1465 the diet at Hamburg renewed the obligation to pay the tax throughout the whole of the Low Countries and reaffirmed the necessity to respect the Bruges staple. When Cologne merchants refused to pay the *schoss* at the fairs of Bergen-op-Zoom and Antwerp, they were arrested at the request of the *Kontor*, but the town authorities soon released them. The Hansa was then foolish enough to appeal against Antwerp to the duke of Burgundy, and Charles the Bold seized the opportunity to summon both Cologne and the Hansa before his court. Realising that she had the duke's support, Cologne in 1467 refused to make any concessions; two years later the court declared against the *Kontor* and ordered it to pay the court fees, without, however, giving a final decision on the question at issue.

It was at this point that the Anglo–Hanseatic war broke out. The English had been expanding their trade with Iceland, thus infringing a monopoly which the Danes claimed for themselves. In retaliation they seized seven English ships in the Sound. The English accused the Hanseatics of having encouraged the Danes, and on 28 July 1468 the Privy Council ordered the arrest of all Hanseatic merchants in England and the seizure of their goods. In London the mob attacked and partly destroyed the Steelyard. To safeguard her own interests, Cologne dissociated herself ostentatiously from the common cause and requested and obtained from Edward IV, at least for a short time, the recognition of her special privileges. The Cologne merchants formed their own association, whose members had to produce documents attesting that they were transporting only wares from Cologne. But she was joined in her secession by only a very few Rhenish towns, among them Wesel and Arnhem.

The Hansa did not attempt a counterstroke immediately, but was content to claim compensation and the release of her merchants. The duke of Burgundy interceded on her behalf, as did certain English groups which had been affected by the measures. A petition from the clothiers of Gloucestershire has been preserved, setting forth the services rendered by the Hanseatics to the English economy.* The merchants were released after nine months' detention, but as no lasting accord seemed possible the Hansa towns resolved on a firm policy. This time there was none of the usual dissension between the Wendish towns and the Prussian towns. On the contrary, in spite of Cologne's efforts to enlist her support, Danzig showed herself the most partisan of all the towns. She was the first to follow the example of the Bruges *Kontor*, which had officially opened hostilities by equipping two warships, and as long as the war lasted, Danzig played the leading part in privateering.

The Hansa was all the less ready to yield since the international situation was in her favour. She had the support of Denmark and Poland; she could count on the friendly neutrality of Charles the Bold, who for a while opened the ports of the Low Countries to her raiders; she was being courted by the Lancastrian party, which promised, in return for her support, to confirm her privileges in England; Louis XI appeared anxious to restore peaceful relations with her once more. The *Hansetag* of September 1470, at which each of the three thirds was well represented, therefore felt strong enough to acknowledge openly the state of war with England which had in fact existed for more than a year. The Bruges *Kontor* was authorised to begin discussions with France, which were, however, abortive. There was no question of dealing gently with Cologne. She was summoned to submit under pain of being excluded from the community. Against a minority vote the diet strengthened the Bruges staple, listing the products which were subject to the staple regulations,† and continued to levy the *schoss* throughout the Low Countries, the revenue being paid to the *Kontor*.

The war, which lasted four years, had economic, military and political repercussions. The Hansa tried to enforce a rigorous ban on the import of English cloth into the Hansa towns, and succeeded in persuading Denmark and Poland to accept it. But for it to be really successful it would have been necessary to forbid the import of English cloth into the Low Countries as well, and this the duke of Burgundy refused to do. He even gave the Cologners a special safe-conduct, granting them freedom to transport English cloth through Flanders. Cologne tried to persuade

* Document No. 40.
† Document No. 27.

him to denounce the conduct of the *Kontor* in respect of the *schoss*, and obtained from England confirmation of the Hanseatic privileges for her merchants only, for a period of five years. Faced with these major attacks on its solidarity, the Hansa hesitated no longer: on 1 April 1471 Cologne was formally excluded from the community.

In the political field the Hansa was less successful. She had at first favoured the Lancastrian party, also supported by Louis XI, but when Edward IV was driven out of England by Warwick and took refuge in the Low Countries, she agreed out of regard for Charles the Bold to change sides and support the Yorkists. In fact it was with the help of ships from Danzig that Edward IV regained his throne, but he straightway forgot his promises and favoured Cologne.

The war at sea was essentially one of piracy. English and French ships attacked one another, and the Hanseatics preyed on both. Lübeck and above all Danzig were especially active. The *Saint-Pierre de La Rochelle*, still lying unclaimed in Danzig habour, was fitted out and armed by the town. Then, commanded by the town councillor Pawest, the ship, rechristened the 'Great Caravel' (*Der grote Kraweel*), crossed the North Sea and raided down the Channel as far as Camaret. She impressed the enemy more by her size than by her success. Damaged, and then immobilised in the Zwijn by mutiny, she was not able to go to sea again until the last year of the war. The privateer Paul Beneke, meanwhile, was covering himself with glory, capturing first John of Salisbury, then the lord mayor of London and finally, in April 1473, a Florentine galley sent to England by the agent of the Medici at Bruges, Thomas Portinari. This exploit, which was later embellished with many apocryphal details, caused a great stir, mainly because of the value of the cargo, which amounted to 60,000 pounds groschen. In addition to a great quantity of alum, the ship was carrying furs, silks, gold brocades, tapestries, crimson velvets and satins, and Memlinc's *Last Judgement*. There was, however, cause for anxiety as well as satisfaction, for the ship had been sailing under the Burgundian flag and there was good reason to fear the anger of Charles the Bold. However he contented himself with sending some threatening letters to the Danzig council. Portinari was forced to go to law, but the case was not concluded until forty years later, with the payment of the last of a series of indemnities, each smaller than the previous one.

This success could not compensate for the defeats suffered in 1472. During the summer French ships had inflicted losses on a Hanseatic fleet and driven it back into the Flemish ports, and a little later the English destroyed the greater part of a Lübeck fleet off Flushing. However the Hanseatics were fairly successful in protecting their merchant ships and their trade with the Low Countries.

Both sides finally wearied of the war, and the efforts of the duke of Burgundy led to the initiation of peace talks in 1472. These made rapid progress in the following year when the Hansa was able to conclude a truce with France, and in spite of Cologne's intrigues the negotiations finally culminated in February 1474 in the Treaty of Utrecht.

This marked a resounding and almost unhoped-for triumph for the Hansa. In England king and Parliament confirmed the Hanseatics in all their privileges and promised compensation of £25,000, which was later reduced to £10,000 after the return of the buildings of the London, Boston and Lynn *Kontore* to be held in fee-simple. London again entrusted the Steelyard with the custody of Bishopsgate, and pledged herself to deal justly with the legitimate complaints of the German merchants. In return the English demanded the same liberties in Prussia which they had enjoyed before the war. This clause nearly wrecked the negotiations. Danzig rejected it outright and did not withdraw her objections until two years later, with the reservation that the English should enjoy only the rights granted to other foreigners. Some Pomeranian and Livonian towns, who were afraid of the expansion of English trade in the Baltic, were equally reluctant to accept this clause.

Peace with England was supplemented by an agreement between the duke of Burgundy, the Hollanders and the Hansa, which was much less favourable to the Hanseatics. Although they obtained the confirmation of certain privileges, they had to release the Hollanders from the Bruges staple and to allow them once more access to the Baltic.

The chief result of the Peace of Utrecht was the surrender of Cologne, which now found herself completely isolated. Edward IV had secretly promised to deny her merchants the Hanseatic privileges in England, and Charles the Bold turned against her because she had aided his enemies at the siege of Neuss. In order to be readmitted into the Hansa, Cologne was obliged to accept all the penalties laid on her by the diet of Bremen in 1476, and to pay heavy indemnities for the losses to the Bruges and London *Kontore* caused by her disobedience. She pledged herself to pay annually for six years a sum of 100 guilders, representing her unpaid share in the *schoss*, after which she would have the choice between paying this tax or compounding at the same rate. Thus Cologne accepted what she had fought against so fiercely, namely the Hansa's right to levy taxes in favour of the Bruges *Kontor*. In London she had to return to the Steelyard the charters, archives and valuables which she had seized in 1468, submit again to the statute of the *Kontor* and pay a double impost not exceeding £250 sterling. Feelings ran so high at the Steelyard that Cologne merchants were further humiliated by being excluded for two more years and then being readmitted only on the payment of a further indemnity of £150.

The re-establishment of good relations between the Hansa and France can also be attributed to the Peace of Utrecht. The armistice concluded in 1473 was periodically renewed and in 1483 transformed into a 'perpetual peace', by which the Hanseatic privileges in France were extended without any political conditions being attached. The collapse of the Burgundian power and the reconciliation between Louis XI and Edward IV had removed all cause for conflict.

The Peace of Utrecht was one of the great events in the history of the Hansa. It came at a critical moment, when the community was threatened with dissolution by the disintegration of its economic system, by the irresistible rise of its rivals, by attacks made in almost all countries on its privileges and by the increasing separatist tendencies of the towns. Consequently the victory had far-reaching effects. The Hansa recovered her international status and strengthened her commercial position in England for the next hundred years while at the same time preventing English expansion in the Baltic. The submission of Cologne had proved her strength and solidarity and would serve to discourage further tendencies towards secession among her members. The main causes of weakness were still there, but their harmful effects were not to become apparent for some time.

CHAPTER THIRTEEN

Decline (1475-1550)

THE favourable outcome of the Anglo-Hanseatic war could not prevent the continual decline of the Hansa, which became very evident towards the end of the fifteenth century and the beginning of the sixteenth. The political and economic causes of this decline continued to operate – the decay of the *Kontore*, the refusal to accept collective discipline, isolationist tendencies and successful competition from outside. A new factor was the spread of the Reformation, which intensified internal dissension and caused conflicts with the princes.

The Hansa's period of decadence coincided with the age of great discoveries. Earlier historians tried to establish some connection between the two, but it has long been evident that no such interpretation is feasible. The changes in the great commercial sea routes and the increased importance of the Atlantic ports were not in themselves prejudicial to the Hansa towns. On the contrary: towards the end of the sixteenth century trade with Lisbon and the Spanish ports led to a new period of Hanseatic expansion, and Europe still needed the goods supplied by the Hansa, especially cereals. The most that can be said is that the development of the Newfoundland fisheries contributed to the decline of the Bergen fish trade.

However by causing the European markets to expand until they became world markets, the great discoveries resulted in an extension and transformation of business enterprises. In spite of its expansion into the Atlantic and the Mediterranean, the Hanseatic sphere of influence was too small, and Hanseatics were no match for great business houses like that of the Fuggers, conceived on a vaster scale and enjoying imperial support. In this sense it would be true to say that the great discoveries were prejudicial to the Hansa, but its decline was due mainly to internal weaknesses which were already present in the fifteenth century.

1. THE DECLINE OF THE *Kontor*

The end of the fifteenth century saw the collapse of the two main pillars of the Hanseatic system, the *Kontore* at Novgorod and Bruges. The fate of Novgorod was sealed when Ivan III made himself master of it in 1478. The grand duke of Moscow was anxious to encourage his own merchants and could hardly be expected to tolerate a privileged German establishment in their midst. He also looked unfavourably on the Hanseatics' collusion with the Teutonic Order in Livonia, with which he was at war, and which was blocking Russian expansion in the Baltic.

In 1494 Ivan III took action. Although investigations were pending, he made the murder of some Russian merchants in Livonia the pretext for the sudden arrest of some fifty Germans in the *Kontor* and the confiscation of their possessions, assessed at 96,000 marks. The merchants were released three years later, but the *Peterhof* remained closed for twenty years. But it is as well not to overestimate the importance of this brutal act. The *Kontor* had been steadily declining since the mid-fifteenth century, as had Novgorod itself, and the tsar's action was only the final blow. In 1514, after a period of hardship, the Hansa was allowed to reopen the *Kontor*, her merchants were granted fresh charters and a revision of the statute of the *Peterhof* was begun. But such measures could not bring back the trade that had been lost, for Novgorod was no longer the great market of north-eastern Europe. By the mid-sixteenth century the *Kontor* buildings and the Church of St Peter were in ruins; in the seventeenth century visitors to the town no longer mention them. Trade between Russia and the west, in so far as it was re-established, shifted to other commercial centres, to the Livonian towns, especially Narva, to the Finnish towns and, a little later, to Archangel and southward to Poland and Leipzig. More and more of it passed into the hands of south Germans, Hollanders and Swedes.

Although the fall of Novgorod inflicted irreparable damage on the traditional commercial system of the Hansa, its consequences were not wholly bad. The three Livonian towns, Reval, Riga and Dorpat, benefited greatly from the new situation. Clinging to their former selfish policies, they strictly enforced the ban on trade between foreign merchants, which applied even to Hanseatics from the western towns. In spite of protests from Lübeck, the Livonian merchants remained the only intermediaries in trade between the Hanseatic west and Russia. Consequently they enjoyed great prosperity during the first half of the sixteenth century, and their wealth became proverbial. But this expansion was short-lived, and one of the factors which brought it to an end was dissension among the Hansa towns.

A similar though less abrupt decline is evident at this time in the Norwegian emporia. In the fifteenth century, particularly after the charters granted to it by Christopher of Bavaria in 1447, Rostock retained control over the trade of eastern Norway through its factories in Oslo and Tönsberg. But the inhabitants of these two towns and the kings remained resentful of their economic dependence, and the rise of Dutch trade gave them the opportunity to free themselves from it by degrees. In 1508 King Christian II, after hearing bitter complaints by the burgesses of Oslo against the Germans, proclaimed the abolition of Rostock's privileges. Germans were henceforth to be allowed to trade only within the town and with citizens of the town, not with foreigners or Norwegian peasants. Rostock tried in vain to get her former charters confirmed. All she could get was permission for her merchants to trade in Oslo and Tönsberg on one day in the week – Saturday – with peasants, a privilege they were not able to make regular use of. Rostock's trade with the two ports, although it remained active, diminished noticeably, while that of the Danes, Hollanders, Scots and English increased. Those Germans who had settled in Norway were gradually assimilated into the native population.

In Bergen the position of the Germans was more secure, but here too they came under severe attack and the commercial supremacy of Lübeck and the other Wendish towns was undermined in various ways. Merchants from the Hansa towns on the North Sea coast, Hamburg and Bremen, who had hitherto been excluded, began to compete with the Lübeckers, bringing to Norway grain and beer, both indispensable and both imported also by the Hollanders. In addition the burgesses of Bergen were acting as middlemen in the trade in fish and furs, interposing themselves between the Hanseatics and the inhabitants of the northern districts. Finally the development of the Icelandic fisheries encouraged merchants from Bremen and Hamburg to sail there regularly, without calling at Bergen, and to bring back cod first to England and then to Germany. This undermining of its position as a fish staple was very damaging to Bergen and also to the Wendish towns.*

However it is as yet too soon to speak of a decline of Hanseatic trade in

* Document No. 42.

Bergen, though the number of houses on the 'German quay' steadily diminished. In 1400 there were about 300 of them; by 1450 there were only 200, and by 1520 the number had dropped to 160. But Hanseatic trade in Bergen had a fresh period of expansion in the second half of the sixteenth century, and did not receive its death-blow until the time of the Thirty Years War.

In the Low Countries the gravest symptom of Hanseatic decadence was the weakening position of the Bruges *Kontor*. This resulted from the decline of the town itself, as its role as a great international market was taken over by Antwerp. There were many causes for this shift in trade. One was the silting up of the Zwijn, a factor whose influence was at one time somewhat exaggerated; but it should not therefore be underestimated. No doubt both merchants and seamen were alarmed by the increasing risk of running aground off Sluys and preferred the deeper channel of the Scheldt. Moreover Antwerp attracted merchants from all nations by the generous privileges granted them and by a less rigorous interpretation of the regulations governing trade relationships. The growing activity of the Brabantine port was encouraged by the fairs held there and in Bergen-op-Zoom, which the Hanseatics visited regularly. For nearly fifty years Antwerp had been the main centre for buying English cloth, whose importation into Bruges was forbidden. As a result merchants from Cologne, the Rhineland and south Germany flocked to Antwerp in increasing numbers. Finally the troubles and revolts which rocked the Flemish towns towards the end of the fifteenth century struck a deadly blow at the prosperity of Bruges. Most of the foreign merchants and consulates, Portuguese, Italian, French and English, moved to Antwerp. Only the Spaniards remained loyal to Bruges, which became the main centre for the import of Spanish wool into the Low Countries.

The decline of the Hanseatic *Kontor* in Bruges had begun about 1450. After the transfer to Deventer many merchants disobeyed the orders of their native towns and did not return to the banks of the Zwijn. The Anglo–Hanseatic war did nothing to improve the situation and in 1472 the council of the *Kontor* had to be reduced from 24 members to 18. In 1486 it was still further reduced to 9, and the number of aldermen from 6 to 3. After the death of Mary of Burgundy, the Bruges revolts against Maximilian led to further departures. In 1485, on the regent's instructions, the Hanseatics who had been buying at the fairs in Antwerp and Bergen-op-Zoom for the first time did not return to Bruges. There was a second exodus in 1488, after Maximilian had been taken prisoner by the citizens of Bruges. However the *Kontor* was officially reinstated in 1493, jointly with other 'nations'. But, as had happened previously, a large number of Hanseatics followed the example of other foreign merchants and elected to stay in Antwerp.

In these circumstances the Hansa considered moving the *Kontor* to Antwerp, where merchants enjoyed long-standing privileges, granted in 1315 and 1409. The community had even bought a house on the corn-market in 1468. But its privileges had not been confirmed for a long time, and the town, which did not need the Hanseatics as much as Bruges did, showed little inclination to extend them. The Hanseatics opened nego-tiations early in the sixteenth century in the hope of obtaining a precise definition of their status, but without success. Most of the Hansa towns, moreover, remained loyal to Bruges, since they were firmly convinced that only the restoration of the Bruges *Kontor* could bring back the vanished prosperity. Even Cologne was lukewarm, since she did not want to see her own position in Antwerp weakened to the advantage of Lübeck and her merchants subject to hampering regulations.

In the end the *Kontor* stayed in Bruges, and with the prince's approval the Hansa reissued the staple regulations, which however remained ineffectual. The managers of the *Kontor* remained in the house of the Easterlings and did their best to prevent the properties of the com-munity from falling into ruin. In 1520, however, they decided to move to Antwerp, though retaining their traditional seal and the title *Kontor von Brügge*. But the Hanseatics of Antwerp were unwilling to obey the instructions of their aldermen and refused to pay the tax which alone would have made possible the continued existence of the *Kontor*. It there-fore grew smaller and smaller and by 1539 was reduced to three aldermen, of whom ten years later only one remained. It had for all practical pur-poses ceased to exist when in 1546, at the instigation of Heinrich Sudermann, the Hansa undertook its restoration.

The situation of the Hanseatics in England was very much more satisfactory. While the privileges confirmed in the Peace of Utrecht were continually being challenged or flouted, the English still complained that they had not regained their commercial franchises in Prussia and that they had been hampered in their business there, for instance by being excluded since 1491 from the *Artushof* in Danzig. Relations were par-ticularly strained during the rule of Cardinal Wolsey (1515–21), who did all he could to cut down the privileges, initiating lawsuits, increasing dues and claiming indemnities for ships seized. In 1522 it seemed as if the charters would be revoked, but matters righted themselves again, probably on the initiative of Henry VIII.

While the *Kontore* on the Continent were declining, the London Steelyard retained its position, benefiting from the city's rising prosperity and expanding commerce. However business at the other German establishments dwindled, especially at Boston, which was no longer visited by Hanseatic merchants from Bergen; but in spite of the concentration of their business in London the Hanseatics continued to prosper.

Hanseatic trade in England remained very much as it had been in the fifteenth century. The north Germans exported more English cloth than any other group of foreigners, as much as 20,000 lengths annually during the first quarter of the sixteenth century and up to 44,000 lengths in 1548. Hamburg's share rose from 12 per cent in 1513 to more than 20 per cent by the mid-century. During this period English merchants dispatched their cloth in increasing quantities to the Continent, but do not appear to have increased their trade in the Hanseatic zone. Only about forty English ships passed through the Sound during the second quarter of the sixteenth century. As for imports into England, the Hanseatics appear to have kept more or less intact their monopoly of wax, which rose to the record figure of 8,455 hundredweights in 1529, nearly all of it being brought to London. By contrast the trade in furs appears to have been to a large extent captured by south German merchants. Lastly the Hanseatics continued to import French wine into England. About forty of their ships made annual round trips between the coasts of Poitou or Gascony and the English ports. In England – and only in England – there was as yet no sign of decline in Hanseatic trade.

As the *Kontore* declined, a further alarming symptom made itself felt – the indifference of many towns in regard to their rights and duties as members of the Hansa. Despite reminders and exhortations they no longer participated in any way in Hanseatic activity. The community could not in the long run tolerate these repeated lapses. The diet of 1518 had therefore to proclaim officially that thirty-one towns were to be excluded from the Hansa, since they no longer availed themselves of the privileges, no longer sent delegates to the diets or were no longer able to keep the deliberations of the diet secret from their territorial rulers. Among the towns excluded were many important ones such as Stettin, Frankfurt-on-the-Oder, Berlin, Breslau, Cracow, Halle, Halberstadt, Groningen, Stavoren, Arnhem and Roermund. Although several of them later asked to be readmitted to membership, their indifference bears witness to the decay of the community.

2. THE HANSA AND THE FUGGERS

While Dutch trade was making sweeping advances in Scandinavia, Prussia and Livonia, the south Germans were expanding their trade in the very homelands of the Hansa.

Merchants from Nürnberg had been the first to settle in Hansa towns, in Cologne, Lübeck and Danzig. By the end of the fifteenth century the most active of their firms was perhaps that of the brothers Mulich, securely established in Lübeck and trading with Prussia, Denmark and Frankfurt. But this was nothing in comparison with the economic domination which the Fuggers of Augsburg, operating also through Nürnberg firms, were beginning to exercise.

The Fuggers moved into the northern markets more rapidly than had the Nürnbergers. They also advanced on a wider front, attacking the Hanseatic economy from all sides at once. In 1491 they were engaged in financial dealings and the sale of cloth in Posen. In 1494 they settled in Antwerp, which soon became their most important centre of operations. In the following year they set up a branch in Breslau. In 1496 they established a bank in Lübeck, managed by Lübeckers, which was at first exclusively concerned with financial operations and transactions on behalf of the papacy but soon embarked on commercial ventures. By 1502 they had gained firm footholds in Stettin and Danzig, later in Hamburg and lastly in Livonia.

The Fuggers first came into the Hanseatic orbit through their large-scale trade in copper. They had been exploiting the Slovakian mines, particularly those at Neusohl, in partnership with Johann Thurzo since 1494, and in a few years they succeeded in monopolising the copper trade of northern Europe, previously an important branch of Hanseatic trade. In Danzig they took into partnership a burgess of the town called Jacob Vetter, a wholesale trader in copper, who represented their interests on the town council. Through his mediation with the king of Denmark the firm obtained business facilities in the Sound (1515) and in Scandinavia. Consequently Slovakian copper, in much larger quantities than previously, was transported through Cracow to Danzig, and from there to Antwerp, to be sold eventually in Portugal. Similarly, with the help of the Teutonic Order, the Fuggers gained a footing in the east and established contacts with the Russians. Of course they dealt not only in copper but in many other Hanseatic commodities. Everywhere they made large purchases of wax and furs, and sold spices, silver, cloth and metal goods.

For some time the leaders of the Hansa remained unaware of their danger. A century earlier Hanseatic merchants had been quick to take alarm at the advance of the Nürnberg merchants, but now they made no prompt effort to hinder the progress of the Swabian firm. The Lübeckers seem to have regarded the Fuggers principally as bankers, engaged in transferring funds on behalf of the papacy. Their blindness can be explained perhaps by the cunning of Jacob Fugger. Acting on good advice, he concealed his real intentions, doing business through his Hanseatic and Nürnberg correspondents, buying their complicity where necessary, retreating when it seemed advisable.

It was not long, however, before the effect of the Fuggers' hold over the copper trade began to make itself felt. Hungarian copper was soon seen to be a dangerous rival to Swedish copper, exported by the Hanseatics to the west. The Lübeck factory, on the initiative of the burgess Godert Wiggerinck, had recently undertaken widespread commercial operations in the east, especially in wax. In 1511 therefore the diet of Lübeck, acting on complaints from Dorpat, resolved on counter-measures. The passage through Hansa towns of goods belonging to great non-Hanseatic firms was forbidden. Augsburg, Nürnberg, Ulm, Leipzig and the duke of Pomerania were called on to withdraw goods belonging to these firms from Hansa towns, and a complaint was filed at the imperial court that contrary to imperial law an attempt had been made to set up a monopoly.

Everyone knew that these measures would prove ineffective, so the use of force was decided on at the same time. Since 1509 the Wendish towns had been at war with Denmark and her allies, the Hollanders. In August 1511 Lübeck attacked a Dutch fleet off Danzig, sank some of the ships and captured the rest. Among the goods seized was a shipment of 102 lasts of copper belonging to the Fuggers, estimated to be worth more than 9,000 Lübeck marks.

A retaliatory blow was soon struck. To get back his copper, Jacob Fugger persuaded the king of Hungary to protest, and begged Pope Julius II, though in vain, to lay Lübeck under the papal interdict. He also appealed to the Emperor Maximilian, who could not refuse to help his own banker. The emperor twice ordered Lübeck to return the shipment and threatened to seize her goods throughout the Empire. Lübeck temporised by suggesting that the case should be brought before the imperial diet and reserved her defence – a denunciation of the Fuggers' creation of an illegal monopoly. Not wishing to find themselves brought to trial, the Fuggers resigned themselves to buying the copper back for 8,000 marks.

This was a success for the Hansa, but the only one. Supported by Danzig, the Fuggers continued their activities in the Baltic. In Livonia they imported silver and exported wax bought from the nobles. The Russians sold them furs, wax and pitch in exchange for silver, spices and glassware. Christian II of Denmark granted them his protection and gave them the right to build a copper mill at Oldesloe, at the very gates of Lübeck. In return they equipped six ships for his war against Gustavus Vasa, and they managed to retain the friendship of the new king, Frederick I. Charles V was even more kindly disposed towards the Fuggers than his grandfather Maximilian had been, and there was no hope of Lübeck being able to reopen their case in the supreme imperial court.

Neither Lübeck nor the Hansa was capable of profiting from the weakness of their enemies. They made no move when in 1525 the king of Hungary seized the copper mines or when Jacob Fugger died. In any case, since Cracow and Breslau were no longer members of the Hansa, a vigorous policy in their area was hardly possible. Under the direction of Anton Fugger the firm continued to invade the Hanseatic domain. The traffic on the river Elbe, passing through Lüneburg towards Hamburg, became increasingly important to the Fuggers. Lübeck, poorly supported by the other towns in her attempts to resist this advance and weakened by internal crises during the Wullenwever period, had to face the hard fact that in forbidding the Fuggers to cross her territory, she was helping her rivals without noticeably hindering her enemies. Lübeck therefore resigned herself to signing a convention with the Fuggers in 1538, authorising them 'to transport freely and without hindrance all merchandise, including copper, from Danzig or elsewhere, in and through our town, harbour and inshore waters, and to forward it as they wish to Hamburg or elsewhere'. This was a confession of failure, the abandonment of a long campaign conducted against the powerful Augsburg firm. The latter, however, was approaching its own downfall. Eight years later Anton Fugger abandoned the lease of the Neusohl mines and gradually withdrew from northern Europe, concentrating on trade with the Low Countries and Spain.

The struggle between the Fuggers and the Hansa was only an episode, but it illustrates the latter's inferiority. The intrusion of firms from Nürnberg and Augsburg – which continued for some time after the withdrawal of the Fuggers – had dislocated the economic system of the Hansa. New trade routes had been created along the frontiers of the Hanseatic orbit. In trade between eastern Europe on the one hand and western Europe and the Mediterranean on the other, the Hansa was no longer a valued intermediary. The influx of south German trade, which contributed in some ways to the prosperity of certain Hansa towns, accentuated the divergences of interest within the community. Danzig, Stettin and Hamburg had refused to help Lübeck in her struggle against the newcomers, who found willing helpers in every town. Hanseatic solidarity had suffered another setback. In this sense Claus Nordmann was perhaps correct in saying that 'the era of the Hansa was succeeded by the era of the Fuggers'.

3. THE REFORMATION AND ITS CONSEQUENCES

The Reformation, which began at almost the same moment in all the north German towns, around 1522, was clearly detrimental to the Hansa, for it introduced an additional cause of dissension into the community and even into the individual towns. The spread of the new faith often led to social and religious troubles. The town councils and the patriciate were, at least at the beginning, hostile to Lutheranism, but the guilds supported it enthusiastically. The patriciate were backed by the Church and the princes, who for some time remained loyal to the old faith. This gave them a new pretext for intervention in the internal affairs of the towns and for asserting their authority over them. Finally the suppression of Roman Catholicism had the effect of bringing the Hansa into conflict with Charles V at a time when imperial support would have made possible an expansion of commercial relations between north Germany and Spain, to the detriment of the Hollanders.

Faced with the religious and social conflicts which broke out in different towns, the Hansa, as usual, failed to adopt a uniform policy. Because the Hansa was essentially the organ of the town councils, it was at first hostile to any religious reform. In 1525 the diet at Lübeck passed measures against Luther's supporters and against the teaching of his doctrine, but only Hamburg, Rostock and Lüneburg drew up an ordinance embodying this decision. The other delegates argued that they had no authority to decide in such matters. The ordinance expressed hostility towards the

'Martinian sect', forbade the printing and sale of Luther's writings, and banned secret meetings of his followers, on pain of imprisonment.

The rapid spread of Lutheranism soon caused a change of attitude. In the same year a second diet proclaimed that in religious matters each town must decide for itself, avoiding only all revolt against established authority. In fact the Hansa, in accordance with her traditions, intervened no further in religious affairs, except in 1535 when she adopted an actively hostile policy towards the Anabaptists, and in 1563 towards Calvinism, which had become established in Bremen. These interventions merely served to demonstrate once more the weakness of the Hansa. Bremen, excluded from the community, had to be readmitted fourteen years later without any serious concessions having been made.

The Reformation established itself most easily in the east. It was introduced into Prussia by the Grand Master Albert of Hohenzollern, who secularised the Teutonic Order in 1525, to his own advantage. As the bishops declared for the new faith it was established peacefully, even in the Baltic districts, where the Land Master had remained faithful to Catholicism.

In Danzig, under the suzerainty of the Polish king, the Protestant tide was checked by the opposition of the burgomaster Ferber, the council and the king, who in 1526 deposed the council and re-established Catholicism by force. However this reaction was only temporary. The spread of Lutheranism was irresistible and in 1557 the king granted a charter permitting religious freedom.

In the west Catholicism put up a better defence, especially in the ecclesiastical principalities. In Cologne and other Rhenish towns it was never seriously threatened. In Westphalia, on the other hand, the Reformation had a fairly easy victory in Dortmund and later on in Soest, though the latter was to some extent forced back to the old faith. In 1531 the Reformers obtained a footing in Münster, despite the resistance of the bishop. But Anabaptists from the Low Countries carried the day and established the 'kingdom' of the twelve apostles of the prophet Mathys, whose place was taken after his death by Jan of Leiden. Terrorism and biblical communism reigned for a year, after which the town was taken by storm and Catholicism restored. This famous episode was not without consequences for the Hansa. The fright it caused helped to maintain or restore the patrician regime in other towns and accelerated the collapse of Lübeck's democratic government.

In the Saxon and Wendish towns the Reformation was introduced by

Bugenhagen, a disciple and friend of Luther. He left Wittenberg to organise the new Church first in the town of Brunswick (1528), then in Hamburg (1529), Lübeck (1531), Pomerania, Denmark (1537) and lastly in the duchy of Brunswick.

In most of the towns religious reform was accompanied by political and social demands. The middle and lower-middle classes seized the opportunity to limit and control the powers of the councils. The opposition usually worked through a commission of between forty and sixty members, supported by a larger assembly elected by the Lutheran parishes. As early as 1524 a commission of this kind, numbering forty members, had been set up in Wismar; its powers were largely financial. It contained twenty-three burgesses who were not members of a guild, including eight brewers, a ship-owner, a merchant, a miller and eleven men described merely as 'burgesses'. Among the twenty guild members there were retailers, weavers, smiths, bakers and four municipal officials. It is evident from these figures that the revolutionary movement was entirely confined to the guilds. As in the urban conflicts of the fourteenth and fifteenth centuries, some of the merchants joined in the struggle against the patricians. The Rostock commission of 1533–5, which numbered 64 members, was similarly constituted. It contained 10 brewers and at least 5 merchants, some of whom were related to members of the council. With regard to the seven classes of tax-payers, 12 members of the commission were in the first three classes, 41 in the fourth and fifth and 10 in the two last.

In Bremen the religious change was of a more radical character. Probably because of its hostility towards the archbishop, the feudal lord of the town, the council was favourably disposed towards Lutheranism. Even so, as early as 1526 the Reformers were demanding political reforms, and five years later the council was forced to work in collaboration with a commission of 40 members, replaced later by one of 64 members, elected by the parishes. Most of the councillors fled from the town as the revolutionaries showed open hostility towards the great merchants. The new regime prohibited the export of more than ten lasts of grain by any one citizen, or five lasts to Portugal. The participation of all foreigners in the export of grain and timber was forbidden. Meanwhile the archbishop made common cause with the exiles and in 1534 attacked the town, which soon gave in. The two commissions were suppressed, their leader executed, the powers of the council restored and the guilds rendered ineffective. But in spite of all this it was not possible to restore Catholicism.

The spread of the Reformation and even the social troubles which resulted from it offered no real threat to the Hansa. But as in the early years of the previous century, events in Lübeck, affecting the town's foreign policy, led to a crisis within the community.

From the beginning the Lübeck council had been strongly opposed to the new religion. This was partly because of their innate conservatism and their fear of offending the emperor, but mainly because the councillors feared that their cousins might lose their prebends and ecclesiastical dignities. When Lutheranism began to gain ground, the council expelled two preachers, proscribed Luther's writings and fined those who distributed them. But they were unable to prevent the spread of Luther's doctrines. In 1528 the council, needing money for the Danish war, was obliged to agree to a commission of 64 being formed, charged with the supervision of the expenditure of the revenues. Among them was Jürgen Wullenwever, who soon became the leader of the opposition. The commission repeatedly demanded the abrogation of measures hostile to the Reformation, and in 1530 the council had to recall the two preachers and to allow them to 'preach the gospel' in all churches. A few months later the council yielded to popular threats and abolished Catholic ceremonies. Bugenhagen came to organise the new Church, appointing a superintendent, assisted by jurors. The monasteries were secularised. The commission of 64 had all the gold and silver ornaments (amounting to 96 hundredweights) removed from the churches and used them to help finance the war. They also drew up a form of constitution in 26 articles, which gave them control of the council. The council could no longer conclude alliances, promulgate ordinances or contract loans without their consent. In future the town was to be administered jointly by the council, the 64 and an assembly of 100 members elected by the parishes. In the following year the council ratified the new ecclesiastical constitution.

The helplessness of the town's leaders was partly the result of the weakness of the Lübeck patriciate, which at this time was composed mainly of estate-owners and *rentiers*. It had almost ceased to co-opt merchants who had become rich by their own efforts. The opposition therefore had the support of a number of merchants as well as of the guilds. It is significant that the commission of 64 was led by two merchants, of whom Wullenwever was one, as well as by a brewer and an anchorsmith representing the two most influential guilds. If Wullenwever was able to succeed for a time in his great undertaking, it was because he had the backing of the most active elements among the Lübeck citizenry.

4. THE OVERTHROW OF WULLENWEVER

Jürgen Wullenwever was not a native of Lübeck. His family came originally from Perleberg in western Brandenburg and settled in Hamburg at the end of the fifteenth century. Jürgen's father, a great merchant, was a member of the Flanders Company. Of his three sons, the second, Joachim, remained in Hamburg, where he belonged to the England Company and became a member of the council. A zealous partisan of the Reformation, he was instrumental in persuading the town to co-operate in his brother's Danish policy. Jürgen, born about 1488, probably settled in Lübeck in 1526 and became a burgess in 1531, by which time he had already embarked on his political career. His reasons for going to Lübeck are not known; he probably wanted to trade in partnership with his brother. But he does not appear to have been successful, and it may have been this failure as well as his zeal for the Reformation which intensified his hostility towards the Lübeck patriciate.

As a member of the commission of 64 Wullenwever soon became very influential by reason of his eloquence and the sincerity of his religious convictions. In 1531, after the break between the Reformers and the patrician council, which had ratified the new ecclesiastical constitution with great reluctance, he began to play a preponderant part in Lübeck's affairs, particularly after Brömse and Plönnies, two of the four burgomasters, had left the town secretly – followed later by most of the councillors – and lodged a complaint with the emperor. Wullenwever took advantage of their flight to get seven new members admitted to the council, none of them patrician, though all were from the upper class of great merchants, *rentiers* and mercers. He was now effectively the ruler of the town and in 1533, when elected burgomaster, its lawful ruler.

So far events had followed much the same pattern as in other towns, but in Lübeck the triumph of the Reformation and the defeat of the patriciate soon led to an ambitious foreign policy, championed by Wullenwever. It was intended to exploit the dynastic quarrels in Denmark in order to enable Lübeck to gain control of the Sound and so close the Baltic to the Hollanders. Events seemed to favour such an enterprise. Christian II, king of Denmark and Norway since 1513 and brother-in-law of Charles V, had been overthrown in 1523 by his uncle Frederick I. Supported by the emperor and the Hollanders, he had landed in Norway in 1531 in an attempt to regain his crown. As a result Lübeck was able to bring pressure to bear on Frederick I, and she could also hope to form an alliance with Gustavus Vasa, elected king of Sweden in 1521 with her aid. The other Hansa towns were expected to support this policy, and in Lübeck itself Wullenwever was backed by both the merchants, terrified of Dutch competition, and the lower classes, traditionally hostile to the Danes. In Denmark itself, Lübeck could expect to find valuable allies, for here, as in Germany, social and religious antagonism was growing between the Catholic nobility and the townsfolk and even the peasants, who had been won over to the Reformation.

In fact the scheme proved abortive. Frederick I, far from collaborating in a policy of hostility towards the Hollanders, preferred to come to terms with them, on condition that they stopped supporting Christian II. He also contrived, by treacherous means, to capture his rival. The Hansa towns showed themselves lukewarm or even hostile towards Lübeck's plan. The Prussian towns in particular had no wish to exclude the Hollanders from the Baltic and only two Wendish towns, Rostock and Wismar, both of which were under a democratic government, gave it active support. Moreover Lübeck had been tactless enough to ask Gustavus Vasa to pay his debts, thus causing the Swedes to defect, and therefore found himself waging a war of piracy almost single-handed against the Hollanders.

The sudden death of Frederick I in April 1533 made the situation even more complicated. Lübeck and the Danish towns offered the crown to Christian, duke of Schleswig and Holstein, the son of the late king, a convert to Protestantism and a member of the League of Schmalkalden. But he refused to play Lübeck's game, preferring to negotiate his accession to the Danish throne with Charles V. Frustrated in this direction, Lübeck organised a naval demonstration under the direction of Wullenwever's strongest supporter, Marx Meyer – a curious figure, a former smith from Hamburg turned *condottiere* and head of Lübeck's armed forces. Charming, ostentatious, the subject of perpetual scandals, but without any real military talent, his influence over Wullenwever was unfortunate, and led him to make many hazardous decisions.

The naval expedition miscarried, but it had one unexpected result. Marx Meyer landed in England and gained the favour of Henry VIII, who knighted him and promised active support for Lübeck's policies. This was no doubt the reason for Wullenwever's uncompromising stand in the negotiations with the Hollanders which had begun at Hamburg. In spite of his isolated situation he demanded an indemnity of 300,000 guilders, and the negotiations broke down. By this time Wullenwever's position in Lübeck was already precarious. Ecclesiastical circles feared that popular excesses would compromise the Reformation, and the friends of the patriciate took heart. Wullenwever hurried back from Hamburg, had his adversaries condemned and manoeuvred some of his friends onto the council, which from then on included only four patrician members.

Having thus consolidated his position, Wullenwever took an extremely rash decision. He announced that Lübeck would no longer recognise the duke of Schleswig as king of Denmark, but would opt for Christian II, who was still a prisoner. He prepared a large-scale military expedition intended to free the captive, thus allowing Lübeck to pose as the champion of Christian's legitimate claims. The plan was hazardous, mainly because in abandoning the Protestant candidate (Duke Christian) for a man who had been reconverted to Catholicism and was moreover the brother-in-law of Charles V, Wullenwever risked arousing the distrust of the League of Schmalkalden and of the whole Protestant world. However he succeeded in winning over the burgomasters of Copenhagen and Malmö, as well as the Danish peasants who were opposed to the nobility. On the other hand Gustavus Vasa remained hostile and Wullenwever looked in vain for a claimant who could drive him from the Swedish throne. Henry VIII was approached but declined to help. The other Hansa towns also held back. Apart from Wismar and Rostock only Stralsund sent soldiers; Hamburg and Lüneburg were content with a modest financial grant. The strongest card in Lübeck's hand was the alliance with Count Christopher of Oldenburg, who provided the troops needed. Lübeck signed a convention with him, which bears witness to the scope of Wullenwever's grand design.*

Lübeck made the mistake of dispersing her effort. Marx Meyer undertook the conquest of Holstein, but was unable either to free Christian II or to win a decisive victory.

The expedition to Denmark, however, was a brilliant success. Christopher of Oldenburg disembarked in June 1534 in the island of Zealand and rapidly made himself master of Copenhagen and the islands. Malmö rose in revolt and recognised Christian II. The Sound was in the hands of the Germans and the toll was levied from their flagship.

Their triumph was short-lived. Duke Christian, supported by the Danish nobility and by various Protestant princes, among them the

* Document No. 13.

elector of Brandenburg and the dukes of Pomerania and Brunswick, was soon able to command an army stronger than that of his enemies. In July the nobility of Jutland and Fyn proclaimed him King Christian III. Wullenwever searched in vain for fresh allies, even going so far as to offer the crown of Denmark to the elector of Saxony and the crown of Sweden to the duke of Mecklenburg, a Catholic. From Henry VIII he obtained only financial help. The situation altered rapidly; when Christian III seized Travemünde, Lübeck was cut off from the sea. Wullenwever was openly criticised and was obliged to reinstate some of his adversaries on the council, and in November 1534 to conclude a truce, limited to Holstein, with Christian, whose own position had been weakened by a peasant revolt. The Danish expedition was liquidated the following year. Despite the intervention of the duke of Mecklenburg, Lübeck suffered two decisive defeats. The first was on land, in Fyn, the other at sea, off Svendborg in the Great Belt, where the Danish fleet was reinforced by Prussian ships. Christian III reconquered the islands. Only Copenhagen held out for another year; it was defended by Christopher, waiting in vain for help from Charles V.

These successive defeats brought about Wullenwever's downfall. A Hanseatic diet, to which about twenty towns, from Kampen to Riga, sent delegations, called on Lübeck to end the war. Lübeck decided to obey an imperial mandate ordering, under penalty of the imperial ban, the reinstatement of the patrician councillors and the exclusion of their supplanters. In the absence of Wullenwever his nominees resigned from the council. On 19 August 1535 he followed their example. Two days later the former patrician burgomaster Brömse, having promised to recognise the constitution of the Lutheran Church, was restored to office. At first Wullenwever was left in peace. He even began negotiations with Henry VIII with a view to resuming the struggle. But while crossing the territory of his enemy, the archbishop of Bremen, he was arrested and handed over to the duke of Brunswick, who ordered him to be tried. Torture dragged from him the avowal of crimes which he had not committed: expropriation of church property, the planning of armed revolt in Lübeck, a plot to introduce the doctrines of the Anabaptists. On 24 September 1537 he was decapitated and his corpse drawn and quartered.

His eventful and dramatic career and the vastness of his aims have made Wullenwever the best-known in the history of the Hansa. In the nineteenth and twentieth centuries he was made the subject of a number of novels and plays which usually presented him in a favourable light. Historians, however, since Georg Waitz, have criticised him more severely, denouncing his demagogy, his unstable character, his contradictions, his mistakes and the chimerical nature of his enterprise. He certainly lacked the qualities of a great statesman and made many mistakes, of which the least excusable – if indeed it was his mistake – was the alienation of Gustavus Vasa. It was foolish, in that day and age, to base a Hanseatic intervention in politics on the hope of popular support in opposition to the patriciate. Wullenwever moreover failed to realise that the decline of the Hansa was irreparable and that even he could not arrest it. But of course it was not as easy for him to see this as it is for us. The partial success of the Danish expedition shows that his policy was not entirely chimerical. It brought Lübeck substantial, if only temporary, advantages. There remains one further question, to which no definite answer can be given: did Wullenwever really inspire and direct the town's policy during these crucial years, or was he only the town's spokesman?

After Wullenwever's fall the patrician council hastened to bring the adventure to a close as cheaply as possible. They concluded a peace with Christian III, recognising him as king on condition that the Hanseatic privileges were confirmed, and signed a five-year truce with Sweden. But the Danish affair was not yet settled. Charles V quarrelled with Christian III and put up a rival against him, the Count Palatine Frederick, his niece's husband. He even brought in the Hollanders against the Danes. But Lübeck, discouraged by defeat, made no attempt to recover lost ground, and in 1544 Charles V, by the Treaty of Speyer, abandoned his candidate and obtained the right of free passage through the Sound for his Dutch subjects. The trial of strength between the Hollanders and the Hansa, for which the prize was commercial supremacy in the Baltic, ended in a victory for the Hollanders.

Two years later a fresh danger arose. Charles V, having consolidated his power in south Germany, began to extend his authority in the north and combat Protestantism there. Most of the great Hansa towns had joined the League of Schmalkalden and so found themselves directly threatened. They either withdrew into a prudent neutrality or submitted, with the exception of Magdeburg and Bremen. The former was put under the imperial ban, the latter was blockaded by imperial forces on two occasions (March and May 1547) and had her entire fleet seized. However the siege had to be raised shortly afterwards and the imperialists were defeated by the Protestant princes at Drakenburg. In spite of his decisive victory at Mühlberg, Charles V was ready to come to terms, and the Hansa towns were thus freed from the fear of religious reaction and political conquest.

These shocks seriously undermined the strength and stability of the Hansa. The lack of unity among its members had often made itself felt. In 1534 Lübeck had struggled almost unaided against Denmark. The other towns had either abandoned her or, like Danzig, turned openly against her. When one remembers that in 1367 an almost identical situation had resulted in a general enthusiasm which bound the maritime towns together, the contrast needs no further elaboration. It is not surprising that in the eyes of the world the Hansa was profoundly discredited. Up to now Lübeck had been regarded as the head of a powerful confederation. In future she would represent only herself, and foreign powers, notably England under Henry VIII, would cease to accord her any special consideration. In contrast the prestige of Denmark, Sweden and Holland would be enhanced, and the balance of power in the northern seas would be completely reversed.

CHAPTER FOURTEEN

Renewal and Eclipse (1550–1669)

By the mid-sixteenth century the Hansa appeared to be on the point of dissolution. The isolation and impotence to which Lübeck had been reduced by her disastrous adventure of 1534 seemed to herald a complete breakdown. But in the second half of the century there was a genuine Hanseatic revival, which showed itself in serious, and to some extent successful, attempts to strengthen the links of the community. In some Hansa towns there was a remarkable expansion of trade, due to one unfortunate circumstance, the revolt of the northern Netherlands against Spain, which allowed the Hansa, with imperial support, to capture – if only temporarily – some of the trade between northern Europe and the Iberian peninsula which had till then been in the hands of the Dutch.

However this partial and short-lived renewal did not arrest the forces of disintegration. In the east the conquest of Livonia by the Russians and Swedes weakened the community by depriving it of the Baltic towns. In the west English competition, long held in check, became stronger and stronger as the Merchant Adventurers gained an increasing share of the trade between England and Germany. The Thirty Years War struck its final death blow: when peace was eventually restored, the Hanseatic community was no longer able to reconstitute itself.

1. ATTEMPTS AT REORGANISATION

From about 1500 onwards two opposing opinions were often expressed in Hanseatic circles. Some said the Hansa was moribund and that nothing could prevent its decease. Others maintained that it was essential, for the general good, to revive the Hansa, either by old and tried methods or by new ones. Before the Thirty Years War this latter point of view was widespread. Innumerable plans for reform were proposed and discussed at the diets, and several of them were put into operation.

Many thought that salvation could only be assured by outside help.

They saw clearly that the Hansa's weakness derived principally from the lack of support by a strong government such as her competitors enjoyed. In addition the fact that the Hansa towns owed allegiance to so many different rulers could not fail to paralyse the community's activities. This gave rise to the idea that the Hansa should put herself under the protection of some powerful prince. The emperor was a fairly obvious choice, but experience had shown that little in the way of effective support could be expected from that direction. Swayed now this way, now that, by opposing interests within the Empire, the emperor, being based on southern Germany and champion of Roman Catholicism, inspired too much distrust for any appeal to be made to him. The king of Denmark, the hereditary enemy, was out of the question. On more than one occasion Danzig proposed the king of Poland as protector, preserver and defender of the Hansa. But the meetings held to discuss this proposal came to nothing, the interests of the respective parties being too divergent.

Another project envisaged was an alliance with the imperial cities throughout Germany. The suggestion came from these cities themselves and arose from their desire to strengthen their own independence and authority against the princes and the emperor. This was essentially a resumption of the old dream of making the cities one of the constituent elements of the empire, which had come to so lamentable an end with the Rhenish Town League of 1254. Its persistence is striking. It was still leading to a constant exchange of letters in the second half of the seventeenth century. But it was evident that an urban league of this kind was utopian. In fact the attempt to strengthen the Hansa by external support was to achieve only one success, the alliance concluded with the United Provinces in 1616. And even that did not last long enough to bear fruit, being brought to an abrupt conclusion by the Thirty Years War.

These attempts at consolidation from without were all more or less impractical. A far more realistic approach was that of trying to strengthen the community from within. Here again two conflicting concepts were current, between which a clear choice was never made. Some believed that the community should be restored to its former size and that recalcitrant towns should be compelled to discharge their Hanseatic duties. Under urgent and persuasive pressure some towns, which had for a long time abstained from sending representatives to the *Hansetag*, agreed to do so once more and proclaimed officially that they were still members of the Hansa. But such demonstrations were little more than empty

gestures. Others, especially Bremen, believed that it was useless to envisage a large community, as long as most towns refused to carry out their
duties and turned to the Hansa only when their own interests were
threatened. It would be better to group together a few loyal towns,
prepared to make sacrifices for the common good. In accordance with this
concept a tentative alliance was formed at the beginning of the seventeenth
century between the six principal Saxon and Wendish towns, which
intervened on behalf of Brunswick when the latter was threatened by its
duke. But nothing permanent came of this. On the other hand the
alliance concluded in 1630 between Bremen, Hamburg and Lübeck,
though not very effective, was to have a long existence, thus ensuring
that the Hansa should at least appear to survive into the twentieth
century.

By the mid-sixteenth century the general wish to strengthen the community had resulted in two important measures. The first was the
constitution of a league, involving clearly defined financial obligations,
modelled on the *tohopesate* of the fifteenth century, and the second the
appointment of a Hanseatic functionary known as the syndic. This was
a completely new departure.

Discussions about a possible remodelling of the Hanseatic structure had
been going on for a long time, but had come to nothing, owing to the
opposition of Cologne, where it was feared that an urban league would
offend the princes. Eventually Cologne revised her attitude and accepted
a project for a confederation to last for ten years, with members' obligations strictly enumerated. The *Hansetag* of 1557 drew up a constitution
in ten articles (*Konfederationsnotel*), to which the chief towns of the
four quarters (Cologne, Brunswick, Lübeck and Danzig) affixed their
seals, and which was accepted by the sixty-three towns represented at the
diet. This constitution merely repeated ordinances which had often been
agreed upon – obligation to send delegates to the diets and to put the
decisions of diets into execution; obligation to submit any dispute between
two towns to arbitration by the neighbouring towns and as a last resort
to the general diet, but absolute prohibition of resort to any foreign
jurisdiction; common responsibility for the protection of land and sea
routes, for ambassadorial costs, for compensation to victims of aggression;
common armed intervention against aggressors; strict control over
foreigners, loafers and artisans; expulsion of guilty parties who refused
to accept sentence. The constitution also called attention to the respect
and obedience due to the emperor and the princes who were the over-

lords of the various towns, and even authorised separate alliances between members of the confederation and non-Hanseatic powers.

Ten years later, in 1579, the confederation was extended, and on more than one occasion articles were revised or made more precise. The constitution as a whole remained in force until the Thirty Years War. But it could not restore the Hansa to its former vigour, and the ordinances it embodied were often disregarded. The list of sixty-three towns which accepted the constitution is somewhat misleading. Many of them, particularly the Livonian towns and those on the Zuiderzee, as well as Goslar in Saxony, were on the point of withdrawing from the community. The paucity of members in the Brunswick quarter, reduced to seven Saxon towns, none of them lying south of the Harz, bore witness to the growing defection of the inland towns. Half the contingent was made up of Rhenish and Westphalian towns, most of them very small. Nevertheless, in comparison with the preceding period, the Hansa was strengthened sufficiently to allow it to continue for another sixty years.

The most remarkable achievement of the confederation was the general acceptance and partial application of the principle that all member towns should make an annual financial contribution. Never before had the Hansa been able to obtain anything more than exceptional levies for particular purposes. Now the need to raise funds caused the diet, as early as 1554, to levy an annual tax (*annuum*) to be prepaid for five years by the sixty-three towns. The scale was fixed according to the estimated wealth of each town. Cologne and Lübeck were rated at 100 thalers a year, Hamburg and Danzig at 80, Bremen, Lüneburg and Königsberg at 60, and so on down to the smallest towns, which paid 10 thalers. The diet of 1557 approved the levy but did not include the tax scales in the articles of the constitution. From then on, though there were many arguments about the rating, the principle of prepayment was never called in question. The same scale was used as a basis for exceptional levies. As occasion required, members were expected to pay a contribution twice, thrice, ten times and even, in 1591, forty times the normal rate.

Naturally these levies gave rise to bitter recriminations, and could not always be collected. From the beginning most of the Saxon towns were reluctant to pay up, and threats of exclusion had no effect. In 1601 Cologne owed more than 8,000 thalers and Königsberg 3,600. Other towns were in arrears for smaller sums. Only Lübeck, Hamburg and two or three other towns had paid in full. It was soon necessary to concede a disguised tax remission to the smaller communities, who were asked to pay only the basic sum (*annuum*). The augmented exceptional levies (*kontributio*) were required only from the fourteen most important towns.

The institution of regular taxes should have been complemented by the creation of an autonomous Hanseatic treasury, but as in previous centuries, such a measure remained unrealised. In practice Lübeck or some other town or towns were obliged to advance the necessary funds, hoping to be repaid later, after long delays, from the proceeds of the annual contribution. Failing the establishment of a treasury, there should at least have been carefully controlled accounts. At the diet of 1579 thirteen towns did present their accounts, but nothing could be obtained from the others. Some declared themselves insolvent, others presented long-winded memoranda dealing with matters going back more than a hundred years. The accounts to be checked amounted to several hundred thousand thalers, and the attempt to clear up the confusion had to be abandoned.

This state of affairs eventually induced the community to set up in 1612 a common treasury, under strict supervision. But the revenues deposited in it were limited: taxes raised in the *Kontore*, profits from the sale of the ordnance belonging to the Bergen *Kontor* or of the silver plate of the Steelyard, fines, and so on. In fact the treasury seldom appears to have had more than a thousand thalers at its disposal and it could not fulfil its intended function. There is no doubt that the work of restoration undertaken by the confederation was seriously hampered by these financial difficulties.

The desire for reform is also evident in the appointment in 1556 of a 'syndic of the Hansa', both title and function being entirely new. The community had always suffered from not having its own officials, to prepare the agenda for the diets and deal with outstanding matters between sessions. These duties had in fact been undertaken first by the Lübeck council and later on by the Lübeck syndic. In the mid-sixteenth century the need for a permanent official with legal training made itself felt with particular urgency. The post was entrusted to Heinrich Sudermann of Cologne. No better choice could have been made. A member of an illustrious patrician family, the son of a burgomaster, a doctor of law of the university of his native town, on whose behalf he had already been employed as a diplomat, he devoted himself whole-heartedly for thirty-five years to the Hanseatic cause. As legal adviser he took part indefatigably in every diet and in all the negotiations. In fourteen years he made nearly fifty diplomatic journeys, mainly to the Low Countries and

England, but also to all parts of Germany, to Bohemia and Poland. His greatest wish, which he realised in spite of all obstacles, only to see it eventually nullified, was the organisation of the Hanseatic *Kontor* at Antwerp along traditional lines.

Appointed originally for six years, Sudermann was later retained in his post, and in 1576 was appointed syndic for life.* On this occasion, in addition to his diplomatic and legal responsibilities, he was charged with the task of making an inventory of the charters, and of composing a history of the Hansa, and a treatise on maritime law. He was not able to complete any of these tasks. Although in general honoured for his zeal, he was subjected to many indignities. His accounts were criticised, payment of his expenses was often evaded, and only part of the salary and emoluments due to him was forthcoming. But up to his death in 1591 he was ceaselessly active, in very truth the soul of the community and the last of the great Hanseatics.

Sudermann had proved beyond doubt how useful it was to have a Hanseatic syndic. Yet, for petty reasons of economy, he was not immediately replaced, and the post was not filled until 1605, when Johann Doman, syndic of Stralsund, was appointed. Doman, too, was very active. As a diplomat he was less successful than his predecessor and provoked more criticism, but he remained in office, except for an interval of one year, until his death in 1618. After him one of the Lübeck syndics was regularly appointed to the position up to the dissolution of the community. Although the efficiency of the syndics of the Hansa was impaired by the jealous supervision and niggardly interference to which they were subject, the creation and continuity of the office bear witness to the vitality of the community.

The same vigour is shown by the increased number of Hanseatic diets held after 1550. There had been only three between 1535 and 1552. There were fourteen, almost one a year, between 1553 and 1567. The figure then fell to five between 1568 and 1597, but rose to twenty between 1598 and 1621. The diets of the quarters also continued to meet. That of the Wendish towns was often in session, and these continued to play a leading role, often taking the initiative or opening negotiations in the name of the Hansa as a whole. As in the past, Lübeck remained the head of the community, perhaps even more firmly than in earlier days. Neither the Wullenwever episode nor the relative decline of the town, which had been overtaken by Hamburg as regards both population and

* Document No. 29.

the volume of trade, seriously threatened its leading position. On several occasions Lübeck asked to be relieved of this burden, which might, she suggested, be taken over by Bremen or Cologne, but these suggestions were not listened to. As leader of the Hansa, Lübeck was irreplaceable.

The community undoubtedly retained its prestige until the end of the sixteenth century, as is shown by the requests for admission which were still occasionally received. For example on four occasions between 1521 and 1553 Narva applied for admission into the Hansa. Each time Riga and Reval, who feared, not without reason, a rapidly expanding rival, caused the application to be rejected. Emden also made an unsuccessful request for admission in 1597. The town was criticised for her excessive complaisance towards the Dutch. The Hansa also showed that despite her weaknesses she would not tolerate flagrant violation of the constitution by her members. In 1563 Bremen, which had adopted Calvinism and ejected its council, was excluded from the community. But this act of severity miscarried, for the Hansa was not strong enough to force the town into submission, and Bremen eventually brought the matter before the emperor, on whose orders the town was readmitted in 1576, without having made any real concessions. The last sentence of exclusion fell in 1601 on the little town of Stade, guilty of having granted a privileged establishment to English merchants; but the sanction was of no practical consequence.

All in all, the praiseworthy efforts made by the Hansa during the second half of the sixteenth century to strengthen her organisation had no lasting results. The sense of solidarity between her members was steadily decreasing, the towns were evading their financial responsibilities and did not even trouble to send delegates to the diets. Between 1606 and 1628 Cologne was not represented at a single *Hansetag*. Grave external failures, added to weaknesses within, hastened the decline which from now on nothing could arrest.

2. THE DISASTERS: LIVONIA, ANTWERP, ENGLAND

In the mid-sixteenth century eastern Europe was the centre of far-reaching political upheavals which did much damage to the Hansa. At the end of the fifteenth century the Russian drive towards the Baltic had been halted by the Livonian branch of the Teutonic Order. The ruin of Novgorod had brought prosperity to the Livonian towns, which inherited the bulk of Novgorod's trade with the west. However fifty years of peace came to an end when Ivan IV (the Terrible) resumed the policy of Muscovite expansion. In 1558 he suddenly attacked Livonia, which the Teutonic Order was unable to defend. The Russians seized Narva and Dorpat, which was completely destroyed, and most of the country. Only Riga and Reval escaped. The Land Master looked about for allies. Lübeck and the other Hansa towns were content to send money and munitions. In return for territorial concessions, Denmark and Poland gave military support, but they were unable to stem the tide. In 1562 the Land Master Ketteler secularised what was left of his state under the name of the duchy of Courland and Semigallia, and accepted Polish suzerainty. The island of Ösel became Danish, and Swedish protection was extended to Reval. It was the end of the Teutonic state.

The Russian advance had profound repercussions throughout Europe. There was talk of a crusade, then of at least breaking off commercial relations with Russia. But events proved otherwise. Ivan the Terrible had spared Narva, and instead of destroying the town, as he had destroyed Dorpat, he helped it to recover and made it a Russian port on the Baltic. Its trade increased very rapidly and soon it eclipsed Reval, being visited by merchants from the Baltic countries, by Danes, Hollanders, English, Scots, and even by Frenchmen and Spaniards. All these brought in cloth and salt and took out furs and wax, which they could buy more cheaply now that they no longer had to deal with the Livonian middlemen. In a short time hundreds of ships were putting in every year at Narva, which had become an important international port on the Baltic.

Lübeck was not slow to take advantage of this situation. She had been seriously alarmed by the news of Chancellor's journey to the White Sea in 1553, and even more by the charter granted shortly afterwards to the Muscovy Company by Ivan IV. It looked as if the English, with the new route through Archangel, would soon capture the whole of Russian trade with the west. As early as 1556 the Hanseatic diet had strictly forbidden its members to travel by the new route, and as a result Lübeck established relations with Narva as quickly as possible. Ignoring Reval, where her merchants had suffered many vexations during the last fifty years, Lübeck sent her ships in increasing numbers to the new Russian port, to resume their former trade. She was even accused of selling war materials to the Russians, in defiance of the imperial ban, a charge which she rejected indignantly.

The new situation was barely under control when it was threatened by the entrance of Sweden upon the scene. The Swedes, as protectors of Reval and its interests, were anxious to dominate the Gulf of Finland in order to share in the profits from Russian trade. It was inevitable that they should oppose Lübeck. In 1565 they seized thirty-two Lübeck ships returning from Narva. When hostilities broke out in the following year between Denmark and Sweden at the start of the Nordic Seven Years War (or the War of the Three Crowns, as it was called, because it had been declared on the futile pretext that Frederick II of Denmark persisted in displaying the three Scandinavian crowns in his coat of arms), Lübeck ranged herself resolutely on the side of Denmark, reproaching Sweden with aspiring to the *dominium* of the Baltic. She posed as the champion of Hanseatic rights and liberties, an attitude which aroused neither sympathy nor imitation in the other towns of the community, who had no intention of interrupting their commercial relations with Sweden. Ranged on the side of Denmark, Lübeck found herself even more isolated than in the days of Wullenwever.

Nevertheless she conducted the war with surprising energy. She equipped four warships, among them the *Adler,* one of the largest of the period, a 68-gun three-decker of 3,000 tons burden, and was for a time successful. But in 1566 she suffered a decisive defeat off Gotland, when her flagship, the *Morian*, was sunk. From the Hanseatic point of view it is the relentless fury with which two of the community's towns attacked one another which is revealing. In 1569 a Lübeck squadron bombarded Reval and captured or burnt 100 vessels.

The terms of the Peace of Stettin (1570) were not unfavourable, but they remained a dead letter. Lübeck had been unable to safeguard her trade with the Russians. In 1581 the Swedes occupied Narva, and all hope of developing trade with this town was at an end. Reval's trade began to expand as she resumed her function as intermediary. Lübeck's trade with Russia was again dependent on the goodwill of either Sweden or Poland. Once more war had favoured the neutral merchants, the Dutch and the English, and had resulted in a fresh advance by the rivals of the Hansa. It had also demonstrated the lack of unity within the community and shown how impossible it was to reconcile the fundamentally divergent interests of its members. The Livonian towns, subject to either Sweden or Poland, could no longer be considered Hanseatic.

From the military point of view Lübeck had had the worst of it. The sacrifices she had been ready to make had been in vain. She had learned her lesson and now renounced all attempts to forward her commercial interests by the use of force. Thus the War of the Three Crowns marks the end of the Hansa as a naval power in the Baltic.

While the strength of the Hansa was being severely tested in the east by war, great hopes were based on the reorganisation of the *Kontor* in Antwerp. Since the beginning of the sixteenth century the Hanseatic merchants, like those of all other countries, had abandoned Bruges in favour of Antwerp. The town was prosperous and there were as many of them there as there had formerly been in Bruges – more than a hundred in normal times. But they no longer formed an organised community, partly because the Hansa had for so long clung to the fiction of the *Kontor* at Bruges. The three aldermen who formed the *Kontor* council lacked all authority and had at their disposal only a ridiculously small sum of money, since no one except the Cologners bothered to pay the tax on business transactions. The funds necessary for the maintenance of the Hanseatic buildings in Bruges had to be borrowed from the towns. The German merchants, eager to form partnerships with burgesses of Antwerp or with foreigners, allowed them to profit from the Hanseatic privileges and facilitated their trade with northern Germany.

Only one solution could be envisaged. The Hanseatic merchants would have to be regrouped into a community organised on traditional lines. In 1540 negotiations were begun with Antwerp in the hope of obtaining confirmation and extension of the old privileges. After considerable delays the town promised important franchises in the event of a permanent *Kontor* being created, but the project made no progress until the syndic Sudermann was charged with its execution. In 1555 the diet decided to restore the *Kontor*. In the same year a delegation was sent to Antwerp and instituted a new council consisting of three aldermen and four assessors, with authority over all Hanseatic merchants in the town. Its main task was to collect and administer the *schoss*, which was levied once more.

It was not easy to put these measures into execution. Many German merchants had settled permanently in Antwerp, married and gone into business with foreign partners, practices which the Hansa had always forbidden. These *husgesetene* ('house-owning settlers'), as they were called, were ordered to move to a Hansa town of their choice, together with their wives and children, entrusting their affairs in Antwerp to an unmarried agent. Thirteen of them – including some very rich ones – refused, choosing rather to be excluded from all Hanseatic privileges.

It was still not enough. It was obvious that even the merchants who had obeyed the order would continue to carry on prohibited commercial operations in partnership with Antwerp burgesses. In order to keep an eye on them, Sudermann conceived the ambitious plan of building a large centre in which they would be obliged to lodge and to lead a community life, as had always been the rule in the other *Kontore*, but never in Bruges. In 1563 Antwerp agreed, ceded a site on the edge of the new town, took over a third of the construction costs and conceded the Hansa full ownership of the finished edifice.

The work was undertaken by an Antwerp architect and was completed in four years (1564–8). It was the largest of the Hanseatic civic edifices. A painting of it by van Uden has been preserved and gives an idea of its size. It was in the form of a quadrilateral surrounding a great courtyard, covering 5,000 square metres, with a façade 80 metres long; it had 'as many windows as the year has days', 23 store-rooms, 133 bedrooms and 27 cellars, as well as dormitories, refectories and kitchens. It was a fitting symbol of resurgent Hanseatic power, and seemed to presage a brilliant commercial future.

But the Hansa was out of luck. Even before the building was completed, the iconoclastic disturbances which foretold the approach of civil strife had broken out, and the economic activity of the town began to diminish. Soon the *Kontor* was struggling with insoluble financial difficulties, which grew even worse after the sack of the city by the Spaniards in 1576. Its debts, which amounted at that time to 18,000 pounds, could not be paid, as had been hoped, by the revenues of the *schoss*, which were dwindling away. The Hansa towns had to come to the help of the *Kontor* with a 'contribution' of ten times the normal tax, but even this brought in only 5,000 thalers. The siege of Antwerp by Alexander Farnese in 1584 put the last merchants to flight. In 1591 recourse had to be had to a fresh 'contribution', forty times that of the normal annual tax. The Hansa even had to sell the *Kontor* plate; but this did little to ease the situation.

More serious than these financial embarrassments was the complete failure of the attempt to restore Hanseatic trade in the Low Countries through the Antwerp *Kontor*. The consequences of Antwerp's ruin were not all to be deplored. Cologne and Hamburg profited by the immigration of foreign merchants. But from the strictly Hanseatic point of view, the unsuccessful attempt to re-establish a *Kontor* in the Low Countries, which might well have revived the fading sense of solidarity between the towns, was a mortal blow to the community.

In England Hanseatic trade continued to flourish during the first half of the sixteenth century, and the German merchants were on the whole successful in exacting respect for their privileged status. As in earlier times, these favourable conditions were due to the goodwill shown by the crown towards the Hanseatics. But in the second half of the century the situation was changing. The monarchy began to support the Merchant Adventurers, and to favour English commercial expansion on the Continent. In the circumstances Hanseatic trade in England was bound to decline.

In 1553 Edward VI declared the Hanseatic privileges lapsed. The concept of the Hansa was so vague, he said, that anyone could enjoy the benefits of membership. A few months later Queen Mary I officially restored them, but they continued to be disregarded, with the result that the Hansa decreed a suspension of trade. In the following year, however, the community authorised Germans to trade with Englishmen in the Low Countries, and maintained the blockade only against England itself. This was a sure way to make it ineffective.

The accession of Elizabeth I caused a momentary slackening of tension. When war broke out between England and the Spanish Netherlands in 1563, the Hansa displayed its usual lack of resolution. In spite of Sudermann's efforts Cologne and Hamburg, who were chiefly interested in maintaining trade with England, wrecked the attempt to form an alliance with the regent of the Low Countries. Worse still, since the English had fixed the staple for their cloth at Emden – not a Hansa town – Hamburg offered them a privileged establishment in Hamburg. A ten-year agreement was signed in 1567 and Sudermann could do nothing to prevent it. The Merchant Adventurers were granted two houses, legal guarantees and exemption from customs dues on more or less the same footing as native burgesses. They were forbidden only to sell retail, to trade along the Elbe, and to dye and finish their cloth themselves. Although one article specified that this agreement should not adversely affect the Hanseatic privileges in England, it was a real betrayal of the community. Hamburg had put its own interest before that of the other towns. The agreement proved very profitable to Hamburg, but otherwise Hanseatic trade in England diminished while English trade in Germany expanded. The Hansa again gave proof of her own weakness by not daring to take strong measures against Hamburg. She was content to bring pressure to bear on the town to make it cancel the agreement, in which she was eventually successful. Meanwhile German merchants in

England, even those from Hamburg, were continually harassed, and in 1578 the Hamburg council decided not to renew the Merchant Adventurers' privilege. But these continued their operations, making first Emden and then Stade the import centre for their cloth.

English merchants were penetrating not only into western Germany but also into the Baltic, where they were able to turn the rivalry between the Hansa towns to their own advantage. When Danzig, which they visited more than any other town, showed signs of hostility because her merchants were being obstructed in England, they turned to Elbing. After long-drawn-out negotiations the Merchant Adventurers, grouped together in an Eastland Company, were granted a privileged establishment in the town in 1579. Danzig made every possible effort to prevent it, but in vain. All that the king of Poland would do was to refuse to ratify the agreement, a step which did little to retard the growth of the establishment. The Hansa lacked the resolution to condemn Elbing publicly, but thereafter the town was apparently not regarded as a member of the community. This does not seem to have done her much damage. When the question of her readmission was discussed some years later, she laid down such exorbitant conditions that in 1618 her application was rejected.

The English charter in Elbing remained in force until 1628. At first it proved very profitable to the town. More than a hundred English ships called there in 1586 and 1587, and then an average of fifty a year up to 1612. They brought in cloth and took away grain and flax. It was ominous that such prosperity could, as in Hamburg, only be won by the betrayal of Hanseatic solidarity.

In the meantime Lübeck was trying to block the commercial progress of the English, and could find no better way of doing so than by appealing to the Emperor Rudolf II and accusing the Merchant Adventurers of arrogating to themselves a monopoly contrary to imperial laws. She even obtained from the imperial diet a vote decreeing the expulsion of the English, but the emperor failed to sign it. The English were quite unmoved and, particularly after the defeat of the invincible Armada, became increasingly intractable. In 1589, after accusing the Hansa of having supported the Spaniards, they seized sixty Hanseatic vessels off Lisbon. The Steelyard was thenceforward almost entirely deserted by German merchants.

Hamburg, annoyed at the favour shown to Stade by the English, joined the Hansa in a second approach to the emperor, hoping to obtain energetic measures against them. In 1597, after a long period of indecision, Rudolf II, probably urged on by Spain, forbade the admission of the Merchant Adventurers into Germany or dealings with them, under penalty of the imperial ban, on the pretext that they were pursuing monopolistic policies and obstructing the freedom of the seas. The counter-attack came almost at once. On 13 January 1598 Elizabeth I ordered the closing of the London Steelyard and forbade the Hanseatics to trade or even to remain within her realm. Only the merchants of Danzig and Elbing, who were not subjects of the emperor,* were excluded from the edict. Shortly afterwards the buildings of the Steelyard were sequestrated.

This outrage caused a great stir in Germany, but in reality, as in the case of the *Peterhof* in Novgorod a century before, the closing of the Steelyard only confirmed officially the irreparable decline of Hanseatic trade in England. It was simply a form of reprisal, and in 1606 the Steel-yard was returned to its owners. But it was too late to save the *Kontor*.

The Hansa was to suffer an even more serious defeat on the Continent when Stade refused to accept the loss of her profitable English trade and, undeterred by exclusion from the community, successfully negotiated the return of the Merchant Adventurers in 1601. Six years later the emperor confirmed the privileges of the English establishment. In 1611 Hamburg, after some hesitation, also resolved to renew the charter of the Merchant Adventurers on substantially the same terms as in 1567. This agreement proved very profitable to both the English and Hamburg, but it was a heavy blow to the Hansa. Her merchants, who for centuries had controlled north German and Baltic trade with England, now saw them-selves driven out of the country and overtaken by their rivals even inside Germany.

3. COMMERCIAL EXPANSION

The increasing ascendancy of foreigners, the reverses suffered in the east and west, and the marked lack of unity among the towns constitute irre-futable proof of Hanseatic decadence in the second half of the sixteenth century. However the same period is characterised by an unprecedented rise in Hanseatic trade, particularly noticeable in certain great ports. This was essentially the result of a general increase in European trade in this period, clearly seen both in the number of ships and in the amount of merchandise transported, and confirmed by the accounts of the Sound,

* Document No. 14.

which have been preserved more or less intact from the mid-century onwards. The Hansa benefited greatly from this general expansion, although to a lesser degree than her rivals. She profited in particular from the increased demand for cereals in the Low Countries, the Iberian peninsula and Italy; the ruin of Antwerp, which caused some of the larger foreign firms to set up establishments in northern Germany; and the struggle between Spain and the United Provinces, which allowed her to capture, partially and temporarily, the trade normally carried on by the Dutch. It is therefore not a paradox to say that the Hansa in the time of her decline achieved a greater degree of commercial prosperity than in the days of her greatness.

One of the factors in her prosperity was her merchant fleet, which has been estimated by Walther Vogel at 1,000 ships with a carrying capacity of 45,000 lasts (90,000 metric tons) at the close of the sixteenth century; a third of them belonged to Lübeck, another third to Hamburg. This represents an increase of about 50 per cent over the fleet of the late fifteenth century.

Until the time of the Thirty Years War Lübeck had always had a larger fleet than any other Hansa town. In 1595 she had 253 ships, 50 of which exceeded 120 lasts, with a total carrying capacity of about 9,000 lasts. This may have been increased still further in the seventeenth century. The shipyards were always busy and fifteen to twenty vessels were launched each year: from 1608 to 1620, 270 ships of 40 to 50 lasts; from 1621 to 1641, 457 ships, of which 6 were more than 200 lasts and 73 were of 120 lasts. Obviously the yards adapted their building programme to current trading requirements. Before 1608 and after 1621 they produced a higher than average number of large ships, intended for the voyage to Spain. During the truce between Spain and the Netherlands, when the Dutch were once more handling the bulk of the Iberian trade, they built smaller vessels, designed for trade within the Baltic. The Thirty Years War saw no slackening of activity in the Lübeck shipyards. The decline did not set in until after the Peace of Westphalia.

The Hanseatic fleet no longer represented the entire German mercantile marine, as it had in the fifteenth century, for the last thirty years of the sixteenth century were marked by a sudden unprecedented expansion of the merchant fleet of the little town of Emden, which was not a member of the community. According to a list of 1572 Emden was the home port of 572 ships of from 10 to over 100 lasts, representing a total carrying capacity of 21,000 lasts, equal, in fact, to the merchant fleet of

England. This expansion is easily explained. The Dutch, while in revolt
against the Spaniards, could no longer trade with the Iberian peninsula.
They therefore set up numerous business concerns in Emden, so as to
be able to continue trading under a neutral flag. But the changing fortunes
of the town and of the Low Countries brought about Emden's rapid decline. By the end of the sixteenth century the Emden fleet had been
halved and in the early years of the seventeenth century it was reduced to
a quarter. But even this still allowed the port to play an appreciable role
in the commerce of the northern seas.

The Hanseatic fleet was certainly much smaller than that of the
Dutch, which was expanding rapidly. It has been estimated that at the
end of the sixteenth century the latter had a carrying capacity of 120,000
lasts, and at its peak in the middle of the seventeenth century, 250,000 lasts.
In addition the Dutch were clearly superior in the art of naval construction. From 1595 onwards they built a great many cargo ships of a new
type, the *Fluite*, whose overall length was from four to six times its width,
of shallow draught and with an improved suit of sails. The *Fluite* was a
fast ship and could make two trips a year from the Baltic to Spain instead
of one. The Hanseatics had no alternative but to build the new type of
ship themselves; but it was not until 1618 that the first *Fluite* was launched
from a Lübeck shipyard. The superiority of the Dutch was overwhelming
from all points of view. Meanwhile the English navy was developing
rapidly. In 1582 it was estimated at 67,000 tons, in 1629 at 115,000, by
which time it had surpassed the tonnage of the Hanseatic vessels. The
tonnage of the French and Spanish navies cannot be ascertained.

During the sixteenth century the Hanseatics extended the range of their
seaborne trade to a remarkable degree. In the far north about fifteen
large ships from Hamburg sailed every year to Iceland to bring back cod.
In 1602 Christian IV of Denmark forbade them to set out, though this did
not prevent Hamburg from continuing to act as the Continental market
for Icelandic cod. Eastward, a few ships from Bremen and Hamburg
sailed as far as Archangel in the wake of the English; but there was no
regular trade along this route.

What was both new and remarkable, though short-lived, was the
appearance of Hanseatic ships in the Mediterranean. This was the result
of several years of famine suffered by Italy at the end of the sixteenth
century. As Spain was blocking the supplies of grain formerly assured by
the Dutch, some of the Italian princes, among them the grand duke of
Tuscany, the duke of Mantua and even the pope, sent emissaries to

Hamburg and Danzig to buy corn. In 1591 twenty-five Hanseatic ships, of which twenty-one were from Lübeck, passed through the Sound bound for Italy, and similar voyages were made in the following years, the ports of destination being usually Leghorn and Genoa. The Venetians also placed their orders, and for some years ships from Danzig sailed the Adriatic. The Venetians granted the Hanseatics equal rights with the south Germans in the *Fondaco dei Tedeschi*, but the latter kept the newcomers at a distance. On several occasions the Danzigers even sailed as far as Crete, carrying grain, timber and metals, and bringing back wine, oil and fruit.

This Mediterranean trade was very precarious. The Hanseatics often returned home in ballast, and piracy was rampant. Between 1615 and 1629 Barbary pirates captured some twenty Lübeck ships. Following the example of the Dutch, an 'Admiralty' was created at Hamburg in 1623 charged with the suppression of piracy. The next year a fund had been established for the purpose of ransoming enslaved captives, some of whom renounced Christianity in order to escape slavery. One captain from Hamburg sailed in the service of the Barbary pirates under the name of Murad. It was the absence of Dutch ships which had led to the presence of the Hanseatics in the Mediterranean. Once the Netherlands and Spain had signed the truce of 1609, German ships were rarely seen in the area, and vessels from Hamburg seldom sailed beyond Malaga.

Hanseatic participation in European colonial expansion was of no great account. After 1585 a few ships sailed to Brazil, usually calling at Lisbon on the way. In 1590 there were ten ships in Hamburg which had made the direct return trip. But the Spaniards were not anxious to open their colonies to foreigners, and German ships were rarely seen in the New World or along the coasts of Africa.

In the sixteenth as in earlier centuries, trade between east and west was the foundation of Hanseatic commerce. The accounts of the Sound supply a good deal of information about this flourishing trade and its expansion, particularly with regard to the movement of ships.* In 1497, the earliest year for which there is any information, only 795 ships passed through the Sound either from west to east or from east to west. For some years in the first third of the sixteenth century this figure barely rose above a thousand. But the annual average increased to 3,280 in the period 1557–69, to 5,036 in the decade 1581–90, and reached its maximum in 1595 with 6,673 ships. It then diminished to 4,500 a year be-

* Document No. 15.

tween 1601 and 1610, increased again to 4,900 in the following decade – the period of the truce between Spain and the Netherlands – and settled down to an average of 3,500 per year during the years 1621–50, with marked variations from year to year. Thus in comparison with the end of the fifteenth century the number of passages at the end of the sixteenth century had increased sixfold, while the number of ships had increased threefold. In at least 80 per cent of these sailings the ships involved were going either to or from Hanseatic ports on the Baltic, between Lübeck and Reval.

The accounts of the Sound also give some indication, at least for the period after 1557, of the nature and amount of merchandise carried in either direction. However the more they are studied, the more inaccurate they are found to be, usually as the result of false declarations made by merchants and ship owners for their own advantage. They declared less salt and grain and more timber than they were actually carrying, and relatively more rye than wheat. Consequently these apparently precise figures may embody errors of as much as 100 per cent. Nevertheless they allow a better assessment than is possible for previous centuries of the general trend of Hanseatic commerce. But they still do not cover total trade between east and west, as no estimate can be made of trade by the land and river route between Lübeck and Hamburg, which remained very important, especially in periods when relations with Denmark were strained.

The eastern products transported through the Sound to western Europe remained more or less the same as in the fourteenth and fifteenth centuries. The only new element is the export through Danzig of saltpetre and potash, previously unknown. However the relative importance of the traditional wares had altered appreciably. Russian furs no longer occupied the most important place in the trade of Lübeck and the Livonian towns, probably because they were now being exported by a different route, through Leipzig and Frankfurt. Wax, though it had lost its former pre-eminence, remained relatively more important. The timber trade had been falling off perceptibly since the end of the fifteenth century, and this tendency increased towards the end of the sixteenth and in the seventeenth century, perhaps because the timber regions of the Vistula and the lower Dvina were nearly exhausted. On the other hand the by-products of the timber trade, ash, pitch and tar, of which several thousands of lasts were exported every year, retained their importance. Hemp and flax, the demand for which had been stimulated by the increase in the shipping of all countries (rigging and sails,) had become a source of great wealth for the Livonian ports, which fetched them mainly from Lithuania and Belorussia. In the early years of the seventeenth century they represented 60 per cent of the total exports from Riga. Lastly metals, formerly a leading commodity in the operations of south German firms, appear to have passed through the Sound in relatively small amounts; only iron from Sweden and Galicia remained important.

The chief point of interest at the beginning of the modern era is, however, the extraordinary increase in the export of grain to the west. Encouraged by a demand which grew steadily larger and more widespread, the cultivation of grain became the major preoccupation not only of Prussia and Poland, but also of the Ukraine, the Baltic countries and Pomerania. Everywhere the great landowners were intensifying production with a view to export. Danzig, to which rye was brought from regions ever more and more remote,* remained the main centre of the grain trade. In normal times more than 75 per cent of the grain from the east passed through her port, supplying the transhipment ports of Amsterdam, London and Hamburg. The rest was handled for the most part by Königsberg, Riga and Stettin. Although there were considerable variations, exports of Danzig rye, carried mainly in Dutch ships, rose from a maximum of 10,000 lasts per year at the end of the fifteenth century to more than 40,000 between 1562 and 1566, then to more than 65,000 during the last four years of the truce between the Netherlands and Spain, with a record figure of 74,000 lasts in 1618. There was a marked recession at the beginning of the Thirty Years War (a few hundred lasts in 1628 and 1629), but trade rose again to 50,000 lasts in 1640–4 and to 68,000 in 1649.† It would be true to say that the export of rye increased approximately fivefold between 1500 and 1600, and the same applies to other cereals. After 1619 exports of wheat appear to have increased considerably, but this may only be because of a stricter check on cargoes. Barley was relatively unimportant, except in certain peak years in the seventeenth century, while the export of flour, still fairly important in the second half of the sixteenth century, became insignificant in the seventeenth.

Trade in the reverse direction, from the west to the Baltic, retained much the same character as in the fifteenth century. It still remained much lower in volume than trade in the opposite direction, and this imbalance is precisely documented by the accounts of the Sound. Up to about 1600

* Document No. 43.
† Document No. 51.

more than half the vessels entering the Baltic were in ballast. This was especially true of the Dutch grain-ships, for which the proportion exceeded 60 per cent in the years 1590 to 1600, while for ships travelling in the opposite direction during the whole century, from 1557 to 1667, barely 2 per cent were travelling without cargo.

The principal western products exported to the east were still salt and cloth. In the mid-sixteenth century French salt retained the pre-eminence which it had acquired by the end of the fourteenth century, the only difference being that it now came almost entirely from Brouage and not from the Bay of Bourgneuf. In 1557 out of 422 German ships passing through the Sound on their way to the east, 240 had sailed from Brouage. 87 of them had Hamburg as their home port, 65 Danzig, 31 Bremen, 20 Emden, and 13 Lübeck. However as Spain was at this time at war with France, a number of Dutch ships, whose owners were Spanish subjects, were sailing under the Hanseatic flag. But even three years later, when peace had been restored, the number of German salt-ships passing through the Sound was still 197, all coming from Brouage (45 from Danzig, 39 from Hamburg, 31 from Bremen and 31 from Lübeck), together with 84 from the Netherlands. Later, after the wars of religion had broken out in France, the salt trade declined considerably, while commercial relations between the Hanseatics and the Iberian peninsula grew closer. For this reason salt from Portugal took precedence in the Baltic from 1575 to 1600. But the Peace of Vervins in 1598 brought French salt back into first place, where it remained for the first half of the seventeenth century, apart from some exceptional years.

During this whole period the amount of salt brought through the Sound amounted, according to the accounts, to an annual average of about 30,000 lasts, reaching occasional peaks of more than 40,000 (as in 1562, 1568, 1578, 1624, 1647). The maximum, almost 60,000 lasts, came in 1623. It is tempting to assume a correlation between the movement of salt towards the east and of grain towards the west. But no such correlation can be established, the peak years for the two products being quite different. It was demand and availability which determined the amounts to be transported. In the east Königsberg was the principal port for the import of salt, ahead of Riga and Danzig. Lithuania was probably the biggest customer.

In spite of the growth of the Polish textile industry, cloth continued to be imported from the west in large quantities. Imports were mainly of English and Dutch cloth, which even in the Hanseatic area had finally supplanted Flemish and Brabantine cloth. Wine also remained important: Rhenish wine as well as wine from Aquitaine and Portugal was now mainly supplied by the Dutch. Danzig was still the chief distribution centre in the Baltic. In 1583 imports of wine amounted to 6,500 *ohm*, that is, about 10,000 hectolitres. Similarly, at a time when the Skanian fisheries were declining, the shipments of Dutch and Norwegian fish to the east remained considerable. A relatively new product was skins and hides from England and Scotland, now regularly exported to the Baltic.

The most novel factor in the commerce of the Hansa towns after the mid-sixteenth century was the increase in trade with the Iberian peninsula, as a result of the revolt of the Low Countries against Spain and the secession of the United Provinces. Philip II took vigorous economic and diplomatic action against the rebels, and planned a grand alliance, embracing the Hansa, Sweden, Poland and later Denmark, aimed at ruining Dutch trade. Although this came to nothing, Spain, unable to forgo the supplies previously furnished by the Dutch, gave a ready welcome to German traders. The number of merchants engaged in the *Spanienfahrt*, organised principally by Hamburg, Lübeck and Danzig, but also by other ports, increased rapidly. Between 1574 and 1578, 92 Danzig ships sailed to Portugal. In 1590, 300 German vessels called at Iberian ports – mainly Lisbon, Oporto, Setúbal in Portugal, San Lucar, the port for Seville, and Cadiz in Andalusia. On the other hand the Asturian and Galician ports were still less frequented.

Hanseatic exports to the peninsula consisted mainly of foodstuffs, fish and above all grain, but also of products used by the Spanish army and navy: timber, saltpetre, copper for guns and for coinage, flax and hemp for rigging and sails. In exchange the Hanseatics brought back salt from Lisbon and Setúbal, oil and Mediterranean fruits, colonial produce, spices, dye-woods (brazil-wood) from Pernambuco, and especially sugar from San Thomé or Brazil.

Trade with Spain, however, had several disadvantages. The most serious was piracy, particularly at the hands of the English, who were intent on intercepting this trade. In order to minimise the risks, Hanseatic charterers tried to insist that ships should pass west of Ireland, which, at least for ships calling at Norwegian ports, did not involve much of a detour. But captains were usually unwilling to follow this route and preferred to risk the direct passage through the Straits of Dover. Moreover the Hanseatics were distrusted by the Spaniards, because Dutch merchants would often settle in a German town and continue to trade with the peninsula under the Hanseatic flag. In order to prevent this the Spanish government insisted on certificates of origin for both ships and cargoes. Finding it still impossible to prevent fraud, they decided in 1603 to levy an *ad valorem* tax of 30 per cent. This would have ruined trade with Germany, and in 1607 a Hanseatic delegation, whose costs were borne principally by Hamburg, was dispatched to the Spanish court. Hanseatic participation in trade with the New World, and the foundation of a *Kontor* at Lisbon were also discussed. But the only solid achievement of the delegation was the abrogation of the 30 per cent tax.

Relations with the Iberian peninsula appear to have reached their peak in the first years of the seventeenth century. They diminished appreciably after the signing of the truce between Spain and the Netherlands in 1609. The alliance formed in 1616 between the Hansa and the United Provinces, though directed mainly against Denmark, who was blocking passage of the Sound, heralded a change of policy. When in 1621 hostilities broke out again between the Dutch and Spain, however, the Hanseatics did not hesitate to sacrifice their new allies in favour of the *Spanienfahrt*, and there was a fresh boom in Spanish trade. In 1621, 85 ships from Hamburg called at Lisbon. Two years later 101 Hanseatic ships called at Portuguese ports and 56 at Spanish ports. In 1627 47 ships from Hamburg put in at Setúbal. But this revival was of short duration and was soon checked by the outbreak of the Thirty Years War.

Characteristic of Hanseatic commerce at this time was the steadily increasing part played by foreigners. The strong position of the Dutch was particularly evident. Between 1550 and 1650 the number of their ships passing through the Sound was more than half of all passages, except in unusual circumstances. It sometimes reached as much as two-thirds. In all the Baltic ports, with the possible exception of Lübeck, Dutch ships were more numerous than German. The English, through their establishments in Hamburg, Stade and Elbing, controlled the trade in English cloth in Germany. Dutch, Italian and Portuguese firms had meanwhile captured most of the trade in the Hanseatic area after the withdrawal of Nürnberg and Augsburg business firms after 1560.

The results of the foreign invasion were not always disadvantageous for the Hansa towns. They profited from the increase in trade, and some burgesses grew rich by entering into partnership with foreigners. It was most damaging to the Hanseatic merchants who lost their role as middle-men when foreigners began to deal directly with producers, and to the ship-owners who had difficulty in finding charterers for their ships. Many merchants, remembering their former importance, were reluctant to become merely the agents or representatives of foreign firms. Torn between these conflicting interests, each town adopted a somewhat uncertain economic policy. Generally the traditional conservatism of the Hansa, whose most fervent advocates were firmly entrenched in such corporate associations as the *Englandfahrer* of Hamburg or the *Schonenfahrer* of Lübeck, carried the day. Cologne, Riga and Lübeck tightened up their staple regulations, enforced the 'guest law' more strictly, and forbade their burgesses to enter into partnership with foreigners. In other towns, however, especially in Hamburg, a new spirit reigned. The traditional system of a corporative organisation, based on minutely detailed regulations, which had been common to Hansa towns, was replaced by small groups, more flexible, in one sense more local, but more receptive to projects involving international co-operation.

The new spirit is particularly evident in the Loitz firm in Stettin, at its most active from 1550 to 1575. It was a very important Hanseatic firm, the only one to compare with the great firms of south Germany and the Low Countries in the volume of its business, its monopolistic tendencies and its dealings with the princes, from whom it obtained many privileges.

The house of Loitz had been in business since the mid-fifteenth century and had grown rich over three generations in the herring trade. In the mid-sixteenth century the firm was controlled by four brothers and still retained its head office in Stettin. But its main business was carried on in Danzig, and close contacts were maintained with south Germany. The firm's agents were scattered throughout central and northern Europe, in Cracow, Breslau, Leipzig, Prague, Frankfurt-on-the-Oder, Lübeck, Hamburg and Antwerp, Copenhagen and Kalmar.

The firm was anxious to capture the monopoly in the import of salt into the north-east. Stephan Loitz therefore settled in Lüneburg and tried, without success, to corner the output of its salt-pans. The Loitzes managed to acquire privileges from the emperor for the sale of salt in Silesia, from the margrave of Brandenburg for transit through his territory, and from the king of Poland for the exploitation of the Galician rock-salt mines. An important branch of their business was their trade in metals, especially copper, for which they were in partnership with firms in the Harz and in Mansfeld. They also held concessions in Sweden and Transylvania. They were active in many other fields. For instance they had a monopoly of Icelandic sulphur, granted them by the king of Denmark, and a near-monopoly of the products of the Lithuanian forests.

Naturally the house of Loitz participated in the grain trade. For this purpose they maintained close contacts with the Pomeranian and Prussian nobility. Michael Loitz's daughter married a soldier of fortune, Colonel Reinhold von Krockow, who took part in some very risky speculations. Stephan Loitz obtained in 1556 a safe-conduct from Henry II of France for the transport to Marseilles of a consignment of 2,000 lasts of corn, some of which was put into warehouses. Because of their speculative enterprises and the large sums which they lent to monarchs, bad debtors all, the Loitzes were caught up in the wave of bankruptcies which broke over Europe at this time. In 1570 Krockow was owed half a million guilders by Charles IX of France, 200,000 thalers by the margrave of Brandenburg, 100,000 by the Pomeranian princes and nearly 300,000 by the king of Poland. The Polish king's death in 1572 caused the firm to suspend payments. Its liabilities amounted to two million thalers. Stephan Loitz fled to Lüneburg, where he tried in vain to restore his fortunes. Once more speculative ventures had turned out badly for Hanseatic merchants.

4. THE GREAT HANSA TOWNS

Between 1550 and 1650 the principal Hansa towns benefited, though to a different degree, from the rising prosperity characteristic of the period, from the general increase in trade and from the development of commercial relations with Spain.

Cologne seemed to be ideally placed to receive the lion's share of Antwerp's legacy. Its proximity to the Low Countries, its commercial relations with Frankfurt, Italy, England and the Baltic, above all its Exchange, founded in 1556, made it the first refuge for many foreign firms, especially those owned by Catholics, when they fled from the troubles of the Low Countries. Among these refugees the Portuguese were the least numerous, despite the official transfer of the 'Portuguese nation' to Cologne in 1578. Only about fifteen to twenty-five of the great Portuguese merchants were accepted as citizens, among whom the wealthiest were the Ximenes brothers. Taking advantage of their relations with Portugal and the East Indies, the newcomers were soon able to monopolise the trade in spices and part of that in precious metals. They then moved into the grain trade between the Baltic and Spain. Though welcomed at first, their success soon aroused distrust and obstruction within the council, which denounced them as swindlers. After the reconquest of the southern Low Countries by the Spaniards and the restoration of Roman Catholicism, they were only too eager to return to Antwerp. Their stay in Cologne lasted no more than ten years. The city failed to hold them and so to profit from their activity.

More numerous were the Italians who arrived between 1578 and 1585, not only from Antwerp and the Low Countries but also from Italy, following a tradition going back to the thirteenth century. There were about forty Italian firms in Cologne, involving in all about three hundred persons. Their business, carried on by both land and sea, consisted for the most part in the export of English and Flemish cloth to Italy and the import of Italian silk and silk fabrics. But they were interested also in grain from the Baltic, in furs and in ammunition. The excise accounts and the records of the 'hundredth penny', a tax created in 1589 to replenish the town's treasury, bear witness to the volume of their business. In 1583 the value of the cloth which passed through their hands amounted to 480,000 thalers or 120,000 Flemish pounds. During the last decade of the sixteenth century they were responsible for up to 30 per cent of the trade of Cologne, even more perhaps if their bitterly denounced ability to evade taxes is taken into account. Like the Portuguese, the Italians encountered hostility among the citizens, who accused them of ruining the local silk industry, and they were irritated by the petty harassments which accompanied the levying of the 'hundredth penny'. In addition their largest firms went bankrupt: the Navaroli in 1602, the Luchini in 1604, the Moriconi in 1618. Consequently the Italians gradually left Cologne, which had not offered them the opportunities they were looking for. Their stay, though not as brief as that of the Portuguese, remained an episode which had no permanent effect on the economic life of the town.

The most numerous among the refugees were natives of the Low Countries, comprising craftsmen as well as merchants, nearly all of them Catholics, coming from Antwerp and Flanders, and also from Hainault and Artois. The presence of the Italians allowed these Belgian firms to continue in their former line of business, principally the export of grain and cloth to Spain and France and occasionally to Italy. One of the first firms known to us by its account-book is that of Jean Resteau, who came from Cambrai in 1569. It had agents in Liège, Amsterdam, London, Stade, Nürnberg, Rouen, Caen and La Rochelle and one of its ships, the

Black Cat, plied between Königsberg and Bordeaux. It dealt mainly in silk, velvet and satin from Italy, as well as in English and Dutch cloth. In the five years which preceded its bankruptcy (1587–92) the firm bought goods to the value of nearly 50,000 Flemish pounds in Cologne and Frankfurt, for resale chiefly in Stade and Middelburg. The richest of the Belgians appears to have been Nicolas de Groote of Antwerp, who settled in Cologne in 1584. He dealt in cloth and spices, the latter bought for him by agents in Venice and Lisbon. He is remarkable not only for his wealth but for having settled permanently in Cologne. His widow and then his sons carried on his business, and his descendants played a notable part in the affairs of the city.

Though not unique, the case of de Groote is exceptional. In general the Belgians too left Cologne, one after another. The town was not wholly responsible for this desertion. The restoration of peace in the southern Low Countries and, even more, the permanently unsettled state of the lower Rhine as a result of the passage of Spanish armies were contributory factors. But it is none the less true that petty chicaneries by the citizens contributed largely to the departure of the immigrants. Cologne was a typical Hansa town, imprisoned within its own commercial traditions and its own xenophobe mentality, persecuting foreigners instead of welcoming them, incapable of adapting itself to the economic conditions of a new age or of seizing the opportunities for renewal which were offered to it.

By contrast Hamburg adapted itself perfectly to the changed situation, and could thus share Antwerp's legacy with Amsterdam. The town was on the flood-tide of expansion. In 1500 it had barely 15,000 inhabitants, and only 20,000 fifty years later. But at the beginning of the seventeenth century it had risen to 35,000 and twenty years later had reached nearly 50,000, leaving Cologne far behind, with a population that had remained more or less stationary (35–40,000 inhabitants) since the end of the fifteenth century. Hamburg thus became the leading German town.

Commercially and financially Hamburg was well equipped for expansion. Of all the Hansa towns Hamburg, after Lübeck, had the largest merchant fleet, estimated at about 7,000 lasts at the end of the sixteenth century. This fleet was augmented by the arrival of Dutch ship-owners and appears to have more than doubled its tonnage in the first half of the seventeenth century. It also seems that river traffic expanded greatly during this period, though little information is available; it was certainly larger than that of the inland towns, particularly Magdeburg. With the

aid of imperial privileges Hamburg extended its economic influence to
the upper reaches of the Elbe and even towards the Oder, along the
rivers Havel and Spree. In 1588 Hamburg founded an Exchange, at
first merely a meeting place for merchants. In 1619 the Hamburg Bank,
a deposit and clearing bank, modelled on that of Amsterdam, was
established. It supervised foreign exchange, the mint and precious metals,
protected merchants against monetary depreciation and by its credit
facilities gave a considerable stimulus to business.

To a large extent the greatness of Hamburg was the work of foreign
merchants. They came in large numbers and they stayed. The town did
all it could to facilitate their business, consciously rejecting, despite the
opposition of the *Englandfahrer*, the principle of 'guest law'. Foreigners
were authorised to trade freely among themselves and to enter into
partnerships with Hamburg merchants. The same facilities were granted
to ship-owners. One ship which sailed from Brazil into Hamburg in 1590
belonged jointly to three Hamburg burgesses, two Dutchmen and a
Portuguese. In order to encourage ship-building, the town allowed
foreign craftsmen to work in the yards, in spite of the opposition of the
native carpenters. The old corporative system, with merchants combining
in companies each dealing with a specific country – which had in any case
been obsolete here for some time – gradually disappeared. A Bergen company (*Bergenfahrer*) had been founded as late as 1535. Fifty years later
there was no question of founding a Spanish company, in spite of the
importance that relations with this country had acquired in the meantime.
It is significant that at the same period the more traditionally-minded
Lübeck founded a company of *Spanienfahrer*. Finally the Merchant
Adventurers, as has already been mentioned, received privileges in 1567
and 1611 which granted them equal rights with native merchants. All
this was entirely contrary to Hanseatic principles, and it is understandable that Lübeck should have protested vigorously against these new
practices. It cannot be denied that by its realistic policy towards foreigners
the young and powerful city of Hamburg contributed more than any
other to the liquidation of the Hanseatic community.

Among the foreign merchants who came to Hamburg either directly
from the Low Countries or from Cologne were both Portuguese and
Italians. The Portuguese, numbering about a hundred, were presented in
1617 with a constitution, which was later renewed. Their presence greatly
stimulated trade with the Iberian peninsula. They themselves dealt
mainly in the import of spices and sugar. After 1625 they began to

specialise in banking. The Italians were less numerous and did not stay so long, since they were forbidden to hold Catholic services. South Germans, usually Protestants, had settled in Hamburg at the beginning of the century, at the same time as the Fuggers. Later they had opted for Antwerp, but after the ruin of that city several returned to Hamburg, where they dealt principally in copper from the Harz and Bohemia. However, as in Cologne, it was the merchants from the southern Low Countries who contributed most to the expansion of Hamburg. They were generally Lutherans or Calvinists. The latter found integration into the native population more difficult. These Belgian firms had dealings with the whole of Europe, from Livonia to Spain and from Scandinavia to Italy. One of the richest was the firm of Rudolf and Arnold Amsink, whose deposits in the Bank amounted to 641,000 marks in 1619.

The economic preponderance of foreigners in Hamburg was notorious throughout Germany. In a note of protest dispatched in 1609 Lübeck claimed that 'hardly a hundredth part' of Hamburg's trade was carried out by the town's own burgesses, being monopolised by Dutchmen, south Germanns, Italians, Frenchmen, Portuguese, Englishmen and others. This was a manifest exaggeration. However the movement of deposits in the Bank demonstrates foreign supremacy very clearly. In 1619 out of 42 firms having deposits of more than 100,000 marks, 32 were Belgian, 2 south German, 2 Portuguese and 6 native to Hamburg.

Grain was of considerable importance in Hamburg's trade. Beside Amsterdam and Danzig the town had succeeded in becoming one of the great grain-markets of northern Europe, to which buyers came from all quarters. Some of the grain came from Danzig by sea, but quantities came also from Holstein, the lower and middle Elbe, and even from Poland through Brandenburg along the rivers Oder and Havel. In addition Hamburg was the main centre for the import of English cloth into the Continent as well as a distribution centre for Portuguese salt. Trade in copper from the Harz, Bohemia, Sweden and Hungary was one of the most profitable lines for foreign firms. Finally Hamburg remained the principal producer and exporter of beer in the whole of north Germany.

It is not easy to estimate the relative importance of the various European countries in Hamburg's trade. Trade with the Netherlands, and up to about 1575 with Antwerp, probably held first place. From 1537 to 1585, according to the accounts of the anchorage dues of Antwerp and its outer ports, Hamburg's share amounted to 46 per cent of all Hanseatic ships and 43 per cent of their cargoes. In the seventeenth century

Amsterdam replaced Antwerp. It is also certain that Hamburg participated more than any other town in trade with the Iberian peninsula, which appears to have amounted to about 20 per cent of her total trade. It was Hamburg which bore the major part (62 per cent) of the 'Spanish collection' levied from 1606 to 1608. It was Hamburg's increasing interest in trade with Spain and Portugal which apparently caused the diminution in her trade with the Baltic, which happened in no other northern town in this period. From 1562 to 1569, one hundred and fifty ships from Hamburg passed through the Sound each year, but from 1574 to 1583 the number fell to less than thirty, partly as a result of hostilities with Denmark. But when peace was re-established, the number rose to only about a hundred annually for the period from 1584 to 1603.

In the Baltic Hamburg's expansion was rivalled by that of Danzig. Its population, less than 20,000 in the early years of the fifteenth century, was estimated at 30,000 in the second half of the sixteenth (judging from the 4,500 men who could be mobilised in 1577) and it continued to increase considerably right up to the Thirty Years War.

The accounts of the Sound show clearly that Danzig was the leading Baltic port, both in the number of its ships and in the amount of merchandise handled. From 1557 to 1585 an average of 1,025 ships from Danzig, most of them Dutch-owned, passed through the Sound towards the west, that is, about 53 per cent of all ships making the passage.* The figure rose to 1,104 for the period 1586–1621, that is, about 44 per cent of all westward passages. This slight percentage fall can probably be explained by the development of other ports, notably Königsberg and Elbing. The anchorage dues (*Pfahlgeld*) levied by Danzig provide information about the value of the seaborne trade. From 6½ million Prussian marks in 1583 – two-thirds exports and one-third imports – it rose to 16½ million, then dropped appreciably, but rose again in 1622 – after war had broken out again between the Netherlands and Spain – to a maximum of nearly 18 million marks.

It is curious that Danzig ships should have held only a relatively unimportant place in the seaborne trade of the town. As early as 1544 the town council was lamenting that their merchant fleet had fallen in a few years from two hundred vessels to a mere fifty. This can hardly be an exaggeration, since in 1583 there were only fifty-three captains in the town who had sailed the high seas, two-thirds of them westward through the Sound and one-third within the Baltic. Nor does the Danzig fleet,

* Document No. 50.

estimated at 3,500 lasts, appear to have increased after this. This stagnation can perhaps be explained by the low freight charges of the Dutch, as can the decline of the ship-building yards, once so prosperous.

As in Hamburg, foreigners played a preponderant part in Danzig's trade. The Dutch were the most numerous and the most active and after them the south Germans. There were fewer English after the founding of their establishment at Elbing in 1579, and the town never succeeded in luring them back, at least not before 1628. A new factor was the presence of Frenchmen, especially Normans. Although, generally speaking, French ships rarely came as far as Danzig, they were to be seen there in great numbers in certain years, probably to buy grain. For example in 1587 there were 196 of them, and nearly 100 in 1595 and 1608. As a result a French colony was established in Danzig, sufficiently numerous for Henry IV to appoint as consul in 1610 a certain Jean de la Blanque, formerly an officer in the service of Sweden, who remained in office for sixteen years.

Although they were made welcome and were admitted to the *Artushof* on the same terms as local merchants, foreigners did not enjoy as much liberty in Danzig as in Hamburg. Anxious to retain their role as middlemen, the basis of their wealth, the Danzigers clung to the 'guest law'. They were not able to prevent all direct negotiations between Polish suppliers and western merchants, especially in the grain-market, but they refrained from granting foreigners equality of rights with native burgesses. Danzig had no rival as a grain-market and foreigners could hardly take their trade elsewhere. In short the town succeeded in combining traditional Hanseatic economic practices with a readiness to welcome foreigners, to her own immense advantage.

The essential source of Danzig's wealth, ever since the fifteenth century, had been and still was the export to the west of grain from Poland, Prussia and Pomerania. Three-quarters of this trade passed through the Sound. It is perhaps even more remarkable that during the whole of the Thirty Years War, except for a few years around 1630, trade remained prosperous, usually attaining 40,000 to 50,000 lasts annually. However various and important other business activities may have been, Danzig was above all the granary of Europe.

The case of Lübeck is a complex one. It is natural to assume that the manifest decay of the Hansa in the sixteenth and seventeenth centuries must have been paralleled, in the town which was its leader, by a marked decline, as much economic as political. This view is only partially

borne out by the facts. Lübeck maintained her share in the general increase in trade and her situation remained in many respects flourishing.

Up to the beginning of the Thirty Years War Lübeck possessed the
largest fleet of the Hansa towns. Her port was always busy. At the end
of the sixteenth century in some years more than 2,000 ships called there,
that is, at least three times as many as a hundred years earlier. Her trade
was as prosperous as ever, for in spite of the increase in the number of
ships passing through the Sound, the road and river route across the
Holstein isthmus was still essential for the flow of goods from east to
west. The increasing hostility which Christian IV of Denmark displayed
towards the Hansa during the first half of the seventeenth century only
served to strengthen its importance.

In this period Lübeck's trade, which had almost doubled in the previous
century, preserved in the main the characteristics of its heyday. One of its
firmest foundations was provided by its relations with Scandinavia. Although the trade in Skanian herring was declining and the fleet of the
Lübeck *Bergenfahrer* was now smaller than those of Bremen and Rostock,
Norwegian cod as well as Swedish iron, copper and butter were still dispatched in large quantities to Lübeck* and re-exported to the west via
Hamburg. Since 1581 direct trade with Russia had been seriously reduced,
but commerce with the ports of the southern Baltic, especially with
Danzig, continued to flourish. For the most part Lübeck supplied Dutch
cloth and Lüneburg salt and received in exchange metals from Hungary,
flax, hemp and wax. As before, she shared to some extent in the great
Polish export trade in grain. Her exports of beer were by no means
negligible. Brewed in the Wendish towns, it was sent to the Low Countries and inland Germany, while that of Hamburg and Einbeck went to
the Baltic countries. Lastly Lübeck had a large share in the trade with
Spain. The company of *Spanienfahrer*, created in 1575, exported Swedish
and Hungarian copper and timber from Norway to the Iberian peninsula.
By common consent Lübeck was still recognised as head of the Hansa
by the other towns, and her finances must have been healthy, for she
always paid her 'contribution' promptly (which, together with that of
Cologne, was the highest). In fact Lübeck at this time was displaying an
incontestable vitality.

However there were signs of decadence. Lübeck's population, which
was about 25,000 at the end of the fifteenth century, does not appear to
have increased over the next 200 years, and she ranked no more than

* Document No. 49.

fourth among the Hansa towns. Politically, her prestige had been seriously damaged by Wullenwever's defeat and the disasters of the Nordic Seven Years War. Economically, foreign influence was resented more bitterly here than elsewhere. The merchants of Lübeck, who had once dominated the Baltic trade, were being supplanted in their own town by foreign firms and even by firms from other Hansa towns. In a significant memorandum addressed in 1609 to the council of Hamburg, Lübeck drew a comparison between the prosperity of her rival and her own downfall, stressing the loss of her privileged status and of her trade in the Baltic. She reproached the Hamburg merchants for their connivance with foreign merchants and accused them of unfair competition. Their firms had agents in Scandinavia, Livonia and Poland, who were doing their best to drive Lübeck merchants out of areas where they had been active for centuries. They wanted to remain merchants and not to become merely 'boatmen, agents and innkeepers' and Lübeck would not endure being reduced to the rank of a 'mediocre posting-house and forwarding agency'.

It was clear to the Lübeckers that their city was declining, but they were firmly determined to oppose the total domination of the town's business life by foreigners. This gave rise to the 'transit dispute' which broke out in the early years of the seventeenth century and dragged on for 150 years. In 1606 Lübeck ordered the seizure of a consignment of salmon and another of Swedish copper, both belonging to Hamburg firms. Paying no attention to their protests, she promulgated in 1607 a general regulation on goods in transit. Justifying her action by her well-known staple regulations, which dealt with goods coming from or being dispatched to the Baltic, and also by the Hanseatic principle of 'guest law' which prohibited direct transactions between foreigners, she banned the passage of all goods bought outside the town from a foreigner. In particular all foodstuffs from Scandinavia, as well as copper, Swedish iron and Finnish hides, were to be sold only to Lübeckers. Infringement of the regulation would be punished by seizure of goods in transit or by increased dues. In this way the Lübeck merchants would recapture the position they had held unopposed for centuries.

Several foreign towns and countries which suffered under the new regulations protested, but all in vain. Most of the disputes concerned the transit of copper. The emperor himself, having received several complaints, intervened on two occasions, first in 1609, when he forbade the levying of any tax on copper, though he gave no ruling on the vexed question of transit, and secondly in 1620, when he condemned the Lübeck 'innovations'. But even this did not put an end to the dispute. Relations with Hamburg became very strained, as the latter, during this period of tension with Denmark, was obliged to send her goods through Lübeck. Notes, accusations, justifications, appeals to Hanseatic sentiment led to nothing more than a few modifications of detail, and in 1632 Lübeck confirmed the regulation of 1607.

It is difficult to estimate the efficacy of this policy. It apparently failed to check the decline in the trade of the Lübeck merchants, who were reduced to little more than agents for foreign firms in their own town. In the seventeenth century Lübeck was regarded as Hamburg's outer harbour in the Baltic, a reversal of their roles in the fourteenth century. The conflict between these two towns, at one time so closely bound together by their common interests, was a serious symptom of the irreparable decay of the Hanseatic organisation.

5. THE THIRTY YEARS WAR AND THE END OF THE HANSA

The partial resurgence of the Hansa and the desire for union among the towns of the community were eventually nullified by the Thirty Years War.

From the beginning the war lay bare the weakness of the Hansa. In the course of the great confrontation between Denmark, the Empire, Sweden and Poland, the Hansa was approached by all the antagonists in turn, but proved incapable of pursuing a consistent policy. She would have preferred to remain neutral, but was not strong enough to compel respect for her neutrality. Each town therefore endeavoured separately to protect its interests by avoiding open partisanship. Isolationism undermined the desire for solidarity and made the restoration of the Hanseatic community impossible, even after the peace.

The first difficulties came from Denmark. Ever since his majority in 1596 Christian IV had shown his hostility to the Hansa by obstructing the activity of German merchants in Iceland, Norway and Denmark. When he showed equal hostility to the Dutch, first Lübeck in 1613 and then, three years later, the Hansa as a whole formed an alliance with the United Provinces to protect their commercial interests. Christian IV also followed his predecessors' policy in northern Germany, supporting the duke of Brunswick in his efforts to subdue the city. Brunswick escaped this danger in 1615 with the help of men and money sent her by the other towns: the last military action undertaken by the Hansa. In 1617 Christian founded the new town of Glückstadt, at the mouth of the Elbe, richly endowing it with privileges in the hope of damaging Hamburg's trade. Two years later he occupied Stade. But he was not successful in establishing his protectorate over Hamburg, which in 1618 obtained from the supreme imperial court recognition as a free imperial city; nor could he bring under his control the Elbe traffic.

The conflict took a new turn with the ambitious plans of the Habsburgs and of Gustavus Adolphus. In 1621, the truce between Spain and the Netherlands having expired, Philip IV, determined to crush the Dutch, decided on concerted action with the Catholic League and Ferdinand II in northern Europe. Ferdinand, who had been victorious in Bohemia, was anxious to come to grips with the north German Protestant princes, Mansfeld and Christian of Brunswick, the allies of Denmark. Christian IV, alarmed, made peace with the Dutch and entered into an alliance with England, but was defeated by Tilly, the League's general, in the battle of Lutter (1626). Tilly and Wallenstein, the generalissimo of the imperial army, easily made themselves masters of the whole area of the Elbe and Jutland. As a reward Wallenstein received the duchy of Mecklenburg as an imperial fief.

It was at this point that Ferdinand II allowed Philip IV to persuade him to join in an ambitious plan which, if it had succeeded, would have allotted a leading role to the Hansa. In order to overcome the Dutch and the Danes and establish the emperor's authority in north Germany, the emperor was to seize the ports of east Frisia and the estuary of the Elbe, obtain the support of the Hansa towns and Poland, ensure co-operation between the merchant fleets of Germany, the Spanish Netherlands and Spain, create a battle fleet which would protect trade with the Iberian peninsula, and finally carry on a merciless war of piracy against the enemies of Spain.

In 1627 Ferdinand II made the necessary overtures to the Hansa towns. Not wishing them to take fright, he contented himself with a proposal to create a German–Spanish commercial company under imperial patronage, dazzling the Hanseatics with a vision of the destruction of Dutch competition, the removal of the Danish menace and greatly increased trade with Spain. But the Hansa was not to be tempted. She was alarmed by the basically military character of the enterprise and by the financial burdens which it would entail. She was afraid of being dragged into a war against the Protestant countries, Denmark, the United Provinces,

England and Sweden, and of losing her trade with them; and for religious reasons she shrank from entering the Catholic camp. Neither imperial promises nor Spanish threats could move the Hanseatic diet of 1628, in which eleven towns took part. The proposal was rejected.

Some modern historians have thought that by her abstention, by her refusal to collaborate with the empire, the Hansa lost the last chance of getting back her former power and of playing an important role in northern Europe. But the events which followed show how mistaken this judgement is. Resistance to the tide of Swedish expansion, which she would not have been strong enough to check, would only have accelerated the ruin of the Hansa. She was wise to refuse an alliance with the Habsburgs.

In the meantime Wallenstein had taken action. Master of the duchy of Mecklenburg and of Wismar, which provided him with ships, and appointed 'General of the Oceanic and Baltic seas', he attempted to seize Stralsund. The town resisted fiercely, supported first by a Danish garrison and later by a Swedish contingent, and Wallenstein was forced to raise the siege. Soon afterwards the emperor signed a peace treaty with Denmark in Lübeck. Christian IV could once more levy his toll at Glückstadt and again threaten the independence of Hamburg.

At this time Swedish dominion over northern Europe was being consolidated. For fifteen years Gustavus Adolphus had been extending his conquests. In 1617 he resumed his war with Poland. His troops invaded the Baltic countries and within a few years he had made himself master of Riga and of all Livonia. In 1626 he attacked Prussia in order to strike a decisive blow at Poland. He did not succeed in capturing Danzig, but his troops occupied the coast and imposed heavy duties on Prussian exports. From then on Prussian and Livonian customs dues formed Sweden's biggest source of revenue – in some years 50 per cent of the total – and contributed largely to financing the war effort. The Swedes were now in control of the grain trade with the west. The duties they imposed caused a steep rise in the price of corn in Amsterdam, which quadrupled between 1627 and 1630. In 1630 Danzig succeeded in coming to an arrangement with the Swedes. On condition that she maintained strict neutrality during the war, export duties were to be shared, Sweden receiving 3½ per cent and Danzig 2 per cent.

Finally in 1630 Gustavus Adolphus embarked on the conquest of Germany. Stralsund passed under his control, as did Wismar. Lübeck, an imperial city, did not dare to declare openly for him, but loaned him

26,000 thalers and adopted an attitude of benevolent neutrality. Hamburg and Bremen adopted the same policy, Hamburg finding in Gustavus a protector against Danish threats. Only Magdeburg ranged herself openly on the side of Sweden, a step which she was to pay for a year later.

The dramatic events of the last five years had shown clearly that the Hansa towns, unarmed and subject to various rulers, were incapable of a common policy. It was the realisation of their helplessness which induced the *Hansetag* of 1629 to ask the three towns Lübeck, Hamburg and Bremen to assume responsibility for the common interests of the Hansa and to act in her name, since circumstances made it almost impossible to hold general diets. This decision was not unlike that taken by the diet at Lübeck in 1418, when the Wendish towns were asked to take over the direction of the Hansa. Perhaps, by evoking this memory, some delegates succeeded in deceiving themselves as to the true significance of their decision. In reality they had resolved on nothing less than the liquidation of the Hansa. As a result of the resolution Lübeck, Hamburg and Bremen concluded in 1630 a special defensive alliance, to run for ten years. If any one of the three towns were to be attacked, the others were pledged to succour it with 500 men-at-arms and, if necessary, two warships of 100 lasts. The three towns also proposed to work out a common policy. In fact they were setting up the kind of town league which had been common from the thirteenth century onwards, and were undertaking to direct Hanseatic affairs in place of the Wendish towns, which were mere shadows of their former selves now that two of them were under the domination of a foreign power. The great merit of this modest alliance was that it survived. It was periodically renewed right up to the beginning of the present century. The three 'free and Hanseatic towns' thus ensured the apparent survival of the Hansa long after she had in fact disappeared.

The closing period of the Thirty Years War was relatively calm in northern Germany, though the war of 1643–5 between Denmark and Sweden (the latter in alliance with the Dutch) seriously affected the trade of the Hansa towns. Denmark was defeated and was forced to reduce the tolls in the Sound, which proved especially beneficial to the Dutch, and to suppress the toll at Glückstadt, to the benefit of Hamburg.

Sweden's supremacy was confirmed by the Peace of Westphalia. She was given West Pomerania, where Stettin and Stralsund as well as Wismar became Swedish possessions, and on the North Sea coast she acquired the bishoprics of Bremen and Verden, including the town of Stade, where a Swedish custom-house was erected. In addition, having obtained 'licences' from the dukes of Pomerania and Mecklenburg, the Swedes effectively controlled the entire trade of the Hansa towns, which brought them in large profits. The sum raised by all these charges on German commerce has been estimated at about 350,000 thalers per annum, which is not far short of the revenue drawn from the Sound tolls.

Although politically much weakened, economically the Hansa towns did not suffer as much as might have been expected. Only Magdeburg had been laid waste. The population of Hamburg and Danzig may even have increased during this period. The depredations carried out by the conflicting armies had certainly affected the countryside, especially in Prussia, Brandenburg and the regions of the lower Elbe, but Westphalia and the Rhineland had almost completely escaped. The accounts of the Sound show that seaborne trade had been maintained, except for a few short periods. From 1627 to 1647, 150 ships from Lübeck passed through the straits every year, more than in the twenty years before and almost as many as in the most prosperous decades of the later sixteenth century. Although Lübeck's trade with the Iberian peninsula diminished, Hamburg's remained constant. Sixty-five of her ships sailed there in 1647, and about fifty a year in the second half of the seventeenth century. In addition trade with France increased. In 1655 the Hansa signed an advantageous commercial treaty with Louix XIV, which gave the Hanseatics cause to hope that they might to some extent supplant the Dutch in Nantes, La Rochelle and Bordeaux. Although the commerce of the Prussian towns had suffered during the war between Sweden and Poland, it recovered after 1630. In 1649 nearly 100,000 lasts of grain, coming from Königsberg and Danzig, passed through the Sound.

However one traditional source of Hanseatic trade was ruined quickly and irrevocably during the seventeenth century. Norway, for so long dependent on the Wendish towns, finally made herself independent of them, mainly through the growth of Dutch trade and the development of the Dutch and Danish merchant fleets, encouraged by Christian IV. In 1600, 167 Hanseatic ships were still calling at Bergen. In 1625 there were only 103, ten years later about 40, in 1640 about 30. In the sixteenth century three-quarters of the freight between Norway and the Baltic had been carried in Hanseatic ships. By the mid-seventeenth century they kept only a third. This decline seems to have affected Wismar, Rostock and Stralsund more than Lübeck.

All things considered, the economic prospects after the return of peace were by no means wholly unfavourable, and the Hansa tried once more to establish its solidarity. Politically, the situation was not encouraging. Denmark was still trying to gain control of Hamburg and remained hostile. The Dutch were still suspicious of their rivals. Sweden was more inclined to grant privileges to towns which had come under her rule than to the Hansa as a whole, but Lübeck and Hamburg hoped that they would now be rewarded by their neutrality during the war.

The most pressing need if the bonds of the community were to be renewed was the calling of a general diet. None had been held since 1629. Many of the towns made suggestions, for example that the diet should find ways of making the privileges operative once more and so reviving trade; that it should levy a new tax on members, appoint a new syndic and restore the financial position of the *Kontore* in Antwerp and London, which were heavily in debt. In July 1651 Lübeck summoned the towns to a diet to be held three months later. But the outcome was disappointing. Although many towns accepted the invitation at first, several, among them Stralsund, Stettin and even Hamburg, asked for a postponement. Cologne forwarded the summons to fourteen towns in her quarter, but also expressed a doubt as to whether the time was propitious for a meeting. Years passed, and the diet still did not meet. In 1662 further consultations took place, but again nothing came of them. Four years later Magdeburg, which was on the verge of being incorporated into Brandenburg, implored the help of the Hansa. She received nothing but kind words, and was obliged to submit to the great elector.

However in the same year, 1666, a minor incident, the destruction by fire of the London Steelyard, brought the question of a *Hansetag* to the fore again. A unanimous decision on the measures to be taken was essential. After several postponements the diet met in 1668, but as only five towns had sent delegates, it was again adjourned until the following year. This time the summons addressed to the chief towns of the quarters stated explicitly that any town which failed to send a representative would thereby be automatically excluded from the Hansa. Lübeck had agreed to this threat with the greatest reluctance, arguing that 'the Hanseatic association was at the point of death and could not stomach so brutal a remedy'. Anyway the threat had very little effect. Of the six Prussian and Livonian towns to which Danzig forwarded the summons, only two, Riga and Thorn, took the trouble to send a refusal. In the Brunswick quarter only Hildesheim accepted. Among the Wendish and Pomeranian towns, Rostock accepted, but the others, now subject to

Sweden, replied that they enjoyed greater advantages from the treaties granted by their sovereign than they could hope to receive from the Hanseatic alliance. The latter, wrote Wismar, was 'more a shadow than a reality, and there was no hope of restoring it to its former prosperity'. None of the fourteen towns in the Cologne quarter wanted to send a delegate. Some towns declared that though they were not going to attend the diet, they intended to remain members of the Hansa, in so far as membership was not incompatible with their other obligations, and protested against the threat of exclusion.

In the end only nine towns were effectively represented at the *Hansetag* of 1669. Besides Lübeck, Hamburg and Bremen these were Danzig, Rostock, Brunswick, Hildesheim, Osnabrück and Cologne. Proceedings opened at Lübeck in July 1669, and this last Hanseatic diet held no fewer than eighteen meetings. The most varied questions were discussed: the restoration of a closer form of alliance, based on the *Notel* of 1604; a project for an association with the imperial cities of southern Germany; the appointment of a Hanseatic syndic and of a permanent representative at The Hague; the rebuilding of the London Steelyard; the payment of arrears of 'contributions' and the assessment of future annual payments; compensation for expenses incurred by Lübeck for the common good, estimated at 58,000 thalers, and so on.

But on no single point did the often stormy debates lead to a positive result. Each proposal was met by a counter-proposal and the delegates, as in the past, asserted that they were not empowered to take binding decisions. The assembly broke up after issuing a non-committal ordinance, which was in fact merely a confession of impotence.

The *Hansetag* of 1669 was the last assembly of the Hansa towns. At the time probably no one realised that the end had come. Optimists still believed that matters had only been postponed to a more favourable time, which however never came. In later years more proposals were made for meetings and for concerted action, but they all came to nothing. The Emperor Leopold apparently still believed in the existence of the Hansa in 1684, when he asked Lübeck to summon a diet to vote him a subsidy for his war against the Turks. But all desire for unity among the towns had vanished, and the Hansa with it.

All that remained was the 1630 alliance, still operative, between Lübeck, Hamburg and Bremen. To a certain extent this embodied the Hansa, since it had been empowered to represent all the other towns. At the Peace of Nijmegen in 1679 the delegates of the three towns received instructions to negotiate 'in the interests of the entire Hansa'. Legally speaking, they were the heirs of the Hansa, and as such responsible for administering Hanseatic properties, notably the Steelyard in London, which was not sold until 1853, and the house in Antwerp, disposed of in 1862. In Bergen the Church of St Mary had been appropriated by the crown in 1766, and the German *Kontor* was dissolved in 1774. But in reality the three 'free and Hanseatic towns' represented only themselves, and the ties between them had slackened considerably. The clauses in the original pact dealing with military assistance soon lapsed; and for the rest the alliance survived only in consultations and decisions on matters of no particular importance, and in joint representation abroad, notably at the court of the elector of Brandenburg. In fact the Hansa had been dead since the mid-seventeenth century.

Conclusion

It is not surprising that the Hansa disappeared in the seventeenth century. The marvel is that it survived so long. It is indeed extraordinary that so many towns, so different and so remote from one another, should for nearly 500 years have been able to engage in so many corporate activities, and remain so loyal to a community of which they were, after all, only voluntary members.

The community's long existence resulted, in the first place, from the geographical situation of the Hansa towns. Lying as they did between north-east and north-west Europe, they were predestined by nature to form a line of communication and a trade route between the two regions. But the Hansa cannot be explained by geography alone, as is evident if one compares its members with the Italian towns which played a comparable role in southern Europe. They too were intermediaries between east and west, but there was never any question of their forming an association. On the contrary they were usually engaged in bitter rivalry, whereas the members of the *dudesche hense* were united by a strong sense of national, and even more of imperial, solidarity. Although the Empire had lost its authority in this area by the mid-thirteenth century, the title 'merchants of the Roman Empire' still conveyed respect, and the dignity of imperial city certainly contributed to the recognition of Lübeck's pre-eminence within the community. In addition this solidarity was reinforced by one circumstance which had no equivalent in the Mediterranean – the urban colonisation of the east, which was the collective achievement of the western towns. A physical link was maintained between new towns and old, their merchants and leading families often being related to one another by marriage as well as doing business together. Colonisation was thus one of the strongest elements binding the community together.

The Hansa came into being to satisfy the desire of the merchants of the north German towns for mutual aid and support in the defence and advancement of their interests abroad. It was always a very fluid organisation, and although it remained substantially the same from the twelfth to the thirteenth century, it underwent a number of important structural modifications. At first it was an association of German merchants in the Gotland Community as they used the island as the regular meeting place on their business trips. A hundred years later this organisation, which was hardly competent to direct activities which had spread to all shores of the northern seas, disappeared and was never replaced, as far as any formal institution was concerned. Instead groups of merchants trading abroad, linked together by common interests, based themselves on settlements which, as time went on, acquired important privileges, but were not contained within any fixed organisation. It was the towns, who were making contact with each other through regional leagues, which now took the place of the Gotland Community in directing and protecting their merchants abroad.

When in the mid-fourteenth century commercial life was subject to greater risks, those German towns which were interested in foreign trade felt the need for some more binding form of organisation. They therefore joined together and formed the 'Hansa of the towns', whose mouthpiece was the *Hansetag*, the general diet, attended by delegates from all the towns. It met only at irregular intervals, but was nevertheless, from every point of view, the ultimate authority within the community. At the same time the towns asserted their authority of the foreign *Kontore*, which had hitherto been independent, and ruled that only burgesses of the Hansa towns should benefit from their commercial privileges. The Hansa of the towns had taken the place of the Hansa of the merchants. This led directly to attempts to strengthen the community by making it not only an economic but also a military and political organisation. But the different leagues which came into being during the fifteenth century with this end in view remained quite separate from the Hansa, and were in any case not very effective. It was not until the mid-sixteenth century that a final attempt at reorganisation made of the Hansa a league whose members were obliged to pay regular contributions. But it was already so enfeebled that this last attempt at consolidation could not check its decline and final disappearance.

The Hansa was for a long time strong and prosperous, partly because of her own internal strength, but also because Europe had need of her. For centuries the west demanded the products of the east, first furs and wax, then the products of forest and mine, and finally increasing quantities of grain. In return the east needed from the west cloth and particularly salt. The generous privileges which foreign sovereigns granted to the Hansa were the result of these basic and unremitting demands. In addition the Hansa owed its success, at least in the beginning, to the technical superiority of its chief means of transport, the cog, well-adapted to the carrying of bulky commodities; to the excellence of its business methods, modelled on those of the Italians and Flemings, and to the outstanding ability of its artisans, which helped to consolidate the economic domination of the Hanseatics, especially in the north. All these factors combined to give the Hansa the monopoly of commerce in northern Europe, and although its supremacy was threatened as early as the end of the fourteenth century, it stubbornly defended the position it had obtained, and was able to maintain it more or less intact for another 200 years.

However the community carried within itself the seeds of dissolution, which was finally to stifle the sense of solidarity. It was evident from the beginning that the interests of so many different towns could never be completely harmonised. The Hansa had to make allowances for the divergent interests of its members, and therefore set up a fluid organisation, limited to the protection of commercial interests. One serious cause of dissension resulted from the position of the towns in relation to the land and the sea. Whereas Lübeck and the Wendish towns wanted to trade along the land route Lübeck–Hamburg, the Prussian and Livonian towns preferred to use the sea route through the Sound. This led to constant disagreements between the two groups on the policy to be adopted towards Denmark and even towards England. A further source of discord came to light with the expansion of the Dutch merchant fleet. Lübeck wanted to exclude the Dutch from the Baltic, but the Prussian and Livonian towns found it profitable to have them there. The newcomers not only bought part of their grain production but also augmented their supply of salt.

The history of the Hansa is marked by a series of disagreements and disputes, some of them extremely serious. Historians have sometimes ascribed too much importance to the inter-urban quarrels of the sixteenth and seventeenth centuries, regarding them as proof of the community's decadence and contrasting them with the harmony which is supposed to have prevailed in earlier times. This is too simple a conclusion and almost entirely false. Even in the most prosperous period there were always grounds for dispute, as is shown by the exclusion of the Bremen merchants in 1285, the secret understanding between Rostock, Wismar and the *Vitalienbrüder*, and the frequent opposition of the

Teutonic Order to the policies of Lübeck. In 1412 Lübeck herself was seriously threatened with exclusion from the community. At first these internal conflicts ended in reconciliation, dictated by the generally recognised need for unity. But eventually they proved more powerful than the sentiment of Hanseatic solidarity.

Apart from the strain of internal conflicts, another main factor of Hanseatic weakness, as has often been stressed, was that the Hansa was never supported by a powerful state. Except in her early days, she received no effective help from the emperors, who were indifferent to events in an area over which they had lost their authority. They looked on the Hansa as nothing more than a possible source of revenue and were often downright hostile to her, notably in their support of the Fuggers. In times of war the Hansa was reduced to seeking alliances with north German princes. But these, anxious to re-establish their authority over the emancipated towns, were in spite of their occasional support not so much allies as dangerous enemies, who contributed to the weakening of the Hansa towns. Meanwhile in the rest of Europe the great monarchies were consolidating their power, and were more anxious to favour the economic activity of their own subjects than to ratify and renew commercial privileges originally granted to foreigners.

Equally fatal to the Hansa was its continual struggle against Denmark. She was exhausted by it, and only survived as long as she did because of the periodic crises which hindered the Danes in the pursuit of their expansionist policy in north Germany. It has been said that the Hansa towns might have benefited by Danish supremacy. This would have increased their trade with Scandinavia, the vexed question of the passage of the Sound would have been decided in their favour, and among the kings of Denmark they might sometimes have found the powerful protector they always lacked. But if the Hansa had come under Danish sovereignty, Lübeck could certainly not have played the great historic role she did.

Apart from the Danes the chief adversaries of the Hanseatics were the Dutch. They were even more formidable, since their economic development threatened the commercial basis of the community. It is no exaggeration to say that after the beginning of the fifteenth century the Dutch were the Hanseatics' nightmare – which found its symbol in the legend of the Flying Dutchman. Here again one may well ask if this confrontation was really necessary, and whether the Dutch – also nominally subjects of the Empire – could not have found a place within the Hansa to the benefit of the community, which would have been spared an unprofitable conflict. The Cologne Confederation of 1367, to which the Dutch towns adhered, proved that there was no lack of grounds for an understanding. In this matter the Hansa was perhaps the victim of her own conservatism. From the fourteenth century onwards she was willing to accept any town whose merchants could not boast of having previously belonged to the community. This was impossible in the case of the young Dutch towns; and so the Dutch, who could have been the Hanseatics' partners, became their most determined rivals.

The spirit of conservatism, which seems to have been particularly strong in Lübeck, was one of the main causes of Hanseatic weakness in and after the fifteenth century. Attempts were constantly made to maintain or restore those economic conditions which had ensured the greatness of the community in the mid-fourteenth century or even the thirteenth, and to oppose innovations necessitated by changing circumstances. As foreign competition intensified, the only remedy proposed was an even stricter regulation of trade. In striving to limit the business operations of foreigners in her domain, the Hansa hindered the activities of her own merchants, forbidding them to go into partnership with foreigners or to trade on credit. This was bound to increase their inferiority relative to their competitors. It would, however, be unjust to consider these petty regulations as nothing more than the expression of a narrow-minded attitude, imprisoned in the past and incapable of understanding modern requirements. The Hansa could retain her identity as a community only if all her members enjoyed equal rights in their trade abroad. Therefore equality had to be maintained. To allow individuals, whether towns or persons, to decide for themselves what measures to take to meet the demands of the moment, would have been to betray the Hansa itself. In the international situation of the thirteenth and fourteenth centuries an association of merchant cities was able to assume control of the commerce of northern Europe. But in the fifteenth and sixteenth centuries, when increasing competition was supported by powerful governments, such an organisation could no longer compete successfully. It was not the measures taken by the Hansa to ensure her survival which brought about her downfall. On the contrary they delayed it. It was the political and economic transformation of Europe as it passed from medieval to modern times which inevitably destroyed the Hansa. The Hanseatic leaders are hardly to be reproached for not having realised this, and for having tried to save the community as best they could.

The important historic role of the Hansa was for a long time under-estimated, largely because the development of northern Germany in modern times took place within an entirely different framework and over a period which saw the decline of many of the towns which had played a leading part in the community. Among them were Lübeck and the other Wendish towns of the Baltic coast, Rostock and Stralsund, and inland such towns as Dortmund, Goslar and Lüneburg, as well as Kampen and Deventer on the Zuiderzee. The towns then coming into prominence – Berlin, Königsberg, Hanover – had formerly been members of the Hansa, but it was as the capitals of monarchies that they were becoming increasingly important. Even the development of navigation and trade no longer took place under the aegis of the three 'free and Hanseatic towns', but under the patronage of monarchs, principally those of Prussia.

For all this, the Hansa occupies a very considerable place in the history of Europe during the last 300 years of the Middle Ages. Although she did not, as was once believed, create the towns of the east and north, she gave decisive encouragement to their development. She founded the lasting prosperity of Danzig, Riga, Reval, Stockholm and above all of Hamburg and Bremen. Further afield the great markets at Novgorod, Bergen and Bruges were developed by the enterprise of the Hanseatics. For centuries they supplied the peoples of east and west with products essential for their development and often for their very survival. Through her too the ideas and arts of the west, and in particular of the Low Countries, spread to all the countries on the shores of the Baltic.

Admittedly the work of the Hansa did not always have positive results. The heavy traffic in cloth from the Low Countries prevented the growth of a large-scale textile industry in northern Germany, and more often than not the interests of the craftsman were subordinated, even sacrificed, to those of the merchant. One cannot deny that in Norway Hanseatic domination ruined the local agriculture, and, to a large extent, local trade, thus creating an unfortunate economic imbalance. On the whole, however, there can be no doubt that the Hansa benefited the inhabitants of the countries in which its activities were carried on.

Finally the community was inspired by a spirit which, though based on material self-interest, is nonetheless worthy of admiration and respect. Indifferent to nationalistic prejudices and even, to a large extent, to religious differences, the Hanseatics were deeply pacific and had recourse to war only when all else failed. They always did their utmost, both among themselves and in their dealings with foreign countries, to settle their quarrels and remove their grievances by arbitration and negotiation. In this way they offer us a lesson in wisdom which we could well profit by today.

Documents

I. Events, Privileges, Treaties

I

THE FOUNDING OF LÜBECK

1143–1159 – The account given by Helmold, priest of Bosau (Holstein), in his Chronica Slavorum, *compiled circa 1171 (cf. p. 20).*

Adolphe [count of Holstein] began to rebuild Segeberg castle and enclosed it within a wall. But as the country was deserted, he sent messengers into Flanders and Holland, to Utrecht, Westphalia and Frisia with an invitation for all those who were without any land to come with their families. They would receive a fine stretch of fertile land, yielding abundant livestock and fish, as well as excellent pasture land. . . . As a result of this appeal, a vast number of people of different races set off with their families and their possessions and came to Count Adolphe in the land of the Wagrians to take possession of the property he had promised them. . . .

Next Count Adolf went to a place called Bucu and there found the rampart of an abandoned castle built long ago by Cruto, the enemy of God, and a great island flanked by two rivers: on one side the Trave, on the other the Wakenitz. Both rivers had marshy and treacherous banks, but on the side facing towards the land there rose a fairly steep hill, in front of the rampart. Seeing immediately how convenient this site was and how excellent the place was for a port, the count began building a town which he called Lübeck, as it was not very far from the former port and town of the same name built long before by the [slav] prince Henry. . . .

One day in 1152 the duke [of Saxony, Henry the Lion] addressed the count thus: 'Some time ago it came to our notice that our town of Bardowiek was losing its citizens as a result of trade in Lübeck, for all the traders and merchants are setting up there. Likewise the people of Lüneburg are complaining that our salt-mines are running down since you opened one at Oldesloe. I ask you therefore to let us share in your town of Lübeck and your salt-mines so that we might be able to withstand the desertion of our town more easily. If not, we henceforth forbid all further trading at Lübeck, for we cannot allow the heritage of our forebears to be destroyed at the hands of foreign interests.'

But the count, not believing such an agreement to be to his advantage, refused. Thereupon the duke decreed that henceforth there should be no more trading in Lübeck and that the only things that might be bought or sold there were foodstuffs. He also ordered merchandise to be transported through Bardowiek in order to bring back life to his town.

During this period (1157) the town of Lübeck was completely destroyed by fire. The merchants and other inhabitants sent delegates to the duke with this message: 'For a long time now trading in Lübeck has been forbidden by you. Until now we have been staying on in the town in the hope that through your lordship's benevolence we might again have leave to carry on our trade. We could not resign ourselves to leaving behind buildings constructed at such great cost. But now that our homes have been razed to the ground, there is no advantage in rebuilding them where we cannot do our trading. We ask you therefore to be so gracious as to allocate to us a place where we can found a town.' Thus the duke founded a new town on the Wakenitz river, not far from Lübeck, and he began to build and fortify it. He named it after his own name *Lewenstat*, 'Lion's Town'. However this spot was inappropriate for a port and a fortress and only small boats could reach it. So the duke approached Count Adolf again, and again raised the question of the port and island of Lübeck. At long last the count gave way and granted him the castle and island. Straightway the merchants and traders, on the duke's instructions, returned joyfully, leaving behind them the unwanted new town, and started to rebuild the town's churches and walls. The duke sent messengers into the northern towns and states, Denmark, Sweden, Norway and Russia, offering them peace and free right of access through his town of Lübeck. He also established there a mint and a market and granted the town the highest privileges. From that time onwards there was ever-increasing activity in the town and the number of its inhabitants rose considerably.

> *Monumenta Germaniae historica, Scriptores in usum scholarum. Helmoldi presbyteri Bozoviensis Chronica Slavorum*, ed. B. SCHMEIDLER (1909) chs 57, 76, 86, pp. 111, 145, 168.

2

CHARTERS FOR MERCHANTS FROM COLOGNE IN LONDON

1157 – Ordinances of Henry II (cf. p. 6).

(*a*) Henry, king of England by the grace of God, duke of Normandy and Aquitaine, count of Anjou, bids welcome to his mayor, sheriff and aldermen. I grant permission for the inhabitants of Cologne to sell their wine at the price for which French wine is sold, namely threepence per gallon. And I forbid anyone to prevent them from doing this or to do them any harm or hindrance.

(*b*) Henry bids welcome to his judges, sheriffs and all other high officers of England. I command you to guard, care and protect as closely as my own subjects and friends the subjects and citizens of Cologne and their goods and possessions. You will neither do nor allow to be done any wrong or damage to their house in London or Gildhall, their goods or their possessions. For they are loyal to me and I am their safeguard and protection. Let them enjoy complete freedom to live according to their rightful customs. Do not impose upon them any new or unwonted taxation or ruling with which they are not already compelled to comply. And should anyone break any part of these commands, act swiftly and firmly in the name of justice.

Hansisches Urkundenbuch, 1, nos 13 and 14, p. 8.

3

TRADE TREATY BETWEEN THE PRINCE OF SMOLENSK AND THE GERMAN MERCHANTS

1229 — Treaty established between Prince Davidovitch of Smolensk in his name and in the name of the princes of Polotsk and Vitebsk; and the German merchants of Riga, Gotland and other towns. Almost every clause granted to the Germans in Smolensk is balanced by a reciprocal clause for the Russians in Riga and Gotland (cf. p. 30).

5. If a Russian buys on credit, from a German supplier and if he is also in debt to another Russian, the German will have priority in receiving payment. . . .

10. A Russian cannot demand from a German in Smolensk, nor a German from a Russian in Riga or Gotland, settlement by duel. If the Germans should fight among themselves with sword or lance, that is of no concern to the prince or any other Russian, and they will reach agreement in their own fashion. . . .

15. Should the official in charge of ferry transport [*Volok*] learn that a German citizen has arrived at the same time as merchants from Smolensk at the ferrying point, he will immediately send an order by messenger to his men to transport together with their merchandise the German citizen and the merchant from Smolensk.

16. Lots will be drawn to determine which of the two should be transported

first. If another Russian from a different region has arrived at the same time, he will cross after them.

17. Every German citizen on entry into the town is obliged to offer a piece of cloth to the princess and a pair of Gothic-style gloves with fingers to the official in charge of ferry transport. . . .

19. Every German in Smolensk can sell his merchandise without dispute.

20. If a German wishes to take his merchandise to another town, neither the prince nor the people of Smolensk have the right to prevent him.

21. If a Russian buys from a German and takes the merchandise away, he cannot bring it back and he must pay for it [and vice versa]. A Russian must not accuse a German in open public court, but only before the prince. But if a German desires a public court hearing, his wishes will be honoured. . . .

27. If a German purchases a silver mark and has it weighed, he will give two squirrel skins to the weigher, but nothing if he sells it. . . .

29. If the weight used for weighing wax becomes inaccurate, it must be corrected by comparison with the standard weights, one of which is in the Church of the Mount, the other in the Germans' Church. . . .

31. A German does not have to pay toll charges from Smolensk to Riga and from Riga to Smolensk. Conversely a Russian does not have to pay toll charges from Gotland to Riga and from Riga to Smolensk.

32. Should the prince of Smolensk wage war, this is in no way the concern of the Germans unless they ask to accompany the prince in battle.

33. Should – God forbid – a German or Russian ship be shipwrecked, the master should unload his cargo on the shore without hindrance. If there are too few men and he is obliged to enlist others, the latter will not receive more than the agreed wages. This rule applies equally to Germans and to Russians in the territories of Smolensk, Polotsk and Vitebsk.

This act was drawn up in 1229 in the presence of Nicholas, bishop of Riga, Priest John, Master [of the Brethren of the Sword] Volkin, and numerous merchants of the Roman Empire whose seal is affixed. Here are the witnesses: Regenbode, Dethard, Adam, citizen of Gotland; Member, Friedrich, Dummom of Lübeck; Henry the Goth and Ilier of Soest; Conrad Blödauge and Johann Kinot of Münster, Bernek and Volker of Groningen; Arembrecht and Albrecht of Dortmund; Heinrich Zeisig of Bremen; the citizens of Riga Albrecht Sluk, Bernhart, Walter and Albrecht, lawyer of Riga.

Should a Russian or German violate this treaty, he violates divine law and justice.

Hansisches Urkundenbuch, 1, no. 232, pp. 73–9.

4

TRANSFER OF THE *KONTOR* FROM BRUGES TO AARDENBURG

1280 – When Lübeck proposed transferring the Kontor *a large number of towns signified their agreement in more or less identical terms. Here is the reply from Visby (cf. p. 43).*

It is unfortunately only too well known that [German] merchants travelling in Flanders have been the object of all kinds of maltreatment in the town of Bruges and have not been able to protect themselves from this. The said merchants were finally forced to bring their complaints to the attention of His Serene Highness Count Guy of Flanders. Thereupon the said count, having listened to and accepted their complaints, had the graciousness to grant the merchants, together with the town of Aardenburg, charters and various franchises if they henceforth chose to frequent Aardenburg with their ships and merchandise.

It is for this reason that, bearing in mind how all foreigners have the right to buy, sell and trade all their merchandise freely and without discrimination both among themselves and with local citizens, we consider that, as far as we are concerned, the main centre of commerce and trade in [Hanseatic] goods should be established at Aardenburg for as long as the said count together with the citizens of Aardenburg and their successors continue to grant us these privileges, favours and charters. We would retain the right only to make special visits to other ports, cities and territories.

In witness whereof we affix to this document the seals of our city, those of Germans and Gotlanders alike.

Urkundenbuch der Stadt Lübeck, i, no. 156, p. 371.

5

CITIZENS OF LÜBECK AT THE CHAMPAGNE FAIRS

1294 – Ordinance of Philip the Fair (cf. p. 42).

Philip, king of France by the grace of God, bids welcome to the provosts, bailiffs and other officials of our kingdom who will receive this document.

Having seen our court record of the conflict which has arisen between on the one hand the merchants of Lübeck and on the other hand the toll-collectors of Bapaume, it appeared that when these merchants travel to the Champagne fairs with goods acquired or purchased in Germany, they are not obliged to take the Bapaume road. They can come and go with their merchandise where they will, paying the usual tolls in the places where they travel.

On the other hand, should they be transporting merchandise or silver from Flanders to the said fairs or other places mentioned in the said record, they must take the Bapaume road. This is why we command you to oppose vigorously any maltreatment of those aforementioned merchants which is contrary to the spirit of the said record.

Hansisches Urkundenbuch, 1, no. 1140, p. 392.

6

UNDERTAKING GIVEN BY THE ENGLISH CUSTOMS TO A GROUP OF MERCHANTS FROM DORTMUND

1340 – Ordinance from Edward III addressed to 'the collectors of customs duties on wool, leather and woollen cloths' in London and twelve other English ports (cf. p. 58).

The prelates, counts, barons and commons of our kingdom of England having, in our recently assembled Parliament, imposed a levy to cover expenditure incurred in the defence of our kingdom and such expenditure as will be necessary to defend our rights elsewhere, this levy on each bale of wool exported from England to be 40 shillings for the English and Flemish and 40 shillings 40 pence for all other foreigners and to last until Lent of next year.

We through the affection we bear for our distinguished German merchants Henry of Muddenpening, Tidemann of Limberg, Conrad of Afflen, Conrad Clypping, Sefrid Spisenaghel, Alvin of Revele, Johann of Wold, Tir of Wold his brother, Henry of Revele the Younger, Johann Clypping, Hertwin of Bek, Wessel of Bergh, Conrad of Revele and their associates.

And by virtue of the great help and considerable loans they granted us on the Continent, as well as the 3,000 bales of wool and 1,100 pounds sterling for which we and others are indebted to the said merchants through our letters patent, the total of which, with expenses, amounts to 18,100 pounds sterling; and because of the 4,000 pounds sterling – the gold écu being reckoned at 18 Tours groschen – that the said merchants spent or undertook to pay for us in

Brussels, in the 10 days following Conrad Clypping's arrival in Flanders; and because of the other 4,300 pounds sterling likewise payable for us in Brussels in the fortnight following the above payment.

We grant that the said merchants or their agents should receive all the afore-mentioned 'customs' and all other customs and 'subsidies' large or small which we have levied in all the ports in England where the 'custom' should be levied, until the said sums and those they will in future lend us are paid back. And the said merchants or their agents will receive half our seal, which is called the cocket, for raising the 'large custom'; and the seal for the 'small custom', in the custody of the collectors in each port, will be handed to them or their agents.

And the said merchants [here follow their Christian names] have ap-pointed in our presence as their general agents the said Tidemann [of Lim-berg] and Johann of Wold for all the said ports.

> *Hanseakten aus England 1275 bis 1412*, ed. K. KUNZE ('Hansische Geschichtsquellen', vol. 6, 1891) no. 114, p. 78; F. KEUTGEN, *Urkunden zur Städtischen Ver-fassungsgeschichte* (1901) no. 433, p. 524.

7

THE CONFEDERATION OF COLOGNE

1367 – The main military and financial measures which were agreed upon at Cologne, in the name of the whole confederation, by the delegates of the Hansa towns of Lübeck, Rostock, Stralsund, Wismar, Kulm, Thorn and Elbing, together with the delegates of the Dutch towns of Kampen, Harderwijk, Elburg, Amsterdam and Briel, for the prosecution of the war against Denmark and Norway (cf. p. 70).

We ... declare ... that we have agreed ...

1. Firstly that because of the manifold wrongs and injuries which the kings of Denmark and Norway have inflicted and do still inflict upon Hanseatic merchants, we have become their enemies and that we shall loyally support one another in the following manner: namely, that the Wendish towns to-gether with the Livonian towns and with those towns which are associated with them, will fit out ten cogs, manned with able men-at-arms, that is, 100 men to each cog; and a *Schute* and a *Snikke** shall accompany each cog. The

* Light ships.

Prussian towns, that is, the seaports, shall equip five cogs of a like kind . . . etc. [22 cogs in all].

2. Further we are agreed that all cogs and men from the Zuiderzee, from Holland and Zeeland shall arrange to be completely ready on Palm Sunday next, when they shall sail with the first good wind to the Sound, and that they will sail together to Marstrand,* put in at the harbour there and there wait until all are assembled, and then sail from Marstrand into the Sound. And the cogs and the men from the Wendish towns and from Prussia shall with their entire fleet, with all the ships that wish to pass through the Sound, be ready next Easter to sail to Gellen,† to assemble there and to join the fleet from the Zuiderzee in the Sound, as soon as they learn that it has arrived there. And when they are assembled in the Sound, the whole fleet from both districts is to remain with the warships and to do as the commanders bid them, on pain of losing honour, life and fortune, until the commanders give them leave to sail. And anyone who breaks this rule shall be brought before a court in whatever town he enters, and the goods which he has brought there are to be handed over to the town in which he lives or whose burgess he is. . . .

3. If any captain, steersman, sailor, boatswain or any other person, native of a town of this Confederation, go over to the aforementioned kings, they are declared outlaws for all time in all towns and ports of this confederation. If any Wendish town or town of Prussia, of Livonia or of anywhere in the entire German Hansa, of the Zuiderzee, of Holland or of Zeeland does not obey what has been decided by the other towns, then her citizens and her merchants shall have no community with any of the towns which belong to this Confederation, so that no one may buy from them or sell to them, so that they may neither enter nor leave any harbour, neither load nor unload any wares, and this for ten years. . . .

4. Further, to cover the costs, each merchant shall pay poundage on his goods, as follows, for every pound groschen one groschen, for six Lübeck marks four Lübeck pennies, for nine Stralsund marks six Stralsund pennies, for four Prussian marks eight Prussian pennies, for twelve Pomeranian marks eight *vinkenoge*,‡ whatever may be his port of destination. And similarly captains shall pay poundage on their ships. . . .

5. This poundage shall be levied in every town of the Confederation when a ship leaves harbour; and a receipt is to be given which they are to bring to their port of destination. If, however, anyone sails from a harbour where this poundage has not been levied, as, for example, from England, Flanders and other parts, and has therefore no receipt on his arrival [in a port of the Confederation], then he shall pay his poundage at that port. Whoever comes from the Baltic and wishes to go to the Zuiderzee or to the North Sea by the land route from Lübeck to Hamburg via Oldesloe, is excused payment of the

---

* Harbour on the west coast of Sweden.
† Headland on the island of Hiddensee, west of Rügen.
‡ 'Finch's eye', the current term for a Pomeranian penny.

poundage in Hamburg, if he can produce a receipt showing that he has already paid on his departure. [The same applies to journeys from west to east.]

And the aforesaid receipts, which they are to bring with them, shall show how much poundage they have paid, on goods of what kind and in what quantity and at what time.

6. In every town where this poundage is to be levied, it is to be kept at the disposal of all those towns which have fitted out ships of war. And the poundage and the corresponding receipts, which they have received from merchants and captains, shall be brought to Lübeck on St John's Day, Midsummer Day [24 June 1368], where they shall all come together, as is written below, and share out the poundage in just proportion. . . .

7. Furthermore: if the Wendish towns should succeed in persuading the above-named princes [the king of Sweden, the duke of Mecklenburg and the count of Holstein] to become our allies, then we will make an alliance with them for the duration of one year from Easter next and the princes shall not make peace without us nor we without them. . . .

8. The above-mentioned Confederation with all its rules and regulations shall remain in full force for a further three years after the time when we shall make peace with the above-mentioned kings [of Denmark and Norway.]

Hanserezesse, I, no. 413, pp. 373–6.

8

MALPRACTICES AND EXCESSES OF THE HANSEATICS IN NORWAY

1370 – A list of complaints at the behaviour of the Hansa towns presented by Haakon VI of Norway, during negotiations which were to end in a five-year truce. The Hanseatics for their part had presented a similar list of complaints.

Charges and indictments which we, King Haakon, submit in the name of our kingdoms of Norway and Sweden against the [German] maritime towns.

1. Firstly, when one of them commits a crime against a third party, the [German] merchants arrange, if they can, a settlement between the plaintiff and the guilty party and thus deprive the crown and its officials of the right to see justice done. Moreover when murder or other blatant major crimes are committed, they carry off the criminals in their ships so that neither the plaintiff nor the crown achieve redress.

2. Item, the maritime towns have become united and taken into the Hansa other towns which were not formerly part of it, without the consent of our predecessors or ourselves, in order that they might enjoy the benefits of privileges that are only valid for those towns named in the documents of our predecessors.

3. Item, they decided among themselves not to allow the goods and merchandise of our subjects on their ships in order to deprive them of any opportunity for profit.

4. Item, wherever they land in our ports, they buy and sell whatever they please in violation of the laws of the land, even to the extent of retailing their cloth and other commodities in our towns and territories. This has in the past been forbidden and neither we nor our predecessors have ever sanctioned it. . . .

10. Item, the [German] merchants from Bergen have often caused trouble and disorder during which our men and subjects have been killed. For this we have never had redress.

11. Item, the merchants from Bergen entered by force our court at Bergen and made their way to Lord Sigurd. When the latter personally urged them to abide by the law, they forced him to do as they wished. The following day they went to Bergen monastery, carried off one of the servants and decapitated him. They then urged the bishop of Bergen to absolve them from their crime and the council to judge this misdeed according to their wishes. Should these demands be refused, they would burn down the episcopal court and town of Bergen. . . .

14. The Wendish towns entered into a truce with the king of Denmark, excluding our father, ourselves and our territories. As a result of this, he [the king] built castles in Finland and occupied large tracts of our country so that we have suffered losses to the value of more than 30,000 marks of pure silver. . . .

20. Item, the [German] tailors of Bergen assassinated the cousin of the lord archbishop of Trondheim. For this we have had no redress. . . .

23. Item, a merchant named Buk from Kolberg killed an Englishman at Marstrand [on the island of Kattegat]. The murderer was carried off by a certain Foltzkin Nortmeyer, although this was forbidden on pain of death and loss of property. . . .

39. Item, the [German] merchants of Bergen refused to accept our money which had been established by the council for the whole kingdom, and would only accept foreign money, namely that of Lübeck and Stralsund. It is evident that in so doing they did us considerable harm and injustice.

My lord consuls [of the German towns] these are our present complaints. We shall, however, detail many more as soon as they reach us.

Hanserezesse, I 2, no. 4, pp. 11–14.

9

OUTRAGES AND WRONGS DONE TO HANSEATIC MERCHANTS BY THE ENGLISH

1386 – Extracts from a memorandum presented by Prussian envoys in England in support of a claim for indemnities (cf. p. 182).

1. In the year of Our Lord 1375 Hermann Halenbergh, a burgess of Danzig, lost a quarter-share in a ship, worth 15 English pounds, and in the ship were 23 tuns of Bordeaux wine, worth at that time 11 or 12 English marks per tun. Ship and wine were taken from this Hermann Halenbergh by Edward le Despencer. To get them back he has appeared three times before the Privy Council with letters from the Grand Master of Prussia and other sufficient proofs. In this suit, which he has now pleaded three times in vain, he has spent more than 50 English pounds and has nevertheless achieved nothing. Finally after a fourth plea the lord chancellor offered him 200 gold nobles, which he would not accept, and so he has remained without any success. . . .

2. Further, in the year of Our Lord 1381 a ship which merchants from Thorn in Prussia had loaded with various wares, namely, wax, furs, iron, lead and various other things, was wrecked off the village of Romney [Kent] and villages round about, and the inhabitants of those villages have seized and kept all the goods, found on the shore or salvaged from the sea. . . . The goods salvaged had been estimated at 600 pounds sterling, of which about 350 pounds was the share of the above-named merchants from Thorn. The rest was the share of other merchants from Hungary, Poland and other places, which we do not name. . . .

3. Further, in the year 83 the ship's captain Evehard Storm, a burgess of Elbing, had sold to the parish of Scarborough [Yorks] timber, pitch and other goods. When they were to pay him the money, they began to dispute with him, and said he was a traitor and a criminal from Brittany and laid many other slanders upon him; on these grounds they have kept back 55 nobles of his money, which they owe him. . . .

7. Further, in the year 79 Hermann Wulf, a burgess of Elbing, entered the harbour at Ipswich with a ship half of which belonged to this Hermann and the rest to merchants from England. But allegedly in the name of the king, Sir Albert de Ver and Sir John Devereux came and seized the ship, brought it to London and have kept it for eight months, so that he has thereby suffered a loss of 100 pounds sterling, as he has sworn on oath. . . .

9. In a similar way Augustin, a burgess from Königsberg, was seized by the Privy Council, together with his ship, and compelled to transport horses for

our lord the king; and he was to receive 10 shillings sterling a month for each horse, of which 20 pounds sterling is still owing to him, as he has sworn on relics. Moreover burgesses of Boston, by name of Ricer Nerwede and Harssic, brought him and his ship to Lynn, to Hudze Paxman's inn, where he was to take on a cargo of wool for Calais on condition that they should bring aboard sufficient wool for a full cargo; and for every last of wool they promised him 13 nobles, of which the payment for 2½ lasts has not yet been made to him. In addition they promised him that as soon as he reached Calais merchants would unload his cargo within the space of three tides; but they did not do so, on the contrary they kept him there with his ship laden for a fortnight, so that because of the lack of water in the port his ship burst open and fell to pieces. This caused him, as he has sworn upon relics, a loss of 100 pounds sterling. . . .

15. Furthermore, in the year of Our Lord 1378 a ship's captain named Tidemann Stiker from Danzig arrived with many other ships from the Bay [of Bourgneuf] off Penmarch, where there were also English warships whose crews called out to the above-named captain by day in a peaceful and friendly way, and he was well known to them. But when night had fallen the afore-mentioned Englishmen came and boarded the ship and during the assault killed the above-mentioned captain and threw him with three others into the sea; in addition they took various goods from the ship, as well as the ready cash, and in order to get his rings they cut off that captain's fingers. Because of this hostile attack Goswin Grote, to whom the ship belonged, has com-plained of a loss of 150 pounds groschen. . . .

Hanserezesse, I 3, no. 202, pp. 189–92.

10

THE STRUGGLE AGAINST ENGLISH COMPETITION

1404 – Extracts from an English list of complaints against the Teutonic Order and the Hansa towns (cf. p. 192).

Here are the points on which we the subjects of our lord the king offer our complaints against the people of Prussia and other territories of the Hansa, namely

1. Firstly the said English merchants travelling in the said region have for time immemorial been accustomed to selling their cloth in certain lengths, namely the whole roll 42 ells long or the half-roll 21 ells long. But the Prussians recently stipulated that each roll was to measure 44 ells and the half-roll 22 ells, the penalty for failing to comply with this being confiscation.

As a result of this recent ordinance our lord the king's subjects have lost each year upwards of 1,000 pounds. . . .

6. Also they ruled that no Englishman travelling with his English wife may stay in the said territory and must leave it immediately or else risk losing all his goods. . . .

9. Also we subjects of our lord the king had permission to elect governors in Prussia among ourselves and organise assemblies just like the Hanseatics in this kingdom. The Prussians forbade the subjects of our lord the king to form assemblies or any kind of group or to pass ordinances, failure to obey being severely penalised. . . .

11. Also the people of the Hansa, under the pretext of their rights and privileges in England ally themselves to certain foreigners in order to protect them and exempt them from taxes for their own good. As a result of this protection, the said foreigners who ought to pay our lord the king a customs duty of 2 shillings 9 pence per length of cloth, now only pay no more than 12 pence per length of cloth like the people of the Hansa, this to the harm and detriment of the king. . . .

19. Also, on the eve of St George's Day in the sixteenth year of King Richard the Second's reign [22 April 1393], several wrongdoers and bandits from Wismar and Rostock in the Hansa sailed in a large ship to the town of Bergen, took the town by storm, seized the merchants and their goods there, set fire to their houses and demanded a huge ransom from the inhabitants, and as is shown by the letters of safe-conduct delivered to them, the plaintiffs incurred losses of some 5,400 nobles. . . .

24. Also the said English merchants complain strongly of the fact that the Prussian *Schäffers** order all ships' captains to take prisoner any Englishman they might encounter on the seas, with the result that English merchants no longer dare to put in at Skania nor any other place and have suffered losses amounting to more than 2,000 pounds.

26. Also they complain most strongly at the fact that while certain English merchants were in the town of Stralsund with their merchandise on the last day of May past [1404], the said people of Stralsund seized the English merchants and their goods and locked them up in a wretched prison; the goods and merchandise are still in their hands, resulting in a loss to the said English merchants of 820 pounds.

Hanseakten aus England 1275 bis 1412, ed. KUNZE, no. 322, pp. 229–34.

* Administrative officials of the Teutonic Order controlling the trade and shipping of the Order.

II

TRUCE BETWEEN THE HANSA AND CASTILE

1443 – A three-year truce (which could be prolonged by twelve years) con-
cluded at Bruges which put an end to the conflict resulting from the
destruction of a Hanseatic fleet by the Castilians in 1419 (cf. p. 258).

To the glory of the Blessed Trinity and so that their commerce may grow to
mutual advantage, the nations of the German Hansa and Spain, formerly
great enemies under the influence of Satan . . ., have thus reached agreement:

1. First, that the said nations both recognise and ratify a truce for three
years to come.

2. All merchants, sailors and subjects of the German nations and German
Hansa will be free to travel, settle and stay as they will in every region, town
and port belonging to his gracious majesty the king of Castile, and to take
with them their goods, possessions, merchandise and retinues. Whenever
Hanseatic sailors enter a port of the said noble king with a surplus of ships
and foodstuffs, they can sell them. Any merchandise purchased with the
money earned from such transactions can be put on board their own ships and
transported wherever they wish. On the other hand, should the said Hanseatic
sailors carry in their ships goods other than foodstuffs, they will load any
merchandise purchased with the proceeds into Spanish ships, provided these are
to be found in the said ports and that they are prepared to set sail for the
countries and ports to which the sailors and merchants wish to send their
merchandise. . . .

5. Item, should it so happen that Hanseatic sailors, having left a port and
reached the high seas in company with Spanish sailors, encounter enemies
of the Spanish such as the English, they will straightway hoist their flags or
any other signal to indicate that they are not enemies. They will then withdraw to one side so as not to encumber the Spanish sailors in their fight
against their enemies. . . .

8. [Kampen possibly to be excluded from the truce if in case of conflict with
the Spanish the town refuses the summons from the *Kontor* of Bruges, sends no
representative and fails to make reparation.]

9. If merchants and sailors from each nation, together in a port and about to
set sail at the same time, pledge themselves, under oath or by simple promise,
to give mutual aid to each other against their enemies or against pirates; and
if the latter are seen at sea, and one side makes off, refusing their ally aid,
they should be severely punished by the nation from which they come as an
example to others in the future.

10. Item, the two sides agree that the merchants of the German nation, whenever they acquire wine or other commodities at the port of La Rochelle, should give preference to loading them in greater quantities on Spanish ships than on ships of any other nation; always provided that the Spanish ships are located there and are sailing for those ports to which the German merchants wish to send their cargo.

> T. Hirsch: *Danzigs Handels- und Gewerbegeschichte* (1858) pp. 272–4.

12

THE DANZIG CHRONICLE

1470–1486 – Extracts from the chronicle of Caspar Weinreich, a Danzig ship-owner (cf. p. 233).

1470. Item, this same summer there came to Danzig many ships from Holland, Kampen and Frisia and our own Baltic ships, from the Bay [of Bourgneuf] and Brouage, so that salt was in little demand, and was sold at six and a half marks per last.

1471. During this same Lent Paul Beneke took *La Madeleine* of Dieppe and *Le Cygne* of Caen; in the latter the mayor of London, Thomas Kriegk, was made prisoner.

1473. Item, on Easter Monday a fine fleet, well-manned and with many new ships, set sail for Flanders, Holland, Zeeland etc.: about fifty ships in all.

Item, on Easter Eve there died a Lombard living in Danzig who had had a great ship built, 51 ells long in the keel, and on Easter Day they bore him to the Carthusians where he was buried.

Item, the second Tuesday after Easter Paul Beneke in the 'Great Caravel' took a galley with a mast 23 fathoms tall and a double forecastle. She had sailed from the Welinge [Flanders], bound for London. The merchandise taken has been valued and certified at 60,000 pounds groschen; it was divided into 400 shares, either of 100 marks or of 80, in addition to 21 marks prize-money per man. The share-out was held according to custom.

1479. In spring of the same year, 1479, the first Danzig ship, of 70 lasts, sailed to Iceland. The owner was Ludke Wespendorff, in association with others; but the ship was lost on the home journey off Nidingen [Kattegat].

1481. During this summer 1,100 ships, great and small, laden with corn, sailed westwards from Danzig, making for Holland, Zeeland and Flanders. In Zeeland at Whitsuntide rye was worth 48 florins and wheat 54 and 55 florins. But in the autumn the export of rye out of Danzig was forbidden; in the autumn therefore rye was worth 70 to 80 florins.

1485. In the spring the wind blew continually from the north, north-east or east, so that no ship could come to Danzig. It was not until a few days before Corpus Christi [2 June] that any Rhenish wine arrived. Item, in the autumn in Skania about 3,000 lasts of herring or more were caught and salted in all depots; but the fish were rather small: 17, 18, 19 [hundred?] per ton, but of very good quality. Nothing like this had happened in twenty years.

Item, in that same summer and autumn only a single ship was built in the ship-yard (*Lastadie*), of 60 lasts, built by a carpenter to order. Never in the memory of men had the yard been so deserted as in this year; not even in time of war had it been so deserted as it was this year.

Item, in autumn of the same year our ships came home from the Bay in ballast and could get no salt there. At Brouage a hundredweight was worth 10 crowns and so Bay salt was sold in Danzig for 40 marks per last, Trave salt for 38 marks, and Scottish salt for 22 marks.

1486. This summer a vast amount of herring was caught in Skania, but it was bought at a high price so that the merchant, in all towns to which he shipped herring, lost money, even though Flemish herring did not come through the Sound.

Item, this summer and autumn the town of Danzig lost many good ships at sea with valuable cargoes of salt, rye, cloth and other goods, so that she suffered great loss at sea that year, as had not happened within the memory of men.

Scriptores rerum prussicarum, vol. 4 (1870), ed. T. Hirsch, pp. 733–60.

13

WULLENWEVER'S GRAND DESIGN

1534 – Count Christopher of Oldenburg's undertakings (given to Lübeck), as commander of the Lübeck troops in the projected conquest of the Danish islands and the liberation of King Christian II, held prisoner by the duke of Schleswig-Holstein (cf. p. 326).

1. Should almighty God look favourably upon our merciful endeavour to liberate the person, realm, lands and subjects of our dear cousin Christian, at present a prisoner, then we promise for our part and on behalf of our afore-

mentioned dear cousin, that all privileges, franchises and rights, enjoyed of old in the kingdom of Denmark and Norway and in all its dependencies, shall without limitation be confirmed and extended to the town of Lübeck, her inhabitants and her allies.

2. We also undertake to put our dear cousin immediately after his release, as we hope with God's help shall be achieved, in the hands of Lübeck, to treat amicably with him and to come to an agreement, as shall seem good to the town of Lübeck, since we should never have been able to free our cousin from captivity without the help of God and of the town of Lübeck.

3. If it should further happen, that the king of Sweden should refuse to give up his ungrateful obstruction and opposition to the merchants, wares and privileges of the town of Lübeck or to take part in discussions on acceptable terms, then we with our allies will support the town of Lübeck with all our power and will help to bring the matter to a good conclusion, on land and at sea, as shall be considered and desired most profitable.

4. This will also apply to the Hollanders and the Holsteiners, in so far as they do not keep the truce agreed or continue to harass the town of Lübeck after it has lapsed; in that case we shall stand by the town of Lübeck and her allies no less than if these harassments had been made against our own person; furthermore we will make no agreement, alliance or truce with them without the knowledge and consent of the town of Lübeck, much less initiate negotiations ourselves.

5. In particular, neither before nor after the liberation of our cousin Christian, shall we enter upon any negotiations with the royal council of Denmark or permit his highness to do so, without the agreement of the council of Lübeck and of her allies, to whom the affair is of no less importance than to us. . . .

6. In addition the town of Lübeck and her allies have suffered considerable loss, disadvantage, obstruction and expense on account of the kingdom of Denmark and Norway and on account of our dear cousin, . . . amounting at a moderate estimate to 400,000 guilders; furthermore all that we are now doing by way of helping our above-named cousin in his dire need amounts to an additional and considerable sum of money; therefore the town of Lübeck shall retain, as a just compensation for such losses and expenses incurred for the common good, Hälsingborg in Skania and Helsingör in Zealand with both castles, and all tolls and rights appertaining to them, until the sums mentioned above, including those which she is now expending for the sake of ourselves and our cousin, have been collected and paid in full; we are willing to hand over the above-mentioned castles to the town of Lübeck, as soon as they are captured, without any reservations or conditions.

7. However if we should, with God's help and in the name of our cousin Christian, conquer Gotland and hand it over to the town of Lübeck for ever with the enjoyment of all rights . . . then the council of Lübeck and their successors will cede and return the above-mentioned castle of Hälsingborg to

the kingdom of Denmark. However they are to retain for ever Helsingör with half its tolls, but shall account to the kingdom of Denmark for the other half; if it should happen that the town of Lübeck receives in one payment the above-mentioned sum of money together with what they are at present expending on our behalf and on behalf of our cousin, then they will voluntarily hand over either the above-mentioned castles or Gotland.

8. In particular Bornholm, which is at present in the possession of the town of Lübeck, shall remain hers for ever irrevocably with all rights and property, in recognition of the friendly goodwill and aid which she has on many occasions shown to the kingdom of Denmark. In addition they shall receive the castle of Segeberg and it shall always remain in possession of the town, and we together with our dear cousin will help them to obtain it and will spare no trouble to that end. . . .

10. Furthermore, since the two towns of Malmö and Copenhagen together with others are under particular treaty obligations towards Lübeck, we have agreed and do agree herewith that we shall not accept homage from these towns, and shall enter into no treaty with them without the knowledge and approval of the town of Lübeck. We will also, as far as is possible, work to bring it about that both towns agree and pledge themselves, as also our dear cousin will doubtless be ready to do, that after his death no king shall be chosen without the co-operation, agreement and goodwill of the town of Lübeck; when the two towns have agreed to this and have given sufficient pledges on this matter, together with other matters on which the honourable council of Lübeck will perhaps wish to treat with them, then we shall use our best endeavours to ensure that the other towns of the kingdom of Denmark and Norway will discuss and accept similar articles concerning the election of the king. . . .

12. Finally we have also agreed and do now agree in our own name and in the name of our dear cousin, as God in his mercy will help us in freeing his person and restoring his kingdom, that we will completely raze the castle of Bergen, which has caused so many dissensions, or allow it to pass into the possession of the town of Lübeck. . . .

GEORG WAITZ, *Lübeck unter Jürgen Wullenwever*, vol. 2 (1855) no. 7, pp. 259 ff.

14

CLOSURE OF THE LONDON STEELYARD

1598.

Elizabeth, by the grace of God, Queen of England, France and Ireland, Defender of the faith etc. To our right trustie and welbeloved, the Maior and Sheriffes of our Citie of London, greeting.

Wheras there hath bin directed a commandment by the name of a Mandate, from the Romaine Emperour to all Electors, Prelates, Earles and all other Officers and subjectes of the Empire, reciting sundry complaintes, made him by the allied Townes of the Dutch Hanses in Germany, of diuers iniuries committed against them in our Realme, and like wise vpon complaint made by them against the companie of the Merchant Aduenturers, without hearing any answere to be made to the saide Hanse Townes in disproofe of their complaints the same being most notoriously vuniust and not to be mainteyned by any trueth: and yet neuertheles by this Mandate the English Merchants, namely the Merchant Aduenturers are forbidden to vse any trafficke of Merchandise within the Empire, but are commanded to depart from thence vpon paines, and to forbeare openly and secretly from all hauens and landing places, or to vse any commerce by water or by land in the Empire, vpon paine of apprehension of their persons and confiscation of their goods, with sundry other extreme sentences pronounced against our said subiects: herevpon, although we haue sent our letters expresly to the Emperor and to the Electors and other Princes of the Empire, declaring our opinion of this proceeding, to be vniustly prosecuted by the saide Hanse Townes, and therefore haue required to haue the saide Mandate either reuoked or suspended, yet being vncertaine what shall follow hereupon, we haue thought it agreeable to our honour in the meane time, to commaund all such as here within our realme, appertaining to the said Hansetowns, situate in the Empire, and especially all such as haue any residence in our citie of London, either in the house commonly called the *Steelyard* or in any other place elsewhere, to forbeare to vse any maner of trafficke or merchandise or to make any contractes, and likewise to depart out of our dominions in like sort, as our subjects are commanded to depart out of the Empire, vpon the like paines, as are conteyned against our subiectes in the said Mandate. And for the execution of this our said Citie of London and the Sheriffes shall forthwith repaire to the house, called the Steelyarde, and calling before you such, as haue charge there of or do reside there, to giue them knowledge of this our determination and commaundement: charging them by the foure and twentieth day of this moneth (being the day that our merchants are to depart from Stade) they do depart out of this Realme:

charging them also, that they giue knowledge thereof to such as be of any of the Hanse Townes belonging to the Empire, remaining to any part of our Realme, to depart likewise by the said day. And you the Maior and Sheriffes, calling vnto you two of the officers of our Customhouse, to take possession of the said house the said 24 day, to remaine in our custodie, vntill we shall vnderstand of any more fauourable course taken by the Emperour, for the restitution of our subiects to their former lawfull trade within the Empire. And this shall be your warrant for the execution of the premises. In witnesse whereof wee haue caused these our letters to be made patent. Witnesse our selfe at Westminster: the thirteenth of Januarie, in the fortieth yeere of our Reigne.

> *Calendar of State Papers (Domestic) 1598–1601* (1869), no. 14, pp. 5–6.

II. Institutions, Society

15

LÜBECK THE HEAD OF THE HANSA

1294 – (a) Message from the aldermen of Zwolle (Netherlands) to the council at Lübeck, identical to one sent by Kampen (cf. pp. 43, 346).

We address our thanks to you for your tireless and fruitful efforts to restore our former rights which, through inactivity and neglect, had almost been abolished. And this you did not only for our benefit and your own, but also for the benefit of all the merchants of the Roman Empire wishing to sail the seas. You acted, noble supporters, as leaders and guides to us all in making good this neglect. As your letters show, you did not hesitate to assume the onerous duty of forbidding the Frisians and Flemish from sailing in the Baltic Sea to Gotland, as they had formerly been doing in violation of age-old laws. And, too, you are preventing the Scandinavians from sailing hence-forth in the North Sea, as they have been doing unlawfully for some time.

That is why we wish your lordships to know, by this letter, that we are as closely dependent on you as are the limbs on the head, and we shall never fail to undertake and execute anything you may decree in respect of this praiseworthy and necessary task. Furthermore we beg you urgently to forbid absolutely all Englishmen to sail the Baltic sea route.

Urkundenbuch der Stadt Lübeck, I, no. 485.

1418 – (b) Ordinance of the diet of Lübeck, acknowledging that the Wendish towns are under the leadership of the Hansa (cf. pp. 93, 290).

Item, the towns here assembled have pondered on the many harmful things that could befall them and their merchants. Realising that, for reasons of cost, it was very inconvenient to meet as often as was necessary, they straightway and with one voice asked the town of Lübeck and the other honourable towns nearby, to represent as best they could the interests of all the towns and merchants in their place as they had done up to this time. Whatever they decided to do for the welfare of the towns and its merchants would receive their support.

Whereupon the delegates from Lübeck and other noble cities nearby, having conferred, declared that whatever they had been able to do for the welfare of the towns and merchants they would willingly continue to try to do in the future. The united towns thanked them for this most warmly.

Hanserezesse, 1 6, no. 556, § 87, p. 548.

16

PATRICIAN JOUSTS

Late 13th century – A report from the Magdeburg Schöffenchronik, *written between 1360 and 1372, about events of the year 1282 (cf. p. 264).*

At this time there were still *kunstabelen*, 'constables'; they were the sons of rich citizens.* At Whitsun they used to organise tourneys, for example, Roland, *Schildekenbom*, the Round Table and other plays; today these are presided over by the councillors themselves. A well-read man called Brun von Schönebeck, a constable, used to take part in these contests. His companions, the constables, asked him to write a merry play. He composed a Grail and wrote courteous letters, which he dispatched to Goslar, Hildesheim, Brunswick, Quedlinburg, Halberstadt and other towns. In these letters the constables invited to Magdeburg all merchants who wished to exercise themselves in knightly sports. There was a pretty woman there called Feie, who was to be given to the man whose gallantry and valour should win her. All the youths of the towns were afire with enthusiasm.

The men from Goslar came with caparisoned horses, those from Brunswick with green horse-trappings and green clothes, and those from other towns also wore their particular coats of arms and colours. When they arrived before the town they refused to ride in before they had tilted. Their wish was granted. Two constables rode out from the town, confronted them and received the strangers at lance-point. In the meantime the Grail had been prepared on the meadow; many tents and booths had been erected there. On a tree on the meadow hung the shields of all the constables who were in the Grail.

On the following morning, after the guests had heard Mass and broken their fast, they went up to the Grail and contemplated it. Each guest was allowed to strike one shield. The youth to whom the shield belonged came forward to fight with him; and so it happened with all of them.

* In Magdeburg the patriciate, as a privileged class, ceased to exist in 1330; its members were distributed among the five guilds.

In the end it was an old merchant from Goslar who won Dame Feie. He took her away with him, married her and provided for her so richly that she abandoned her old wild ways of life. A whole German book was written about the matter by that Brun von Schönebeck, who later wrote many other German books, a Song of Songs, a Hail Mary and many good poems.

Die Chroniken der deutschen Städte, vol. 7: *Magdeburg* (1869) pp. 168–9.

17

THE ORGANISATION OF THE BRUGES *KONTOR*

1347 – Revision of the statutes of the Kontor *(cf. p. 51).*

In the name of the Lord, amen. Since it is good and profitable to have written down and preserved those things and matters which one should bear in mind, the common merchants from the Roman Empire of Germany in the year of Our Lord 1347 on the day of the Apostles SS Simon and Jude [28 October] came together in the refectory of the Carmelites in Bruges and all those present at that time were agreed that, for the profit of the above-mentioned common merchants, they should have and keep a common book, in which all regulations and ordinances should be entered, which should be decreed and proclaimed among their people, as well as any customs and usages which they should observe.

1. First, be it known that the above-mentioned common merchants are divided into three groups, namely: those from Lübeck, the Wendish and Saxon towns and their dependencies in one third; those from Westphalia and Prussia and their dependencies in the second third; and those from Gotland, Livonia, Sweden and their dependencies in the last third.

2. Further, each year, eight days after Whitsun, two aldermen shall be chosen from each third, and whoever is chosen shall accept the office or pay a pound groschen into the funds of the common merchants, and he must take his chance whether he is chosen a second time or not, at the risk of incurring the same fine.

3. Further, in the event of one of the aldermen going away, the five remaining are to choose a man out of the third to which the sixth alderman belonged and they shall be empowered to do so and to impose the above-mentioned fine.

4. Further, the six aldermen are empowered to bid all common Germans under pain of a fine of three groschen, to assemble within the bidden time at

the place where the aldermen are. . . . [Further regulations about fines follow.]

5. Further, if a matter is of particular urgency, the aldermen may give instructions to whom they will, under pain of such fines as they will.

6. Further, if an alderman fails to attend, he is to pay double the normal fine.

7. Further, if the aldermen cannot agree among themselves, the minority is to accept the decision of the majority.

8. Further, if the three thirds cannot agree among themselves, then the following applies: where two thirds agree, the other third shall accept their decision.

9. Further, in matters which affect the common merchant, whether within or without the gates [of Bruges], the following shall apply: the wisest and most competent of the six aldermen, shall be their mouthpiece to the best of his ability, as instructed by the five others. If the matter concerns one third more than another, then the aldermen of the third which the matter touches most closely shall be the spokesmen. . . .

10. Further, the six aldermen shall choose on the day [of their election], six assessors from each third. . . . [Fine of five shillings in accordance with para. 2.]

11. In addition the six aldermen and the eighteen assessors shall meet as often as the aldermen demand. And they can act in all matters without holding an assembly of the common Germans.

12. Further, those whom the aldermen instruct to appear before a magistrate or in some other place must obey, under penalty of a fine of two shillings within the gates, and under pain of a penalty of five shillings without the gates, whether he rides or goes on foot.

13. Further, when the common Germans or the eighteen assessors meet at the Carmelites, the aldermen, when they go into the refectory, shall tell their boy to walk about the church saying that the aldermen are there, so that they may come in; and if anyone comes later, after the aldermen have begun to speak, then he shall pay three groschen into the funds.

14. Further, if anyone sits down on the bench when the aldermen are standing and speaking in the *Kontor*, or if he begins to talk with another person, whether it be with one, two or any other number, and if they do not listen to what the aldermen say, then each one of them, no matter how many there be, shall pay a groschen into the funds, for each separate offence. And the same fines shall apply whenever a third meets separately.

15. Further, whoever opens the door without permission from the aldermen shall pay five shillings into the funds; and whoever leaves without permission shall pay three groschen.

16. The aldermen are also empowered to administer an oath to speak the truth, on pain of a fine of one pound groschen, when questioning any person on matters concerning German law.

17. Further, if one of the above-mentioned merchants begins a lawsuit, big or small, inside or outside Bruges, he must conduct it at his own cost, and if he cannot or will not conduct his case himself, then let him ask someone else to speak on his behalf. And the Germans are to help him in his suit according to their knowledge and ability.

Hanserezesse, I I, no. 143, pp. 75–7.

18

A TOWN ADMITTED INTO THE HANSA: BREMEN

1358 – Conditions agreed at Lübeck by Bremen in the presence of the Wendish towns for her admission (or readmission) into the Hansa.

We, the council and people of the town of Bremen, express our deepest gratitude towards the honourable councillors of the maritime and other towns, as well as the community of merchants of the Hansa and Germans of the Holy Roman Empire, for having granted us the honour of sharing in the privileges and charters of the said merchants, of which we have in the past been deprived.* We want everyone to know, once and for all, and we publicly proclaim that we will observe exactly, the clauses and conditions that follow:

First, whenever we are required by the council of the aforementioned towns, namely Lübeck, Wismar, Rostock, Stralsund and Greifswald, to protect the said merchants and defend the straits called the Sound we will readily do our duty and send a well-fitted ship with fifty armed men aboard together with other weapons of war, entirely at our own risk and expense. Should God grant our allies and ourselves victory over the pirates or other enemies, we will share the booty with our allies, proportionately to the number of men each of us has.

Item, whenever we are required by the council of Hamburg to defend the Elbe, we will readily send a ship and a hundred armed men, at our own risk and expense. . . . And should it be necessary to send more, we will do so without argument.

Item, we will scrupulously observe and respect all decisions taken by the councils of the said cities in the name of the said merchants. Should one of our citizens make so bold as to undertake to journey to places that are

* Reference to the exclusion from the Hansa of the Bremen merchants in 1275 as a result of their refusal to be associated with the blockade of Norway.

forbidden by the said councils and merchants* and to infringe their decisions, he must lose his life and all his goods, two-thirds of the goods he was transporting into the town where he was arrested reverting to the said merchants, and one-third reverting to the council of that town. His remaining possessions that are located in our town or elsewhere are to be the rightful property of his heirs or kinsfolk.

Item, we publicly promise and pledge ourselves not to cause any harm to the said merchants as a result of the prerogatives and privileges we held in England, Norway and Flanders at the time when we were excluded from the charters of the said merchants, always assuming that there is no trace whatever of malpractice or fraud.

Item, should it transpire – God forbid – that we, one of ours, our citizens or someone acting for us or known to us, act fraudulently in violation of all or part of the aforementioned prescriptions, then we and our successors should in perpetuity be excluded from the Hansa of the aforementioned merchants and their charters and should remain completely outside the authority of the said merchants.

Hanserezesse, I I, no. 216, p. 143.

19

CONSOLIDATION OF THE HANSA OF THE TOWNS

1366 – Ordinance of the Hanseatic diet in Lübeck (cf. p. 68).

11. The towns have resolved and decreed that no man shall enjoy the privileges and franchises of the Germans unless he is a burgess of a town of the German Hansa.

12. Further, no man shall become an alderman in Flanders or in Bergen who is not a burgess of a town of the German Hansa.

13. Nobody shall visit Novgorod who does not share in the privileges or the Hansa of the Germans.

14. Further, those who have renounced their citizenship in times of war shall not be accepted as burgesses in any of the above-mentioned towns. . . .

17. Further, none of the above-mentioned towns shall offer sanctuary to an outlaw from another town, except in an emergency or on request from the council of that town. The delegates from Kiel did not agree to this article. . . .

26. Further, the towns of the Lübeck and Visby thirds have decreed:

* Reference to the blockade of Flanders decreed by the Hansa in the same year, 1358.

1. Merchants sojourning in Novgorod shall make no important or definite regulations without the previous knowledge and agreement of the towns of Lübeck, Visby and those associated with them; they are to inform these towns beforehand in writing.

2. No German merchant shall either buy from or sell to a Russian any goods of any kind, unless payment be made in cash in accordance with the law of the Novgorod *Kontor*, to be enforced by a fine of fifty marks.

Hanserezesse, I I, no. 376, pp. 332–6.

20

A TOWN EXCLUDED FROM THE HANSA: BRUNSWICK

1375 – Decision of the Hanseatic diet in Lübeck occasioned by the overthrow of the patrician regime in Brunswick (1374), the murder of several members of the council and the complaint brought by relatives of the victims (cf. p. 90).

It is known to princes, cities, knights and squires, in fact to the whole country, that the Brunswickers have done grievous wrong to the honourable members of their council. Though they had committed no crime, they have executed them without trial, contrary to all law, they have driven out their friends, outlawed them and fined them. They have unlawfully confiscated the property of both the dead and the living. And when the associated maritime towns demanded that a meeting be held to discuss these matters, they rejected it three times and failed to attend. When the towns eventually held a diet with them in Lüneburg, they refused to return to the reign of law. They remain obstinate and persist in their crime and refuse to make amends. Therefore the common towns of the German Hansa, with full authority from the other towns which share in their privileges, have agreed unanimously and in full concord that they will exclude the Brunswickers from the Hansa and from the rights and franchises of the merchant. No merchant in Flanders, England, Denmark, Norway, Novgorod or in any other place who shares in the merchant's privileges shall have intercourse with them or do business of any kind with them, whether by land or sea, whether buying or selling, under pain of losing both honour and property. Nor shall anyone be allowed to supply goods of any kind to them, or accept goods from them, in so far as it may be prevented. Further, neither they nor their goods shall have safe conduct through any town which shares in the merchant's rights. And if in any town which shares in the merchant's rights there should arrive friends or relatives of those murdered in Brunswick, then shall those who helped in the murders, either by word or deed, be brought to trial for their lives. All the above-mentioned points shall remain in force, until they are ready to atone for the crime of which they are accused, as is right and just.*

Hanserezesse, I 2, no. 92, p. 106.

21

ABSENTEEISM AT THE HANSEATIC DIET

1383 – Letter to the Prussian towns from the delegates at the Hanseatic diet meeting at Lübeck (cf. p. 94).

You know well that a diet was held here after Easter of this year, as had been agreed between your councillors and ourselves. Nevertheless you sent no one. For this reason another diet was resolved on, to be held here at the present time [May], and you were informed of this in writing, so that you might send your delegates: this you failed to do. And yet the delegates of the towns of the Zuiderzee have come to this meeting, and the councillors of Cologne, Dortmund, Münster and many other towns have sent their delegates to this diet.

Therefore we ask you to fix yourselves the date of an assembly which you and the other associated towns will be able to attend without fail, here in Lübeck, between now and next Michaelmas to discuss the same affairs and matters of which you have been informed by letter. Do not fail to fix the date for this diet, for it is of great importance to us all and to the common merchant. Be so good as to give us early notice of the day you choose, so that the other towns can be informed in time to send their delegates. The messenger who bears this is to bring us your decision and reply.

Hanserezesse, I 2, no. 264, p. 319.

* Brunswick was readmitted to the Hansa in 1380 on the following conditions: the rebels must erect a chapel of expiation, send a pilgrim to Rome for each person murdered, make a formal statement of their repentance before the diet in Lübeck, return the property confiscated and reinstate the exiles in their offices. (Ibid., no. 217, p. 259.)

22

A REGIONAL DIET AS PREPARATION FOR A GENERAL DIET

1384 – Ordinance of the diet of the Prussian towns, held mainly to propose a continuance of the conditions imposed by the Peace of Stralsund upon Denmark until 1385 (cf. pp. 72, 96).

In the year of Our Lord 1384 the delegates of the Prussian towns assembled in Marienburg on the Sunday before Christmas and discussed the following articles:

1. First, concerning the general diet to be held on 5 March with the common towns in Lübeck: are we to be represented by delegates or merely by letters? It was unanimously resolved that delegates should be sent to this diet, because of the many matters which concern us, the common towns and the merchants.

2. Further, are the castles in Skania to be surrendered on the date fixed in the treaty? . . .

On this matter it seems best to us to keep the castles as long as we can and not to return them, unless the merchants are compensated for their losses, for the castles were pledged to the towns by the father of the queen and not by the queen. . . .

3. As for the alliance formed by the towns, contained in the Treaty, is it to be continued or not? On this point we believe that the alliance should be continued in its present form. . . .

5. Shall we continue next year to levy poundage as before? We think that it should still be levied as before, under oath.

6. Concerning the warships, shall we continue to fit them out or not, etc.? It seems good to us to fit them out and to pacify the seas as far as is possible, as has been done before, and to ask the common towns to undertake the equipment of them as before, etc.

7. As for the ban on the manufacture of cannon (*geschossbuxen*) in the common towns for the use of foreigners: our opinion is that the decision and consent of our lord the Grand Master be accepted. . . .

10. As for the vessels which sail up and down the Vistula with herring or other cargo, when they are wrecked or ice-bound: on what terms are the skippers and crews to receive wages and subsistence, how long are the crews to be allowed to use wood from the banks, if the channel is blocked? On this question each delegate is to consult his own town council about what is best to be done, and also whether the town has anything written on this matter.

Each delegate is to bring these documents or a reply to the next diet and there report on the matter.

Hanserezesse, 1 2, no. 297, pp. 349–50.

23

A MERCHANT BARRED FROM THE HANSA BY THE LONDON *KONTOR*

1385 – Report to Richard III's secret council, drawn up in 1394, on the disputes between the merchant Christian Kelmer and the London Kontor (cf. pp. 109, 190).

Christian Kelmer, a citizen of Dortmund, one of the principal Hansa towns, humbly addressed a petition to the esteemed council of our lord the king. For more than forty years he has been a merchant and member of the Hansa association, and as such has enjoyed in London and elsewhere the privileges granted by the king's forebears and confirmed by him. However about ten years ago he acquired and imported into London a quantity of ermine furs, for which he paid to our king's customs agents in London the 'custom' appropriate to goods imported into the kingdom by the said association. Then, when Christian could not sell these furs in London he re-exported them abroad to sell them. For this he again paid to the customs officials the tax claimed from him, namely three shillings and one and a half pence, for merchandise exported from the kingdom.

Because this export tax was paid, Wilhelm Borne [four other names follow] and several other merchants of the said association became angry with Christian, a very rich merchant and one well liked by the late queen, the knights and squires. . . . They argued that because Christian had paid three shillings and one and a half pence customs duty, he had violated the Hanseatic privileges and as punishment was henceforth barred from the association. Christian offered to swear that in paying this tax he was not aware that he was causing harm to the said association. The merchants refused this offer, although the swearing of oaths was a custom of the society. Thereupon Christian offered to pay the society, before being barred from it, an indemnity of twenty shillings for each penny, that is, thirty-seven pounds ten shillings. They rejected this offer and refused to allow him to retain his privileges.

Then Christian, declaring that they were wicked and bent on excluding him from the Hansa, made so pressing an appeal to the queen and her entourage that our king, through a special favour and letters patent, granted the said Christian the right to buy and sell in the kingdom on equal terms with the native population, provided that like them he paid the 'customs' and subsidies. Then the mayor and the aldermen of London bestowed on him by letters patent and under the mayoral seal the title of freeman of that town.

Thereupon the merchants, treacherously seeking Christian's downfall, agreed among themselves to send messengers abroad to declare that he had destroyed the Hansa merchants' privileges, that our king had bestowed on him citizenship, that the people of London had granted him freedom of the city, and that henceforth he belonged more to the English merchants than to those of the Hansa. What is more, if he were to retain his goods and merchandise, he would ruin the prosperity of the said association in England: there was no alternative but to confiscate his possessions abroad so that he would be unable to pay his debts in London and would thus lose all his credit. In fact among the petitioner's goods 700 pounds in cash were seized and handed over to a certain Ertmar Ergest, a Hanseatic colleague of Christian's, as is proved by a letter from Ertmar which Christian is prepared to produce. In the same way the merchants of the said association saw to it that the goods remaining in the said Ertmar's possession, to the value of 300 pounds, were confiscated, so that Christian was utterly ruined.

May it therefore please the secret council . . . for the love of God, the interests of justice and the re-establishment of the wretched petitioner's rights, to rule that goods and merchandise to the value of 1,000 pounds of the said association in the town of London be seized and remain confiscated until the said Christian receives satisfaction according to the value of his goods which were confiscated as described above. Further, that in future the said Christian be allowed by the aforementioned merchants to live in peace and proper security.

Hanseakten aus England 1275–1412, ed. KUNZE, no. 277, p. 184.

24

STATUTE OF A MERCHANT ASSOCIATION

Circa 1390 – The oldest version of the statute of Arthur's Court (Artushof) *in Danzig (cf. p. 161).*

. . . Therefore we, the commander and deputy-commander [of the Teutonic Order] in this town, and we, the councillors of the said town of Danzig, have enjoined upon the court the following laws to be strictly observed in good fellowship and discernment.

First, the four men chosen according to long-established custom to preside over the court shall co-opt four of the most senior men who frequent the court; to these eight the council shall add four of its own members who frequent the court. These twelve shall to the best of their ability administer the court and settle all matters which concern it. If the twelve cannot do so, the matter is to be brought before the council and the community, and it shall be done as they decide. All matters concerning the court shall be decided in the morning before mealtime in the court. The court may be opened every day, after the midday meal on Sundays and saints' days, and on workdays at vespers; when the beer-bell is rung, all are to take their leave. But the four aldermen may continue to sit and drink and those who have their permission. Those who sit longer shall present a barrel of beer to the company as a fine. The musicians shall depart when the company breaks up. Musicians may be no more than two couples, paid one and a half pence.

[Here follow regulations about the number and pay of the servants, about lighting, food and drink offered to guests.]

And no one shall invite guests to the court unless he knows that they are worthy to be admitted. The guests shall also be such that they give offence to no one and if they do, their host shall pay a fine of a half-last of beer.

No one shall be admitted to the court unless he owns property to the value of twenty marks and no less. Also craftsmen shall not be admitted, whoever they may be, nor those who sell beer retail, nor those who have worked for wages within the previous year.

Also the court is closed to all those who will not help a man to his rights and to those who have married a woman of bad reputation. Also all those shall be excluded who have knowingly and intentionally voyaged into forbidden regions or have sent goods there, until they have made good their ill-doing and have brought to the aldermen an attestation that they are honourable people as they were held to be before they transgressed the law.

Should anybody for this cause or for any other be accused of breaking the regulations of the court and setting himself boldly against them, he is to pay a fine of two marks, to be shared equally by the court and the town, and shall remain excluded until he has mended his ways. . . .

Should it happen that these regulations are not observed through the fault or negligence of the four men who are in charge of the court at that time, each of them shall pay a half-last of beer as a fine. If anyone hereafter desires to change these laws, this shall be the responsibility of the councillors. . . .

P. Simon, *Der Artushof in Danzig* (1900) pp. 306–9.

25

A PILGRIMAGE

1441 – Extract from the 'Book of Miracles' of St Theobald of Thann (Alsace), which relates in detail numerous similar pilgrimages made by north German merchants (cf. p. 184).

There was a young merchant from Lübeck who sailed overseas on business. Then he fell among pirates, who took him captive and stripped him of all he had and also of three hundred guilders which he had borrowed from honest people. Therefore he prayed to God and St Theobald to help him, that he might escape from the pirates and be able to repay the honest people what they had lent and entrusted to him. He vowed to come here to Thann to St Theobald, the prince of Heaven, with his offering. And straightway he escaped from the pirates. Therefore he pledged his right hand to St Theobald: if he did not carry out his vow and make the pilgrimage with his offering within the year, then St Theobald might plague him as he wished. But it came to pass that he did not carry out his vow within the time fixed: he prospered both in honour and in wealth, so that he paid all to whom he owed money and still had a great sum left over, enough to meet all his needs. Now that he had gone beyond the time fixed and had failed to carry out this vow, St Theobald attacked him and his right hand became paralysed, so that he could not use it. Then he was afraid and remembered his vow and set out on his journey, and as soon as he set out his hand was cured. This he swore when he made his pilgrimage, with all possible solemnity.

Tomus Miraculorum Sancti Theobaldi, ed. G. Stoffel
(1875), no. 65, p. 42.

26

THE LEGAL STATUS OF THE HANSA

1469 – The Hansa's reply to a memorandum from the English Privy Council, which was intended to justify the arrest of Hanseatic merchants and the confiscation of their property (cf. p. 106).

2. . . . . It is incorrect to assert that there has existed in Germany from time immemorial a *societas*, a *collegium* and a *universitas* generally called *Hansa*

Theutonica etc. For, most honourable fathers, with all due respect to the royal majesty, the *Hansa Theutonica* is not a *societas*: for it knows no community of property either in whole or in part, since no common property exists within the *Hansa Theutonica*; neither is it a *societas* for specific commercial enterprises, as within the *Hansa Theutonica* each trades on his own account, and profit and loss from trade falls to each individually. Now as the law knows no other form of society than the said three forms, it has been established that the *Hansa Theutonica* is not a *societas*.

Neither is it a *collegium*, because in law the joining together of several into a single entity is called a *collegium*: the *Hansa Theutonica* is, however, made up of widely separated towns, as the royal letters acknowledge. It is therefore clear that the *Hansa Theutonica* is not a *collegium*. Nor is it a *universitas*, for in both civil and canon law it is required that a community, to merit the name of *universitas*, should hold its property in common, have a common treasury, a common seal, a common syndic and a common business manager; but nothing of this kind is to be found within the *Hansa Theutonica*. It is therefore not a *universitas*.

And furthermore . . . the *Hansa Theutonica* came into being through agreement and alliance of different towns; but it is clear beyond all doubt that a mere grouping of towns can produce in law neither a *societas* nor a *collegium* nor a *universitas*, for which many other qualities are essential.

But the *Hansa Theutonica* is . . . a firm *confederatio* of many cities, towns and communities for the purpose of ensuring that business enterprises by land and sea should have a desired and favourable outcome and that there should be effective protection against pirates and highwaymen, so that their ambushes should not rob merchants of their goods and valuables. [There follows a dissertation on the etymology of the word *Hansa*, suggesting that it is derived from the Latin word *ansa*.]

3. The *Hansa Theutonica* is not controlled by the merchants; on the contrary each city and each town has its own lords and its own magistracy by whom its affairs are directed. For the *Hansa Theutonica*, as has been shown, is nothing other than a kind of alliance between towns, which does not release the towns from the jurisdiction of those lords who ruled over them previously: on the contrary they remain subject in all things to these lords as they were before, and continue to be governed by them.

4. Moreover the *Hansa Theutonica* has neither seal nor council in common. Indeed the situation does not allow the existence of a common seal. But when for essential purposes letters are written in the name of the whole *Hansa Theutonica*, they are sealed with the seal of the town in which they were written, as can easily be seen from the documents and warrants sent to you recently, most honourable fathers, in the name of the whole *Hansa Theutonica*: they were not sealed with some seal common to the whole *Hansa Theutonica*, but with the seal of the town of Lübeck, where they were written.

The *Hansa Theutonica* has no common council; but each town sends delegates, with instructions, who are not called councillors (*consiliarii*) but delegates (*oratores*), whenever it is necessary to deliberate on matters pending. . . .

6. Neither the *Hansa Theutonica* nor any one of the towns has the power to summon assemblies and fix meetings; instead the towns of the Hansa assemble whenever there are questions to be discussed by common agreement in a certain place and decide among themselves what they consider necessary for the good of their merchants. Also up to the present no Hansa town has taken precedence over the others. Rather do the towns decide among themselves which ones are particularly concerned in the matters at issue and these, according to the importance of the matter, notify the other towns that they are to send delegates.

Hansisches Urkundenbuch, vol. 9, no. 584, pp. 463–5.

27

THE HANSEATIC STAPLE IN BRUGES

1470 – Renewal of the staple in Bruges by the Hanseatic diet in Lübeck; the fairs in Antwerp and Bergen-op-Zoom are excepted (cf. p. 203).

§46. . . . And nobody, whoever he may be, whether he is in the Hansa, as a burgess or inhabitant, or whether he does not belong to the Hansa, shall take cloth made in Flanders, Brabant or Holland into any Hansa town or its territory which has not passed through the staple at Bruges or was not bought or offered for sale in Antwerp or Bergen-op-Zoom at the Cold Fair held at Martinmas. . . .

§51. Regarding the other staple goods, which are also to be brought to the staple, the following was decided: all staple goods, such as wax, furs, copper, tin, sheepskins, goatskins and all other kinds of skins, wool, fish-oil, *osmund**
and iron of all kinds, woad, flax, vitriol, butter, linen and all other staple goods, whatever they may be called, except for perishable goods (*ventegut*) such as beer, grain, pitch, tar, beams and planks, are to be taken to the staple in Bruges or to the two fairs in Antwerp or to Bergen-op-Zoom for the Martinmas fair, as is laid down in the previous articles. And if any such staple goods should remain unsold at the fairs in Antwerp and Bergen-op-Zoom, they must be brought back to the staple at Bruges. . . .

§53. Similarly all eastern Hanseatic towns, namely Lübeck, Rostock, Stralsund, Wismar and also the Pomeranian towns, as well as Danzig, Königsberg and other Prussian towns, and also Riga, Reval, Pernau and other Livonian

* Iron from Sweden, considered to be the best Swedish type of iron.

towns, and all other Hansa towns, shall refrain from supplying anyone, whether he belongs to the Hansa or not, with any staple goods for passage through the Sound or the Belt, unless he swears on oath beforehand or gives surety that he intends to take those goods to the staple in Bruges, to Antwerp or to the fair in Bergen-op-Zoom, as is laid down above. . . .

Hanserezesse, II 6, no. 356, pp. 335 ff.

28

THE SEA ROUTE FROM SLUYS TO ROSTOCK THROUGH THE GREAT BELT

Second half of the 15th century — An extract from the 'Book of the Sea', a collection of practical instructions on coastal navigation, from Andalusia to the Gulf of Finland (cf. p. 146).

If you want to sail from the Zwijn to the reef of Jutland, move out from the shore to a depth of 27 fathoms, then sail north-north-east towards the reef and keep this course until you can no longer find bottom, at 40 fathoms; then set course north-east-by-east until you espy Jutland; you can then pick a course which will keep you in sight of land until you reach Skagen.

When you have passed the reef of Skagen and have soft bottom at 14 fathoms, sail due south until the Island of Läsöe is north-east of you; then veer south-east and continue to sound until you find a depth of 10 fathoms; then continue to follow the coast of Jutland in a south-south-westerly direction towards [the island of] Hjelm, and further to the south towards the Weders reef, until you have a depth of 7 fathoms — *no* nearer. There is deep water between the two. When the island of Veiröe lies to the west-north-west of you, set course south-south-west, until Kalundborg comes in sight. Then continue south-east as far as Romsöe and farther in the same direction towards Sprogöe. When Sprogöe lies on the beam and you have soft bottom at 11 fathoms, you will see the island of Vresen; but do not approach closer than 7 fathoms. When you have 16 to 20 fathoms, sail to the south, staying close to the wind, towards the centre of Langeland, and from there onwards south-south-west. When you have passed Trones, sail east-south-east. You will thus arrive off the Warnow [Rostock].

K. KOPPMANN, *Das Seebuch* (1876) p. 52.

29

THE OFFICE OF SYNDIC OF THE HANSA

1576 – Appointment of Heinrich Sudermann to a second period of office as syndic of the Hansa (cf. p. 335).

We, the delegates and representatives of the quarters and other honourable common towns of the Hansa, being met together at this time in the town of Lübeck at a general Hanseatic diet, proclaim and decree as follows:

Since the honourable and learned gentleman Heinrich Sudermann, doctor of both civil and canon law and syndic of the common Hansa, has been bound to us and to the other common and honourable Hansa towns for twenty years and served us even before that time . . . we therefore in the name of the honourable common towns have entered into negotiations with the said Doctor Sudermann and he with us, and we have jointly and lawfully resolved as follows, namely that he, Doctor Sudermann, binds himself again to us and to the honourable common towns, to be and to remain ready and willing to serve us and them, as long as he shall live, to the best of his ability, to give us advice and counsel and serve us in any other way necessary and as we and the honourable common towns will be obliged to use him, and this for as long as God's grace shall preserve to him reason, understanding and health, on the following conditions:

1. The said syndic shall be obliged, on the bidding and command of the honourable towns of the Hansa, as need shall arise, without fail, to act in all business affecting the kingdom of England, the Spanish Netherlands and all other places in which the honourable common towns have need of his services, with the sole exception of the *legationes* to Moscow and Bergen.

2. The said doctor shall without fail attend all Hanseatic diets, whenever his presence is commanded or requested.

3. The syndic is at the moment engaged in preparing an inventory of all the privileges, treaties and negotiations, so that unimpeachable information may be available to assist the general deliberations of the Hansa, and has made good progress in this undertaking; he has also undertaken, in so far as he receives the necessary help from the honourable towns and in so far as lies within his power, to bring together in a history or *chronicon* how this glorious association came into being, how it grew and increased and what happened in times of peace and war and when dissension and rebellion sprang up and all the noteworthy happenings of those times.

4. The syndic is willing and shall be obliged to draw up an inventory of all the privileges, treaties, charters and all other matters of interest to the *Kontore*

which he has in his keeping, and shall dispatch the same to the honourable towns of the quarters.

5. He will apply himself to the task of compiling a clear and coherent version of a permanent sea-law, which the honourable common towns will be able to use in a uniform matter in dealing with skippers and all maritime matters. And the honourable towns shall and will send to the said syndic whatever they have in their keeping and may obtain elsewhere which would be of use in this undertaking. In exchange we, the aforementioned delegates of the common Hansa towns, have pledged and promised to the said syndic on behalf of the honourable common towns, an annual salary, as long as he shall live, of 100 pounds sterling and an additional 100 thalers for the support of his secretary, servants and boys, of which half shall be paid him at Christmas and the other half on the feast of St John the Baptist by the alderman and merchants' council of the London *Kontor*; and in addition 100 thalers from the Bruges *Kontor*, at present situated in Antwerp, similarly paid half at Christmas and half on the feast of St John, all of which shall be done every year and strictly performed for as long as he shall live. But in so far as the expenses and subsistence of the syndic when he is on his travels are concerned, matters shall be arranged as follows: namely, whenever he is employed in some *legatio* on behalf of the Hansa as a whole, he is to diligently write down, from the very first day of his journey, whatever he spends on food, transport or other matters, and send the account to the alderman and merchants' council of the *Kontor* on whose behalf the expenses were incurred; the latter shall reimburse him, after which the syndic shall no further trouble the *Kontore*. These accounts kept by the syndic are to be sent to the honourable council of the town of Lübeck by the *Kontor* concerned, so that they may be checked and justified at the next Hanseatic diet. . . . To validate this agreement two copies with identical content shall be made of this document and both shall be sealed with the privy seal of the honourable council of the town of Lübeck and with the signet of the said Doctor Sudermann, and one shall be given and entrusted to the aforementioned honourable council of Lübeck and the other to the syndic. . . .

Inventare hansischer Archive, vol. 3; *Danziger Inventare 1531–1591*, no. 33, p. 894.

III. Economic Matters

30

TRANSACTIONS OF A LÜBECK FINANCIER IN BRUGES

1290 — Letter from Mornewech, Lübeck's chargé d'affairés in Bruges, to the council of Lübeck (cf. p. 204).

Reinekin Mornewech humbly addresses the right noble burgomasters and councillors of Lübeck. Please note that I have completely settled the account with the citizens of Herford as well as those of Magdeburg, Brunswick and Stendal. However, having settled with these in accordance with their wishes, I have until now been unable to pay the citizens of Ghent, Ypres and others to whom I have commitments in the name of the aforementioned citizens; also I borrowed money to pay off the interest, and this is to be repaid at the fair at Lille: the amount in question is about 800 marks. I will do the best I can in all things. The wax about which you wrote to me has not yet arrived although I have already sold some of it, namely 30 pounds at 6¼ marks, for which I have received payment.

I asked you to pay John Old 300 marks. Since then I have received from him 33 marks which you should give him back together with the 300. I urgently entreat you, honourable sirs, to be so gracious as to pay without delay and on demand, according to their contents, all the foreigners who present to you my letters of credit, rewarding them thus for the civility they have shown me for your sake.

Your messenger came to me on the sixth day after the Assumption of Our Lady, and Gerkin Wollepont's money was exchanged then. This letter, written on the Saturday after the Assumption of Our Lady [19 August], will leave Bruges tomorrow. The said messenger informed me that he took twelve days to get from Lübeck to Bruges. I am at your disposal. Now that your affairs are in order, I will return as soon as possible. If your first letter had reached me in good time before the fair at Thourout, I would have had the necessary money at my disposal.

Urkundenbuch der Stadt Lübeck, 1, no. 156, p. 371.

31

THE STRUGGLE AGAINST CREDIT FINANCE

Circa 1295 – (*a*) *Ban on credit transactions declared by the Novgorod* Kontor *in the second article of its regulations (cf. p. 205).*

No German may purchase goods from the Russians on credit. Anyone who does so shall pay the sum of 10 marks for every 100 marks' worth of goods acquired on credit.

A fine of 50 marks will be imposed on any German who enters into any form of trading partnership with the Russians or who accepts goods from them by way of commission. The same penalty will be imposed on anyone entering into partnership or accepting a commission for handling Italian, Flemish or English merchandise.

Urkundenbuch der Stadt Lübeck, 1, p. 703.

1401 – (*b*) *The diet in Lübeck forbids buying on credit in Flanders.*

First credit buying, such as takes place in Flanders, was discussed. As the common merchant has suffered and still suffers great loss by this practice, the towns have agreed that nobody shall buy or sell any goods in Flanders on credit, on pain of forfeiting the goods and his rights as a merchant; of the goods confiscated, two-thirds shall become the property of the towns and one-third that of the common merchant [i.e. the *Kontor*]. This regulation shall come into force next Martinmas and shall be valid against all appeal for three years.

Hanserezesse, 15, no. 23, §1, p. 16.

1411 – (*c*) *Regulations of the Livonian towns implementing the ban on credit transactions.*

Be it known that at the diet which the towns of this country have held in Pernau we have agreed that no wares from Flanders, such as salt, cloth, wine and all kinds of fruit, as are usually taken to Russia, shall be brought into this country if they were purchased in Bruges on credit; for we hold this practice to be harmful to the merchant. Therefore whoever wishes to bring such goods into the country is to take an oath before the *Kontor* in Flanders or before the council of the Hansa town from which he intends to sail that he did not buy them in Bruges [on credit]. He must obtain letters which he can show here or dispatch with the goods. [Otherwise the goods will be confiscated and become forfeit if the proof demanded is not forthcoming within a year and a day.]

Hanserezesse, I 6, no. 7, p. 6.

1462 – (d) Letter from the London Kontor *to the Hanseatic diet on abuses of credit.*

The *Kontor* begs you in your wisdom to take measures to deal with the abuse which the merchant in London encounters every day, namely that cloth may be bought from the English on credit at a higher price than if one paid cash or in kind, and indeed at times as much as 2, 3 or 4 pounds more per bale. This is an evil practice, and all too often it leads to spurious and dishonest merchants coming from the Hansa to London, buying on credit and then absconding, so that respectable people are swindled out of their due, and because of which we are abused and harassed in many towns. It also has the result that the English Commons accuse the merchant in Parliament so that he cannot get his privileges confirmed. It would therefore be good to suppress buying on credit and to allow payment only in cash or in kind so that business and businessmen remain honest.

Hanserezesse, II 5, no. 263, § 49, p. 190.

32

FRAUDULENT TRADING

Circa 1300 – Letter from the council of Eisenach (Thuringia) to the council of Lübeck.

Further to your letters to us, we should like to emphasise that we will willingly grant your request concerning fraud in the hop trade and will take action immediately.

For our part we humbly and earnestly request you to join with the lords and cities in your territory in directing that the herrings placed in the middle of barrels should be of the same quality as those on the outer edges. Many complaints have in fact reached us, from both our own citizens and from foreigners, that the herrings that come from your territory are tasty and fresh on the edges of the barrel but rotten and tasteless in the middle. We ask you therefore to guard against such malpractice in future.

We will do for you all that is in your interest, just as we desire to be worthy of similar or greater favours that you might confer on us or our fellow-citizens.

Urkundenbuch der Stadt Lübeck, 1, no. 736, p. 666.

33

DIFFERENT TYPES OF TRADING PARTNERSHIPS

1311 – (a) Commission (sendeve) *(cf. p. 166).*

Hermann Wacherowe received from Floreco [of Münster] 83½ silver marks. Any profits or losses resulting from this will be assumed solely by Floreco.

1358 – (b) Business partnership between a sleeping and an active partner.

In the year of Our Lord 1358, on All Saints' Day, Arnold Lowe paid 800 Lübeck guilders into a 'true partnership'. Rudolf Wittenborch paid nothing in but received the 800 guilders from the above-mentioned Arnold in order to trade with it to the profit of both. If Rudolf were to die in the meantime, Arnold will have a prior claim on the 800 guilders out of the assets of the firm. All profits gained by the grace of God belong in equal parts to the two partners. If losses are incurred – which God forbid – they also fall equally upon the two partners; they have both pledged themselves to this freely and in full accord as the Book of Debts bears witness.

P. Rehme, 'Die Lübecker Handelsgesellschaften in der ersten Hälfte des 14. Jahrhunderts', in *Zs. für das gesamte Handelsrecht*, 42 (1894) no. 1, p. 396; no. 64, p. 408.

1441 – (c) Partnership into which all members put funds.

In the year 1441, on 24 June, Friedrich Depenbeke, burgess of Reval, and Ludwig Greverode, burgess of Lübeck, announced before the Book of Debts that they had founded a free partnership with Alf Greverode, brother of the above-mentioned Ludwig and burgess of Stralsund, to do business together, without incurring liability for expenses other than the duty upon the wares, under the following conditions:

Alf is to buy honey in Stralsund and send it to Reval, the partnership bearing the cost and accepting the risks, as soon as the other two have provided him with the money needed to buy the honey. It was also agreed that Ludwig and Friedrich should each keep a special account-book, to be used only for matters affecting the partnership. . . . In addition Alf is to inform Ludwig straightway what he has sent to Friedrich. Ludwig and Friedrich shall settle up between themselves, and all three shall circulate written accounts every spring, so that all shall know what each one is holding and what capital the partnership has. Each of the three has invested 400 Lübeck marks in the business, 1,200 marks in all, at present in the care of Ludwig. The partnership shall continue unchanged until spring three years from now. If anyone then wants to withdraw, he must make a declaration by word of mouth or in writing that he does not wish to continue in the partnership for a fourth year. Each shall then receive his share back, a third of the profits and of the capital. Finally it was decided that each of them should work zealously on behalf of the firm, by standing surety on its behalf or by any other means, without any double-dealing.*

C. W. PAULI, *Lübeckische Zustände im Mittelalter,* vol. 3 (1878) no. 90, p. 159.

34

COST OF FITTING OUT A COG AND PROFITS MADE FROM ITS FREIGHT

1374–1380 – Extract from the account-book of the Hamburg merchant Vicko van Geldersen (cf. p. 152).

I, Vicko van Geldersen, master Heyne Crowel and Helmich van der Heyde have entered into partnership with Swartekop for him to buy a ship in which

* A note in the Book of Debts says that the partnership was dissolved after five years.

each one of us is to have a quarter-share. Each of us has contributed 75 marks. The total is 300 marks. This took place at Easter in the year of Our Lord 1374.

Item, I paid out 31 marks 4 shillings and master Heyne Crowel did likewise. This we sent after him [the skipper Swartekop] in the form of salt to Prussia. This took place on the day of the Twelve Apostles [15 July 1374].

Item, I spent 25 marks 7½ shillings, which I paid to Tymme Ghulsowe in exchange for 5 pounds groschen, which Swartekop had bought in Flanders on the first Sunday in Lent in the year of Our Lord 1375.*

The total of my expenses amounts to 131 marks 11½ shillings.

Item, I paid out 26 shillings, which I gave to Semmeke van Munster for an anchor, which he [Swartekop] had lost in England.

In exchange I received 10 Lübeck pounds and 5 shillings, and each partner received the same amount, from the 10 pounds groschen which Swartekop gave to Albert Lüneburg in Flanders on St James's Day [25 July] 1376.

Item, I received 14½ marks, 4½ shillings and 3 pence; this money came from the 37 nobles which he [Swartekop] left in Danzig. I received this money on the Thursday before St Thomas's Day [18 December] 1376.

Item, I received 2½ tons of herring, from the last† of herring which Henneke Puster brought back from Skania in 1376.

Item, I received 16 marks from 3 lasts of herring, which Lange Hermann had received from Bremen.

Item, I paid 1 mark and 3 pence against the nobles which Johann Diderkes was to collect in Prussia.

Item, I paid out 8 marks less 3½ shillings as my share for 2 cables, ropes, horsehair and cordage.

Item, I received 2 marks in herring on Circumcision Day [1 January] 1378.

Item, I paid out as my share 11½ pounds groschen for refitting the cog.

Item, I received in the year 1378 13 marks and 2 shillings.

Item, I received in 1379 60 marks less 2½ shillings.

Item, I received 15 marks in the same year at Martinmas [11 November].

Item, I received 29½ pounds groschen, which he [Swartekop] had given to Vicko Elbeck in 1380.

[Total: Expenses 199 marks, 10 shillings, 3 pence; Receipts 284 marks, 13 shillings, 3 pence. This gives a gross profit of 42 per cent or 6 per cent annually.]

H. NIRRNHEIM, *Das Handlungsbuch Vickos von Geldersen* (1895) no. 711, p. 109. Cf. W. VOGEL, *Geschichte der deutschen Seeschiffahrt* (1915) pp. 383–4.

* This doubtless refers to a bill of exchange drawn by Swartekop.
† This last of herring equalled 12 tons, that is, about 2,000 kg.

35

A BILL OF EXCHANGE DRAWN BY LÜBECK ON DANZIG

1378 – Transfer of poundage raised to combat piracy (cf. p. 204).

To the honourable gentlemen, the mayor and councillors of Danzig, their loyal friends.

First, our respectful greetings, dear friends. We ask you out of the 1,000 marks which you have collected as poundage in your sector, as you recently told us by letter, to pay the bearer of this letter, our burgess Heinrich Ricboden, as soon as he presents this letter to you, 60 Prussian marks, which we have received from him in form of a draft. You will thereby do us a great service.

May God keep you, as we pray.

Written at Lübeck, on the day of the Blessed Pope Calixtus [14 October], under our seal.

The council of the town of Lübeck.

Hanserezesse, I 2, no. 181, p. 194.

36

COMPETITION FROM NÜRNBERG MERCHANTS

1399 – (a) Letter from the Prussian towns assembled in Thorn to Nürnberg.

. . . Dear friends. We wish to inform your worships that some of your fellow-burgesses have this year sent copper and other goods by sea to Flanders, which has never happened before and has no precedent. Therefore, dear friends, we warn you and yours in all friendship and beg you to ban and forbid this practice in the future, as we fear – if this practice should continue – that you and yours would thereby suffer loss, for which we would be very sorry. . . .

Hanserezesse, I 4, no. 540, p. 495.

1405 – (b) Petition from the Lübeck retailers to the council (cf. pp. 196, 229).

Dear sirs, your burgesses and merchants complain generally against the Nürnbergers, who here hold open shop, so that they sell all kinds of goods, for example Flemish articles in quantities both great and small, all kinds of goods from Cologne such as yarn and silk, goods from Frankfurt and goods from Venice, all sold by pennyworths. They also sell pearls and gold by the ounce.

Dear and gracious sirs, this causes great loss to your burgesses and merchants; for one Nürnberger can sell by himself as many goods as twenty other people, and he disposes of more goods and sells more in one day than your burgesses and merchants in a year. Therefore the merchants believe that they [the Nürnbergers] should not be allowed to sell goods in their shops other than those that are manufactured in the town of Nürnberg. Therefore, dear councillors, have a care of your fellow-burgesses, as you have always been ready to do in the past, that they may not be ruined by foreigners.

C. NORDMANN, *Nürnberger Grosshändler im spätmittelalterlichen Lübeck* (1933) p. 5.

37

TRADE WITH VENICE

1411 – Letter addressed by Peter Karbow from Venice to his partner Hildebrand Veckinchusen in Bruges (cf. pp. 175, 258).

Friendly greetings! May I remind you, dear Hildebrand, about the 1,000 ducats which, as I wrote to you, I borrowed from Hans Reme of Augsburg: I informed you that you must pay him for this on 19 March.* I beg you for the sake of our friendship to pay him punctually, as I have given him guarantees and also letters with our company's seal on them. If he should lose by this, I would have to compensate him, together with my associates. – I further inform you that a week ago I dispatched spices to the value of 10,000 ducats, namely Indian and Arabian ginger, nutmeg, mace, cloves and whatever else I could get on favourable terms: I shall dispatch further consignments within the next week. For this I need money, unless I am to leave the amber rosaries,

* The text of the bill of exchange is no. 3 in the same publication: Hildebrand, in Bruges, was to give the payee 1,263 francs and 5 groschen, 1 franc being reckoned at 33 groschen.

the cloth and ermine [in pawn] until St James's Day. In addition I have paid out 12,000 ducats in cash since Christmas, and every day I receive more bills of exchange from [our partner] Hans von Mynden.

Dear Hildebrand, may God help us so that we can carry on for another year and so that things turn out as I have written to Sievert:* I said that I was confident that with God's help I should be able to present as favourable a balance-sheet as the last one.

We must bear in mind that we must not give up the trade in rosaries, because even if they are slow to sell, one gets a year's credit with them. I cannot write more about this. Farewell in Christ. Written on 19 January.

Concerning the shipment of furs which you sent me, I make the total 2,000 pieces. They were supposed to be lynx, but they turn out to be a very inferior variety. Let me know what has happened.

Peter Karbow.

W. STIEDA, *Hansisch-venetianische Handelsbeziehungen im 15. Jahrhundert* (1894) no. 4, p. 126.

38

A MERCHANT IN FINANCIAL DIFFICULTIES

1418 – A letter from Sievert Veckinchusen in Cologne to his brother and partner Hildebrand in Lübeck (cf. p. 176).

My dear brother, your six lots of fish and the small barrel of furs arrived here safely. But I think we shall have difficulty in selling them. No one will pay 28 guilders for *rakelvysch*† or 35 guilders for *lotvysch*† and the furs are not worth 80 guilders in cash; no wares can command a cash sale here. To judge by your letter you have paid too much for the fish. Today I have sold 2,000 'beautiful furs' (*schonwerk*) on credit, to be paid for before the next Lent Fair [at Frankfurt] at 87 guilders per thousand. I have had them on my hands here since summer, because nothing can be sold here for cash. I would have gladly sold the furs for 80 guilders in cash, because I can raise no money at all.

When I think of what I owe, I do not really know how I could come to Lübeck, and I fear that I shall have to stay here the whole winter; this worries me, as I should suffer much damage and loss, while I should have been glad to go to Lübeck for many reasons; but I will do my best. In all my life I have never been in such financial difficulties, and I really do not know how I shall

---

* Sievert Veckinchusen, Hildebrand's brother, in business in Cologne and a partner in the Venetian enterprise.

† Varieties of dried fish.

get away from here. May God help us all in our need. Remember me to all friends. Written on the eve of SS Simon and Jude [27 October] in the year 1418.

W. STIEDA, *Hildebrand Veckinchusen* (1921) no. 191, p. 214.

39

A FREIGHT CONTRACT

1416 – Contract between two Hanseatic merchants and a skipper from Kampen for the journey to the Bay (cf. p. 156).

In the name of God, amen. Be it known to all who see or hear this document read, that Hans Strateken and Claes Ubbyes, both merchants and members of the German Hansa, have chartered the *pleyte** of the skipper Jan Claessoen of Kampen, at present at anchor in the Zuiderzee, to sail with the first ships, with good wind and weather, as God shall grant them, to the Bay [of Bourgneuf]. And there the aforesaid merchants are to load 7 hundreds of salt† into the above-mentioned good ship . . . namely, the above-named Hans Strateken 4 hundreds, to be delivered to Hermann Vogelsanck at Reval in Livonia, and in addition Claes Ubbyes 3 hundreds, to be delivered to Gherwen Borneman. As soon as the said ship is loaded with this salt, the skipper is to sail for Reval in Livonia, by the direct route, bypassing the Zwijn. And when he arrives there, with God's help, he is to receive 15 Riga marks for every last of salt which he delivers from the ship out of the aforesaid 7 hundreds. . . . But if the above-mentioned skipper should die – which God forbid – on the homeward journey, then his next of kin is to receive the money. . . .

Therefore the said merchants are pledged to collect the cargo, to dispose of it and to pay the freight charges. The skipper for his part shall put himself at the disposal of his merchants according to the tradition of the sea, in all good faith.

In knowledge of the above-mentioned facts, agreements and conditions, two identical documents have been drawn up, one cut from the other along the ABCD line, one copy being handed to the said skipper and the other to be kept by the said merchants. Drawn up at the Cold Fair in Bergen-op-Zoom in the year of Our Lord 1461, on the fourth day of December. . . .

Hansisches Urkundenbuch, vol. 8, no. 1089, p. 653.

* A flat-bottomed ship.
† The hundred of salt, usually reckoned at 7½ lasts, i.e. about 15,000 kg.

40

SOLIDARITY BETWEEN ENGLISH CLOTHIERS AND HANSEATICS

1468 – Petition to Edward IV from the clothiers of Gloucestershire on behalf of the imprisoned Hanseatic merchants (cf. p. 245).

The petitioners, the clothiers and citizens of your county of Gloucester, address their complaints to your majesty regarding the trade in cloth which up to now has been sold most profitably for them and thousands of your subjects to the Baltic merchants from Germany residing in your kingdom. Indeed the manufacture of cloth is conditioned by this trade. Several hundred of your loyal subjects were employed in its production and their livelihood was ensured by it. In this way – praise be to God – unemployment and many other undesirable things were avoided among the people.

Then, your highness, in reply to the seizure by the king of Denmark of ships belonging to merchants in London and other ports, the said merchants were some time ago arrested and their goods confiscated. The result has been considerable harm to us petitioners and many more of your faithful subjects. Whereas the sale of cloth was usually carried on principally at St Bartholomew's Fair for large sums of money, as well as at other times during the year, at the last St Bartholomew's Fair the cloth could not be sold and could only be cleared now at a loss. This has led to a marked reduction in the manufacture of cloth, much to the distress of us petitioners and many others.

If this should continue, there will inevitably be a decline in the said manufacture and irreparable unemployment – Lord preserve us – among your faithful subjects. Besides, as a result of their arrest and the seizure of their goods, the said merchants had to defer payment of their debts to us petitioners. The total sum owed exceeds 5,000 pounds and this will probably be entirely lost if this situation is allowed to continue. Thus we petitioners, the said Baltic merchants and your majesty, by losing the rewards of our customary exports, which ought in the future to expand, are being greatly harmed.

May it please your majesty therefore to consider these matters and to acknowledge that the said merchants are and have always been among the most trustworthy friends of your kingdom. How can they be suspected of being responsible for seizing our ships? We believe, in all respect to your majesty, that this crime was attributed to them as a result of an evil and cunning plot to force your majesty to banish them from your kingdom – heaven forbid – and deprive them of their charters. That is why we beg your majesty to take the measures necessary for the prosperity of us petitioners and of your kingdom, namely to give back to the said merchants their former charters, to set them free and return their possessions, and to look favourably on their activities so that they may be more inclined to return to your kingdom.

Hansisches Urkundenbuch, vol. 9, no. 525, p. 380.

41

A SHIPOWNER'S MOVABLES

1494 – Hermen Mesman and his heirs acknowledge that they owe the sum of 4,000 marks capital plus a yearly interest of 200 marks to the Convent of St John in Lübeck. A councillor from Lübeck and five other persons acting as guarantors of this debt, Mesman pledges to them all his movable effects (cf. p. 152).

Hermen Mesman, burgess of Lübeck, has, of his own free will, on his own behalf and on behalf of his heirs, made an agreement with the said guarantors, and pawns to them by means of this document all his disposable assets, his silverware, furniture and household utensils, his pots, kettles and cauldrons, his assets, all his ships and shares in ships, with their tackle, anchors, cables, rigging and all fittings wherever or in whosesoever possession they may be, nothing excepted, to wit:

of Marten Quante's hulk, a quarter-share	400 marks
of Hans Holste's ship, an eighth-share	200 marks
of Hans Blank's ship, a three-eighths share	600 marks
of Peter Ruter's ship, a quarter-share	300 marks
of Hermen Burscop's ship, an eighth-share	200 marks
in addition a half-share in Hans Vranke's ship	85 marks

These ships all lie at the present time at Lübeck.

In Hans Schakel's ship, which at present lies at Reval, at least 625 marks.

Another hulk, to which he has now appointed Hanke Brandt as skipper and which is at present in port at Stockholm, is worth a good 1,300 marks. In addition another whole ship, at port in Stockholm, of 60 lasts, which is worth more than 200 marks.

Total: 3,900 marks.

In addition the said Hermen . . . has agreed: if the Lord God should summon him to himself and the above-mentioned pledges should not be sufficient, then the guarantors or their heirs shall be entitled to claim his entire property in land, that is, the houses which he owns, as well as all other movable and real property inside or outside the town of Lübeck.

PAULI, *Lübeckische Zustände im Mittelalter*, vol. 3, no. 25, p. 117.

42

THREAT TO THE TRADE IN NORWEGIAN FISH

1514 – Memorandum from the Hanseatic Kontor *in Bergen to the Norwegian government regarding negotiations in Oslo (cf. p. 313).*

First, since the position of the *Kontor* in Bergen had declined in the past because of the Hollanders and other non-Hanseatics, his most serene highness King Christian [I] gave the *Kontor* fresh privileges [1469 and 1471]. Accordingly the merchant begs that the Hollanders and other non-Hanseatics should be forbidden to trade illegally or to sail to the said kingdom, and that they be allowed to come to Bergen only, with one or two ships . . . and that they shall live in two courts only, on the south shore of the port, and that there they shall trade only wholesale, and not in ells or small weights. . . .

Even in ancient times no other place, but only Bergen, was recognised as the legal market in Norway: fishermen brought fish from many districts and from many islands, but it was all brought to Bergen. And as long as things were kept in this way, all was well in Norway and the merchant brought all kinds of wares into the kingdom; and when he came with his fish to Lübeck, it was in demand and sold well and many merchants could live well in Bergen.

But then the Hamburgers began to make an annual voyage to Iceland, with one ship or occasionally with two, and to sail from there with their fish to England. At that time this fish was hardly known in Germany. Now, however, they sail there with six, eight and often with ten ships and take the fish not to England but to Hamburg, and merchants from Bremen have also begun to make the journey and sail back to the Weser, and the Hollanders and others follow their example and take their cargo back to Amsterdam. They make large profits from the fish, so that there is little demand for fish from Bergen and as a result it is now almost worthless.

In addition the south Germans, who at one time bought and dispatched Norwegian fish, no longer require it. They have learnt a special technique, beating the Icelandic fish to make it soft. This has spread so far and become so established that they greatly prefer Iceland to Bergen fish. Therefore the Norwegian fish finds no buyers and the merchant cannot make a profit and must give up making the journey since it is no longer profitable.

The merchants of Hamburg and Bremen can sell more cheaply, because they can load more fish in three ships than we can carry in five, and in Iceland they need not pay so much for houses and courts as the merchant has to pay in Bergen; if therefore this great and growing evil is not checked now, the *Kontor* will be ruined – which God forbid.

Therefore the merchant humbly requests that the towns of Hamburg and Bremen and the others, in accordance with the privileges mentioned, be strictly warned to stop sailing to Iceland and returning direct to their own ports, contrary to the long-established law of Norway, and that they be allowed to carry Icelandic fish only to England and not to German or other ports or lands, under pain of forfeiting the royal privileges and the right to trade in the rivers, harbours and provinces of this kingdom.

Finally the merchants of Hamburg, Bremen and Amsterdam, as well as the Hollanders and others, visit the Shetlands and the Faroes and bring from there, contrary to custom, butter, tallow, wool and feathers, thus causing no small loss and damage not only to the merchant but also to the kingdom of Norway. The merchant therefore begs that this also should be forbidden in future. . . .

F. BRUNS, *Die Lübecker Bergenfahrer und ihre Chronistik* ('Hansische Geschichtsquellen', n.s. 2, 1900) pp. 211–13.

43

EXPANSION OF THE GRAIN TRADE CARRIED ON BY THE NOBILITY

1534 – From a report by the imperial secretary Maximilian Transsilvan to the regent of the Low Countries, describing, apropos of certain matrimonial projects, the prosperity of Poland (cf. pp. 198, 232, 348).

The whole profit and growth of the kingdom of Poland and of the said town of Danzig lies in this, that the Hollanders come once or twice every year with 200 or 300 ships, and within a fortnight buy and carry off all the grain which is to be found in the said town of Danzig. For all the great lords and noblemen of Poland and Prussia have in the last twenty-five years found out how to send by certain rivers all their grain to Danzig and there to sell it to the men of that town. And therefore the kingdom of Poland and the said lords have become very rich and are becoming ever richer. For in former times they did not know what to do with their grain and left their land fallow, and the town of Danzig, which was at one time a mere village, is now the most powerful and richest town on the whole Baltic Sea.

Niederländische Akten und Urkunden, vol. 1, no. 178, §28, p. 200.

IV. Trade Statistics

44

TRAFFIC IN THE PORT OF LÜBECK
18 MARCH 1368–10 MARCH 1369

*1. Volume of goods imported or exported by sea, including those travel-
ling through Hamburg (grouped under the heading 'West'): values in
thousands of Lübeck marks, according to place of origin or destination
(cf. p. 198).*

Imports		Origin, Destination	Exports		Total	%
150		West	38		188	34·4
44		Livonian towns:	51		95	17·4
	10	Riga		14		
	34	Reval		14·3		
	—	Pernau		22·7		
49·4		Skania	32·6		82	15
52		Gotland–Sweden	29·4		81·4	14·9
19		Prussian towns:	29·5		48·5	8·9
	16	Danzig		22·8		
	3	Elbing		6·6		
17·2		Wendish and Pomeranian towns:	25·2		42·4	7·8
	5·5	Stettin		7		
	4	Stralsund		7·5		
	2·2	Rostock		4·6		
	5·5	Wismar		6·1		
4·3		Bergen	—		4·3	0·8
3		Small Baltic ports	1·2		4·2	0·8
338·9		Total	206·9		545·8	100

2. *Goods imported and exported by sea: values in thousands of Lübeck marks.*

Goods	Principal origin	Imports	Exports	Total
Cloth	Flanders	120·8	39·7	160·5
Fish	Skania	64·7	6·1	70·8
Salt	Lüneburg	—	61·6	61·6
Butter	Sweden	19·2	6·8	26
Skins, furs	Russia, Sweden	13·3	3·7	17
Grain	Prussia	13	0·8	13·8
Wax	Russia, Prussia	7·2	5·8	13
Beer	Wendish towns	4·1	1·9	6
Copper	Sweden, Hungary	2·2	2·4	4·6
Iron	Sweden, Hungary	2·4	2·2	4·6
Oil	Flanders	2·7	1·5	4·2
Flax	Livonia, N. Germany	0·4	3	3·4
Various foodstuffs	—	2·2	1·2	3·4
Silver currency	?	0·7	2	2·7
Wine	Rhineland	1·3	0·9	2·2
Linen	Westphalia	0·2	1·1	1·3
Various		39·9	16·6	56·5
Unclassified		41	49	90
Total (to nearest whole number)		338·9	206·9	545·8

3. *Movements of the 680 ships which entered and left the port.*

Arrivals	%	Origin, Destination	Departures	%
289	33·7	Mecklenburg–Pomerania	386	42·3
250	28·8	Skania	207	22·8
145	16·8	Prussia	183	20·1
96	11·2	Sweden	64	7
35	4·3	Livonia	43	4·7
28	3·2	Fehmarn	27	3
12	1·6	Bergen	—	—
3	0·4	Flanders	1	0·1
858	100		911	100

G. Lechner, *Die Hansischen Pfundzollisten des Jahres 1368* (1935) pp. 48, 53, 66.

45

THE TEUTONIC ORDER'S TRADE WITH FLANDERS

1390–1405 – Exports and imports of the 'great treasury' (Grossschäfferei) of the Teutonic Order in Königsberg: values in pounds of Flemish groschen (cf. p. 212).

	Exports to Flanders						Imports			
	Amber	Copper	Wax	Furs	Various	Total	Cloth	Spices*	Total	Total Turnover
1390	690	—	—	—	—	690	—	—	—	690
1391	1,089	105	100	—	326	1,620	56	5	61	1,681
1392	826	—	702	—	—	1,528	1,125	29	1,154	2,682
1393	810	—	734	293	342	2,179	2,378	27	2,405	4,584
1394	756	251	886	409	14	2,316	1,360	23	1,383	3,699
1395	1,348	365	565	508	140	2,926	2,614	27	2,641	5,567
1396	876	326	1,776	408	—	3,386	3,248	44	3,293	6,678
1397	823	—	—	835	—	1,658	2,381	20	2,401	4,059
1398	900	—	211	1,009	—	2,120	1,491	20	1,511	3,631
1399	759	209	850	960	—	2,778	2,011	299	2,310	5,088
1400	646	—	1,500	560	—	2,706	—	—	—	2,706
1401	—	40	1,800	380	—	2,220	—	—	—	2,220
1402	602	—	—	—	—	602	—	—	—	602
1403	211	46	900	460	40	1,657	—	—	—	1,657
1404	370	120	1,800	480	27	2,797	1,754	445	2,199	4,996
1405	90	—	—	146	—	236	—	—	—	236
Total	10,796	1,462	11,824	6,448	889	31,419	18,418	939	19,357	50,776
Average†	720	184	985	538	148	2,575	1,842	94	1,936	4,521

F. RENKEN, *Der Handel der Königsberger Grosschäfferei des Deutschen Ordens mit Flandern um 1400* (1937) p. 165.

* Under the heading 'Spices' are included also fruit from the Mediterranean, almonds, grapes and figs.

† In calculating the averages years with no entry were not included.

46

SOME PRICES

*1400 – Prices of various articles sold by the Teutonic Order in Prussia in
1400: the prices, in Prussian marks, all relate to the standard quantity of
1 last (cf. p. 216).*

Saffron	7,040	Hungarian iron	21
Ginger	1,040	Trave salt	12½
Pepper	640	Herring	12
Wax	237½	Flemish salt	8
French wine	109½	Wismar beer	7½
Rice	80	Flour	7½
Steel	75	Wheat	7
Rhenish wine	66	Rye	5¾
Oil	60	Barley	4⅕
Honey	35	Ash (woad)	4¾
Butter	30		

After W. BÖHNKE, 'Der Binnenhandel des Deutschen
Ordens in Preussen', in *Hansische Geschichtsblätter*, 80
(1962) pp. 51–3.

47

EXPORT OF ENGLISH CLOTH BY HANSEATIC MERCHANTS

Yearly averages, mostly over a five-year period, of lengths of cloth exported by Hanseatic merchants (cf. pp. 212, 245).

1366–1368	1,690	1451–1455	7,682
1377–1380	2,028	1456–1460	10,176
1392–1395	7,827	1461–1465	8,734
1399–1401	6,737	1465–1470	5,733
1401–1405	5,940	1471–1475	3,360*
1406–1410	6,160	1476–1480	9,820
1411–1415	4,990	1481–1482	15,070
1416–1420	5,686	1510–1514	21,607
1421–1425	7,238	1515–1520	20,400
1426–1430	4,495	1521–1525	18,503
1431–1435	4,016	1526–1530	20,372
1436–1440	9,044	1531–1535	24,266
1441–1445	11,480	1536–1540	30,740
1446–1450	9,292	1541–1545	27,329
		Jan–Sept 1554	27,903†

E. Power and M. Postan, *Studies in English Trade in the Fifteenth Century*, 2nd ed. (1951) p. 407; G. Schanz, *Englische Handelspolitik gegen Ende des Mittelalters*, vol. 2 (1881) p. 103.

* This drop was caused by the Anglo-Hanseatic War of 1469–74, during which trade continued only with Cologne.

† Figure from K. Friedland, 'Der Plan des Dr Heinrich Sudermann zur Wiederherstellung der Hanse', in *Jahrbuch des Kölnischen Geschichtsvereins*, 31–2 (1956–7) p. 244.

The first three figures for the fourteenth century are taken from H. L. Gray, 'The Production and Exportation of English Woollens in the 14th Century', in *English Historical Review* (1924) p. 35.

48

IMPORTS OF WAX INTO ENGLAND BY HANSEATIC MERCHANTS

Yearly averages in hundredweights (cf. pp. 219, 245).

1476–1479	1,107
1480–1483	2,750
1510–1514	4,064·6
1515–1519	3,658·2
1520–1524	2,798·4
1525–1529	6,361·2
1530–1534	2,561
1535–1539	1,630·6
1540–1544	926·6

SCHANZ, *Englische Handelspolitik gegen Ende des Mittelalters*, vol. 2, p. 155.

49

EXPORTS FROM STOCKHOLM TO LÜBECK AND DANZIG

Exports of butter, copper, osmund (*i.e. high quality iron*) *and pig-iron: figures for the fourteenth and fifteenth centuries from the* Pfundzoll-bücher *of Lübeck, those for the sixteenth and seventeenth centuries from the customs accounts of Stockholm; the percentages refer to the total quantity of each product exported from Stockholm. The quantities of* osmund – *given in the sources in lasts – have been converted into* shiffspfund, *reckoning 12 schiffspfund to the last (cf. p. 360).*

	Butter (tons)				Copper (*schiffspfund*)			
	Lübeck	%	Danzig	%	Lübeck	%	Danzig	%
1368	c.2,000				460			
1369	c. 900				530			
1400	247				45			
1492	76				2,250			
1493	53				2,849			
1494	—				1,806			
1495	—				435			
1559	1,254	89	150	11	—			
1572	1,350	74	252	14	564	94	3	0·5
1574	1,294	80	105	10	803	85	59	6·2
1576	1,659	79	158	7	1,362	88	94	6·1
1582	1,224	86	47	3	2,031	81	2	0
1583	1,133	77	165	11	2,153	70	122	4
1584	909	74	177	14	2,425	69	49	1·4
1591	742	74	170	17	1,487	74	247	12
1600	—	—	56	5	—	—	1	0
1610	64	47	7	5	1,411	83	18	1·1
1620	659	76	50	6	7,434	86	12	0·1

	Osmund (*schiffspfund*)				Pig-iron (*schiffspfund*)			
	Lübeck	%	Danzig	%	Lübeck	%	Danzig	%
1368	1,680							
1369	3,080							
1400	2,964							
1492	5,976							
1493	7,320							
1494	5,316							
1495	1,380							
1559	—							
1572	4,620	32	7,428	51	1,851	59	259	8
1574	8,304	34	8,918	46	2,250	62	308	8
1576	5,508	29	11,844	62	2,019	48	886	21
1582	6,228	36	9,960	58	2,669	56	574	12
1583	4,032	27	9,948	66	2,389	55	1,104	25
1584	4,728	28	11,436	67	3,304	58	728	13
1591	6,468	33	11,636	60	3,402	49	1,334	19
1600	—	—	5,424	31	—	—	332	3
1610	1,524	14	8,280	73	1,562	33	610	13
1620	1,308	11	8,448	73	3,842	29	1,969	15

After K. KUMLIEN, *Sverige och Hanseaterna* (1953)
pp. 303, 309, 313, 314.

50

DANZIG'S TRADE

1560–1661 – The number of cargo-ships, grouped by country of origin, which sailed from Danzig and passed westwards through the Sound.

Year	Danzig	Other Hanseatic ports	Emden	Netherlands	Denmark	Norway	Scotland	England	France	Total sailing from Danzig	Total sailing from the Baltic
1560	138	80	30	420	8	3	23	9	0	711	1,409
1565	3	27	72	1,029	4	0	15	17	6	1,173	1,674
1569	52	97	311	349	55	4	36	60	3	967	1,583
1575	55	55	256	554	37	9	58	74	4	1,105	1,878
1580	29	37	121	465	13	5	23	10	13	717	1,876
1585	26	18	116	523	63	2	14	3	9	776	1,967
1590	40	41	134	596	33	15	39	6	25	931	2,496
1595	68	76	134	825	47	11	51	32	83	1,330	3,143
1600	66	68	102	529	26	4	24	12	11	842	2,154
1605	46	51	65	624	65	0	23	21	11	924	1,955
1610	20	40	51	614	36	1	16	6	13	816	2,044
1615	17	48	61	732	45	27	22	47	17	1,018	2,479
1620	9	35	47	892	18	18	12	12	0	1,072	2,614
1625	19	32	16	284	1	12	18	14	6	403	1,444
1630	4	13	7	186	4	4	10	4	17	249	1,165
1635	18	32	16	432	26	25	26	78	6	662	2,077
1640	50	103	3	340	86	48	10	86	0	740	1,705
1646	44	77	0	342	44	40	9	33	3	618	1,772
1650	17	51	45	587	12	22	9	20	0	774	2,182
1655	29	63	29	320	4	12	12	13	0	473	1,608
1661	4	8	16	197	1	4	1	15	3	251	1,069

N. ELLINGER BANG, *Tabeller over Skibsfart og Varetransport gennem Øresund 1497–1660,* 1: *Tabeller over Skibsfarten* (1906).

51

EXPORTS OF GRAIN FROM DANZIG TO WESTERN EUROPE

Yearly averages, in lasts *taken from the accounts of the Sound.*

Period	Total exports of rye through the Sound	Exports from Danzig			
		Rye	Wheat	Flour	Barley
1490–1492		8,473	128	95	
1562–1565	50,676	42,720	4,826	4,424	603
1566–1569	43,771	34,089	2,258	1,390	495
1574–1575	35,773	28,796	3,493	1,750	277
1576–1580	25,297	14,071	1,437	1,259	41
1581–1585	24,431	19,860	2,258	1,305	187
1586–1590	39,295	28,633	2,982	1,472	498
1591–1595	45,290	29,080	2,097	1,082	676
1596–1600	50,070	38,585	4,773	1,221	474
1601–1605	37,818	32,283	1,664	903	208
1606–1610	55,472	38,980	3,258	255	796
1611–1615	44,378	34,765	1,941	227	507
1616–1620	68,326	51,778	5,679	263	1,418
1621–1625	48,576	32,845	3,704	109	475
1626–1630	20,973	8,139	690	150	37
1631–1635	45,466	31,004	6,807	210	114
1636–1640	45,251	31,778	8,011	232	2,067
1641–1645	53,910	42,090	12,383	377	4,676
1646–1650	53,056	34,554	11,162	158	1,541
1651–1655	28,745	17,788	4,550	35	947

ELLINGER BANG, *Tabeller over Skibsfart og Varetransport gennem Øresund 1497–1660*, II: *Tabeller over Varetransporten A* (1933).

BIBLIOGRAPHY

List of Abbreviations

Annales E.S.C.

HGbll.
VSWG

ZHambG.

ZLübG.

Annales: Économies, Sociétés, Civilisations
Hansische Geschichtsblätter
Vierteljahrschrift für Sozial- und Wirtschaftsgeschichte
Zeitschrift des Vereins für Hamburgische Geschichte
Zeitschrift des Vereins für Lübeckische Geschichte und Altertumskunde

I. General Works

1. GENERAL SURVEYS

K. PAGEL, *Die Hanse*, 3rd ed. (1963): useful and comprehensive, but confusingly arranged. W. VOGEL, *Kurze Geschichte der deutschen Hanse* (1915): best short survey. D. SCHÄFER, *Die Deutsche Hanse*, 4th ed. (1943): standard monograph, intended for the general public.

2. IMPORTANT MONOGRAPHS

D. SCHÄFER, *Die Hansestädte und König Waldemar von Dänemark. Hansische Geschichte bis 1376* (1879): the only comprehensive work, though now partly out of date, on the earliest period of Hanseatic history. E. DAENELL, *Die Blütezeit der deutschen Hanse. Hansische Geschichte von der zweiten Hälfte des 14. bis zum letzten Viertel des 15. Jahrhunderts*, 2 vols (1905–6): still essential. W. VOGEL, *Geschichte der deutschen Seeschiffahrt, I: Von der Urzeit bis zum Ende des 15. Jahrhunderts* (1915): excellent; only the first volume has appeared. W. VOGEL and G. SCHMÖLDERS, *Die Deutschen als Seefahrer* (1949):

a summary of the preceding work, with additional chapters on the modern period. P. JOHANSEN, 'Umrisse und Aufgaben der hansischen Siedlungsgeschichte und Kartographie', in *HGbll.* 73 (1955): wider in scope than its title suggests, examines many problems. A. VON BRANDT, P. JOHANSEN, H. VAN WERVEKE, K. KUMLIEN and H. KELLENBENZ, *Die Deutsche Hanse als Mittler zwischen Ost und West* (1963): symposium of German, Flemish and Swedish historians. R. HAEPKE, *Der Untergang der Hanse* (1923): brief popular survey.

3. THE TOWNS

J. SCHNEIDER, *Les villes allemandes au moyen âge* (1955). *Deutsches Städtebuch*, ed. E. KEYSER (1939 ff.). H. PLANITZ, *Die deutsche Stadt im Mittelalter* (1954). F. RÖRIG, *Die europäische Stadt und die Kultur des Bürgertums im Mittelalter*, 4th ed. (1964). W. STEIN, 'Die Hansestädte', in *HGbll.* 19–21 (1913–15). W. SPIESS, *Braunschweig als Hansestadt* (1929). G. BESSELL, *Bremen, Geschichte einer deutschen Stadt*, 3rd ed. (1955). P. SIMSON, *Geschichte der Stadt Danzig*, vols 1, 2, 4 (1913–18). E. KEYSER, *Danzigs Geschichte*, 4th ed. (1941). Z. SNELLER, *Deventer, die Stadt der Jahrmärkte* (1936). L. VON WINTERFELD, *Geschichte der freien Reichs- und Hansestadt Dortmund*, 2nd ed. (1956). E. CARSTENN, *Geschichte der Hansestadt Elbing* (1937). E. WISKEMANN, *Hamburg und die Welthandelspolitik von den Anfängen bis zur Gegenwart* (1929). E. VON RANKE, *Das hansische Köln und seine Handelsblüte* (1925). W. REINECKE, *Lüneburg als Hansestadt*, 2nd ed. (1946). F. TECHEN, *Geschichte der Seestadt Wismar* (1929).

4. HANSEATIC REGIONS

Der Raum Westfalen, ed. H. AUBIN, II 1 (1955): important; II 2 (1934); IV 1 (1958); IV 2 (1964). B. SCHUMACHER, *Geschichte Ost- und Westpreussens*, 4th ed. (1959). P. JOHANSEN, 'Die Bedeutung der Hanse für Livland', in *HGbll.* 65–6 (1941).

5. COMMERCIAL AND POLITICAL RELATIONS WITH OTHER COUNTRIES

C. NORDMANN, *Oberdeutschland und die Hanse* (1939). F. SCHULZ, *Die Hanse und England von Eduards III. bis auf Heinrichs VIII. Zeit* (1911). E. POWER and M. POSTAN, *Studies in English Trade in the Fifteenth Century*, 2nd ed. (1951). J. H. A. BEUKEN, *De Hanze en Vlaanderen* (1950). F. VOLLBEHR, *Die*

Portugal na idade media (1959). L. K. Goetz, *Deutsch-russische Handelsge-Holländer und die deutsche Hanse* (1930). A. de Oliveira Marques, *Hansa e schichte des Mittelalters* (1922). L. Musset, *Les peuples scandinaves au moyen âge* (1961). M. Gerhardt and W. Hubatsch, *Deutschland und Skandinavien im Wandel der Jahrhunderte* (1950). O. A. Johnsen, *Norwegische Wirtschaftsgeschichte* (1939). K. Kumlien, *Sverige och Hanseaterna. Studier i svensk politik och utrikeshandel* (1953). J. Schreiner, *Hanseatene og Norges nedgang* (1935); *Hanseatene og Norge i det 16 århundre* (1941). W. Stieda. *Hansisch-venezianische Handelsbeziehungen im 15. Jahrhundert* (1894).

6. MAIN COLLECTIONS OF SOURCE MATERIAL

Hanserezesse, series I, 1256–1430, ed. W. Junghans and K. Koppmann, 8 vols (1870–97); series II, 1431–76, ed. G. von der Ropp, 7 vols (1876–92); series III, 1477–1530, ed. D. Schäfer, 9 vols (1881–1913); series IV, vol. I, 1531–5, ed. G. Wentz and K. Friedland (1941 ff.). *Hansisches Urkundenbuch*, ed. K. Höhlbaum and others, II vols, 975–1500 (1876–1939): vol. 7 ii, 1442–50, is missing. *Hansische Geschichtsquellen*, ed. Verein für hansische Geschichte, 12 vols (1875–1922); continued as 'Quellen und Darstellungen zur hansischen Geschichte' (1928 ff.). 'Abhandlungen zur Verkehrs- und Seegeschichte', ed. Verein für hansische Geschichte, 10 vols (1908–22); continued as 'Abhandlungen zur Handels- und Seegeschichte, 5 vols (1933–7), and as 'Abhandlungen zur Handels- und Sozialgeschichte' (1958 ff.). *Urkundenbuch der Stadt Lübeck* [to 1470], II vols and index (1843–1932). *Veröffentlichungen aus dem Staatsarchiv der Freien und Hansestadt Hamburg* (1910 ff.). *Quellen zur Geschichte des Kölner Handels und Verkehrs im Mittelalter*, ed. B. Kuske, 4 vols (1918–34). J.-M. Pardessus, *Collection de lois maritimes antérieures au XVIIe siècle*, 3 vols (1828–34): includes French translations. *Niederländische Akten und Urkunden zur Geschichte der deutschen Hansa und zur deutschen Seegeschichte*, ed. R. Häpke, 2 vols, 1531–1669 (1913–23). *Inventare hansischer Archive des 16. Jahrhunderts*, ed. P. Simson, 3 vols, Cologne and Danzig (1896–1913). N. Ellinger Bang, *Tabeller over Skibsfart og Varetransport gennem Øresund 1497–1660*, 2 vols (1906–33).

7. USEFUL AIDS

K. Schiller and A. Lübben, *Mittelniederdeutsches Wörterbuch*, 6 vols (1875–1881). F. Bruns and H. Weczerka, *Hansische Handelsstrassen*: atlas and text ('Quellen und Darstellungen zur Hansischen Geschichte', n.s. 13 i, ii, 1962–7).

II. Bibliography to Individual Chapters

Chapter One

1. L. Musset, *Les peuples scandinaves au moyen âge* (1951). O. A. Johnsen, 'Le commerce et la navigation en Norvège au moyen âge', *Revue historique*, 178 (1936). A. Hofmeister, *Der Kampf um die Ostsee vom 9. bis 12. Jahrhundert*, 3rd ed. (1960). S. Mews, *Gotlands Handel und Verkehr bis zum Auftreten der Hansen* (1937). W. Koppe, 'Schleswig und die Schleswiger (1066–1134)', in *Städtewesen und Bürgertum, Gedächtnisschrift F. Rörig* (1953). R. Rohwer, *Der friesische Handel im frühen Mittelalter* (1937). R. Doehaerd, *L'expansion économique belge au moyen âge* (1946). A. Joris, 'Der Handel der Maasstädte im Mittelalter', *HGbll.* 79 (1961). W. Stein, *Handels- und Verkehrsgeschichte der deutschen Kaiserzeit* (1922). H. J. Seeger, *Westfalens Handel und Gewerbe vom 9. bis 14. Jahrhundert* (1926).

2. E. Jordan, 'L'Allemagne et l'Italie de 1125 à 1273' (*Histoire générale: Moyen Âge*, IV 1) (1939). B. Gebhardt, *Handbuch de deutschen Geschichte*, vols 1–2, 9th ed. (1954–5). A. Hauck, *Kirchengeschichte Deutschlands*, vols 3–4, 5th ed. (1925). K. Hampe, *Der Zug nach dem Osten*, 5th ed. (1939).

3. R. Latouche, *Les origines de l'économie occidentale* (1956). H. Planitz, *Die deutsche Stadt im Mittelalter* (1954). Y. Dollinger-Léonard, 'De la cité romaine à la ville médiévale dans la région de la Moselle et de la Haute-Meuse', in *Vorträge und Forschungen*, vol. 4, ed. T. Mayer (1958). W. Schlesinger, 'Städtische Frühformen zwischen Rhein und Elbe', ibid. H. Ludat, *Vorstufen und Entstehung des Städtewesens in Osteuropa* (1955). P. Francastel (ed.), *Les origines des villes polonaises* (1961). W. Neugebauer, 'Das Suburbium von Alt-Lübeck, *ZLübG.* 39 (1959). H. Schwarzwälder, *Entstehung und Anfänge der Stadt Bremen* (1955). E. Keyser, *Städtegründungen und Städtebau in Nordwestdeutschland im Mittelalter*, 2 vols (1958).

Chapter Two

1. Rörig's thesis: F. Rörig, *Wirtschaftskräfte im Mittelalter* (1959), containing 'Der Markt von Lübeck' (1921) and 'Die Gründungsunternehmerstädte des 12. Jahrhunderts' (1928). Critical opinions: L. von Winterfeld, 'Gründung, Markt und Ratsbildung deutscher Fernhandelsstädte', in *Westfalen, Hanse,*

Ostseeraum (1955); T. MAYER, 'Die Anfänge von Lübeck', in *Westfälische Forschungen*, 9 (1956); A. VON BRANDT, 'Stadtgründung, Grundbesitz und Verfassungsanfänge in Lübeck', *ZLübG*. 36 (1956).

G. FINK, 'Lübecks Stadtgebiet', in *Gedächtnisschrift F. Rörig* (1935). F. RÖRIG, 'Die Schlacht bei Bornhöved', in *Vom Wesen und Werden der deutschen Hanse* (1940).

2. F. RÖRIG, 'Reichssymbolik auf Gotland', in *HGbll*. 64 (1940); also in *Wirtschaftskräfte im Mittelalter*. N. YRWING, *Gotland under äldre Medeltid* (1940). F. FRENSDORFF, 'Das Stadtrecht von Visby', in *HGbll*. 22 (1916). W. VOGEL, *Geschichte der deutschen Seeschiffahrt* (1915).

3. F. RÖRIG, 'Die Entstehung der Hanse und der Ostseeraum', in *Wirtschaftskräfte im Mittelalter*. L.-K. GOETZ, *Deutsche-russische Handelsgeschichte des Mittelalters* (1922). P. JOHANSEN, 'Die Bedeutung der Hanse für Livland', in *HGbll*. 65 (1941); 'Novgorod und die Hanse', in *Städtewesen und Bürgertum, Gedächtnisschrift F. Rörig* (1953). Z. LIGERS, *Histoire des villes de Lettonie et d'Estonie* (1946). H. VON ZUR MÜHLEN, *Studien zur älteren Geschichte Revals* (1937).

4. H. PLANITZ, *Die deutsche Stadt im Mittelalter* (1954). E. KEYSER, *Deutsches Städtebuch*, I (1939). W. BÖTTCHER, 'Geschichte der Verbreitung des lübischen Rechtes' (Ph.D. thesis, Greifswald, 1913). K. KÖTZSCHKE and W. EBERT, *Geschichte der ostdeutschen Kolonisation*, 2nd ed. (1944). K. JAZDEWSKI, 'La genèse de la ville de Gdansk', in *L'Artisanat et la vie urbaine de la Pologne médiévale* (1962).

5. L. MUSSET, *Les peuples scandinaves au moyen âge* (1951). A. SCHÜCK, 'Die deutsche Einwanderung im mittelalterlichen Schweden und ihre kommerziellen und sozialen Folgen', in *HGbll*. 55 (1930). S. TUNBERG, 'Die Entstehung und erste Entwicklung des schwedischen Bergbaues', in *HGbll*. 63 (1938). O. JOHANNSEN, 'Das Aufkommen der Bergerzverhüttung in Schweden,' in *HGbll*. 66 (1941). A. CHRISTENSEN, 'La foire de Scanie', in *Recueils de la Société Jean Bodin*, 5 (1953). O. A. JOHNSEN, *Norwegische Wirtschaftgeschichte* (1939).

6. K. KUNZE, 'Das erste Jahrhundert der deutschen Hanse in England', in *HGbll*. 6 (1889). L. VON WINTERFELD, *Dortmunds Stellung in der Hanse* (1932). K. WAND, 'Die Englandpolitik der Stadt Köln und ihrer Erzbischöfe im 12. und 13. Jahrhundert', in *Aus Mittelalter und Neuzeit, Festschrift G. Kallen* (1957). J. H. BEUKEN, *De Hanze en Vlaanderen* (1950). W. STEIN, 'Uber die ältesten Privilegien der deutschen Hansa in Flandern', in *HGbll*. 10 (1902). H. REINCKE, 'Die Deutschlandfahrt der Flandrer während der hansischen Frühzeit', in *HGbll*. 67–8 (1942–3). R. HÄPKE, *Brügges Entwicklung zum*

mittelalterlichen Weltmarkt (1908). H. van Werveke, *Bruges et Anvers* (1944). H. Ammann, 'Untersuchungen zur Geschichte der Deutschen im mittelalterlichen Frankreich', in *Deutsches Archiv für Landes- und Volksforschung*, 5 (1939).

Chapter Three

1. U. Kleist, *Die sächsischen Städtebünde zwischen Weser und Elbe im 13. und 14. Jahrhundert* (1892). H. Mendtal, *Die Städtebünde und Landfrieden in Westfalen* (1879). P. Kallmerten, 'Lübische Bündnispolitik (1227–1307)', (Ph.D. thesis, Kiel, 1932).

2. J. A. Gade, *The Hanseatic Control of Norwegian Commerce during the Late Middle Ages* (1951). O. A. Johnsen, 'Le commerce et la navigation en Norvège au moyen âge', in *Revue historique*, 178 (1936). J. H. Beuken, *De Hanze en Vlaanderen* (1950). W. Stein, 'Die deutsche Genossenschaft in Brügge und die Entstehung der deutschen Hanse', in *HGbll.* 14 (1908). K. Bahr, *Handel und Verkehr der deutschen Hanse in Flandern während des 14. Jahrhunderts* (1911).

3. D. Schäfer, *Die Hansestädte und König Waldemar von Dänemark* (1879). I. Andersson, *Erik Menved och Venden. Studier i dansk utrikespolitik 1300–1319* (1954).

4. K. Kunze, *Hanseakten aus England 1275–1412* (1891). F. Schulz, *Die Hanse und England von Eduards III. bis auf Heinrichs VIII. Zeit* (1911). A. Schaube, 'Die Wollausfuhr Englands von Jahre 1273', in *VSWG* 6 (1908). J. Hansen, 'Der englishe Staatskredit unter König Eduard III. und die hansischen Kaufleute', in *HGbll.* 16 (1910).

5. H. Reincke, 'Bevölkerungsprobleme der Hansestädte', in *HGbll.* 69 (1951); 'Hamburgs Bevölkerung', in *Forschungen und Skizzen zur Geschichte Hamburgs* (1951). E. Peters, 'Das grosse Sterbern des Jahres 1350 in Lübeck', in *ZLübG.* 30 (1940). W. Abel, *Die Wüstungen des ausgehenden Mittelalters*, 2nd ed. (1955).

Chapter Four

1. H. Pirenne, *Histoire de Belgique*, vol. 2, 3rd ed. (1922). J. H. Beuken, *De Hanze en Vlaanderen* (1950). W. Friccius, 'Der Wirtschaftskrieg als Mittel hansischer Politik im 14. und 15. Jahrhundert', in *HGbll.* 57 (1932). K. Bahr,

Handel und Verkehr der deutschen Hanse in Flandern während des 14. Jahrhunderts (1911). G. H. VON DER OSTEN, *Die Handels- und Verkehrssperre des deutschen Kaufmannes gegen Flandern, 1358–60* (1886).

2. D. SCHÄFER, *Die Hansestädte und König Waldemar von Dänemark* (1879). E. DAENELL, *Geschichte der deutschen Hanse in der 2. Hälfte des 14. Jahrhunderts* (1896). D. K. BJORK, 'The peace of Stralsund 1370', in *Speculum*, 7 (1932). B. EIMER, *Gotland unter dem Deutschen Orden* (1966).

3. H. PALAIS, 'England's first attempt to break the commercial monopoly of the Hanseatic League 1377–1380', in *American Historical Review*, 64 (1959). F. KEUTGEN, *Die Beziehungen der Hanse zu England im letzten Drittel des 14. Jahrhunderts* (1890). L. K. GOETZ, *Deutsch-russische Handelsgeschichte des Mittelalters* (1922).

4. W. VOGEL, *Geschichte der deutschen Seeschiffahrt*, vol. 1 (1915). P. GIRGENSOHN, *Die skandinavische Politik der Hansa 1357–95* (1898). H. CORDSEN, 'Beiträge zur Geschichte der Vitalienbrüder', in *Jahrbuch des Vereins für Mecklenburgische Geschichte*, 73 (1908). K. KOPPMANN, 'Der Seeräuber Klaus Störtebeker in Geschichte und Sage', in *HGbll.* 2 (1877).

Chapter Five

1. E. DAENELL, *Die Blütezeit der deutschen Hanse*, vol. 2 (1906). W. STEIN, 'Die Hansestädte', in *HGbll.* 19 (1913). K. FRIEDLAND, 'Kaufleute und Städte als Glieder der Hanse', in *HGbll.* 76 (1958). L. VON WINTERFELD, 'Das westfälische Hansequartier', in *Der Raum Westfalen*, II 1 (1955). H. STOOB, 'Dithmarschen und die Hanse', in *HGbll.* 73 (1955).

2. H. LAUBINGER, 'Die rechtliche Gestaltung der Hanse' (Ph.D. thesis, 1930).

3. P. JOHANSEN, 'Novgorod und die Hanse', in *Städtewesen und Bürgertum, Gedächtnisschrift F. Rörig* (1953). M. SZEFTEL, 'La condition légale des étrangers dans la Russie novgorodo-kiévienne', in *Recueils de la Société Jean Bodin*, 10 (1958). F. TECHEN, *Die deutsche Brücke in Bergen* (1923). P. NORMAN, 'The Hanseatic settlement at Bergen in Norway', in *Archeological Journal*, 71 (1914). C. KOREN WIBERG, *Hanseaterne og Bergen*, 2nd ed. (Bergen, 1941). K. ENGEL, 'Die Organisation der deutsch-hansischen Kaufleute in England im 14. und 15. Jahrhundert', in *HGbll.* 19–20 (1913–14). M. WEINBAUM, 'Stalhof und deutsche Gildhalle zu London', in *HGbll.* 53 (1928). W. STEIN, *Die Genossenschaft der deutschen Kaufleute zu Brügge in Flandern* (1890). L. VON WINTERFELD, *Dortmunds Stellung in der Hanse* (1932). W. STEIN, 'Vom

deutschen Kontor in Kowno', in *HGbll.* 22 (1916). O. A. Johnsen, 'Der deutsche Kaufmann in der Wiek in Norwegen', in *HGbll.* 53 (1928). F. Schulz, *Die Hanse und England von Edwards III. bis auf Heinrichs VIII. Zeit* (1911). A. Leroux, *La colonie germanique de Bordeaux*, vol. 1 (1918).

4. W. Friccius, 'Der Wirtschaftskrieg als Mittel hansischer Politik', in *HGbll.* 57–8 (1932–3). W. Bode, 'Hansische Bundesbestrebungen in der ersten Hälfte des 15. Jahrhunderts', in *HGbll.* 45, 46, 51 (1919, 1920, 1926). H. Reincke, *Kaiser Karl IV. und die deutsche Hanse* (1931).

Chapter Six

1. W. Stein, 'Die Hansestädte', in *HGbll.* 19–23 (1913–17). A. von Brandt, 'Hamburg and Lübeck, Beiträge einer vergleichenden Geschichtsbetrachtung', in *Geist und Politik in der lübeckischen Geschichte* (1954). H. Westphal, 'Die Verhältnisse der wendischen Hansestädte untereinander, zu den Landesherren, zur Hansa' (Ph.D. thesis, 1911). W. Spiess, *Braunschweig als Hansestadt* (1926). F. Wiegand, 'Über hansische Beziehungen Erfurts', in *Hansische Studien* (1961). E. Müller-Mertens, 'Berlin und die Hanse', in *HGbll.* 80 (1962). L. von Winterfeld, 'Das westfälische Hansequartier', in *Der Raum Westfalen*, II 1 (1955). Z. W. Sneller, *Deventer, die Stadt der Jahrmärkte* (1936). H. Pirenne, 'Histoire de la constitution de la ville de Dinant au moyen âge', in *Les Villes et les Institutions urbaines*, vol. 2 (1939). F. Petri, 'Die Stellung der Südersee- und Ijsselstädte im flandrisch-hansischen Raum', in *HGbll.* 79 (1961). P. Therstappen, 'Köln und die niederrheinischen Städte in ihrem Verhältnis zur Hanse in der 2. Hälfte des 15. Jahrhunderts' (Ph.D. thesis, 1901). B. Schumacher, *Geschichte Ost- und Westpreussens*, 4th ed. (1959). O. Stavenhagen, 'Die Anfänge des Livländischen Städtebundes', in *Baltische Monatschrift*, 52 (1901). K. Kumlien, 'Königtum, Städte und Hanse in Schweden um die Mitte des 14. Jahrhunderts', in *Städtewesen und Bürgertum* (1953).

2. E. Keyser, *Bevölkerungsgeschichte Deutschlands*, 3rd ed. (1943). H. Reincke, 'Bevölkerungsprobleme der Hansestädte', in *HGbll.* 70 (1951). E. Krüger, 'Die Bevölkerunsverschiebung aus den altdeutschen Städten über Lübeck in die Städt des Ostseegebietes', in *ZLübG.* 27 (1935). O. Ahlers, 'Die Bevölkerungspolitik der Städte des wendischen Quartiers der Hanse gegenüber den Slawen' (Ph.D. thesis, Berlin, 1939). T. Penners, *Untersuchungen über die Herkunft der Stadtbewohner im Deutsch-Ordensland Preussen bis in die Zeit um 1400* (1942). H. von zur Mühlen, 'Versuch einer soziologischen Erfassung der Bevölkerung Revals im Spätmittelalter', in *HGbll.* 75 (1957). R. Mols, *Introduction à la démographie historique des villes d'Europe du XIVe au XVIIIe siècle*, 3 vols (1954–6).

3. H. Planitz, *Die deutsche Stadt im Mittelalter* (1954). F. Bruns, 'Der Lübecker Rat, Zusammensetzung, Ergänzung und Geschäftsführung', in *ZLübG.* 32 (1951). G. Wehrmann, 'Das lübische Patriziat', in *ZLübG.* 5 (1888). A. von Brandt, 'Individuum und Gemeinschaft im mittelalterlichen Lübeck', in *Geist und Politik* (1954); 'Die gesellschaftliche Struktur des Spätmittelalterlichen Lübeck', in *Vorträge und Forschungen*, XI (1966). H. Reincke, *Forschungen und Skizzen zur Geschichte Hamburgs* (1951). J. Schildhauer, 'Die Sozialstruktur der Hansestadt Rostock', in *Hansische Studien* (1961). M. Hamann, 'Wismar-Rostock-Stralsund-Greifswald zur Hansezeit', in *Vom Mittelalter zur Neuzeit* (1956). H. Koeppen, *Führende Stralsunder Ratsfamilien* (1938). L. von Winterfeld, *Handel, Kapital und Patriziat in Köln bis 1400* (1925).

4. C. Wehrmann, *Die älteren lübischen Zunftrollen*, 2nd ed. (1872). E. Thikötter, 'Die Zünfte Bremens im Mittelalter' (Ph.D. thesis, 1929). F. Techen, 'Etwas von der mittelalterlichen Gewerbeordnung, insbesondere der wendischen Städte', in *HGbll.* 9 (1897); 'Die Böttcher in den Wendischen Städten, besonders in Wismar', in *HGbll.* 50 (1925). W. Stieda, 'Hansische Vereinbarungen über städtisches Gewerbe im 14. und 15. Jahrhundert', in *HGbll.* 5 (1886). A. von Brandt, 'Die Lübecker Knochenhaueraufstände von 1380–1384', in *ZLübG.* 39 (1959). K. Czok, 'Zum Braunschweiger Aufstand 1374–1386', in *Hansische Studien* (1961).

Chapter Seven

W. Vogel, *Geschichte der deutschen Seeschiffahrt* (1915). W. Vogel and G. Schmölders, *Die Deutschen als Seefahrer* (1949). P. Heinsius, *Das Schiff der hansischen Frühzeit* ('Quellen und Darstellungen zur hansischen Geschichte', n.s. 12, 1956); 'Dimensions et caractéristiques des Koggen hanséatiques dans le commerce de la Baltique', in *Le Navire et l'Économie du Nord de l'Europe* (1960). B. Hagedorn, *Die Entwicklung der wichtigsten Schiffstypen bis ins 19. Jh.* (1914). K. F. Olechnowitz, *Der Schiffbau der hansischen Spätzeit* (1960). W. Vogel, 'Zur Grösse der europäischen Handelsflotten im 15., 16. und 17. Jahrhundert', in *Festschrift Dietrich Schäfer* (1915). T. Kiesselbach, 'Grundlage und Bestandteile des älteren Hamburgischen Schiffsrechts', in *HGbll.* 10 (1900). K. Koppmann, *Das Seebuch* (1876). H. Reincke, 'Simon von Utrecht', in *Forschungen und Skizzen zur hamburgischen Geschichte* (1951).

Chapter Eight

1. H. Reincke, 'Hamburgische Vermögen, 1350–1530', in *Forschungen und Skizzen zur Geschichte Hamburgs* (1951). P. Simson, *Der Artushof in Danzig*

(1900). F. Bruns, *Die Lübecker Bergenfahrer und ihre Chronistik* (1900). D. Schäfer, *Das Buch des Lübeckischen Vogts auf Schonen*, 2nd ed. (1927). J. Bolland, 'Die Gesellschaft der Flandernfahrer in Hamburg', in *ZHambG*. 41 (1951).

2. E. von Lehe, 'Der hansische Kaufmann des 13. Jahrhunderts', in *ZHambG*. 44 (1958). P. Rehme, *Geschichte des Handelsrechts* (1913). A. von Brandt, 'Ein Stück aufmännischer Buchführung', in *ZLübG*. 44 (1964). F. Rörig, 'Das älteste erhaltene deutsche Kaufmannsbüchlein' and 'Grosshandel und Grosshändler im Lübeck des 14. Jahrhunderts', in *Wirtschaftskräfte im Mittelalter* (1959). F. Keutgen, 'Hansische Handelsgesellschaften vornehmlich des 14. Jahrhunderts', in *VSWG* 4 (1906). W. Ebel, *Lübisches Kaufmannsrecht, vornehmlich nach Lübecker Ratsurteilen des 15/16. Jahrhunderts* (Göttingen, 1953). E. Maschke, *Die Schäffer und Lieger des Deutschen Ordens in Preussen* (Hamburg, 1960).

3. C. Mollwo, *Das Handlungsbuch von Hermann und Johann Wittenborg* (1901). L. von Winterfeld, *Tidemann Lemberg* (1925); *Hildebrand Veckinghusen* (1929). W. Koppe, *Lübeck-Stockholmer Handelsgeschichte im 14. Jahrhundert* (1933). C. Nordmann, 'Die Veckinghusenschen Handelsbücher', in *HGbll*. 66 (1942). M. P. Lesnikov, 'Die livländische Kaufmannschaft und ihre Handelsbeziehungen zu Flandern am Anfang des 15. Jahrhunderts', in *Zs. für Geschichtswissenschaft*, 6 (1958); 'Lübeck als Handelsplatz für osteuropäische Waren im 15. Jahrhundert', in *HGbll*. 78 (1960). G. Neumann, *Hinrich Castorp* (1932); *Nürnberger Grosshändler im spätmittelalterlichen Lübeck* (1933). F. Rörig, 'Das Einkaufsbüchlein der Nürnberg-Lübecker Mulich auf der Frankfurter Fastenmesse des Jahres 1495', in *Wirtschaftskräfte im Mittelalter* (1959).

4. G. von der Ropp, *Kaufmannsleben zur Zeit der Hanse* (1907). R. Häpke, *Der deutsche Kaufmann in den Niederlanden* (1911). P. Johansen, 'Novgorod und die Hanse', in *Städtewesen und Bürgertum* (1953). J. Bühler, *Bauern, Bürger und Hansa nach zeitgenössischen Quellen* (1929). W. Stein, 'Handelsbriefe aus Riga und Königsberg von 1458 und 1461', in *HGbll*. 9 (1898). W. Stieda, *Hildebrand Veckinghusen, Briefwechsel* (1921).

Chapter Nine

1. K. Bahr, *Handel und Verkehr der deutschen Hanse in Flandern* (1911). F. Schulz, *Die Hanse und England* . . . (1911). L. K. Goetz, *Deutscherussische Handelsgeschichte des Mittelalters* (1922). V. Niitema, *Das Strandrecht in Nordeuropa im Mittelalter* (1955).

2. M. Postan, 'The economic and political relations of England and the Hansa from 1400 to 1475', in E. Power and M. Postan, *Studies in English Trade in the Fifteenth Century*, 2nd ed. (1951). K. H. Ruffmann, 'Engländer und Schotten in den Seestädten Ost- und Westpreussens', in *Zs. für Ostforschung*, 7 (1958). F. Vollbehr, *Die Holländer und die deutsche Hanse* (1930). N. W. Posthumus, *De geschiedenis van de leidsche lakenindustrie*, 3 vols (1908–39). C. Nordmann, *Oberdeutschland und die deutsche Hanse* (1939). M. Małowist, 'Über die Frage der Handelspolitik des Adels in den Ostseeländern im 15. und 16. Jahrhundert', in *HGbll.* 75 (1957).

3. W. Stein, *Beiträge zur Geschichte der deutschen Hanse bis in die Mitte des 15. Jahrhunderts* (1900). H. Rogge, 'Der Stapelzwang des hansischen Kontors zu Brügge im 15. Jahrhundert' (Ph.D. thesis, 1903). E. Daenell, *Die Blütezeit der deutschen Hanse*, vol. 2 (1905).

4. M. Neumann, *Geschichte des Wechsels im Hansagebiet bis zum 17. Jahrhundert* (1863). C. Nordmann, *Nürnberger Grosshändler im spätmittelalterlichen Lübeck* (1933). R. de Roover, *The Rise and Decline of the Medici Banks, 1397–1494* (1963).

5. W. Jesse, 'Die Münzpolitik der Hansestädte', in *HGbll.* 53 (1928); *Der wendische Münzverein* (1928); 'Lübecks Anteil an der Münz- und Geldgeschichte Deutschlands', in *ZLübG.* 40 (1961).

Chapter Ten

1. M. Mollat, 'Les sources de l'histoire maritime en Europe, du moyen âge XVIIIe siècle' (4th Conference on Maritime History, 1962; including also articles by M. Postan and E. Carus Wilson for England and by M. Małowist for Poland). G. Lechner, *Die hansischen Pfundzollisten des Jahres 1368* (1935). W. Stieda, *Revaler Zollbücher und Zollquittungen des 14. Jahrhunderts* (1887).

2. M. Postan, 'The trade of medieval Europe: the North', in *Cambridge Economic History*, vol. 2 (1952). W. Vogel, *Geschichte der deutschen Seeschiffahrt*, vol. 1 (1915). W. Abel, *Geschichte der deutschen Landwirtschaft* (1962). F. Semrau, 'Der Getreidehandel der deutschen Hanse bis zum Ausgang des Mittelalters' (Ph.D. thesis, 1911). G. Franz, *Der deutsche Landwarenhandel* (1960). M. Lesnikov, 'Lübeck als Handelsplatz für osteuropäische Waren im 15. Jahrhundert', in *HGbll.* 78 (1960); 'Der hansische Pelzhandel zu Beginn des 15. Jahrhunderts', in *Hansische Studien* (1961). H. Hartmeyer, *Der Weinhandel im Gebiete der Hanse im Mittelalter* (1905).

3. H. Nirrnheim, *Das hamburgische Pfundzollbuch von 1369* (1910); *Das hamburgische Pfund- und Werkzollbuch von 1399–1400* (1930). F. Bruns, 'Die Lübeckischen Pfundzollbücher von 1492–96', in *HGbll.* 11–14 (1905–8); Lübecks Handelsstrassen am Ende des Mittelalters', in *HGbll.* 8 (1896). C. Higounet, 'Lunebourg capitale du sel au moyen âge', in *L'Information historique*, 24 (1962). W. Fellmann, 'Die Salzproduktion im Hanseraum', in *Hansische Studien* (1961). A. Braun, *Der lübeckische Salzhandel bis zum Ausgang des 17. Jahrhunderts* (1926). M. Barth, *Der Rebbau des Elsass und seine Absatzgebiete* (1958). H. Ammann, 'Von der Wirtschaftsgeltung des Elsass im Mittelalter', in *Alemannisches Jahrbuch* (1955). R. van Uyten, 'Die Bedeutung des Kölner Weinmarktes im 15. Jahrhundert', in *Rhein. Vierteljahrsbll.* 30 (1965). F. Techen, 'Das Brauwerk in Wismar', in *HGbll.* 21–2 (1915–16). H. Hohls, 'Der Leinwandhandel in Norddeutschland vom Mittelalter bis zum 17. Jahrhundert', in *HGbll.* 51 (1926). C. Nordmann, *Oberdeutschland und die Hanse* (1939). A. Dietz, *Frankfurter Handelgeschichte*, vol. 1 (1910). W. Koppe, 'Die Hansen und Frankfurt am Main im 14. Jahrhundert', in *HGbll.* 71 (1952). B. Kuske, 'Die Kölner Handelbeziehungen im 15. Jahrhundert', in *VSWG* 7 (1909).

4. V. Lauffer, 'Danzigs Schiffs- und Warenverkehr am Ende des 15. Jahrhunderts', in *Zs. des westpreussischen Geschichtsvereins*, 33 (1894). H. Samsonowicz, 'Le commerce extérieur de Gdansk pendant la seconde partie du XVe siècle', in *Przeglad historyczny*, 47 (1956); in Polish, with summary in French. P. Simson, *Geschichte der Stadt Danzig*, vol. 1 (1916). T. Hirsch, *Handels- und Gewerbegeschichte Danzigs* (1857). E. Carstenn, *Geschichte der Hansestadt Elbing*, 2nd ed. (1937). K. A. Anshel, *Thorns Seehandel und Kaufmannschaft um 1370* (1961). C. Sattler, *Handelsrechnungen des deutschen Ordens* (1887). W. Böhnke, 'Der Binnenhandel des deutschen Ordens in Preussen', in *HGbll.* 80 (1962). F. Renken, *Der Handel der Königsberger Grosschäfferei des deutschen Ordens mit Flandern um 1400* (1937). A. Rohde, *Bernstein, ein deutscher Werkstoff* (1941). M. Małowist, 'L'approvisionnement des ports de la Baltique en produits forestiers pour les constructions navales aux Xve et XVIe siècles', in *Le Navire et l'économie maritime du nord de l'Europe*, ed. M. Mollat (1960). L. K. Goetz, *Deutsch-russische Handelgeschichte des Mittelalters* (1922). P. Johansen, 'Der hansische Russlandhandel', in *Die deutsche Hanse als Mittler zwischen Ost und West* (1963). B. Geremek, 'Le commerce de Novgorod avec l'Occident', in *Annales E.S.C.* (1964). W. Koppe, 'Revals Schiffsverkehr und Seehandel in den Jahren 1378–1384', in *HGbll.* 64 (1940). K. H. Sass, *Hansischer Einfuhrhandel in Reval um 1430* (1955). H. Laakmann, *Geschichte der Stadt Pernau in der Deutschordenszeit* (1955). M. Lesnikov, 'Die livländische Kaufmannschaft und ihre Handelsbeziehungen', in *Zs. für Geschichtswissenschaft*, 6 (1958).

5. K. Kumlien, *Sverige och Hanseaterna. Studier i svensk politik och utrikeshandel* (1953). W. Koppe, *Lübeck-Stockholmer Handelgeschichte im*

14. Jahrhundert (1933). B. Boëtius, *Kopparbergslagen fram till 1570-talets genombrott* (1965). L. Schwetlik, 'Der hansisch-dänische Landhandel und seine Träger', in *Zs. . . . für Schleswig-Holsteinische Geschichte*, 85–6 (1961), 88 (1963). A. Christensen, 'La foire de Scanie', in *La Foire, Recueils de la Société Jean Bodin*, 5 (1953). G. Weibull, *Lübeck och Skånemarknaden* (1922). D. Schäfer, *Das Buch des lübeckischen Vogtes auf Schonen*, 2nd ed. (1927). O. A. Johnsen, *Norwegische Wirtschaftsgeschichte* (1939). J. A. Gade, *The Hanseatic Control of Norwegian Commerce during the Late Middle Ages* (1951). F. Bruns, *Die Lübecker Bergenfahrer* (1900). J. Schreiner, 'Bemerkungen zum Hanse-Norwegen Problem', in *HGbll.* 72 (1954). E. Baasch, *Die Islandfahrt der Deutschen* (1889).

6. E. Carus-Wilson and O. Coleman, *England's Export Trade 1275–1547* (1963). F. Schultz, *Die Hanse und England von Eduards III. bis auf Heinrichs VIII. Zeit* (1911). E. Power and M. Postan, *Studies in English Trade in the Fifteenth Century*, 2nd ed. (1951). H. L. Gray, 'The production and exportation of English woollens in the 14th century', in *Eng. Hist. Rev.* (1924). G. Schanz, *Englische Handelspolitik gegen Ende des Mittelalters*, 2 vols (1881).

7. J. H. Beuken, *De Hanze en Vlaanderen* (1950). K. H. Bahr, *Handel und Verkehr der deutschen Hanse in Flandern während des 14. Jahrhunderts* (1911). H. van de Wee, *The Growth of the Antwerp Market and the European Economy, 14th–17th century*, 3 vols (1963). H. van Werveke, *Bruges et Anvers. Huit siècles de commerce flamand* (1944). W. Stein, 'Über den Umfang des spätmittelalterlichen Handels der Hanse in Flandern und in den Niederlanden', in *HGbll.* 23 (1917). H. Ammann, 'Deutschland und die Tuchindustrie Nordwesteuropas im Mittelalter', in *HGbll.* 72 (1954). *Algemeene Geschiedenis der Nederlanden*, vols 3, 4 (1951–2). J. F. Niermeyer, *Dordrecht als handelsstad in de tweede helft van de 14 eeuw* (1941–3). E. Daenell, 'Holland und Hanse im 15. Jahrhundert', in *HGbll.* 11 (1903). G. Schellenberg, *Hamburg und Holland. Kulturelle und wirtschaftliche Beziehungen* (1940). F. Vollbehr, *Die Holländer und die deutsche Hanse* (1930). Z. W. Sneller, *Deventer, die Stadt der Jahrmärkte* (1936). F. Petri, 'Die Stellung der Südersee- und Ijsselstädte im flandrisch-hansischen Raum', in *HGbll.* 79 (1961).

8. A. Agats, *Der hansische Baienhandel* (1904). O. Held, 'Die Hanse und Frankreich von der Mitte des 15. Jahrhunderts bis zum Regierungsantritt Karls VIII.', in *HGbll.* 18 (1912). A. Leroux, 'Bordeaux et la Hanse teutonique au XVe siècle', in *Revue historique de Bordeaux* (1910). R. Dion, *Histoire de la vigne et du vin en France des origines au XIXe siècle* (1959). J. Craeybeckx, *Un grand commerce d'importation: les vins de France aux anciens Pays-Bas* (1958). Y. Renouard, 'Le grand commerce des vins de Gascogne au moyen

âge', in *Revue historique*, 221 (1959). M. DE DAINVILLE, 'Les relations de Bordeaux avec les villes hanséatiques', in *Mémoires et Documents J. Hayem*, 3rd series (1912). M. MOLLAT, *Le commerce maritime normand à la fin du moyen âge* (1952). R. VOLLAND, 'Die Rolle Bordeauxs im Handel zwischen den Hansestädten und Westfrankreich' (Ph.D. thesis, 1962). A. DE OLIVEIRA MAGQUES, *Hansa e Portugal na idade media* (1959); 'Navigation entre la Prusse et la Portugal au debut du XVe siècle', in *VSWG* 46 (1959) and *Revue du Nord*, 164 (1959). R. HÄBLER, 'Der hansisch-spanische Konflikt von 1419 und die älteren spanischen Bestände', in *HGbll.* 8 (1894).

9. W. STIEDA, *Hansisch-venezianische Handelsbeziehungen im 15. Jahrhundert* (1894). B. KUSKE, 'Die Handelsbeziehungen zwischen Köln und Italien im späteren Mittelalter', in *Köln, der Rhein und das Reich* (1956). A. SCHULTE, *Geschichte der grossen Ravensburger Handelsgesellschaft*, vol. 2 (1923).

Chapter Eleven

1. A. BACH, *Geschichte der deutschen Sprache*, 6th ed. (1956). W. HEINSOHN, *Das Eindringen der neuhochdeutschen Schriftsprache in Lübeck* (1933). K. SCHILLER and A. LÜBBEN, *Mittelniederdeutsches Wörterbuch*, 6 vols (1875–81). A. LASCH and C. BORCHLING, *Mittelniederdeutsches Handwörterbuch* (1956 ff. – in progress.

2. H. DE BOOR and R. NEWALD, *Geschichte der deutschen Literatur*, vols 1 and 2, 2nd ed. (1955). G. EHRISMANN, *Geschichte der deutschen Literatur bis zum Ausgang des Mittelalters*, vol. 2 (1935). A. VON BRANDT, 'Lübeck in der deutschen Geistesgeschichte', in *Geist und Politik* (1954). R. FOLZ, *Le souvenir et la légende de Charlemagne dans l'Empire germanique médiéval* (1950). W. LEXIS, *Das Unterrichtswesen im deutschen Reich*, vol. 1 (1904). E. ENNEN, 'Stadt und Schule, vornehmlich im Mittelalter', in *Rhein. Vierteljahrsbll.* 22 (1957). R. SCHMIDT, 'Die Anfänge der Universität Greifswald', in *Festschrift zur 500-Jahrfeier der Universität Greifswald*, vol. 1 (1956).

3. K. PAGEL, *Die Hanse*, 3rd ed. (1963, ill.). G. DEHIO, *Geschichte der deutschen Kunst*, vols 1 and 2, 4th ed.; vol. 3, 2nd ed. (1930–1). W. PINDER, *Vom Wesen und Werden deutscher Formen*, 3 vols (1935–43). G. DEHIO and E. GALL, *Handbuch der deutschen Kunstdenkmäler*, 3rd ed: 1. *Niedersachsen und Westfalen* (1949); 2. *Rheinlande* (1949); 3. *Nordosten* (1928). A. RENGER-PATZSCH, *Norddeutsche Backsteindome* (1930). K. WILHELM-KÄSTNER, 'Der Raum Westfalen in der Baukunst des Mittelalters', in *Der Raum Westfalen*, vol. II 1 and IV 2 (1955–64). C. G. HEISE, *Lübecker Plastik* (1926). H. BUSCH, *Meister des Nordens, 1450–1550* (1940). W. GREISCHEL, *Der Magdeburger*

Dom (1939). H. VOGTS, *Köln im Spiegel seiner Kunst* (1950). Many monographs in the collection 'Deutsche Lande, Deutsche Kunst': e.g. H. GRÄBKE and W. CASTELLI, *Lübeck*; E. KEYSER, *Danzig*; N. VON HOLST, *Baltenland*, etc.

4. S. H. STEINBERG, 'Die bildende Kurst im Rahmen der hansischen Geschichte', in *HGbll*. (1928). H. PLATTE, *Meister Bertram in der Hamburger Kunsthalle* (1959). W. PAATZ, *Bernt Notke und sein Kreis*, 2 vols (1939). C. HABICHT, *Hanseatische Malerei und Plastik in Skandinavien* (1926). P. O. WESTLUND, *Die Stockholmer Hauptkirche St Nicolai* (1958). F. BRUNS, 'Der Dreikönigsaltar der Marienkirche und die Familie Brömse', in *ZLübG*. 32 (1951). H. REINCKE, 'Probleme um den "Meister Francke"', in *Jahrbuch des Hamburger Kunstvereins* (1959). P. HEINSIUS, 'Schnitzereien am Novgorodfahrer-Gestühl zu Stralsund', in *Zs. für Ostforschung*, 11 (1962).

Chapter Twelve

1. E. DAENELL, *Die Blütezeit der deutschen Hanse*, 2 vols (1905–6). W. VOGEL, *Geschichte der deutschen Seeschiffahrt* (1915).

2. C. WEHRMANN, 'Der Aufstand in Lübeck 1408–1416', in *HGbll*. 3 (1878). V. NIITEMA, *Der Kaiser und die Nordische Union bis zu den Burgunderkriegen* (1960). W. BODE, 'Hansische Bundesbestrebungen in der ersten Hälfte des 15. Jahrhunderts', in *HGbll*. 45 (1919).

3. E. WEISE, *Das Widerstandsrecht im Ordenslande Preussen und das mittelalterliche Europa* (1955). B. SCHUMACHER, *Geschichte Ost- und Westpreussens*, 4th ed. (1959). K. L. GOETZ, *Deutsch-russische Handelsgeschichte des Mittelalters* (1922). G. HOLLIHN, 'Die Stapel- und Gästepolitik Rigas in der Ordenszeit', in *HGbll*. 60 (1935).

4. J. A. GADE, *The Hanseatic control of Norwegian commerce* (1951). A. NIELSEN, *Dänische Wirtschaftsgeschichte* (1933). M. HOFFMANN, 'Lübeck und Danzig nach dem Frieden zu Wordingborg', in *HGbll*. 10 (1901). M. GERHARDT and W. HUBATSCH, *Deutschland und Skandinavien im Wandel der Jahrhunderte* (1955).

5. J. BEUKEN, *De Hanze en Vlaanderen* (1951). W. STEIN, 'Die Burgunderherzöge und die Hanse', in *HGbll*. 10 (1901). W. FRICCIUS, 'Der Wirtschaftskrieg als Mittel hansischer Politik', in *HGbll*. 58 (1933). F. VOLLBEHR, *Die Holländer und die deutsche Hanse* (1930). E. DAENELL, 'Holland und die Hanse im 15. Jahrhundert', in *HGbll*. 11 (1903).

6, 7. E. Power and M. Postan, *Studies in English Trade in the 15th Century*, 2nd ed. (1951). F. Schulz, *Die Hanse und England von Eduards III. bis auf Heinrichs VIII. Zeit* (1911). W. Stein, 'Die Hanse und England beim Ausgang des hundertjährigen Krieges', in *HGbll*. 46 (1921); *Die Hanse und England. Ein hansisch-englischer Seekrieg im 15. Jahrhundert* (1905). O. Held, 'Die Hanse und Frankreich von der Mitte des 15. Jahrhunderts bis zum Regierungsantritt Karls VIII.', in *HGbll*. 18 (1912).

Chapter Thirteen

1. P. Johansen, 'Novgorod und die Hanse', in *Städtewesen und Bürgertum, Gedächtnisschrift F. Rörig* (1953); 'Die Bedeutung der Hanse für Livland', in *HGbll*. 66 (1941). G. Mickwitz, *Aus Revaler Handelsbüchern* (1938). O. A. Johnsen, *Norwegische Wirtschaftsgeschichte* (1939). O. Röhlk, *Hansisch-norwegische Handelspolitik im 16. Jahrhundert* (1935). H. van Werveke, *Bruges et Anvers* (1944). J. Maréchal, 'Le départ de Bruges des marchands étrangers', in *Annales de la Société d'Émulation de Bruges*, 88 (1951). J. van Houtte, 'Anvers aux XVe et XVIe siècles', in *Annales E.S.C.* 16 (1961). F. Schulz, *Die Hanse und England* (1911). K. Friedland, 'Hamburger Englandfahrer 1512–57', in *ZHambG*. 46 (1960).

2. R. Ehrenberg, *Le siècle des Fugger* (1955). G. von Pölnitz, *Fugger und Hanse* (1953); *Jacob Fugger*, 2 vols (1949–52). P. Jeannin, 'Le cuivre, les Fugger et la Hanse', in *Annales E.S.C.* 10 (1955). L. Bechtel, 'Die Fugger in Danzig und im nordeuropäischen Raum' (Ph.D. thesis, 1943). G. Nordmann, *Oberdeutschland und die Hanse* (1939).

3. R. Häpke, *Die Regierung Karls V. under europäische Norden* (1914). E. Wolff, 'Bugenhagen', in *Neue Deutsche Biographie*, 3 (1957). J. Schildhauer, *Soziale, politische und religiöse Auseinandersetzungen in den Hanstestädten Stralsund, Rostock und Wismar im ersten Drittel des 16. Jahrhunderts* (1959). M. Hamann, 'Wismar-Rostock-Stralsund-Greifswald zur Hansezeit', in *Vom Mittelalter zur Neuzeit, Festschrift H. Sprömberg* (1956).

4. G. Waitz, *Lübeck unter Jürgen Wullenwever und die europäische Politik*, 3 vols (1855–6). R. Häpke, 'Der Untergang der hansischen Vormachtstellung in der Ostsee 1531–1544', in *HGbll*. 18 (1912). G. Wentz, 'Der Prinzipat Jürgen Wullenwevers und die wendischen Städt' in *HGbll*. 56 (1913). H. Pannach, 'Einige Bemerkungen zu den sozial-ökonomischen Problemen um Jürgen Wullenwever', in *Vom Mittelalter zur Neuzeit, Festschrift H. Sprömberg* (1956).

Chapter Fourteen

1. P. Simson, 'Die Organisation der Hanse in ihrem letzten Jahrhundert', in *HGbll*. 13 (1907). G. Fink, 'Die rechtliche Stellung der Hanse in der Zeit ihres Niederganges', in *HGbll*. (1936). R. Häpke, *Der Untergang der Hanse* (1925). K. Friedland, 'Der Plan des Dr Heinrich Sudermann zur Wiederherstellung der Hanse', in *Jahrbuch des Kölnischen Geschichtsvereins*, 31–2 (1956–7).

2. W. Vogel and G. Schmölders, *Die Deutschen als Seefahrer* (1949). W. Kirchner, 'Die Bedeutung Narwas im 16. Jahrhundert', in *Hist. Zeitschrift*, 172 (1951). P. Jeannin, 'L'économie française du XVIe siècle et le marché russe', in *Annales E.S.C.* 9 (1954). A. Dreyer, *Die lübisch-livländischen Beziehungen sur Zeit des Untergangs livländischer Selbständigkeit 1551–63* (1912). F. Lindberg, 'La Baltique et l'historiographie scandinave', in *Annales E.S.C.* 16 (1961). W. Evers, 'Das hansische Kontor in Antwerpen' (Ph.D. thesis, Kiel, 1915). H. van Werveke, *Bruges et Anvers* (1944). K. Friedland, 'Die Verlegung des Brüggeschen Kontors nach Antwerpen', in *HGbll* (1963). P. Jeannin, 'Les relations économiques des villes de la Baltique avec Anvers au XVI siècle', in *VSWG* 43 (1956). J. Denucé, *La Hanse et les compagnies anversoises aux pays baltiques* (1938). R. Ehrenberg, *Hamburg und England im Zeitalter der Königin Elisabeth* (1896). L. Beutin, *Hanse und Reich im handelspolitischen Endkampfen gegen England* (1929). E. Wiskemann, *Hamburg und die Welthandelspolitik* (1929). P. Simson, 'Die Handelsniederlassung der englischen Kaufleute in Elbing', in *HGbll*. 22 (1916). E. Carstenn, *Geschichte der Hansestadt Elbing* (1937).

3. W. Vogel, 'Zur Grösse der europäischen Handelsflotten im 15., 16. und 17. Jahrhundert', in *Festschrift Dietrich Schäfer* (1915). R. Davis, *The Rise of the English Shipping Industry in the 17th and 18th Centuries* (1962). B. Hagedorn, *Ostfrieslands Handel und Seeschiffahrt im 16. Jahrhundert* (1910). K. F. Olechnowitz, *Der Schiffbau der hansischen Spätzeit* (1960); *Handel und Schiffahrt der späten Hanse* (1965). H. Brunschwig, 'L'expansion coloniale allemande du XVe siècle à nos jours', in *Études coloniales*, 9 (1957). A. Friis, 'La valeur documentaire des comptes du péage du Sund', in *Les Sources de l'histoire maritime en Europe* (1962). P. Jeannin, 'Les comptes du Sund', in *Revue historique*, 231 (1964); 'Lübecker Handelsunternehmungen um die Mitte des 16. Jahrhundert', in *ZLübG*. 43 (1963); 'Le tonnage des navires utilisés dans la Baltique de 1550 à 1640', in *Le Navire et l'Economie maritime du nord de l'Europe* (1960). M. Małowist, 'L'approvisionnement des ports de la Baltique en produits forestiers', ibid. J. Zoutis, 'Riga dans le commerce maritime en Baltique au XVIIe siècle', ibid. H. Thierfelder, *Rostock-Osloer Handelsbeziehungen im 16. Jahrhundert* (1958). H. Kellenbenz,

'Spanien, die nördlichen Niederlande und der skandinavisch-baltische Raum in der Weltwirtschaft und Politik', in *VSWG* 41 (1954). J. PAPRITZ, 'Das Handelshaus der Loitz zu Stettin, Danzig und Lüneburg', in *Baltische Studien*, n.s. 44 (1957). L. BEUTIN, *Der deutsche Seehandel im Mittelmeergebiet* (1933).

4. H. THIMME, 'Der Handel Kölns am Ende des 16. Jahrhunderts', in *Westdeutsche Zs. für Geschichte und Kunst*, 31 (1912). H. KELLENBENZ *Unternehmerkräfte im Hamburger Portugal- und Spanienhandel 1590–1625* (1954). E. BAASCH, 'Hamburgs Seeschiffahrt und Warenhandel vom Ende des 16. bis Mitte des 17. Jahrhunderts', in *ZHambG.* 9. (1893). P. SIMSON, *Geschichte der Stadt Danzig*, vol. 2 (1918). E. KEYSER, *Danzigs Geschichte*, 4th ed. (1941). P. JEANNIN, 'Le commerce de Lubeck aux environs de 1580', in *Annales E.S.C.* 16 (1961). E. BAASCH, 'Die "Durchfuhr" in Lübeck', in *HGbll.* 13 (1907).

5. M. HROCH, 'Wallensteins Beziehungen zu den wendischen Hansestädten', in *Hansische Studien* (1961). H. C. MESSOW, *Die Hansestädte und die habsburgische Ostseepolitik im 30jährigen Kriege* (1935). A. HUHNHÄUSER, *Rostocks Seehandel von 1635–1648* (1914). G. JENSCH, *Der Handel Rigas im 17. Jahrhundert* (1930). F. DICKMANN, *Der Westfälische Frieden*, 2nd ed. (1965). A. WOHLWILL, 'Die Verbindung der Hansestädte und die hanseatischen Traditionen seit der Mitte des 17. Jahrhunderts', in *HGbll.* 9 (1899); 'Wann endete die Hanse?', in *HGbll.* 10 (1900).

INDEX

NOTE. In the case of countries (England, France, etc.), main references only are given.

48920